SURRENDER
IS NOT AN
OPTION

DEFENDING AMERICA
AT THE UNITED NATIONS
AND ABROAD

JOHN BOLTON

THRESHOLD
EDITIONS

New York   London   Toronto   Sydney

Threshold Editions
A Division of Simon & Schuster, Inc.
1230 Avenue of the Americas
New York, NY 10020

First Threshold Editions hardcover edition November 2007

THRESHOLD EDITIONS and colophon are trademarks of
Simon & Schuster, Inc.

For information about special discounts for bulk purchases,
please contact Simon & Schuster Special Sales at
1-800-456-6798 or business@simonandschuster.com.

Designed by Joy O'Meara

Manufactured in the United States of America

10   9   8   7   6   5   4   3   2   1

Library of Congress Cataloging-in-Publication Data

ISBN-13: 978-1-4165-5284-0
ISBN-10:   1-4165-5284-7

For Gretchen and Jennifer Sarah

CONTENTS

CHAPTER ONE

EARLY DAYS

De l'audace, et encore de l'audace,
et toujours de l'audace, et la patrie sera sauvée.

—GEORGES JACQUES DANTON, SEPTEMBER 2, 1792

Election night in 1964 found me at the local Goldwater for President headquarters in Catonsville, Maryland, just outside Baltimore. I had done volunteer campaign work there during the summer after the Republican Convention, and on weekends. Having obtained permission to be absent from high school on Election Day to hand out Goldwater leaflets at a nearby precinct, I was in Catonsville when Maryland's polls closed to await the national returns. Although Lyndon Johnson seemed to have a large lead going into the election, I remained optimistic that Barry Goldwater would run well, and might even pull off an upset.

So much for the early signs of a promising political career. Goldwater was crushed, in what was then the worst presidential election defeat in American history. At the Catonsville office, which had become quite crowded, many of the adult volunteers (I was just about the only teenager there) were weeping, something I had never seen before in public. I was somewhat puzzled by this display of emotion, but I was more puzzled by the election results, which were going from bad to worse. Dean Burch, Goldwater's chairman of the Republican National Committee, said, "As the sun sets in the West, the Republican star will rise." I believed that for a while, until it became ever more obvious that "down" was the only direction in which Goldwater was headed.

It took weeks for the extent of the defeat to penetrate fully into my be-fuddled brain. When a few brave souls, just weeks afterward, printed bumper stickers that read "AuH₂O '68," I was ready to sign up again. After all, the American people could not really vote in overwhelming numbers for a candidate who said things like, "I want y'all to know that the Democratic Party is in favor of a mighty lot of things, and against mighty few." I had read Goldwater's *Why Not Victory?* and *The Conscience of a Conservative,* and fiercely admired the Arizonan's philosophy and candor. He was an individualist, not a collectivist, who said without reservation, "My aim is not to pass laws, but to repeal them."[1] He was against "the Eastern Establishment," which conservatives saw as a major source of our misguided statist policies at home, and what Barry called "drift, deception, and defeat" in the international struggle against Communism. I cheered when Barry said we should cut off the eastern seaboard and let it drift out to sea, even though my own state of Maryland would have been drifting out there as well. Later, after he returned to the Senate, Goldwater began a letter to the CIA director, "Dear Bill: I am pissed off." (How many times in my own government career did I long to write a letter like that, although I never did.) In my heart, I knew Barry was right.

While I thought the 1964 presidential election was a no-brainer, I was obviously part of a distinct minority, even though others would bravely say of Goldwater's popular vote total that "twenty-six million Americans can't be wrong." It would have been entirely logical after 1964 to give up politics as completely hopeless, and go on to a career, say, in the Foreign Service, as I seriously contemplated. Or I might have drifted off to the left in college, as so many of my contemporaries did. But like many others whose first taste of electoral politics came in the Goldwater campaign, I had exactly the opposite reaction. If the sustained and systematic distortion of a fine man's philosophy could succeed, abetted by every major media outlet in the country, overwhelmingly supported by the elite academic institutions, to the tune of negative advertising like Johnson's famous "daisy commercial," which accused Goldwater of being too casual about nuclear war, and slogans like "Goldwater for Halloween," it was time to fight back. If the United States was in such parlous condition that people who showed off

---

1. Barry Goldwater, *The Conscience of a Conservative* (New York: MacFadden Books, 1960), p. 23.

their appendectomy scars in public and held up beagles by their ears could get elected president, something had to be done. Surrender was not an option.

Thirty-six years later, election night 2000 was a very different affair. Beginning in 1968, Republicans had dominated American presidential politics. Only the unfortunate elections of two failed southern governors had intervened, and the objective in 2000 was to prevent the second Democratic interruption from being extended. Unlike 1964, however, the 2000 election was excruciatingly close, and I didn't stay around to await the outcome. I left for Seoul the morning after the election to participate in a conference on Korea-related policy issues at Yonsei University, which was cohosted by the American Enterprise Institute (AEI), where I was senior vice president. When I checked into my hotel in Seoul late on Thursday, Korea time, the Florida outcome remained up in the air. After a long day on Friday, I turned on the television in my hotel room and found that chaos still reigned in Florida, with no final result.

Most significantly for me, Governor George W. Bush had named Jim Baker, my former boss at the State Department during the previous Bush administration, to lead his effort to salvage Florida's electoral vote. No one at that point had the slightest idea of what might be involved, or how long it would take to decide the evolving contest. Before I collapsed into bed early that Friday evening in Seoul, I left a voice message for Baker at his Houston law firm. I explained that I was in South Korea, but offered to fly to Florida to help. At about 2:00 A.M. Seoul time, the phone rang, and I picked it up to hear Baker's unmistakable Texas twang saying, "Get your ass on a plane and get back here."

Just a few days later, I was in West Palm Beach, part of the great "chad" exercise. I stopped first in Tallahassee, but Baker immediately dispatched me to Palm Beach where he thought a "heavyweight lawyer" should be added to the team already diligently at work. Ken Mehlman, later Republican Party chairman, called me "the Atticus Finch of Palm Beach County," but there were many, many people volunteering. Hour after hour we sat, psychoanalyzing ballot cards. This was the process Democrats hoped would produce a change in Florida's popular vote totals and award them the state's electoral vote, and therefore the national election. One of my AEI colleagues, Michael Novak, a former Democrat, feared the worst, as he

watched on television a battle between "the street fighters and the prep-
pies." It turned out we won despite our rosy cheeks. I tried to go home for
Thanksgiving, but I was called back to Palm Beach just as I arrived in
Washington. My family couldn't face weeks of eating turkey without me, so
I returned ours to the local grocery store on Thanksgiving morning, which
was certainly a first for me, and flew back to Palm Beach. On the evening of
December 12, the Supreme Court ended the struggle in Bush's favor, and
quite correctly, as a matter of law, I might add. I was in Baker's office when
he called Texas to tell the candidate the good news, saying to Bush, for the
first time legitimately, "Congratulations, Mr. President."

After more than a month in Florida, one of the great emotional
roller-coaster rides of my professional life, I flew back to Washington on
a private plane with Margaret Tutwiler, a long-time Baker aide. We agreed
it had been a completely different experience from our time in the State
Department during the first Bush administration. It was only a matter of
time, however, before both of us found ourselves back at the State Department, where Chad was a country in Africa, not a tiny bit of meaningful
paper.

Between the 1964 and 2000 elections, a lot had happened to me,
demonstrating in my own experience the definition of "history" as "one
damned thing after another," with a few preliminary events before 1964 to
get me to that unhappy Goldwater election headquarters in Catonsville.

I started out in Baltimore on November 20, 1948, a baby boomer by any
definition of the term, the son of a Baltimore firefighter, Edward Jackson
Bolton ("Jack" to everyone) and his "housewife," as we used to say, from
Wilmington, Delaware, Virginia Clara Godfrey, or "Ginny." Neither had
graduated from high school, but I have no doubt that my own academic
record was based on the genes I inherited from them, since it certainly did
not come from our social contacts or standing in society. All four of my
grandparents, who were mostly Scotch-Irish or Irish, emigrated to the
United States in the early 1900s, so my parents were first-generation
Americans who had grown up during the Depression and been steeled by
World War II. They didn't need anyone to tell them that they had been
through tough times, and they were determined, like most in their generation, that their children were not going to repeat their experiences.

Jack lied about his age to join the Coast Guard once World War II
started, eager to go to sea, not a surprising aspiration for a Baltimore boy,

living in the East Coast's second-largest port after New York. Unfortunately, first assigned to land duty, he made it to sea by dropping a pan of fried eggs on the shoes of an officer who had pushed him a little further than he wanted to go. The ships on which he'd served looked like big hunks of ice, escorting cargoes across the North Atlantic, or so I thought years later when my father showed me the tiny photographs he'd kept. Wounded on D-Day off the coast of France, Jack spent the rest of the war recuperating in Florida, tending to the morale of the stateside female population, or at least that's how he described it. Back in Baltimore, after 1945, he knocked around for a while, and then got married, starting out as a plumber. The union rules, which resulted in what seemed to him to be endless hours of sitting around, finally prompted him to seek something more exciting, perhaps never having shaken the peculiar hold of wartime experience. He became a firefighter for the city of Baltimore, a decision that did not thrill his wife, Ginny, and certainly did no wonders for the family finances.

Shortly after taking his new job, Jack also decided to register to vote, which he did, listing himself as a Republican. The City Hall clerk, reviewing the registration form, said there must be some mistake because Jack was a city employee, and yet he had registered Republican rather than Democrat. When my father said there was no mistake, the clerk explained to him again that city employees registered as Democrats, which my father was still not buying. The story of my father's response undoubtedly grew with the telling over the years, but suffice it to say that Jack registered as an Independent, and no fried eggs were dropped on the clerk's shoes, or worse.

Jack loved being a firefighter, was a good union man, became a shop steward, and held other union offices over the years, attending conventions in what for us were exotic places like Puerto Rico. Make no mistake, he was not a "fireman"; they were the people who shoveled coal into locomotive engines, which was not his job. Although he was probably unaware of Calvin Coolidge's suppression of the Boston police strike of 1919, Jack would have absolutely agreed with Coolidge's admonition that "there is no right to strike against the public safety by anybody, anywhere, anytime." Although we all felt that firefighter and police salaries were too low, it was inconceivable to my father that he would ever go out on strike and leave Baltimore's citizens at risk. When it became fashionable in the 1960s for teachers to strike, he deeply resented it, considering them spoiled for having gone to college and having cushy jobs, which they certainly were compared to his.

We lived for most of my young life, joined by my sister Joni Rae in 1957, in a southwest Baltimore row-house development called "Yale Heights," just off Yale Avenue, complete with a small baseball field: "Yale Bowl." Psychologists, I guess, can use this to explain my later disinclination to attend Princeton or Harvard. We lived next to a policeman and his family on one side, and a machinist at Westinghouse on the other. Nearby were roofers, bartenders and waitresses, stevedores, and even a few people who worked in offices. To me, Baltimore was a city of industry and manufacturing. I faithfully watched a weekend television program called *The Port That Built a City,* hosted by Helen Delich Bentley, a newspaper reporter and later a Republican congresswoman, soaking up its explanation of Baltimore's trading and seafaring connections with the wider world. The city had benefited greatly from institutions like the Enoch Pratt Free Libraries (which I frequented), the Walters Art Gallery, and the Peabody Conservatory, all created by far-seeing individuals, not by the government.

Whereas Jack was naturally a quiet man, who generally kept his opinions to himself, except when agitated by government officials, Ginny was not a quiet woman. She explained to me that she had been a socialist in her Delaware youth. That notwithstanding, attractive blonde that she was, she'd also dated du Ponts. Ginny decided that I was not going to be educated forever in Baltimore public schools, which she regarded as inadequate, and she focused on getting me into McDonogh, one of Maryland's most prestigious private schools, in Reisterstown, just outside Baltimore.

As a sixth grader, I sat for the McDonogh scholarship examination, an event so prominent in Maryland at the time that it was advertised on Baltimore television stations. McDonogh then had an eight-hundred-acre campus, luxurious by my standards, and quite a change from city life. I found the day-long exam somewhat lonely and intimidating, but I passed that round and was called in for interviews. My parents were interviewed as well, which wasn't pleasant for Jack, but Ginny was more than happy for an opportunity to sing my praises. My father worked two jobs at the time in order to earn enough income for an adequate living. After fighting fires on the night shift, and working at his machinist's job during the day, he was not usually in a talkative mood. Our interviews apparently went well, and I was accepted into the seventh grade on scholarship. I spent the next six years at McDonogh as a boarding student, which all scholarship students were at the time, coming home on weekends and for vacations. That's why being allowed out of school on Election Day 1964 was so special. Not only was I skipping class, I was off campus on a weekday!

McDonogh had been founded with the legacy of John McDonogh, a Baltimore native who had made a fortune in pre–Civil War New Orleans, and who had divided his wealth between the two cities for the education of the poor. New Orleans used its share to create its public school system, but Baltimore, which already had public schools, and was starting to benefit from the contributions of Pratt, Walters, and Peabody, founded McDonogh in 1873 for orphan boys. So successful was the school that the wealthy wanted their own sons to attend, and paying students were later admitted. By the time I attended, the graduating classes were just under a hundred boys. Typically, between fifteen and twenty boys were on scholarship. McDonogh was a "semimilitary" school, which meant we all wore uniforms and did our share of drilling, but it was not a "military academy" of the southern sort. Two successive headmasters named Lamborn, father and son, were Quakers, and the uniforms originated at McDonogh's founding when the students didn't arrive with many clothes. Over the years, the uniforms had mitigated the disparity between the sons of the wealthy and those of us on scholarship because there was no opportunity for competition in clothes or other ostentatiousness, as at many other schools. Competition was in the schoolroom, on the athletic fields, and in extracurricular activities, and it was intense.

Indeed, the competition was sufficiently intense that it enabled me to get into Yale College, where I started in the fall of 1966, still on scholarship. I traveled to New Haven on a Trailways bus because the ever-benevolent Baltimore government would not let my father have the time off to drive me there himself. Yale was also intense, especially in the late 1960s when anti–Vietnam War sentiment was growing around the country. I was just as much of a libertarian conservative at Yale as I had been in 1964, and given the prevailing campus political attitudes, I might as well have been a space alien. By senior year, students at Yale and elsewhere had decided that "striking" by not attending classes was an effective way to protest whatever was the flavor-of-the-day political issue. I didn't understand or approve of students' striking any more than my father had liked teachers' striking, and I especially resented the sons and daughters of the wealthy, of whom there were many, telling me that I was supposed to, in effect, forfeit my scholarship. I had an education to get, and the protesters could damn well get out of my way as I walked to class.

Yale was filled with extracurricular activities, and I spent a lot of time in the Yale Political Union and the Connecticut Inter-Collegiate Student Legislature (CISL). The Political Union, founded in the 1930s, was modeled after the Oxford and Cambridge Unions and brought in prominent speakers and held debates during the school year. I joined the Conservative Party and found the opportunity to listen to Republicans from "outside" a welcome relief from Yale's relentless, smug, self-satisfied liberalism. The highlight for me was a debate between William F. Buckley, Jr., and Yale's chaplain, William Sloan Coffin, on the proposition "Resolved: that government has an obligation to promote equality as well as preserve liberty." Buckley argued the negative, and cleaned the floor with Coffin, although I have to admit that Coffin had the best line of the evening. As he started, Coffin noted that he had been in Yale's Class of 1949, and Buckley in the Class of 1950. "Back then," said Coffin, "Bill was only a year behind me." After graduation, at the start of the Cold War, both Buckley and Coffin had joined the CIA. Those were the days.

The Political Union did have its more frivolous moments. One issue that consumed Yale in the late sixties was whether the college, all male since its founding in 1701, should become coeducational. This debate may have been more intense than the debate over the Vietnam War, although I doubt the antiwar students would ever admit it, because the outcome could have a profound and immediate impact on our lives. I was against coeducation, thinking instead that Vassar should move to New Haven from Poughkeepsie and join with Yale. Many questioned whether Vassar was up to Yale's academic standards and I suppose at Vassar they had similar concerns. In time, the Political Union addressed this momentous question in a debate on the proposition "Resolved: that in any Vassar-Yale merger, Yale men will always come out on top." In an unusual display of open-mindedness (or perhaps with other motives), the Yalies invited Vassar girls to participate in the debate, which drew an especially large crowd at the Political Union's house on fraternity row. One Vassar girl, who said her name was Ophelia Bust, surprisingly argued the affirmative of the proposition, basically on the grounds that Yalies had no imagination. I forget who won the debate, but Vassar kept its daisy chains in Poughkeepsie, and Yale went coed in 1969, making my Class of 1970 the last all-male class to graduate from Yale College.

CISL was a training ground in political maneuvers. Delegates from about twenty Connecticut colleges and universities met every spring in Hartford, the state capital, to pretend they were the two houses of the legislature. The Yale delegation drew largely from the Political Union, across the ideological spectrum. Unlike Union debates, which were about philosophy and policy, our CISL activities were strictly about getting our candidates and those of our allies elected to key offices. I was ultimately the head of the Yale delegation, and was elected Speaker of the House in 1970, a peculiarity, to say the least, when many college campuses, Yale's included, were beset with protest movements.

Like many Yale institutions, CISL had its own difficulties with coeducation. Our delegation meetings were usually pretty boisterous, with no-holds arguing, unlike the more decorous Political Union. One of our traditions was that a delegation member who had made a political mistake had to raise his arms to the heavens in front of the delegation and plead in a loud voice "give me shit," which the rest of us were happy to do. Our politics were no holds barred as well, as we conspired to build coalitions with other schools to achieve our objectives. We had "seduction squads" to deal with recalcitrant girls' schools, we bargained relentlessly over political deals, and we were expert at sharp parliamentary practices. In a House committee meeting in Hartford, I once had the contents of an entire bill deleted and replaced without a vote as a "typographical error." In preparation for our first delegation meeting with new Yalies in 1969, I called a preliminary meeting of the returning delegates, where we vowed to be a little more refined than usual, so that we wouldn't deter potential female delegation members. When the first regular delegation meeting ended, I knew we had succeeded because one of the girls came up to me afterward and said she knew we were trying to be on our best behavior, which she and the other girls appreciated. Nonetheless, she continued, we were all Yalies now, and we should simply be ourselves. The CISL veterans internalized that advice, and followed it at the next delegation meeting. None of the girls returned after that.

The Vietnam War eventually consumed Yale, as it did the entire country. In New Haven in spring 1970, we also faced the trial of Bobby Seale, a Black Panther accused of murdering Alex Rackley, another Panther.

Rackley's body was found in a swamp near New Haven, his body covered with scars from stubbed-out cigarettes and scalding water poured over him before he died. Thousands of radical protesters and their hangers-on, including the Chicago Seven's Abbie Hoffman, converged on New Haven to shut Yale down. I felt that all of this activity, which grew more and more intellectually and, at times, physically coercive, was completely contrary to the community of free expression that a university should be. At "town hall" meetings in Calhoun College, my residential college, I argued to the liberal Yale faculty that this intolerant radicalism posed an even greater challenge to intellectual freedom than the hated Joe McCarthy in the 1950s. Then, at least, the threat came from outside the university; this time, the barbarians were inside the gates. Some of the deeply unsettled faculty liberals, who seemed overwhelmed by the scorn and hostility from the generation they had spawned intellectually, responded favorably to my arguments, but most students simply swept them aside.

Apart from the particular issue of Vietnam, the incessant politicization of every aspect of Yale life was the most dangerous consequence of the late sixties. This really was the American version of China's "Cultural Revolution." Not as damaging as China's, it was still pernicious intellectually, with consequences that continue to damage the fabric of American society as the baby boom generation has aged, but too often not matured. One example was at our Class Day exercise, a traditional part of Yale's graduation ritual. In 1970, our Class "leaders" decided that Class Day would be all about Vietnam, rather than about graduation, which I didn't like at all. I liked it even less when I saw the list of speakers, all of whom were from the far left. I protested this imbalance to the organizers, who replied snippily that their program was balanced, because a student who supported Hubert Humphrey for president in 1968 would represent the conservative side.

That was the last straw. These rich kids might enjoy perverting Class Day, but my mother and firefighter father were not coming to their son's graduation for a political seminar. I shoehorned my way into the Class Day program, determined to have my say, at least to the Class of 1970's parents, if not to the students. Class Day, like graduation, is held on Yale's Old Campus where we had all lived as freshmen, before departing to our residential colleges for the last three years of college life. There were thousands of people present, the largest audience I had addressed, and as I started my few minutes of remarks, I was greeted by hecklers, the only speaker so graced. I had faced this sort of thing many times from the liberals at Yale, who saw themselves as brave and oppressed dissenters from U.S. national policy, but who couldn't stand encountering dissent in their own little sandbox. "What you have over there," I said, pointing to the hecklers, "is a typical example of liberal 'tolerance.'" This very Class Day program, I went on, was "a typical example of liberal self-congratulation," and I called for "an end to the politics of this weekend and a return to the joy and happiness that commencement is supposed to be." I assured everyone that "the conservative underground is alive and well here; if we do not make our influence felt, rest assured we will in the real world." I received a nice reception from the parents, and mostly silence from my classmates. Par for the course.[2] Both my mother and my father lived until the mid-1990s, but I never had any doubt they thought my graduating from Yale justified all of the hardships they had been through.

Before graduation, I joined the Maryland National Guard, finding a position by driving from armory to armory in the Baltimore area and signing up on waiting lists until a slot opened up. I had concluded that the Vietnam War was lost, and I made the cold calculation that I wasn't going to waste time on a futile struggle. Dying for your country was one thing, but dying to gain territory that antiwar forces in Congress would simply return to the enemy seemed ludicrous to me. Looking back, I am not terribly proud of this calculation, but my World War II veteran father, who still risked his life daily for his fellow citizens as a firefighter, approved of it, and that was good enough for me.

I graduated *summa cum laude,* and was elected to Phi Beta Kappa in December of my senior year. I especially liked the Phi Beta Kappa certificate, which read "for excellence in liberal scholarship," where the word "liberal" clearly meant the free and open search for knowledge so threatened by the intolerance of the late sixties student radicals. I also assigned it a secret meaning, showing that I had beaten Yale's liberals at their own game. I was an "intensive" major in political science, and the main requirement was writing a senior essay, mine being on international relations. My opus (376 pages), on decision-making in the British, French, and American governments during the 1956 Suez Crisis, was sufficiently interesting to others

---

2. *Yale Alumni Magazine,* July 1970, pp. 27–28.

that it won Yale's James Gordon Bennett Prize for the year's best essay in international relations.

I went on active duty for training to Fort Polk, Louisiana, where I spent eighteen weeks from July to November 1970. The highlight was on election night 1970, after taps, when I listened illegally to the returns on a static-filled transistor radio. In between detailed reports of various liquor-by-the-drink referenda in East Texas were national results, including the startling news that Jim Buckley had been elected senator from New York on the Conservative Party line. His more famous brother Bill had run for mayor of New York in 1965 as a Conservative, winning all of about 14 percent of the vote, but after the Goldwater defeat of 1964, Buckley's mayoral campaign, quixotic though it was, had been a welcome relief. Now, however, in 1970, we had his older brother in the Senate, and that promised real conservative intellectual force at the national level.

All of my academic glories were enough to get me into Yale Law School, where I started in 1971. Ironically, this small professional school had more conservative faculty members—three to be precise—than all of Yale College. I studied antitrust under Robert Bork, whose then-scorned law-and-economics theories are now the predominant source of antitrust law, an intellectual triumph of stunning proportions in an amazingly short time. I took courses from Ward Bowman, another Chicago School member, and the first tenured professor at any major American law school who was not a lawyer. I was also a research assistant for, and student of, Ralph Winter, later chief judge of the Second Circuit Court of Appeals, yet another member of the law-and-economics school. Only one other student and I considered ourselves real conservatives, although our classmate and good friend, Clarence Thomas, now an outstanding Supreme Court justice, later more than qualified. So few were our numbers that when Bork was named solicitor general, Ralph Winter said the *Yale Daily News* lead should be, "Yesterday, President Nixon nominated 20 percent of all of the conservatives at Yale Law School to be solicitor general." I also took constitutional law from Alexander Bickel, which affected me deeply, but Bickel was still a New Deal liberal, not a libertarian as Winter, Bowman, and Bork were at the time. I was never a "big government" conservative, not then, and not now. Both Bill and Hillary Clinton were also then at Yale Law School, but I didn't run in their circles.

While slogging through law school, I spent the summer of 1972 as a

White House intern for Vice President Spiro Agnew, Maryland's former Republican governor, a political anomaly right there. I had been attracted to Agnew because of his criticism of the Legal Services Program, about which Steve Holzer (the other conservative Yale Law student) and I were writing a Note for the *Yale Law Journal*.[3] In many respects, my job options for that summer represented a career high point, since I had three ideal offers: to go with Agnew, to be Alexander Bickel's research assistant, or to be an intern at Buckley's *National Review*. Showing that my political judgment remained as unerring as when I predicted that Goldwater might win the 1964 election, I chose Agnew, but I never regretted it. He was a kind and humorous man, a real middle American, for all that he was bound up in the Maryland political culture that eventually led to his downfall.

My major activity that summer was working to defeat a proposal by what was left of the liberal wing of the Republican Party to change the formula that allocated delegates among the states at the national nominating conventions. Historically, delegation size was based on Electoral College voting strength, with bonuses for states carried by the preceding GOP presidential candidate. The Ripon Society wanted to award convention delegates based only on each state's percentage of the national popular vote. Ripon's formula would enhance the influence of populous states such as New York and Pennsylvania in selecting presidential candidates, even though their electoral votes were most likely to be cast for Democratic nominees.

To most conservatives, the Ripon plan was political suicide, but the liberals hoped to prevail at the Miami convention, by persuading Governor Ronald Reagan to side with them. A big state like California would benefit proportionately from their approach, but Reagan was shrewd enough to see that the broader effect would be to dilute conservative strength in the national party. He kept California aligned with the western and southern states, and the Ripon plan was defeated. After the final vote, I went out to celebrate with Dave Keene, the former chairman of Young Americans for Freedom who had hired me as an Agnew intern. As we were leaving our hotel, we got on the same elevator as Frank Sinatra and his guards. Sinatra asked about us, and when we said we worked for Agnew, one of his great

---

3. Note, "Legal Services and Landlord-Tenant Litigation: A Critical Analysis," 82 *Yale Law Journal* 1495 (1973).

buddies, that was all he needed to hear to invite us to have a beer with him at the hotel bar. As part of the Sinatra entourage, we were whisked right up to the bar, where the three of us each ordered a Budweiser. We did not have an extended conversation with Sinatra, however, because every female in the place rapidly elbowed us aside.

After surviving law school, I became an associate at Covington & Burling, then the largest and one of the most prestigious law firms in Washington. I yearned to join the Nixon administration full-time, but Ralph Winter had wisely advised me to go into private practice first, become a partner in a law firm, and then go into politics. His advice proved exactly right, as first Agnew and then Nixon were forced to resign in disgrace, Nixon just days after I started at C&B in August 1974. Then Ford lost the 1976 election to Carter. Had I been a political appointee in the government, I would have been looking for a job. Having followed Winter's advice, I was happily ensconced making money as a lawyer and was well situated to endure the long night of the Carter administration.

In fact, I had the best of both worlds, since I spent a large part of 1974–76 working on *Buckley* v. *Valeo*,[4] challenging the constitutionality of every major provision of the post-Watergate campaign-finance "reform" legislation. Overreacting to Watergate, as in other laws such as the War Powers Act and the Independent Counsel statute, Congress had set strict contribution and expenditure limits on federal campaigns; tried to limit drastically "independent expenditures" separate from campaigns; imposed sweeping reporting and disclosure requirements; created a system of public financing for presidential elections; and established a new regulatory body, the Federal Election Commission, to oversee the law. Ralph Winter had already written extensively about why this entire construct violated the First Amendment's protection of freedom of speech, and we initially hoped President Ford would veto the legislation. Given the weakened state of the Ford presidency and the overwhelming pressure to "reform," that proved impossible.

Instead, Jim Buckley, on whose Senate staff Dave Keene, my friend from the Agnew internship, worked, decided to challenge the statute's constitutionality, and enlisted Ralph Winter as the lead counsel. I persuaded Covington & Burling to take the case *pro bono*, and we set off assembling a

---

4. 424 U.S. 1 (1976).

broad coalition of plaintiffs to help demonstrate the law's unfairness as well as its unconstitutionality. Keene had already lined up the New York Civil Liberties Union, which had challenged other statutes purporting to limit independent expenditures, and which probably didn't agree with Buckley on much of anything else. Eugene McCarthy, who had campaigned for the 1968 Democratic presidential nomination as a Vietnam War opponent, and who was running again for president in 1976 as an independent, also joined. McCarthy challenged both the contribution and expenditure limits, which he knew from his own experience could cripple a dissident political campaign before it could even get started, and he opposed the public funding for presidential campaigns because of the overwhelming advantage such subsidies provided to the two major parties, to the detriment of independent and third-party candidates. Although I had obviously not agreed with McCarthy in 1968, I grew to admire him immensely for his candor and integrity. He liked to say that the word "reform" should be banished from the English language because it meant everything and therefore nothing, which sounded right to me.

Everyone knew the decision in *Buckley* v. *Valeo* could determine the election in 1976, not to mention the future shape of American politics. Buckley had inserted into the legislation a special provision for expedited judicial review of constitutional challenges, precisely to help facilitate an early answer, one way or another, to avoid the potentially catastrophic consequences of a decision in the middle of the campaign. Ralph and I personally went to federal district court in Washington to file the case on January 2, 1975, the first business day after the new law's effective date, where it received docket number 75-0001. We were off. Predictably, we were wiped out in the D.C. circuit, where the judges' liberal instincts prevailed, and we appealed almost the entire decision to the Supreme Court.

There, the Court held a nearly unprecedented four hours of oral argument, rather than the one hour most cases received. Ralph argued against limits on contributions and expenditures, including limits on independent expenditures, fittingly, since he conceived the First Amendment theories underlying our arguments. Opposite him on these issues was Harvard law professor Archibald Cox, former special prosecutor and the very embodiment of the "reform" cause. Under President Nixon's orders, and after Attorney General Elliott Richardson and Deputy Attorney General Bill Ruckelshaus had resigned, Solicitor General Bork had fired Cox in the

"Saturday Night Massacre." Little known then or now, Richardson and Ruckelshaus felt they had to resign, having committed to do so in their confirmation hearings if they saw any White House interference in Cox's investigations. Bork had been confirmed before Watergate was an issue, and had made no such commitment. All three knew that if Bork resigned, the rest of the Justice Department might go, too, provoking an even more serious constitutional crisis. In a pivotal meeting, Richardson said, "You've got the gun now, Bob. It's your duty to pull the trigger." Bork did so to his detriment, as the controversy made Ford afraid to nominate him to the Supreme Court. Instead, Ford selected John Paul Stevens, another Republican mistake that perpetuated our inability to get a sound Supreme Court majority.

For Ralph and me, therefore, Cox had special meaning. Moreover, since this was Ralph's first Supreme Court argument, I wanted him to be relaxed and his usual jovial self. Just before he rose to begin his argument, I slipped him a note that said, "Go Yale! Beat Harvard!" It must have worked because Ralph was superb. The Supreme Court's decision, in January 1976, was mixed, striking down as unconstitutional the expenditure limits and limits on independent expenditures but upholding contribution limits and public financing. Significantly, the Court also struck down the Federal Election Commission, accepting our argument that vesting the appointment of four of its six voting members in Congress violated the separation of powers doctrine (and laying the basis for a later decision that invalidated the legislative veto). We hoped that by hacking away large portions of the statute, we had made the rest unworkable, but Congress quickly responded by recreating the FEC in a constitutional way, and the still-weakened president Ford signed it into law. Legal scholars will continue to debate for decades who won and who lost in *Buckley,* but the Supreme Court itself gave its interpretation by ruling that the parties defending the statute had to split fifty-fifty the cost of preparing the record for appeal, which we had initially borne as appellants. That satisfied us, although having the entire sloppy statute declared unconstitutional would have satisfied us more. Ralph later asked me, "How does it feel that your first case was the biggest case you'll ever have?" It was a good question, and one that I never resolved satisfactorily. Truly, after *Buckley,* it was hard to get as excited about anything else in litigation.

Sadly, Jim Buckley lost in 1976 to Daniel Patrick Moynihan, largely because of the attention and publicity Moynihan justifiably attracted as ambassador to the United Nations. In particular, Moynihan had led our unsuccessful effort against the General Assembly's 1975 resolution equating Zionism with racism. He had famously torn up the resolution at the General Assembly podium, declaring, "The United States ... does not acknowledge, it will not abide by, it will never acquiesce in this infamous act." Running in heavily Democratic New York, that was all Moynihan needed to overwhelm Buckley. *National Review* had named Moynihan as its first "man of the year" in 1975, but ended the award in 1976, fearing it had already caused enough trouble. I was despondent on Buckley's behalf, but had no inkling that my path would later cross Moynihan's.

Although I attended the 1976 Republican Convention in Kansas City, hoping that Reagan could seize the nomination from President Ford, it was not to be. Watergate gave the November election to Carter, but proved the wisdom of Ralph's advice: As long as we were in the political wasteland, I might as well pursue my legal career. For the next several years, I immersed myself in private practice and had some interesting times, such as a Supreme Court case involving New York City's decision to declare Grand Central Station a landmark.[5] The Penn Central bankruptcy trustees wanted to construct an office tower above it, which was not as outrageous a plan as many thought. The architects had contemplated an office tower in the terminal's original design, and the building's architectural structure could accommodate the large tower the Penn Central wanted without significant change.

Nonetheless, as in *Buckley*, this was another case where the High Minded were on the other side, although this time it was not Archibald Cox but Jackie Kennedy Onassis who was the center of attention. We had not handled the case in the lower courts, but the Penn Central asked Dan Gribbon, Covington's preeminent litigator, to take the appeal to the Supremes, and he in turn asked me to work with him. I thought we had an excellent argument under the Fifth Amendment's Takings Clause, but we lost 6–3 in the Supreme Court. During my later residence as UN ambassador in the Waldorf-Astoria Hotel, just down the street from Grand Central, I walked or drove near the terminal almost every day. Constitutional questions aside, I still think it would look better with an office tower above it.

---

5. *Penn Central Transportation Co.* v. *City of New York*, 438 U.S. 104 (1978).

CHAPTER TWO

THE REAGAN REVOLUTION AND THE BUSH 41 THERMIDOR

Be always sure you're right—THEN GO AHEAD.

—Davy Crockett, 1831[1]

As the Carter administration careened erratically along, I hoped again, as in 1976, for the nomination of Ronald Reagan to lead us out of the wilderness. During most of 1980, I was engaged in a major case representing the Kerr-McGee Corporation in a dispute over the pricing of nuclear fuel Kerr-McGee had contracted to sell to a number of Ohio and Pennsylvania utilities, a case that was in trial in Oklahoma City by election night 1980. I arrived late at a small gathering of friends, and by that time, even the liberal commentators could not conceal that Reagan was winning by a landslide.

Many times that evening, I thought about 1964 and Goldwater's defeat. Almost certainly, Reagan would not have won had Goldwater not shown the courage of his convictions by running in 1964, so soon after the Kennedy assassination that no Republican could hope to win. Goldwater had been willing to suffer the opprobrium heaped upon him, not just in opposition to his policies but personally as well, probably knowing from the very beginning of his campaign he had almost no chance of winning. In a

---

1. Quoted in William C. David, *Three Roads to the Alamo: The Lives and Fortunes of David Crockett, James Bowie, and William Barret Travis* (New York: HarperCollins, 1998), p. 313.

real sense, Reagan's victory in 1980 was Goldwater's as well. Although Goldwater had been scorned and derided, Reagan brought the contemporary equivalent of his foreign and domestic policies back from the wilderness. The Reagan administration would force the final confrontation with, and victory over, Communism, and by enacting massive tax cuts, would preclude the growth of government at the federal level that had been almost uninterrupted since the New Deal. This truly was a revolution, and all conservatives knew it. So did the liberals, when they dared to state the obvious.

So exhilarating was Reagan's win that I abandoned Ralph Winter's advice and decided to try to join the Reagan administration. I had been at Covington six and a half years, just eighteen months away from the firm's critical decision whether to make me a partner, but I wasn't about to miss the fun. As I said to one uncomprehending liberal partner, "Now I know how the Democrats felt in 1932!" Nonetheless, getting a political appointment in an incoming administration is always "an experience." Among other things I did in 1980 was to contact Jim Baker, whom I first met in 1978 when he ran unsuccessfully for attorney general of Texas. Several friends were working on that campaign, and they came to me with a question of Texas election law. After *Buckley* v. *Valeo,* I was building a small election law practice, and they thought I might be able to lend a hand. I met Baker again through Dave Keene, who had worked with Baker on George H. W. Bush's campaign for the 1980 Republican presidential nomination, and after the election, Reagan had named Baker to be his White House chief of staff. Baker was never a favorite on the right because he was seen as a "pragmatist" rather than a true "Reaganaut." I always thought, however, that his political instincts were correct, trying to maximize the yield in any given battle, rather than just opining about it, however satisfying opining might be. One of Baker's soundest pieces of political advice was, "Keep your eyes on the prize," which is frequently harder to do than it sounds.

Baker urged me to join the White House Counsel's office after the inauguration, which I was glad to do, having worked with the Transition Team after returning from Oklahoma. Baker wanted me to stay with Fred Fielding, the incoming counsel, as did Fielding, but I was lured away by Peter McPherson, counsel to the Transition Team and acting White House counsel in the hectic days right after the inauguration. Being on the White House staff was fun, but I wanted "line" responsibility, to manage something and to change it, not simply to be "staff," even at the White House. Fielding gently explained to me that everyone except the president himself was "staff," wherever we served, which I see in retrospect to be correct, although I didn't at the time. Instead, I accompanied McPherson to the Agency for International Development (AID), our main program of bilateral foreign economic assistance, in effect the descendant of the Marshall Plan. I was first general counsel, and then assistant administrator for program and policy coordination, the number-three job at AID. It was my first presidential appointment.

I was attracted to AID because it involved both U.S. foreign policy and domestic policy in the recipient countries. Our goal was to make AID's programs more market-driven, to induce recipient countries to foster private enterprise, and to turn AID away from a welfare-oriented approach known as "basic human needs." This rubric disguised a belief that poverty in developing countries was caused by a lack of resources and that poverty could be overcome by developed countries' transferring the missing resources. I regarded this as essentially backward: The creation of wealth by developing countries was the long-term cure to their poverty, which they could accomplish by market-oriented policies that rewarded rather than penalized domestic and foreign trade and investment. Simply transferring resources to countries that pursued misguided economic policies was only a prescription for waste and frustration. However good it made the High Minded feel, it wasn't going to eliminate Third World poverty. While at AID, I first worked with Cary Weil (later Barnett), Matthew Freedman, and Sarah Tinsley, all of whom were to rejoin me much later in the George W. Bush administration, and Michelle Laxalt, who remained a close friend and political adviser, especially in my subsequent confirmation battles.

Early on, we made a key point by returning to the U.S. Treasury $28 million that was obtained by canceling AID projects around the world that were failing. This was not a huge amount of money in Washington, but it was a shock to a government culture of spending that *never* returned money to the Treasury. We made up a big check, like the ones seen on game shows, and convinced Jim Baker that Peter McPherson should present it to Reagan in a Rose Garden ceremony. On a hot August afternoon in 1981, McPherson made the presentation, which Reagan obviously loved. After receiving the check, Reagan said, "Anyone who's familiar with the Washington scene—as so many of you are—knows that it is far more normal at this stage of the fiscal year, only a couple months to go, that anyone that finds $28 million unspent in their department says to everyone, 'Rush out and buy new furniture or do something. We must spend this money before the end of the fiscal year.' Twenty-eight million dollars—I can't wait to hand this to Don Regan." Although we made only a start in the 1980s at AID, the collapse of Communism seemed to show that proliberty, promarket forces essentially won the debate. I believed that until, in August 2005, I arrived in New York, where I saw that, in the UN's Twilight Zone, we were still in the 1980s, if not before, on economic policy.

While I was at AID in late 1981, I had my first professional contact with the UN system, when McPherson asked me to lead the U.S. team for the second "replenishment" of the International Fund for Agricultural Development (IFAD). Founded in 1977, IFAD was Henry Kissinger's brainchild, a way to recycle OPEC (Organization of Petroleum Exporting Countries) petrodollars into Third World economic development, thus in part relieving U.S. budgets strained by the Vietnam War. The original concept was that OPEC members collectively would pledge half of IFAD's resources and the world's industrial democracies (the members of the Organization for Economic Cooperation and Development, OECD) would pledge the other half. IFAD in turn would make grants and highly concessional loans to developing countries to help alleviate rural poverty. As it turned out, however, both in IFAD's original funding and in the first "replenishment" in the late 1970s, OPEC's commitments failed to equal the OECD's pledges. For the new Republican Senate, getting OPEC back to a fifty-fifty share was a high priority.

The endless hours I spent working on IFAD's second replenishment taught me a lot about the workings of international organizations. For example, countries with which the United States has close bilateral relations are not always helpful in such bodies. El Salvador, for one, was very critical of the "insufficient" U.S. pledge to the replenishment. I thought it was pretty cheeky of Salvador to turn around and bite our ankles at IFAD when we were providing enormous military and economic aid to help it fend off a vigorous, Cuban-backed Communist insurgency, but I came to see this was just business as usual at the UN. I also thought the rhetoric of other countries was a little extreme. Mali was also not happy with our replenishment pledge, and at one point took the Governing Council floor to say that its meagerness amounted "to killing the poor people of the world." Veteran

European diplomats took all of this in stride—especially when the criticism was directed against the United States rather than themselves—but I never got used to it. I never understood why the United States was expected to be a well-bred doormat.

I left USAID in the summer of 1983, tired of beating my head against the wall. I returned to Covington & Burling as a partner, and to be executive director of the 1984 Republican Platform Committee, chaired by Trent Lott, then the House Republican whip. The platform was a fascinating task, allowing me to attend my third Republican Convention, this one in Dallas. From outside the government, I garnered more insights into the tenacity of bureaucracies defending their policies. While one might expect the executive branch's "political" leadership to enthusiastically support the platform in order to carry forward unfinished elements of the Reagan Revolution, almost the exact opposite was true. Even loyal political appointees worked to shape a platform that would endorse what they had done in the first term, regardless of whether those efforts conformed to Reagan's 1980 campaign promises. I found this phenomenon very discouraging, as it demonstrated the power of bureaucracy to co-opt, over a relatively short period, even ardent political appointees to the bureaucracy's own agenda. This was disappointing not only as a matter of philosophy, but also in its implications for democratic theory: Voters might think they were voting for change, but the prevailing reality of bureaucratic stasis meant that change was not really being delivered, and perhaps could *not* be delivered without superhuman effort. That was depressing.

One of the highlights of the 1984 Republican Convention was UN ambassador Jeane Kirkpatrick's speech, which I listened to from the convention floor. During most of the pro forma sessions before the presidential nomination and acceptance speech, the convention delegates and alternates are often doing something other than paying attention. In Jeane's case, however, everyone on the convention floor was listening, and listening carefully, as she explained how the Democratic Party had left her and many others in its rush to the left, and how she became a Reaganaut. Two of her lines in particular have gone into the history books: her characterization of the foreign policy follies of "the San Francisco Democrats" (where they held their 1984 convention), and her telling criticism, "They always blame America first." This was good stuff, and later helped inspire a "Draft Kirkpatrick" movement for the 1988 presidential nomination.

The Reagan Justice Department

With Reagan's subsequent landslide election to a second term in 1984 effectively reversing Goldwater's defeat twenty years earlier, Ed Meese moved from the White House to become attorney general and asked me to join the Department of Justice as assistant attorney general for legislative affairs. This turned out to be an arduous proposition, in part because of the massive Senate Democratic assault against Meese and his personal integrity, as they tried to block his confirmation immediately after Reagan nominated him on January 3, 1984. Meese, a long-time Reagan confidant and adviser, going back to Reagan's days as California governor, was White House counselor in the first term, a position expressly created for Meese, as one of the troika (along with Jim Baker and Mike Deaver) of aides closest to Reagan. Conservatives saw Meese as the "keeper of the sacred scrolls," the linchpin of philosophical fidelity at the White House, and Senate liberals targeted him for exactly that reason.

Although Meese was ultimately confirmed on February 6, 1985, the long battle delayed all the other personnel changes that inevitably follow from the selection of a new cabinet officer. The ripple effect, combined with continued opposition to some of the nominees in the Senate, dragged the process out even longer, but, finally, most of the rest of us were confirmed easily late in 1985, and I started at Justice in December. Although I certainly hadn't planned to change every major aspect of my life simultaneously, I also married Gretchen Smith Brainerd on January 24, 1986. She was the Washington chief of mission of the International Committee for Migration (ICM), a non-UN body dealing with migration issues, founded after World War II to help resettle Jewish Holocaust survivors and other displaced Europeans, including those fleeing Communism. ICM's relatively small membership, and the absence of Soviet-bloc members, made it far more effective than many UN agencies, and I used to joke that its only Communist member was Nicaragua. Both of us had been married before, and divorced, and neither of us had children from these prior marriages.

My first "official" act after being sworn in was to send a letter congratulating Jim Buckley, who had been confirmed at the same time to be a judge on the D.C. circuit. Not only was this a justly deserved appointment for Buckley, it was also a sweet revenge against those on the D.C. circuit who had savaged our constitutional case against the campaign "reform" laws ten years earlier. Buckley became part of Reagan's most important domestic achievement, a fundamental reshaping of the American judiciary.

In fact, it was the Reagan judicial nominations on which I spent the bulk of my time at Justice. Many nominees encountered little or no opposition, largely because of long-standing senatorial courtesies for nominees to federal district courts, who were as much picked by Republican senators from the states in question as by the president. Where there were no Republican senators, Reagan had more leeway, but in every case Justice lawyers carefully screened potential nominees philosophically. Reagan declared a new policy for federal appellate judgeships, considerably reducing the senatorial role in the selection process. This caused some initial political turmoil, which subsided as Reagan's determination to assert presidential prerogatives became clear. As more and more federal judges became Reagan appointees, however, Democratic scrutiny grew more intense, and the level of political combat in the Senate intensified.

The big event in Reagan's second term was the expected Supreme Court nominations, and the first arrived when Chief Justice Warren Burger announced his retirement. Reagan decided to elevate Associate Justice William Rehnquist to the chief's job, and in turn nominated D.C. circuit judge Antonin Scalia to the slot opened by Rehnquist's move. This was a truly epic battle, more like a political campaign than the "world's greatest deliberative body" deliberating, but that's what the confirmation process had become. There were several days of hearings, including long discussions about opinions written by Rehnquist when he was assistant attorney general for the Office of Legal Counsel (OLC) in the Nixon administration, before his 1971 nomination as an associate justice. We argued repeatedly that this questioning was overtaken by Rehnquist's fifteen years on the Court, and that if it was appropriate to question him on his days at Justice, that opportunity had arisen in 1971, not fifteen years later. Nonetheless, the opponents were determined to bury Rehnquist, whatever way possible.

The hearings took a potentially dispositive turn when Democrats Kennedy and Metzenbaum demanded access to Rehnquist's Office of Legal Counsel opinions. The current head of OLC, Chuck Cooper, a former Rehnquist law clerk, was also a strong believer in defending executive prerogatives. The idea of turning over files from the office known as "the president's lawyer's lawyer" naturally aroused his intense opposition, as it did for all of us at Justice. Although we sought ways to avoid a confrontation with the Democrats, in some ways both sides wanted a fight. Rehnquist's opponents knew they had us in a tight spot, and were in effect forcing us to choose which we cared about more: getting Rehnquist confirmed or protecting the OLC documents.

Our side wanted to assert "executive privilege," as part of the overall effort to repair the damage to the executive branch caused by the combined ravages of Watergate and the anti-Vietnam protests of the 1970s, so the battle was joined. Executive privilege, a doctrine originated by George Washington, protects the confidentiality of communications among the president and his top aides, so that the president receives the fullest range of advice, and his staff is not chilled by the prospect of having the political opposition second-guess them. Of course, our opponents relished the opportunity to paint us all as a bunch of Nixonian stooges, who were back in the days of Watergate cover-ups. It wasn't easy to explain the Constitution in a "debate" that resembled street fighting.

One of our key decisions was how actually to assert executive privilege, in part because we didn't want this struggle to drag out forever and imperil Rehnquist's nomination through protracted litigation or filibuster. Late one morning during the hearings, after Rehnquist had concluded his testimony before the Judiciary Committee, I provided a brief explanation of why we could not be compelled to produce the documents, but I stressed in open session there was no final decision on whether to claim executive privilege. Afterward, committee chairman Strom Thurmond and Senator Paul Laxalt, Reagan's "best friend" in the Senate, pulled me aside to say we were at the decision point on claiming executive privilege, and could not delay any further. I carried this message back to Meese, who in turn asked to see Reagan to get the decision one way or the other on how to proceed. In the meantime, Chuck Cooper and I raced around feverishly pulling together remarks I could give before the Judiciary Committee later that evening if Reagan decided to hold the line.

That's exactly what Reagan did. In the early evening, Thurmond convened the committee and invited me to the witness table. My testimony consisted of pieces of memos and handwritten notes assembled during the afternoon, which I used to explain why the OLC documents should not be produced. I ended by saying that the president had authorized asserting executive privilege with respect to the documents requested, and Thurmond responded, "Well that's it," hoping to bring the hearing to a close. It was not to be, as the Democratic senators were pouring into the hearing room. Sure enough, on cue, Kennedy was claiming we were "back in the days of Watergate," and away we went. Thurmond, Laxalt, and Orrin Hatch were very helpful in the ensuing melee, but the Democrats clearly smelled Rehnquist's blood, implying that his memos had titles like "How to Suppress the First Amendment Rights of Antiwar Protesters," or "Illegal Arrests and Detentions for Fun and Political Profit." This was about as far from the truth as one could imagine. Having already read several of the memos in dispute, I knew they were as dry and boring as most products of the Justice Department, not that anyone was taking our word for it.

We eventually negotiated a compromise allowing senators and a few staffers to review the documents, but we did not make the documents public. As I expected, after all the fuss, Rehnquist's opponents found the files as boring as we had. The issue disappeared. Democrats made one last stab, asking the FBI to conduct interviews about allegations that as a young lawyer in the 1950s, Rehnquist had harassed black voters in Arizona. To be sure, this was a highly unusual use of the FBI, but we wanted Rehnquist confirmed, so we agreed. This also turned out to be a dry hole, and the Senate confirmed Rehnquist on September 17, 65–33, Goldwater and Garn not voting due to illness.

While the fireworks over Rehnquist were exploding, the stealth Scalia nomination moved inexorably toward success. Nominating the first Italian-American to the Supreme Court promised about as precooked a result as you could get, and certainly nothing like the Rehnquist battle. We even had Italian-American Peter Rodino, an iconic Watergate hero, and the House Judiciary Committee's Democratic chairman, asking to testify on Scalia's behalf, which we graciously accepted. Sometimes, even Republican nominees catch a break. In retrospect, history might have been very different had Reagan nominated Bork to fill in behind Rehnquist and saved Scalia for the next vacancy. The fire would still have been concentrated on Rehnquist because of the importance of the chief justice's position, and the difficulty of conducting two negative campaigns at the same time would have been just as great. Of course, at the time, there was no guarantee there would be another vacancy, and Scalia was younger than Bork, a central consideration in our necessarily cold-blooded effort to remake the federal judiciary.

So easy was Scalia's path that at one point Chuck Cooper asked, in response to my explanation that I had missed a department meeting on Rehnquist because I was attending a White House meeting on Scalia: "You left the beaches of Normandy on D-Day to go be in a fistfight?" That was about the right comparison, as Scalia was confirmed 98–0, with Goldwater and Garn again not voting. The vote took place in the evening, and I called Scalia at a large banquet he was attending, as we had prearranged. "Congratulations, Nino," I said, "the vote was ninety-eight to nothing." There was silence on the other end, and Scalia finally asked who hadn't voted. When I answered, Scalia burst into laughter, asking, "You mean we lost Goldwater and Garn!" This was too good to be true.

In fact it was. The relative closeness of the Rehnquist vote whetted the liberal appetite to do better the next time, a task made immeasurably easier when Democrats retook control of the Senate in 1986, and Joe Biden became chairman of the Judiciary Committee. When Biden had been simply the ranking Democrat on the committee, he had often appeared accommodating, pointing literally and figuratively at the likes of Metzenbaum and Kennedy and saying, "I can't control these guys." Now, however, all eyes would be on Biden as chairman, a plus from his perspective, as he was preparing to run for the 1988 Democratic presidential nomination. In fact, with 1988 near and the Senate in Democratic hands, the stakes on Supreme Court nominations were as high as they could get. By that time, Reagan had appointed three justices (Rehnquist as chief, Sandra Day O'Connor, and Scalia), and the possibility of additional nominations before the end of his presidency, and the consequent effect on the Court, guaranteed that any future nominations would be bloody.

Things looked bleak, at least until Friday, February 13, when our daughter Jennifer Sarah was born. As Trent Lott had said when I told him that Gretchen was expecting, "This will change your life," and indeed it did. JS turned out to have many talents I did not, including musical ability (mastering the piano and the oboe), a flair for mathematics, and an outgoing personality, not to mention good looks, all of which I am reliably informed she inherited from her mother.

In any event, when Justice Lewis Powell retired in 1987, many in the White House thought the administration should try to avoid a bruising battle. That was not the view at Justice, where transforming the judiciary remained a central objective. Besides, it was Bob Bork's turn, indeed, long overdue. Bork was the nation's finest legal analyst, representing everything

that Reagan wanted in the judiciary. Bork had persuasively argued why judicial authority had to be limited in a representative government, and why
the Constitution had to be interpreted consistently with the original intent
of the framers. Such an analytical approach, of course, spelled death for the
liberal vision of judges as Platonic Guardians, dispensing contemporary
justice as they saw fit, unconstrained by quaint words on a fading piece of
parchment. The battle began even before Bork's nomination went to the
Senate on July 7, 1987, and continued through weeks of brutal Judiciary
Committee hearings in September. Bork insisted on pushing for a floor
vote, although by then, it was clear the nomination was doomed. The Judiciary Committee reported the nomination unfavorably on October 6, and it
was rejected 42–58 in a Senate floor vote on October 23. Bork resigned
from the D.C. circuit shortly thereafter.

Bork's nomination has been recounted in detail elsewhere, where I had
a chance to tell my side of the story,[2] so I will not repeat here the entire
dreadful saga. Clearly, however, key conclusions emerge from the theatrics
of distorting a nominee's record and vilifying him personally, a process now
known as "borking." The most important lesson was that the Reagan administration, certainly the White House, was caught totally by surprise at
the force of the opposition to Bork. They should not have been, given the
recent record in the field of judicial confirmations, and I certainly tried to
tell everyone what I thought was about to happen. As I patiently explained
what Bork's opponents would do, listeners nodded in agreement and then
repeatedly failed to take the necessary steps to counter the opposition. The
administration was conducting a confirmation process, while the opponents were waging an election campaign. We studied Bork's law review articles and judicial opinions and wrote scholarly rebuttals to expected
criticisms. The street fighters prepared for a neighborhood brawl, playing
for time until they were ready, while we were dressed for the debating society. Even a political novice should have foreseen the inevitable result. That
was why living through the Bork nomination, for me, and I expect for him,
was like living through a recurring nightmare. It was so perfectly obvious
what the outcome could be, and yet our side let it happen.

2. Ethan Bronner, *Battle for Justice* (New York: W.W. Norton & Co., 1989), and Mark
Gitenstein, *Matters of Principle* (New York: Simon & Schuster, 1992). Bork told his side, at
least in part, in *The Tempting of America* (New York: Free Press, 1990).

We lost Bork's confirmation battle, but Biden's presidential aspirations also collapsed because he plagiarized from the then–British prime minister—certainly an unlikely source of material for an American presidential candidate—in one of his campaign speeches. After Bork's defeat, Doug Ginsburg's nomination blew up on the launching pad, very unfairly, Ginsburg being an outstanding judge and lawyer. I thought this was the opportune moment to nominate Ralph Winter, then sitting on the Second Circuit, to the Supreme Court, and there was a fierce debate at Justice about what to do. On November 30, 1987, Reagan nominated Ninth Circuit judge Anthony Kennedy, who sailed through the Senate with only three days of hearings, and was confirmed 97–0 on February 3, 1988. Perhaps both sides were simply exhausted from all of the effort—I certainly was—and this confirmation was the last judicial battle of the Reagan years.

Unfortunately, especially for Meese, the 1986–88 fighting over the Judiciary was not the only battle in town. The "Iran/Contra" controversy made Meese and others at Justice central figures in yet another Democratic assault on the Reagan presidency. In late 1986, Meese uncovered the connection between Middle East "arms for hostages" deals the administration had denied and efforts to provide clandestine funding "off budget" to the anti-Communist "Contra" rebels in Nicaragua. I had only a peripheral role in uncovering the Iran/Contra connection, and none at all in the underlying events relating either to Iran or to Central America, but I was heavily involved once the inevitable Hill investigations began. Meese was a principal target because his opponents had never given up, and because of his role in uncovering the Iran/Contra connection and his legal opinions on the "arms for hostages" program. Perhaps the only bright spot was that I got to know Dick Cheney, who was serving as a member of the combined Senate-House Iran/Contra committee. Cheney, having been Ford's last chief of staff at the White House, provided invaluable political and tactical advice to a very beleaguered presidency. We certainly needed it. Moreover, Cheney always seemed calm and low-key, which was a welcome relief from the turmoil within the administration.

By early 1988, I had moved over to head Justice's Civil Division, a litigator's dream job. "Civil" then had about four hundred lawyers and close to twenty thousand cases, both numbers being substantially higher today. I argued several cases myself, including one before the First Circuit in fall 1988, styled *Dukakis* v. *Department of Defense*. In the midst of the Bush-

Dukakis presidential campaign, I couldn't have invented a better name. Governor Dukakis had sued to enjoin Reagan from ordering troops of the Massachusetts National Guard to active duty in Central America. Justice had responded that the National Guard had two capacities, one of them as an element of the national armed forces under the president's constitutional commander in chief authority, and that, in its federal capacity, the Guard was not subject to orders by state governors. Rita Braver, the CBS News Justice Department correspondent, covered the oral argument in Boston, right in the heart of Dukakis-land, and I said in her postargument interview that his position showed he didn't know how foreign and national security policy was made in Washington. Of course, since there are no politics in the Department of Justice, I was only making a constitutional observation. (After the election, we won the appeal, 3–0.)

Although I had moved to the much quieter Civil Division, life for Meese did not improve. His opponents never forgave him, not for his alleged misdeeds, but because he just kept escaping their grasp. Finally, however, he came to a point where he believed he would serve President Reagan best by resigning, which he did in July 1988, after the report of yet another independent counsel. Dick Thornburgh, Meese's successor, took office on August 12, bringing a very different management style to a department staffed with Meese loyalists. I learned several lessons from this experience, most notably that when a new boss comes into a bureaucracy, one should not expect existing working relationships to continue. Things will change, often to your dissatisfaction, not because one regime is better or worse than the other, but because different leaders do things in different ways. If you were comfortable with the "old ways," it may well behoove you to move on to a different position, regardless of whether you are happy about it. I was also taken by one of Thornburgh's mantras: "no surprises." It was better to hear bad news early than not to hear it until it was too late.

The Baker State Department

When Bush defeated Dukakis, Thornburgh was not immediately sure if he was staying on as attorney general, which left the Justice Department in turmoil. Bush's announcement immediately after the election that Jim Baker would be secretary of state made my decision easy: I asked Baker if I could join him at State, and he welcomed me there. My goal at that time was to become AID administrator, to finish what I'd started in the Reagan years, but, sadly, the incumbent AID administrator had cancer. Baker justifiably had no intention of moving him from his position. Instead, Baker proposed that I become assistant secretary for International Organization Affairs (IO), responsible for overseeing the entire UN system, which I accepted, since almost any job with Baker at State would be interesting. First, of course, I had to get confirmed, and I found myself in a scrape with Senator John Kerry. He believed that my signing a Justice Department letter denying him access to the files of ongoing criminal investigations of allegations of Contra drug smuggling and gun running had thwarted his own inquiries and also his 1988 presidential aspirations (there was a lot of that going around). In fact, my letter simply repeated a long-standing policy that Justice did not open the files of ongoing investigations because outside interference could jeopardize the investigations and their confidentiality, and might even put lives at risk.

Fortunately, Kerry's efforts were derailed, largely because his fellow Democrat Daniel Patrick Moynihan, another Foreign Relations Committee member, had his own ulterior motive in getting me confirmed quickly. In early 1989, the PLO (Palestine Liberation Organization) had launched a major effort to join several specialized agencies in the UN system, yet another example of the PLO's perennial strategy to improve its position vis-à-vis Israel by doing anything other than negotiating directly with the Israelis. The membership campaign followed the PLO's late 1988 decision to change its name card at the UN from "Palestine Liberation Organization" to "Palestine," apparently under the theory that if you sound more like a country than an organization, people will treat you more like a country. This was what the PLO got away with at the UN. Even the United States allowed it to slip by. The next "logical" step was to have "Palestine" become a member of various UN agencies, thus further attesting to its status as a "state" in international circles. Beneath the charade of appearances, however, lay the political fact that membership in UN bodies was typically limited to "states." Raising the PLO from the status of "observer organization" by admitting it to full membership as "Palestine" would reflect a decision of sorts that the PLO had achieved a status equal to that of Israel, which was manifestly already a state.

There was no doubt the United States would oppose the PLO effort, but the issue was how to do so effectively. The PLO had wide support among Third World countries, and the Europeans were typically flaccid in opposing Third World causes. The PLO's first target of opportunity was the World Health Organization (WHO), whose annual general meeting, the World Health Assembly, meets in Geneva in early May, kicking off a "season" of such meetings throughout the UN system. If the PLO was admitted by one UN agency, it was a precedent for other agencies to admit the PLO as well, exactly what the PLO intended. Moreover, WHO's health mandate made it attractive, since opposing the PLO could be portrayed as opposing better health for Palestinians, a nonsensical argument but nonetheless effective propaganda in the UN system. While I concentrated on my confirmation, the PLO campaigned around the world for WHO membership. So great was our concern that I secured informal acquiescence, because of Moynihan, to do the unthinkable, and actually engage in anti-PLO lobbying even before I was confirmed.

I was completely certain what congressional reaction would be to a PLO success, and it would cut right at the heart of the United States' 25 percent assessed contribution to WHO's budget. Drastic measures were required. I concluded, however, that pointing to Congress as "the bad guys" was not going to be effective. The only way to get anyone's attention to stop the PLO was for the Bush administration itself to threaten to withhold the U.S. assessment. Accordingly, I worked out with Baker a statement making it unmistakably clear that the highest levels of the administration opposed upgrading the PLO's status, even a little bit. Released on May 1, Baker's statement said: "I will recommend to the President that the United States make no further contributions, voluntary or assessed, to any international organization which makes any change in the PLO's status as an observer organization." I still feared it was not enough to stop the PLO's onslaught at WHO. At a minimum, however, I hoped to avoid a rolling withdrawal of U.S. funding from almost the entire UN system by cutting off WHO, thus cauterizing the wound. Once we defunded even one specialized agency, I hoped the rest would get the message.

I flew to Geneva in early May, as soon as I was confirmed, and saw that the PLO's lobbying campaign had been very effective, and no one really believed the United States would defund WHO if it admitted the PLO. Other countries ascribed our threat purely to domestic political purposes, and said that while we might not like the PLO's joining, we would learn to live with it. Fortunately, however, the defunding threat ultimately worked—an important lesson—and the PLO was defeated. Even so, it was a wild ride at the decisive meeting, with the Libyan delegate standing on his desk screaming, and the Sandinista from Nicaragua causing all kinds of trouble.

From Geneva, I went to Paris, headquarters of the UN Educational, Scientific, and Cultural Organization (UNESCO), where the PLO was planning its next move. Even though Reagan had withdrawn the United States from UNESCO to protest its blatant anti-American bias, mismanagement, and corruption and general irrelevance (except to left-wing intellectuals), we were under constant pressure to rejoin. With the WHO experience just a few days old, I was able to tell key UNESCO delegations straightforwardly: Don't even think about the United States' rejoining if the PLO were admitted. UNESCO could have America back (maybe, someday), or it could have the PLO, but it couldn't have both. Delivering this happy message, I thought Paris in the springtime had never been more beautiful.

With the PLO campaign in a ditch, I turned to other matters, and particularly to the ineffectiveness, corruption, and mismanagement that characterized so much of the UN system. During the mid-1980s, with tacit encouragement by the Reagan administration, Congress withheld substantial amounts of U.S. assessed contributions to protest the enormous problems within the UN system. Withdrawal from UNESCO (from which Singapore and Mrs. Thatcher's Britain also withdrew) was the most dramatic example, but the funding cuts, especially their size, made a telling point. By the end of the Reagan years, State had concluded the UN had sufficiently reformed that we should begin repaying the arrearages built up during the 1980s. Incoming president Bush endorsed the plan, which contemplated repaying the arrearages at the rate of 20 percent a year, over a five-year period, a presidential policy decision I inherited as I took over IO.

As I saw it, however, little had really changed at the UN, other than economies that necessarily resulted from American withholdings, and its lackluster performance in many areas had not been cured. I had no doubt that Bush, a former U.S. permanent representative to the United Nations, who had called it "the light that failed," had a thoroughly realistic view of both the UN's potential and its problems. The issue, though, was to translate our intentions into a strategy that was more than just perpetual dissatisfaction with contribution levels. I created a conceptual framework called the "Unitary UN" for this purpose, hoping to take a global view of the entire UN system, to compare performance levels so we could allocate funds based on real accomplishments. No other country paid as much attention to what the UN actually achieved, as opposed to its aspirational rhetoric, especially in New York, home of the UN's huge regular and peacekeeping budgets. Of course, no one else paid anything like our assessment levels, which were 25 percent of the UN's regular budgets and 31 percent of UN peacekeeping. Japan, the next-highest contributor, had an assessment rate only half ours. I tried to enhance the "Geneva Group," an association of major UN contributors so named because it originated in Geneva, the headquarters of many UN agencies. The theory was that as part of a group of other large contributors the U.S. would have a greater say in budget and management questions, thereby allowing us to better manage the size of the dollar assessment we would face annually and have to justify to Congress. It was a nice theory.

Within the State Department, which I knew well from my AID days, I found that an inordinate amount of time was spent arguing with other bureaus over who had "the lead" on everything from broad policies to the drafting and clearing of memoranda to the secretary of state or other "Seventh-Floor Principals," as we called State's top management. Most assistant secretaries had offices on the department's sixth floor, and their staffs worked on lower floors. This arrangement once prompted Goldwater to suggest that you could fix the department by "firing the first six floors," a comment I took careful note of. The department, then and now, consisted of "regional" and "functional" bureaus, the former dealing with bilateral relations with individual countries, and the latter dealing with broad policy areas like economies, human rights, and arms control. Indeed, "turf fights" inside State often seemed more important than dealing with foreigners, a striking contrast to Justice, where turf fights were rare and usually resolved quickly. I decided quickly I just was not going to play the game as it had been played before. I also assembled an excellent team, including, once more, Cary Weil, and Christine Samuelian, Jackie Sanders, and Terry Miller, all of whom would join me again at State after the 2000 election.

I decided to avoid the day-to-day turf fighting by finding allies on the Seventh Floor, particularly Larry Eagleburger, the deputy secretary, and Bob Kimmitt, undersecretary for political affairs, State's number-two and -three officials. When I ran into problems with the rest of the building,

I was usually able to go to them or other friendly officials, like Margaret Tutwiler, Baker's long-time aide, or State's counselor, Bob Zoellick, the other key member of Baker's inner circle, to get a resolution of whatever the issue was in a timely fashion. Even when the decision went against me, at least things didn't drag on endlessly. In fact, I learned a lot of bureaucratic skills in the Baker years that I was later able to use many times to confound the bureaucracy, to its continued amazement. While not exactly scintillating to outsiders, surviving and flourishing in a federal bureaucracy is often the difference between failure and success, which I define as implementing the president's policies. Since the bureaucracy defines success differently—who sat where at the daily morning staff meeting, whose name appeared first on the "from" line of a memo to the secretary, who went on what trip, and other such weighty questions—I often got what I wanted by giving the bureaucracy what they wanted. This approach was also consistent with Baker's general rule to yield on process issues in order to hold the line on substantive questions. I thought it was like buying Manhattan for beads and shells.

State was incredibly busy during what we later called "Bush 41" (to distinguish the forty-first president from his son, the forty-third), with the collapse of Communism in Eastern Europe, and then the Soviet Union itself. Many of these events required careful managing by Bush, Baker, and Dick Cheney, Bush 41's secretary of defense, but the groundwork for these momentous changes had been laid previously by Reagan and many others in the long war against Communism. I saw the evidence in places as far removed as Namibia, where I traveled in November 1989 to watch UN-supervised elections. For example, in the small mining town of Tsumeb, founded during German colonial times, Senator Edmund Muskie, appointed by President Bush to lead the U.S. observers, took us into what looked like a German beer garden for some refreshment after a hard day on the road. We saw a group, which had obviously been there for a while, sitting near a tree with a West German flag draped over its branches. I went over to ask what the celebration was about and was told that the Berlin Wall had fallen the night before. When I relayed this to Muskie and the others, there was just silence, so overwhelming was the realization of what had happened. In the summer of 1990, Gretchen, JS, and I were in Berlin, and walked along and through the by-then-disappearing wall, again overwhelmed by what American leadership and persistence during the Cold War had accomplished.

By contrast, Iraq's unprovoked invasion of Kuwait in August 1990 was a matter entirely for Bush's team to handle, and was his presidency's defining national security issue. In both diplomatic and military terms, Bush's preparations for Desert Storm cannot be faulted, although historians will debate for years whether his war aims were too limited, and whether Bush stopped too soon, before toppling Saddam Hussein. On the diplomatic side, we marched through a series of Security Council resolutions, starting with Resolution 660 immediately after Iraq invaded Kuwait and culminating in Resolution 678, authorizing the use of force by the U.S.-led coalition to oust Saddam Hussein's armies and restore Kuwaiti sovereignty. I worked minute by minute with Baker, Kimmitt, and others on these resolutions, following a strategy that evolved in small meetings in the White House and was conveyed to us by Baker. Bush loved getting involved in the specifics of drafting resolutions. On two occasions, I was in Baker's office as he spoke to Bush by telephone with the phone held out to me so I could take notes directly on what Bush wanted: "If I were back in New York, I would . . ." Those were instructions from the man Baker liked to call "the guy who got elected," and that was all we needed to hear. Moreover, Bush did a lot of the diplomacy himself, calling foreign leaders, and earning the title "the mad dialer" from a frustrated State Department bureaucracy that was not always in the loop, which is probably the most irritating thing in the world for a bureaucrat.

But the day-to-day tactical command of the diplomacy for Desert Storm was in Baker's hands. He knew what Bush wanted, and he brooked no interference or second-guessing on what could determine not just the future of Kuwait but the future of Bush's presidency. Accordingly, it drove him to near distraction when Tom Pickering, our UN Ambassador in New York, decided he had a better plan. Of course, these days, I have a better feeling for Pickering's perspective, but at that time I, too, believed that all wisdom came from Washington. "What's that cowboy doing up there?" Baker would ask me repeatedly on the direct line connecting our offices, expecting I would keep USUN under control so he could resolve more pressing matters. Moreover, Baker knew that the critical resolution authorizing the use of force would have to be negotiated directly among foreign ministers, and not left to the ambassadors. Having formed a particularly close relationship with Soviet foreign minister Shevardnadze, Baker had used it effectively from the earliest days after Iraq's invasion of Kuwait.

After we formulated the key phrase describing the authorization to use force ("all necessary means"), Baker took these few words around the world as he met face-to-face with every one of the foreign ministers of the Security Council's other members, seeking their personal commitment to support a Council resolution containing those words. The most fascinating meeting was in New York, on the eve of the actual vote, which was to take place at the ministerial level, a very rare event in those days, chaired by Baker, since the United States had the Council presidency in November 1990. For the first time in over thirty years, a U.S. secretary of state met formally with the foreign minister of Cuba, in this case Isidoro Malmierca, an old-line Communist. Baker made his pitch, but Malmierca did not respond, barely moving a muscle as Baker spoke. Baker wasn't about to let go easily, however, and he kept trying to find a way into Malmierca's brain, saying, "This resolution is about preventing big countries from invading small countries," wink, wink. No response from Malmierca. Baker leaned forward, with a tight smile, and tried again: "To keep big countries to the North from invading small countries to the South." Still no response from Malmierca. Maybe the translator was getting it wrong, but it was hard to imagine what else Baker could say.

The big uncertainty was China. While we thought China would abstain from voting on the resolution, we couldn't dismiss the risk that China would veto it, which would have brought the entire Security Council strategy to a crashing halt. The day of the Council vote, a few of us gathered in Baker's suite, and there were recommendations to try one or another further incentive to shift the Chinese to a "yes." I thought we had China where we wanted them: An abstention would allow the United State to use military force, whereas if we spooked China and it vetoed, we had no Plan B. "Bolton, you're very silent today," Baker said after a few minutes, and I urged him not to go back to the Chinese and risk upsetting the apple cart. I think that was his instinct all along, and that was what he decided to do.

The vote came out the right way, 12–2–1, with Cuba and Yemen against and China abstaining. Yemen sat next to the United States, and Baker tried to win its vote up until the last minute. When Yemen went the wrong way, he leaned back to the Americans sitting directly behind him and said, "That's the most expensive vote they ever cast." U.S. foreign assistance to Yemen was thereupon cut dramatically, something I have wished was more widely known. Bush and Baker had scored an enormous diplomatic victory in the Security Council, obtaining the authorization to use force against Saddam Hussein even before Congress had voted to do so. In fact, in the immediate aftermath of the Iraqi invasion, as Congress was leaving Washington for the August recess, many members were asked if they could support the use of force to expel the Iraqis from Kuwait. Not a few had paused, and then said, in effect, "Yes, if the UN Security Council will authorize the use of force," fully expecting that that would never happen. Now it had, and Bush used Resolution 678 to good effect domestically, as plans for the war shifted to their final phase.

With diplomacy in the UN now essentially over, IO's pace slowed dramatically. My last mission before the war was to travel to Europe in January 1991 to talk to the IAEA (International Atomic Energy Agency) and several European allies, including the foreign minister of Luxembourg, then holding the EU presidency, about what might happen after the war, and specifically our efforts to destroy Saddam's nuclear, biological, and chemical weapons programs, as well as his ballistic missiles. I was in Vienna when Baker had his dramatic meeting in Geneva with Iraqi foreign minister Tariq Aziz, what many called the "last chance" for peace, where Aziz refused even to accept a letter from Bush explaining the inevitable consequences if Saddam did not withdraw from Kuwait. Listening to Baker's press conference after the meeting, there could be no mistaking that war was only days away.

Desert Storm's air campaign commenced on January 17, 1991. Given the time difference between Kuwait and Washington, we fully expected the ground war would begin in the late evening on the East Coast, early morning in the Persian Gulf, so we were prepared with assignments of people to call to tell them once the liberation of Kuwait actually started. Gretchen and I were at dinner at the Watergate residence of Egyptian ambassador Rauf el-Reedy and his wife, when State's Operations Center called with instructions to return at once to the department for what could only be the last diplomatic gestures before the ground war began. My assignment was to call UN secretary general Pérez de Cuéllar to tell him the war was starting. The information certainly did not take him by surprise.

The ground war ended on February 28 with the total defeat of the Iraqi forces, and we immediately launched negotiations on what became Resolution 687, "the mother of all resolutions," so dubbed by Soviet "permanent representative" Yuli Vorontsov. Among its provisions, this "cease-fire resolution" created UNSCOM, the UN Special Commission, to be used to discover and destroy Saddam Hussein's weapons of mass destruction; modified the economic sanctions imposed on Iraq by Resolution 661; and created a boundary commission to demarcate the Iraq-Kuwait border, Saddam's trumped-up *casus belli*. But even as we concluded the mother of all resolutions, events on the ground were moving rapidly. Acting in response to the Bush administration's calls, Kurds in Iraq's north and Shi'ites in the south rose to overthrow Saddam, and he responded swiftly and harshly with decisive use of his remaining military forces. We did nothing for the Shi'ites, which I believe they have never forgotten. Kurdish refugees began moving toward and into the mountainous border area with Turkey in difficult winter conditions, and a humanitarian disaster loomed.

The Security Council quickly passed Resolution 688, the first to declare a country's internal repression, and its consequences, such as cross-border refugee flows, a threat to international peace and security. It authorized the coalition that had liberated Kuwait and others to address the needs of the rapidly growing numbers of Kurdish refugees. As with the expulsions of foreign workers by Iraq after it invaded Kuwait, which also imposed an enormous burden on the UN's humanitarian agencies, we were concerned that the UN system's response was slow and inadequate. Baker sent me to Geneva, headquarters of the UN high commissioner for refugees, WHO, and the International Committee of the Red Cross (ICRC) to try to help expedite and coordinate their efforts. Baker himself decided to interrupt the shuttle diplomacy he was doing on the renewed Middle East peace process to travel to Turkey to discuss the Kurdish problems, and to travel to southeastern Turkey where the refugee problem was greatest. I joined Baker and his traveling party in Ankara, where he met with Turkish president Turgut Özal, a firm American ally.

The next day, we flew to a joint U.S.-Turkish Air Force base at Diyarbakir, where the first U.S. air drops of humanitarian assistance were being prepared, and then we helicoptered off to a Turkish military base close to the Iraqi border. During the flight, one of the crew members, tethered to the wall of the large transport helicopter for safety, slithered back and forth across the tail end looking out the open portion of the rear door. When we landed, I asked him what he had been doing and he said "looking for small arms and rocket fire," which I was happier to find out after we landed rather than before takeoff. After a briefing by the Turks at their base, we drove to the border. We arrived at a small ridge and looked out over hilly countryside that was simply covered with people. This was one of the gathering points for tens of thousands of Kurdish refugees, where they were without food, shelter, or sanitation facilities. There was clearly trouble in the making if humanitarian assistance and some basic order were not rapidly provided. By this point, as I learned from Baker's diplomatic security detail, we were actually inside Iraq, a situation the agents must have had nightmares about.

Back at Diyarbakir, Baker made it clear he thought that the UN was not going to be able to handle the humanitarian burdens being imposed upon it. I had the same uneasy feeling and spent a considerable amount of time over the next several months on this issue, and other postwar problems. Indeed, the work of UNSCOM and other elements of Resolution 687 were important priorities right until Bush left office.

Inevitably, however, other matters intruded, including the breakup of Yugoslavia, dealing with issues like who would hold the USSR's Security Council seat when there was no longer a USSR, the U.S. intervention in Somalia,[3] and many others too numerous to cover here at any length. Nonetheless, a few more IO "war stories" serve as a useful prologue for my later experience as UN ambassador.

Most important for future reference was the effort to repeal General Assembly Resolution 3379, the infamous 1975 text equating Zionism with racism, and a clear effort to delegitimize Israel. Passage of "Z/r," as we called it, had instead delegitimized the UN in the minds of many Americans, because it convinced them that the UN was the hopeless captive of Soviet manipulation and Third World radicalism, both of which perceptions were accurate. Repeal of "Z/r" had become a priority for Israel and many pro-Israeli groups in the United States, and a test of whether the United Nations could ever hope to regain even a hint of the moral authority that its founders envisioned for it in 1945. During the Cold War, there was essentially no chance that the Soviets would give up their hard-won victory, or that the Arab states and the PLO would back away from their efforts to affect Israel's diplomatic position in the UN General Assembly

---

3. See my "Wrong Turn in Somalia," 73 *Foreign Affairs* 56 (January–February 1994), Number 1.

(UNGA). Accordingly, while there was a lot of rhetoric about repeal, that was all that it was for many years.

With the advent of *glasnost* and *perestroika* in the Soviet Union, however, I saw the possibility of righting the historic wrong represented by "Z/r" and also demonstrating that the United States might actually be able once again to win highly contentious votes in the General Assembly, something long out of fashion. During 1989–90, I consulted with the Israelis and with many private American groups, several of which were lobbying foreign governments to support repeal of Resolution 3379. I thought that the time was right in late 1990, and that it was symbolically important to repeal the "Z/r" resolution on its fifteenth anniversary, during the global effort to liberate Kuwait. Israel, however, was nervous, fearing that a losing effort would do more damage than not acting at all, and urged delay until 1991. Baker and Bush were also reluctant, although for a different reason. They understandably didn't want to do anything that might jeopardize Saddam Hussein's isolation.

After the liberation of Kuwait, however, the political environment changed dramatically, as the United States launched the "Madrid process," which opened the prospect of direct talks between Arabs and Israelis. Since it was certain that the United Nations would have no role whatever in a changed Middle East as long as "Z/r" was on the books, Baker agreed with my importunings in early 1991 to start laying the necessary diplomatic groundwork for repeal. As a cautious vote counter, however, he made it clear that a final decision would not be made until later in the year. Accordingly, I increased the frequency and detail of our contacts with close allies, from whom we would want not only their votes, but also active lobbying of other UN members to maximize our chances. Sadly, many countries, including close NATO allies, responded in much the same way as the Soviets: Yes, Resolution 3379 was a shameful thing, but it would be a huge effort to repeal. "Let it lie on the shelves and gather dust" was the way one Soviet diplomat put it to me, which was an unfortunately common response to problems in the UN system.

In September, as the General Assembly opened, I was convinced we had the votes necessary. Firing the opening shot in the campaign in his annual UN address, President Bush included a call for repeal, signaling that this year we were serious indeed. During the fall, I pressed for the signal to launch the all-out repeal campaign, because I knew, despite our vote count, that we had to overcome an enormous amount of inertia. With the Madrid Middle East peace process still shaky, however, Baker declined to pull the trigger, although he said we should do everything else necessary to be sure we could move out quickly once the word was given. I grew more nervous as the weeks passed.

Then, on December 3, Baker said it was time to launch, and we began a round-the-clock, round-the-world diplomatic campaign to obtain support and cosponsorships for the repeal resolution. In the UN, private expressions of support are cheap and easy to come by, but when countries declare publicly by becoming cosponsors of a resolution, there is no going back, and everyone at the UN knows it. Since we expected Arab and other "Z/r" defenders to try either to amend our resolution to death or to sidetrack it procedurally, the gathering of cosponsors made it increasingly evident that these diversionary tactics would not work. We "demarched," the fancy diplomatic word for lobbying in foreign capitals, we pressed hard in New York, and we called in ambassadors in Washington. Bush and Baker were both "mad dialers" by this time, as was I. Persistence paid off. As each new cosponsor fell into place, we moved inexorably toward the magic halfway point of total UN membership where it would be clear not only that we had a majority for repeal, but that there was no way the resolution could be blocked procedurally.

Because Baker was unavailable, Deputy Secretary Larry Eagleburger gave the American speech on December 16, the day of the vote. I wrote an op-ed piece in the *New York Times* that morning,[4] and media attention on the General Assembly was higher than it had been at any moment since "Z/r's" original passage. Senator Moynihan and leaders of many of the groups that had worked actively for repeal were in the galleries, and expectations were high. Our cosponsorship strategy was successful, and our vote count was accurate. As one of its last official acts before it dissolved, the Soviet Union voted to repeal the resolution it had inspired, and the Third World countries were badly split over repeal, another side benefit. Europe and Latin America were almost unanimous cosponsors for repeal, Cuba being a notable exception. "Z/r" was dead. I was a happy man.

---

4. Bolton, "Zionism Is Not Racism," *New York Times*, December 16, 1991, p. A19, col. 4.

After the celebrating, however, there was still much to be done to have Israel treated equally with other UN members. Even as late as 2005 when I became U.S. ambassador, Israel was not fully a member of the UN regional groups, a critical omission when it came to membership on important UN bodies, such as the Security Council, and other potentially important indicia of full membership. Moreover, the incessant pounding on Israel through the repetitive passage of General Assembly resolutions that blamed Israel for every problem imaginable in the Middle East, not to mention the level of anti-Israeli and anti-American rhetoric, did not disappear simply with the repeal of "Z/r." In fact, so deep-seated was the problem of anti-Israeli bias in the UN that it occupied a considerable amount of time and effort during my entire tenure in New York.

Other problems that cropped up in 1991 would also recur later. For example, Japan felt it should be a permanent member of the Security Council, which the United States had endorsed back in the Nixon administration. In 1991, under rising domestic political pressure, Japan got serious about its aspiration and turned to us to develop a strategy. While we agreed on the merits, there were enormous political obstacles. We also worried that adding more permanent members would cripple the Council's decision-making capability by making it too large and unwieldy. Since we had just finished awakening the Council from its long Cold War slumber, the last thing we wanted was to make rapid, radical changes before we could evaluate just how effective the Council could be. Despite numerous consultations with Japan, the effort never went anywhere.

Another issue that would recur later was selecting a new secretary general to succeed Javier Pérez de Cuéllar of Peru, whose second five-year term expired at the end of 1991. The political buzz in New York was that it was "Africa's turn," since there had never been an African SG, and since the African Group's large membership formed a powerful voting bloc. The United States never approved the idea of the regional rotation of the secretary general's job, or other high-level jobs, but altering the political realities in New York often took an enormous amount of work, as the effort to repeal the "Z/r" resolution was demonstrating. Baker's marching orders were typical of his subtle style: It was okay to frustrate the "Africa's turn" argument, as long as we didn't get caught. Boutros Boutros-Ghali, a senior Egyptian diplomat (all of North Africa being part of the UN's African Group), appeared at the top of the Africans' list of candidates largely because the names were listed in alphabetical order, and only the Egyptians knew that their man's last name was actually "Boutros-Ghali," not "Ghali".[5]

French foreign minister Roland Dumas loved the Boutros-Ghali idea, calling him "the candidate of my dreams" (which Dumas said only in French, of course): an Arab, an African, and—best of all—a very fluent French speaker. I explained the evolving political situation to Baker, who told me that Egypt's president Mubarak had pressed Bush and Baker to support Boutros-Ghali. Baker saw a key role for Egypt in his emerging Middle East process, and he didn't want to provoke a disagreement over what he frankly considered to be less than an earth-shattering priority. This exposed another lesson about the UN within the U.S. government, namely, that it was often simply not important enough to matter compared to other pressing priorities.

Boutros-Ghali ultimately emerged as a compromise between the Anglophone and Francophone countries, and he took office on January 1, 1992. I met him in Paris (how fitting) on the day he was elected in New York, and he cleared everyone else out of the room to tell me that he was deeply committed to making the UN more efficient. He said he knew the Egyptian bureaucracy, with its thousands of years of accumulated baggage, and he thought he could find ways to keep the UN from following the same route. These were comments made after his election was a done deal, so I took them as sincere, and not made as pure politics.[6] In fact, in his early days, he made a number of changes in the bureaucracy, such as eliminating several high-level positions, which were encouraging.

In January 1992, at a luncheon he hosted for heads of state attending the Security Council Summit, Boutros-Ghali offered the United States the position of undersecretary general for management and administration. This would be a position central to our "Unitary UN" efforts, and after the lunch, President Bush mused about whether we should take the position, and whom we might select to fill it if we did. I strongly supported taking it, as did Baker. Bush suggested Dick Thornburgh, who had just lost a tough

---

5. The family had adopted this combined name decades before, in honor of the first Boutros Ghali, who had been assassinated.

6. Boutros-Ghali described several of our meetings in his book *Unvanquished: A U.S.-U.N. Saga,* (New York: Random House, 1999).

Senate race in Pennsylvania, after resigning as attorney general. National Security Adviser Brent Scowcroft asked if Thornburgh were qualified for the job, and Baker observed witheringly, "Brent, he was governor of Pennsylvania." That pretty much ended the discussion. I was deputized to call Thornburgh to see if he might be interested, which he was. Once in New York, he immediately grasped the extent of the UN's problems and concluded that only the most sweeping changes could possibly rescue the organization from inertia. Unfortunately, the incoming Clinton administration purged Thornburgh in 1993, and his changes were lost to history. Rereading his suggestions in 2005, I was amazed to find they were still quite relevant, since almost nothing had changed in the intervening years, except to get worse.

Exile and Return

During the Clinton years, I again wandered the political wilderness. In 1997, I joined the American Enterprise Institute (AEI) as senior vice president, renewing relationships I had started at Yale Law School with Ralph Winter and Bob Bork. At AEI, an oasis during the Clinton years, I had the chance to write and speak extensively on a wide variety of foreign policy issues, such as what was wrong with the International Criminal Court and other Clinton-era mistakes, which I thought would reduce America's global influence, and on challenges to American sovereignty, which I saw not in abstract terms, but in the actual reduction of control over decisions directly affecting our own well-being. While there, I met fellow AEIers Mark Groombridge (a Chinese-speaking Asia scholar) and Dave Wurmser (a Middle East scholar), who would later join me in the Bush 43 State Department.

I also had the opportunity to work *pro bono* for the United Nations during 1997–2001. Kofi Annan asked Jim Baker to become his personal envoy to help resolve the long-standing dispute over the future of the Western Sahara, a former Spanish colony on the west coast of Africa where a guerrilla war had been festering for over twenty years. Baker's mission was to bring about a referendum the UN Security Council had resolved to hold in 1991 to determine whether the Western Sahara would be annexed by Morocco, which had held de facto control of the territory since 1975, or achieve independence. Despite Baker's leadership and our strenuous efforts to get the disputing parties to agree on the voting rules for the referendum, we did not succeed and the Western Sahara matter was still pending when I arrived in New York in August 2005.

Fortunately, the 2000 Florida recount, although at times it seemed liked guerrilla warfare, did not last as long as the dispute over the Western Sahara. By mid-December 2000, although somewhat delayed by the length of the election dispute, the Bush Transition Team turned its full attention to the new administration's staffing and policies. And so did I.

CHAPTER THREE

CUTTING GULLIVER LOOSE: PROTECTING AMERICAN SOVEREIGNTY IN GOOD DEALS AND BAD

Treaties, you see, are like girls and roses:
they last while they last.

—Charles de Gaulle[1]

Two for T

John Bolton, my very, very determined Under Secretary.

—Colin Powell[2]

Colin Powell called me on Monday, January 29, 2001, to offer me the job of undersecretary of state for arms control and international security affairs. Contrary to a favorite media myth, I was not forced on Powell against his will, to be an agent of influence for the nefarious Dick Cheney and Donald Rumsfeld, or the tribe of "neoconservatives." Both Powell and I knew exactly what we were getting into, and both of us were realists, although of differing philosophies and careers.

---

1. Quoted in Tony Judt, *Postwar* (New York: Penguin Press, 2005), p. 241.
2. Secretary Powell's remarks to the press in the airport lounge in Manaus, Brazil, en route to Santiago, Chile, November 17, 2004, http://www.state.gov/secretary/former/powell/remarks/38357.htm.

Nonetheless, much of the internal national security politics in Bush 43's first term is illuminated by how I became "T," which is how that undersecretary job is known in State's alphabet soup of abbreviations. The Secretary is "S," the deputy secretary is "D," and so on. Even Ian Fleming's "M" exists at State, but it stands only for the undersecretary for management. "T" reflects the first person to hold the job in 1972, former director of selective service Curtis W. Tarr, or the original name of the office "Science and Technology," depending on who you ask. Why not another letter? Who knows?

I first discussed returning to State with Jim Baker in Florida, a few days before the dispositive Supreme Court decision, and expressed interest in either deputy secretary (D) or undersecretary for political affairs (P, the number-three job). Confirming what everyone had been speculating, Baker said Powell would be secretary and would have great independence and flexibility in his personnel selections. After flying home to Washington, I attended the annual dinner for AEI's board of trustees, scholars, and their spouses on Friday, December 15, which was honoring Dick Cheney, one of the trustees. Not surprisingly, the mood was jubilant. Both Dick and Lynne Cheney spoke, thanking various AEIers who had worked on the campaign. Dick also thanked me for my time in Florida, which generated a great round of applause, and he then said: "And the answer to your next question is . . . anything he wants," provoking more applause and hilarity.

The next day in Austin, with Cheney present, Bush announced he would nominate Powell as secretary of state. Two days later, Powell's office called to set up a meeting, which we fixed for Wednesday, December 20. I met Powell in the same Transition office at State where I had talked with Baker almost twelve years before about the IO job, and Powell opened the conversation by saying, "Jimmy Baker told me last night that you kicked some ass down there in Florida." Powell then turned quickly to the business at hand, saying he was doing his "commander's assessment" of things at State. I raised my interest in the D and P jobs, and Powell said he expected D to be an "inside" managerial position, with none of the special tasks of the last Clinton D, Strobe Talbot. He expected P to be supervisor of State's regional bureaus, one of its traditional roles. Although we discussed how a secretary could allocate responsibilities between D and P, I had no sense I was in the running for either one, which Powell in effect confirmed by asking if I had an interest in any of the other undersecretary jobs. I did not. He then raised the possibility of the counselor position (C), which I didn't bite on. C did not fit into the regular chain of command, and, as the secretary's "consigliere," his portfolio depended entirely on what the secretary assigned. Henry Kissinger once said, "Never take a government job without an in-box," and with no prior relationship with Powell, I worried about having a big title and no responsibilities. I had no interest in sitting in an office watching the paint peel, but I could not figure out a gracious way to tell Powell that I doubted he would make very much of C, especially since I hadn't expected it. The meeting ended inconclusively.

The December 28 announcement of Don Rumsfeld as secretary of defense changed a lot of plans in Washington, especially for Rich Armitage, who badly wanted to be deputy secretary of defense. As Armitage later said to me, Rumsfeld had no interest in him, and the feeling was mutual. By early January, it appeared that Armitage, who was like a brother to Powell, would become D, meaning that P would likely go to a Foreign Service careerist, the traditional pattern. I began to think I would remain at AEI, when Fred Iklé, a national security scholar and senior defense and arms control official in prior Republican administrations, called to urge that I take T. Iklé said he and Reagan's first national security advisor, Dick Allen, had concluded that, given the importance of missile defense, T required someone who would get us out of the 1972 Anti-Ballistic Missile (ABM) Treaty. They thought I was it. I told Iklé I had basically already turned T down, but his pitch had definitely been persuasive. I called Cheney, who was heading the Transition Team, to ask his advice, and he said, "I don't want to get between you and Colin on this, but I think he's about to call you. I'm surprised he hasn't already." This left me feeling uneasy that Powell was going to offer me C, so I asked Cheney if the UN ambassador job remained open, and he said, "Yes, that is still open, and you should raise that with Colin. The action is with him on that and the other jobs as well."

I heard nothing more until after the inauguration, when Powell called on January 24 to say he had picked Armitage for D, to be in charge of "systems management," which State badly needed. A careerist would be P, said Powell, but he had now heard I might be interested in T. I said that Iklé had raised the issue, but that I would also be interested in the UN job. When we continued our discussion the following week, Powell told me, "We've been having a lot of conversations over the past twenty-four hours, discussing with Dick Cheney and the president what to do with you. On UN ambassador, we are moving in a different direction, but I would like you to take the T job instead. With missile defense and everything else, this is going to be central, and I think you would have a lot of fun doing it. Dick thinks you would be great and the president is supportive as well." Reading this to mean that Bush and Cheney had already signed off on the deal, I agreed enthusiastically. I was just happy it wasn't C. (T had been Jim Buckley's job under Al Haig in the Reagan administration, and I had been in that office many times during the intervening twenty years.) Powell also seemed very pleased, and said, "You'll check me and I'll check you, but it will be fun and productive." I agreed. During his entire time at State, Powell never filled the C job.

Although my nomination did not go to the Senate until March 8, it leaked into the press, generating speculation about how contentious the confirmation process might be. Jesse Helms, chairman of the Senate Foreign Relations Committee (SFRC), whose re-election committees I had represented in private practice, offered his full support. His staffer, Marshall Billingslea, predicted a "wild ride" as some liberal devotees of arms control theology tried to pin me down on commitments that could later constrain what I would be able to do. As my AEI colleague Richard Perle put it to me, "The Democrats invented arms control, and they feel they have a right to that job. They can't believe that someone like you would get it." While I waited for the Senate to act, I received briefings and met others on Powell's incoming team. On February 9, in midafternoon, I met Armitage for the first time. He apologized that our meeting had started five minutes late and said he was trying to instill some discipline about starting meetings on time. I wished him good luck. We talked about a wide range of things, and I found Armitage to be blunt and unreflective, speaking in short sound bursts. At 3:30 P.M., the time of his next appointment, he rose from his chair in midsentence (his own) and started toward the office door. I took this as a sign the meeting was over, as indeed it was.

Connecticut senator Chris Dodd was already opposing Otto Reich's nomination to be assistant secretary for Western Hemisphere affairs. Reich, a Cuban-American immigrant, had often crossed Dodd's pro-Castro path, and there was no love lost between them. I wanted to avoid the same fate, and Helms and his staff tried to schedule a prompt confirmation hearing. I had written a large pile of articles, and some unfortunate staffers were plowing through them to see what "outrageous" things I had said over the years that could be used against me. The more time they had, doubtless the more they would find, and a delaying game would ensue, to a nominee's distinct disadvantage, as in Bork's failed confirmation fight. Sure enough, the Democrats postponed my hearing until the end of March. Joe Biden, who had years before ceded his ranking Democratic position on Judiciary to become the ranking SFRC Democrat, nonetheless promised Helms on March 23 that, while he was "not a John Bolton kind of guy," he would not try to block the nomination. He agreed to a vote in the SFRC on April 3, before the Easter recess.

The confirmation hearing on Thursday, March 29, lasted about three and a half hours, and was uneventful. Unquestionably, the high point came when Biden said to me:

> I agree with your competence in this area. And I want to make it clear, this is not about your competence. My problem with you, over the years, has been, you're too competent. I mean, I would rather you be stupid and not very effective. I would have had a better shot over the years. . . . I think you're an honorable man and you are extremely competent.

Biden did most of the questioning for the Democrats, but John Kerry, Barbara Boxer, and Bill Nelson of Florida also participated briefly. Kerry allowed as how "you're a very smart fellow, and I respect the career you've had." The other four Democrats did not appear, and only Helms and Brownback attended for the Republicans. Dodd did not come to the hearing, but said during the floor debate, "There is no question that Mr. Bolton is an individual of integrity and intelligence."[3] The hearing's most bizarre point came when Nelson asked if Powell supported the nomination. I assured him he did, but I wondered where such a question could have come from. Powell and Armitage both called me on Friday to say they were glad the hearing had gone well, and they looked forward to confirmation being completed before the Easter recess.

Given this uneventful course, I expected the SFRC to report the nomination to the Senate on April 3, with a floor vote a few days later. Late on April 2, however, Steve Biegun, Helms's chief of staff, called to say that Biden wanted me taken off the SFRC agenda because he had to be in

---

3. Statement of Senator Dodd, *Congressional Record,* May 8, 2001, p. S 4454.

Delaware that day for a Bush speech on education. Under the SFRC's rules, a senator could ask to "hold over" a nomination to the next business meeting, for any reason or no reason. Because of the Easter recess, the effect was a three-week delay until the next SFRC business meeting on April 26.

While Biden's request sounded innocuous enough, there were signs that something more complicated was afoot. A former Kerry staffer told us that Biden's staff was encouraging press opposition. Biegun found that Biden had told Dick Lugar that I opposed Lugar's signature "Cooperative Threat Reduction" program to dismantle former Soviet weapons systems (commonly known as the "Nunn-Lugar program," after its sponsors). Fortunately, I had met with Lugar before the hearing and discussed this very issue, suggesting we needed more financial support for weapons destruction from Europe and Japan in order to complete the task more expeditiously. Then, a friend of mine who attended a small reception on April 2 told me that Biden had said some unusual things about Bush's foreign policy team. Biden had observed that Powell might not be in charge of the State Department, given, for example, one high-level nomination the SFRC would be taking up shortly. His interest piqued, my friend, who had never met Biden before, worked his way into a one-on-one conversation in which Biden said, "John is a very smart guy, and I've worked with him for sixteen years," but he also said, "A number of senators on my side think they would be doing Powell a favor by voting against John." Biden didn't say or imply he personally believed it, but the substance of his remarks was obviously troubling.

To avoid problems after the recess and ensure Republicans were ready, Helms's staff went into high gear. Nebraska's Chuck Hagel agreed to be the point man supporting the nomination during the April 26 SFRC business meeting, a significant signal to the Democrats. Hagel, unlike Helms, had supported all of Clinton's nominees before the SFRC, and could therefore make a strong argument for allowing the president to pick his own team. To rebut any contrary gossip, Powell signed a letter "endorsing" my nomination, an unusual step, but one Helms thought important. In addition, the American Israel Public Affairs Committee and other pro-Israel groups were working key Democratic senators in support of the nomination. The full Senate was split fifty-fifty, the SFRC having nine senators from each party, so a party-line vote would mean a tie, blocking the nomination from being reported to the floor. We needed at least one Democrat to get out of the committee.

Powell called Biden the night before the SFRC business meeting. While Biden conceded that the full Senate would confirm me, he said seven of the nine Democrats would vote against me on arms control grounds. Fortunately, in the increasingly bitter atmosphere of an equally divided Senate, the SFRC vote went the right way, 10–8 in favor of the nomination, with Wisconsin's Russ Feingold breaking Democratic ranks, voting "yes" because he believed, then at least, that presidents should get their nominees, absent some debilitating ethical or personal problem.

Safely out of the SFRC, the next issue was whether the nomination could come swiftly to a floor vote, or whether a Democrat would put a "hold" on it, thus delaying it, possibly indefinitely. Unknown to us at the time, the Democrats were negotiating secretly with Vermont's Republican senator Jim Jeffords, hoping to persuade him to switch parties or at least caucus with them, thus shifting Senate control into their hands. That, of course, was exactly what happened, making it clear that delaying nominations was intended to prevent Senate decisions until control had shifted. Moreover, Strom Thurmond's health was a source of constant speculation, so the Democrats saw several different ways in which Senate control might shift to them. Since we had no inkling of the secret negotiations, we could do little except wait for Republican leader Trent Lott to work out a "time agreement" with the Democrats that would govern floor debate on the nomination. In the meantime, on May 1, I attended former senator Paul Laxalt's Nevada "lamb fries" dinner, an annual event since the Reagan administration's first year. Laxalt had been a friend and mentor of mine on political issues for many years, and he had seen his share of tough confirmation battles. He sat me next to Dick Cheney, which allowed me to brief Cheney on my Senate travails.

I also spoke to Helms to find out what he thought about the prospects for floor action, and what Biden and other Democrats might be up to. Helms said, "There's no one more eager to get you confirmed than yours truly," and said of Biden, "Sometimes Joe behaves like a long-tailed cat in a room full of rocking chairs." Lott worked tirelessly to get the necessary time agreement, and the floor vote was finally scheduled for Tuesday, May 8. The debate began with North Dakota's Byron Dorgan generally assaulting the Bush administration, arguing that I was qualified to dismantle the arms control system but not to build it up, the heart of the opposition's case. Minnesota's Paul Wellstone said that my presence in Powell's inner circle would undercut Powell. Biden concluded for the Democrats, saying that I was an honorable and decent man, that Powell supported me (an important public admission), and that his opposition was based entirely on the issues. Biden read his speech in an unemotional and hurried fashion, as if going through the motions, and said he had not lobbied for other negative votes. Helms spoke briefly, and then the voting started, seemingly lasting forever but concluding after forty minutes. The vote was 57–43, meaning we had held all fifty Republicans (including Jeffords) and picked up seven Democrats. As Haley Barbour, former chairman of the Republican National Committee, said later, "That's a landslide in my line of work."

A Bad Deal—the ABM Treaty—Travels to the Ash Heap

> You do cover my right flank, and it needs covering.
> —COLIN POWELL, DECEMBER 19, 2002

I started at T on Friday, May 11, 2001, beginning immediately to prepare for the impending Washington visit of Russian foreign minister Igor Ivanov. The central topic of Ivanov's meeting with Powell would be the post–Cold War Russian-American strategic relationship, a subject that had not been adequately addressed during the 1990s, but which now required action, given the growing threats we saw from rogue states seeking to acquire weapons of mass destruction (WMD) and the ballistic missile capabilities to deliver such weapons to their targets. We needed to prepare, together we hoped, defenses against the increasing threat of WMD proliferation, even as we moved to a more normal bilateral relationship and developed what National Security Adviser Condi Rice was calling "a new strategic framework" since both of our Cold War nuclear postures had become obsolete.

Our initial focus was the ABM Treaty of 1972, a Cold War relic that essentially precluded both Russia and the United States from developing national missile defense systems. In the 2000 campaign and in speeches early in his presidency, Bush made it clear he wanted to be free of the ABM Treaty's constraints, either by unilateral U.S. withdrawal or by mutual U.S.-Russian consent, so we could develop defenses against threats posed by rogue states with relatively small numbers of ballistic missiles, and against the risk of accidental launches by Russia or China. Bush also wanted to reduce our offensive nuclear forces, either in agreement with Russia or unilaterally. To this end, Bush ordered a "nuclear posture review" to determine what our actual level of offensive nuclear forces should be, given current global circumstances. In many respects, however, the "new strategic framework" was still somewhat dreamy and academic, and debate within the administration focused on how to make it concrete and practical, both on the strategic offensive and defensive sides of the equation.

This Bush administration thinking ran squarely contrary to existing arms control theology, which had been painstakingly developed during the Cold War, and kept on life support during the Clinton presidency by devotion and prayer rather than hard reality. While always receptive to reducing the number of offensive nuclear weapons, often regardless of the impact on U.S. military capabilities, the arms control crowd believed that scrapping the ABM Treaty was heresy, a desecration of their sacred scrolls. Preventing Russia and the United States from having national missile defenses was at the heart of "Mutual Assured Destruction" (MAD), Robert McNamara's 1960s strategy, and intended to dissuade the Soviets from initiating a nuclear exchange that would prove terminally destructive to both sides. In MAD's upside-down logic, defense was provocative: national missile defense would upset the strategic "balance of terror" and actually make nuclear war more likely. This arms control canon was reflected in the benediction that the ABM Treaty was "the cornerstone of international strategic stability." I used to joke that one had only to type in "ABM Treaty" in computers in foreign ministries and editorial boards around the world, and the "cornerstone" mantra would automatically appear on-screen.

Breaking out of this formulaic approach was necessary because it was both flawed in theory and no longer reflected strategic reality, if it ever had. This was more than the arms control theologians could handle, and they dug in their heels against the new administration. At the outset, I actually suggested to Powell that we replace the ABM Treaty with one barring Russia and the United States from building missile defenses against first strikes by the other, thus defeating the arms controllers' central argument for keeping the existing treaty. Bush had no intention of building such a capability, as conceived in Reagan's Strategic Defense Initiative (SDI, derided by its critics as "Star Wars"). Instead, he wanted to create a defense against strikes by "handfuls not hundreds" of missiles, the levels of forces Iran or

North Korea might acquire in the near future, or by accidental launches in Russia or China. "Giving up" something we didn't want was thus not a concession, but it could head off the nearly infinite variety of bad ideas bubbling up from the arms control bureaucracy. Moreover, I worried about speculation from anonymous "Bush advisers" that "we want to keep the possibility alive that nobody has to walk out of the [ABM] treaty, and that you can actually use it to move to a new relationship with Russia."[4] This was what was dreamy to me: Whatever else we did, it was absolutely critical to get out of the ABM Treaty unambiguously. Then, whether we succeeded or failed in broader negotiations with Russia, we would be free to pursue a missile defense system to protect Americans from current threats.

Powell agreed with my approach, but as early as May 14, my first one-on-one meeting with him after being sworn in, he criticized the Department of Defense (DoD) and the National Security Council (NSC) staff for underestimating how much work needed to be done to make missile defense viable. In Powell's mind, what to do about the ABM Treaty was a hypothetical question, remote rather than practical. Powell was relaxed and cordial, and emphasized he was glad I was finally on board and able to take up these issues, especially with Ivanov's visit at the end of the week.

I went to the White House to see Steve Hadley, just back from a trip to Moscow (which I had unfortunately missed because of the delays in confirmation) with Deputy Defense Secretary Paul Wolfowitz to explain the administration's position on missile defense. While I was waiting in the West Wing basement for Hadley, whom I had first met during Bush 41 when he was at the Defense Department working for Cheney, a stream of friends passed by on their way to other meetings, including Karl Rove, who said, "You know, I gave blood for you last week!" Bob Joseph, NSC senior director for proliferation strategy, and an experienced national security scholar and government official, escorted me to Hadley's tiny office next to Rice's on the West Wing's first floor. Although he spoke in his usual low-key manner, Hadley was clear that the White House would take the lead in relations with Russia, and that Powell's role would be limited. That didn't seem to be Powell's expectation, however, so I just listened, taking due note.

On Thursday I went with Powell to an NSC "Principals Committee"

---

4. Jim Hoagland, "The Stage Is Set for a Bush-Putin Summit," *Washington Post,* Sunday, May 13, 2001, p. B7, col. 1.

meeting (a "PC"), my first such interagency encounter where the departments are represented by their secretaries. On the ride to the White House, I laid out the NSC's plan to have Bush explain the "new strategic framework" at the first Bush-Putin meeting in mid-June, in Slovenia. I worried that broaching the concept cold at the Summit, with no prior preparation, would confirm the Russian bureaucracy's worst fears, which was all that Putin would hear beforehand. We drove through the White House complex's Southwest Gate, pulling up at the awning-covered basement entrance to the West Wing, and then walked through the cramped NSC quarters into the Situation Room, where several participants were already present. Cheney called out, "The man with the mustache is finally here!" which Powell still thought was funny. Rice opened the meeting outlining the NSC "cold call" approach to the Summit, but Powell quickly reoriented the discussion by talking about the first Reagan-Gorbachev encounter. He urged that in the two to three hours the two presidents might have together, they should spend a substantial period just getting acquainted, which would be highly important for their future relationship. Moreover, if the main focus was "the new strategic framework," and Putin disagreed with it, the ever-ready media would quickly spin the Summit as a failure, whereas a get-acquainted meeting could hardly "fail." All agreed. Instead of taking the NSC head-on, Powell had made his point by changing the subject, prevailing without generating any opposing argument.

Although the group was unanimous on tanking the ABM Treaty someday, the meeting ended in confusion. Rumsfeld argued for a better understanding of Russia's political agenda, and he also worried about congressional attacks on missile defense budget requests. I agreed, pointing out the risk of "Boland amendment"–style restrictions on funds appropriated for missile defense, as had been done to the aid Reagan tried to provide to the Nicaraguan Contras. These points were never answered, and the meeting drifted to something else, even though funding restrictions could cripple missile defense. Riding back to State, Powell was satisfied because the meeting's inconclusive outcome was consistent with his view that Defense had not progressed far enough operationally on missile defense for us to tank the ABM Treaty now. By contrast, I wanted the treaty out of the way immediately, precisely because we should not risk foreign or congressional obstacles that could prevent us from ever making progress on a missile defense system.

Later in the day, Armitage called me to his office, a few dozen yards down the hall from mine, and asked how the meeting went. After I described it, he said he had just spoken with Powell, who gave a similar account, emphasizing that he was pleased with the outcome. This was an early demonstration to me of the almost continuous contact between Powell and Armitage throughout the day on every major issue. It was a closeness of communication between a cabinet secretary and his deputy I had never seen before, and it meant they had the capacity to react with surprising speed to unexpected developments. This was one reason why Powell was such an agile bureaucratic infighter.

The Russians arrived on May 18. Powell hosted Foreign Minister Ivanov for lunch in his personal dining room on State's ceremonial eighth floor (which, although quite ornate, was privately donated, since Congress would never have funded the glitz). Ivanov knew English, but preferred to speak Russian, and he seemed a genial enough man. With him was Georgi Mamedov, my counterpart who had held his job for ten years. Mamedov, whose English was excellent, was a Cold War Soviet arms controller, but he was wearing a Heritage Foundation tie. He gave me a colored chart, in Russian, showing their view that the ABM Treaty was "the cornerstone of strategic stability." The discussion at lunch, with about eight participants per side, was mostly about Iraq and its continued violation of multiple Security Council resolutions covering its WMD programs. Strategic issues were to be discussed after Ivanov saw Bush at the White House. Bush did in fact raise the issue of missile defense with Ivanov, and Powell opened the afternoon meeting by noting that Bush had spoken "passionately" about it, and said that we needed to discard years of strategic thinking because circumstances were now so different. This was as chilling to many State careerists there as it was to the Russians.

After a Powell-Ivanov press conference, Mamedov, Russian deputy chief of staff Colonel-General Yuri Baluyevsky, and the rest of their delegation came to my office to continue the discussions. Getting down to specifics, Mamedov emphasized the importance of predictability in strategic matters. Our missile defense ideas were a radical departure from Clinton's proposal to reinterpret or slightly modify the ABM Treaty to permit "theater" (or local area) but not full nationwide missile defenses. I responded that the Clinton ideas were dead. We had something very different in mind, namely, a "new strategic framework," including much more than just scrapping the ABM Treaty. I explained that the new threats from rogue states were not amenable to the Cold War logic of deterrence, nor the constraints of the ABM Treaty. Mamedov kept returning to the Clinton ideas, and I explained each time they were no longer in prospect, finally saying, "That was then and this is now." The Russians were plainly having a hard time processing our election results, but I made it absolutely clear the ABM Treaty was not going to limit our missile defense efforts, and I thought they got the point. We also covered Iran's nuclear weapons program, a good example of a rogue state threat, and our worries about Russian-Iranian cooperation. Mamedov didn't deny Iran was pursuing nuclear weapons, but lamented instead that we did not treat all such programs other than those of the Security Council's five permanent members the same way, at last admitting implicitly what Iran was doing, a candid observation other Russians rarely repeated.

The pace of our activity quickened as the June 16 Bush-Putin Ljubljana Summit drew near. Rumsfeld requested a "PC" meeting on June 1 to discuss an upcoming gathering of NATO defense ministers, and asked if he shouldn't inform them that the United States was commencing a robust missile defense testing-and-development effort, thereby imminently breaching the ABM Treaty. Rumsfeld didn't ask to give the six-month notice the treaty required for withdrawal, but said we owed our allies the courtesy of telling them we would very shortly be exceeding treaty limits. This was an interesting gambit. Powell had just finished a NATO foreign ministers' meeting at which several allies complained about the potential loss of "the cornerstone of international strategic stability," and he had said nothing about timing. Rumsfeld was pushing because he didn't see much enthusiasm for missile defense at State, so why not go a different route? I thought Rumsfeld's ploy might be the only way to get things rolling toward withdrawal, but that was not Powell's reaction. He was practically jumping out of his chair at this proposed end run, if you can call something that is presented so frontally an end run. Powell was laid back on substance, but adamant on turf, the opposite of Jim Baker. He observed wryly that Rumsfeld's comments would certainly make big headlines once they leaked out of the NATO meeting. Nonetheless, while Powell obviously didn't like Rumsfeld's approach, neither did he really dig in against it. I thought that

Powell, intentionally or not, was signaling he wasn't so upset that it made any difference. In fact, Rumsfeld said at NATO pretty much what he wanted, which I thought represented progress.

The Ljubljana Summit produced no news on missile defense. It was noteworthy mostly for Bush's comment about Putin: "I looked the man in the eye. I found him to be very straightforward and trustworthy. We had a very good dialogue. I was able to get a sense of his soul." Putin stood firm on missile defense, saying squarely, "We proceed from the idea that the 1972 ABM Treaty is the cornerstone of the modern architecture of international security."[5] As I predicted, we had not done enough groundwork with Russians at lower levels, and there was no Russian movement. Time was passing, grousing about leaving the treaty was growing in Congress and overseas, and we weren't making any progress with Russia, no matter how many internal U.S. meetings we had.

While Powell was content with the endless meetings, Rumsfeld was growing increasingly impatient. As he said to me at a small lunch in his office on June 25, "We have all of these meetings which never seem to decide anything, they just get scheduled one after the other, and, my goodness, the president's never there." Moreover, bureaucratic turf fighting drove relations between State and Defense downhill, exacerbated by Armitage's visceral dislike for Rumsfeld, after he was rejected for DoD deputy secretary. Providing a break in these festivities was the president's reception for foreign ambassadors on June 28, a prelude to the Fourth of July. Bush said to me, "The fact you were confirmed proves there's justice in the world," which was certainly the way I felt. On missile defense, Bush said, "We're making progress on our favorite issue with the Europeans, Big John," but, "we need to get out there and push some more," which is what I wanted to do, rather than go to interagency meetings.

On July 10, there was yet another missile defense Principals Committee meeting, in advance of the upcoming Genoa G-7 gathering (seven nations representing nearly two-thirds of the global economy), which Russia would attend as a guest and where a second Bush-Putin meeting would take place. After a long introduction by Rice, Cheney said we should get out of the ABM Treaty, "the sooner the better," and that we would end up with the worst of both worlds if we tried to cut and trim it. Powell responded that

5. Found at http://www.whitehouse.gov/news/releases/2001/06/20010618.html.

Bush's program was to create a missile defense system, not simply to get out of the treaty. He saw two options: withdrawal, or negotiating to modify or replace it. He rejected a concept the NSC had been developing—a concept I never understood—to "set aside" the treaty to allow testing and development. Powell did not favor Bush's "pulling the trigger" in Genoa, or at Putin's expected visit to Crawford in November. Powell rarely went head to head with Cheney in these meetings, but there was one enjoyable exchange at an August 2 PC, when Cheney correctly explained how arms control agreements could actually force us to keep more weapons systems than we needed. Powell said, "You're incorrigible!" to general laughter.

Rumsfeld said we had to get out of the treaty as soon as possible because its provisions were already restricting what we could do, describing it as a "uniquely presidential" job. In Genoa, Bush should raise it one-on-one with Putin, saying we planned to announce withdrawal in, say, three months, thus triggering the six-month notice period. Otherwise, Rumsfeld said, the Hill would tie us in knots with budget restrictions, which I had been warning about for months. Rumsfeld's proposal was, in effect, to "give notice of giving notice" in Genoa, to avoid being too abrupt to the Russians, but creating a path to withdrawal nine months thereafter, which was eminently reasonable. To my surprise, Powell jumped in to say, "As a P.S., I would just say if you give notice, you can still cut a deal. You have nine months total to do it. What this really says is: We've got to be out in nine months. Do you want to figure out a way for both of us, or not?" The group then turned to what an alternative treaty might provide; at one point I explained the concept of "novation," which in contract law extinguishes one deal and replaces it with another. Rumsfeld smiled and said, "I thought that was an apprentice nun."

Powell's acquiescence to Rumsfeld's suggestion allowed Rice to summarize that there was a unified PC recommendation to the president that he tell Putin in Genoa that, while we could discuss a new or amended treaty, we were giving notice of withdrawal in three months. For a second time in the meeting, however, Powell shifted, saying, "I want to ponder this, because it's the story of the decade. The story in Genoa would be, 'We're out, and the consultations are over.' " On the other hand, Bush could stress that "the treaty is of another time, and let's see if we can work together to come up with a way of codifying strategic stability." There was more back and forth, but Rice's summary of the meeting stood. Riding back to State with Powell,

I was surprised by how upbeat he was, focusing on the nine months we had to negotiate something new. The next morning, when the NSC's Bob Joseph showed me a draft Rice-to-Bush memo presenting the PC recommendation I was even more surprised to see that the three-month interim period had become one of two options for giving the six months' notice, the second option being to wait until the end of the year before doing so. The second option was an idea Rice had come up with, after the PC to give the allies more time to appreciate that the ABM Treaty was disappearing. Powell had already agreed, but Rumsfeld was unaware of it.

Bush himself chaired a full NSC meeting on July 12. We all stood as he entered the Sit Room and took a seat at one end of the table, with Cheney to his right and Powell to his left; I sat behind Powell along the wall. Rice was opposite the president and started off by saying we would discuss the new strategic framework and the timetable of events leading to the Bush-Putin November Summit in Crawford. Cheney explained his strong desire to get out of the ABM Treaty as soon as possible, and Powell said we could do that either by U.S. withdrawal or by mutual agreement with Russia, at which point Bush interrupted to ask, "To ditch the Treaty?" and Powell agreed. Rumsfeld said we needed relief from the Treaty and strategic relief generally, and paraphrased what Bush might say to Putin in Genoa: "Let's talk for three months or so, until Crawford, but then I'm giving the six months' notice." Bush nodded affirmatively. "I can't see Putin stiffing you," said Rumsfeld, and Bush nodded again: "I'm going to convince the guy," he said. With respect to Rice's concern about notifying our allies, Bush said, "We've already told the allies; how many times do we have to?"

Rice asked later in the meeting if Bush should raise the ABM Treaty with British prime minister Blair during a stopover in London on the way to Genoa, to get "a buy-in on the concept," but Bush responded, "I've already done that. . . . I've already told Tony Blair that if we can't strike a deal, we're getting out." Bush summed up: "I'm glad we've got consensus. I think we'll get a deal. We're moving on this but we'll give Putin a choice. He knows the Europeans look at him as this little poor guy standing over here needing help, but we're his friends. We'll get an agreement, and then we'll go after the Europeans in a pincer movement." Everyone laughed, and then Bush said, smiling, "I didn't say that." Over the weekend, a test of our "hit-to-kill" missile defense system succeeded over the Pacific, providing an excellent backdrop to the Bush-Putin meeting in Genoa.

Powell flew to Rome for a G-8 foreign ministers' meeting before Genoa. During the plane ride, he and I discussed a long NSC paper on a "grand bargain" with Russia, a "term paper" in Powell's phrase, that Bush might hand to Putin, and that, ironically, neither he nor Rumsfeld liked because it was both abstract and complex. The draft was still being hashed over, but Powell was uninterested. His seeming indifference to much of government's "paper chase" was a real bureaucratic strength, because it allowed him to stay focused on larger objectives. He described this as his "bull ring" technique for handling Rice: wave a red flag at her on unimportant issues until she got tired, and then go after what he really wanted, rather than doing it head-on. On July 18, at 8:00 A.M. at the Excelsior Hotel in Rome, Powell and Ivanov had a twenty-minute one-on-one, followed by breakfast with their staffs. As breakfast started, Powell handed me a note that indicated Ivanov had said that "mutual withdrawal is impossible." Much harder than before, Powell pressed Ivanov to understand that we were going to leave the ABM Treaty unless we found some other way to create a national missile defense system. Mamedov responded by asking again about Clinton's "theater missile defense" ideas, and I repeated what I had said in May: Those ideas were off the table.

The Genoa G-8 meeting turned out to be surprisingly positive. Putin told Bush, "I'm ready to move [on the ABM Treaty], but my people are not." On this basis, Rice decided Bush should not hand over the "term paper," yet another vindication of Powell's "bull ring" technique (although Rice did subsequently give it to Russian defense minister Sergei Ivanov). On Sunday, July 22, Bush told Putin unequivocally that the United States was proceeding with missile defense preparations, so we needed to reach an understanding on what would transpire on the ABM Treaty sooner rather than later. Putin answered that several advisers had urged him to let the Americans walk out of the ABM Treaty, but he disagreed. Whatever the overall strategic balance, his main concern was preserving Russia's security, which Bush acknowledged. Their brief joint statement, however, was disturbing. It linked strategic offensive and defensive issues in a way that could allow Russia to condition elimination of the ABM Treaty on a new offensive weapons treaty. The linkage was unfortunate both because it reflected Cold War strategic thinking and because it could wrap the ABM Treaty withdrawal issue into endless arms control negotiations, which we certainly did not want.

My first trip to Moscow as undersecretary came on August 11 when I flew with Rumsfeld and his DoD team. During in-flight meetings he was firm that he had as little use for the NSC's "grand bargain" as Powell. We wanted a new relationship, including economic as well as strategic issues, which couldn't be codified in a "bargain" any more than our overall relationships with many other countries. On August 13, at the Ministry of Defense, Rumsfeld and Defense Minister Sergei Ivanov, formerly Russian national security adviser, met one-on-one for an hour and forty-five minutes, while their delegations milled around and chatted. Rumsfeld liked small meetings, and we thought that Ivanov, the first civilian Soviet/Russian defense minister, wanted to see Rumsfeld without a lot of his own "uniforms" around. The substance of the meeting provided little that was new. "SBI" (as our Moscow Embassy called him, for his full name "Sergei Borisovich Ivanov") did not give an inch on withdrawal from the ABM Treaty, and he wanted to know what our offensive nuclear weapons levels would be, and the proposed timing on reductions from present levels, essentially so that Russian weaponeers could do their own calculations on the potential impact of the ABM Treaty's demise.

A subsequent meeting between Putin and Rumsfeld followed this same line. While he had no interest in maintaining MAD as such, Putin said he would be deemed a "national security traitor" if he simply accepted our withdrawal from the ABM Treaty without long negotiations over a successor treaty and a new treaty on offensive levels, since our withdrawal would shift the balance of forces. Putin raised the prospect of Russia's joining NATO, saying, "We are being pushed out of the system of civilized Western defense." The only light moment in the talks came at dinner that evening when General Baluyevsky asked if we knew who actually originated Reagan's Strategic Defense Initiative, happily informing us he had learned on the internet that it was "an economist named Lyndon Larouche." The Americans found this hilarious, since Larouche was a political crank with a career of seeming to wander from the extreme left to the extreme right, but we tried to handle it graciously. In fact, it was frightening that Russia's second-highest military officer seriously believed such a story.

The overall Russian response indicated we had made no progress on the ABM Treaty and showed the Russians engaged in Cold War–style calculations about the impact of U.S. missile defense on their second-strike capabilities, even though we had repeatedly said that our plans were to protect against strikes by "handfuls not hundreds" of incoming warheads. One had to wonder if the Russians were not listening to what we were telling them at these meetings, or if they still simply couldn't believe we were serious about withdrawing from the ABM Treaty. Of course, many at State and in the "arms control community" couldn't believe it either, so the latter possibility was not unlikely. Indeed, Putin told Rumsfeld several times that while Russia would not stir up international criticism if we unilaterally withdrew, they could if they wanted to, and someone else surely would, a not very subtle threat, in Rumsfeld's view. I concluded we needed a complete break with the ABM Treaty, with no further talk of a replacement.

I then met with Mamedov at the Foreign Ministry's Osobnyak compound in Moscow, owned in pre-Soviet days by a wealthy industrialist sympathetic to the Communists. We actually met in a building that was originally servants' quarters, but was now set up for meetings. Our delegation was embarrassingly Cold War sized (sixteen on each side) because none of the agencies involved trusted the others enough to be left alone with the Russians. Mamedov and I led off with general statements of our positions, although mine was about ten minutes, and Mamedov's, in two parts, was about fifty, a good portion of which was for the benefit of Baluyevsky and the Russian uniforms present.

Finally, however, I decided to do a little performing myself. Mamedov had said Russia worried about the changeability of American views (that is, those pesky presidential elections), so I assured him that even if Bush lost in 2004, there would be no change in U.S. views of the ABM Treaty, because by then there wouldn't be a treaty. I said they needed to understand that the ABM Treaty was not a permanent agreement with a six-month withdrawal clause, but a six-month-long treaty being renewed on a daily basis. That definitely got the Russians' attention, and led the DoD contingent to declare privately that I had won the "line of the day" award, even though it was still well before lunchtime. After explaining the rogue-state threats that had led us to conclude we needed a limited but nationwide missile defense capability, we broke to have lunch in the Morozov House, named for the Communist-sympathizing industrialist. Just to make me feel at home, Mamedov recalled that Lenin, Trotsky, and the Bolsheviks had had a disdainful view of treaties, renouncing most of the czarist treaties after they took control in 1917. I noted they had also abolished the Foreign Ministry because they considered nation-states to be obsolete political manifestations of capitalism, to be replaced by direct relations among the world's working classes. Mamedov agreed that, indeed, times had changed.

Unfortunately, back in the carriage house, nothing changed. The Russians continued to reject both unilateral U.S. withdrawal and mutual withdrawal by jointly abrogating the ABM Treaty. I made it clear that we were open to other suggestions, but we would soon be announcing withdrawal, thus giving the treaty's required six months' notice. Two days later, I met with Foreign Minister Igor Ivanov to say we were ready to meet anytime, anywhere on the ABM Treaty, but that time was growing very short. Ivanov said they were considering everything we had said, and that he looked forward to meeting Powell on September 19.

In preparation for that meeting, Mamedov and I agreed we should talk in London on September 13. On the morning of September 11, I came to State with my bags packed ready to fly to London to meet with the Brits on the twelfth and Mamedov the next day. The Al Qaeda attacks ended all that and consumed Powell's attention once he returned late on September 11 from Peru. After a large meeting in Powell's office at 7:00 A.M. on September 12, he asked me to stay behind, observing that I was obviously not meeting with Mamedov in London. Powell said I needed to find a way to rendezvous somewhere with Mamedov before September 19. It was now all the more important to find out whether Russia was prepared to break from its high level of opposition to ending the ABM Treaty. "I know you understand you have a hunting license to get whatever you can from him," said Powell, "and you need to keep at it." I called Mamedov, and we agreed to meet in Moscow on Monday, September 17. Of course, at this point there was no way of telling what would be happening with commercial air travel, so I set about getting a Pentagon plane to Moscow. Defense came though with an Air Force Gulfstream V, and my small delegation departed on September 16 from Andrews Air Force Base, headed for Moscow.

As we flew east of Manhattan, we watched in silence the cloud of smoke and dust still blowing from where the World Trade Center had stood. There was simply nothing to say, but I will never forget it, as I will not forget the scene from my office at State on September 11, when I could see the flames and smoke rising from the Pentagon. Although some long-time critics of missile defense concluded that the September 11 attacks proved it was unnecessary, I concluded precisely the opposite. If Al Qaeda possessed nuclear, chemical, or biological weapons, or if rogue states like Iran, Iraq, or North Korea used these weapons with ballistic missiles, the death and destruction would be far worse. Our intelligence had missed the preparations for this devastating attack, and there was no telling what else they were missing. I was reinforced in my view that we needed to proceed even more quickly to establish a new relationship with Russia, so we could turn our attention urgently to the broader threat of WMD proliferation.

On Monday, September 17, surrounded by a large media gaggle, we met the Russians at Osobnyak. Mamedov said in an opening one-on-one that Russia wanted "a true alliance against terrorism," which was "a real and present danger" because "we are at war." September 11 created "a new sense of urgency" for Russia strategically because they felt insecure, as did we. They wanted to know what our military response would be to September 11, particularly given media reports it would have a "nuclear element," which I explained was simply press speculation. The attacks "created a new window of opportunity in our relationship," said Mamedov, and "what is really important is that strong people unite in the face of tragedy." Igor Ivanov, he said, would have a reaction to Rice's "term paper" when he met with Powell, but not a "complete response," because real progress could be made only when Putin and Bush met in Shanghai in a few weeks. The real key for them was that they expected us to have our projected level of offensive weapons by then, so that the discussions could get more serious.

The meeting with the full delegations covered this same ground at greater length, as was so often the case, but emphasized possible cooperation that would be tangible evidence of a "new strategic framework." Of course, that went only so far. When one of the Americans noted we had just given their ambassador in Washington a tour of our Nevada nuclear test site, I suggested they give me a tour of theirs. "No, John," said Mamedov, "you're too dangerous." In the afternoon, I met with Igor Ivanov, who said he would bring proposals personally approved by Putin, and that he looked forward to a serious discussion with Powell in Washington. He also related that, on September 11, he was with Putin watching events on television when he was told Rice was calling from Washington. He picked up the phone, and heard Rice say, "Sergei?" to which he responded that she did have an Ivanov, but not the right one. Ivanov suggested that Rice talk directly to Putin, which she did, explaining that the military steps the United

States was taking that day were not directed against Russia. Rice's fascination with SBI, who had been her counterpart but was now defense minister, led to endless turf squabbles with Rumsfeld and Powell.

After Powell's September 19 meeting with Ivanov, Powell wrote me a note saying Ivanov had brought Putin's proposed "political statement" for Crawford that Powell thought contained "elements we can work with." (Later, when I read the documents I found them disappointing because they didn't say anything new.) Powell and Ivanov discussed possible counterterrorism cooperation, as Ivanov acknowledged the significant link between terrorism and WMD proliferation, possibly signaling developments in their thinking, especially on Iraq and Iran. Powell explained that "it is not in your interest to be seen as a friend of Iraq," which obviously took Ivanov by surprise. Powell also stressed that when Bush spoke Thursday to a joint session of Congress, he would emphasize we would be going after not just the terrorists themselves, but also the states that sponsored or harbored them. Indeed, during his meeting with Ivanov, Bush linked terrorism, WMD proliferation, and ballistic missiles, especially Iran, which showed that his instincts were on target. Even better, Bush told Ivanov, "Let's not wait for the Europeans, let's lead them," and that he was "holding out his hand" to Putin, which was already reflected in their frequent telephone calls about our response to 9/11.

Shortly thereafter, while I was in Uzbekistan arranging basing and access rights for our imminent military operations against the Taliban in Afghanistan, Rumsfeld was prodding Powell. He noted on September 24 that the Pentagon had canceled three ABM tests because State "had failed to get out of the ABM Treaty," a comment that definitely increased Powell's blood pressure. In fact, State-Defense relations continued downhill, the atmosphere at State being particularly corrosive. Missile defense was only a tiny part of the emerging hostility, especially from Powell and Armitage. They complained about the disorganization they saw at Defense, especially within Defense's civilian political leadership. The attacks sometimes got personal, as on October 9 when Armitage opined that perhaps Rumsfeld's memory was not what it once was. Armitage liked to gossip, and what was wrong at Defense was a frequent topic of his discourse. The Foreign Service heard all of this as well, and the hostility was reflected in interagency dealings. I explained the deteriorating situation to Karl Rove at a small dinner hosted by the Cheneys at their residence in early October, and he fully understood the negative implications for the administration as a whole.

I flew with Powell to Pakistan and India for short visits before we landed in Shanghai on October 17 for the APEC (Asia-Pacific Economic Cooperation) meeting where Bush would raise the issue of the ABM Treaty with Putin. During the flight, Powell and I discussed the Pentagon's evolving offensive warhead numbers, based on what he was hearing from Rice. Powell was very unhappy, complaining about the long delays in Defense's nuclear posture review, which had produced results only days before the Bush-Putin meeting. "Rumsfeld's up," said Powell, "but he won't be for long. The QDR [Quadrennial Defense Review] is crap and his budget sucks, and that will all come out." He wasn't much happier with Rice: "I can't figure Condi out anymore," Powell complained, citing several examples of her indecisiveness. "She's always positioning herself."

During an October 18 dinner with Igor Ivanov, Powell was quite firm in explaining we either had to make progress quickly on "moving beyond the ABM Treaty," or, "we're getting out." The Bush-Putin meeting focused largely on strategic issues and went quite well from my perspective, as Bush explained to Putin we were leaving the ABM Treaty. Putin responded that he would not object if we withdrew, but he did not see that the treaty actually limited what we wanted to do, or so his experts told him. If so, why withdraw? Bush candidly explained that our military had not had a full opportunity to decide on offensive numbers, but that we would do so shortly. In the subsequent press conference, Bush called the treaty not only "outdated," but "dangerous."

Bush returned from Shanghai determined to decide the issue of offensive numbers, and Powell had the distinct impression Bush wanted a treaty to announce in spring 2002. In fact, what the White House wanted was not clear, as Powell and Rice resumed discussions in which withdrawal from the ABM Treaty blurred into negotiating offensive weapons limits. All of this sounded like a return to the "grand bargain" approach that I thought had been discarded. Powell also happily told me that Counselor to the President Karen Hughes thought that "unilateral withdrawal" from the ABM Treaty was not good in domestic political terms. DoD finally came up with its offensive numbers, a range between 1,700 and 2,200 or 2,300, quite close to what we had expected. Nonetheless, Powell told me Cheney was grumbling about the whole direction he and Rice were taking, and Rumsfeld felt the same way. It was certainly the way I felt.

Although Powell and Rice seemed to agree on substance, they continued to diverge on process, with Powell asking Igor Ivanov to come to Washington, and Rice preparing to invite Sergei Ivanov. I told Powell what I had heard, and he exploded about Rice and SBI: "She's going with her hormones again!" Rumsfeld's reaction was to announce the cancellation of three tests the ABM Treaty precluded, his way of trying to break free from this quasi-academic exercise. At one point as we discussed a document to give to Igor Ivanov, now coming to Washington on November 1, Powell yelled over the phone, "Condi, you don't have the faintest idea what's going on! Rumsfeld and those guys over there don't want any deal! Don't you see that?"

Igor Ivanov arrived at State on November 1, and Powell handed over an arduously drafted "declaration" we hoped the two leaders could deliver. Since the Russians needed time to read it, Powell and Ivanov adjourned for a one-on-one. There, Powell told Ivanov that our offensive number was 1,800 to 2,300, and that, at Crawford, we would give notice of withdrawal from the ABM Treaty, effective in six months, saying we were prepared to defer deployment of a missile defense system for two years.

When Powell and Ivanov returned, I explained the draft declaration, which Mamedov said they considered to be "very serious." Ivanov said the essence of the draft was withdrawal from the treaty. They did not dispute our sovereign right to withdraw, but announcing it while Putin was in America could hardly make his visit a success. Ivanov pointed out, correctly and tellingly, that we had not even begun negotiations on any of the issues presented by the draft. Ivanov was unknowingly highlighting the problem on the American side, namely that we had been circling around at abstract levels and not concentrating on the most important concrete issue, namely withdrawal from the treaty, which we had to do whether or not there was to be a "new strategic framework" with Russia. Our "term paper" approach had not gotten us what we needed, nor had it resolved Russia's concerns, effectively leaving us both at square one.

The next day, Friday, November 2, I flew with Rumsfeld from Andrews AFB to Moscow. After Ivanov's departure on Thursday, Rumsfeld had pushed Rice and Powell on the withdrawal point, saying, "We should have withdrawn from the ABM Treaty six to eight months ago." Powell urged further discussions, but Rumsfeld asked, "Why don't we just put the notice of withdrawal in an envelope tomorrow? When does Putin want it? Tomorrow? At Crawford? In three weeks? Why don't I just ask him?" Rice and Powell talked Rumsfeld out of this approach, and Powell called Igor Ivanov on Friday morning to say I was available to stay behind to talk further after Rumsfeld met with Putin. This could be important, Ivanov said, because Putin's reaction to his report on the Washington discussions had been, "Don't jab me in the eye while I'm in the United States." We arrived at the Defense Ministry at 9:00 A.M. on Saturday, and Sergei Ivanov met with Rumsfeld, accompanied only by notetakers. Rumsfeld started by saying that there were three options for receiving the formal notification of withdrawal: before, during, or after the Crawford Summit, which certainly resolved what Rumsfeld thought his negotiating latitude was. SBI reacted with some horror to the idea that we would give notice before or during Crawford, which may well have been the shock therapy that Rumsfeld intended, because SBI focused entirely on the "when" of the notice, not the "whether."

Just before 11:00 A.M. we rode to the Kremlin for Rumsfeld to meet Putin. We entered near the Kremlin museum, circled the perimeter, and stopped at the elaborate presidential building. We were ushered into a large, ornate, lime-and-white room where Putin greeted Rumsfeld, and where the media got their "photo op." We then sat down at a white, inlaid conference table. Accompanied by SBI, Baluyevsky, and a notetaker, Putin, who was thoroughly relaxed and confident, said he and Bush had had a very useful time in Shanghai, and their dialogue was developing nicely. Putin launched into a long monologue on Afghanistan, saying our cooperation against the Taliban had reached unprecedented levels. He said their "security forces" had recently detained a foreigner who had entered Russia using false papers. "Let me go," the man said, "I'm a CIA agent. I'm on your side. I can prove it," and asked to call a number that turned out to be our embassy. Putin said in Russian, "Seriously, we must succeed. We cannot afford to lose in Afghanistan." The Taliban had urged Russia to assist them, but, said Putin *in English*, "We gave them only one answer," gesturing with the Russian version of "the finger." We all laughed, and Rumsfeld said, "We do it a little differently, but I get the point!"

Shortly after noon, Putin turned to strategic issues and his upcoming U.S. visit. Missile defense was "a huge problem" for him, but he said, "I assume we should think about the future. We are ready to agree that there are some threats" from rogue states, but they were decades away. Perhaps we could agree to "additions to the treaty," which Putin said was vastly different from their position in the Clinton years, as we should recognize. If America wanted to withdraw, that was our sovereign right, even if they did not understand our logic. In addition to being "contrary to our philosophy," Putin said his political situation made "mutual withdrawal" impossible, because it would be seen as caving in to us: "It would be our last agreement, and they would replace us here," Putin said as both he and SBI chuckled. As to our announcement of withdrawal, Putin said, "We will work honestly and openly with you as a partner. We are not trying to create difficulties for you, but don't put us in a difficult situation. For us, American withdrawal during our visit would not be the best background." Rumsfeld said, "I understand."

Putin said that eliminating all restrictions on testing and development would eliminate the treaty *de facto,* which I thought was worth responding to. I said we thought the Russians had agreed to this, and Putin responded, "I know I am dealing with a colleague. I am a lawyer, too, but the fact is the guts of the treaty would be gone without those provisions. This is almost like talking to a relative, so I do not need to explain further." Rumsfeld said we did not object to further discussions among "experts," noting that he was "a law school dropout." "Then you are even more dangerous," said Putin to general laughter.

For the next three days I had frequent phone conversations with Powell and many discussions with Igor Ivanov and Mamedov in which I assured them we would not announce withdrawal from the ABM Treaty while Putin was in Crawford. Powell then told me to tell Ivanov and Mamedov we would disclose all of our testing programs to the Russians so they would know exactly what we had in mind, thus putting them at ease, which I did later that day. The Russians thought we were back in negotiations, whereas I knew we had bought the necessary time to finally bring this matter to a head. Hadley called to say Bush spoke by phone with Putin on November 8, and to confirm we should give the Russians the briefing they wanted. Hadley said the discussions in Moscow had gone just right: "I know you've been cold steeling them over there, and everyone here is very happy with the way things have gone."

While the Pentagon scrambled on November 9 to put together the briefing, I flew with Powell to New York, where he would attend the postponed opening of the UN General Assembly, but where the real agenda was dealing with the Russians. If we could convince them that our testing program was in violation of the treaty, which it clearly was, then we would be back on the road to withdrawal. I communicated all of this to Joseph and J. D. Crouch, an assistant secretary of defense, and an academic when he wasn't in government service. Crouch was honing the briefing so we could show just how violative of the treaty DoD's plans were. This briefing, scheduled at the Russian UN Mission for 3:00 P.M., was now even more crucial than before. Baluyevsky and the other Russians present had many questions, but by the end there could be no doubt in their minds that we would be massively violating the ABM Treaty in very short order. The Russians were silent by the end of this seventy-five-minute discussion, signaling that they knew exactly where things now stood.

Powell and Ivanov met the next morning, November 11. After discussing other aspects of the Crawford Summit, which were easy compared to the ABM Treaty, Powell asked about their reaction to the Saturday briefing. Baluyevsky said it was clear we contemplated tests not in a "gray zone" but that were clear violations of the ABM Treaty. I whispered to Rice, "We have been telling them this for three months," and she whispered back, "I know, and they just started listening yesterday." Ivanov said that Putin had earlier made their position very clear, and there was no possibility of compromising away from it. Ivanov could only ask, "What is the hurry to leave? Is it really technical, or is it political?" This was the first time I really believed we had won the battle, and that the ABM Treaty was history. The meeting ended just before noon, and so did the ABM Treaty, for all practical purposes.

We still needed agreement, however, on the text of what the two presidents would say. Back in Washington on November 13, I left with Powell at 8:30 A.M. on the thirteenth to ride to the White House, waiting in the West Wing basement lobby while Powell went to the Sit Room for the daily Afghanistan meeting and the news that the Taliban had just fled from Kabul. Rumsfeld came by and asked, smiling, "Have we given up anything yet today?" I said, "Not yet, but we're working on it!" Putin and his delegation arrived around 10:00 A.M., as the opening Bush-Putin meeting (with only Powell and Rice attending on our side) got under way.

At about eleven-twenty, there was the unmistakable agitation of people coming out of the president's secretary's office, and I could hear Powell saying, "Where's Bolton?" as he and Ivanov emerged into the hallway outside the Cabinet Room, Hadley trotting behind them. I followed, as we raced toward the West Wing's southwest corner, and then down to the basement into a suite of windowless rooms off the lobby, where Powell, Ivanov, Hadley, and I sat around a small conference table. Powell said the missile defense statement would say only that both sides were continuing to explore their options. "President Putin fully understands, however, that we are withdrawing in December," said Powell, "but we just won't say so." That was it. I concentrated on keeping my game face on. Powell said that, on offensive weapons, we would announce the U.S. range of 1,700 to 2,200, down from about 6,000, and the Russians would "welcome it."

With President Bush's announcement of the U.S. withdrawal from the ABM Treaty on December 13, a dangerous relic of the Cold War was officially put to rest.

The Treaty of Moscow and the End of Arms Control

> The alternative to arms control and détente is the bankruptcy and death of civilization.
>
> —George McGovern[6]

During the ABM Treaty negotiations, the Russians repeatedly asked for our offensive numbers, following the Cold War logic of calculating the impact of Bush's missile defense system. In arms control negotiations going back to the 1920s, fixed limits and targets of different kinds of weapons had been central. In the minds of arms control theologians, these limits did not require calibration with strategic reality because their ultimate objective was disarmament—the Holy Grail. Arms control opponents disagreed strongly, and this fundamental rift never closed. For the Bush administration, the end of the Cold War, and pursuing a "new strategic framework" with Russia, meant it was time to end prior arms control fantasies. Strategic weapons should be only one facet of relations with Russia, and certainly not the dominant one, as during the Cold War.

First, we wanted to determine what an adequate level of strategic forces would be for us, and then negotiate with Russia, rather than picking arbi-

---

6. Quoted in Eugene V. Rostow, "The Case Against SALT II," *Commentary*, February 1979, p. 23.

trary targets and hoping we could get Russian agreement. Rumsfeld had in mind a very different role for nuclear weapons in our overall defense posture. This role would reflect changed international circumstances and threat levels, and result in the reduction of deployed warheads over the next several years. Russia was, in fact, no longer a strategic threat (whatever other problems it might pose), and we projected that its nuclear capacities would be dropping like a stone over the next decade. Accordingly, a treaty that simply embodied our own planning levels was hardly a burden, especially if it also provided "exit ramps" to allow for rapid changes in its terms as the strategic threats we faced evolved or increased.

Next was targeting: How many strategic warheads were needed for conflicts that were sufficiently foreseeable to plan against? This was, to say the least, a complex military exercise, but with important political overtones, which explains why we ended up with a range of 1,700 to 2,200 deployed warheads, rather than a single number. Moreover, numerical limits addressed only visible areas of military competition, not others that might actually be more important, such as weapons production capabilities, levels of tactical nuclear weapons, intelligence, and total economic strength. Russia and America did not have "symmetrical" capabilities, but treaties with specific warhead limits gave the illusion that they did, hiding important differences.

Then, there was "counting." In prior negotiations, enormous amounts of time and attention were devoted to "counting rules," ways of imputing nuclear levels to the parties, because of the inadequacies of verification and each side's unwillingness to reveal exactly what it had. To overcome these difficulties, "counting rules" imputed capacities that "counted" against a treaty's limits even if they were not fully used. For example, a Russian SS-18 missile can carry ten warheads, so it "counts" as ten, even if a given missile only carries five. We wanted to count only "operationally deployed strategic nuclear warheads," thus replacing "counting rules" with the actual numbers. Not only was this approach more accurate, it would free up large numbers of delivery systems for conventional warheads, making them more useful against the non-nuclear threats we were increasingly facing.

The first U.S.-Russia negotiating session was in Washington on January 29, 2002. Mamedov knew Putin was determined to have an agreement by the May Summit, although in true Cold War style, the Russians demonstrated an uncanny ability to make lengthy speeches and say little. They

knew the impatient Americans well; we would grow eager to actually negotiate rather than speechify, which would work to their advantage, as it had so
many times before. Mamedov handed over two drafts, one containing the
elements of an offensive weapons treaty, and one on the overall strategic relationship. That evening, the president gave the State of the Union address
describing Iraq, Iran, and North Korea as an "axis of evil," which gladdened
my heart. In the near term, however, my focus was on the May Summit.

On February 11, Powell spoke privately with Bush, saying there was a
PC meeting the next day to resolve interagency disputes, which Bush said
he was "ready" to hear, given the short time until the May 18 Summit:
"When do things get out of tolerance?" asked Bush. Powell said I had negotiations in Moscow on February 19, and Bush said, "Tell John not to worry,
he'll know what he needs to do." Still, Powell was unhappy with Rice's unwillingness to act decisively, and her constant "positioning" to avoid criticism, saying to me, "I don't have a future after this job, and neither does
Rumsfeld. Neither does Cheney," implying that the three of them said exactly what they felt regardless of the consequences. Powell said he was generally tired of Rice's thinking that she "has two cabinet secretaries to fuck
with." Rumsfeld was also not happy with Rice's style, and he asked specifically that the principals meet directly with the president, an indirect slap at
what he and Powell separately complained about, namely lack of face time
with the president. The February 12 PC meeting turned out to be no more
than reciting established positions on whether the offensive weapons levels
should be fixed in a "legally binding document" (a treaty or an executive
agreement) or something else, such as a joint statement. Powell and Rice
favored the former, while Rumsfeld and Cheney favored the latter. Since I
saw treaties as essentially only political documents, and the whole debate
over what was "legally binding" in "international law" as just another theological exercise, I didn't care about the answer. Most important, Putin had
asked Bush for a treaty, and Bush appeared to agree. "Keep your eyes on the
prize," Jim Baker would say.

Bush told Powell later, "Don just wants to be provocative, but I'm thinking geostrategically on this issue. I know what I have to do with my buddy
[Putin]. We need the ability to get out [of any treaty] and the response
force, and I know that. But I can get what I need and still be faithful to the
Russians." Powell was thus very confident how the February 15 NSC meeting would turn out, and it was, in fact, decisive. Powell opened with Bush's

campaign pledge to reduce nuclear weapons levels, unilaterally if need be, and noted that Russia strongly preferred to have the new limits in a treaty. He noted the number of provisions for withdrawal, consultation, and amendment we had proposed, and also stressed that START I (the existing strategic weapons treaty) verification would remain in place. Rumsfeld said he wanted to maintain flexibility in our nuclear posture, as Bush interjected, "I really think that the reliability of the warhead stockpile over time is the bigger issue." After hearing everyone out, Bush said, "I believe we must have something that lasts beyond our presidencies. The strategic relationship with Russia is something that's important for the next ten years. So, to cement relations, I'm willing to throw the guy [Putin] some bones." Bush related to Putin's domestic political vulnerability, since he "is on thin ice in his own mind. I want to give him a document he can hold up," to help Putin "bring her [Russia] West. I view this paper, frankly, as part of the larger strategy to link Russia with us. We need a document that he can hold up and say, 'Time is on our side' in May."

Looking at Powell and me, Bush said: "We should push hard for an agreement with the right numbers and with flexibility that we can give to Congress for approval, not necessarily a treaty. We would just have an up-or-down vote in Congress, no changes. This is only a letter agreement, and it ought not be complicated. We should work toward our words on our philosophy, laying out the target numbers with thirty or forty-five days' notice to change, and the transparency things." He stressed, "I am willing to have no deal." He said to Rumsfeld, "I am just as frustrated as you by all of those negotiations in Geneva. That's not going to happen again." Bush asked, "Who's going over there next week," and Powell said "Bolton," Rumsfeld chiming in, "Mr. Hanging Chad!" Bush laughed and said, "That's why he's here!" Pointing at me, Bush said, "Now look, John, this piece of paper is important from our strategic perspectives. Putin is at huge risk, and he needs to fight off his troglodytes. Without a treaty, however, there is no discipline, but we're not going to have any changes by Congress; this will be a straight up-or-down vote. I want you to be tough with them, because Putin needs this agreement." I said only, "It will be my pleasure, Mr. President." "*We* don't need an agreement," Bush went on. "If they won't deal, I will fade to heat," repeating a few seconds later he would "fade to heat" before signing a bad agreement. "I am really more worried about the quality of our warheads, rather than their number," he said as he rose to leave, shaking my hand on the way out, saying, "Go get 'em, John." "Yes, sir," I said in a burst of inspiration.

Rumsfeld said good-bye with his trademark, "Now don't screw this up, John." Cheney said, "The only mistake you can make is to come back with a bad agreement," which was just right. Powell pulled Rice aside and urged, in light of what Bush had said, "I expect now that there will be no more trench warfare from DoD on the offensive warhead issue," and Rice agreed the president had been very clear. "You got what you needed" were Powell's last words to me as we headed off to separate meetings. The main point coloring all of these discussions, evident to me in any event, was that Bush wanted an agreement to announce at the May Summit.

That launched three months of intensive negotiations in Moscow and Washington, where, unfortunately, we seemed to be spinning our wheels. While that was no different from countless other negotiations where the opening foreplay stretches out almost interminably, we didn't exactly have an eternity to fool around. Russia's basic position was that it could accept our proposed range of 1,700 to 2,200 warheads, but only according to START II counting rules, in a "legally binding document," as well as proof that some of our delivery platforms (such as submarines and heavy bombers) were being converted to non-nuclear weapons. It was clear that differences over "counting rules" masked the more fundamental problem that the Russians felt extremely uncomfortable with "operationally deployed strategic nuclear warheads" as a basis for the treaty. This was not the way arms control had been conducted in the past, and the Russians saw no reason to abandon the old-time religion, thus allying themselves revealingly with American arms control acolytes. On March 13, Rumsfeld said explicitly, "We are at a fork in the road," and SBI responded, "We are not ready to go cold turkey." While the metaphors were mixed, the disjunction was clear.

Back to serial meetings, we started with a March 21–22 Bolton-Mamedov meeting in Geneva, the site of so many Cold War arms control efforts of long and fruitless days and nights. Mamedov and I met again in London on April 2, followed by Powell and Igor Ivanov, accompanied by Mamedov and me, in Madrid on April 10–11, then another Mamedov-Bolton meeting in Moscow on April 22–24. The London meeting with Mamedov was actually something neither of us had mentioned widely within our own governments, in order to avoid dragging along our massive arms control delegations. Powell told Rice about the meeting as it was happening, saying, "Bolton is out doing good things that you don't want to know anything about." "Like what?" she responded, and Powell said again, "You don't want to know, but he'll be back tomorrow." At that point, Rice laughed and said, "Okay, I don't know anything." Bush said to Putin in an April 2 phone call that he was very pleased that we had made progress, although he understood there were many issues yet to resolve. So happy was Powell that, when I briefed him after my return from London, he rose from his chair, laughing heartily, to give me a high five, and asked, "Who's your daddy?" Thus is serious diplomacy conducted.

The turning point came on April 23, when Sergei Ivanov invited me to his office. I arrived just before 6:00 P.M., and Baluyevsky took me to SBI's suite, which seemed very quiet compared to the customary level of activity in Powell's or Rumsfeld's office. Ivanov's office followed the Russian pattern of long, relatively narrow rooms with a large desk at one end and a conference table on one side. We sat in a small seating area near Ivanov's desk, just the two of us, and Ivanov spoke in his accented but nearly perfect English. "Igor and I met yesterday to discuss the strategic issues, because we are obviously stuck. We have almost no time left until the Summit, and at our present pace, we will not reach agreement. Please forgive me for being so blunt, because I am not a diplomat . . ." I broke in to say, "That's okay, I'm not a diplomat either. I'm a lawyer." SBI smiled and said, "But at least officially you are a diplomat," and we both laughed. I said we had not made progress even that morning on the existing draft, and Ivanov said, "Yes, I am not surprised. I have spoken last week with Condoleezza Rice on this point."

They had prepared an alternative draft, much shorter than what we had been working on, in an effort to reach agreement. Igor would have given it to me, Sergei said, but he was traveling with Putin to Turkmenistan for the Caspian Sea Summit, so he was handing over the new text, in Russian, only three pages long. "We thought someone named 'Ivanov' should give it to you," he said, laughing. He translated the key provisions as limiting "strategic offensive weapons" to the 1,700 to 2,200 range, and also providing: "Both sides shall separately define the structures of their strategic offensive forces within these limits." SBI explained, "This means each side reaches the limits in its own way. If you want 4,600 warheads [i.e., our range plus our "response force"], that's okay with me. That's your plus. Our plus is that this language doesn't mention 'operationally deployed warheads.' We can then eliminate [weapons] platforms if we choose, and you can keep them if you choose." I concluded to myself that SBI was basically accepting our concept without wanting to endorse it specifically, which, while awkward, was certainly fine with me. The new Russian draft eliminated our "off ramps" to increase the permissible warhead limits but still stay within the treaty, but it contained a withdrawal provision that left the required notice period blank, meaning the time was open for negotiation.

These proposals, after months of gridlock, meant that agreement was now possible by the May Summit, one month away. Ivanov said, "Please tell your colleagues, no public statements about this until you are ready to respond to it. Our president knows about this, but few others. Both presidents want something they can sign at the Summit, and our press cares only about this treaty." Back in Washington on April 25, I briefed both Powell and then a Hadley-chaired meeting on the breakthrough. When DoD picked at the text, Hadley responded, "We often have a problem reacting to 'yes' as an answer, and I think we need to be careful of that here." No one doubted there was still much to do, but the Russians had moved three-quarters of the way toward our basic positions.

The next key event was a Rumsfeld–Sergei Ivanov meeting at Sheremet'yevo Airport near Moscow on April 29. It was certainly unusual to have the two defense ministers rather than the two foreign ministers negotiating, but it was typical of the way the NSC allowed this negotiation and withdrawal from the ABM Treaty to proceed, with all of the attendant turf fighting. Rumsfeld arrived in Moscow on Monday, April 29, and Ivanov hosted a lunch for him. Rumsfeld was in good humor, noting how closely he was working with Powell and Rice on the negotiations, and he said at one point: "John has really been working for both State and Defense on this," which I knew would thrill Powell if he heard it. Rumsfeld added, "In fact, John's only real defect is that he is a lawyer," always a good laugh line for him. Rumsfeld and SBI went through the draft agreement paragraph by paragraph, but didn't actually change anything. At the joint press conference afterward, Ivanov said, "I want to divulge to you a small secret concerning our joint work. The fact is that literally a few days ago, actually four to five days ago, we submitted to the U.S. side a number of new ideas, which in our view could provide the basis for an agreement." That certainly opened the curtain. Later that day, Igor Ivanov and Mamedov told me Sergei believed the meeting had been a disaster because Rumsfeld had rejected everything in their recent draft. I assured them that they were misreading our position, which they were. I called Powell to tell him that "Igor is one unhappy puppy," but Powell agreed he was overreacting. In fact, on May 3 in Washington, Igor basically conceded on our counting rules and the concept of "operationally deployed warheads," although we still had the "exit ramps" and several smaller issues to resolve. After Ivanov and Mamedov left Powell's office to go to the White House for a courtesy call on Bush, Powell and I shook hands in his small inner office, because we knew at that point there would be a treaty to sign in Moscow.

There remained the cosmic question of what the treaty would be called. In arms control, names using acronyms like "SALT" and "START" were common, and therefore every instinct was to come up with something analogous. I preferred a radically different name, such as "Treaty of Moscow," where most of the agreement was negotiated and would be signed, and showing emphatically it was a different kind of treaty. That's what I have always called it, even though the Russians found words conforming to the old arms control style, which made them happier. On May 13, after Mamedov and I worked out the last details, the two presidents made essentially simultaneous announcements in Moscow and in Washington. I was back in Moscow on May 20 for final preparations. Referring to the treaty and the Summit political declaration, Igor Ivanov said, "There are sentences in these documents that only you and Mamedov understand," which was unfortunately probably true!

Bush arrived on the evening of May 23, and the next morning, the presidential caravan rolled into the Kremlin to the Great Kremlin Palace. After a longer-than-expected private Putin-Bush meeting, their entourages moved into a holding area, where, one last time, I looked over the English version of the text Bush and Putin were to sign, bound in formal treaty style. Then we proceeded to St. Catherine's Hall where we lined up so that the two presidents could greet each other's delegations. "Nice to see you again," Putin said to me.

The actual signing was in St. Andrew's Hall, which had formerly been a throne room, and which Yeltsin had restored a few years earlier to its opulent czarist splendor, tearing out an ugly Stalinist auditorium. The signing was everything that a photo op could be, followed by a press conference on the U.S.-Russian relationship. After a ceremonial lunch, President and Mrs. Bush took a walking tour of the Kremlin's Cathedral Square, which was unexpectedly filled with tourists. Since our advance people had emphatically told all of us to stay out of the pictures, Powell and I dodged around the square, not really knowing where the tour was going next. As with many Bush tours, this exercise lasted all of seven minutes, not the scheduled thirty minutes. That pretty well summed up the end of arms control.

The G-8 Global Partnership: A Different Kind of Multilateralism

In early 2002, while negotiating the Treaty of Moscow, an idea arose that could further cement U.S.-Russian cooperation, and also spread the cost of destroying Russia's Cold War arsenal of nuclear and chemical weapons and ballistic missiles. Under existing programs, including the original Nunn-Lugar legislation, we were spending roughly one billion dollars a year to destroy these weapons (and we still do). Most of our allies, however, spent little or nothing, despite the enormous benefits they and we derived from eliminating Russia's Cold War weapons stockpile. Why shouldn't the others help bear the costs and contribute to programs from which they clearly benefited? With the annual G-7 meeting approaching at Kananaskis, Canada, we suggested the G-7 double the amount of funding for these programs during a ten-year period. Given what the United States was already spending, the idea's first iteration was called "10 plus 10 over 10," meaning we would continue spending at that rate for ten years, and the other G-7 members collectively would put up an equal amount during that period. Bush liked the idea immediately, and Congress, especially Senator Lugar, was enthusiastic as well. The Canadians concurred and saw it as a major potential "deliverable" from Kananaskis.

Russia, eager to join the G-7 (which they did at Kananaskis, thus making it "the G-8"), was at first cool to the idea, focusing instead on a higher economic priority, namely debt relief, which it thought had been promised by German chancellor Schroeder and others. G-7 central bankers, however, did not like debt relief because they considered the outstanding debt a potentially useful hedge against the uncertain future of Russia's nascent democracy. While they were willing conceptually to consider swapping "debt for proliferation," this was hard to do operationally. We turned instead to programs funded directly by G-7 countries, modeled on the Nunn-Lugar approach. But the other G-7 members remained skeptical.

The Canadians did not present "10 plus 10 over 10" to Russia until mid-May, when I was in Moscow preparing for the Moscow Summit. Unfortunately, the Russians still viewed new assistance through the prism of economic policy rather than counterproliferation, and they still wanted debt relief, not weapons destruction. Nonetheless, they at least were willing to make a political commitment to the idea and put up more of their own money, which was enough for us to push for agreement at Kananaskis. The Soviet Sherpa for the Summit, Andrei Illarionov, was a brilliant and sometimes charming free-market economist, but he had no interest in destroying economically irrelevant weapons stockpiles with resources he would rather see invested in economic development.

We faced very tight time constraints, since Kananaskis was scheduled for June 26–27, 2002, just a month away. Canada decided to pledge a billion dollars Canadian, a disproportionately high share, but others were reluctant to pledge much or to pledge at all. Moreover, though the money wasn't even there, Russia resisted G-7 efforts to establish "principles" for administering the funds. Russian obstreperousness, in turn, simply made everyone else more nervous. I flew to Moscow on June 19, with just one week remaining before Kananaskis to meet with Illarionov and others, trying to convince them that their many objections, such as insisting on taxing grant aid and subjecting our contractors to liability in Russian courts, was going to torpedo the entire effort. Illarionov was on his worst behavior, blaming everyone else for "10 plus 10" collapsing. I kept thinking, as I sat in his Kremlin office listening to his tirade, how hard it was to give away billions of dollars.

Thanks to the around-the-clock work of all the negotiating teams at the Kananaskis Summit and Bush's diplomatic efforts with the other G-8 leaders, the Global Partnership was created at the funding levels we had been seeking, even if agreement didn't come until the Summit's final hour.

So Many Bad Deals to Kill, So Little Time

> I have not yet begun to fight.
>
> —JOHN PAUL JONES, SEPTEMBER 23, 1779

With the creation of the Global Partnership, our massive effort with Russia came to a logical pause. But during this intense activity in 2001 and

2002, we also faced a significant number of decisions on other national security issues highlighting how different Bush 43 was from past presidents. I was not involved in the decision to reject the Kyoto Protocol on global warming, but I was active in many others that the True Believers characterized as Bush's "unilateralist" approach. In fact, we were simply rejecting inferior policies and agreements, and replacing them with greater American independence and fewer unnecessary constraints. It was just that there were so many unnecessary constraints that everywhere we turned there was something to eliminate.

Comprehensive Test Ban Treaty (CTBT). The CTBT, which sought to ban all nuclear weapons testing, was a hangover signed in the Clinton administration; Bush said during Campaign 2000 that he had no intention of submitting it to the Senate for ratification. Nonetheless, State Department arms controllers and the wider congregation of arms control True Believers worked diligently to make the new leadership succumb to their relentless efforts, as so many previous "conservative" administrations had done, and accept the "inevitability" that the CTBT would enter into force. After all, the Europeans favored it, including Britain and France, Europe's two nuclear weapons states. Why should we have a problem with it, notwithstanding that Republican efforts in the Senate had led to a majority vote actually rejecting the CTBT on October 13, 1999, the first major such action since the defeat of the Treaty of Versailles on March 20, 1920. In this case, the administration outlasted the bureaucracy, and the CTBT candle-lighters resolved simply to wait until the barbarians departed, which they hoped would be after the 2004 elections. Now, they can only await the CTBT's resurrection, which they hope to see in 2009. May they wait in vain.

The real issue was not what to do with the CTBT, but whether and when we would take the steps necessary to resume nuclear testing, both to ensure the continuing safety and reliability of our existing nuclear stockpile and to test weapons designs that could address problems such as the hard or deeply buried targets favored by terrorist groups and rogue states. Any mention of resumed testing, breaking the moratorium Bush 41 had instituted, was heresy to the True Believers, but the inconvenient truth was that the long failure to test could leave the United States vulnerable in the future. An unsafe nuclear stockpile could cause disaster if a weapon detonated accidentally, while unreliable weapons could reduce or even eliminate the deterrent effect—the "nuclear umbrella"—that had protected us (and our allies) for decades during the Cold War. As one nuclear scientist put it to me, our warhead stockpile was like a huge garage filled with cars: We didn't want any of them to start unless we turned the ignition, but if we did, we expected the car to start the first time. When I left the administration, the future of testing was unresolved, but a decision will not wait much longer. By derailing the CTBT, Bush will leave his successor free to make that decision, and not bound by a treaty that constrains the United States, unlike our principal opponents and rogue states that will ratify the CTBT and then ignore it.

Unsigning the Rome Statute. My happiest moment at State was personally "unsigning" the Rome Statute that created the International Criminal Court (ICC). The ICC purportedly has authority to try individuals for crimes against humanity, and its advocates see it as the heir to the post–World War II Nuremberg Tribunals. I viewed it instead as an unaccountable prosecutor, possibly politically motivated, posing grave risks for the United States and its political and military leaders. Here, too, Bush campaigned against the ICC, so there was no question of our supporting it; the question was whether we would eliminate any ambiguity about our views by removing our signature, which I advocated. State's lawyers and others vigorously disliked the concept of "unsigning," let alone doing it to this treaty, but I was determined to establish the precedent, and to remove any vestigial argument that America's signature had any continuing effect.

As a professional soldier, Powell had no love for the Rome Statute, but his bureaucrats urged at every turn that foreign governments would be extremely upset if we unsigned. In fact, only sundry High Minded Europeans cared even slightly, which was simply further evidence that unsigning was the right thing to do. But State's bureaucrats used every conceivable excuse to delay the unsigning, in hopes our resolve would disappear. When Rumsfeld finally objected to all of the State-created delays, Bush reacted by saying we should get out of the statute immediately, and we did, on May 6, 2002, in a letter I signed. I told Powell that I felt like a kid on Christmas Day. The reaction from the High Minded was entirely predictable, but my only regret is that we didn't unsign more bad treaties, like Kyoto and the CTBT, during the Bush administration.

As well as unsigning, we launched a global campaign for agreements with other countries to ensure they never surrendered any Americans into ICC custody. Authority for such agreements came in Article 98 of the Rome Statute itself, and we sought "Article 98 agreements" from both signatories and nonsignatories of the statute, to ensure we were covered as broadly as possible. Congress was also sufficiently aroused that it passed the American Servicemembers Protection Act (ASPA), cutting off several types of military assistance to countries that did not sign Article 98 agreements.

By contrast, Beth Jones, the career assistant secretary for European and Eurasian Affairs (EUR), didn't like our ICC policy, didn't like our Article 98 campaign, and didn't like pressing the European Union to stop its negative campaign against us. Where the other regional bureaus used ASPA to good effect to help get Article 98 agreements, Jones concentrated instead on getting waivers for affected EUR countries. In fact, Jones's biggest offense was early in the Article 98 campaign, before the EU had gotten its act together in opposition to our efforts. Because she didn't agree with our policy, she and her bureau did not move aggressively to sign up even a few EU countries, thus preventing them from arriving at a consensus against us.

Although we had signed over thirty Article 98 agreements by April 2003, Jones then tried to limit the scope of Article 98 coverage, as the EU wanted, only to "official" Americans, essentially just service members and diplomats, which, she said, existing conventions and agreements already protected. These were important people to protect, but our campaign was devoted to covering *all* Americans: private citizens such as missionaries, journalists, NGO members, businesspeople, even tourists, who could be swept up in a conflict and used as scapegoats simply because they were Americans. Jones's main point, however, was much broader, namely that we were wasting political capital on our campaign, which she wanted to terminate or dramatically scale back. She wrote a memo to Powell urging us to reverse course, which she convinced the other five regional bureaus to sign.

When Powell asked about the memo, I said it ignored the strategy we had agreed on long ago and were pursuing successfully. Powell said, "I don't like petitions," and I thought the matter was ended. Undersecretary Marc Grossman, however, decided to hear the regional bureaus out at one of his regular weekly meetings, even as President Bush met in the Oval Office with Uruguayan president Jorge Batlle, urging him to sign an Article 98 agreement. Grossman invited Linc Bloomfield, assistant secretary for

Political-Military Affairs and me to attend as well, to make our case for continuing the Article 98 effort. Grossman opened the April 30 meeting by asking Jones to explain her position. She basically argued that the Article 98 campaign had topped out, and that we were wasting our time pursuing it.

I then pointed out that Jones was wrong in her fundamental point about how much protection was afforded to diplomats and service members, and that in any event none of the agreements she cited covered *former* diplomats or service members, who were likely to be in jeopardy of ICC prosecutions years after the events in question. I handed out a recent EU statement *rejecting* coverage for such persons, which Jones had conveniently ignored. I handed out charts of each bureau's performance, and the prospects for future Article 98 agreements, showing good progress and good prospects ahead. I concluded by pointing out that the Rome Statue had taken over four years to negotiate, four years from its signing to its entry into force, and fifteen months more to pick the judges and the prosecutor. This was a more-than-nine-year process; why should we get tired after only nine months of effort in the Article 98 campaign?

There was essentially no reply. Grossman, a careerist himself, ended the meeting by saying, "I gave the speech the day John unsigned the ICC treaty, and I was glad that I had that chance. There are a lot of bad things that this administration has opposed, like the Kyoto Protocol and the ICC, and we have to carry through on them." The regional bureau people were stunned, because they knew it was unlikely Grossman would have been so strong in support of the Article 98 campaign if he had not already talked to Powell. Thus, Powell stood firm in support of Bush administration policy on this issue, despite dissension in the State Department ranks, and signaled his view unmistakably through this meeting. On the other hand, Jones stayed in her important position for four years, doing who knew what else to undermine the administration.

Bloomfield later sent me an email reading, "That was smashing. I haven't seen such great lawyering since the Florida recount. Hope you were satisfied with the outcome." Indeed I was. We went on to roll up over a hundred Article 98 agreements, a testament to the virtue of persistence.

Foiling International Gun Control at the UN. One cloud that appeared on the horizon early in my tenure at T was the UN conference on small arms and light weapons, scheduled for July 9, 2001. Ostensibly, the conference

aimed at a political declaration on illicit trade in small arms, especially as
they flowed into local "conflict zones." Although this was innocuous
sounding, like many UN events, I nonetheless wondered what hidden
agendas were floating around. As I better understood the likely proceedings, it was increasingly clear that many of the "nongovernmental organizations" (NGOs) orchestrating this gathering (such as the umbrella group
International Action Network on Small Arms) actually had an agenda focused on domestic U.S. gun control issues. Although it might seem unusual
for Americans to expend their efforts in an international forum rather than
lobbying at the federal, state, or local levels, in fact, the international approach was an increasingly popular one with the American left, which felt
that its agenda was constantly being frustrated by the "vast right-wing conspiracy" or worse in the United States.

The left's strategy, although counterintuitive, actually was quite inspired. By building international support for their proposals, each in its
own field, they could, over time, leave the United States feeling "isolated,"
an anathema to the career diplomat, and thus induce our delegations to accept language they would prefer not to in order to "join consensus." Expro-
priating the legitimate term "civil society" from the national context, they
used it to describe NGOs, as opposed to nation-states, in the international
context. Thus, at UN meeting after UN meeting, there would be delegations from member governments, and then delegations from "civil society,"
as if "civil society" existed outside of nation-states.[7] While in some cases,
this might provide a way for oppressed citizens under authoritarian governments to be represented, most of "civil society" consisted of American and
Western European NGOs, for whom oppression meant having to put up
with conservatives and libertarians, and now the Bush administration.

Of course, in many instances during the Clinton administration, U.S.
delegations actually shared NGO policy preferences, making it even easier
to succumb. This was the way leftist groups such as Greenpeace and
Human Rights Watch had successfully worked to "isolate" the United
States on the Kyoto Protocol, the Rome Statute, and the Ottawa Land-
mines Convention, and they used it with increasing frequency on domestic

---

7. I have previously discussed the role of NGOs in a broader context: John R. Bolton,
"Should We Take Global Governance Seriously?" 1 *Chicago Journal of International Law* 205
(2000), pp. 215–18.

policy issues like "rights of the child," the death penalty, and now gun control. This approach, often called "norming," meaning, in a neutral sense, creating international norms of behavior, could be helpful, especially if it meant raising standards in intolerable regimes. What it increasingly came to mean, however, was whipping the United States into line with leftist views of the way the world should look. Many U.S. leftists found "European values" more appealing than Republican values, so they were happy to debate these issues in international organizations and conferences where there were so many fewer uncongenial conservatives, and so many more nice social democrats who thought the way they did. Rightist Americans were not generally attuned to this troubling development, but one group that saw the danger and took action was the National Rifle Association (NRA).

The NRA, which, unusually for a "conservative" group, had become an accredited UN NGO, had been watching the unfolding UN small-arms conference with increasing unease, sensing that while "illicit trade" in such weapons was the initial focus, it was only a first step toward a network of international treaties that would deeply affect U.S. domestic policies. In fact, the very rubric of "small arms and light weapons" covered everything from hunting rifles to antiaircraft guns and crew-served mortars, lumping together unquestioned weapons of war with firearms for legitimate personal sport and protection, thus starting with a rhetorical and propaganda victory for the gun control NGOs. As I learned more, I saw that the real problem posed by the upcoming conference was not a new treaty on small arms, but an unending "program of action" (another pet phrase in the international conference world) for the delegates to endorse, thus giving essentially perpetual life to the issue, and creating endless headaches down the road.

I decided that one way to set the tone of our participation in the UN conference was for me to make the U.S. opening statement, which I worked on extensively over the 2001 July Fourth weekend. Once I had laid down our red lines, through a fully cleared text, it would be hard even for the most determined bureaucrat to compromise them away. Moreover, I also hoped to signal that the Clinton era's deference to "norm setting" by huge international conferences was over. Just the fact that Powell was not delivering the U.S. statement was a powerful indication we had other things to do. Cary Barnett, an adviser since my USAID days, and I flew to New York on Monday, July 9, and rode to the U.S. Mission to the United Nations at First Avenue and Forty-fifth Street, the closest mission to the UN complex, just across from its main entrance. Since John Negroponte's confirmation as UN ambassador had been held up in the Senate (he was not confirmed until September 14, right after the terrorist attacks), I used the permanent representative's office, which still had Richard Holbrooke's speed-dial lines on the telephone.

At about 11:15 A.M., I walked across First Avenue to deliver the speech, proceeding to the podium of the General Assembly right after the speaker from Iran. My basic point was that the conference should concentrate on the real international problem of the flow of small arms and light weapons (which I defined as "strictly military arms") to regions of conflict, rather than to questions of domestic gun control laws. I said we believed "that the responsible use of firearms is a legitimate aspect of national life. Like many countries, the United States has a cultural tradition of hunting and sport shooting, but with a *constitutional* foundation." Although there were many aspects of the draft political declaration we could support, I said, there were several we could not. The most controversial point I made was to say: "We do *not* support measures that prohibit civilian possession of small arms. This is outside the mandate for this Conference. . . . The United States will not join consensus on a final document that contains measures contrary to our constitutional right to keep and bear arms."

The horror! Invoking the American Constitution, and relying on Attorney General John Ashcroft's recent opinion about the Second Amendment, in an international forum to explain the U.S. position! This was not good norming, and the NGO criticism was intense, thus proving I had made one point I wanted to make: This was not the Clinton administration. During an afternoon press conference one of the first questions I was asked was whether I was a member of the NRA and how many NRA members were on the U.S. delegation. Seeing this as a McCarthyite tactic, I responded by paraphrasing the response of many McCarthy targets in the 1950s: "I am not now and never have been a member of the NRA," adding that I had no idea how many NRA members were part of our delegation. Back in Washington the next morning Armitage called to say that Rice and Hadley were surprised by the amount of coverage the speech had received. At Powell's morning staff meeting, he turned to me with a chuckle and said, "John?" and I explained what I had said. Armitage chimed in, "The speech was policy, and it was fully cleared," which was why I had insisted everyone sign off on it before I delivered it, which they had. This was a bureaucratic lesson that stood me in good stead throughout my days at State.

In New York, however, the UN conference droned on, as the tedious negotiations over the final document continued until the end of the following week. Jack Straw, the new British foreign secretary, came to Washington, and Powell hosted a lunch for him on State's eighth floor on Wednesday, July 11, which I attended. Among other subjects, the British complained about our position on the small-arms/light-weapons conference, as well as on a continuing debate about biological weapons, and there was general merriment around the table (at least I thought it was funny) when it became clear to the Brits that I was the source of the problem on both issues. The conversation moved on, but when Straw departed, he said to me, "They told me you had horns and a tail, but I haven't noticed any." I said I kept them hidden from visitors, which Straw found amusing, even if his handlers from the Foreign Office did not.

Linc Bloomfield headed our delegation at the end of the two-week conference (New York has a lot of shopping and cultural opportunities that cannot be fully enjoyed in a one-week conference) and held our red lines against a ferocious assault by the pro–gun control NGOs. I kept Powell and Hadley informed as things went late into the evening on Friday, July 20, and basically all night into early Saturday, July 21. By 5:30 A.M. on Saturday, when I spoke to Bloomfield, the two issues most important to the United States—restrictions on civilian ownership of weapons and transfers of weapons to "nonstate actors," aka "freedom fighters" such as the Contras—were still unresolved. This was a familiar tactic: wear the United States down until only its key issues are unresolved, declare it isolated, and then use the sleeplessness and frayed tempers of many late-night sessions to press us to "join consensus" and avoid "isolation." Fortunately, I was not sleepy and I did not feel isolated, and Bloomfield wasn't having any second thoughts either. Two hours after our conversation, the conference accepted our red lines. Our only setback came in our having to accept yet another one of these conferences in five years, in 2006, to "review" what had happened in the interim. I suspect that many gun control NGOs fervently hoped that Bush would no longer be president then, and they were simply making a tactical retreat until that happy day. NSC senior director Elliot Abrams, and an old friend, told me later that, after describing the conference at an NSC staff meeting, Hadley had said: "All of this is due to John.

If he hadn't given his speech, for all the flak that he took, they never would have understood how serious we were."

Even worse for the NGOs, five years later, not only had Bush been re-elected, but I was the American ambassador to the UN. In June 2006, my successor at T, Bob Joseph, gave the U.S. opening speech at the conference, and I concentrated on one thing: making sure that there was not going to be another review conference in 2011. Renick Smith of my staff and I were even more successful than in 2001. Many countries, including India, China, and Pakistan joined the United States in objecting to the draft final document. There was so much disagreement that, in the end, no final document could be agreed upon, and there was therefore no decision to hold another review conference, meaning we accomplished the one major objective that had eluded us in 2001. We had achieved the almost unachievable in UN terms, breaking the endless cycle of meetings that the NGOs used to numb us into submission. Now, the domestic gun control groups were left only with working in the UN General Assembly, a far less visible forum than a large UN conference. For once, the United States had truly outlasted the normers!

Spurning Illusory Arms Control: Tanking the BWC Verification Protocol. Because of the nature of biological weapons (BW) research and production, BW arms control agreements are inherently unverifiable. What looks like and could well be a university research facility or a pharmaceutical manufacturing plant can be converted easily to and from BW use in ways that would foil even the best BW expert. Unlike, for example, a uranium-enrichment facility, which cannot be disguised, BW facilities are dual-use by definition. Accordingly, the 1972 Biological Weapons Convention (BWC) and earlier efforts at prohibiting BW were aspirational, depending on the good faith of the treaty parties for compliance. Significantly, the underlying BWC of 1972 stemmed from Nixon's *unilateral* decision to renounce the use of biological warfare, one of those inconvenient facts about unilateralism that the High Minded like to forget. Needless to say, many governments cheated, leading arms controllers to conclude that some kind of verification was necessary, even though real BW experts told them it was impossible. In fact, pursuing the illusion of verification diverted attention from the more important task of using national intelligence to detect and confront those that were actually cheating.

By spring 2001, international negotiations on a verification protocol to the BWC had been under way for almost eight years, in one form or another. The negotiations had been long, and much remained in disagreement, but there was especially intense pressure from Europeans to conclude an agreement in summer 2001, in order to submit it to the BWC's five-year review conference in November. The current negotiating vehicle was an "Ad Hoc Working Group" that had been laboring away since the 1996 BWC review conference, and that faced its decisive meeting in July. Their draft was largely British work, operating under then foreign secretary Robin Cook's "moral" foreign policy, but was masquerading under the guise of a "chairman's text" from the Ad Hoc Working Group, which was another aspect that I disliked, as if the chairman had autonomy from, or a position above, the national governments actually doing the negotiating.

As a practical matter for the Bush administration's political leadership, we had little time to get our act together. The interagency process had identified thirty-seven separate, substantial problems with the current protocol draft (all of which were deemed "must have" changes before the text would be acceptable). Our objections were, in fact, insurmountable, and fell into three broad categories. In the first place, the inspection provisions of the draft protocol were most unlikely to uncover a real BW program, given the ease with which the inherently dual-use nature of BW could be concealed or camouflaged. If anything, the protocol would endanger our extensive export control mechanisms, which sought to limit the export of dual-use items that could be used to develop an offensive BW program. In short, the protocol would not accomplish its purported basic objective. Second, its inspection provisions would have the negative effect of exposing our defensive BW preparations to international scrutiny, thus defeating their very purpose. Defenses against biological warfare were legitimate under the BWC, but if our preparations were known and understood, hostile countries could design their offensive BW programs to defeat our defenses. Third, our legitimate pharmaceutical industry greatly feared the intrusion into their laboratories and production facilities, and the potential loss of important intellectual property to international inspectors over whom we had little or no control. These were objections that could not be satisfied merely by "tweaking" language in the draft protocol or by "constructive alternatives" (which had in any event been explored to death during the long years of negotiation). These were real problems.

Another problem came from State's arms control bureaucracy. While they knew as well as anyone that the current draft protocol was unacceptable, they could not bear being separated from their EU arms control brethren who wanted to adopt the protocol. This disjunction caused them a fearful angst. Although Powell had said publicly that the draft protocol was unacceptable, I worried that intense pressure from State and the British, and Rice's and Hadley's equivocating on the issue, would change his position.

At a July 15 PC, Rice opened the meeting by turning to Powell, who said that in all his years in senior national security positions, he had never encountered an arms control treaty that was so widely disapproved within the U.S. government, and that had essentially no real advocates. Powell said that the chairman's text was "fatally flawed," that it brought us "no benefit," that we "can't fix it," and that "we shouldn't keep people dangling, but we should let them know now where we stood." He concluded that we should take the "clean break" option, the one I favored. While taking notes, sitting behind Powell and Rumsfeld, and therefore just a few feet away from Rice, I watched Rice's face, noting the expression of amazement and incredulity that spread over it. Of course, I was amazed, too, but I kept my courtroom face on, or at least I hoped I did. Rumsfeld and Spence Abraham, the secretary of energy, also came out for a clean break, and Ken Dam of Treasury said "there is no question we must reject" the chairman's text.

Rice tried to roll everyone back, but Powell absolutely refused to budge, saying flatly three more times that we should reject the text and move on. Rice, who herself agreed that the current draft was "a tremendous turkey," finally retreated to discussing the media and legislative strategy for announcing our position, ending the meeting after only twenty minutes. I rode back to State with Powell, and he asked, "You happy?" I said I was, and he laughed and said, "I'm slow, but I always get there." I thought it was Powell's finest hour at State. In fact, in subsequent days, when Rice tried to back away from the PC decision, Powell repeatedly resisted, working to ensure that when we spoke at the July Ad Hoc Working Group, there would be no ambiguity in what we were saying. On July 25, we announced our decision in Geneva, producing a few days of moaning and groaning by the protocol's advocates, but most countries understood our position was not going to change.

Resurrecting the protocol, however, turned out to be a sustained EU project as the BWC's five-year review conference in Geneva approached. The EU hoped to extend the Ad Hoc Working Group until the next five-year review conference in 2006, as with the UN's small-arms/light-weapons conference, hoping that the Bush administration would be history by then. Not only did I want to inter the protocol and its drafting vehicle permanently in Geneva, I also wanted to use the conference to "name names" of countries violating the BWC, including Russia and China, in large part to show that we had a global BW problem not for lack of treaties but because several important governments were simply lying about their compliance with a treaty we already had. The arms control bureaucracy worried that such an approach was too provocative, but I asked how it could not be appropriate to raise the issue of compliance with a treaty at a once-every-five-years meeting to discuss how the treaty was doing. There was no answer.

I gave the "naming names" speech on Monday, November 19, identifying Iraq, North Korea, Iran, Libya, Syria, and Sudan, noting that the list was not exhaustive. I wanted to name others, but the level of bureaucratic opposition was too intense, and the time to work out the differences too short, so I was content, for the moment, with naming just a few violators. Although those I had fingered protested, most other governments had to agree that discussing compliance with the BWC at this meeting was entirely sensible. If not here, where?

For the media, however, which hadn't realized what had happened in July when we made it clear that the verification protocol was dead, the protocol was the real issue. In press encounters, I made it clear that we supported the BWC itself, but not the protocol, a distinction many media types didn't get. With the help of J. D. Crouch at Defense and Bob Joseph of the NSC, we continued to oppose the Ad Hoc Working Group's existence and put the final nail in its coffin.

Facing Up to Failure at the OPCW. Too often, once a treaty is negotiated, diplomats conclude the hard work is done, and that mere "implementation" remains. The Chemical Weapons Convention (CWC) provides an example of this mentality at work. Negotiated in the early 1990s, the CWC created the Organization for the Prohibition of Chemical Weapons (OPCW) to administer weapons destruction programs. The first OPCW director general, José Bustani of Brazil, was in the U.S. view a management disaster, whose performance called into question the OPCW's credibility and indeed the CWC itself. State's arms controllers complained repeatedly about Bustani's incompetence, and the harm he was causing at OPCW, but their only strategy was to ask Brazil to handle this unhappy problem. I had several meetings with senior Brazilians, but they had no interest in fixing the problem. I also spoke directly to Bustani, but the only result was that he began an aggressive campaign to rally support to keep his job.

Powell became worried that our efforts were not succeeding, an assessment I fully shared. I explained that the career arms controllers hoped that Bustani would resign "voluntarily" and avoid an open fight, which, win or lose, was hard for consensus-style diplomats to imagine. I said that if we wanted Bustani out, we were going to have to work for it. Powell clearly felt this approach was more likely to succeed, but he said, "If you're going to go after this guy, you've got to win."

I directed that we begin explaining to others that the U.S. contribution to the OPCW might well be cut if Bustani remained, which Germany and Japan were also considering, so concerned were they about Bustani's mismanagement. Hans-Joachim Daerr, my German counterpart, was particularly determined, because, as he said to me on March 13, 2002, "Everyone knows it can't go on," and, "there's no way back" if we were to avoid the OPCW's financial collapse. Our lobbying campaign picked up steam in advance of the OPCW Executive Council meeting on March 19, and I went to The Hague myself. I met with Bustani to tell him he should resign, as the EU, Canada, and Japan had already said. If he left now, we would do our best to give him "a gracious and dignified exit." Otherwise, we intended to have him fired. Bustani said he would fight on, so we shook hands and left, the entire affair taking less than five minutes.

We pushed forward with a March 22 Executive Council vote on our "motion of no confidence" against Bustani, which carried by a vote of seventeen in favor, five against, and nineteen abstentions or not voting. Since we did not have the requisite two-thirds vote of the entire Council, we called for a full Conference of States Parties to the CWC at the earliest possible date. The Brazilian press was having a field day with all of this, quoting Bustani attacking me, saying what I "lack in competence is more than made up with a fanatical antidisarmament ideology. He is against all the international organizations. It was him that launched the campaign against me." Armitage wrote me a note that said, "You're known by your enemies as much as by your friends."

Sunday, April 21, was the date for the Conference of States Parties, and we lobbied around the world for our second motion of no confidence in Bustani. He tried to "compromise" by offering the United States the position of deputy director general of the OPCW, which I rejected. We wanted Bustani out even more than we wanted an American in, which I thought was a powerful argument to the undecided CWC governments, as it indeed turned out to be. The only opposition to spreading the word about Bustani's crude effort to buy us off came from State's Brazil Desk, a truly grotesque example of clientitis, and I immediately overruled them. I returned to The Hague on April 21 for one last check, but had to leave for Moscow the next day, when the vote actually took place. There were 105 states parties registered for the conference, and we prevailed 48–7, with fifty countries abstaining or not voting. The seven who voted with Bustani were Brazil, Belarus, China, Cuba, Iran, Mexico, and Russia, quite a collection. Only France among the major industrial democracies abstained.

Rogelio Pfirter, an Argentine, replaced Bustani as director general of the OPCW and has performed well. What should have been an easy personnel decision had turned into a world-class diplomatic battle, albeit not one that many people paid attention to outside of the small world of arms control and international organizations.

What conclusions can we draw from these struggles?

In the case of the ABM Treaty, the CTBT, the small-arms/light-weapons issue, and the ICC, the True Believers, both inside the career bureaucracy and outside it, flatly disagreed with the Bush administration's position and worked to reverse it. With persistence and hard work, President Bush's position prevailed. The ABM Treaty is dead, the CTBT Treaty will never come into force, the small-arms/light-weapons issue has been put in its proper place, and the United States has kept its independence from the ICC. On the Treaty of Moscow, while the True Believers didn't much like it, they knew they couldn't stop it.

By contrast, with Bustani and the BWC verification protocol, the career bureaucracy suffered from a terrible and paralyzing intellectual schizophrenia. They knew there were severe problems, but they could not bring themselves to take action. They knew that the verification protocol could not provide adequate verification, but they could not bring themselves to kill it. On Bustani, they knew that he was undermining the CWC, but, on their own, they could not do what was necessary to fire him. When I stepped in to tank the protocol, and then to tank Bustani, their frustration was probably due more to antipathy to the administration taking the action than to the actual decisions. Nonetheless, their own continuing inability to resolve their contradictory feelings meant that the problems were continuing, and not being resolved, thus revealing one of the State Department's gravest cultural defects.

CHAPTER FOUR

FOLLOWING THE YELLOW CAKE ROAD ON NORTH KOREA

You deny agreements you entered into not an hour ago, in fact you yourself offered.

—COLONEL JAMES C. MURRAY, USMC, PANMUNJOM, NOVEMBER 1951[1]

The lesson of North Korea policy under George W Bush is fundamentally the lesson of the Risen Bureaucracy. Their catechism was always the same: North Korea can be talked out of its nuclear weapons program. Although the 2000 elections posed an obstacle to continuing this Clinton administration policy, the bureaucracy and their High Minded leaders on the outside persevered. They lost many battles, but won the ones that were critical. They ignored or misrepresented distasteful realities and hard issues. They picked up some allies among Bush's political appointees, distracted a few, and seduced others. They whispered to the press against the infidels in the new administration who advocated a harder line. They even watched a few of their own go over the side, but they always persisted. And in the Seventh Year, Bush and his team rested. The bureaucracy's persistence prevailed so overwhelmingly that Bush himself did not even realize it.

Ironically, Bush is blamed for following confrontational policies he didn't follow, rather than the bureaucracy's policies, which he partially adopted, and were precisely the ones that led him to failure, just as his orig-

---

1. Quoted in Chuck Downs, *Over the Line: North Korea's Negotiating Strategy* (Washington, D.C.: The AEI Press, 1999), p. 61.

inal instincts told him. Had Bush's persistence—and that of all the president's men and women—been as stout as the bureaucracy's, history would have been different. My own involvement in North Korea policy extended from 2001 to 2006. I struggled against bureaucratic inertia to put in place a tougher, more realistic policy, which culminated in two epic but successful battles in the Security Council. The worst happened after I left, but was well in train before then.

The Democratic Peoples Republic of Korea (DPRK) will never give up nuclear weapons voluntarily. It often *promises* to do so, as it did in the Clinton administration's 1994 Agreed Framework. It will even more readily *bargain* over that promise, especially in exchange for items of tangible economic and political value, such as fuel oil, nuclear reactors, "security assurances," or removal from our list of state sponsors of terrorism. The DPRK will gladly "engage" with us, accept our concessions, and then violate its own commitments. As Fred Iklé once said, "The only thing truly reliable about North Korea is its boundless mendacity."[2] The DPRK has followed this game plan successfully many times, and it has every reason to believe it will continue to succeed into the future. Ironically, North Korea's policies have often been more sensible than our own, where the hope of the High Minded seems always to triumph over contrary experience.

In this chapter, I recount key aspects of the Bush administration's North Korea policy in its first term, and in Chapter XI, I consider what we did in the Security Council in the second term, thus largely preserving the narrative's chronological flow.

Driving a Stake Through the Agreed Framework

The signs are becoming clear that the North Korean nuclear-weapons program has never stopped.
—AMBASSADOR JAMES R. LILLEY, NOVEMBER 9, 1998[3]

When Bush took office in 2001, the outgoing Clintonites, State Department careerists, and the High Minded lived under the happy and danger-

---

2. Ibid., back cover.
3. James R. Lilley, "New Rules in Korea," *Newsweek*, November 9, 1998, p. 19, col. 1.

ous assumption that the 1994 Agreed Framework was on track and being implemented. This bilateral DPRK-U.S. deal provided that the North would abandon all efforts to acquire nuclear weapons, including freezing the reactor and other facilities at Yongbyon under the inspection of the International Atomic Energy Agency (IAEA). In exchange, North Korea was to receive two bundles of carrots: an annual supply of five hundred thousand tons of heavy fuel oil and the two light-water nuclear reactors to be built by South Korea and Japan. The North violated the deal almost before the ink was dry. In short, the Clinton policy and the Agreed Framework were classic illustrations of the delusion that a rogue state could be coaxed out of nuclear weapons, and were embarrassments to the United States. Former secretary of state Jim Baker correctly characterized it as "a policy of appeasement."[4]

The heavy fuel oil was "intended" as a short-term substitute for the "lost power" from the frozen Yongbyon reactor, which was a joke since Yongbyon wasn't even hooked up to what North Korea laughingly referred to as its "power grid." A famous photo from space of the Korean peninsula at night shows the South shining brightly, and the North just as dark as the seas on either side of it, depicting just how extensive the North's "grid" was. That heavy fuel oil supported the DPRK police state by subsidizing the regime and its military-industrial complex. The light-water reactors were sold to the American public and Congress as less risky from a proliferation standpoint (actually sold as "proliferation proof") than the Yongbyon reactor, which was also a fanciful notion. While not as efficient in producing plutonium as heavy-water reactors, light-water reactors do produce plutonium as part of the nuclear fission process. (The plutonium in a reactor's spent fuel rods is chemically reprocessed to be available for nuclear weapons.) Having two light-water reactors, both larger than Yongbyon, would barely slow a determined North Korea. I always found this aspect of the Agreed Framework the most incomprehensible, as if one should treat a heroin addict by shifting him to cocaine. The Clinton negotiators later said privately that they never actually expected the light-water reactors to be completed or put into service, because they assumed Kim Jong-il's regime would collapse long before that time. I would have thought the negotiators would be

---

4. James A. Baker 3rd, "North Korea Wins Again," *New York Times*, Friday, March 19, 1999, p. A21, col. 2.

embarrassed to make this point, since it showed their skills as political prognosticators were no sharper than their appreciation for the DPRK's skills at cheating.

The Clintonites also tried to persuade the North to give up its ballistic missile program in exchange for other nations' launching its satellites. At the start of the Bush administration, when I learned about these negotiations, I gasped, "You're joking, aren't you?" because the DPRK didn't have satellites and couldn't use them anyway except for military purposes, so impoverished is the country. Sadly, my briefer was serious. State's bureaucracy wanted simply to continue down this road, endorsing the South's "sunshine policy" toward the North, which Colin Powell was perfectly prepared to do. On March 6, 2001, he said the administration planned "to engage with North Korea, to pick up where President Clinton left off. Some promising elements were left on the table."[5] The very next day at the White House, Bush made it clear to South Korean president Kim Dae-jung that that was not at all our policy. Powell confessed, "I got a little too far forward on my skis."[6] Even five years later, Kim did not understand Bush: "He didn't talk about what we had agreed upon, but began to criticize North Korea by saying that a regime that couldn't even feed its people was making nuclear weapons. . . . From that time on, things began to go wrong."[7] For Kim, things had gone wrong even before that, starting with a Putin visit to Seoul shortly before Kim's U.S. visit. Kim had opposed missile defense and supported the 1972 ABM Treaty, not a way to warm Bush administration hearts.

In 2001, the NSC launched a "policy review" on North Korea, an open invitation to intragovernmental warfare that consumed months of time and effort. Academic as it was, at least it was better than proceeding "to pick up where President Clinton left off." Throughout the review, the State Department's Bureau for East Asian and Pacific Affairs (EAP) used every opportunity to press relentlessly to restart talks with North Korea: on any subject, at any level, at any time, for any objective.[8] Although Rumsfeld and

---

5. Quoted in Michael Hirsh, Melinda Liu, and George Wehrfritz, " 'We Are a Nuclear Power,' " *Newsweek*, October 23, 2006, p. 36.
6. Colin Powell, May 14, 2001, interview with Andrea Koppel of CNN.
7. See note 2.
8. Such was the extent of their campaign, they even used Bush 41, and one of his advisers, Don Gregg, as a channel to Rice. Jane Perlez, "Fatherly Advice to the President on North Korea," *New York Times*, Sunday, June 10, 2001, p. 1NE, col. 6.

Cheney tried to preserve a strategic perspective, we had our own proliferation problem, as one idea for talks after another poured forth, including a suggestion from Rice that Hadley go to Pyongyang to speak with Kim Jong-il directly. Powell shot that idea down on turf grounds (the NSC staff shouldn't be negotiating), but by early June, Bush authorized lower-level bilateral talks with the DPRK, without preconditions. This meant we would be open to talk about everything from their WMD programs to their missiles, to their conventional force posture on the Korean peninsula. With any luck, the DPRK would have rejected this approach, thus saving us from ourselves

September 11 pushed North Korea to the side, but by year's end I was able to move onto the offensive toward dismantling the failed Agreed Framework and its various manifestations, such as the Korean Peninsula Energy Development Organization (KEDO), through which, incredibly, the North was receiving the carrot deliveries of fuel oil and the light-water reactors. Congress had imposed conditions on providing assistance to North Korea, notably requiring that the president annually make various "certifications," including that North Korea was meeting its obligations under the Agreed Framework, and that it was making progress in denuclearization and reducing ballistic missile exports. Under Clinton, these certifications had been made routinely, even though they were completely contrary to reality. As I had testified in an exchange with Senator John Kerry during my 2001 confirmation hearing for undersecretary, North Korea's manifest noncompliance with its Non-Proliferation Treaty and IAEA Safeguards Agreement made it impossible to say the North complied with the Agreed Framework. I instructed Mark Groombridge, a China expert on my personal staff, to tell EAP we would not "clear" the decision memo asking Powell to recommend that Bush make the required certifications. This started an enormous, months-long policy struggle.

At the outset, I was willing to be accommodating to the bureaucracy, but Bush's January 29, 2002, "axis of evil" State of the Union speech convinced me to take a harder line. Actually, it was not just the speech, but also the reaction to it the next morning at the State Department staff meeting. Jim Kelly, EAP assistant secretary, announced that his bureau would be preparing press guidance explaining that *Bush's speech did not represent a change of policy on North Korea.* Kelly was not the only careerist who recoiled at the speech, and opposition from State leaked out through the media all day long. It was so bad that Powell himself had to say, at the January 31 staff meeting, that Bush believed strongly in his speech, and that no one in the department "should try to take the edge off what the president said, or try to spin it." The room was deathly silent, because so many people realized they were being rebuked precisely for what they had been doing since the moment the State of the Union speech had ended. I sensed that Powell had made a conscious decision that no reporters were going to be writing stories about "daylight" between Bush and Powell on this one.

Of course, the mere fact that Bush held this view of the "axis of evil" didn't stop the bureaucracy from doing precisely the opposite of what Powell had just told them, but they did shift to more covert methods.[9] I believed there was no way, even in State weasel words, we could now urge Bush to certify DPRK "compliance" with the Agreed Framework, though I recognized we would likely invoke the statute's waiver provisions to allow assistance to continue flowing even without certification. I could accept this outcome, because, for the first time, we would break the chain of "compliance" certifications, thus laying a basis to say in the future that North Korea's manifest noncompliance required us to tank the Agreed Framework once and for all. This put me in a distinctly moderate position, between EAP, which wanted business as usual, and Defense, which wanted to end the Agreed Framework immediately. I agreed with DoD, but their position was not achievable, and pressing it heedlessly might result in simply falling back to EAP's default position of business as usual. On Monday, March 4, Kelly and Jack Pritchard, his DPRK negotiator, finally agreed to my approach, based on my argument about the North's violations of the Non-Proliferation Treaty. "You're too good a lawyer for me on that, John," Kelly said. DoD also agreed, and the deed was done. This major shift from Clinton administration policy was the first critical U.S. step toward eliminating the charade that the Agreed Framework was somehow still viable.

EAP, however, continued to press for direct negotiations with Pyongyang, and was at times supported by the NSC, which in the spring of 2002 was pushing for a "bold approach" to the Korean issue. Hadley had apparently read a *Washington Post* opinion article to this effect and picked up on it, which mystified even Powell and EAP. At several NSC meetings

9. See, generally, Charles L. Pritchard, *Failed Diplomacy* (Washington, D.C.: Brookings Institution Press, 2007).

in early May, the whole thing was punted back for further staff work. Delay and uncertainty were fine with me because I was consumed with wrapping up the Treaty of Moscow and was happy to avoid distractions. According to Bob Joseph, Rice was saying that our policy had to be "180 degrees" different from the last administration's policy, that the DPRK's regime was "abhorrent," and that we could have no more "business as usual." That was certainly what I thought Bush's view was, as when he told the visiting president of Finland on May 31 that if North Korea ever used military force, it would become a "smoking, smoldering ruin."

EAP's persistence nonetheless paid off, and Kelly was authorized to travel to the North in mid-July, 2002, assuming the DPRK agreed. The North's response in late June was an unprovoked attack by their naval forces against South Korean patrol boats near their disputed maritime boundary, killing four South Koreans. That incident alone should have tanked the idea of Kelly flying to Pyongyang. While the trip was indeed canceled, the "EAPeasers" tried to spin the press that the DPRK simply hadn't extended a timely invitation. Their thinking was that a mere logistical mixup could easily be corrected later and the trip could be scheduled again, whereas canceling because North Korea was killing people made it much harder to justify rescheduling. EAP's logic was certainly correct, and this vignette demonstrates graphically the extent to which bureaucracy will go to pursue the policy *it* wants to pursue, inconvenient facts be damned. Groombridge did an excellent job in killing the trip, causing Kelly to call him down to his office and curse at him. That is something, one should note, I never did when I reprimanded the sensitive INR analyst Christian Westermann for lying to me, and Senator Chris Dodd would depict as pressuring a career intelligence officer during my 2005 confirmation hearing. Kelly later admitted to me that the DPRK attack made the trip impossible, and cast grave doubt on the viability of the South's "sunshine policy."

During the fallout over the naval attack, the intelligence community (IC) was coming to the conclusion that the North was actively attempting to acquire a production-scale capacity for uranium enrichment. Considerable evidence had accumulated over the years, but by mid-July the IC became convinced that the DPRK was pursuing this alternative route to nuclear weapons, a clear violation of the Agreed Framework. Pressed by other business, I didn't appreciate the significance of the IC's judgment until July 10, 2002, when I was at the CIA for meetings about Fulton Armstrong, the national intelligence officer for Latin America, who incorrectly alleged that I hadn't received IC clearance for a speech I gave about Cuba's BW program. After we finished those meetings, Alan Foley, who headed the CIA's WINPAC (Weapons Intelligence, Non-Proliferation and Arms Control) office, walked me out to the CIA headquarters' cavernous, white-marble lobby and stressed the salience of what they had concluded. Standing there under the twelve-foot-long biblical quotation carved in large letters on the marble walls—"And ye shall know the truth and the truth shall make you free"[10]—Foley said it was as if A. Q. Khan, the Pakistani head of a large, profitable, illicit nuclear proliferation network, had written a cookbook for uranium enrichment, and North Korea was out purchasing the ingredients. He urged me to examine what the IC had recently written on the subject, which I did, finding it dramatic indeed. Within roughly a week's time, more information fell into place, all of it underlining what Foley had said.

This was the hammer I had been looking for to shatter the Agreed Framework. The reaction of EAP and its allies around Washington, such as Jack Pritchard at State and Jim Moriarity at the NSC, was twofold. First, they argued that a uranium-enrichment program didn't actually violate the Agreed Framework, and second, they said that the new evidence was inconclusive. The first argument was laughable and quickly swept aside. The second argument crumbled before the IC's conclusions, conclusions many analysts, including State's INR Bureau, had resisted but now acknowledged were inescapable. A variation from the DPRK sympathizers was that the North had only started its uranium-enrichment program in anticipation of our abrogating the Agreed Framework. This, too, was laughable, but it at least accepted the basic fact of what North Korea was up to. Subsequent evidence indicated that the DPRK's uranium-enrichment activities extended well back into the 1990s. We still lacked considerable information about the uranium-enrichment program, such as where it was located, and these facts were difficult to obtain given the extraordinarily secretive nature of the DPRK, but the underlying reality was not debatable. Even the Russians shared our view of the North's procurement activity, as my counterpart Georgi Mamedov would later describe to me in Moscow on November 10,

---

10. John 8:32.

although at that point the Russians did not believe North Korea had actually finished construction of an enrichment facility. Mamedov also said at that meeting that China essentially shared Russia's analysis, which showed, of course, that Moscow and Beijing were comparing notes on what the DPRK was up to.

My chief objective was to bring the matter to a head, and I selected an upcoming July 19, 2002, meeting, arranged after the North's naval attack, among Undersecretary Marc Grossman (P), Kelly, and me, to sort ourselves out and develop a consistent State position. I planned to argue that we had reached a critical moment in dealing with the DPRK, and that it was time to blow the whistle on the North's manifest, substantial, and continuing violation of the Agreed Framework. Coming out of the meeting, I wanted a decisive conclusion that the Agreed Framework was dead, and not another endless, debilitating internal debate. On Friday morning, to lay the proper groundwork, I first briefed Armitage on what I intended to say to Grossman and Kelly, knowing Armitage would tell Powell as soon as I left his office. Armitage said we should see how the afternoon meeting went and bring Powell into the process in the first days of the coming week. I also told representatives of the IC what I planned to do with their analysis—go straight for the Agreed Framework's jugular—and none of them blanched. In fact, they believed their information would only get stronger as time went on.

We met just after 3:30 P.M. in Powell's conference room, across the hall from his office, and Kelly started by trying to table a long agenda of items to discuss, which I thought would be a waste of time. I intervened, saying we had reached a turning point in history, and that the new information we now had on North Korea's uranium-enrichment activities could lead to only one conclusion, namely that the Agreed Framework was dead. I reviewed the framework's policy goal, which was to resolve the "nuclear question on the peninsula," which it plainly had not done. We faced not merely a technical violation of the framework, but a gross breakdown of the entire policy it reflected. Accordingly, I said, we needed to reach a common understanding that the framework was in the tank, and then move promptly to address the range of policy issues that would immediately emerge: how and when to tell Congress and the American people; how and when to brief our friends and allies (and the IAEA); and what military and other contingency plans to make in the event of an irrational North Korean reaction. I said that I had views on all of these issues, but that, at this meeting, I was only pressing for consensus that the Agreed Framework was dead.

Kelly responded that there was still disagreement about exactly when North Korea would have enough highly enriched uranium to make a warhead, which was true but irrelevant to the point that the DPRK was violating the Agreed Framework. He also said that the North might begin reprocessing plutonium if we announced the demise of the framework, and that South Korea and Japan would certainly be surprised. I answered that it was incontrovertible that procurement for an industrial-scope level of uranium enrichment was under way, and that any new information we obtained could only make us more concerned. Grossman said that the INR analysis he had seen was indisputable. As for plutonium, I said it was a top matter for contingency planning, but not a reason to save the Agreed Framework. Consultations with Japan and South Korea needed to be at the top of our "to do" list once we decided that the framework was in fact in the grave. Grossman agreed and said we needed to move quickly or we would be in the unfortunate position of responding to a crisis instead of managing it. Kelly essentially went silent, agreeing that the uranium-enrichment program was a real problem, and that we should make an unambiguous decision that the framework was history. Grossman was leaving that day for two weeks of annual leave, and as our meeting broke up, he said to me, "You have my proxy." In turn, I asked Grossman to brief Powell on our meeting before he left.

I expected that when the EAP staff heard about the meeting, they would erupt into paroxysms and produce a sharp counterattack. In a draft memo for Powell summarizing the meeting, however, Kelly made very few changes. On Monday, Armitage said he had briefed Powell, who wanted a small meeting the next day. I told the NSC's Joseph of our meeting's unanimous outcome, secure in the knowledge he would act on it, briefing Rice within a day or two, which he did, reporting back that she was generally comfortable with the approach we were taking. I gave Powell a copy of the memo at 7:00 A.M. on Tuesday, July 23, and told him it reflected our meeting's unanimous conclusion that the Agreed Framework was dead. I then walked down the hall to Armitage's office to give him the memo, and in neither case did I detect any resistance to the death notice.

Throughout the day, I had over a dozen separate meetings on this issue, the most important scheduled for 10:00 A.M. with Powell, Armitage, and others. We started late because Powell was late returning from a White House event, with Powell reading one of the many reports on DPRK enrichment efforts. When he finished, he turned to me, and I said again I thought we were at a turning point in history. I ran through the conclusions of the Friday meeting, saying we had very little time to make decisions, given the CIA view that it had to start briefing Congress and the risk of press inquiries, which had already commenced. Kelly agreed with my comments, but worried about the impact of the news on Japan and South Korea. Powell said he had just met briefly with Bush and Rice in the Oval Office and told them what was up, and Bush's instant reaction was, "We cannot sit on this intelligence." Rice fretted about managing this issue and Iraq at the same time, as Saddam Hussein continued to resist international efforts to determine if he had complied with Security Council resolutions concerning his WMD programs. Powell asked Kelly about the press, and Kelly said Vicki O'Hara at NPR had asked for comment on what "Defense sources" were telling her about a new DPRK weapons program. Powell reacted predictably, interpreting the leak as a Pentagon effort to kill the Agreed Framework and tie the president's hands. My heart sank, fearing that if this became a turf war rather than a policy matter, all was lost. Fortunately, Powell said only, "Let's not make any decisions here today," and then, "Of course, there's no doubt in my mind what the result will be, but we need to buy ourselves some time."

Joseph later said Rice's account of the Oval Office meeting that morning was the same as Powell's. Rice, however, was still focused on Iraq, which continued to refuse to cooperate with UN weapons inspectors and grant them full and unimpeded access inside Iraq, as numerous Security Council resolutions demanded. She told Joseph to prepare press guidance in case the DPRK information started to leak. Joseph had asked, "As part of our exit strategy [from the Agreed Framework]?" and Rice responded affirmatively. Crouch reported from DoD that Rumsfeld was fully convinced the Framework was history, and the only issue was where State would come out, about which I made encouraging noises. Cheney's office clearly felt the same way. On Thursday, July 26, Powell asked to see me, talking mostly about North Korea. He described a lunch he, Cheney, Rumsfeld, and Rice had had that day, at which the question of Iraq had hung over all of their discussions, the "eight-hundred-pound gorilla sitting in the corner," as both he and I called it. Powell wanted to be sure that the DPRK intelligence was as clear as it seemed, and I noted that full briefings were being given to Cheney and Rice on Wednesday, and one could be arranged for him upon his return from his imminent South Asia trip. Powell asked if I would have ended the Agreed Framework without the new information, and I said I had simply been waiting for the North to do something so un-ambiguous that no one could in good conscience defend what I viewed as a policy of pure appeasement. Powell reminisced that, after he had become a civilian in the 1990s and was giving speeches around the country, he used to say that if North Korea ever used WMDs, we would turn the country into "a charcoal briquette," which definitely got his audience's attention.

By mid-August, however, there was still no definitive decision that the DPRK had violated the Agreed Framework. In part, not reaching a deci-sion benefited the EAPeasers who were still in denial, and in part it re-flected Powell's desire to postpone any decision until after South Korea's December elections to choose Kim Dae-jung's successor. I left on an al-ready scheduled trip for Japan and South Korea on August 23, my first dur-ing the Bush 43 administration, which would obviously involve discussions about the DPRK, but with great uncertainty whether to address the uranium-enrichment issue. In Japan, on August 26, I met for the first time with Deputy Chief Cabinet Secretary Shinzo Abe and was heartened at how tough a line he took against North Korea. (I kept up with Abe in suc-ceeding years, meeting with him on almost every trip to Tokyo, and I was delighted in 2006 when he became prime minister.) Howard Baker, our ambassador to Japan, and I discussed the DPRK uranium-enrichment ef-fort and when and how to tell Japan about it. Baker had stressed from his first awareness of the issue that we had to brief the Japanese before they read about it in the press, and that was still his view. I said a decision had been made that I would not brief them on this trip, in part because NSC principals had still not met to make a definitive decision that the Agreed Framework was dead.

As it turned out, Baker learned that Japanese prime minister Junichiro Koizumi planned to announce on August 30 a visit to the DPRK on Sep-tember 17 to discuss a number of issues, notably the "abduction issue," a matter of intense political interest in Japan, involving the North's kidnap-ping of Japanese citizens over the years. We had to decide what to tell Japan before Koizumi's announcement, and whether we should try to convince him not to go at all, given the DPRK's enrichment activities. I called Powell that evening Tokyo time, and he said he thought Baker would be author- ized to tell Chief Cabinet Secretary Fukuda some of what we knew before Koizumi's announcement. I pointed out that we could hardly tell Japan without telling South Korea. Powell agreed, but when I called again the next morning, August 28, while driving to Narita Airport to catch a flight to Seoul, he said no decision had yet been made on what to say to Japan, even though a Koizumi-to-Bush call was being arranged as we spoke. In South Korea, as I rode to our embassy, I found out I had just missed an anti- Bolton demonstration by all of five students, carrying a banner reading, "Reject U.S. hard-line policy toward North Korea." "If only" was my reac- tion. Our ambassador, Tom Hubbard, was a clear example of clientitis, wholly reflecting Kim Dae-jung's view on almost every issue.

On Thursday morning, August 29, I spoke again with Powell, who said Baker had mentioned the uranium-enrichment issue briefly to Fukuda. Bush, as expected, had not raised it with Koizumi, although it reminded me what Bush had said about Kim Jong-il at the Kananaskis G-8 meeting just before seeing Koizumi: "I can't wait to tell him what I think of that little tyrant." I wondered if Bush had made that observation again during the call, but didn't ask. Powell said I should brief the South Koreans, which I did after a speech that morning. I was quite pleased with the response to the speech, including the DPRK's calling me the "envoy of evil." The NSC's Mike Green later found that Kim Dae-jung personally intervened to keep ROK television stations from covering my speech live or broadcasting any of it in their news programs.

I first briefed Deputy Foreign Minister Lee Tae-Sik, explaining that I had not done so the day before in my meeting with the foreign minister be- cause I had only just been authorized to convey the information. Lee was such a strong apologist for the DPRK that, before I filled him in, he sided with the North over the IAEA in estimating how long it would take the IAEA to complete its verification obligations under the framework, as- suming the North ever let it start. Lee was not happy with what I told him, because he understood even without my saying so that the North's actions would plunge the Agreed Framework into crisis. I later briefed Minister of National Defense Lee Jun, who immediately grasped the significance of the information. In between, I visited the underground headquarters of U.S. Forces Korea (USFK), which was conducting our annual joint exercise with South Korean forces, and helicoptered to and from the DMZ. I was struck by the motto of South Korea's First Infantry Division: "Liberators of Pyongyang." I was also struck by the comment of General Leon LaPorte, the four-star USFK commander, in reaction to a possible North Korean attack: "We will kick his ass." I wondered what the diplomats from EAP and the South Korean foreign ministry thought of all that.

On September 10, the NSC principals finally met and concluded that the DPRK had effectively killed the Agreed Framework. Very little else was decided, but at last the critical line had been crossed. Joseph filled me in over a public telephone while I waited at JFK to board a flight to Moscow, so our conversation was highly elliptical. I asked how Kelly and Moriarity looked when the meeting was over, and he said "sick," which told me everything. In the meantime, the House appropriations subcommittee dealing with KEDO voted to cut our annual contribution from $75 million to $50 million, and to eliminate the waiver authority we had used after deciding not to certify DPRK compliance with the Agreed Framework, clearly indicating where Congress was headed. Moreover, when the IC briefed the Hill on the uranium-enrichment program, there was no doubt of its impact. A Senate staffer told me that Biden's reaction, on hearing what the North was up to, was to say, "Those fuckers!" Biden also said the enrichment activity represented a "clear violation" of the Agreed Framework. I later shared Biden's remarks with several foreign officials, just so they would know the commonality of the American reaction.

Undeterred, EAP still focused on getting Kelly on an airplane to Pyongyang, particularly since Koizumi had announced after his DPRK visit that he would normalize relations with the North. Although Koizumi experienced a short-term public opinion boost, families of the abducted Japanese citizens were outraged, reflecting the rising salience of the abduction issue across Japan. Bush himself ultimately authorized Kelly to go to North Korea in the fall of 2002, largely to avoid distracting from Iraq, and called Kim Dae-jung on September 25 to give him the "good news." Rice said the trip would show we were "reaching out" to a rogue state, unlike the way we were about to deal with Iraq.

My first reaction was dismay, but the more I thought about it, the more positive I became. The North would have to react to what we knew about their uranium-enrichment program, and that raw reaction could not be later disguised or "interpreted" by their apologists. Above all, I had real faith in the North Koreans. They were what they were, and no amount of

EAP spin could overcome that. After a huge interagency struggle, the NSC staff drafted very sound talking points, and essentially forced them on Kelly and EAP, to ensure we sent a clear message. Essentially, they read: Change your policy 180 degrees, or we have little to say to you. Incredibly, EAP wanted to host a banquet for the North Koreans in Pyongyang, which Rice canceled, saying we were hosting no banquets for "those bastards." As Kelly, Pritchard, and Green boarded their flight for Asia, EAP began to realize that perhaps this trip wasn't such a good idea after all.

The North's initial response to Kelly's message, on Thursday, October 3, 2002, via Vice Foreign Minister Kim Gye-gwan, was that everything was a fabrication by "anti–North Korean forces." The next day, Joseph called me early to say that Kelly was sending a classified cable from the British Embassy in Pyongyang (since we obviously had no embassy there), and that it would be "significant." Powell asked me to his office at 9:20 A.M. and handed me Kelly's cable via the Brits. Incredibly, First Vice Foreign Minister Kang Sok Ju, who was personally close to Kim Jong-il, unmistakably admitted they did have a uranium-enrichment program under way, claiming it was a direct response to Bush's naming them in the "axis of evil." Indeed, all their security efforts were in direct response to our threats, and everything would be fine between us if we just backed off. Kelly reported that the North Koreans had had an all-night meeting to discuss what he had told them, and to decide how to react, which our Asia hands thought almost surely meant that Kang's statement had been run past the Dear Leader himself. As Kelly said, to his credit, the DPRK had now "shredded" the Agreed Framework.

Powell was reeling from the news. I was as surprised as he about the directness of North Korea's admission, since their knee-jerk denial the first day was much more predictable. Later in the morning, in addition to the cable, we received a transcript our notetakers had made of the meeting, which fully corroborated the cable. Kang, reading from prepared talking points, said several times that his comments reflected the position of "the party and the government," which we all understood for the North Koreans was freighted with significance. It is worth noting that all eight Americans present had reviewed both the transcript and the cable, and there was *no dissent* from either document. Opponents of Bush administration policy later tried to rewrite history by pretending the confession hadn't actually happened, and wasn't contemporaneously recognized as such: "Bush officials later said the North Koreans had confessed. But diplomats now say that was a translation error."[11] This is flatly wrong. No one in October 2002 had any doubts about what the North Koreans had said and done.[12] They had killed the Agreed Framework both by their deeds and by their words. We had truly reached a turning point in history.

I was jubilant, but many EAP types just didn't get it. The NSC's Moriarity read the two documents and concluded that North Korea's position constituted "a desperate cry for help." Although Rumsfeld and others had suggested I lead the U.S. delegation on the Pyongyang trip, which Powell had rejected, I was now actually quite happy I had not gone. The U.S. delegation was all Asia hands, who were all pro-"engagement," and all pro–Agreed Framework. No one could accuse them of ulterior motives or blame them for "provoking" the DPRK, which some would have said had I led the mission. The North Koreans had done this to themselves, cleanly and unmistakably. In fact, as Kelly briefed Seoul and Tokyo on his way back to Washington, the magnitude of the DPRK confession began to sink in. ROK foreign minister Choi Sung-hong said he was "astounded at the seriousness" of the North's admission. Unification Minister Lim Dong-won, a real DPRK apologist, must have coordinated with Moriarity, because he said the North was signifying "a willingness to negotiate." Kelly made it clear the ball was in the DPRK's court, which must have truly disheartened the South Koreans. Of course, their mood was bad to begin with. They were also being pummeled by allegations that Kim Dae-jung's government had arranged approximately $400 million in bribes to bring Kim Jung-il to the "Pyongyang Summit," which had been trumpeted as a huge breakthrough. For Japan, which had been incredibly supportive of the Agreed Framework and "normalizing" relations with North Korea, as exemplified by Koizumi's trip, the revelations of DPRK cheating sparked a turnaround in their position, so that, by 2005, they were as hard-line as many of us in the Bush administration, or more so, a most welcome turn of events.

On Monday, October 7, Powell called me to his office. "There's no

---

11. See Hirsh, Liu, and Wehrfritz, "We Are a Nuclear Power," n. 2, p. 38.
12. See Pritchard, *Failed Diplomacy*, n. 7, pp. 37–40, especially his description of the U.S. delegation's tasking of its three Korean speakers, one of whom serves as the translator for the president of the United States, to recreate what they had heard from Kang in Korean, without relying on what the DPRK translators had said.

question it's over," he began, referring to the Agreed Framework. He was uncertain what to replace it with, and I said there was no need to replace it with anything. Kelly and I met later that morning with Powell, Grossman, Pritchard, and others so Kelly could debrief Powell on the Pyongyang meetings. Kelly and Pritchard pitched for "suspending" the framework, arguing that if we said it was dead, the North might begin reprocessing plutonium. I said the only intellectually honest conclusion one could draw was that the Agreed Framework *was* dead. Since we judged the North had already reprocessed enough plutonium to make several weapons even before all this news, I didn't see that even the "worst-case reaction," as Kelly called it, would make the slightest difference. Besides, we could predict with a high degree of certainty the congressional reaction to the news of the DPRK's alternative route to nuclear weapons, and it would be politically foolish for the administration to try to keep alive a failed—indeed humiliating—diplomacy. Powell asked about the consequences of cutting off our shipments of heavy fuel oil (five hundred thousand tons per year), and Pritchard said he did not think there would be adverse humanitarian consequences.

I was convinced Powell knew what had to be done, even though EAP did not yet realize that its worldview had collapsed around it. Indeed, the next morning, Armitage told me privately that Bush, on hearing of the Pyongyang meetings, said he wanted to control the timing of the announcement so that there would be no adverse effect on Iraq matters, but that the Agreed Framework was "kaput." That sounded synonymous with "dead" to me, but EAP still wasn't getting it. Even the Energy Department was arguing now that the North could not be trusted to live up to any agreements they might sign in the future. Powell ultimately made clear his position, and therefore State's, at an NSC meeting chaired by Bush on October 15 that the Agreed Framework was dead, and that EAP's "suspension" idea was just as dead. Kelly and I were to go to Beijing to brief the Chinese on our conclusion, with Kelly splitting off to go to Seoul and Tokyo, while I proceeded to Moscow, Paris, London, and Brussels (for the EU), but there would be no public announcement for at least several weeks because of Iraq issues. My only worry was that Bush's legitimate concern about not having a Korea crisis in the middle of the Iraq crisis would be used by EAP for mischief, which, of course, they were at incessantly. (Intense Security Council negotiations on Iraq were then under way, and on

November 8, the Council unanimously adopted Resolution 1441, deciding that Iraq was in "material breach" of prior resolutions, providing a "final opportunity to comply" fully with those resolutions, and warning that Iraq "will face serious consequences" if it did not.)

When Kelly and I left for Beijing on October 16, however, the story broke in the media. While the leak probably came from EAP and its friends, I didn't hesitate to return the innumerable incoming press calls and explain that the North was in material violation of the Agreed Framework, and had, for all intents and purposes, tanked it. Joseph was doing the same in Washington. The EAPeasers were spinning merrily to the contrary—after all, it was only the president who had declared it "kaput"—and it was left to the common sense of the American people to decide what the facts were. Needless to say, that was finally the end of that debate, as I made clear not only in Beijing but also in the follow-on meetings with the Security Council's other permanent members and with the EU. In Beijing, the consultations took place only a week before the Bush-Jiang Zemin Summit meeting in Crawford, so a lot was at stake for both sides. I read from a prepared script to brief the Chinese, so there would be no misunderstanding. Kelly followed, stating that everyone in the administration saw the DPRK issue the same way, thus emphasizing why we were appearing together in Beijing to deliver the message. The other capitals all heard the same message, and no one disputed that the North had been caught in a serious violation of the Agreed Framework.

This was especially important in Moscow, with a Bush-Putin meeting coming shortly after the Crawford Summit with China. So important was it that Russia understand exactly what had happened in Kelly's Pyongyang meetings that I gave Igor Ivanov a copy of the British Embassy cable. I decided I should confess this to Jack Straw when I was in London, saying, "Better to ask for forgiveness than to ask for permission." Fortunately, Straw responded heartily, "Good for you, John!" EU commissioner Chris Patten said publicly before I arrived in Brussels, "It is difficult in present circumstances to see how we can continue with our contributions to KEDO," showing that even he was out in front of State's bureaucracy. France, as a nuclear weapons state, was especially interesting on how it wanted the United States to deal—and not to deal—with the European Commission, a contributor to KEDO. Particularly sensitive that the EC have no role on real strategic matters, the Quai d'Orsay's political director, Stanislas de Laboulaye, said casually but earnestly to me in Paris, "Just stay in touch with us and the British on the key issues." Very French.

In fact, the North Koreans made a signal contribution to the debate over the status of the Agreed Framework by asserting that our actions had "nullified" it. Powell used the DPRK stance as a comfortable crutch on the Sunday, October 20, talk shows, saying, "an agreement between two parties, one of whom says it's been nullified, makes it sort of a nullified agreement." Rice was more direct, saying the North had "blown a hole in this political arrangement," which led CNN to headline its Web story: "U.S.: N. Korea arms pact effectively dead." After a few further EAP-caused bumps in the road, our shipments of heavy fuel oil to the DPRK were terminated after the November delivery, thus ending the last practical aspect of the Agreed Framework. Thank God that was done.

Launching the Proliferation Security Initiative

> PSI is an activity, not an organization.
>
> —British Foreign Office diplomat

The next three and a half depressing years brought an endless series of IAEA discussions, and those related to the "Six-Party Talks," an embarrassing series of failures I will be happy to describe at greater length when circumstances permit. During these years, the State Department bureaucracy attempted to do exactly what it had been doing in the last years of the Clinton administration, and what it had tried unsuccessfully to do in Bush's first two years. No matter what the facts were, and no matter what the DPRK did, the catechism was always a prayer to negotiate the North out of its nuclear weapons. Fortunately, for most of this period, EAP made no visible progress, essentially because North Korea had a fundamentally different objective from what EAP and the High Minded thought. Additionally, the evolving Japanese position was moving steadily toward a harder-line approach, thus substantially limiting EAP's ability to give away important policy positions. This at least prevented State from compromising one central objective of mine, which was to prevent North Korea from repeating its

1994 flim-flam, the Agreed Framework, thereby preserving its nuclear weapons program while extracting tangible economic benefits from the United States and other countries.

By the same token, however, State's bureaucracy and its allies were able to block or weaken my efforts to bring the North Korean nuclear weapons program to a halt by increasing real international economic and political pressure, such as through stringent sanctions. The outcome, in many respects, was an unsatisfactory stand-off, as noted by outside commentators. This was deeply frustrating, but I saw no alternative to incessant bureaucratic combat unless realists were simply to surrender the field to the High Minded accommodationists and EAPeasers. The stand-off's most unfortunate aspect was the spin many critics gave it, slamming Bush administration policies as if we were actually doing what I was trying to achieve. Attacked for being unilateralist, interventionist, preemptive hardliners, in fact we were nowhere close. We were locked in trench warfare against the Crusaders of Compromise. EAP was thus blocked in the first term, as were the hardliners, but as key players like Rumsfeld, Libby, Crouch and Joseph moved to different positions after 2004 or left the administration, the balance shifted, and the permanent bureaucracy took its shot.

We did have a few good moments, such as a 2003 speech I gave in Seoul, where I roundly criticized Kim Jong-il and his totalitarian regime and tried hard to raise South Korean concerns about the grotesque police state oppressing their fellow Koreans across the DMZ. I knew we had struck home when the DPRK's news agency denounced me as "human scum," probably the highest accolade I received during all my service in the Bush years. This speech, another successful effort by Groombridge and others in my office to follow the bureaucracy's process imperatives to the letter in the clearance process, while trumping them on substance, also gained notoriety during my 2005 confirmation battle. When Biden asked Powell about it at a closed SFRC briefing on September 9, 2003, Powell told me later that day he pointed to Jim Kelly, sitting with him, and said, "Jim's right here, and he can tell you that he cleared it."

The internal U.S. government stand-off on North Korea meant we had to focus our activity elsewhere to prevent their nuclear capacity, and their ballistic missile and chemical and biological weapons programs, from growing at an alarming rate. Indeed, one of the central deficiencies of the Six-Party Talks from the outset was that the talks concentrated only on nuclear weapons, and not the North's other WMD programs. This was no consolation to USFK forces and South Korean civilians, whose main risk would come from chemical weapons fired by the North's massive artillery forces in the opening hours of any military conflict. Since the Six-Party Talks were doing nothing to slow the DPRK, and indeed provided it cover while it progressed on an alarming variety of fronts, we needed to take more decisive action elsewhere. For example, some of North Korea's uranium-enrichment program, although by no means all of it, came from the DPRK's association with the A. Q. Khan proliferation network. Khan successfully sold nuclear technology, including weaponization plans, to the DPRK, Iran, Libya, and perhaps others, before being exposed. Nonetheless, it was North Korea's aggressive efforts to proliferate ballistic missiles components and technology, and to acquire the materials and technology necessary for their own WMD programs, that led to one of the most profound of Bush's innovative policies, the Proliferation Security Initiative (PSI).

In late November 2002, we became aware of a ship, the M/V *So San*, making its way from North Korea toward an unknown destination, and likely carrying a shipment of concealed ballistic missiles. This was "real-time" information, which we might actually be able to do something about, although the environment was complex. We were then trying to persuade the IAEA board of governors to condemn the North's nuclear weapons program and refer it to the Security Council for action, and the DPRK threatened to expel IAEA inspectors from Yongbyon if, as they feared, we cut off heavy-fuel-oil shipments. EAP was still not getting the message that our policy had changed, as one anecdote from an NSC meeting to discuss the cut-off neatly exemplified: Rice asked Moriarity what steps we were taking to persuade Japan and South Korea to agree with us on the cut-off. Moriarity was stunned by the question, and it rapidly became clear that our diplomats were doing precisely nothing to change Tokyo's and Seoul's views. Why should they? They were waiting for the ROK and Japan to change *our* views, not the other way around. Bush and Rice blew past that obstructionism, but it was one more issue to resolve as the *So San* and its concealed cargo of ballistic missiles sailed on its way.

Moreover, at the IAEA, we and other concerned board members were negotiating with ourselves, watering down the condemnatory resolution to the point of vapidity, even before we circulated it to countries like China and Russia, which would of course only try to water it down still further. What we ultimately agreed to on November 29 was a pale imitation of the explicit condemnation we wanted, with no referral of the DPRK to the Security Council. We had concluded by then that the *So San* was actually headed to Yemen, in flat violation of Yemen's mid-2001 agreement with us not to purchase such missiles from the DPRK or anyone else. At a Deputies Committee meeting (DO) chaired by Hadley on November 20, we all agreed that the Multilateral Interdiction Force (MIF) conducting operations under the Iraq sanctions regime should interdict the *So San* and inspect its cargo. (A DC is an interagency meeting one level below a PC, which cabinet secretaries attend. DCs meet in varying configurations, depending on the issue involved, to help formulate national security policy. There are interagency meetings below the DC level as well.) Not surprisingly, Moriarity, still hearing that "desperate cry for help" from North Korea, argued against an interdiction, but he was ignored. Bush fully approved the operation, and a Spanish vessel in the MIF boarded the ship on December 9 and took control. We had clear authority to do so, since the ship had repeatedly obscured its name and registration markings, making it a "stateless" vessel; we had other authority as well, including Cambodia's (one of the several places the vessel was registered) not objecting to a boarding. The *So San*'s master claimed he was only carrying cement, until the Spaniards dug through several layers of cement bags and found over a dozen crates of Scud missiles.

Unfortunately, what should have been a clandestine operation was by this point probably known by thousands of people in government because it was conducted through regular military channels. I flew to Copenhagen on other matters, arriving the morning of December 11, only to find the story breaking wide open in the media, which produced the usual feeding frenzy of inquiries we simply were not ready for. This vacuum allowed the implication to develop that somehow we had done something in violation of (say this in a slow, deep voice) "international law," which of course would be a Bad Thing. That was entirely incorrect. We had the authority not only to conduct the boarding, but to seize the missiles as well, given the *So San*'s obvious and multiple violations of its obligations as a "commercial" vessel. Nonetheless, with a snow-and-ice storm keeping many people from their offices, and a rising tide of near hysteria in Washington among the weak-kneed, things got out of control. I thought we should have seized the missiles for our own use, but the decision was somehow made, based on Yemen's cooperation in the war on terror, to allow the *So San* to proceed there to offload its cargo. Ironically, my Danish hosts were all in favor of the interdiction, their only regret being that it was not a Danish vessel undertaking the mission. Jim Wright of Canada told me a few days later that they would have fully supported us if we had seized the Scuds.

I traveled on to Brussels, and in the early evening separately called Joseph and Crouch, who were both quite depressed that the operation, so carefully prepared and initially so successful, had fallen apart. Many pointed to weakness from the NSC's lawyer, John Bellenger, his typical reaction to difficult circumstances, but the larger issue was the general chaos and confusion within the administration, in which fear from the lawyers had caused panic. Simultaneously, the DPRK was torquing up the pressure by threatening to restart the Yongbyon reactor, which they had wanted to do for a long time anyway. At a minimum, they were, in their own inimitable way, trying to influence the upcoming December 19 South Korean presidential elections, and given the closeness of the margin by which Roh Moo-Hyun ultimately won, they might well have. I just hoped the North Koreans were not encouraged by our inability to prevent the *So San*'s cargo from actually being delivered to Yemen, and didn't view our failure as a sign of weakness.

In fact, the DPRK began removing IAEA seals and cameras at Yongbyon, including those from the spent fuel rods in the cooling ponds, within forty-eight hours of Roh's victory, which showed exactly how much opposition they thought they would face from his administration for even the most outrageous behavior. Removing the seals from the spent fuel rods also showed clearly that North Korea was preparing to reprocess additional plutonium, which was a direct challenge to the United States. A few days later, the DPRK began expelling IAEA inspectors, as it had earlier threatened, and, predictably, announced its withdrawal from the Nuclear Non-Proliferation Treaty. Just as predictably, therefore, EAP started pressing for what became the Six-Party Talks, which went through many permutations before emerging in their current form. I couldn't see what the agenda would be for such a gaggle, other than to get us in the same room with North Koreans, which was EAP's answer to everything.

We had endless conversations after the *So San* incident, trying to understand how the interdiction had gone wrong, and what we could do to make similar efforts go right. Fortunately, the publicity that swirled around the incident, despite my initial misgivings, left many people around the world with the impression that we had a larger WMD interdiction capability than we actually did. Of course, covert action against proliferation had been around for a long time, but here we had real potential for something new. Joseph and his staff, which were responsible at the NSC for issues such as Khan's network, did much of the conceptual thinking, and Cheney, Rumsfeld, and many others contributed to thinking about PSI. Basically, we felt that better advance coordination among diplomatic, military, and intelligence components of like-minded governments would result in better planning and therefore better implementation of future interdiction efforts. Moreover, if active interdiction had a higher political priority, there would surely be a significantly greater number of operations, and hence a significantly enhanced actual and deterrent effect against proliferation. There was more, of course, and we had actually had some very preliminary discussions with the Brits about enhanced interdiction efforts, but the *So San* affair was what catalyzed and drove the process forward.

Our focal point became Bush's announcement of PSI, which he delivered in Krakow, Poland, on May 31, 2003. In order to turn the president's speech into something concrete as soon as possible, we needed to assemble the countries that would form PSI's "core group." Bush's stop in Krakow came just before the Evian G-8 Summit, which meant it was critical that the G-8 not say anything that would get in the way of the new initiative, a diplomatic goal I was able to achieve at Evian.

I turned my attention immediately to the first meeting of the PSI Core Group, which Spain agreed to host in Madrid on June 12. Eleven countries attended: Australia, France, Germany, Italy, Japan, Netherlands, Poland, Portugal, Spain, United Kingdom, and the United States. We needed to flesh out the two sentences in Bush's Krakow speech and make PSI real as soon as possible, both because it was the right policy, and because Bush had put his prestige on the line. These were strong incentives, although we had no road map for how to proceed. Joseph and I agreed that we wanted a strong Madrid political statement that Core Group members were fully prepared to engage in WMD interdictions, and that if we found ourselves hamstrung by voices of timidity, we would be prepared to ice them out of future PSI activities. I already had a call from Javier Gil Caetana, the Spanish Foreign Ministry's secretary general, who would be chairing the Madrid meeting, asking about the EU participating. I said we were interested in countries with real operational capabilities—intelligence services and militaries—neither of which the EU had, not more diplomatic personnel. That didn't bother the Spanish, who might well have been as tired of constant calls from Brussels as many others. I also rejected the idea of including a NATO representative, for reasons similar to those for not wanting the EU involved: NATO had a ponderous bureaucracy and carried enormous baggage. To start off a completely new endeavor by immediately importing all of that baggage, without at least thinking it through, struck me as pure cost and no benefit.

Although initially concerned that the Core Group's first meeting could get lost in a diplomatic miasma, we were encouraged by the practical, operational approach the group took. Even France said we should not engage in abstract discussion but approach interdiction issues on a case-by-case basis. Very Burkean, and very welcome. Our DoD people had drafted a two-page document on "rules of the road," intended to describe the rights and obligations of sovereign nations concerning WMD interdictions, which we hoped the Core Group would adopt. If they did, we intended to distribute the text more generally, encouraging others to adhere to it for cooperation in future interdictions. We were surprised and encouraged at how constructive was the discussion of the "rules of the road," which showed interdiction was widely, indeed enthusiastically supported within the Core Group. I said that, before the next meeting, we encouraged further comments on the "rules," which we would revise and distribute in advance, and we should all focus on integrating such existing antiproliferation regimes as the Nuclear Suppliers Group (NSG), the Missile Technology Control Regime (MTCR), and the Australia Group (dealing with chemical and biological weapons) into PSI's work. As a practical matter, we expected to use their export control lists, rather than have PSI countries go through the needless and duplicative exercise of coming up with their own. I left Madrid to meet with Egypt, Yemen, and other Arab countries to discuss why they should not meet their defense needs by procuring from North Korea. This was another aspect of our diplomacy, and not a public one, but intended to complement PSI by eliminating North Korea's revenue sources even before interdiction became necessary by cutting off its customers.

A later meeting of EU political directors decided to have the next PSI meeting in Europe. How gracious of them to decide where to hold the next meeting of *our* initiative, and, what a coincidence, how convenient it would be for them! That confirmed my desire to head Down Under, and in fact the second PSI meeting was in Brisbane (pronounced with a short "a," I learned), on July 9–10, 2003. I arrived in Sydney on the morning of Tuesday, July 8, having left Washington on July 6, watching an entire day disappear simply by crossing the International Date Line. I hope others enjoyed July 7, 2003, but I never lived it. After quick consultations in Canberra, I flew to Brisbane and settled in for three rounds of expert meetings (diplomatic, military, and intelligence) on July 9, as we had agreed to do in Madrid. Although I concentrated on PSI, Washington was fixated on the "Niger uranium" issue, which soon developed into the "Valerie Plame leak." During my later confirmation battle for UN ambassador, many from the left's conspiracy-minded fever swamps were convinced I was involved in concocting the Niger uranium story or leaking Plame's name to the press. Probably fortunately, I never met Valerie, didn't know Joe Wilson, had never been to Niger, and was in the Antipodes when the whole thing blew up. As the Aussies say, no joy there!

The three expert groups went well, although a "conference" of representatives from eleven intelligence agencies was clearly an unnatural act for them. While we felt comfortable about intelligence sharing with those present, the intel types didn't often meet in large gatherings. They preferred quiet, bilateral contacts, and I had the feeling when I entered their meeting that their real inclination was to slink off into corners to have more traditional conversations. Even so, our objective was greater coordination not only among intelligence agencies, but with military and other operational actors as well, to facilitate interdictions, and the discussions made considerable progress. The military experts agreed on PSI's first operational exercise, piggy-backing on an already-planned September naval exercise in the Coral Sea, marking an important milestone to prove that PSI would be the real thing, not just chitchat. Australian foreign minister Alexander Downer hosted a dinner that evening for the Core Group delegations, during most of which he and I discussed American and Australian politics. Throughout the Bush administration, Australia, under John Howard and Downer, was our closest ally, the most like us and the most sympathetic to our policies, as their work on PSI demonstrated.

"Outreach" was a constant subject of Core Group discussion. Obviously, the more countries that supported PSI, the more successful our interdiction efforts could be, so there was no lack of ideas on how to enlist the broadest possible support, especially from major powers like China, Russia, and India. We kept China fully briefed on PSI as part of our regular consultations on strategic issues, hoping to gain its support. Similarly, I explained PSI at my first meeting with Sergei Kislyak, Mamedov's successor as deputy foreign minister handling U.S. and arms control issues, in Washington on August 18. Like China, Russia worried that PSI would effectively become a blockade of North Korea (which wouldn't have bothered me in the slightest). Nonetheless, I stressed to both that PSI was directed against all WMD proliferation threats. Most encouraging was that Russia, as opposed to China, wanted *in* to PSI, an attitude we took seriously. India hung back at the outset, and because of India's own activities regarding nuclear weapons and ballistic missiles, we initially worked simply to keep it informed.

On August 8, 2003, we had a PSI-like interdiction by Taiwan, which seized cargo from a DPRK ship, the *Be Gaehung*, in Kaohsiung harbor. The vessel had loaded in Thailand a dual-use chemical that could be used as a precursor for VX nerve agent, but without obtaining permission to transit Kaohsiung with a dangerous cargo. This was the hook used by Taiwanese customs officials to stop the vessel, at our request. The *Be Gaehung's* captain refused to cooperate, which was hardly surprising given the cargo he was carrying, and there was a brief impasse as Taiwan refused to allow the vessel to sail. Hundreds of barrels of the dangerous cargo were ultimately offloaded and seized by Taiwan. This was a marvelous example of how interdictions could work, not as dramatic as an interception on the high seas, but just as effective. Once again, a North Korean cargo was interdicted, this one on its way *to* the DPRK to support its WMD programs, rather than a shipment out, but the actual and deterrent effects on DPRK commerce were just as great.

The Paris Core Group meeting on September 3–4 was significant because we reached agreement on the "Statement of Interdiction Principles," endorsed by all Core Group members. (The leftist newspaper *Libération* had a headline reading *"France et Etats-Unis dans le même bateau,"*[13] a play

---

13. Jean-Dominique Merchet, *"France et Etats-Unis dans le même bateau," Libération*, September 4, 2003, Quotidien premier edition, p. 3, col. 4.

on the naval interdiction idea.) We wanted to make the statement public immediately and start soliciting other countries to sign up so we could begin operations, but Germany and France were hesitant, arguing that we should first consult Russia and China. We had already been doing that, as had the Brits, but one reason Russia and China were not in the Core Group to begin with was that we wanted to get something going that was not wishy-washy or watered down, and then bring others on board. We wanted "an activity, not an organization," as one of the Brits properly characterized PSI, meaning that gaining adherence to our statement was less important as a first step than a strong statement, which we had now achieved. Time enough now to go after China, Russia, and others, which in fact French political director Stanislas de Laboulaye and I did immediately, calling Kislyak in Moscow and sending him a copy of the statement. In response to Kislyak's question whether the statement was open to changes, I said it was not carved in stone, but neither should he treat it as still being in the word processor, which was the gentlest way I could think of to say we were satisfied with what we had.

The Paris meeting showed the benefits of planning and U.S. determination not to leave PSI's fate in the hands of others, a sharp contrast with our continuing diplomacy on North Korea and Iran, where we were outsourcing our diplomacy to the Six-Party Talks and the EU, respectively. Paris also showed the importance of keeping the president's agenda clearly in sight at State, and not letting it get lost. The contrast on North Korea had become particularly acute with Pritchard's resignation in late August as our chief North Korea hand. This caused quite a press flap, demoralizing as it was to the "engagers" and to Powell. Interestingly, Pritchard seemed to be angry with Powell as much for not defending the EAP perspective effectively as for anything else, which was an interesting take on what the permanent bureaucracy thought the proper role of the secretary of state should be. Groombridge heard this because several people in EAP told him that Pritchard had paid me the backhand compliment of saying, "At least Bolton has a policy," even though Pritchard disagreed with essentially all of it. It should have been quite a lesson for Powell, who had tried to embrace the bureaucracy, but was instead bitten by it.

One tangible success that showed how PSI would operate came in late September, when we began tracking the course of a German-owned vessel, the *BBC China* (which was unrelated to either the BBC or China), on its way through the Suez Canal. We believed the vessel was carrying centrifuge components from A. Q. Khan's network to Libya, and it was an invitation to put PSI concepts into action. By October 6, with the owner's consent, the *BBC China* was diverted from its course to Tripoli, and docked in southern Italy, where it offloaded five large containers filled with centrifuge equipment (including such things as motors and pumps), which were seized by Italian customs officials. (And, as one wag put it, once Italian customs had it, it would never depart.) The containers were labeled as containing such things as "used auto parts," typical of Khan's smuggling skills, but this time we had foiled them, in effect using this seizure to open up what we knew of the Khan network. What to do about the network had been under discussion for some time, with some in our government arguing to shut it down earlier, while others thought we should allow it to operate in order to learn even more about it. This was a complex and difficult judgment. Obviously, once we moved against what we knew of the network, we would lose the possibility of tracking whatever remained in operation. On the other hand, waiting too long could mean, for example, that Libya's nuclear weapons program might proceed too far to stop. Although one can never be sure, I think the administration acted at the right time against Khan's network.

I wanted to publicize the *BBC China* seizure widely, but CIA director George Tenet and the Brits resisted fiercely because they were talking to Libya about renouncing its nuclear weapons program, discussions started after Muammar al-Qaddafi watched the ease with which we overthrew Saddam Hussein, and worried he might be next. The intelligence types feared that publicizing a PSI-type success might spook Qaddafi, which was reasonable, but in fact seizing the *BBC China* was the second major step (after deposing Saddam) in convincing Libya that we already knew what they were up to. The final step was Saddam's capture in Iraq in December, which was all Qaddafi needed to see before making the final decision to allow us to transport his entire nuclear weapons program to Oak Ridge, Tennessee, where it now rests, and where there is ample room for the DPRK and Iranian programs if these states ever see the light. In fact, State's decision to allow settlement of the Pan Am 103 murders, Libya's subsequent renunciation of terrorism, and Qaddafi's decision to abandon his nuclear weapons program, subject to full and complete inspection by the CIA and the U.K.'s Secret Intelligence Service (MI-6), opened the path to normal relations with the United States. That same path is also open to North Korea and Iran, but they have not taken it.

Subsequent PSI Core Group meetings in London on October 9–10, and Lisbon, Portugal, on March 4–5, 2004, allowed us to expand the Core Group to include Canada, Norway, and Singapore. Bush underlined our determination on WMD proliferation at his annual address to the UN General Assembly on September 23, 2003, mentioning both PSI and the G-8 Global Partnership, saying: "The deadly combination of outlaw regimes and terror networks and weapons of mass murder is a peril that cannot be ignored or wished away. If such a danger is allowed to fully materialize, all words, all protests, will come too late. Nations of the world must have the wisdom and the will to stop grave threats before they arrive." The real progress was on the operational front, where cooperation among military, intelligence, and law-enforcement agencies moved steadily ahead, buoyed by the *BBC China* incident as details became public. We fended off multiple efforts, especially by EU states, to bog us down in legalistic and diplomatic negotiations that would have sapped the vigor from PSI. In fact, with the adoption of the statement of interdiction principles, there was not really much more for the diplomats to do except hand over responsibility to their operational colleagues. This was why PSI really was "an activity not an organization," as opposed to the UN, which one Brit said was "an organization, not an activity." The White House thought that the initiative was well launched, and in fact Rice joked to me in December, "You and Joseph can retire now," to which I responded, "Some people want us to!"

By the time of the U.S.-hosted, G-8 Sea Island Summit in 2004, we had also brought Russia into the Core Group, at the May 31–June 1 meetings in Krakow, Poland, celebrating the first anniversary of Bush's speech launching PSI. The Poles held that meeting deep underground, in a salt mine that is now a tourist attraction, with fantastic rooms and statues carved out of salt. "We have a history of doing things underground," said the Polish host, to the evident discomfort of both the German and the Russian delegations, but the rest of us found it most amusing. Unfortunately, Russia's participation in PSI's operational activities remained sporadic, and their commitment to PSI principles very uncertain. If they had been more "engaged," and China more supportive, we might not have encountered what was to come from the DPRK.

In October 2004, just before the U.S. presidential election, I participated in a PSI exercise in Tokyo Bay, in which French, Japanese, Australian, and American vessels practiced interdictions. Because this and other PSI activities rarely receive media coverage, few critics of Bush administration "unilateralism" fully understand PSI. But make no mistake, PSI is real multilateralism, and definitely not the "multilateralism" of the chattering class.

CHAPTER FIVE

LEAVING THE DRIVING TO THE EU: NEGOTIATIONS *ÜBER ALLES* WITH IRAN

I have a simple principle in foreign affairs.
I see what the Americans are doing and I do the opposite.
That way I'm sure to be right.

—JACQUES CHIRAC[1]

Throughout George W. Bush's presidency, Iran's nuclear weapons ambitions were a constant problem. Iran's goals never changed, but the administration's goals were too often in flux, and not pursued as consistently or as relentlessly as they might have been. Whether, after his re-election, President Bush wavered personally remains unknown, but too many of his subordinates did, and he allowed them to do so. As a result, Iran continued to make progress toward its goal, while we watched.

I certainly did not accomplish what I wanted to do on Iran. I was not able to convince enough other people above me of the seriousness of Iran's threat; I suggested early on a multilateral diplomatic course that others hijacked and ran in slow motion, to my dismay and to our detriment; and finally, time just ran out on me as I left State. There were many other reasons,

---

1. Chirac is quoted as having "told colleagues [this] on several occasions," according to Franz-Olivier Giesbert's *"La Tragédie du Président,"* a political obituary of Mr. Chirac published last year. Matthew Kaminski, "France's Anti-Anti-Americans," *Asian Wall Street Journal,* January 17, 2007, p. 12, col. 3.

not least that the "global test" mentality carried far more weight inside the Bush administration than I anticipated. (Senator John Kerry, during his September 30, 2004, debate with Bush had said of preemptive military action, "If and when you do it, you've got to do it in a way that passes . . . the global test where . . . you can prove to the world that you did it for legitimate reasons.") After Iraq, the fear of being separated from the Europeans was too great to overcome, even within an administration of supposed unilateralist cowboys.

As with North Korea, I divide the Iran saga into two parts, the first dealing with Bush's first term, and the second with events in the Security Council in 2005–6.

Russia's "Czarist" Policies in Iran

I first saw Iran's proliferation efforts through the prism of creating a new strategic framework with Russia. Although the problem was clear in 2001—one of my early conversations with the NSC's Steve Hadley and Bob Joseph concerned the nuclear power plant Russia was building for Iran at Bushehr—our negotiations with Russia concentrated on strategic defenses first, then on strategic offenses, as described earlier. When we raised the subject of Iran's aggressive nuclear weapons and ballistic missile programs during these talks, the Russians said unequivocally that they were just as worried about Iran as we were. Powell specifically flagged Iran for Foreign Minister Ivanov in Moscow on December 10, 2001, as we gave notice of our exiting the ABM Treaty, saying, "I want to lay down a marker on this," and, "We are troubled by the nature of the regime." Moreover, the administration was also debating how to administer various sanctions statutes (e.g., the Iraq-Iran Non-Proliferation Act of 1992 and the Iran-Libya Sanctions Act of 1996), which had withered and almost died for lack of use under Clinton. I pressed for vigorous enforcement of these laws, but met unrelenting bureaucratic opposition.

In fact, our roundabout approach on Iran worried Israel, since it seemed to imply that Iran and other proliferation issues were far down on our list of priorities. In mid-January 2002, for example, I visited Israel and explained we had now concluded our principal discussions with Russia on strategic defenses and were turning to offensive issues. There were pained reactions from the Israelis, perhaps because they remembered Cold War arms control negotiations, which dragged on for years, meaning we wouldn't be turning to Iran any time soon. Even so, Israel's major recommendations at that time were rather limited, such as "just-in-time" shipments of fuel rods from Russia to the Bushehr reactor and the immediate return of spent fuel, both of which would minimize the amount of nuclear material present in Iran at any given time. These were positions similar to what our Department of Energy was advocating.

Within our government, Cheney and Rumsfeld held tougher views, insisting that Russia should cease all nuclear and missile cooperation with Iran, including Bushehr, and stop all sales of advanced conventional weapons (ACW). As a February 15, 2002, Principals Committee meeting on our Treaty of Moscow negotiations ended, Rice raised the Russia-Iran proliferation issue. Powell let me advance my idea, not yet agreed to within State, to tell Russia we weren't even prepared to discuss Bushehr or possible U.S.-Russian cooperation on nuclear matters until they ceased all WMD and ACW relations with Iran. If they weren't willing to do so in a way that gave us confidence they were adhering to their commitments, I explained, there really wasn't much to talk about. Rice said, "Well, John has certainly put this in a different way, what do we think about that? I like that approach." Cheney said, "I agree with the way John would approach it. That's really exactly right." Rumsfeld still wasn't buying, but Rice said, "John's going to be in Moscow on Monday, and he needs instructions, Don. Can you at least agree that John can open conversations with the Russians?" Rumsfeld was still grousing, when Cheney laughed and said, "Come on, this is Bolton, he's tough." Rumsfeld finally smiled and said, "Oh, all right" as the meeting broke up.

Within the Russian government, there were various opinions on Iran. The most knowledgeable about Iran's activities, and therefore probably the most worried, was Aleksandr Rumyantsev, head of the Ministry of Atomic Energy (Minatom). His predecessor had been widely suspected of corruption, so we were quite interested in getting to know Rumyantsev, a nuclear physicist who obviously knew the ins and outs of both civil nuclear power and weapons production. In my second meeting with him, in Moscow on February 18, 2002, Rumyantsev, a large, jovial, very direct man, said there simply was no cooperation with Iran on weapons-related matters, a position the Russians adhered to consistently. My next meeting that day was with Yuri Koptev, general director of Rosaviakosmos, their equivalent of NASA, who stoutly denied his agency had any dealings with Iran and said we should bring any information to the contrary to his attention. Less clear were the activities of Russian firms, such as Energomash, which had important contractual relationships with Iran, but which also denied currently assisting Iran's ballistic missile program. Since such U.S. firms as Boeing and Lockheed purchased launch vehicles for American satellites from Energomash, and engaged with it in other business ventures, many of which required U.S. government approval and licenses, we tried to leverage these relationships to reduce Russian cooperation with Iran.

Although Rumyantsev's and Koptev's responses sounded reasonable, they posed difficult problems for us, given our concern not to compromise sensitive intelligence sources and methods, which could be revealed simply by the nature of the information we might disclose. I met with CIA director George Tenet on this question on April 19. Accompanying him was one of his deputies, John McLaughlin, who said unequivocally that Russian behavior with Iran in nuclear weapons and ballistic missiles was as bad as or worse than it had been for some years. Nonetheless, he resisted any idea of confronting Russia with what we knew. I certainly didn't want to disclose intelligence promiscuously, which too many others at State had done many times before, but to develop better advocacy with the Russians to make them either confront the problem, or if they continued to deny it, for there to be attendant consequences in our bilateral relations.

I made the point about bilateral relations with Rumyantsev and Koptev on April 30, 2002, in Moscow, which neither of them liked hearing. In the last days before the Moscow Summit, I told my counterpart, Georgi Mamedov, that Bush would raise the matter of Iran with Putin, because we had failed to resolve the problem at lower levels. Interestingly, Mamedov responded, "You're not going to try to bribe us, are you?" He said Moscow no longer looked favorably on receiving financial "cooperation." "Cash for performance" was patronizing, he said, which it was. In any event I didn't think we should be paying them with "carrots" to stop doing what they shouldn't have been doing in the first place.

Bush did raise the matter of Iran with Putin right before signing the Treaty of Moscow, and they were asked about Iran at the press conference afterward. Putin denied that Russia was doing anything untoward, or anything different at least from what we were doing in supporting the construction of light-water reactors in North Korea, which I thought was a telling point against us. As we were milling around before the next meeting, Bush correctly expressed disappointment with Putin's unhelpful answer. While Putin had agreed in their private meeting that Iran was a security threat to Russia, nothing concrete developed from that. The Bush-Putin discussion in Moscow was largely repeated at the June 2002 Kananaskis G-8 meeting, but once again Putin failed to say precisely what steps Russia would actually take to act on its concerns about Iranian proliferation activities.

Russia actually moved in the opposite direction, announcing in late July that it planned to build up to five new reactors in Iran similar to Bushehr. Rice heatedly called Sergei Ivanov to protest, but Ivanov said the stories were inaccurate, reporting only internal Russian government discussions. This was slightly better news. Secretary of Energy Spence Abraham, whom I had known for many years, and I were in Moscow a few days later to see Rumyantsev, giving us a perfect opportunity to further express our displeasure. Abraham and I consciously played a "good cop, bad cop" strategy with the Russians, which we used to good effect in these Moscow meetings. We met Rumyantsev on July 31, and he assured us that new reactors would be discussed with Iran only after Bushehr was finished. Russians had operated it long enough to train Iranians, and they had agreement on the rapid "take-back" of the spent fuel as soon as practicable after it was removed from the reactor. In addition, said Rumyantsev, Iran would have to refrain from developing its own fuel cycle, and accede to the IAEA Additional Protocol, so there was adequate provision for IAEA inspection of Iran's compliance with its Safeguards Agreement. All of this was positive, but it took an hour and a half to resolve the problem caused by the earlier announcement, which set back progress on other issues.

The problem with Bushehr was that once the reactor became operational, Iran could reprocess enough plutonium from spent fuel rods for sixty or more nuclear weapons, if they decided to seize all the nuclear material on the reactor's premises. Requiring Iran to ratify the IAEA Additional Protocol, which gave IAEA enhanced inspection rights, was little additional protection against a determined cheater like Iran. Moreover, Russian insistence on a "take-back agreement" was also not sufficient, given the time that the spent fuel had to stay in cooling ponds until it could actually be transported. Further meetings with Rumyantsev and Koptev in September,

October, and November were unproductive, and by this point the looming war in Iraq began to choke out other subjects with the Russians. We stressed to Rumyantsev in particular our concerns over Iran's construction at Arak of a heavy-water production facility and a heavy-water reactor, but our focus on Bushehr and the possibility of Russia's constructing additional reactors in Iran did not diminish. The Israelis also remained quite concerned about Iran's activities, which were steaming right along regardless of Russia's level of involvement.

How Many IAEA Meetings Does It Take to Screw in a Lightbulb?

Now, however, the focus began to shift from Russia to Iran directly. When IAEA director general Mohamed el Baradei visited Iran in mid-February 2003, he was shown an operating 164-centrifuge cascade, and he and the IAEA team saw components for up to one thousand additional centrifuges. Moreover, Iran also revealed it had received UF_6 (the gas used in the enrichment process) from China years earlier, the prior concealment of which obviously violated Iran's Safeguards Agreement. The disclosures raised more questions than they answered. This was powerful information, dramatically corroborating what we already believed, and only increased my level of concern. I thought Iran might be employing a "bait and switch" approach, disclosing part of its nuclear program, thereby hoping to divert attention from other activities. Armitage's reaction when I briefed him was right on point: "We caught them."

Abraham and I met with el Baradei in Vienna, on March 11, and stressed that he should be very circumspect in his remarks about what he did or didn't know about Iran's activities, a point el Baradei never listened to. He was a career international bureaucrat from Egypt, first elected to head the IAEA in 1997, who made excuses for Iran the entire time I was in the Bush administration. He was constantly hunting for "moderates" in Iran's leadership who did not want to pursue nuclear weapons, a nonexistent group, in our judgment, and more interested in trying to cut a deal than in faithfully reporting what IAEA inspectors were telling him. I told el Baradei that "the Iranians are trying to play with our heads," but the point didn't sink in. He didn't want to hear it.

One thing increasingly different in the diplomacy toward Iran and North Korea was the level of French and British interest. I had tried to insert France and Britain into the Six-Party Talks on North Korea, noting to Powell that as Security Council permanent members and legitimate nuclear weapons states they were more likely to be helpful than not, especially when we later sought Council sanctions against the North. Powell never bought the argument, and Britain and France had only minor roles until the DPRK issue actually reached the Council. Nonetheless, I tried to keep them informed, and they often brought up Iran. Britain thought we were being too hard on poor el Baradei, an attitude I tried unsuccessfully to change. In addition, U.K. foreign secretary Jack Straw had developed an interest in Iran, and approached Powell in late March 2003 to request we reconsider our refusal to license aircraft parts that Rolls-Royce needed to build engines for Airbuses Iran wanted to buy. When we investigated the matter, it appeared that Rolls-Royce was a lot less interested in making the sale than Straw, and the issue faded away.

I wanted to pursue Iran in the IAEA board of governors (BOG, as accurate an acronym as there ever was), using Iran's continued intransigence, which I fully expected, to move the entire matter to the Security Council, where we could try to impose sanctions. I wasn't confident about the Security Council, but at least we would check the IAEA/UN box, and could then go on to do whatever might actually be necessary to stop Iran from achieving a nuclear weapons capability. The IAEA board met quarterly, and I expected it would perhaps take us two, or at most three IAEA meetings, starting in June 2003, to get our referral resolution. Little did I know the process would last over three years. I first raised this approach at a Paris Perm Three meeting (U.S., U.K., and France) on April 8, well ahead of when we would need to start a lobbying campaign in the IAEA board, but their initial reaction was tepid. Russia was also not enthusiastic, and still not excessively concerned, although there was one positive sign. Rumyantsev came to Washington on April 10, bearing a letter from Putin to Bush, stating, in part, "We share the concern of the U.S. about Iran's intentions to create production of their own nuclear fuel for which, in our opinion, there will be no economic necessity in the foreseeable future." I took this to mean not simply that Russia wanted to be the source of Iran's nuclear fuel, but also, more important, that Russia didn't accept Iran's fatuous argument that it needed to develop "civil nuclear power" because it was running out of oil and gas. To me, the very inanity of Iran's point was evidence of mendacity, and its intention to develop nuclear weapons. Rumyantsev very candidly said that he, too, was now very troubled by Iran's activities, which he acknowledged were at least consistent with a nuclear weapons program.

By mid-April, the IAEA knew from "swipes" taken at the Natanz enrichment facility that Iran had introduced UF_6 into the centrifuges shown to el Baradei in February. Iran's failure to inform the IAEA about this step was another Safeguards Agreement violation, further evidence that Iran was more advanced than we had thought or they had admitted. This sort of revelation came up time and again in the next three-plus years, reinforcing my view that Iran was lying, and with good reason, since it clearly had something to hide. On May 5, I met again with Rumyantsev in Moscow. All the work we had been doing began to pay off, as he confirmed that Russia simply would not ship fresh fuel to Bushehr until the questions about Iran's nuclear programs were resolved. This was a substantial step, perhaps indicating that the entire Bushehr project was in jeopardy, because a reactor without fuel was simply an expensive pile of concrete. I asked Rumyantsev specifically if Russia was now considering cutting off all nuclear cooperation with Iran, and his reply was, "Yes, of course," as he reminded us that he was a nuclear physicist.

Just to be sure we hadn't missed the point, Mamedov asked me later that day if I appreciated the significance of Rumyantsev's comments. With evident displeasure, Mamedov said he "gave that to you entirely for free." "I know," I responded, "with you it would have taken six or seven meetings." "At least six," Mamedov replied, laughing, clearly not contesting Rumyantsev. "Putin himself has largely concluded that Iran has a nuclear weapons program," said Mamedov, although he described the conclusion as "not entirely 100 percent. There are still a few pieces missing in the jigsaw puzzle." I asked what these were, but Mamedov deferred to Minatom. I offered to send experts back to discuss the issue, and he agreed. Mamedov said expressly they were close to a "watershed" decision on Iran. When I returned to our embassy, I immediately called Armitage on a secure line to relay all of this, and suggested he tell Powell and Rice, because I did not intend to put in the reporting cable Rumyantsev's and Mamedov's most important comments, in order to prevent them from leaking prematurely. Armitage, who was leaving for South Asia later that day, concurred, and suggested I call Powell, which I did the next day. Armitage had filled him in, and Powell said he had already told Rice and would be telling the president when he saw him in half an hour.

I wanted to refer Iran to the Security Council at the June 2003 IAEA board meeting. If we couldn't do it then, we could at least lay the basis to do so in September. Reports from IAEA headquarters in Vienna were encouraging because Iran was having no success in convincing other delegations its program was peaceful. After one question-and-answer session in early May, the Mexican IAEA perm rep said to our delegation, "There must have been something wrong with the translation today, because nothing the Iranians said made any sense." At the experts' meeting in Moscow, Russia admitted that Iran's enormous interest in centrifuges, heavy-water production facilities and reactors, and even the advanced atomic vapor-laser isotope separation approach, combined with Iran's utter lack of transparency and the substantial number of IAEA questions to Iran that remained unanswered, were all troubling. At the expert level, however, the Russians did not go as far as Rumyantsev, clearly indicating it would take political leadership from the top, which Putin might well provide, to bring them to a decisive point. Unfortunately, China was less forthcoming. The United States was sanctioning one after another of China's military-industrial complex companies, such as NORINCO, for providing ballistic missile equipment and technology to Iran, in violation of our statutes. Bushehr, NORINCO, and other commercial arrangements made clear that neither Russia nor China yet fully understood, as we did, that profits from short-term business deals did not nearly make up for the risks inherent in proliferating sensitive technologies to Iran and other rogue states.

The June IAEA meeting produced nothing worthwhile on Iran, largely because neither our mission nor the Europeans were willing to do the heavy lifting necessary to take strong action. We weren't asking for much, simply a referral to the Security Council, where the real battle within the UN system would take place, but even this was impossible. The "spirit of Vienna" held that all IAEA board decisions should be by consensus, a rule reminiscent of the League of Nations, and one likely to leave the IAEA in the same historical ditch as the League. The Brits in Washington told me that, for a change, the instructions to their mission in Vienna were very strong, and that Jack Straw personally said they should try to get "all that the traffic would bear." That was fine at a declaratory level, but in the Vienna woods, the Western ambassadors essentially convinced themselves they couldn't get a Security Council referral, and therefore did next to nothing. This continuing UN weakness motivated me strongly to make PSI a success, because we certainly needed something more than what the IAEA membership was able to produce. In fact, neither our ambassador to the IAEA, Ken Brill, nor his British counterpart followed their instructions to get a board resolution, instead concentrating on a much weaker "chairman's summary" of the board's discussions. I was traveling in the Middle East when Armitage finally agreed that a chairman's summary was the best we could get, but I knew he was not happy with Brill's performance. I certainly wasn't. Nonetheless, I declared victory in the press, recognizing that most reporters couldn't tell the difference between a resolution and a chairman's summary, but I knew privately that we were in real trouble at the IAEA. We had come nowhere close to getting "all that the traffic would bear."

I continued to press for action before the IAEA board's next regular session in September, but our mission sent back at least two cables saying that vacation schedules made any action before then impossible. Are nuclear weapons really more important than vacations, they seemed to be asking? El Baradei was even less interested in having the matter referred to the Council, because he would drop out of the media spotlight, a typically shortsighted attitude. Reporters called the IAEA the "UN's nuclear watchdog," but it was no wonder U.S. skeptics called it instead "the UN's nuclear watchpuppy."

Unfortunately, in early August, a plan by the United Kingdom, Germany, and France—the EU-3 as we came to call them—emerged that would derail our efforts on Iran for the next three and a half years. It was inspired in part by Straw's effort to carve out his own niche separate from Blair's dominance of foreign policy, and also by Franco-German desires to show that the EU could handle Iran differently from the way those unilateralist Bush administration cowboys had handled Iraq. If they could stop Iran's nuclear program by diplomacy, they felt, in effect, they could justify their opposition to the Iraq War. Britain went along, in my view, to burnish its EUroid credentials, and to show it was not a complete "poodle" of the United States, as many critics described Blair's relationship with Bush.

In fact, I thought Bush had killed the EU-3 idea in an August 1 conversation with Blair. Bush had said he was worried about the message Blair was sending to Iran ("the big enchilada in the war on terror") "because of its geography and because of its absolute and clearly stated aim of the destruction of Israel." Bush stressed that their shared objective was "to free Iran," and then related a conversation he had had with Israeli prime minister Ariel Sharon. Sharon said, "We are a tiny country and Iran is a big country, and it doesn't take much to blow up a tiny country." Then came Bush's most basic and most important insight on Iran: "I thought, we are just beginning to watch the beginning of a Holocaust. There has to be no ambiguity, and no rewards unless there is a complete dismantlement." I remembered these words over the following years as I fought the internal government fights on Iran policy because they clearly indicated what the president thought. And, as Jim Baker liked to say, he was "the guy who got elected."

The EU-3 wrote to Iran proposing that it give up its nuclear program in exchange for unspecified but implicitly generous carrots from them. I didn't like the idea, but Powell would not stand in its way when Straw raised it with him. Fortunately, or so I thought, Iran's response was complete mush, which I hoped would be enough to persuade the EUroids that they were not going to accomplish anything substantial. Indeed, Iran's answer underlined why we needed to have the IAEA refer Iran to the Security Council in September, which we set about making the necessary diplomatic preparations to do. We had interesting information from the IAEA that its recent inspection of Iran's Kalaye electric facility showed that the Iranians had repainted and retiled several rooms just before inspectors arrived, although the IAEA was still confident their "swipes" would indicate whether radioactivity was present. This was precisely the kind of dissembling and concealment that demonstrated Iran was trying to hide something. We wanted to get this information out in public so others could also see the pattern of Iran's behavior, but the ever-unhelpful el Baradei heavily edited the draft report prepared by the IAEA staff, deleting many revealing details about Iran's continuing cover-up. Nonetheless, Australia, Britain, and Canada were with us, and we began lobbying to get others on board early. Timing was getting very tight, as Israel continued to express concern, through officials such as Gideon Frank, the head of its atomic energy agency, that Iran was nearing "the point of no return," when it would have complete domestic mastery over the nuclear fuel cycle, after which we could not stop their progress toward nuclear weapons without using force. The Israelis were not advocating force, but were pointing out that failure to take strong diplomatic action now might leave us with no other option, and sooner rather than later.

Unfortunately, on September 2, 2003, the EU-3 foreign ministers decided to write back to Iran, saying essentially, "Your letter didn't answer our letter," which I thought was a complete waste of time. Two days later, William Ehrman, my U.K. counterpart (and hard-line compared to Straw), and I had breakfast in Paris before a PSI Core Group meeting, and he gave me the bad news: Straw had rejected our effort to get a September IAEA board referral of Iran to the Security Council. I suspected Germany and France had turned Straw around because of the EU-3 initiative, and because of internal disarray in Blair's government after the recent suicide of a British expert over the issue of Iraq's prewar WMD capacities. With the Brits out of the IAEA effort, there was little prospect of success. Walter Schmid, head of the German PSI delegation, reaffirmed that the EU-3 ministers didn't want to proceed at the IAEA in September, although he said, "[Joschka] Fischer is more hard-line than you" on Iran, which I doubted. At a Perm Three meeting on September 5, after the rest of the PSI Core Group had departed, I expressed dismay to Ehrman and de Laboulaye, my U.K. and French counterparts, that they had climbed down from a Security Council referral, but they assured me we would lay the basis at the September BOG to obtain a referral in November. I gritted my teeth and agreed, based on their assurances they would not turn back again. This meeting demonstrates precisely how the EU-3 effort worked repeatedly over the following three years to postpone effective action on Iran. I find it painful to write about it even now.

When the BOG convened on September 8, el Baradei actually did reveal some of what the IAEA inspectors had found at Kalaye Electric, namely evidence of UF_6 enriched up to a 5 percent concentration of U_{235} (basically, reactor-grade level), demonstrating enrichment activity (subsequently, there would be even more about Kalaye, including evidence of highly enriched uranium). Nonetheless, the "tough" resolution we sought from the IAEA was under assault. Brill was doing little to defend it and was certainly not following his instructions. My only consolation was attending a dinner at the VP's residence on September 9, where, as we discussed life at State, Rumsfeld put his arm on my shoulder and said, laughing, "I don't know how you survive over there!" I kept Powell and Armitage informed, saying specifically to Armitage after the September 10 staff meeting that I thought Brill was badly mishandling matters in Vienna. By this time, the NSC staff and DoD were up in arms at what was happening, namely Brill's near total surrender of our "tough" position in negotiations with other board members.

Armitage was now sufficiently worried about the collapse in Vienna that he was making calls to foreign ministries, trying to lobby them to our side. He described Brill's efforts in Vienna, or lack thereof, as "bullshit," a pretty accurate assessment in my view. The final flap, a typical UN battle, was whether we continued to insist that the IAEA reach "definitive conclusions" about Iran at its November meeting, a code phrase for a referral to the Security Council, or whether we would accept Russian wording simply mentioning "conclusions," thus reducing it to mush. I thought we had already conceded too much, and I told Brill so. He appealed to Armitage and set up a conference call at about 6:45 A.M. Washington time on Friday, September 12. Brill argued that if we didn't agree to this Russian change there would be chaos, and that for the sake of "the spirit of Vienna" we should accept it and reach consensus. Armitage asked my view, and I said that we had already given up too much, that we hadn't gotten what we wanted elsewhere in the resolution, and that I didn't care about "the spirit of Vienna" if it stopped us from reining in Iran. We had the votes for "definitive conclusions" and we should reject Russia's change and ask for a show of hands on our text. Armitage said, "I'm pretty much where John is," but Brill kept arguing, simply irritating Armitage, who thought he had already given Brill his decision. Armitage finally said, "We need to stiffen the IAEA's spine here," to which Brill responded condescendingly, "It's not the IAEA itself; it's the member governments we're talking about." "I understand that, Ken," Armitage said icily, and told Brill to inform the other delegations about our position.

It transpired that when Brill told others of our position, the board immediately decided to break for two hours for lunch, this being a UN agency, after all. I called Armitage, who said, before I could even start, "The IAEA isn't worth a bucket of warm spit," and then, "the IAEA ought to stand for something," which sounded right to me. By 10:30 A.M., word came back from Vienna that Russia and the nonaligned countries had collapsed, the phrase "definitive conclusions" would stay in, and chaos would not engulf Vienna. This was the kind of "definitive" win we could achieve much more often in our negotiations if our diplomats stood firm. Joseph said an NSC staff meeting broke into applause when he told them about our victory, but I wondered if any of this sank into the minds of the permanent bureaucracy.

In any event, Brill had certainly sunk himself in Armitage's mind, more profoundly than anything I could have ever done. It was one reason Armitage ensured that Brill did not receive an onward ambassadorial assignment once his tour in Vienna ended. The rest of the administration also concluded that we simply could not repeat the experiences of the June and September IAEA board meetings, and that we needed much stronger, more effective representation in Vienna.

It Gets Worse, for Over Three Years: The EU Lost in Space

> The EU can therefore be regarded, in some senses at least, as a new European empire.
>
> —Professor Dominic Lieven,
> London School of Economics, July 5, 1999

I wanted to turn immediately to the November IAEA board, determined to do all of the necessary preparatory work, mostly in member governments' capitals rather than Vienna, to get a Security Council referral. However, the EU-3 gobsmacked those plans, as the Brits say, by sending Iran another letter that went much further than the others, basically offering nuclear reactor technology if Iran effectively renounced its nuclear program by ceasing uranium-enrichment activities. Central to EU-3 thinking was that such a cessation would prevent Iran from making progress on the nuclear front, thus allowing negotiations to proceed at whatever pace they might without increasing the risk of Iran's achieving nuclear weapons status. Ironically and disastrously, the renewed EU-3 effort produced exactly the opposite result. Over the next three and a half years, it gave Iran precisely what it needed most: time to overcome the difficulties of mastering the nuclear fuel cycle. It brought the EU-3 and the United States little in return except the greater risk posed by more advanced Iranian nuclear weapons and ballistic missile programs. The EU-3 gambit was a classic example of diplomacy based on nothing but air, creating the illusion of security, but actually undermining it. We can only hope that the United States, Israel, and the Europeans themselves escape its negative consequences before Iran achieves the weapons capabilities it has sought so persistently, opposed by little more than feckless diplomacy.

Britain's Ehrman told me about this recharged EU-3 effort when we met on September 29, 2003, to plan for the London PSI Core Group meeting scheduled for early October. I expressed my dismay, but Ehrman said he fully expected Iran to reject the offer, giving us an even better argument for an IAEA referral to the Security Council. I didn't think Ehrman actually believed this, although I bet Straw did, obviously a terrible portent for the future. De Laboulaye told me a few days later that he was of the same view as the Brits, even though he acknowledged Iran might misinterpret the offer of carrots as a sign of weakness. Even worse, Iran invited the EU-3 foreign ministers to Tehran, an offer they rejected, instead offering to send undersecretaries, but implying that ministers might follow. At breakfast with Ehrman at London's Royal Yacht Club in Knightsbridge on October 9, I told him in no uncertain terms what a bad idea I thought this was, and how adversely I thought it could affect our November efforts to have the IAEA board refer Iran to the Security Council. At the most basic level, it was poor bargaining. Even if I agreed with seeking a deal with Iran, which I definitely did not, what was gained by pushing to engage now? Why not wait until Iran was referred to the Council, where we could put some pressure on them, rather than agreeing to talk beforehand.

I waited until the sun rose in Washington, and then called Powell. Straw and he had spoken the week before (they talked all the time, usually without notetakers) and mentioned the possibility of the EU-3 ministers' visiting Tehran. Powell said he asked what possible use such a trip could have. Straw's lame response convinced him the idea wasn't going anywhere, but I said it clearly was going somewhere unless we stopped it, and that Straw was the driver within the EU-3. Powell wasn't so sure, but said he would call Straw immediately. Within an hour, Powell reached me to say that indeed Straw, French foreign minister Dominique de Villepin, and German foreign minister Joschka Fischer, whom Powell was calling "the three tenors," were packing their bags for Tehran. Powell said he gently suggested that Straw perhaps speak to me directly, since I was in London, which I was certainly ready to do. Instead, Ehrman called me at about 3:20 P.M. to relay Straw's side of the conversation, to say, "Tell John that I won't go to Tehran to be made a fool of," and that he did not want a U.S.-EU split over the issue. That was all well and good, I replied, but a visit by three undersecretaries was going to get into the press, and it would precisely be portrayed as a split with the United States, which it manifestly was! Ehrman swallowed

and said Straw thought keeping the French and Germans close was important, because otherwise they would wander off and make bad deals with the
Russians. All of this reaffirmed that Straw was the driver within the EU-3,
although Ehrman concluded by saying that Straw wanted to underline he
had made no decision himself on going to Tehran. He would wait and see
what happened to the undersecretaries (whom Powell and I soon started
calling "the three little tenors").

Joseph called later to say Rice thought the idea of any size tenors going
to Tehran was "insane," which she conveyed to the Brits. The EU-3 undersecretaries went anyway. I reached Ehrman in Brussels on October 19,
right after his return, and he said things "had not gone off the rails, but neither had they advanced very far along the rails." The Iranians swore up and
down they were fully cooperating with the IAEA (which we both knew
was flatly untrue) and planned to sign the Additional Protocol shortly. As
for suspending uranium enrichment, which had been a prerequisite raised
earlier by the EU-3, Hassan Rouhani, the head of Iran's National Security
Council, simply had no answer. Rouhani did not, however, reject out of
hand ceasing uranium enrichment if Iran could be guaranteed a fuel supply
for its reactors, asking how such a guarantee would work. In Vienna, the
three little tenors briefed el Baradei, who was about to go to Iran, with the
EU-3 foreign ministers likely evaluating that trip before making any decision on their own. (El Baradei reported afterward that Iran was "shocked"
by the September 12 IAEA board resolution and its widespread support,
and "Iran knows the noose is tightening around it." If only.) Putin also
weighed in publicly, saying he couldn't see why Iran would not make full
disclosure of its nuclear program if it were truly peaceful, which was assuredly the right tack.

Not surprisingly, the three big tenors couldn't resist the bait, and off
they flew on October 21. I tried to persuade Powell to call Straw to stop the
trip, but he declined. This was a critical failure, which permitted years to
pass and gave Iran breathing space to advance its nuclear and ballistic missile programs. Once launched on a diplomatic frolic, foreign ministers and
their bureaucrats are very difficult to restrain, as this lengthy, unproductive
detour was to prove. Straw was accompanied to Tehran by John Sawers, the
new U.K. political director, who, like Straw, decided that making a deal
with Iran was his Holy Grail. Sure enough, Sawers reported afterward, Iran
agreed to everything from signing the Additional Protocol to suspending

uranium enrichment to full cooperation with the IAEA. In the joint press conference in Tehran, however, Rouhani was more accurate regarding suspending enrichment: "We voluntarily chose to do it, which means it could last for one day or one year. It depends on us. As long as Iran thinks that this suspension is beneficial for us it will continue, and whenever we don't want it we will end it." What wonderful candor; too bad the Europeans couldn't match it!

So euphoric were the EU-3 that I concluded being a voice of reason was just a waste of time. Let the discussions play out for a while, until Iran acted like itself, I thought, bringing the whole thing into a ditch, and then we could step in to set things right. The problem with this approach was allowing the November IAEA board meeting to pass, thus losing yet another opportunity to get off square one. I still preferred to squeeze Iran harder, as Joseph said Rice wanted to do, but the EU-3 had outmaneuvered us, with Powell's at least tacit support. At a minimum, however, we had to avoid becoming complicit with the EU-3, such as by having an IAEA resolution endorsing their effort, which would be the worst of all worlds. Powell basically agreed with my laid-back approach, perhaps because he knew Bush's real views.

Bush spoke to Blair on November 6, saying Iran was trying to wiggle out of the nuclear issue, and Blair, astonishingly, professed not to know much about it. Later that day, Bush also pressed on Iran when he stopped by Rice's office, where Rumyantsev was visiting, to say there would be a "Nuclear Holocaust" against Israel if Iran ever got nuclear weapons, and that Israel might have to strike first in self-defense. Bush said that Iran was clearly lying about its nuclear intentions, and, moreover, that we didn't really trust the IAEA to ferret out what was going on. The IAEA, said Bush, was unwilling to challenge Iran and looked the other way in the face of obvious violations of Iran's Safeguards Agreement. This was a historic moment, said Bush, and we needed to seize it to reduce the Iranian threat. Later, when I saw Rumyantsev in my office, I underlined that he had now heard directly from Bush on Iran (and North Korea), several aspects of which I repeated, not for Rumyantsev, but for the State Department types in the meeting. I wish they could have heard it more often directly from the guy who got elected.

Needless to say, however, the EU-3 felt it was unnatural not to seek a resolution, a point Straw made to Powell in Washington on November 13.

Rice also met with Straw, and expressed her displeasure with the EU-3's weakness, arguing that referring Iran was an "obligation" under the IAEA statute. Powell later asked me about this, and I said that the "statutory obligation," like most things in UN circles, was an issue of political will, not legal correctness, and the EU-3 were distinctly lacking in political will. Nonetheless, said Powell, Rice was "flying around the rafters" and "dripping testosterone" over this "statutory obligation," which she had argued to Straw. Joseph also called, and said that Rice urged Bush "to go over Straw's head" to Blair to correct the exceedingly weak U.K. position, exemplified by the limp-wristed draft resolution Straw was peddling. I was delighted. The British Embassy later told Joseph they had been surprised by the strength of Rice's message because "Straw didn't hear that from Powell," and that, in the U.K., Iran policy was entirely Straw's, implying they didn't like it any better than we did. On November 17, Rice met with Fischer in Washington and argued strongly that the EU-3 draft was so weak it would encourage Iranian noncompliance. She pushed to refer Iran to the Security Council, but there was no chance given what the EU-3 had done, and their desire not to upset Iran. Powell, in turn, complained that Rice dropped in and out of negotiations, making her opinions known and then departing, which was not terribly helpful. Of course, this was also our pattern on other negotiations, and would be later as well, with people stepping all over one another rather than having one focal point.

At the IAEA, Australia, Canada, and Japan gave up on the EU-3 and introduced their own resolution, stating flatly that Iran was in "noncompliance" with its Safeguards Agreement, yet another effort at a "trigger mechanism" to force action on a Security Council referral at the next IAEA meeting. By this time, India, Malaysia, and Egypt were arguing that the EU-3 draft was too weak, the three of them being less worried about upsetting Iran than Britain, France, and Germany, whom State careerists were now calling the "T-3" (for "Tehran Three") rather than the EU-3. Still worse, after seeing another T-3 draft, which Iran said it could accept, even Ken Brill thought it was hopelessly weak! By dint of enormous effort, as I worked over de Laboulaye and Sawers (Michael Schaeffer, the German political director, being hopeless), and Canada, Australia, and Japan simply refusing to accept the EU-3's weakness, we avoided a complete debacle in Vienna. Nonetheless, this was tangible evidence that the EU-3 gambit had preempted other, more serious efforts to bring Iran to account. It was *not* simply a complementary approach, but one that precluded forward progress on tougher measures, thus providing Iran with that most precious of all resources, time—time in which they continued to advance their nuclear weapons and ballistic missile programs.

Within days of the IAEA board resolution, Iran accepted the EU-3 terms, or so the EU-3 thought. For example, Iran finally signed the Additional Protocol, which induced euphoria in Europe and parts of State, even though Iran never ratified it, and, in any event, didn't abide by it. Even so, the signing alone was taken as another sign that the Millenium was close at hand. A similar reaction greeted Rouhani's announcement that Iran had "voluntarily and temporarily suspended" its uranium-enrichment activities, even though no one really knew what he meant by that.

Finally, however, reality intruded, as the "agreement" the EU-3 thought they had broke down. In Washington, on January 22, 2004, de Laboulaye expressed concern that Iran was resisting EU-3 efforts to agree on a clear definition of "suspension of uranium-enrichment activities," which Iran now wanted instead of "cessation," the original EU-3 demand. Moreover, Iran was clearly still assembling centrifuge parts, a necessary step in the enrichment process, even though they were not then spinning UF_6 in centrifuges. Still, as long as Britain and France were invested in their deal, there was no chance the IAEA would refer Iran to the Security Council. (Germany, as usual, thought everything was fine.) By mid-February, despite overwhelming evidence of Iran's violations, which the EU-3 didn't dispute, they were still absorbed trying to save "the Paris agreement," trying to find "fixes" that could resuscitate the deal. This sent even Powell through the roof, saying to Blair's foreign policy adviser, Nigel Sheinwald, on February 20: "You've already got a deal that the Iranians are violating, and there shouldn't be a new one." Bush made similar points to Sheinwald in a separate White House meeting. Sheinwald did not react. Moreover, the EU-3 political directors did strike another deal with Iran in Brussels in late February, with just as many holes as the previous one. So inadequate was it that Bush called Blair to complain on February 24, saying things like, "I told Nigel we should not go down this path. We need to be tough. As soon as you're not tough on them, they beat you." Once again, Blair professed ignorance about what Straw was up to, leading us to wonder if Sheinwald had reported Bush's objections to Blair.

I checked with Armitage that same day and found him livid about the

EU-3. While we were talking, Powell called me to his office, where I described a very detailed letter being prepared to explain to the EU-3 what was wrong with both the original deal and the latest modification. Powell asked if he should sign the letter, and I said it would be so detailed that, at this stage, I should probably send it. If the response was inadequate, we could escalate. Powell agreed, asking to see the letter before it went out, which I thought would allow him to approve and be comfortable with it. I then met with French ambassador to Washington Jean-David Levitte on a number of subjects, and of course Iran came up. I described generally what the letter would say, especially about Iran's violations of the EU-3 agreement, and in a classic of European diplomacy, Levitte responded nonchalantly, "I tell you, having been Chirac's adviser on the Middle East for five years, the Shi'ites lie all the time. We know that." I was tempted to ask, "Then why are you dealing with them?" but I bit my tongue. Later on February 24, Powell called to say the letter looked fine, and that Bush was unhappy his conversation with Blair had been so inconclusive. Powell told Bush about the letter to the EU-3, and Bush thought it was a good idea. Earlier, I had told Hadley that Powell and I addressed the issue of who should sign the letter, which satisfied Hadley, who liked the text of the letter.

Once delivered, the letter made the EU-3 most unhappy. Fischer called Powell to complain, and according to the reporting cable, Powell said he no longer had any concerns about the EU-3/Iran deal, giving the impression he disagreed with the letter, which expressed those very concerns at length. This was amazing. Armitage, for example, had just told Michael Jay, the Foreign Office's highest-ranking careerist, that "Bolton and I don't see eye to eye on much, but on the Iran issue, there's no difference between us." Accordingly, I showed Armitage the reporting cable on the Fischer-Powell call. Although he first tried to wish the problem away, he finally conceded it was real and blamed it on Powell's being preoccupied for three days and nights with Haiti (during this time President Jean-Baptiste Aristide had been flown out of the country). Powell, however, said simply at his regular 8:30 A.M. staff meeting that we should try to get a tough resolution at the March IAEA board meeting, but that he didn't plan any further involvement. That was more than a little strange, so I cornered Armitage again after the staff meeting and found him without any explanation, other than Powell's continuing fatigue over Haiti. I filled in Joseph on all of this, and he was speechless, which was close to my reaction.

I departed for London to meet with Ehrman and Sawers on March 2, urging them that the EU-3 had to have a point at which they realized the deal with Iran had failed. What would it take to convince the EU-3 of Iran's duplicity? Weapons design information? Evidence of a previously undisclosed enrichment facility? "Yes" to both questions, Ehrman and Sawers both answered, although I had the uneasy feeling that Sawers was so obsessed with the intelligence failures of Iraq, and the particular harm that had befallen Tony Blair as a result, that he was on a different wavelength from the intelligence-savvy Ehrman. I read the transcript of Bush's February 20 drop-by to the Sheinwald-Rice meeting, mentioned above. To dispel any doubts about our view on the UN, I quoted Bush saying, "In the second term, and there will be a second term, we can try to figure out how the UN can be made more effective. It just isn't now." The Brits were silent.

The calendar then brought us to the March 8 IAEA board meeting, at which chaos reigned. Rouhani said publicly, "We told them [the EU-3] that if you don't fulfill your promise, everything will return to day one," which looked to be exactly where Iran was headed. Certainly there was no progress at the IAEA in March, and Bush complained again to Blair in midmonth. Blair could only say that he would try to work through the issues still dividing us. One idea I floated with Ehrman and Sawers in London on April 5 was that if we didn't get an IAEA referral at the June board meeting, we should just walk away from the IAEA and go directly to the Security Council. We didn't need IAEA action, and after a year of beating our heads against the wall, maybe a little pain relief was in order. I also stressed that the United States had a presidential election coming up in seven months. The Brits, like Iran, could sit around hoping that John Kerry (the near-certain Democratic nominee) would be elected over Bush, or they could face up now to the prospect that the Bush cowboys would be around for another four years. These points certainly got their attention, but their description of the policy review Blair had ordered after his unhappy conversations with Bush showed that they hadn't moved one iota away from their laserlike focus on trying to make the EU-3 process work, carrots *über alles*.

Emboldened by our disarray and ineptitude, Iran mounted a major effort for the June IAEA board meeting to "close the file" on their program, which would have truly signaled the collapse of the EU-3 effort, not to mention our own. Fortunately, however, the Iranians returned to form, threatening to resume enrichment, and after several days, the IAEA adopted another meaningless resolution, allowing us to say with a relatively straight face that Iran would remain under IAEA scrutiny, and that we intended to push forward with a referral to the Security Council at the September BOG.

Imagine my delight, therefore, when Iran came through for us, just before a June 24, 2004, House hearing, with letters to the EU-3 withdrawing from the February "agreement," saying it intended to resume the manufacture, assembly, and testing of centrifuge equipment. I sought permission from the Brits to release the letter and also asked if they had any objection to my characterizing the letter as the Iranians' "thumbing their nose at the international community." Edward Oakden, one of Ehrman's deputies, and someone I always considered a solid citizen, concurred, saying, "It would be no more than the truth." I opened the hearing with this late-breaking news, thus guaranteeing maximum coverage, due to Iran's ever-exquisite timing. The Iranian Parliament was also indicating there was no chance it would ever ratify the Additional Protocol, significantly undercutting the notion that Iran had at any time been serious about these negotiations. The EU-3 sent a letter in response that contained one crucial sentence: "We will only be able to make progress in the context of a full suspension." I recalled for the Brits on July 1 in London what Chirac had said a few weeks before at the G-8 Sea Island Summit even before any Budweisers (his favorite drink, which must have embarrassed other Frenchmen), namely that you could never trust the Shi'ites, that he didn't believe they would really adhere to the EU-3 deal, and that there was little we could do to keep nuclear weapons out of their hands. This remarkable burst of candor, Ehrman observed, tracked with what Blair said, namely that he didn't see that either of the current Iran or DPRK regimes could be persuaded to give up the pursuit of nuclear weapons. This was definitely a point worth remembering, because if diplomacy with the *current* regimes wouldn't work, we needed to try something else, including military force if need be. To have so concluded publicly, however, would have meant undercutting the central rationale for the entire EU-3 effort, namely that they could prevent WMD proliferation better than the United States, and without force.

My main point was to refer Iran to the Security Council at the September IAEA board meeting. I said that unilateral U.S. pressure alone had not stopped Iran, but obviously neither had the EU-3 effort. It was time to overcome what I charitably called "the tactical gap" between us and reunite our efforts. I was trying to find a way for the EU-3 to support taking Iran to the Security Council without making it look as if they were conceding defeat and admitting that those damned Americans had been right all along. Rather than rubbing their noses in it, I argued instead that the only way their diplomatic effort would have a chance of succeeding was to ratchet up the pressure on Iran, such as by getting to the Council. Of course, we still had Russia and China to persuade, but only by uniting our efforts was there a chance they would also concur, rather than sitting back watching our separate efforts fail. Ehrman and Oakden said they found my arguments "compelling," but it was clear they couldn't agree to anything until they talked to Straw.

On July 13, in Paris for a G-8 meeting, I made essentially the same pitch to de Laboulaye, and he seemed very receptive. De Laboulaye said that France was looking at the specifics of possible economic sanctions the Security Council might adopt, an important and revealing comment, which, along with other comments, indicated that France fully understood the EU-3 deal was in serious jeopardy. I also worked on other G-8 countries, including Canada, whose Jim Wright agreed that Iran had simply been "ragging the puck," and that it was time to torque up the pressure.

After taking the Eurostar train through the "Chunnel" back to London, I met with Ehrman and Sawers at the Foreign Office on July 15. We agreed the United States would draft a brief scenario of what the Council could do once the Iran issue was lodged in New York. As diplomatic matters go, this was real progress, because it meant the Europeans were starting to think ahead. They were also optimistic that the Germans were close to their positions about going to the Council, providing some evidence that "the tactical gap" might in fact be closing. On July 23, in Tokyo, I briefed Yukiya Amano, which was important because Japan would likely be a nonpermanent member of the Security Council in 2005–6. Japan was also moving closer to an important step, namely a dramatic drop in its capital commitment to develop Iran's Azadegan oil field, which they later took, thus reducing exposure to Iran's using its oil and natural gas resources for blackmail or coercion. Countries like Japan, China, and India, with large and growing demand for energy, sought assured sources of supply from oil- and natural-gas-producing countries like Iran, Sudan, and other undesirables. No country was better than Iran at using its underground assets as weapons, so any indication that Japan was preparing to distance itself from an extensive, long-term capital commitment was good news.

The EU-3 hadn't really given up yet, but on July 22, at a meeting in London, Iran flatly refused to budge from resuming the manufacture of centrifuges, insisting it had a right to uranium enrichment. When the Brits repeated the key point of the recent EU-3 letter, namely that there would be no progress on other issues without full suspension leading to cessation, the Iranians turned to threatening bad things if the Brits didn't offer them more carrots. Specifically, the Iranians said that a "tough" IAEA resolution in September would provoke Iran to resume production of fissile material within one year, with the ability to produce a weapon within three years. On July 27, just days before another meeting with the EU-3, the press reported that Iran was breaking the IAEA seals related to its centrifuge program. What else did the Europeans need to hear and see?

The EU-3 met again with Iran on Friday, July 30, unfortunately, Ehrman's swan song, as he left to become chairman of the Joint Intelligence Committee, one of those shadowy institutions of Whitehall mandarins, succeeding John Scarlett, who was to be the new head of the Secret Intelligence Service. Unlike Sawers the European, Ehrman was an Atlanticist, a diminishing breed at the Foreign and Commonwealth Office, and he would be missed. Joseph called Ehrman on Friday to wish him well in his new job, and Ehrman said Iran was "poorly behaved" at their meeting: It would not ratify the Additional Protocol, which would certainly be a shock to the treaty-bound German mentality, and its real bottom line was that it had no intention of giving up enrichment activities. This left the EU-3 with exactly what their approach had long deserved: nothing. France gave us essentially the same report, conceding that the EU-3 effort had now "run into the sand." Our paper on Security Council options, discussing sanctions and stronger steps, was now about ready, but I was surprised when the American Israel Public Affairs Committee's (AIPAC) Howard Kohr told me of a recent conversation in which Rice had expressed uncertainty about what the Council would actually do once we got there. Of course, I had no illusions on that score either. I just wanted to finish checking the boxes (first the IAEA and then the Council), either to get the real and substantive support we needed, or to show the "multilateralists" that we had tried their route and were now going outside the UN system to do what we needed to do.

Iran was now saying that it would suspend uranium-enrichment activities only if the EU-3 would agree to "close the file" on Iran at the September IAEA meeting, which everyone else knew was a nonstarter. Fortunately, by this point, Brill had been moved out of Vienna, and I was able to install as head of our delegation to the September board meeting Jackie Sanders, then our ambassador to the Conference on Disarmament (CD) in Geneva. Since Jackie had worked for me as far back as Bush 41, I was confident she could read the tactical situation in Vienna correctly, and that her assessments would not rest on a propensity to surrender at the first sign of trouble. France's CD ambassador joked to her that their mission in Vienna, on hearing of her appointment, had asked in a panic who this "terrible iron woman" was? I was glad they were getting the message.

It was not clear, however, that Straw was getting it. Powell said he told Straw "three separate times" that the EU-3 deal had run its course at a barbecue Straw hosted in Britain on Sunday, August 15, 2004. "Jack didn't really respond," Powell mused, which further convinced me that Straw was our problem in London. He was not ready to go to the Security Council in September, Powell said, but hoped we might tee up a referral in November. At this rate, we would never reach the Council. To British and French dismay, the Germans at this point were practically on their knees begging Iran to resume suspension for fear that U.S. hard-liners would take stronger action, which was exactly what I did want to do. This was the central EU-3 problem. Their position was constantly watered down to the lowest common denominator, typically Germany's. In fact, Straw's idea for the September BOG turned out to be asking el Baradei for a comprehensive report on Iran, hardly a helpful suggestion when we were then actively trying to stop el Baradei from getting a third term as IAEA director general! I saw no alternative at this point except to try yet another Bush call to Blair to see if he had any better idea on what his government was doing on Iran than before. I later suspected that Straw did not keep Blair adequately informed, perhaps a key reason why Straw was sacked in May 2006.

Powell Weakens, as His George C. Marshall Legacy Project Grows

By the end of August, Iran announced plans to test its 164-centrifuge cascade at Natanz, proving it was moving further and further from its EU-3 "deal." The EU-3 dithered. Again. We didn't know whether Iran would spin the centrifuges in a vacuum, with an inert gas, or with UF_6, but the news was still significant. On August 30, Powell told me he had agreed with Straw to seek only a "trigger" resolution at the September IAEA board meeting, and a referral in November (i.e., after our election), bowing to Straw's weakness and playing for time to resurrect the EU-3 deal. I argued to Powell that such tactics would guarantee yet another bucket-of-mush resolution, of which we already had an ample supply. As at the past *five* IAEA board meetings, I felt we had to at least try for a referral, and not simply yet again push the issue into the uncertain future. Powell agreed to talk to Straw, to underline the latest IAEA report, buried within which was the finding that Iran planned to convert thirty-seven tons of yellowcake (U_3O_8, a solid) into the gas UF_6 as an "experiment," a curious characterization of such extensive conversion, which obviously allowed enriching the UF_6 in the new cascade. Converting to UF_6 and then subsequently enriching thirty-seven tons of U_3O_8 would produce approximately one hundred kilograms of highly enriched uranium, enough for four or five nuclear weapons. Some "experiment"! (We now know, of course, from Hassan Rouhani's subsequent speech, that Iran used the passage of time during the negotiations to perfect the conversion process. This revelation was most embarrassing to the EU-3 when it emerged during subsequent Security Council negotiations, but it had been foreshadowed by Israel's telling us all along that Iran was jiving us, or more precisely, jiving the EUroids.)

Unfortunately, this new reality did not dissuade the EU-3 foreign ministers, but the draft resolution produced by their Vienna missions was not even a weak "trigger" resolution; instead, it called for another el Baradei report, Straw's original proposal to Powell, rejected even by Powell! I wondered if anyone in the EU-3 cared about the damage being done to institutions like the IAEA by their continuing inability to affect events in the real world, wondering as well how EU diplomats could be so content to chew over problems rather than solving them. Clearly, the EU-3 believed that even whispering about Security Council action would derail their efforts to resuscitate their deal with Iran, so there was no doubt where the dispute between us would be at the IAEA board meeting. The candid Rouhani was saying in public that he knew exactly how to jerk the EU-3's chain: "Whenever Iran gets practically close to enrichment issues, the sensitivity of the Europeans rises, and whenever we practically distance ourselves from enrichment, their tone changes and you see a smile on their faces." I was mystified that the Europeans weren't mortified at this sort of thing, but susceptibility to shame was apparently not one of their virtues.

I continued to press, unsuccessfully, for more at the September IAEA board meeting. One of Rouhani's deputies, Hossein Musavian, said publicly that "the reason the Europeans are asking us to continue [the suspension of enrichment] is that they want cessation, and this will never happen."[2] By September 14, even Powell was discouraged, saying he thought the Europeans would "collapse like a cheap suit" in Vienna as the week wore on. As if to prove the point, the Aussies and Canadians threw up their hands at the EU-3 and decided to draft a real "trigger" resolution on their own, a very helpful development. The EU obviously didn't like the tougher U.S. negotiating style, leaking their discontent and causing a malicious little wire story that we had "flown in a team close to U.S. Undersecretary of State John Bolton for the board meeting—effectively sidelining the Vienna-based U.S. mission that usually handles such conferences." An unnamed "senior Western diplomat" "suggested the Washington team 'doesn't perhaps have a good sense of what the Vienna audience can accept.' " They were, of course, referring to Sanders and others who had replaced the emollient Brill. I was pleased, however, because it showed that Sanders and her team were following their instructions, and doing the job they had been sent to do, which was a big change in the Vienna Woods. I frequently recalled this story in later days at the UN when "unnamed diplomats" had their say about my diplomatic style, and what "the New York audience" could accept.

Straw called Powell on September 15 to say how much the United Kingdom missed Brill, and how difficult our new people were. Powell told me he listened for a while, and finally said, "Jack, if you want to bring the Iranians around, you have to hold an axe over their heads." Straw worried what would happen if we actually got to the Security Council, and Powell said in that case it would be better to ask why we wanted to go to the Council on anything. The conversation ended with Straw blaming most of our problems on Germany, his most accurate observation. In fact, in Vienna, our negotiations with the EU-3 were proceeding well for a change, except

---

2. Gareth Smyth, "Iran Seeks Wider Deal on Security in Nuclear Dispute," *Financial Times,* Monday, September 13, 2004, p. 8, col. 7.

with the Germans, who alternated between intransigence and belligerence in defense of Iran. Even the French were now complaining privately to us that Germany's position was hopelessly weak. Because of the EU-3's desire to stick together, however, we followed their lowest common denominator, meaning the Germans were effectively running American foreign policy.

Powell called Fischer, who ducked responsibility by saying he was out on the campaign trail, tired and not up to speed on developments in Vienna. Finally, however, Berlin erupted in anger against its Vienna perm rep (who was married to an Iranian!), and he more or less ultimately fell into line with what we wanted. The Brits told Sanders that the message Germany understood from Powell's call was, "Who is that asshole you have in Vienna, and why is he always saying he has no instructions?" Even so, considerable damage had already been done, and we were not able to recoup. Helpfully, Rouhani angrily rejected the weak resolution adopted on Saturday, September 18, almost immediately, referring to it as an "ultimatum" that Iran could never accept. Early the next week, Iran announced that it had commenced converting the thirty-seven tons of yellowcake (U_3O_8), thus in fact proving convincingly that the "suspension" was well and truly dead.

That evening, Jonathan Karl of ABC News broke a story about Iran's weapons-testing facility at Parchin, and the possibility they were testing detonation devices for high explosives that surrounded a uranium or plutonium "pit" in the "physics package" of a nuclear weapon. When the explosives detonated, the "pit" imploded, forming a critical mass setting off an uncontrolled nuclear chain reaction. Whatever anyone might say about Iran's conversion or enrichment activities, work on detonation devices and high explosives was manifestly weapons-related, something neither el Baradei, nor Germany, nor Iran could explain away. Everyone knew it. In Vienna, the press was all over a lead that el Baradei had edited a reference to Parchin out of the IAEA staff's report, which was par for the course for him. The IAEA refused to confirm or deny that inspectors had requested Iran's permission to visit Parchin, and that the request had been denied.

With yet another IAEA meeting behind us, attention turned to New York and the annual General Assembly opening festivities, where I joined Powell. On September 22, I met with Sawers and Wright and continued to press for the EU-3 to finally recognize that their deal had failed. Right before a G-8 foreign ministers' dinner that evening, I briefed Powell that

Sawers still wasn't ready to accept this reality, figuring it might come up. Since we were near the end of the U.S. G-8 presidency, I didn't expect much from the dinner, so I was amazed the next day to run into Glyn Davies, an official in the European Bureau (EUR), who had attended with Powell. Davies said he had looked for me the night before to say that Powell and the other foreign ministers (including Sergei Lavrov from Russia) agreed to present Iran with a "package of carrots and sticks." This was astounding, since a Principals Committee meeting a few weeks before had reaffirmed our present course. It was equally astounding when Davies said Fischer had recommended the issue be given to G-8 political directors, diverging from the pattern followed for close to two years, in which G-8 nonproliferation officials had worked the issue.

I found Powell in his suite, where he was leaving for another event. He said only that everyone else at the dinner wanted to offer "carrots and sticks," and that he had gone along only after pointing out we had offered Iran humanitarian assistance after the Qum earthquake, and had been rejected. I said, "We're going to participate in giving carrots to the Iranians?" but Powell was ducking out. I immediately called Washington to fill in Joseph, and he was stunned, saying he did not believe Rice had a clue about what Powell had done. Joseph said later that day he had spoken with Rice, who was completely in the dark. I also saw a draft reporting cable of the G-8 dinner, written by an EUR notetaker who almost surely had no understanding of the significance of what he was reporting, as close to verbatim as possible, which read that it was Powell who said the offer to Iran should consist "mostly of carrots." The next day, IO assistant secretary Kim Holmes, a conservative political appointee, told me that German political director Schaeffer had cornered him and regaled him with the wonders of the G-8 dinner, appalling Holmes, given the substance. By this time, the reporting cable on the dinner was all over our government, and bells were ringing at the NSC, DoD, and the Office of the Vice President, all of which were amazed by Powell's latest frolic, which I saw as reminiscent of "leaning too far forward over his skis" early on concerning the DPRK.

We were, of course, in the middle of a closely contested political campaign. The idea that we would start talking about carrots for Iran, which Israel correctly called the world's leading terrorist state since the fall of Saddam Hussein, and which had just slapped the EU-3 in the face by repudiating their deal, was beyond me. I stopped Davies from doing anything to follow up on the dinner until Joseph geared up the interagency process, and until I could talk at greater length to Powell. I worried that Powell's negative comments on the Sunday talk shows about the situation in Iraq and his mind-boggling offer to hold a round of Six-Party Talks on North Korea in October, thus handing an enormous lever to North Korea within weeks of our election, meant he was consciously distancing himself from the administration. Given the polls, it was a coin toss how the election would come out. I had already worried for some time that Powell had a different agenda, namely his own "legacy." There were a number of additional indications, such as the whispering campaign that he was, contrary to our policy, giving tacit support for el Baradei's re-election, which was certainly what el Baradei was telling everyone, and which uncomfortably called to mind Biden's comments to a friend of mine that senators would be doing Powell a favor by not confirming me in 2001. Powell had also resurrected and was aggressively pushing the idea that we should negotiate a multilateral Fissile Material Cut-Off Treaty (FMCT), a dog of an idea we had put on the sidelines at the start of the administration, where, we hoped, it would mildew away.

Powell's pattern of behavior was widely discussed at State, some calling it the "George C. Marshall legacy project," because Powell's acolytes were backgrounding the press that Marshall was Powell's idol, and that Powell had emulated Marshall's career. Indeed, the anonymous backgrounders suggested that Powell's tenure as secretary of state was much like Marshall's, the old soldier called back to duty (both of them being former chairmen of the Joint Chiefs of Staff), implying that Powell was loyal to Bush as Marshall had been loyal to Truman, despite grave doubts about the wisdom of many administration policies. The example of Marshall's loyalty these minions often cited was his acceptance of Truman's recognition of Israel, even though Marshall thought it was a bad idea. This was a curious choice, showing a political tin ear, despite the Powell machine's reputation for bureaucratic sagacity. Although my relations with Powell had often been complex, they did not turn seriously bad until the George C. Marshall legacy project really got rolling, in large part because success in that project turned precisely on distancing Powell from Bush. This had to do mostly with Iraq, but the legacy project was far broader in its implications, with far greater dangers, especially in the perilous weeks before the November election. Only at this relatively late date, and because of the implications of the legacy project, did my tensions with Powell rise perceptibly, and remain high, for me at least.

Back in Washington following the G-8 dinner, I had several conversations with Powell, but he did not bring up Iran. I didn't either, since I knew nothing was going on. If Powell wanted something to move, he would have to tell either Davies or me, and he wasn't saying anything. Rice and Powell finally spoke on October 5. Rice told Joseph that Powell claimed the reporting cable on the G-8 dinner was "distorted" and agreed with Rice there was no change in our Iran policy. I checked again with Davies, and there was simply no way to reconcile what Powell said at the G-8 dinner with his conversation with Rice. I decided to follow the famous "Cuban Missile Crisis" model, when the USSR sent the United States two inconsistent messages, and Kennedy responded to the more encouraging one. If Powell had told Rice there was no change in our Iran policy, I was satisfied, and on that happy note, off I went to my other responsibilities.

Further proof of what had actually happened at the G-8 dinner came in the form of a letter from Canada's Jim Wright, which I saw on October 6. It read, "As suggested by Secretary Powell, we have focussed [sic] on 'carrots' rather than 'sticks.' " I had still not spoken to Powell about it by this point, and did not until his next regular staff meeting on October 8, when he asked me about the state of play on Iran. I mentioned the October 15 meeting, and Powell responded, "Let me review what we have committed to here. I said at the G-8 dinner that we felt we needed to go to the Security Council, but that we would listen to others if anyone else had any other ideas. We are obligated to listen, but that's all. If the Iranians don't comply with their obligations, we go to the Security Council." I was amazed because this rendition of the G-8 dinner was the same as what Powell had told Rice. I had the wit, if I do say so myself, to agree this was exactly where we were headed. I then brought staff from the Bureau of Nonproliferation Affairs to my office and repeated what Powell had said. I felt my backside was now sufficiently covered to begin blasting away at the EU-3 for deviating from the previously agreed-upon road to the Security Council.

On October 12, the EU-3 paper that had been expected since the September 22 G-8 dinner finally arrived in advance of a G-8 meeting we had scheduled for October 15 in Washington. It was as bad as one might have anticipated, with fewer sticks and even more carrots than I had thought possible. "European diplomats" were already deliriously leaking to the press in Vienna that the United States had changed its position to that of carrot deliverer, but Iran responded by reaffirming that it would never give up the right to enrichment. At a large October 12 meeting in Powell's office that dealt mostly with the EU's troubling efforts to lift its embargo on arms sales to China, a weaker counterpart to the U.S. embargo, Powell asked me about the upcoming G-8 meeting on Iran. I said we were preparing a script for interagency clearance, which would have us listen to the EU, but lay out our objections to their proposals, now that we finally had them, and maintain our position to go to the Security Council. Powell expressed general agreement with this approach, saying, "Okay, let me know how the meeting goes on Friday." The script later approved in the interagency process followed what I had said to Powell, although it did not get into specifics on the EU-3 proposal, meaning it was fairly short. Cheney actually thought the script was too weak, according to his staff, but he was too occupied with the presidential campaign to worry more about it. Nonetheless, at Rice's request, Hadley talked with Cheney, who explained we should simply tell the EU we didn't like their carrot approach at all, and gave Hadley some specific changes. Joseph called me with those changes late Thursday afternoon and said I should show them to Powell as "NSC changes," since Hadley also agreed with them.

I still hadn't heard from Powell about the script, which I had sent to him despite his comment that he wanted to hear about the Friday G-8 meeting only after it happened. I wanted him to approve or modify the text before the meeting, so there would be no ambiguity he had approved what I was to say. At about 6:50 A.M. on October 15, Powell called to ask me down to his office, where he started to look at the script and make small changes in it. I had been typing up the NSC changes, and handed them to Powell to look at while reviewing the basic draft. He accepted all of them. I could not have wished for a happier outcome. Not only did I have Powell's clearance, I had fifteen or twenty words in the text that he had drafted himself. Back in my office, I called Hadley at about 7:25 A.M. and said that Powell had accepted the NSC changes, and had a few himself, which Hadley accepted as I read them over the phone. Hadley and I also talked about exactly what we would do once we were in the Security Council, which showed his focus. We also worked on press guidance, preparing responses to questions we anticipated from the media, which Powell reviewed at about 9:15 A.M., making a few mostly stylistic changes. I called Hadley back to read him the last changes on the press guidance, and he confirmed to me that DoD had signed off on the script I would actually use in the G-8 meeting, which meant our clearance process was now finally complete.

And not a moment too soon, as I walked down to the Ops Center's seventh-floor conference room where nearly everyone was gathered for the meeting, scheduled to start at ten o'clock. I let Sawers start by reporting at great length on the EU-3's latest cavalcade of carrot trucks for Tehran, and I then turned to Wright, since Canada was the only other country that had sent in a written suggestion. Wright was helpfully quite critical of the EU-3 paper and said Iran should have been referred to the Security Council long ago. I let everyone else around the table speak and only then turned to our long-labored-over script, which I read word for word, slowly, for my usual manner of speaking. (Although he wasn't there, British ambassador David Manning later complained to Armitage that I "raced through" the text, as if that were sinful.) Sawers then had a long response to everyone's earlier remarks. Wright broke in to ask Sawers exactly what the EU-3 meant to achieve in terms of the "cessation" of Iran's enrichment and reprocessing activities. Sawers tried to answer, but then Schaeffer interrupted him, and in turn de Laboulaye interrupted him, each having somewhat different answers to this very basic question. Wright asked another related question and provoked almost exactly the same three-way split reaction. I could not have made up this scene of disarray among the EU-3, in plain and very painful view of the rest of the G-8, which alone was worth the agony of going through this meeting. The EU-3 themselves knew they were not ready for prime time, as Schaeffer tried to joke lamely about "the virtues of trilateralism."

I didn't participate much in the discussion that followed, because I didn't have anything cleared except the script, and I wanted to be careful not to be more of a target for the postmeeting leaks than was inevitable, other than to rebut, from time to time, comments by the EU-3 about how different Powell's position had seemed at the New York G-8 dinner. I noted that I had spent an hour with Powell that very morning going over what I had read, and that Powell had actually dictated passages to me. Apparently what I actually said was, "I dictated to him," instead of "he dictated to me," which Davies corrected. "Thank God Glyn is here," I joked, to general merriment, but Schaeffer said dourly, "A Freudian slip, John." I said at another point that Powell saw no disjunction between what he had said in

New York and what I was saying, which I didn't believe but which I knew Powell hoped to be true. I sensed that the EU-3 were most upset not by what I said, but by what I didn't say: I wasn't engaging on specific points in their paper, because, of course, I had nothing cleared to say. What I *had* read was cleared, and if the meeting was going to tank, it was going to tank on that basis, and not on the basis of something I said that hadn't already been approved by half the U.S. government.

After a while someone asked what we would say to the press, so I read the cleared press guidance that we had prepared for U.S. use, which Sawers and Kislyak wanted to change! I said politely the guidance was for our use, was cleared internally, and that they were of course free to say whatever they wanted in their national capacities. Someone suggested that we have a joint G-8 press statement, and I declined, explaining that Powell had already rejected that idea; each country should speak on its own. We broke around 1:00 P.M., which had been agreed upon earlier. I immediately went to Powell's office to brief him, Armitage, and Boucher on what happened, giving them pretty much a blow-by-blow account. Powell seemed satisfied, and we made modest changes in the press guidance to conform to what actually happened. After a previously scheduled meeting with Kislyak back in the Ops Center conference room, I called Hadley at 3:45 P.M. and reported to him. He said he was now prepared to move to the Security Council, which was certainly where I was. So angry was Sawers with the outcome of the G-8 meeting that he canceled an afternoon meeting with DoD's Doug Feith, which I am sure made Feith's day. Press reports also began to come in, on the basis of which Powell decided he would not say anything himself. He called at 6:30 P.M. to say that he was quite satisfied with the press coverage so far, and that none of the three big tenors had yet called him, although he expected they would over the weekend.

On Monday, October 18, Powell told me that Straw had called, unhappy with Friday's meeting. The EU-3 could hardly base their frustration on a "breach of promise" argument, since that would expose Powell. Instead, the bad news would be blamed on me and the meeting's "tone," a factor impossible to measure, but often more damaging than admitting to a substantive policy disagreement. By contrast, Joseph said Rice and Hadley were very pleased with the meeting, and its complete lack of impact on the campaign. As Powell suggested, I called the three little tenors, who were quite relaxed, focused on their own meeting with Iran in a few days. Sawers even said they were satisfied with press coverage of the meeting. Indeed, if the EU was distraught about anything, it was precisely that I had simply restated existing U.S. policy.

Nonetheless, I found the three weeks after the G-8 dinner the hardest of my entire tenure as undersecretary of state for arms control and international security affairs, and indeed of my entire tenure in the Bush 43 administration. Powell had violated our long-standing Iran policy, colluded with the EU-3 against it, and come out nearly endorsing Kerry's Iran position only weeks before our election. All of this, I thought, was part of the George C. Marshall legacy project, which I decided could not be permitted to distort administration policy so dramatically. Along with others, I had foiled Powell's legacy gambit. I knew it, and he knew I knew it.

CHAPTER SIX

WHY DO I WANT THIS JOB?

I thought the people who voted against him were nuts.

—Former New York Mayor Ed Koch, September 27, 2005

On December 14, just over a month after the 2004 election, I had a pleasant thirty-minute meeting with Condi Rice and Steve Hadley in Rice's West Wing office. Bush had already named Rice to replace Powell at State, and Hadley to replace Rice as national security adviser, so this was one of many conversations she was having to staff her new position, a dance almost as complex at the beginning of a second presidential term as in the presidential transition. Rice asked what role might interest me, and I said I would like to be considered for deputy secretary of state. We discussed the deputy's function, and especially how "D" related to the undersecretary's responsibilities. In a tip-off that D was unlikely, Rice asked if I was interested in anything else, and I said I thought deputy national security adviser was a place I could "make a contribution," as they say. In yet another tip-off, after a few minutes, Hadley said, "I think I know the answer to this, but are you interested in becoming an ambo?" and I said I was not. Rice asked, "What about staying at T?" and I responded that the law of diminishing marginal returns had a real logic to it. Rice smiled and responded warmly, "I understand that!"

Powell's departure from the administration was inevitable, given his increasingly open disagreements with Bush on many issues, especially Iraq. I played no significant decision-making role on Iraq policy, because Powell and Armitage largely excluded me from these issues, no doubt fearing my views would be similar to Cheney's and Rumsfeld's rather than their own. It was the greatest favor Powell ever did for me, utterly unintentionally, to be sure, and my Iraq-related activities were only at the margins of the central decisions. Ironically, therefore, my personal difficulties with Powell did not arise over Iraq or arms control matters, but over nonproliferation issues, especially how to handle Iran and North Korea from 2002 to 2004. There was little doubt, however, about the extent of the White House–Powell divide. White House Chief of Staff Andy Card told one administration staffer in January 2004, "You know, John Bolton is the *only* person in that building that the president trusts completely."

Bob Zoellick's selection as D leaked in the *Wall Street Journal* on January 6. Rice called later that day to say she had tried to reach me before I read it in the papers, which was a considerate gesture. She continued, "I've liked working with you, in the G-8 and so on, and I'll try to be supportive [for another slot] because I don't want the administration to lose you," which was encouraging. Zoellick's selection was unexpected because he would be stepping down from a cabinet-level job as U.S. trade representative, and it was followed quickly in early February by the decision that J. D. Crouch, who had been with Rumsfeld at Defense, would be Hadley's principal deputy. That looked like the door closing on options in the administration, so I reconsidered life in the private sector more closely. Nonetheless, I had taken Rice to be serious in saying she wanted to keep me in the administration, so I continued to wait, and found that she was indeed serious.

Although Rice and I met many times after her January arrival at State to discuss policy, on February 25, we met to discuss my situation. Rice herself raised the question of the UN job, saying she knew me well and thought I was an excellent negotiator, but she wanted to ask what impression might be created were I to be nominated for "USUN," the acronym for the U.S. Mission to the United Nations. I described the repeal of the "Zionism is racism" resolution in 1991, and the long string of Security Council resolutions adopted after Iraq's 1990 invasion of Kuwait, and concluded by saying I had written a lot that was very critical of the UN. Rice responded, "So have I," and then stressed that she wanted the UN ambassador to "be a part of my team," not just a lonely outpost in New York. I told her I thought that was the only productive way to proceed and told her my favorite joke about

USUN: "Looks good to me, let me see if I can sell it in Washington." She laughed appreciatively.

Rice's third point was that she wanted a coordinated press policy, which I suspected stemmed from Powell's and Armitage's criticism during Bush 43's first term. Obsessed by their own press coverage, they searched constantly for who might be the source of what they perceived as unfavorable media stories. Their eye often fell on me, incorrectly, given the number of opponents they had in other parts of the administration. Rice went on to say, "You are the obvious movement conservative in the department, and I'd like to work with you on the conservative press." Here, I thought, Rice showed herself to be more Jim Baker than Colin Powell, so I said, "I'm not blaming anyone but myself here," and reviewed the hard times in my relationship with Powell, especially on Iran and North Korea. At Rice's request, we met again in the early afternoon, and she said that she had spoken to Bush about the UN job during his recent European trip: "The president wants you to do this," she said.

The following Monday, I met with Dina Powell, head of Presidential Personnel. While waiting to go to her office, I stood in the West Wing basement lobby as a stream of people came by, including Hadley, who said, "This is a great day, really a great day." The real purpose of the meeting with Powell (no relation to Colin) was to kill some time until the president was ready to see me, and we trotted down to the Oval Office after about ten minutes. Bush greeted us and took us to the familiar seating arrangement in front of the fireplace, he in his usual chair, me on the sofa to his left, and Powell on the other sofa. Bush said, "I just wanted to have a chance to talk to you about your interest in U—S—U—N," drawing out the initials. "Why do you want it?" I answered that I thought it was a critical job in U.S. foreign policy; it was something I was familiar with, having been International Organization Affairs assistant secretary during the Bush 41 administration; I had studied and written extensively about the UN since then; and I thought it was a great opportunity to continue to serve the country.

"Do you want to withdraw from the UN?" he asked, and I said, "Absolutely not." The UN could serve U.S. foreign policy interests, as during the Persian Gulf Crisis of 1990–91, but there was an enormous amount that needed to be fixed. "Bolton, you have strong opinions—and there's nothing wrong with that—but are you up there to talk about your opinions," he asked, "or to get things done? No, that's a loaded question," Bush said, "let me ask it differently. You make waves—and there's nothing wrong with that either, you wouldn't be here if I thought it were. But my father thought of the job when he did it as basically keeping everything flowing smoothly and not getting anyone upset. How do you see it?" I said that the critical point was to advance the president's policy agenda, and not to get lost in the UN environment. The job was to get the best deal we could. I told the story of Secretary of State Dean Rusk's not wanting to let Adlai Stevenson have fallback instructions when he was in New York, because Stevenson would already be at the fallback position before Rusk could turn around.[1] Diplomacy, I said was "advocacy; advocacy for America."

Contrary to advice from friends before this meeting, I decided to go further: "As I said, though, I've written a lot about the UN, and I hope the Democrats aren't still hung up on Florida, as they were back in 2001 when I was being confirmed for this job." Bush responded instantly, "Don't worry, I'm not going to back away from you," and I said, "I'm not worried about that at all. I just don't want to be a problem for you with so much else going on." Bush shrugged it off, saying, "Nyeah," and went on: "We need to get things done up there whether we like it or not, and our allies need it for political cover. There's going to be a lot of big issues coming at you, like Iran for instance. It's an important job." Then he added: "Nice digs, too," concluding, "Well, look, I appreciate your coming by. I just wanted to sniff you out a little bit, and let me think about it some more, and I'll get back to you. I want you to know you've done a terrific job, and I thank you for your service." And with that, Powell and I left the Oval Office, as she tried to reach White House Counsel Harriet Miers to do the customary ethics interview that somehow had gotten lost in the shuffle.

Rice was in Europe by this point, and I didn't hear anything back from Dina Powell. However, Zoellick and Brian Gunderson, Rice's chief of staff, were already talking to me about the roll-out strategy for the nomination's announcement, which was certainly a lot more preparation than there had been in 2001. Rice told me on Friday, March 4, that the White House wanted her to make the announcement on Monday, in order to avoid leaks, and to show that key jobs were being filled. Gunderson convened a meeting of Rice's press and speechwriting people to talk about her Monday remarks

---

1. See Thomas J. Schoenbaum, *Waging Peace and War: Dean Rusk in the Truman, Kennedy and Johnson Years* (New York: Simon & Schuster, 1998), p. 285.

and mine, and how to handle the media, both immediately before and just after the actual public announcement. During the morning of March 7, Rice, Zoellick, and I, and others, made numerous calls to former secretaries of state, UN ambassadors, and other eminences, Hill people, several foreign ministers, reporters and editorial writers, think tankers, and "interest group" leaders, to alert them to the coming announcement. Rice told me that SFRC chairman Lugar had said that he would be helpful, but that she had not been able to reach Biden, the ranking Democrat. The early reactions were very positive, with Tom Lantos of California, the ranking Democrat on the House International Relations Committee, saying he was "delighted" at the news, and Brad Sherman and Howard Berman, also Democrats from California, being supportive as well. Rice said she had had to calm Kofi Annan down, but that he seemed okay by the end of the call. Sean McCormack, a career Foreign Service officer who was to become head of Public Affairs, and Jim Wilkinson, a politico who was Rice's communications guru, both backgrounded the press. The wire services and news networks almost immediately started to run the story.

Rice reached Biden right before the 1:00 P.M. announcement, and he laughed when he heard the news, and not in the way Paul Gigot of the *Wall Street Journal* or Rich Lowry of *National Review* laughed when I told them. Deb Fiddelke, of the White House legislative affairs shop, my Hill handler during the confirmation, said Biden's chief of staff told her that Democratic reaction to my nomination "was not overwhelmingly positive, but it was too early to say how strong the opposition would be or how it would manifest itself," an understatement if ever there was one. Gretchen and JS arrived at about 12:45 P.M., and we walked down to Rice's office to ride the elevator to the eighth floor, where the announcement would be made in the Ben Franklin Room. JS was then finishing her freshman year at Yale, having graduated from high school in 2004, and the proximity of New York to New Haven was a nice side benefit of being UN ambassador. I noted to Rice that JS had been accepted at Stanford, but had nonetheless decided to go to Yale, prompting Wilkinson to joke to Rice, "You can still change your mind!" JS had chosen my Yale college, Calhoun, mostly to avoid being assigned in the random pool for freshman to one of the other colleges whose rooming arrangements were not to her taste. (Although Calhoun had been partially remodeled since my days there, so that the room layout was not exactly the same, JS and nine other girls chose in their sophomore and junior years to live in essentially the same suite of rooms I had lived in during my junior and senior years almost forty years earlier. That is a coincidence others can explain.)

Rice's announcement to the press and my brief statement went well, feeding the growing story, and we both returned to our offices to continue working the phones. I spoke with Linc Chafee (R., R.I.), reminding him that in 2001, he had actually been the first senator to vote in my favor on the floor roll call for the T job, and he replied, "Ah, a pioneer." I spoke with many other Republican senators as well, setting up meetings and listening to their assessments of what the Democrats might do, and a few Democrats as well, such as Ben Nelson of Nebraska, who said he was looking forward to supporting me again, as he had in 2001, and didn't even need a meeting with me to make his decision. On the other hand, Zoellick spoke to Chuck Hagel, whom he thought would be "a tough sell," which I also expected, given his closeness to Powell and Armitage. Nonetheless, Republican Hagel said that he would withhold comment until he had spoken with me. Democratic leader Harry Reid, who just a few days before had called Alan Greenspan a "political hack," issued a critical statement, although neither he nor several other Democrats, such as Kerry and Dodd, said flatly that they would oppose the nomination.

Colin Powell sent me an email, the subject line of which read, "On to the Waldorf!!!" with the text reading: "JB, Congrats! All the best in NYC. cp." Jeane Kirkpatrick told me that she was telling the press that I was "one of the smartest people I had ever met in Washington." Jim Baker said, "You're one of the brightest people in Washington, and you were always a good, loyal soldier for me. Throw my name out there, and I'll be happy to talk to the media." Rice also moved decisively to counter media speculation, as had developed concerning Powell, that I had been forced on her, telling the *Washington Times*, "John Bolton was my first choice." Democrats could no longer argue that attacking me was not equivalent to attacking Rice.

Various foreign officials also spoke out, starting with Australian foreign minister Alexander Downer, who endorsed the nomination, and Jean-Marc de La Sablière, now France's perm rep, who said that France had worked well with me on nonproliferation matters. Stanislas de Laboulaye, the French political director, called me to say that his minister had told him, "Your friend Bolton is going to New York," the first congratulatory call I received from any foreign diplomat. As Rice predicted, Annan issued a statement by late afternoon, saying he "warmly congratulates Bolton, and looks forward to working with him on UN reform, among other issues." Indeed, when Annan called me, on March 28, he said, "I look forward to having you up here," because, "we have a lot of work to do." Cathy Bertini, an old friend who was UN undersecretary general for management, said that when my nomination was announced at a UN senior staff meeting earlier in the week, many people had "rolled their eyes" at the prospect, which just delighted her.

The next morning, Gunderson convened the first of a series of almost daily strategy sessions in Rice's conference room, which were helpful. Even so, I worried that none of those present, from the White House or State, had ever been through anything quite like the Bork experience, which Democrats had run as a political campaign and Republicans had treated as a confirmation process, thereby losing. While no one minimized possible Democratic opposition, I worried there was not a visceral appreciation for how rough this process might be, a point I emphasized at several meetings. In fact, the central problem was my unwillingness to repeat endlessly the catechism of support for the UN, which Bill Buckley had called my violation of the rule we learn as children, "No jokes in church."[2] In the UN church, I was at it over and over again, and this was frowned upon.

As these early days passed, information flowed in from a variety of sources, much of it contradictory, and little of it clear. A Biden staffer told a former Helms staffer, for instance, that "Joe really likes John," and that he thought I was "going to get through, no better and no worse than last time." Bob Kimmitt, a friend of Hagel, called to say that the two of them had spoken, and that Hagel was "looking for ways to support the nomination." Chuck Schumer said that Democrats would certainly give me "what for" on Iraq, as a convenient administration target, but that he would keep an open mind. Many moderate Republicans expressed support, such as Representative Chris Shays of Connecticut and Oregon's Senator Gordon Smith, who said, "You've got a lot of friends up here, and Lugar should be willing to fight on this thing."

---

2. William F. Buckley, Jr., "Pity Rhode Island: Bolton in Chafee's Hands," *National Review Online*, April 12, 2005, http://www.nationalreview.com/buckley/wfb200504121339.asp.

Almost immediately, I began the ritual of Senate courtesy calls, starting with Norm Coleman, a freshman Republican from Minnesota, who was leading efforts to uncover the full story of the Oil for Food scandal, and who had called for Annan's resignation. Coleman, an SFRC member, was to be my chief Senate defender throughout the confirmation process, and he was eager to move the nomination ahead quickly, something we were also pressing Majority Leader Bill Frist and Lugar to do. I met with Chafee on March 10, and much of our discussion was about his vote against the Iraq War. When I explained the rationale for fears about Saddam Hussein's weapons program and his long-term WMD strategy, Chafee said, "I wish we had had that debate instead of the one we did have." The more I responded to Chafee's questions, the more confident I became that the meeting was going well. At the end, Chafee said he had never voted against any of the president's nominees, and recalled his days as a mayor, when he never much liked the City Council "messing around" in his affairs. Among others, I also met with Joe Lieberman of Connecticut, who was very supportive.

I saw Hagel on March 14, and we talked for forty minutes on UN reform, the importance of my working closely with Rice and Zoellick, and his desire that I stay in close touch with Congress. At the end of the discussion, which only his chief of staff, Lou Ann Linehan, attended, Hagel said he would support me, a major step forward, and he issued a press release to that effect just a few hours later. That same day, I also met with Ohio's George Voinovich, who turned out to be intensely interested in UN management reform, which we discussed at some length, and quite cordially. John McCain urged me to "speak softly and carry a big stick," and said he would be helpful, which he was throughout the battle. All the other Republican senators I saw were enthusiastic: Allen of Virginia, Martinez of Florida, Murkowski of Alaska, Sununu of New Hampshire, Alexander of Tennessee, Ensign of Nevada, Inhoff of Oklahoma, Craig of Idaho, Specter of Pennsylvania, Sessions of Alabama, Graham of South Carolina, Kyl of Arizona, Vitter of Louisiana, and more. I spoke with many others, such as former national security adviser Brent Scowcroft, who said, "Congratulations, old friend, you don't shirk the hard ones, do you?" I had lunch with former senator Tim Wirth, who was noncommittal, and breakfast with Clinton UN ambassador Dick Holbrooke, who was as well. Wirth warned me to be careful what I said to Holbrooke, because it would surely end up in the press.

The formal nomination papers went to the Senate on March 17, and the next question was how soon Lugar would schedule an SFRC confirmation hearing after the Easter recess, which began the next day. A White House check of Republicans showed "soft" support from Chafee and Lugar, Hagel undecided, and Pete Domenici of New Mexico opposed. (The White House did not check the Democrats because they didn't think they would turn up anything that wasn't already obvious, but I was nonetheless surprised that they did not even ask.) Domenici's "opposition" was caused by obscure problems with Russia's plutonium disposition program, a high priority for New Mexico given the Los Alamos and Sandia National Laboratories there. I thought it could be resolved, which it was, with Domenici subsequently giving me a warm endorsement in a floor speech. Hagel and Chafee were now on board, in my view. Lugar's softness reflected his earlier disputes with Helms, going back twenty years, over who would be the SFRC's ranking Republican, and was more a problem for Lugar's staff than for Lugar himself, in part because the staff were still exacting "payback" on people associated with Helms. In fact, as Jeff Bergner, a former Lugar chief of staff, told me, the increasing shrillness of the opposition and its nonexistent factual basis hardened Lugar's support, as it also did for other Republicans not on the SFRC. Lugar said at one point to one of his staffers, "Maybe I should act more like Jesse Helms, and remind Biden he's not chairman of the committee." Lugar noticed the confirmation hearing for Thursday, April 7, a date relatively soon after the Easter recess. Nonetheless, the three-week gap between nomination and hearing provided plenty of opportunity for mischief makers.

Once again, I pored through all of my articles for potential grist for opposition questions. During my preparations, on March 29, Paul Volcker issued his report on Kofi Annan's role in the Oil for Food scandal. It was devastating. What had been intended as a program to provide humanitarian assistance to Iraq had been riddled with corruption and mismanagement, and contributed significantly to increasingly negative views about the UN, at least in the United States. In the immediate aftermath of the 1991 Persian Gulf War, in Security Council Resolutions 706 and 712, we had created a mechanism to use the revenues from limited sales of Iraq's oil supplies to provide sustenance to the Iraqi population, and to do so under firm international control in a way we hoped would undercut Saddam Hussein's hold on power. Perhaps not surprisingly, Saddam rejected Resolutions 706 and 712, and the program never became operational. In the Clinton administration, however, as in so many areas, the U.S. position weakened, and in April 1995, Security Council Resolution 986 created an "Oil for Food" program that Saddam found to his liking. Even then, he insisted on negotiating a "memorandum of understanding" with the UN, signed in May 1996, which weakened UN oversight over the program, and which Saddam promptly set about exploiting. The first food shipments arrived in Iraq in early 1997, by which point Kofi Annan had succeeded Boutros-Ghali as UN secretary general, so almost all of the implementation of Oil for Food took place on Annan's watch. As we learned from the Volcker report, Annan had essentially paid no attention to the administration of the program.

Both Coleman and Shays, who had followed the scandal closely, called for Annan to resign, highlighting why massive UN reform was necessary. The Democrats were silent. Then, on April 2, Pope John Paul II died, and the April 7 hearing was postponed to accommodate members of Congress who wished to attend the Rome funeral. Biden asked for two days of hearings, starting on Monday, April 11, agreeing to an SFRC vote on the nomination on Thursday, April 14. It was probably the best deal available, if the April 14 vote held. I continued my courtesy calls, meeting on April 5 with Barack Obama of Illinois for around fifty minutes, much longer than scheduled. He said several times that if we were colleagues on a university faculty, he would doubtless enjoy having a beer with me and discussing UN issues, on many of which we agreed. What bothered him was Bush policy on Iran and North Korea, but he planned to attend the hearing, and, he thought, if confirmed, I would do a good job representing the administration. I also met with a noncommittal Hillary Clinton, who was likewise concerned about Bush's North Korea and Iran policies.

On April 11, Gretchen and I rode to Capitol Hill. Dick Lugar greeted us behind the Hart Building's media-friendly hearing room, and we walked in at 9:30 A.M. This was a Washington spectacular, with mobs of photographers and reporters, and it continued that way through much of the morning. Lugar and I each gave brief opening statements, and then the fun began. As Fiddelke told me later, her report to the White House described the Democrats that day as "take two questions and repeat them endlessly for eight hours." Only a few Republicans showed up for long, although Lugar, Coleman, and Allen stayed most of the day. Perhaps the most important thing I said that day, which I had said to Lugar a few days before, was that I was prepared to have every document and every interview the SFRC staff had done on every issue made completely public.[3] I had nothing to hide, and everything to gain, by allowing all of the facts to come out. Perhaps it was not as important, but probably my best line of the day came in the late afternoon, when Barack Obama, who sat through almost the entire hearing, observed that he had thought of a number of interesting questions while listening to the exchanges. I said, "I've thought of a few things, too," which brought a good laugh from the steadily dwindling audience and press contingent.[4]

The centerpiece of the Democratic attack was a speech I gave at the Heritage Foundation on May 6, 2002, entitled "Beyond the Axis of Evil: Additional Threats from Weapons of Mass Destruction," and specifically, a brief passage dealing with Cuba's involvement with biological weapons. The context of the Democrats' "concern" was their massive effort to criticize the Bush administration for having "politicized" intelligence by trying to bend it to conform to our preconceived conclusions, and specifically what had been said about Saddam Hussein's weapons of mass destruction before the military campaign to overthrow him. The Democrats had dug and dug and dug to see if I had done anything with respect to Iraq that they could latch on to, but having found nothing, they instead focused on Cuba's BW activities. Here, they concentrated on complaints from two careerists, one an analyst with the State Department's Bureau of Intelligence and Research (INR), Christian Westermann, and the other a CIA analyst whom John Kerry named publicly in the hearing as Fulton Armstrong. Given the hunt to identify who in the administration had "outed" Valerie Plame as a CIA employee, I was happy to call Armstrong "Mr. Smith," to Kerry's evident dismay. Democratic staffers also desperately tried to prove I had some involvement in the Plame affair, convinced I had to be part of the conspiracy, but, alas for them, that was just fantasy, too.

---

3. "Hearing on Nomination of John R. Bolton to Be U.S. Representative to the United Nations," Monday, April 11, 2005, reprinted as Annex E to the Report of the Senate Foreign Relations Committee on the nomination, May 18, 2005, Exec. Rep. 109-01, 109th Congress, 1st Session, p. 164 (cited hereinafter as "Report").
4. Dana Milbank, "Nominee Reacts Mildly to Democrats' Barbs," *Washington Post*, Tuesday, April 12, 2005, p. A10, col. 4.

The Heritage WMD speech gave examples of the "junior varsity" axis of evil—Syria, Cuba, and Libya—but Senator Dodd's focus was Cuba alone. I had pointed out that, in 2001, Castro visited Iran, Syria, and Libya, all state sponsors of terrorism like Cuba, and at Tehran University had said, "Iran and Cuba, in cooperation with each other, can bring America to its knees." I quoted Clinton secretary of defense William Cohen's 1998 statement, "I remain concerned about Cuba's potential to develop and produce biological agents, given its biotechnology infrastructure." This was an important point, given that a Cuban spy, Ana Belen Montes, had been for years the senior Cuba analyst at the Defense Intelligence Agency (DIA), and was a key player in intelligence community assessments of Cuban capabilities. On March 19, 2002, she pleaded guilty in federal court to espionage charges, and on October 16 was sentenced to twenty-five years in prison, "acknowledging that for 16 years she provided Fidel Castro's government with top-secret information, including the true identities of four American undercover intelligence officers."[5]

The portion of the speech that dealt with Cuba ended as follows:

> Here is what we know: The United States believes that Cuba has at least a limited offensive biological warfare research and development effort. Cuba has provided dual-use biotechnology to other rogue states. We are concerned that such technology could support BW programs in those states. We call on Cuba to cease all BW-applicable cooperation with rogue states, and to fully comply with all of its obligations under the Biological Weapons Convention.

This language, and how it was derived, was the source of the controversy.

To fit the Democratic narrative about Bush administration efforts to distort intelligence and pressure intelligence analysts to change their views, SFRC staff focused on the INR analyst Westermann, asking to interview him before my confirmation hearing. There was one major problem with their entire approach, however, namely that the head of INR had used these very words in Senate testimony *before* I gave the speech. As the *Washington Post* reported the day after the Heritage speech: "As it happens, Bolton was

---

5. Tim Golden, "Pentagon Aide, a Cuban Spy, Is Described as Unapologetic," *New York Times*, October 12, 2002, p. A4, col. 1.

not the first official to make a public statement on the subject. Carl W. Ford Jr., assistant secretary of state for intelligence and research, used identical language in March 19 congressional testimony that largely went unnoticed."[6]

In fact, when I read that *Post* article early on May 7, 2002, I was astounded that Ford had already used the language. I was completely unaware of his March testimony, which, as the *Post* said, apparently attracted little attention, and certainly no controversy. Ironically, just before the Heritage speech, I read the Cuba language to Representative Lincoln Diaz-Balart, and he had what I thought was a curious reaction: "I think that language has been used before." I politely told him he was mistaken, but when I saw the *Post* story, I was perplexed, not to say irritated. The Cuba language had been specifically cleared for the Heritage speech, originally planned for March, but postponed to May due to the press of other business. Given how difficult and deceptive Westermann had been in the clearance process, I was especially surprised that his boss would have preempted me by using this language without even telling me! On May 7, I asked Ford before Powell's 8:30 A.M. staff meeting what was up, and he said that since INR had given final clearance on the language in February, he assumed I had already given the speech in question. Accordingly, he didn't think twice about including it in his Senate testimony.

Ironically, Ford's use of the language in question, two months before my Heritage speech, largely insulated me from criticism in 2002 by the pro-Castro spectrum. After all, if Ford had used the same words, how could they criticize me? Chris Dodd tried to make something of it shortly after the speech, calling Ford and me to testify on the issue, having doubtless heard from some insider about the incident. I suspected it was "Mr. Smith" (or Fulton Armstrong, as Senator Kerry called him), a friend of Ana Belen Montes. Dodd was always on the alert for slights against Castro, but the administration stood firmly behind me. In Moscow, in a May 12 joint appearance with Igor Ivanov on Victor Posner's television show, Colin Powell said my remarks were entirely appropriate, and that both the United States and Russia had an interest in WMD nonproliferation. Rice said in a May

---

6. Peter Slevin, "Cuba Seeks Bioweapons, U.S. Says," *Washington Post,* May 7, 2002, p. A18, col. 1.

13 interview on the *News Hour with Jim Lehrer,* "There is plenty of reason to be very concerned about what the Cubans are doing in this area. And what Undersecretary Bolton was doing was putting it on the agenda. Now, how it's dealt with will depend in part on what Castro is willing to do."

Powell decided that only Ford would testify, because the sole issue Dodd had raised in his letters of invitation to testify was what facts were known about Cuba's BW program, not their policy implications. Dodd was furious, but he acquiesced because he didn't want to cross Powell, although he clearly blamed me for making his hearing much less newsworthy. Dodd also tried to make something of the remarks about the Cuba BW effort ascribed in a Reuters story to Southern Command's head, General Gary Speer. I called Lieutenant General George Casey, then the J-5 at the Pentagon, to ask him to check into this, which he did. Casey called me back to say that Speer had told Casey's deputy, Major General John Dunn, that he had been misquoted in the Reuters story, and that he fully supported what I said in the Heritage speech. Three years later, however, Dodd was back at it because of the Iraq WMD issue, which many Bush administration opponents saw as a way to cripple the presidency, even though it had failed in the 2004 presidential election. Westermann, with whom I had spent three minutes during my previous four years at the State Department, became their instrument.

The facts, however, don't fit Dodd's fantasy. The intelligence community (IC) had granted final clearance for the intelligence aspects of the speech, and specifically the Cuba BW language, on Friday, February 22. Part of the clearance effort was to get permission from the IC to declassify an intelligence estimate about what Cuba was up to, a procedure followed with some regularity to explain the basis for policy decisions or positions, but which required concurrence from the IC to avoid revealing intelligence sources or methods, or compromising other IC equities. Fred Fleitz, a career CIA officer detailed to my staff, had found the language in question in intelligence assessments, and on February 12 had followed the routine procedure for seeking declassification by sending it to INR, the "intelligence" office in the State Department, and asking INR to circulate it within the IC. As I learned later, Westermann had at first refused to circulate the language, and when he had finally done so, he attached a note to it saying that INR did not concur with the language that Fleitz had essentially copied from the existing analysis. Westermann had turned what should have been a clerical exercise into an effort to revisit intelligence conclusions, and had made no effort to tell Fleitz.

Fleitz learned of Westermann's note when a CIA colleague asked him what INR was up to, since the note was entirely out of line. I thought so, too. I called Westermann to my office to find out what happened. At first, he denied writing the note, but when Fleitz confronted him with the hard copy of an email containing it, he became flustered and began to argue about what he had done. I finally said something like, "I don't care what your opinion is, but I do care about being lied to," and sent him away. I then called Ford, who had left for the day. In his absence I called in Tom Fingar, his principal deputy, and told him I thought Westermann's conduct was duplicitous and unprofessional. Fingar said he would check into it and get back to me, which he did in an email. Referring to INR, he wrote, "We screwed up," that Westermann's behavior was "entirely inappropriate," and "it won't happen again."[7]

I took this to be a vindication by the highest-ranking INR official physically present. Dodd instead tried to spin the incident as an effort to browbeat a career intelligence officer and to politicize intelligence. In fact it was just the opposite. I had found an INR staffer attempting to impose his own policy views on what a policy official could say, a clear violation of that "wall" between intelligence and policy that Dodd and others talked so much about. And this was not the only time that INR or elements of the IC had been guilty of violating the "wall" from their side, a fact Dodd and others were never able or willing to contemplate. Because Westermann had lied to my face, I completely lost confidence in his veracity and judgment on the sensitive area of WMD proliferation. I wanted him moved to another position, where his deception and bad judgment could not adversely affect our foreign policy, but INR never moved him. I frankly lost interest because I had other things to do, but this also became part of Dodd's complaint. The bottom line is that I never tried to change a single line of intelligence reporting or analysis that Westermann said or wrote. I only wanted him to be honest with me, and he had failed that test.

This issue was what the bulk of the contentious SFRC hearing was about, which was broken up briefly by the "Ladies in Pink," a "peace" group

---

7. Quoted in Report, op. cit., n. 3, p. 286.

protesting Bush's foreign policy. Lugar ended the hearing at 5:40 P.M., and told me afterward he thought I had done very well. The next day, the Democrats brought in Carl Ford, himself a former Democratic Senate staffer. Ford told SFRC staff before the hearing he agreed that the final Heritage speech had been cleared, that no intelligence analysis had been changed, and that no one had been fired. Lugar's staff characterized Ford's likely testimony as a "dry hole" on the Cuba BW issue. That was true, but Ford instead made a savage personal attack on me, based on nothing except the Westermann incident, using broad, vitriolic, and vicious language. My personal reaction was that Ford was so over the top that no one could take him seriously, an assessment others shared. During the hearing, Coleman later told me that Chafee had leaned over and whispered to him, "Bolton got tubed and he got angry; what's the big deal?" Lugar's press aide, Mark Helmke, emailed a friend later in the day about Ford's testimony that "if I were a Democrat, I'd be depressed that the wrong witness blew his top." I thought that was about right.

There was even less to the story of "Mr. Smith," a well-known IC apologist for Cuba, who at the time was the national intelligence officer (NIO) for Latin America, on the staff of the National Intelligence Council (NIC), a small interagency body under CIA director George Tenet. Otto Reich, assistant secretary for Western Hemisphere affairs, had been trying to get Fulton Armstrong moved out of the NIC almost from the day he took office. (Ultimately, Reich's successor, Roger Noriega, with the full cooperation of Jamie Miscik, then CIA deputy director for intelligence, did succeed in removing Armstrong from the NIC's Latin American account.) Not only was Armstrong biased and inaccurate about Cuba, he was deficient in many other professional respects, in Reich's view. He worked assiduously to bring Montes from DIA to the NIC, which would have put her into even more sensitive territory.[8] Senate Republican staff also knew Armstrong well and believed that the real problem was Armstrong's imposing his own pro-Castro biases on Cuban-related intelligence. They did not suggest that he was complicit in any of Montes's criminal activity. Others, such as Representative Lincoln Diaz-Balart of Florida, characterized the

---

8. See Scott W. Carmichael, *True Believer: Inside the Investigation and Capture of Ana Montes, Cuba's Master Spy* (Annapolis, Md.: Naval Institute Press, 2007). Carmichael was the DIA's senior security and counterintelligence investigator.

affair as part of the "Dodd battle" that Cuban-Americans had waged against Dodd for years.

To this day, I have never met Armstrong, or even laid eyes on him. I first learned about him when he started claiming that the Heritage speech had not been fully cleared by the IC, which was contrary to fact, and which we quickly came to learn actually meant "not cleared by him." In reality, as Alan Foley, the head of the CIA's nonproliferation and arms control office, told me, Larry Gershwin, the national intelligence officer for science and technology (and the NIC official responsible for biological weapons) *had* cleared the speech. Armstrong had not, but he had neither the responsibility nor the knowledge to do so. In fact, it began to look like a classic bureaucratic turf fight. Armstrong had been excluded from something, and there is no worse hell for a bureaucrat. Of course, I had had absolutely nothing to do with selecting which NIC official reviewed the text, which was entirely up to the IC. That should have been the end to the Armstrong matter, since it obviously had nothing to do with trying to change intelligence analysis or reporting.

My opponents, however, had a different view. Finding that there was simply no substance to the allegation that I had tried to distort intelligence, they shifted the debate to whether I was a nice person, thereby inviting every person in government whom I had ever defeated in a policy battle, of whom there were many, to turn the issue into one of personal disparagement, which, in a city of massive egos, was not hard to do. Carl Ford was a good example. I never paid much attention to him during Bush's first term, finding him slow, pedestrian, and bureaucratic. His public testimony was not his only effort at sabotage, since he and others in INR complained to the SFRC Democratic staff that I was getting intelligence directly from other agencies, and not through INR. Of course, that's what everyone at State did, but INR tried to make it into a security issue, which even the Democrats wouldn't bite on. Another obvious INR leak emerged in questions Dodd raised at the hearing about intercepts I received in the normal course of my daily intelligence "take," and why I had asked for the identities of a number of individuals. This was a fairly routine practice, but any public mention of "intercepts" and the National Security Agency was enough to make the conspiracy theorists salivate. In fact, since Westermann himself had handled some of my requests for identities, I was almost certain it might be Westermann trying to help out the Democratic staffers. Moreover, I think that my efforts to build closer ties to the CIA and other intelligence agencies had infuriated the turf-conscious Ford and other INR staff, who used the confirmation hearing as payback.

However, responding to another Democratic request for delay (for more time to formulate questions for the record, QFRs), Lugar postponed the SFRC vote until Tuesday, April 19. Perhaps realizing that their various efforts were dead-ending, Dodd's QFRs centered on the NSA intercepts he had raised earlier. All procedures had been properly followed in the few instances in which I had asked for identities, a practice required because NSA routinely "minimized" the names of U.S. and U.K. persons who might show up in intercepts, describing them as "a named U.S. person," rather than actually naming the name, as NSA did for all other nationalities. Obviously, knowing who was saying what could be important to understanding the intercept, and the regular procedure at State was to ask INR to ask NSA to pass back the name that had been "minimized," by showing a reason why it was needed. Armitage later said that he had told several senators that the NSA issue was "chasing the wrong thing," and that "there's nothing there," concluding, "I bet I asked for names over a hundred times while I was at State." By contrast, I had made a total of ten such requests during my four years there.

State careerists were also leaking, and several reporters decided to go after me, including Dafna Linzer of the *Washington Post*. On April 18, the day before the SFRC vote, she reported, based on unnamed sources, that I had withheld information from Powell and Rice, in an article typical of her sloppy and inaccurate approach to journalism.[9] Rice was furious about the leak, and opened the morning staff meeting by saying, "I don't like fratricide. . . . I don't like hearing from the *Post* what I did or did not know from John Bolton before my European trip. That article wasn't just wrong, but unhelpful," she continued, as emphatically as I ever heard her. "I'm not pointing fingers, but I want everyone in here to communicate this to your people, and I don't expect it to happen again." Linzer went on to coauthor a story discussing Rice's comments, which were relayed to her by a staffer in State's Nonproliferation Bureau, which was filled with people who had never liked Bush administration policies. Significantly, Linzer told this

---

9. Dafna Linzer, "Bolton Often Blocked Information, Officials Say," *Washington Post*, Monday, April 18, 2005, p. A4, col. 1.

staffer that Armitage was one of her sources, evidence of Linzer's lack of professionalism.[10] Armitage himself, however, broke his public silence on May 5 to say, "John Bolton is eminently qualified. He's one of the smartest guys in Washington."

April 19 was unquestionably the low point in the confirmation battle, and also the low point in my entire government career. The SFRC met at 3:15 P.M., and faced an unrelenting barrage of criticism and hype from Biden, Dodd, and Kerry, lasting for over an hour, while the Republicans sat and listened. At about four-twenty-five, Lugar said that it was time to vote, with everyone fully expecting that the vote would be 10–8, along party lines, to report the nomination to the floor favorably. To everyone's complete astonishment, however, Voinovich, admitting he had not attended any of the hearings, announced that he was not ready to vote. What had been a one-sided and rancorous proceeding now descended into chaos, with the Democrats demanding that the SFRC record be reopened, and the confirmation vote postponed until the first week in May. Lugar agreed to their demands, and adjourned the committee at about 5:00 P.M. There were a number of alternatives, such as recessing the SFRC to see if Voinovich could be persuaded to vote to report the nomination without recommendation (which is what ultimately happened), or simply to recess without making any decisions, regroup, and come back the next day with a new plan. Instead, the Democrats, doing little more than rabble-rousing, had swept the field. Norm Coleman summed it up well when he called me the next day to say, "The Democrats come in loaded for bear, and we just sit there and get discouraged. Our silence was taken as acquiescence in their charges, and we looked just awful."

Several weeks then passed during which the Democrats encouraged every rumor, every speculation, and every dissatisfied bureaucrat to emerge. We had to refute all of this, although in fact there was really very little, despite the media frenzy, sustained by selected leaks from the SFRC Democratic staff. Since most of the accusations bore only a coincidental relationship with the truth, I was not demoralized by the attacks, although they were hard on my family and friends. We distributed point-by-point rebuttals and letters signed by hundreds of former coworkers at AID, the

---

10. Charles Babington and Dafna Linzer, "Panel Delays Vote on Bolton Nomination to U.N.," *Washington Post*, Wednesday, April 20, 2005, p. A1, col. 3.

Justice Department, Bush 41's State Department, AEI, and others, including former secretaries of state and defense and other senior officials, all based on reality rather than the fantasy the critics were trying to create. We also made sure that SFRC staffers interviewing witnesses heard from those who knew the facts in response to the various charges. As a result, the colorful press accounts that I was not a nice person all fell out of the Democratic playbook. Sadly, they did not fall out of the files of the media, which repeated them even when the nomination's opponents were too embarrassed to bring them up. The headline of a *National Review* editorial captured the real story: "The Disappearing Case Against John Bolton." [11]

Just one example was the refutation of Melody Townsel, who alleged I had chased her down a hotel hallway in Moscow ten years earlier, throwing things at her and saying unkind things about her. In fact, I had met her once in a room full of people, thus constituting our entire personal contact. The SFRC interviews showed that, while in Kyrgyzstan on behalf of an AID contractor called International Business and Technical Consultants, Inc. (IBTCI), she had engaged in what could most kindly be called inadequate financial and accounting reporting, for which inadequacies she had been fired. I did some legal work for IBTCI, and she associated me with her firing. There was little doubt to me and others her accusations were payback. Once the witnesses were heard, especially IBTCI president Jay Kalotra, a bearded, turbaned Sikh naturalized citizen from India, the story evaporated. Kalotra laid out the many problems he and IBTCI had had with Townsel, and several others who worked for IBTCI at the time fully supported him. Not only was Kalotra entirely credible and truthful, there was no way Democrats were going to allow someone like him to defend me in front of the cameras. This pattern repeated itself again and again.

After this long ordeal, the Republican SFRC's majority report on the nomination summed up exactly how I felt about things:

> The end result of all this is that Secretary Bolton emerged looking better than when it began. Some allegations turned out not to be as serious as they first appeared, new information had cast others in a different light, most have proven to be groundless, or, at best, highly

11. "The Disappearing Case Against John Bolton," *National Review Online*, May 11, 2005, http://www.nationalreview.com/editorial/editors1200505110914.asp.

overstated, while some were apparently judged by the Democratic Members as not even worth looking into. The interviews and documents showed Secretary Bolton to be a hardworking public servant, a pro-active policymaker eager to implement President Bush's agenda, with strong views and a blunt style that, frankly, rubbed some people the wrong way.

But there was no evidence to support the most serious charge, that Secretary Bolton sought to manipulate intelligence. He may have disagreed with intelligence findings, but in the end, he always accepted the final judgment of the intelligence community.

The majority report also noted, "The ethical inquiry into Secretary Bolton's background was pressed by members who planned to vote against him even before the committee began interviewing witnesses," and, "at times the inquiry followed a more prosecutorial path than most nominees have to endure." [12] All too true.

Despite the difficulties, President Bush spoke very strongly in support of the nomination, saying to a group of insurance executives on April 21, "Welcome to the nation's capital, where sometimes politics gets in the way of doing the people's business." After explaining the situation, Bush said, "John's distinguished career and service to our nation demonstrates that he is the right man at the right time for this important assignment. I urge the Senate to put aside politics and confirm John Bolton to the United Nations." Many senators spoke on the Senate floor, and John McCain was especially memorable, breaking out in laughter when he compared the allegations about my temperament to what everyone saw from senators every day of the week. When I called McCain to thank him, he joked about an aphorism he attributed to Chairman Mao: "It's always darkest just before it's totally black." I spoke with former secretary of state Al Haig, who had been defending me in the media, and he said we had to stick together against "weak-kneed Republicans who flutter in the heart," which put it all in one phrase. Unfortunately, the one person on whom Democrats seemed to be making an impression was Voinovich, and he was basically the only one who mattered.

---

12. Report, op. cit., n. 3, p. 3.

I met with Rice on April 22 and told her that she and the president should use the SFRC debacle on Tuesday as an opportunity to reconsider whether to proceed with the nomination. This was the time to make the political cost-benefit analysis, because if the administration did not want to invest the political capital necessary, better to make that decision now rather than later, when giving up would be worse for Bush. I felt it was my duty to raise this option, although I was in no mood myself to give up. Recalling unfounded criticism of her tenure as Stanford's provost, when she was accused of not supporting enough women for tenure, Rice thanked me for raising the issue and noted that it showed why she and the president trusted me. She said she saw no reasons to pull back now but would talk to Andy Card about it. Card called me on Saturday morning, and I said, "Hi, Andy, how are you?" to which he replied "I'm fine—and so are you." He said the White House legislative assessment was that "we're in good shape, although we're disappointed that Lugar decided to keep this open until May 12." He went on to say, "We don't want to do a cost-benefit analysis, we want you at the UN." That was that.

By the time of the May 12 meeting, Voinovich had been called by Bush, Cheney, Rice, Card, Jeane Kirkpatrick, Larry Eagleburger, and countless senators, but without success. I met with Voinovich in his Senate office on May 10, and he said that he was not going to support the nomination, essentially because he was worried that, despite calls from Cheney and Rice, he thought I would end up reporting to the VP rather than the secretary. I tried to turn Voinovich around, and the meeting went on for nearly an hour, but I think his mind was made up before I entered his office. Deb Fiddelke and Sarah Tinsley of T were waiting for the one-on-one with Voinovich to end, and we immediately went to Lugar's office to report the bad news. Lugar subsequently met with Voinovich, convincing him that if he could not vote favorably on the nomination, he should at least vote to send it to the floor without recommendation. This approach would avoid a 9–9 vote on a favorable recommendation, with a tie meaning defeat. With this commitment in hand, we at least knew that I would be liberated from the SFRC on a party-line vote on May 12, which was exactly what happened. It was like crossing the River Styx in the right direction.

The next issue was how exactly the Democrats would prevent the nomination from coming to a vote in the full Senate. Democratic leader Harry Reid told a friend of mine right after the SFRC vote, "Your guy's going to make it. Joe [Biden] doesn't want a filibuster." The term "filibuster" by this point in history encompassed not only the traditional Senate "talkathon," but also a variety of delaying tactics on the Senate floor that were designed to drag out a nomination long enough to kill it. Biden, however, was not the initial problem on the floor; it was Dodd who was still pursuing the NSA intercepts. Moreover, there was another floor complication. The battle over Bush's judicial nominations was coming to a head, and Republican majority leader Bill Frist wanted to conclude that before setting a date for my vote. As the controversy over the judicial nominations played out, and as time dragged on, my nomination simply stalled.

By this point, the NSA intercept question had been fully explained to White House Counsel Harriett Miers, and was really now an executive-legislative issue. The administration now had to decide what to do about the larger question of congressional access. Left entirely to myself, I would have disclosed the intercepts and the identities of the names that had been "minimized." There was so little involved here that any fair-minded person reading the intercepts would understand this, and full disclosure would have taken away the Dodd argument that there was some kind of cover-up going on. Personally, I would have had no objection to printing everything in the newspapers, because I had everything to gain by a broader understanding of what Armitage and I, and many others at State and other agencies, had done over the years.

Recalling the executive privilege fight over Rehnquist's OLC documents in 1986, I kept hoping that something could be negotiated; Frist, Roberts, McCain, and others made many efforts to find a solution, but they were all unsuccessful.

In part, the problem arose from the ever-escalating conspiracy theories about why I had asked for the names: I was spying on Colin Powell; I was fronting for Halliburton in Iraq; I was retaliating against my opponents in the State Department. It could easily have been shown that these conspiracy theories were without basis simply by producing the intercepts and the names involved. In part, however, the problem continued because Dodd kept increasing his demands, which simply made the White House even less sympathetic to compromise. At one point, Dodd suggested that he provide the White House a list of names, and the White House in turn would say whether the intercepts contained any of the names. Since I knew what the names in the intercepts were, I liked the idea, but Dodd kept increasing the number of names he wanted to submit, and finally rejected his own proposal, saying that he would only be satisfied with seeing the actual intercepts. Since this was something that the Senate Select Committee on Intelligence did not plan to allow, there was no way Dodd would get what he wanted. Of course, in truth, what he really wanted was not to see the intercepts or find out the names, but to block the nomination from ever receiving an up-or-down vote, which he knew he would lose. In this respect, he later received unexpected help from Republican senator John Thune of South Dakota, who was upset over the decision to close a major Air Force base in his state, as a result of the Defense Department's base-closure review process. In protest, Thune would not agree to a "time agreement" on my nomination, so Frist had to bring the nomination up and schedule a cloture vote to break the filibuster just before the Memorial Day recess.

The chosen day was Thursday, May 26, and Frist was confident he would obtain "cloture," with sixty votes needed under Senate rules to shut off debate, because Reid assured him we would have enough Democratic votes. Not everyone was so confident. Coleman said at 9:00 A.M. he was "not sure how it will play out tonight," and Lugar said, "I just hope the Democratic cooperation is there with Dr. Frist, as he says it is, and we get cloture." John Warner told me, "Don't be discouraged. The Democrats are just running a media show, and you're the only act in town today." Of course, a large part of the struggle within the Democratic Party arose from Dodd's unsuccessful run against Reid for the Democratic leader's position, which neither of them ever forgot. Whatever the reasons, Frist's vote counting went awry, and we fell four votes short of the sixty required, 56–42. Senator Arlen Specter was on his way to a medical appointment in Pennsylvania, which one might have thought we would have known about, and Frist switched his vote at the last minute in order to be on the "prevailing" side in order to move for reconsideration. Thus we actually had fifty-eight votes, just two short, and Lieberman had voted against cloture only at the specific request of Dodd, his fellow Connecticut senator. The White House believed we were still very much in the game. Moreover, it was now clear to everyone that if there were a straight up-or-down vote, I would be confirmed.

Nonetheless, given the continued Democratic obstructionism, I thought it was about time to begin considering a recess appointment, a power vested in the president by the Constitution to fill vacancies in the executive branch without Senate action. The downside was that a recess appointment would end with the adjournment of the following session of Congress (meaning the end of 2006 in this case), and by statute and longstanding legal interpretation could not be renewed on a salaried basis. Nonetheless, it was better than sitting around waiting for the Senate, and there was always the possibility of getting confirmed after the recess appointment took effect. Especially in my case, we had a strong predicate because a minority of the Senate was preventing the majority from expressing its opinion on a nomination to an important position, which was thus tailor-made for the president to exercise his recess appointment power.

Unfortunately, the White House legislative affairs office reported that Reid had unequivocally committed to Frist that there would be enough Democratic votes for cloture after the Memorial Day recess, and urged therefore that we not proceed with a recess appointment. I was amazed, since Frist had received a similar commitment from Reid on this last vote, and there were no signs Dodd was backing away from his effort. In any event, the decision was made: no recess appointment during the ten-day-long Memorial Day recess, a classic missed opportunity. Nonetheless, the White House remained confident I would be confirmed when the Senate session resumed the week of June 6. That didn't happen, because Frist brought up additional judicial nominations, because there were no signs of movement on the NSA intercepts, and because Reid didn't do anything more than he had before in terms of providing Democrats to support a cloture vote. For reasons I couldn't see, the White House still remained confident I would be confirmed the following week.

On June 14, McCain, who was working hard on my behalf, called just before 6:30 P.M. to describe separate conversations with Biden and Dodd during the day. While Dodd was "hard over" on the issue, said McCain, Biden "wanted out." He needed a "fig leaf," but the White House line on the intercepts allowed Dodd to poison the atmosphere by saying we were being unreasonable. McCain recalled Violeta Chamorro's 1990 inauguration as president of Nicaragua, after she defeated Sandinista Danny Ortega, where Dodd and Bianca Jagger had been publicly hugging and crying over the Sandinista defeat. No surprise there. With McCain's and Karl Rove's help, a one-on-one meeting was set up for me and Biden.

When I went to Biden's office on June 16, we agreed that our meeting should stay out of the press. He confirmed that he had said to McCain that he "wanted out" of this matter, but we had two issues to resolve: the NSA intercepts and a new red herring, the issue of classified testimony I had given the year before on Syria's WMD programs. Biden described the NSA issue as being Dodd's concern, whereas he was more interested in Syria. I explained the background of the testimony and said that I would be willing to have senators see email exchanges and comments about drafts of the testimony, on the condition that all agree on a time certain for a vote that would follow automatically thereafter. We reached agreement on this issue, which would be based, he suggested, on his signing a document with McCain. Biden concluded by saying, "I'm not the lawyer you are, but surely we can do that."

On the NSA intercepts, Biden described some of the conspiracy theories floating around. He acknowledged he had spoken to Armitage ("No friend of yours," said Biden), and that Armitage had told him there was nothing to the issue (matching what Armitage had said to me, although he hadn't mentioned that his conversation had been with Biden). Biden also mentioned a recent dinner he'd attended, hosted by former secretaries of state, in honor of Rice, at which Kissinger had lit into him for causing me so much trouble. Biden said he was trying to explain, when Powell interjected, "If I were ever in a foxhole again, I'd want John there with me, but I wouldn't put him in New York." If nothing else came of the Biden meeting, these were interesting data. I explained to him how the distribution of intel worked, why it was logical to ask for the identities of minimized names, and so on. In particular, I explained that I didn't ask for anyone's name as such; it was actually exactly the opposite, since I was only asking for the name of someone identified in an intercept as "a named American person," all of which seemed new to him. Biden asked if I minded his inviting Dodd to our meeting, and I said I had no objection. When Biden got Dodd on the phone to explain, it was clear from Biden's side of the conversation that Dodd was stunned to hear that the two of us were talking. He agreed to come to Biden's office.

Dodd walked in, looking sullen. Biden summarized our discussion, and Dodd launched into a Senate-floor-style speech describing how unhappy he was, and his particular displeasure with Pat Roberts. Roberts had taken seven of the most obvious names Democrats might have listed (such as INR analyst Westermann) and sent them to John Negroponte, the new director of national intelligence, who confirmed that none of them were among the minimized names whose identities I had requested. I said I bet at least six of Roberts's seven names were on Dodd's list of thirty-six. Dodd didn't respond, just glowering instead. I also said thirty-six names would never fly, given that Dodd himself had started at "two or three," which had climbed to "five or six," and which was now thirty-six and growing. Dodd left twenty minutes later, and I repeated to Biden that thirty-six names was unreasonable. Biden said he would work with Dodd to try to get a lower number and assured me "The apartment is yours," if we could resolve these issues, and, "You have between fifty-two and fifty-seven votes for confirmation," which I knew was low, but didn't dispute.

The proposed deal Biden and I reached was agreeable to Rove and Card, although it took more negotiating with Biden to tie down the specifics. The NSA issue would depend on how many names Dodd insisted upon, but Biden and Card had a good discussion of the issue. Even though negotiations with the Democrats were in full swing, Frist decided to schedule another cloture vote on June 20. The White House urged postponement to Frist, which he unaccountably did not do, even knowing a number of Republicans would not be in Washington in time to vote. I didn't understand why we were proceeding, but with eight senators out of town, cloture failed 54–38, which was really only one vote worse than before, as was generally understood, but still short of sixty. The *Washington Post* headline the next day read: "Democrats Block Vote on Bolton," [13] which demonstrated the predicate for a recess appointment.

Republican Arizona senator John Kyl, who had been doing an enormous amount of work on my behalf, both behind the scenes and in the media, called to say there had been a lot of frustration against the White House the night before, and there would be much second-guessing that the nomination had been bungled all along the way. Kyl thought we should simply make a recess appointment now, although he asked whether the upcoming Fourth of July recess was long enough. In an interview, Frist blamed Democrats for repeatedly moving the goalposts, which was partially true, but he stressed, after meeting with Bush at a lunch for all Republican senators, that Bush still wanted an up-or-down vote. McCain called

---

13. Charles Babington and Jim VandeHei, "Democrats Block Vote on Bolton," *Washington Post*, Tuesday, June 21, 2005, p. A1, col. 6.

to urge making the recess appointment as soon as possible, saying it was "like winning an election by two votes; people care about it for a while, then they forget it."

I decided I should talk to Cheney to see what he thought, and a meeting was scheduled for Wednesday morning, June 29. Cheney said, "The president, Condi, and I are all solid on [a recess appointment]. It will happen if we don't get a Senate vote." I urged that the appointment be made over the Fourth of July recess, since waiting until August would lose a valuable month in New York. Cheney worried whether the Fourth of July recess was long enough, and I joked with him about defending executive branch prerogatives. He then explained what had been uppermost in their minds at the White House for taking such a hard line on the NSA intercepts: "We have a lot of equities in reserving our channel on intelligence matters to Roberts and the Intelligence Committee, and we want to make sure that Biden and Dodd and the rest of them can't start messing around there. Then . . . we don't want Armed Services in the intel any more than we want Foreign Relations." Cheney said they were all willing to continue the confirmation battle, but continuing the battle was by no means inconsistent with a recess appointment, emphasizing again why sooner was better than later in terms of what was happening in New York.

When Cheney and I concluded, I waited in his secretary's office to have a word with Scooter Libby on the issue of the timing of recess appointments, explaining that the ten-day recess was a Senate preference, not an executive branch one. We called Cheney's lawyer, David Addington, who completely agreed. Nonetheless, as Rice told me on Thursday, June 30, she and others wanted to make one more try with Biden, right after the Fourth of July recess, and felt that any recess appointment should come only then. Whatever slight possibility there was to argue for further consideration of a recess appointment, however, was then blown away by Sandra Day O'Connor's resignation from the Supreme Court, which concentrated attention on selecting her successor. Further troubles came the week of July 11, with the Valerie Plame issue erupting again, and the revelation that Rove was the source for a *Time* magazine reporter. The Rove story was also enough to cause another ripple of interest in the press about whether I was involved in the Plame matter, which I was not. The NSA intercept issue nonetheless provided a hook for the media to fantasize, even though those intercepts could not have been further away from the Plame affair. MSNBC, for example reported that I had testified before the Plame grand jury, which was completely untrue, although it did provoke another letter from Biden asking about it.

Rice's final conversation with Biden was futile, and we began moving toward a recess appointment. The Senate adjourned on Friday, July 29, and a new phase was about to begin.

CHAPTER SEVEN

ARRIVING AT THE UN: FEAR AND LOATHING IN NEW YORK

I am not much of a carrot man.

—JOHN BOLTON, FROM TIME TO TIME, AS APPROPRIATE

On Monday morning, August 1, Gretchen and I arrived at the White House for the president's announcement of my recess appointment. Shortly before the appointed hour of ten o'clock, we were ushered down the hall toward the Oval Office where Chief of Staff Andy Card greeted us warmly, escorting us through the secretary's space into the Oval Office, where Rice, Hadley, and Crouch were already with the president. I thanked Bush again for standing by me during the confirmation fight and for the decision to make the recess appointment. He responded as if they were "givens" in his mind. Bush said, "You're going to have a big, bright target on your back in New York, even bigger than it has been. I know you know what you need to do, but just be aware that some liberal bureaucrat with a grudge is going to be looking for a chance to make trouble." I said that I appreciated the advice, and Bush responded, "They're going to be gunning for you, no question about it." Then he said, "The chain of command obviously runs from me to Condi to you, but you need to stay in touch with us here," which was comforting because it showed Bush understood the difficulties of operating in the State Department. He showed me the cards on which he had written his remarks, and asked if I had anything prepared. I took out the half page or so of remarks I had written and held it out to him. "Is that all?"

he asked, obviously happy it was short. Hadley, whose daughter had been a classmate of JS's at Holton-Arms, asked where JS was. I explained that she was a counselor at Interlochen Arts Camp in Michigan where she had spent many summers as a camper, and getting ready to start her sophomore year at Yale, which Bush had also attended, graduating two years ahead of me.

Without further ado, we walked into the Roosevelt Room, right at 10:00 A.M., and gave our respective remarks. Bush used his to explain the need for the recess appointment: "Because of partisan delaying tactics by a handful of senators, John was unfairly denied the up-or-down vote that he deserves." He also made it clear that I would "be an important member of my State Department team. . . . I am sending Ambassador Bolton to New York with my complete confidence. . . . He will speak for me on critical issues facing the international community." After we trooped back into the Oval Office, Gretchen's cell phone rang, prompting Card to say, relatively humorously, "Uh-oh, major security violation." At least it hadn't rung during the announcement. The caller turned out to be JS, who had just watched from Interlochen. Bush motioned to Gretchen to give him the phone, which she did, and he said, "JS, do you know who this is? So did you see me on TV with your old man? I thought I limped through it okay for a Yalie." History does not record how JS answered, and she doesn't remember, but at least the White House photographer got a picture of our side, which Bush later signed for JS.

Although the public announcement was obviously a critical moment, both for the president and for me, my mind had raced ahead of it to the impact of taking over at USUN in New York. I wanted to waste no time, and had decided that I would leave on the next possible shuttle flight to New York and head immediately to the mission to have an "all-hands meeting" to introduce myself to the USUN staff. Now accompanied by a detail from State's Diplomatic Security (DS) Bureau that would be with me for the next sixteen months, I arrived at the mission on Forty-fifth Street and was greeted by Anne Patterson, a career Foreign Service officer, who was the deputy perm rep. There was a mob of television cameras, and all of seven protesters shouting "Booo!" After all the fuss, I was disappointed: only seven? They turned out to be the first and last anti-Bolton demonstrators I ever faced at USUN.

Once in my new office, which was then and remained pretty nondescript, we discussed what should be done in the first few days, including a wave of courtesy calls on other perm reps, which was an important element in getting started. One formality was the customary reporting cable sent to the State Department by a new "chief of mission," using the traditional language: "Ambassador Bolton arrived post on Monday, August 1, 2005, at 2:00 P.M. and assumed charge." The all-hands meeting went well, as did a later tour, office by office, of the entire mission. I thought this kind of personal introduction was important, given the negative publicity that had accompanied the confirmation battle. The USUN personnel could at least verify firsthand that I did not have horns and a tail. I stressed in this and subsequent staff meetings that we should not be protective in our reporting to Washington about what the UN was doing. We were not here to argue the UN's case. That kind of defensiveness had long been endemic to USUN, a multilateral form of the "clientitis" afflicting State's regional bureaus. I wanted to eliminate clientitis, at least during my tenure. I also stressed the "Dick Thornburgh rule" of management: no surprises. Bad news was always welcome, but not surprises. Ric Grenell, the USUN director of communications, told the voracious press that I had "said all the right things," which was the impression everyone seemed to have. I stayed at USUN until 7:00 P.M. before going to my new residence in New York, Apartment 42-A at the Waldorf-Astoria Towers, the long-time abode of U.S. perm reps, complete with a security guard outside the entrance, and a full-time staff, who were to prove most helpful.

The next day, I turned to the most pressing problem, the fast-approaching "World Summit" to be held in mid-September, and more particularly the prosaically named "Outcome Document" that had been under negotiation for several months. The Summit was to mark the fifth anniversary of the 2000 Millennium Summit, as well as the UN's sixtieth anniversary, and was part of a chain of similar extravaganzas that had paraded through the 1990s, starting with the Rio Summit on the environment in 1992, the 1994 Cairo Conference on Population and Development, the 1995 Social Summit in Copenhagen, the 1995 Women's Summit in Beijing, and the 2000 Millennium Summit, among others. I had long believed that these gatherings, and the declarations that they invariably adopted, were potentially quite pernicious, since their decisions, although generally little-noticed in the United States, were part of the "norming" exercise that many thought was a critical role for the United Nations. The broad statements that emerged from these summits, couched in seemingly vague and general language, were often filled with buzz phrases that were far too often used later against the United States. I preferred the democratic expression of opinion in free societies like ours to make policy, rather than obscure international negotiations by the High Minded, but I was swimming against the tide in UN circles.

These sprawling, often-incoherent mass meetings, however, symbolized broader problems within the UN system, which had metastasized so far away from what the 1945 drafters of the UN Charter had in mind that the organization was almost unrecognizable except in outward form. Conceived fundamentally for collective security, the charter's preamble reflected the basic mission that had embodied so many hopes: "to save succeeding generations from the scourge of war, which twice in our lifetime has brought untold sorrow to mankind." Indeed, the very name "United Nations" was the phrase Roosevelt used in the January 1, 1942, "Declaration by the United Nations" (twenty-six in number) to describe the ultimately victorious World War II military coalition led by the United States. By calling the new organization the "United Nations," Roosevelt and the other founders advanced the implication that the successful wartime alliance would proceed seamlessly from winning the war to protecting the peace. For many Americans, the United Nations to this day remains the UN of UNICEF trick-or-treating on Halloween, and of famine-relief efforts in natural disasters, or combating diseases in developing countries.

Very quickly, however, the UN was sidelined by the Cold War, and it never regained its footing. Instead, after the wave of decolonization starting in the 1950s, the UN, which originally had 51 member states (and now has 192), was increasingly a sounding board for anti-Western and specifically anti-American criticism, used quite effectively by the Soviet bloc and its accessories. In addition, developing countries saw the UN as a place to press for increased foreign assistance, another "spigot," which was the term they revealingly used to describe sources of such aid. Americans in larger and larger numbers wondered what any of this had to do with the ideals motivating the founding of the organization and had turned away from the UN, as one offense or scandal after another piled up. By the time of my arrival, the UN was widely viewed in America as ineffective at best, and adverse to U.S. interests and deeply corrupt at worst. The audience I hope to reach with this book is not only these disillusioned Americans, but also those who still think glowingly of the UN as they had imagined it on Halloweens long ago.

Another important formality was presenting my credentials to Secretary General (SG) Kofi Annan, which I did the day after arriving in New York. Annan had just had shoulder surgery, his arm was in a sling, and he seemed very unanimated, perhaps due to his medication. Before the inevitable picture taking for the press, we traded stories about the Western Sahara, a problem still unresolved even after fifteen years with a UN peacekeeping force there. Annan advised me to ignore everything that had happened in the confirmation process, since no one in New York would care about it anyway, which turned out to be correct. Whatever else they thought, the other perm reps really wanted someone who could speak authoritatively for the United States, and they now had that.

The following days were consumed by courtesy calls on other perm reps, which I used for substantive discussions about the Outcome Document, learning their priorities and concerns, on which I could base an appropriate U.S. strategy in response. As I told the press, borrowing a line from George Shultz, "Listening is vastly underrated as a means of obtaining information." The real problem, however, was more basic. For most of 2005, the United States had been supporting Annan's version of "UN reform," which included some things of interest to us (such as a more-efficient, better-managed UN and replacing the discredited Human Rights Commission), but which also included many ideas only tangentially related to what America really wanted. In fact, there were major disagreements between Annan and the United States even in the realm of management reform. Mark Malloch Brown, Annan's chief of staff (or "chef de cabinet," as we say in UN circles), said in our first meeting on August 3 that Annan wanted more management power so that UN members could act more like a corporate board of directors. EU members accepted this analogy since it reminded them so much of their beloved European Commission, but I had no intention of allowing the UN to evolve in that direction. My aim was to increase the authority and influence of the United States, not to reduce it even further in order to enhance the SG. On this issue, we found common ground with the Third World countries, which also did not want to surrender sovereignty to the Secretariat, which they saw, most ironically, as being dominated by "the North."

Moreover, more fundamental reforms we should have been advocating—such as top-to-bottom change in how the UN is funded and
how much America pays—were not even on the table. While waiting for
weeks and months for the recess appointment, I had written out my own
"UN reforms," waiting to inject them into State's bureaucracy once I became official. At this point, however, less important than the contents of
those ideas was the ever-clearer fact that we were careening toward a September Summit and an "Outcome Document" that would allow Annan
and others to say that "reform" had been successfully achieved, and then to
go back essentially to business as usual. If that strategy succeeded, the far
more fundamental changes I believed were necessary would never even get
a hearing. All this reminded me why Gene McCarthy had been so wise in
recommending that the word "reform" be banned from the English language.

What emerged from my seemingly endless series of introductory meetings was how happy the Europeans seemed with the way things were going,
and how unhappy were the Third World countries, sometimes referred to
as "the Group of 77" (G-77), although there were actually about 130 of
them (this being the UN, who was counting?). Essentially this same group-
ing also went by the now-anachronistic Cold War name "Non-Aligned
Movement," or "NAM." Of course, we would never accept many substantive policies that countries like Pakistan, India, Egypt, and South Africa
wanted, but many European Union views weren't all that palatable either.
Although USUN had been working hard for months to get our positions
reflected in the Outcome Document, they had clearly been unsuccessful,
and I struggled to understand why.

In my first days in New York, the member governments were waiting
for the third draft of the Outcome Document to emerge from the office of
Jean Ping, foreign minister of Gabon, and the current president of the
General Assembly. Ping's unhappy responsibility was to present the Outcome Document's final draft for adoption by the September Summit, since
no one had any expectation that the heads of state and government attending the Summit would actually negotiate the text, or even read it, for that
matter. This exercise in hypocrisy was one of the real problems with the
Outcome Document (and the declarations of the prior Summits as well),
the third draft of which turned out to be almost forty single-spaced pages.
This was the product of bureaucrats, not leaders, and yet, once adopted,

many would treat its every word as secular gospel, which concerned me greatly.

Although I would be criticized later for offering hundreds of amendments to the draft that Ping produced in early August ("Ping III," as we called it), these proposed changes were written and cleared in the interagency process in Washington and were not substantially different from what the United States had been pressing in earlier iterations of the Ping draft. When I began launching these amendments, however, what really aggravated both Annan and the EU was that I went after the process they had been using, which I found to be the real source of concern. This process was not unique, and, indeed, as I complained about it during August, the puzzled response from many in the Secretariat and from European missions was that this was exactly the same process that had been used in the Millennium Summit in 2000 and many other international conferences in the past ten years. Indeed. Now I knew I was on to something.

The Outcome Document had been broken down into subject-matter sections, being handled by working groups of interested countries, each led by a "facilitator." In compiling the first draft ("Ping I"), UN members had submitted ideas of proposed language to the facilitators, each of whom produced a draft of his own section, which was then, in theory, consolidated by Ping in his capacity as president of the General Assembly. The endless meetings among delegations were not drafting or negotiating sessions, but only the presentation of prepared statements. The facilitators were doing the real drafting, deciding what to include and what not to include. In reality, Ping's facilitators were too few to undertake such a task, and substantial portions of the real work were being done by the UN Secretariat, under Annan's direction. No wonder our amendments were being regularly and routinely rejected. I am not talking here about typing and copying, but about the actual drafting of the Outcome Document, which I considered a particularly perverse approach. Member governments should draft such documents, with clerical help from the Secretariat, and perhaps even some technical advice, but no more. They worked for us, not the other way around, although that was a hard lesson for many of Annan's top people to learn.

I concluded that I had to break the "facilitator" process, which was fostering exactly the kind of substantive result we wanted to avoid. When I first floated the notion that the Outcome Document process was not entirely to our liking, the EU was not happy. Emyr Jones Parry, the U.K. perm rep (also serving as EU president, since the United Kingdom held that office for the second half of 2005), protested that people had been working hard on the Outcome Document for eight months, and that we could hardly shift now. I pointed out that people had worked hard for almost eight years on the draft verification protocol to the Biological Weapons Convention before the Bush administration had tanked that in 2001, and Jones Parry physically cringed. I could tell our relationship was off to a good start, but the British problem was not confined to Jones Parry. His deputy perm rep, Adam Thomson, in one discussion, said plaintively, "But that's the way we do things at the UN," which was not an argument to make to me. Behind his back, staffers at UKUN called Thomson, the son of a British diplomat, "Harry Potter" because of his resemblance to the character from the series of children's books. Sadly, thereafter, I could never look at or listen to Thomson without immediately thinking of Harry and all his little friends.

In my first meeting with Ping, on August 3, I proposed direct negotiations among member governments, which he obviously didn't like. Ping struck me as a sincere man, but not one likely to break out of the UN mold, especially when I heard he was leaving for vacation the next day and not returning until August 22. Like many others at the UN, Ping thought August was for vacation, and that the draft Outcome Document was in good shape. I obviously disagreed on both counts. If we didn't start changing things around, the United States would be faced with rejecting the Outcome Document on the very eve of the Summit, which many thought would make it less likely for us to take such a step. Of course, that prospect didn't bother me in the slightest, because I thought that the overhanging threat that there wouldn't be any pretentious Outcome Document at all was the biggest single piece of bargaining leverage that we had.

Back in Washington on Friday, August 5, I met with Nick Burns, the careerist who had replaced Marc Grossman as undersecretary of state for political affairs (P) and IO assistant secretary Kristen Silverberg. I had known Burns slightly in a number of prior incarnations, and I worried about his personal political preferences. There was a story circulating that, at the 2004 Wehrkunde Conference in Munich, Dick Holbrooke, after consuming several measures of the local specialty, had introduced Burns as the man who would be P when Holbrooke became secretary of state. A funny thing happened to Holbrooke, but there was Burns, nonetheless, on schedule as Holbrooke had predicted. I had first met Silverberg during the Palm Beach County recount in November 2000, and she had served in the White House in Bush's first term, advising on domestic policy.

As I explained my first week in New York, it emerged that we had a common problem in the person of Shirin Tahir-Kheli, Rice's senior adviser for UN matters. Appointed before Silverberg or I arrived, Tahir-Kheli, a naturalized citizen originally from Pakistan, had handled the reform negotiations. She supported all of Annan's proposals, but had none of her own, and her operating style in New York left USUN staff shaking their heads in dismay. Without a US perm rep around, however, no one was going to challenge someone obviously close to Rice personally, and as a result she had had a free hand. Tahir-Kheli believed, and had routinely assured Burns, that Ping would "deliver" for us, and that we would have no problems with the Outcome Document final draft. I told Burns and Silverberg that whatever Ping's intentions, it was beyond his capability to "deliver" for us, and that we were very close to being sandbagged in September. Burns and I agreed that the best thing was to put Tahir-Kheli on an airplane and get her out of New York. I also tried to explain to Burns that the real issues of "UN reform" that motivated conservative Republicans had little to do with what we were debating in New York, but I could tell I was not getting through on that point. I also tried to describe what was wrong with the overall process in New York, and why the Outcome Document was headed in the wrong direction, which Silverberg at least understood. She had said earlier, "Kofi thinks that he will give us a few things that we want in exchange for a lot of stuff we don't want." That's exactly what I intended to prevent.

Burns, Silverberg, and I later attended a Deputies Committee meeting (DC) in the White House Sit Room. I was delighted to have as many DCs as possible, because the officials attending from the NSC, OMB, Defense Department, the vice president's office, and other agencies were likely to be far more philosophically sympathetic to what I thought Bush wanted done at the UN than the State Department. J. D. Crouch chaired the meeting, and he asked Burns, as the State "deputy," to lead off the discussion of the Outcome Document. "Let's be clear," Burns opened, "we all hate this document." Burns and I offered the suggestion I had made in our earlier meeting that we replace the thirty-seven-page draft Outcome Document with something that was two to three pages long. This would be a more "leaderly" declaration, one the leaders might even read themselves, and it could be supplemented if need be by disaggregated papers on the various topics under discussion. The DC quickly agreed on this approach, as well as on the proposition that at least part of Bush's September 14 speech to the opening of the UN General Assembly should focus on the "next stages" of UN reform, to make it clear that whatever the Outcome Document said, it was only a small beginning, and not the end, as Annan and others seemed to want. With the successful conclusion of this DC in my back pocket, I returned to New York to rejoin the battle in progress, which continued for some days in one meeting after another.

During the days following my initial arrival in New York, I called dozens of senators who had been involved in the confirmation battle, starting with Chairman Lugar, to thank them for their support and to urge that we stay in touch. I also spoke with John McCain, who said, "My advice to you is kick ass and take names. Ninety percent of the American people think that that place up there needs to be massively overhauled, and you are the one to do it." Similarly, Mel Martinez said, "Don't change. Don't forget why the president sent you up there." Joe Lieberman said that, if there had ever been an up-or-down vote on my nomination, he would have voted for me since "we are very much of like minds on the key foreign policy issues." Lincoln Chafee said, "I'm grateful you reached out to me," and John Warner said I should "go at it with complete zest." There were many more to similar effect. Of particular importance, I spoke with George Voinovich on August 18, in response to a book he had sent me on Christian principles of management. I thanked him for the book and the nice letter he sent with it, and we talked about UN and USUN management and personnel issues. He concluded by saying, "I genuinely appreciate the call, and let's stay in touch," which I assured him I would do.

While all of this was swirling around, the Volcker Commission, appointed by Annan to investigate the Iraq Oil for Food scandal, issued its third report on August 8. Volcker's investigation, though limited, produced a devastating analysis, and criminal probes by the Justice Department, as well as several congressional committees, were already homing in. I met Volcker a few weeks later, in his Rockefeller Center offices, and he said that his next report would be ready right after Labor Day, just before the start of the September Summit. Volcker's findings, modest in scope though they were, combined with the prospect of a failed Summit, gave rise in the Secretariat to fears that a "perfect storm" was about to descend upon them. If the final Outcome Document was as negative from the U.S. perspective as Ping III, there would indeed be a perfect storm, but that was precisely what I was working to avoid. As for the Volcker Commission, Annan's reaction would be a real test of whether he understood just how gravely the UN had been wounded by fallout from the Oil for Food debacle. Some perm reps believed that things were so bad that Annan might resign after the September Summit, but I am unaware of any evidence that he seriously considered doing so, more's the pity.

Although the EUroids, as we called them privately, were satisfied with the Outcome Document's progress, others were not. Australian ambassador, John Dauth, for example, shared the U.S. view both on substance and on process, although he despaired of making any significant improvements. From a different direction, the Russians made it clear on August 15 they would not support the proposed new "Human Rights Council" to replace the existing commission, and the G-77/NAM were also growing increasingly restless. Munir Akram, the smooth-as-silk Pakistani perm rep, was saying that it was time to get down to line-by-line negotiation, and other Third Worlders were as well. Thus, while I had no doubt that the EU intensely disliked what I was up to, the United States was not the only dissonant voice. It finally sank in on the EU that their dream of having the rest of the UN membership somnambulantly proceed toward adopting the Outcome Document was just not going to happen. In any case, we were simply not going to accept a process in which Ping and the facilitators drafted on their own. We needed a real multilateral negotiation, during which sovereign governments could come to grips with their differences, or not, and not just endorse documents produced by facilitators, however much the EUroids liked that approach. I strongly believed they liked it precisely because they knew it would force us to swallow many provisions we otherwise would have rejected.

I resisted pressures from many countries urging the United States to lay out our "red lines," the positions we would not compromise on. They seemed to think that if only we tipped our hand, the hard negotiations would be over. I saw it differently. The Outcome Document contained a considerable amount of junk that might not violate U.S. red lines, but that we should not accept substantively. Language we accepted once would inevitably be forced upon us in the future, or would be the predicate for even worse language. Moreover, no one else wanted to reveal their red lines, and I knew exactly what would happen if we did. We would not find our positions protected. Instead, we would engage in extended discussions to see how far below our red lines we could be pushed before we finally called a halt.

I met Ping again when he returned from vacation on Monday, August 22, and by this time near panic was setting in, as the media began to appreciate that the entire pre-Summit process was in trouble. I stressed that we needed to find a new process that would allow the member governments to reach agreement on the specific words of whatever the Outcome Document turned out to look like. Silverberg said Washington was satisfied with where we were, which meant we had turned a decisive corner, away from the unacceptable facilitator process and toward real multilateral negotiations, a fairly ironic development given all of the criticism the Bush administration had received over the years for being so incorrigibly unilateralist. Many conservatives who had been ignoring the developments in New York, quite reasonably hoping they would just go away, started to express their concerns as well. In a *Washington Times* op-ed on August 23, Frank Gaffney compared my efforts to John Wayne riding to the rescue in a classic Western movie,[1] which was flattering, and almost certainly the exact opposite of Annan's view of my efforts. This was supposed to be the Summit that extricated him from the Oil for Food morass, and I was not cooperating.

The day after meeting with Ping, I sent out by fax and email the first of several "Dear Colleague" letters to all of the other missions in New York, explaining the U.S. position on negotiating the final text of the Outcome Document and urging that we move forward quickly. This "Dear Colleague" letter was an unusual thing to do, but I thought it important for the United States to communicate, in its own words, directly with every other government, rather than relying on word-of-mouth interpretations of what we were saying. When the letter leaked to the press, as was probably inevitable, it also required the reporters to report our exact words, rather than whatever spin might otherwise have suited them. I subsequently sent out "Dear Colleague" letters on the Millennium Development Goals, carefully explaining what the U.S. position was, as well as letters on our positions on

---

1. Frank Gaffney, "U.N. AmBush," *Washington Times,* August 23, 2005, p. A15, col. 1.

terrorism, the proposed Peace Building Commission, arms control and nonproliferation, and ultimately on each of the draft paragraphs that composed the Ping III draft. The letters were very well received by the other governments, precisely because they said explicitly what the U.S. position was. Terry Miller, our UNESCO observer during Bush 41, who was now in IO, was a key actor in all these efforts, and later became an ambassador at USUN dealing with economic and social issues.

While some Europeans seemed to be getting our message, others were not. Jan Eliasson, incoming president of the Sixtieth General Assembly, Ping's successor, who would be responsible for handling General Assembly action on the Outcome Document, was one of the latter. A former Swedish ambassador to Washington and former senior Secretariat official, Eliasson was in full, dreamy Dag Hammarskjöld mode when I met him in late August. When I explained our views on the Outcome Document, he actually asked me how we planned to handle American public opinion on the subject, which he had been "discovering" by giving speeches around the country. Obviously, Eliasson had not merely an ethereal Hammarskjöldian vision problem, but also a Gunnar Myrdal problem, yet another foreigner who "understood" us better than we did ourselves. I should have introduced Eliasson to the Republican senators I had been talking to for further discussion on American public opinion about the UN. Moreover, what neither Eliasson nor many others yet seemed to realize was the devastating impact the Volcker Commission's findings were having on the real American opinion about the UN. When Claudia Rosett wrote on the *Wall Street Journal*'s website that "John Bolton has a chance to be the Eliot Ness of Turtle Bay,"[2] she was talking much less about me and much more about the predominant view of what the Oil for Food scandal meant for the UN.

Rice gave me clear marching orders on Thursday, August 25, just before she departed for vacation, via a secure video transmission system. I explained that for almost four weeks I had been saying in New York that the United States had real substantive difficulties with the current draft of the Outcome Document, that we had proposed various alternative formats, including the two-to-three-page "leaderly" approach, and that we had particularly urged the commencement of real negotiations. Rice listened

---

2. Claudia Rosett, "The U.N.-Touchables," WSJ.com Opinion Journal, August 24, 2005.

carefully and said plainly she wanted to move in the direction of the two-to-three-page approach. This was obviously significant, because it would mean losing about thirty to thirty-five pages of rhetoric. Speaking with Rice just a few days later, even Annan agreed we should have a three-page document for the heads of state to agree upon, and said Ping agreed as well, although he later tried to forget he had made these observations. Although much of my negative assessment of the state of play in New York seemed new to Rice, she did not object to my overall take. In fact, after the conference call, Silverberg told me separately that she thought Rice's overall expectations for the September Summit had been usefully lowered.

Rice then wanted to discuss Tony Blair's proposal for the Security Council to have its own Summit to discuss a U.K.-drafted resolution condemning activity amounting to the incitement of terrorism, a particular problem in the United Kingdom. We had already been discussing this idea in New York, selling it to the Philippines, whose president, Gloria Macapagal-Arroyo, could chair the Summit, since the Philippines would hold the Council presidency in September. I found the British focus on the problem of inciting terrorism too narrow and was happy to hear that Washington wanted us to cover more ground, given the wide attention a Summit-level Council meeting would get.

This call with Rice was very timely. The next afternoon, Ping called a General Assembly meeting to announce he was convening a "core group" consisting of about thirty countries, to engage in genuine negotiations of the Outcome Document's seven most "controversial" (in his view) substantive areas: terrorism; the proposed Peace Building Commission; the proposed new Human Rights Council; the "responsibility to protect," a moveable feast of an idea that was the High Minded *cause du jour;* economic development, the key focus of the G-77/NAM; management reform, the key focus of the "North"; and nonproliferation and arms control, my own personal favorite. Although there was still disputation about which countries would be in the core group, Ping's idea won wide support, from both the NAM and yours truly. That got everyone's attention, especially the EU, which was still trying to process what U.S. agreement with the NAM might mean. I joked from then on that the United States should apply to join the Non-Aligned, since after all, in the UN context, we weren't aligned with anyone either.

Ping convened his first "core group" meeting on Monday, August 29, which I looked forward to so we could start substantive negotiations, rather than spinning around on purely process questions. This group was to discuss the terrorism issues, but we ran immediately into disagreement over the very definition of terrorism, which the draft Outcome Document had until then avoided. The United States believed there was no "acceptable" form of terrorism, whereas for many others, whatever steps "national liberation movements" took, especially Palestinians against Israel, were not "terrorism." That obviously wasn't going anywhere for me, and I had already coordinated our tactics with Dan Gillerman, Israel's ambassador, who saw this whole exercise as one long threat to Israel. In fact, the problems with the terrorism section were inherent in the very idea that meaningful agreements were possible, given the Outcome Document's scope. More progress might have been possible if the Summit's scope had been limited. Such a limitation, however, would have undercut the web of pretension on which the entire exercise rested.

The pretension that the UN was the right vehicle for member states to use to opine on virtually everything originated fundamentally with Annan and the Secretariat, but it was also supported by the EUroids, or at least enough of them to make a difference. They all knew, deep down, that real international agreement on so many key issues was not likely unless differences could be obscured, which was a key role for the facilitator process. If the UN could be kept in the declaration-generating business over time—and it would have to be over a *long* time—even if many of the declarations were mush, the centrality of the UN could be enhanced and the independent leeway of the United States in particular reduced. Sadly, the core group discussion dissolved into yet another process debate, which was fortunately enlivened when Venezuela's representative pounded the Venezuela name card on her desk until she was recognized. Lord, this was fun!

Ping finally decided to spin off from the "core group" a "working group" to do the actual negotiation of the terrorism section of the Outcome Document, a pattern he followed for the rest of the week. As the core-group discussions wended along, he also set up working groups for his other six substantive areas, as well as one group for all the rest of the Outcome Document. The real locus of activity shifted to the eight working groups. All of this activity was reported back to Washington in emails and cables. This intensive reporting, which was almost as taxing to the USUN staff as the actual negotiations, was necessary so that all of the myriad offices around the entire executive branch couldn't complain later that they weren't being kept in the loop.

Annan asked to see me on August 31 to discuss the Outcome Document, but it was a very perfunctory conversation. Annan looked completely preoccupied, which I ascribed to his growing concern over the next report of the Volcker Commission, drafts of which on his own conduct Volcker had allowed him to review. Chris Burnham, the relatively new undersecretary general for management, a friend from State, and a close ally in New York, showed me a copy of the executive summary of Volcker's report a couple of days later. I could understand why Annan was so preoccupied. Although Volcker did not accuse Annan of criminal conduct, he was scathing in his assessment of Annan's "management" of the Oil for Food program.

By now, more general agitation among the EUroids had started to grow, as they stirred up press stories and increased the frequency of appeals to Washington. The French, for example, tried to persuade Rice and Hadley to endorse a tax on international airplane tickets to fund Third World development projects, which was a way for France to pander to its former colonies. Elliott Abrams assured me that both Rice and Hadley felt very comfortable with the way things were proceeding in New York, and that they understood that many of the press stories had personalized my role because of that target on my back that Bush had mentioned when he announced the recess appointment. "They know it's not your fault," said Abrams, "and there are several of us down here watching your back," which was fortunate for me, and much appreciated. Some of the criticism came from our supposed friends. Several EU perm reps told me that, at an EU meeting on August 31, Jones Parry had said, "Bolton is playing his own game," and that my instructions were coming from Cheney and Rumsfeld rather than Rice. During a conversation with French deputy perm rep Michel Duclos and me a few days later, Jones Parry complained about our lack of cooperation with the EU. I thereupon confronted Jones Parry with his remarks to the EU meeting, which I said were untrue and unhelpful, and he turned whiter than normal. Duclos remained noticeably silent, but certainly did not come to Jones Parry's defense.

Much of the negative press commentary on USUN (and me personally) dealt with the changes we proposed to the text relating to the Millenium Development Goals (MDGs). These goals had been adopted by heads of state at the 2000 Millenium Summit, and we did not question them. Subsequently, the UN Development Program had created quantitative measures for the goals, which were never accepted by heads of state. Nonetheless, there was a widespread tendency to refer both to the general goals and the quantitative targets as MDGs, confusing two very different things and leading to a misapprehension of what the United States had agreed to. Before the Gleneagles G-8 Summit in 2005, State had sent out a cable explaining this distinction, and the positions we took in New York all derived from this earlier explanation. In fact, we succeeded in having the Outcome Document define MDGs according to *our* understanding of the term. So defined, we endorsed them. Criticism of us on this issue was a complete red herring, but many lazy reporters and leftist NGOs couldn't have cared less.

By the time Labor Day weekend arrived, perm reps reluctantly concluded they would have to cut into their leisure time to have any chance of finishing the Outcome Document, thus giving new meaning to the term "Labor Day," as some complained. Many working groups, which were meeting simultaneously in various conference rooms around the UN building, were getting nowhere, and the EUroids were showing signs of reverting to "facilitatorism" in their anxiety to get a document their leaders could adopt (not read, just adopt). My impression was that we were sweating out of the document a lot of the garbage language that we hadn't wanted, but that little progress was being made on resolving the really key issues. I worried throughout that Annan and the Secretariat were preparing their own draft (a "Ping IV"), which might be sprung on us without warning as a "take-it-or-leave-it" proposition. I would have "left it" in a heartbeat, given its likely content, but the pressure to have the leaders adopt *something* at the September Summit, if only to justify showing up, was intense, and at some point I worried that Washington would cave in to peer pressure on the subject.

I kept in touch with Rice by phone over Labor Day weekend and found she had been hearing from Jack Straw, doubtless relaying Jones Parry's growing frustrations. Many Brits believed that their role in life was to play Athens to America's Rome, lending us the benefit of their superior suaveness, and smoothing off our regrettable colonial rough edges. During and after World War II, there was a popular rhyme (in London at least):

> *In Washington, Lord Halifax*
> *Once whispered to Lord Keynes:*

> *"It's true they have the moneybags*
> *But we have all the brains."*[3]

Jones Parry was obviously of that ilk, but I was content to allow Athens to take a breather on this one. Rice was still quite determined, noting, "If this thing is going to collapse, I'd rather go to the wall over management reform than anything else," which was good news. I filled Rice in on the general state of play in New York, which was useful before the last week of difficult negotiations before the Summit actually convened. The *Wall Street Journal* had an editorial called "The Bolton Edit," fully supporting what I was trying to do, which was obviously quite helpful in getting around the broader explanation of what we were trying to accomplish, and the befuddling folkways of the UN.[4]

I worked through a cloud most of the weekend, first worrying about Chief Justice Rehnquist's increasingly grave condition, and then learning that he had died. Having known him and worked with him during his own 1986 confirmation battle when I was at Justice, I admired Rehnquist and thought that he would be greatly missed.

As everyone returned from Labor Day, we found that the UN and the larger press corps were focusing on Volcker's scheduled September 7 report to the Security Council on Oil for Food, rather than the arcana of our continuing negotiations over the Outcome Document. This being the UN, even on something as important as Volcker's report, process questions dominated Council preparations. The Secretariat acknowledged that Volcker would have to report in a public session, but they wanted the Council to retreat behind closed doors for "informal consultations" for the ambassadors to react to what they had heard. This was not an untypical format, where the Council would hear from the Secretariat in a public session, while the Council members remained silent, speaking only in private. I was having none of this stage-managing. The Security Council members were

---

3. Quoted in Tony Judt, *Postwar* (New York: Penguin Press, 2005), p. 160, n. 11.
4. "The Bolton Edit," *Wall Street Journal*, September 7, 2005, p. A16, col. 1. The editorial concluded: "For years, the U.N. has got by on the assumption that nobody, at least nobody in the U.S., is paying much attention. Its defenders have spun Mr. Bolton's efforts as a last-minute rogue operation designed to hurt the U.N. But in fact Mr. Bolton is doing Turtle Bay the favor of taking its words seriously. Those who want something more than a feckless and corrupt world body should welcome his efforts."

not potted plants, stage props for the Secretariat, and I had been insisting that if the Secretariat wanted to brief in public, Council members should reply in public. If the briefing was sensitive enough that it should be in private, so be it, and Council members could also respond in private. I let it be known that I planned to respond to Volcker in the public session, as each Council member had the right to do, and let the rest of them decide on their own how they would respond. Once it had become known I was going to speak, it followed, almost inevitably, that every other Council member also spoke in public.

Volcker's presentation to the Council was a blistering critique of the Secretariat's performance in Oil for Food, and was also highly critical of the Security Council for forfeiting its oversight role, which I felt was also largely justified. Established in 1995 by Resolution 986, the Oil for Food program was intended to use Iraq's oil revenues for humanitarian assistance to the Iraqi people. Instead, Saddam Hussein had used the oil revenues for bribery and corruption to manipulate the programs for his own ends, perverting it to enhance his own power by controlling the distribution of the assistance. Moreover, just days before the report, the U.S. attorney in Manhattan indicted a top UN budget official, Vladimir Kuznetsov, on corruption charges, highlighting the basic thrust of the Volcker report, not that anyone at the UN paid much attention. In fact, one senior UN official of the Oil for Food program had said in November 2004, "The scandal, quote, unquote, is, in my view, nonsense."[5] In Congress and among the American people, the reaction was exactly the opposite, highlighting a key disjunction between daily life at the UN and daily life in the United States. While the Volcker report reverberated throughout congressional debates, it sank without a trace in Turtle Bay, the picturesque name for the UN's location in Manhattan.

By Wednesday afternoon, the core group started nearly continuous drafting sessions, not that lengthening the amount of work time seemed likely to improve the quality of the finished product. During all of this, the U.S. priority on management reform was being completely obscured. Dutch perm rep Dirk Jan van den Berg, the chair of the management work-

---

5. "Oil for Food as Usual," *Wall Street Journal,* September 15, 2005, p. A16, col. 1. The *Journal*'s editorial highlighted that "the U.N.'s worst critics couldn't invent what the Volcker report reveals."

ing group, explained that their efforts were gridlocked because of "two fundamentally different views on the role of the secretary general." I tried to explain to the G-77 that the United States had no intention of transferring power from the General Assembly to the SG; surely they should recognize I would be the last person in their midst to favor reducing national sovereignty to enhance the position of the SG. What we did want was a leaner, more effective Secretariat, and one not burdened by positions like the undersecretary general and high representative for the least developed countries, landlocked developing countries, and small island developing states. Of course, what we really wanted was not more authority in the secretary general, or more authority in the General Assembly, but more responsiveness to the United States throughout the UN system. I wasn't exactly handing out leaflets to that effect. Try as I might, however, I could not get through to them, even on the severe damage the UN's reputation would suffer in the United States if we didn't address the Volcker Commission's devastating reports. The response from Stafford Neal, the Jamaican perm rep and spokesman for the G-77, was to say that references in the draft to the "Oil for Food scandal" should be changed to the "Oil for Food matter," because we shouldn't be "prejudicial." It was as though he were a UN official himself, rather than an ambassador of a sovereign nation.

The negotiations were now at an obviously critical point, with just days remaining before the Summit opening and huge swaths of the Outcome Document nowhere near agreement. With tensions rising, there were moments inexplicable to those unfamiliar with the UN's folkways. At one point, a senior U.S. careerist said of our efforts, "The time for negotiation is finished; it's time to start giving." I could only hope that that sentiment wasn't too widespread among our negotiators. By Saturday, September 10, the media were reporting deep divisions within the UN membership, but noticeably not pointing the finger at the United States. For once, the reporting had the virtue of being accurate.

On Sunday, September 11, we were back at it at 8:20 A.M., still not making any progress, and I started to worry again that Annan and the Secretariat were preparing their own alternative draft that would emerge as a "take-it-or-leave-it" proposition that we would find most unhelpful. Then two positive developments occurred. First, the Brits had prepared "harvest texts" on terrorism, and the proposed Human Rights Council and Peace Building Commission, which were in fact "honest broker" drafts that left out all of the contentious points on terrorism, the HRC, and the PBC, and they were quickly agreed to. Second, since there were still large areas of the Outcome Document in brackets, with almost no time left, Akram of Pakistan and I both argued that the only way to finish in the other areas was to start throwing overboard text where there was no agreement, which approach an informal caucus of perm reps agreed to. We worked until nearly midnight, and did succeed in tossing aside more language where we were never going to agree, but we were still a long way from being finished.

On Tuesday, September 13, President Bush was due to arrive in the afternoon for the start of the Summit, and we still had no Outcome Document. I called Jones Parry at 8:30 A.M., and he said he had never been this close to such an important event without a final text, and that the "prospect of a text from somewhere" might still arise. That was all I needed to hear. I immediately called Annan, who equivocated on what Ping and Eliasson were up to. Quite obviously, Ping, Eliasson, and the Secretariat had already been working away on "filling in the gaps," as Annan had put it. Annan said that perhaps he and Ping could explain to me how they could "build on the text that has been agreed," and suggested that I come to his office.

I reached the thirty-eighth floor at about 9:15 A.M., and was immediately ushered down to Annan's office where he, Ping, Eliasson, and Robert Orr, an American Secretariat staffer who had once worked for Clinton UN ambassador Richard Holbrooke, were assembled. They clearly had a new text already prepared, which was largely Orr's work, and Annan asked him to explain what he had done to produce a "clean text." Orr said that the Secretariat had basically accepted all of the language the United States wanted on management reform issues, and had not crossed any of our red lines on trade, debt, climate change, or any other major issue. The section on non-proliferation, arms control, and small arms/light weapons had been completely eliminated. I asked what the text said on the International Criminal Court (ICC), and Orr said they had a favorable reference to it in a larger paragraph on "impunity," saying that Annan would take a beating if there were no ICC reference. I made it clear that I wanted the ICC language out entirely, and the group reluctantly agreed. I also insisted on removing all references to national liberation movements in the terrorism section, which Annan also agreed to.

On the document overall, however, I obviously couldn't agree until I had a chance to review the whole thing, and I asked when a copy might be available for inspection. "Noon," said Eliasson, but Annan quickly interjected that they would give me a copy as soon as our meeting broke up. That was the right answer. Annan said they would make the additional changes I wanted during the rest of the morning and try to persuade everyone else to accept the inevitable. I didn't entirely like this method, because even here at the end, nameless, faceless drafters in the Secretariat were still drafting, hoping to produce something they could sell as a victory for Annan. Substantively, though, it appeared as if we were coming out better than I might have predicted, so I decided to hold my fire on the process points. I raced back to the mission with the text that Orr had given me and distributed it for copying to the many U.S. experts working on the different sections. We found several passages that still caused us heartburn, which we called to Orr's attention, and which he agreed to fix. As the morning wore on, however, Jones Parry—who had quite likely seen Annan's latest draft well before I did—called to say that Ping was waffling on what to do next, obviously under withering G-77/NAM pressure, given that the text now tilted so far away from what they wanted.

Ping finally started the final core group meeting at 1:25 P.M., handing out the "final" version of the text, which our experts immediately pored through, finding that every fix or change we had asked for had in fact been made. After Ping finished explaining what "he" had done to come up with this text (meaning, of course, what the Secretariat had done), Jones Parry took the floor for the EU to rhapsodize about how wonderful the text was, which was more than the traffic would bear for me. I left the large conference room where we were meeting just before 3:00 P.M. to meet Bush and Rice, instructing Anne Patterson not to say anything on behalf of the United States. As other delegations expressed their support for Ping's draft, in one final telling anecdote, Jones Parry came over to where the United States was sitting to try to persuade Patterson to say something. He even wrote out talking points for her to use until the Conference on Disarmament ambassador, Jackie Sanders, who was in New York working on the nonproliferation section, said, "Anne, I don't think John wants you to say anything." With that Jones Parry retreated to his delegation. While it was clear this had not been the first time he had written speeches for the United States to give, I was determined that it would be the last, and it was. Athens could take the rest of the day off.

Looking back over the seemingly endless saga of the Outcome Document negotiations (even though I was only involved for a month and a half), I judged that we had put the shoe on the other foot for a change, turning the normal dynamic in the United Nations, which worked against the United States, back against those who disagreed with us. We had made the desperation of Annan and the EU to have an agreed-upon Outcome Document work in our favor, rather than against us. Instead of the United States' being jammed into accepting language it did not like, many of the others had been jammed into accepting a declaration that had little that they found helpful after nine long months of effort.

The Outcome Document looked like nothing the United States would have written on its own, and it still contained a lot of ash and trash, but we had at least held our red lines. We even made a few advances, such as re-establishing our clear opposition to the foreign aid target of 0.7 percent of donor-country GNPs, a decades-old NAM/G-77 Holy Grail intended to keep up high levels of foreign aid flows without regard to their desirability or effectiveness.[6] This minimal achievement had taken almost seven weeks of continuous, often late-night and early-morning, efforts by dozens if not hundreds of U.S. government employees, all resulting in a lengthy document with far more words than meaning. Moreover, little or nothing had been accomplished toward what the United States really needed as "reform," and it was clearer than ever that we needed an *American* reform plan, not simply something that Annan had come up with to increase his own independence. After this long struggle over the Outcome Document, I can say only that we achieved the UN's most common benchmark: "It could have been worse." I certainly never plan to read it again. I doubt many others will either.

In any case, I had an arriving president to worry about. I waited at the base of the escalators just inside the delegates' entrance to the UN, as security had requested. Bush and Rice, accompanied by the Secret Service and others, swept in just after 3:00 P.M. This was the first time I had seen Bush

---

6. We did have one reservation to make, on the document's "reproductive health language." Although the Bush administration had agreed some years earlier in some statement somewhere, the language in question still bothered right-to-life groups. Accordingly, with Rice's personal approval, I made the "explanation of vote" (EOV) containing the standard Bush administration reservation in the early-evening proceedings of the General Assembly on Tuesday, September 13.

since the August 1 ceremony in the Roosevelt Room, so I was curious whether he had any advice or criticism of the past several weeks. After the standard photo opportunity with Annan, we headed to the SG's tiny ceremonial office behind the General Assembly stage for Bush's annual courtesy call. As everyone sat down, Bush asked Annan, "How's Bolton doing? Has he blown the place up yet?" I thought this was hilarious, but Annan only smiled wanly, perhaps thinking of the wringer I had just put him through on the Outcome Document. In fact, Annan told the press later in the day I had been "very constructive" during the Outcome Document negotiations, which certainly made it hard to blame the U.S. government for its minimal substance.

In any event, Bush was only warming up. After the pleasantries, he said that, for most Americans, the real question was whether to be in the UN at all. Unlike New York, said Bush, out where he came from, that's what people actually thought, not that he himself believed it, you understand, but he just wanted to let Annan know that's where things stood. The smiles on the UN side of the tiny meeting room were growing more forced. Bush then turned to Iran, noting that "we need to solve this diplomatically," or the Israelis would solve it some other way. By this time, Annan had recovered enough to say he had recently spoken with Mohamed el Baradei, director general of the International Atomic Energy Agency, to encourage Iran to be more cooperative. After describing North Korea as one of the worst examples of repression in history, Bush then raised the question of Iraq, saying that he wanted a greater UN presence there to help out on the pending constitutional referendum. Annan fell back to his perennial excuse since the bombing of the UN compound in Baghdad—that there was not enough security—which Bush and Rice both refuted. Bush criticized Syria for continued interference in Lebanon, but Annan seemed to lose focus and was unable to discuss the situation coherently.

After some additional desultory chatter, Bush went to the nearby office of General Assembly president Eliasson, for yet another annual courtesy call. Bush reiterated what he'd said to Annan about the lack of American public support for the UN, which prompted Eliasson, Swede extraordinaire, to explain American public opinion back to Bush. Bush just looked at him and said patiently, "If there were a referendum today, I don't think the UN would win," which pretty much ended that discussion, other than for Bush to say, "That's why we sent Bolton up here, to get things fixed." Bush visibly lost interest in further conversation with Eliasson, so the discussion wrapped up. That evening, Bush gave his reception for other heads of state and government in the Waldorf's Starlight Roof room, where Gretchen and I served as greeters. We rubbed shoulders with the kings and queens of Spain and Jordan and other lesser lights, until Bush spoke briefly and then left at 8:20 P.M., bringing a long day to an end.

The next morning, at nine o'clock, Gretchen and I waited for Rice in the small lobby of the Waldorf Towers, and then climbed into jump seats in the presidential limousine to wait for the president and Mrs. Bush to arrive, and then we were off, tearing down Fiftieth Street on the way to the UN, then going the "wrong way" down First Avenue to make the trip as quick as possible. As Bush waved at a group of Falun Gong demonstrators protesting against the repressive policies of the Chinese leadership, the subject of Bill Clinton somehow came up, and I observed that both Bill and Hillary Clinton had graduated a year ahead of me from Yale Law School, and Bush said, "Before you had the mustache?" to the general merriment of the ladies in the car. I would have explained that actually I already had the mustache in law school, but by that time we were arriving at the UN.

We went to the holding area behind the General Assembly podium, where Bush reviewed his remarks one more time before addressing what the White House staff called "the wax museum," because of the Assembly's annual lack of enthusiasm for Bush, particularly in contrast to Clinton. Rice, Hadley, and I walked out to the U.S. seats in the General Assembly Hall, and Gretchen joined Mrs. Bush and Mrs. Annan in the observer section. As predicted, Bush's speech was greeted politely, but no more than that. Afterward, we headed to the Security Council chamber for the Summit on terrorism, where Bush would deliver another set of remarks. The forgettable British draft resolution on terrorism and an equally forgettable African resolution on conflict prevention were both adopted unanimously, with the customary raising of hands. On the first vote, Bush raised his arm only slightly, so I leaned forward and whispered firmly "higher." Realizing in nanoseconds what I had just done, I quickly whispered just as emphatically, "sir," which at least gave Rice and Hadley a laugh.

Bush spoke fourth among the fifteen Council members, and then followed the sequence of events soon to be known worldwide as "the Bush bathroom break." Perhaps not having been briefed that press cameras were above and behind him in the Council chamber, Bush had written a note asking where the bathrooms were. Ambassadors have many duties, not all of which are written in their formal letter of instructions, and I didn't shirk mine. Not knowing that all of this was on film, I explained that I could get the president to the desired location, and that Rice could take his chair at the Council table. Bush waited until Tony Blair finished speaking, and then the two of us got up and I led him to the private bathroom in the SG's tiny office near the Council chamber, which the diligent Secret Service had already scoped out.

While we were waiting for a polite moment to return to the Council table, after the president of Benin had finished speaking, Bush asked, "How do you like it up here? Are you having fun?" I responded, "It's a target-rich environment," and we went back into the chamber for Bush to resume his seat. The less-than-scintillating meeting broke at about noon and off we raced to a basement UN conference room for the first meeting of the heads of state of Bush's Democracy Initiative. Security was intense throughout Bush's visit, but we learned later that someone had made his way into the crowd of heads of state assembled for the "class picture" customary at such events, which was disconcerting to say the least; as for the picture, the prankster was airbrushed out. After the secretary general's annual lunch at the start of the General Assembly, Bush left New York, and my new life as an ambassador returned more or less to normal.

CHAPTER EIGHT

SISYPHUS IN THE TWILIGHT ZONE[1]: FIXING THE BROKEN INSTITUTION, OR TRYING TO

Our guest today has one serious disadvantage . . . [compared to] Hercules. The disadvantage is that the stable he has been sent to clean is not standing empty of the animals that once lived there. It is still very full.

—MIDGE DECTER, INTRODUCING JOHN BOLTON AT THE MANHATTAN INSTITUTE, DECEMBER 7, 2005[2]

A Limit on Spending Money? At the UN?

Bolton Agitates Audience.

—*YALE DAILY NEWS* HEADLINE, OCTOBER 4, 2005

Although the Summit's Outcome Document should have launched a major UN reform effort, that did not happen. As Gene McCarthy had observed, because "reform" means so many different things to so many different people, effectively it means nothing. That was right on target at the UN. Kofi Annan had produced his version of "reform" in March 2005, en-

---

1. See Brett Stephens, "Our Man in the Twilight Zone: The Weekend Interview with John Bolton," *Wall Street Journal*, Saturday, September 17, 2005, p. A14, col. 3.

2. http://www.manhattan-institute.org/html/past_events_2005.htm.

titled "In Larger Freedom: Toward Development, Security and Human Rights for All," a grab-bag of ideas ranging from enlarging Security Council membership to management reform, and everything in between, including creating a new "Human Rights Council," dealing with terrorism, economic development, and almost anything else one could imagine at the UN. The report's central premise reflected UN theology: Everything is related to everything else, and therefore everything is a priority. Annan's report went so far as to say all its reforms had to be accepted as a "package," all or nothing, which was as unrealistic as it was presumptuous from a UN bureaucrat. "In Larger Freedom" was really pursuing "In Larger Kofi," the continuing legacy project for rescuing Annan's diminished reputation from the Oil for Food scandal. In fact, the Secretariat intended the Outcome Document to validate "In Larger Freedom." Once endorsed, "In Larger Freedom" would be hailed as Annan's vindication, and sweetness and light would return to Turtle Bay, "a new San Francisco moment," as Annan himself described it in a further burst of presumptuousness.[3] My interference with these happy plans explained the outrage that greeted my suggestion that UN member nations might actually negotiate what their heads of state would later "agree to," rather than leaving it to facilitators and the Secretariat to tell us what they decided.

In fact, Annan's report dealt only in part with what, for the United States, was the true objective of UN reform: changing the governance and management of a thoroughly discredited and dysfunctional institution that had changed little since the Bush 41 administration. What we wanted from "reform" was a more effective, responsive, and transparent UN—like the "Unitary UN" concept I'd developed when I was IO assistant secretary—not, as Annan recommended, one that would ignore its current failings by tackling even more challenges beyond its competence. Thus, from the outset of my tenure, there was a disconnect between what Annan wanted and what the UN needed.

Having at least blocked the worst excesses of the Outcome Document, and with that paper chase behind us, I wanted to get on with "real reform." The Oil for Food scandal had raised tempers in Congress, and the prospects were very real for another wave of legislative withholdings of our

---

3. Kofi Annan, " 'In Larger Freedom': Decision Time at the UN," 84 *Foreign Affairs*, Number 3, May/June 2005, p. 65.

assessed contributions, as happened in the mid-1980s and mid-1990s. (In 2006, our assessments for the regular UN budget were just under $423,464,855, and for peacekeeping operations, $1,399,027,000.) In fact, Henry Hyde's bill would cut our assessed contributions by 50 percent if thirty-two of thirty-nine specified reform conditions were not met, and it had passed the House on June 17. Even if its fate in the Senate was uncertain, the bill was a sign of Republican rumblings of mutiny against the administration position that we should pay our full assessments. Hyde, Norm Coleman, Chris Shays, and others had also been investigating the Oil for Food scandal, and Hyde's staff told me that Richard Goldstone, a South African jurist and member of the Volcker Committee, had argued that the committee should apply a different standard of culpability to Annan than to mere mortals under investigation. While Volcker properly rejected this argument, the anecdote reflected the prevailing UN mind-set, one that could be devastating if discontent in Congress became too advanced.

Leading our reform charge, Rice presented the annual U.S. address to the General Assembly opening session on Saturday morning, September 17, stressing that the UN needed a "revolution of reform," a striking statement from an American secretary of state, one that would prove extremely useful in the upcoming debates. Nonetheless, it was clear from all of my study of the UN, before and after my nomination, as well as my intense activity while in New York, that no "revolution" would emerge from the Outcome Document's "reform" goals. In fact, even those limited objectives were not achievable unless we focused on broader, more sweeping changes to the UN beyond the limited field of "management reform." This, in turn, required me to move the U.S. government away from the largely passive approach it had been following thus far in Bush's second term, following and not leading. I had, after all, said years before, "If the UN Secretariat building in New York lost ten stories, it wouldn't make a bit of difference," and that still seemed true to me. In fact, on September 19, just before the annual SG lunch for the Perm Five foreign ministers, the Secretariat building lost power when a generator blew, requiring UN employees to be sent home, leading Annan's chief of staff Malloch Brown to say, "This will be a test of your theory, John, to see if anyone notices." Jack Straw said to me after the lunch, "They'll never live this down," and de La Sablière joked that undoubtedly the power failure would be blamed on me.

In the meantime, however, I was more worried about a power failure among the UN's member governments, and losing what little political momentum there was in New York. My first thought was to enlist the Brits and the French, so I arranged a meeting on September 22 with Jones Parry and de La Sablière at the French Mission, located near the UN. We agreed that the Secretariat had to provide very promptly the management reports required by the Outcome Document, and we agreed to meet Malloch Brown to develop a schedule. I was astounded at that meeting, on September 27, to hear that the first reports wouldn't arrive until February 2006, which demonstrated a lack of Secretariat seriousness. Moreover, Annan wanted to bring in someone from "the outside" to lead the management reform effort, as if it were some extraneous task that the UN's existing managers were too busy to undertake. I said this was hardly the "revolution" Rice had called for. We needed to undertake substantial reforms in fall 2005, and reflect them in the two-year budget adopted by December 31 (the current two-year budget expiring on that date). Reform would be stillborn if we waited until after adoption of the next budget. I also said that importing an outsider to do the heavy lifting meant everyone else in the Secretariat would resume "business as usual," precisely the opposite of what we wanted. There was an uncomfortable silence, but then both Jones Parry and de La Sablière agreed with my assessment.

At this same time, I was working on testimony to be delivered to the House International Relations Committee (HIRC), chaired by Hyde, where I planned to lay out for the first time as UN ambassador the only reform that mattered: shifting the UN system from assessed contributions to voluntary contributions. The NSC staff fully supported this approach, but Nick Burns was trying to rewrite it. I testified to HIRC on September 28, and despite enormous difficulties in getting the testimony cleared by Burns, I was able to make this fundamental point:

> I also note, as this committee has observed, that there are differences in performance based on the way different entities were funded. UN agencies are primarily funded through assessed contributions, while funds and programs are typically funded through voluntary contributions. Catherine Bertini, former UN secretary general for management, and former head of the World Food Program (WFP), noted that "voluntary funding creates an entirely different atmosphere at WFP than at the UN. At WFP, every staff member knows

that we have to be as efficient, accountable, transparent, and results-oriented as is possible. If we are not, donor governments can take their funding elsewhere in a very competitive world among UN agencies, NGOs, and bilateral governments."

I concluded that we needed "to help break the sense of entitlement that is pervasive in some quarters." This was a pale shadow of what I wanted to say, and what NSC staff would have supported, but I had at least gotten the assessed-versus-voluntary-contributions debate started. I also made this point in a speech at the Yale Political Union on October 3, which helped prompt the headline at the start of this section. (JS was a Union member, and later, as a Junior, became chairman of its Tory Party.)

Malloch Brown briefed the HIRC after I finished, and argued against voluntary contributions on the ground that countries would then only pay for what they wanted. No kidding! Even in its watered-down version, however, my testimony produced a stunning outcome. Malloch Brown called Burns, a frequent channel of communication, and Burns later sent IO assistant secretary Silverberg a handwritten note reading: "Kristen—I do not believe we should speculate on voluntary funding in public comments. Kofi + MMB are unhappy." This was an extraordinary comment by an American official, submitting to direction from "unhappy" UN bureaucrats, but it fully reflected the difficulties inside State in getting a really *American* reform agenda rolling. By contrast, when Silverberg and I met privately with Josh Bolten, then OMB director, on December 9, he immediately understood why a shift to voluntary contributions would be entirely sensible. I have never wavered from the view that voluntary funding is the only meaningful UN reform, the mere discussion of which in UN circles would be enormously helpful in pushing through lesser reforms, just as a strong wind cleanses as it blows.

Critical to our management reform efforts within the Secretariat was Chris Burnham, who had become undersecretary general for management on June 1, after leaving his previous Department of State position as chief financial officer. In my first meetings with Jones Parry, Duclos, and Malloch Brown in early August 2005, they all complained about Burnham's remarks in a press interview that his primary loyalties lay with the United States, arguing that these comments undermined reform. Of course, Burnham had only said about the United States what many Secretariat officials felt about their own countries, and his sin had simply been to say it publicly. Moreover, the complaints said more about the complainers and the UN mind-set than they did about Burnham. What did Burnham's patriotism have to do with management reform? Nothing, of course, except to provide one more excuse why it was never going to happen.

Annan's continuing inability to deal with someone like Burnham was magnified by the political direction he and General Assembly president Jan Eliasson wanted to take. Despite Rice's emphasizing that management reform was the top U.S. priority, Eliasson and Annan barely had it on their radar screens. "Reform" to them meant stressing UN economic development activities, creating a "Peace Building Commission," and replacing the discredited Human Rights Commission. I told Eliasson in late September that dropping management reform into the basement on the priority list would mean we never got to it. Burnham's exclusion from Annan's inner circle and Eliasson's leftist tilt and excessive view of his own importance were powerful early indicators that the status quo was going to prevail in our reform battle.

The Peace Building Commission (PBC), which Eliasson decided to push first, hoping to build "goodwill" with the G-77, was a classic example of UN thinking. Based on the blinding insight that there were always nonmilitary issues associated with trying to solve either a civil war or an international conflict, Annan's response was to propose a new institution to handle the "peace building" activities, which were rarely discussed with any specificity. One might think that the Security Council had the wit to understand that resolving conflicts involved more than just military issues, but that would imply a larger Council role than the G-77 wanted. In fact, the UN's operations in Namibia, El Salvador, and Mozambique had already involved the successful conduct or monitoring of elections in order to end conflicts, so this was hardly new or different from the Council's perspective. In addition, one might turn to ECOSOC, the Economic and Social Council, a UN "principal organ," after all, although it had barely functioned since its creation in 1945. However, instead of using the Security Council, which sometimes functioned, or fixing ECOSOC, which didn't, Annan proposed creating a third body.

As I and others predicted, the debate over creating the PBC turned almost entirely on how its members would be selected, and therefore who would have the dominant influence in its deliberations. The United States was determined that the PBC not become a backseat driver for the Security Council, while others had exactly the opposite objective: lessening the Council's role in UN affairs. The main problem, however, was the basic idea of creating a new entity, which could be listed as an achievement in Annan's legacy project, rather than repairing what already existed, which would attract much less media attention. Most important, there was a fundamental conceptual divide over whether the PBC would be advisory (our view) or operational (the G-77 view), which in part reflected its morganatic origins and the continued fuzziness in Annan's thinking.

While we were dithering at the UN, however, life went on elsewhere, including another opportunity for me to make the point about moving from assessed to voluntary contributions in an SFRC hearing on October 18. My testimony was essentially the same as what I had given to the HIRC, but I found I was beginning to enjoy testifying on the Hill again. The Democratic staffers based their questions on recent press stories, many of which were distorted, such as on the Millenium Development Goals, thus giving me a chance to make full, on-the-record explanations of my position. It was wonderful. Equally intriguing, Voinovich, who stayed for most of the hearing, wished me well in New York, thanking me for a recent phone call. Our very pleasant exchange on management reform issues jolted the press out of their slumbers.

But more important, Paul Volcker briefed the SFRC on his investigation of the Oil for Food scandal. Volcker testified about the "deep-seated systemic problems in UN administration" and stressed that "the importance of maintaining high ethical standards has been lost." Norm Coleman asked if he thought there was a "culture of corruption" at the UN, and Volcker replied there was not, although there was corruption, and that the real problem was "a culture of inaction." I could not have said it better. Indeed, by early November, Natwar Singh, India's foreign minister, resigned because of the Oil for Food scandal, a sensation in India, but barely a ripple in New York. Another mere ripple was the story of Annan's son, Kojo, avoiding Ghanaian taxes on a new Mercedes under the pretense it was for Kofi. So offended was Annan at even being asked questions about his son's misuse of his official UN position that he refused to answer, calling James Bone from the *Times* of London a "schoolboy" for being so uppity as to ask. "No jokes in church," Bill Buckley had said, and certainly not about the "secular pope" as Annan's staff had tried to characterize him in earlier press backgrounders.

In the meantime, in New York, things were going nowhere, except on the PBC, where President of the World Eliasson was chugging right along. On November 1, I had a very tough conversation with him, stressing we were very displeased that our reform priorities were disappearing. At our present rate of speed, our only achievement by the end of the year would be creating one new institution, the PBC, and failing to change anything else. Fortunately, the Perm Five were holding together in their determination to keep the PBC role limited and advisory, except for Jones Parry. I couldn't tell if this was due to personal weakness, or was the institutional Foreign Office view that the best way to keep alive Britain's tenuous claim to permanent member status was by constantly abasing itself before the G-77. Watching Jones Parry in action, I often wondered how Britain had acquired an empire, although he proved why they had lost America.

With December 31 looming, and no reports from the Secretariat in sight, I began proposing the idea of an "interim budget," perhaps for the first quarter of 2006, rather than a regular two-year budget. This approach would allow us more time to evaluate the mandate reforms that might be possible, and then reflect whatever changes we made in the final two-year budget. This had never been done before, reason enough for many G-77ers to oppose it, but Japan and others increasingly saw the "interim budget" concept as an important way to leverage real management reform. We certainly weren't going to get it any other way. Paul Volcker saw the dangers in a business-as-usual approach and told a luncheon audience at New York's University Club that adopting a regular two-year budget would send the wrong signal about reform efforts. President Bush, after seeing a press story with my statements on the UN budget, called Rice to tell her he liked my approach, which helped stiffen even Burns in his public comments.[4]

Annan, however, continued to agitate that we were planning to leave the UN without a budget, which I repeatedly explained was not correct. Our whole point in proposing an interim budget was to allow the UN to con-

---

4. Frederick Kempe, "The U.N.'s Bolton Moment," *Wall Street Journal*, November 29, 2005, p. A4, col. 1.

tinue operating while we worked out the key reforms. We wanted reform to drive the budget, not the other way around, an idea obviously foreign to Annan's bureaucratic universe. Although Annan made public statements about "boldness" and "speed" in the reform effort, his words were not backed by actions, especially as time dragged on and he failed to provide the critical information we needed. After one meeting in Annan's thirty-eighth-floor office at which we went through this drill, I sat next to Annan at the monthly Security Council–SG lunch. I noticed that Annan could not seem to keep his hands still, patting his lap with both hands from time to time, and continually fiddling with his note cards, which he always spoke from, even in informal settings such as the lunch. I thought perhaps Annan might be suffering from a medical condition, but my wife, Gretchen, said his fidgeting was undoubtedly caused by having to sit next to me.

Indeed, while Annan wailed that he had to have a regular two-year budget, Chris Burnham told me privately that the UN could live with a nine-month or even a six-month budget. The only real problem with a three- or six-month interim budget was concern about cash flow, caused by uncertainty about the assessment mechanism, which ran on an annual basis. A one-year budget, said Burnham, by definition eliminated the cash-flow problem. I pocketed this information and continued to push for something less than a full year, to signal more dramatically that reform was more than just empty rhetoric. I had by then privately concluded that an acceptable compromise was a one-year budget, but with the Secretariat's authorization to spend funds ending after six months, which would require a General Assembly vote to turn the money back on.

I worked with increasing optimism to round up support for our linkage of the budget and reform issues, starting with Japan, and bringing along the "CANZ" group, so named from the initials of Canada, Australia, and New Zealand, three other former British colonies more likely to side with us than with the colonial master. Japan and the United States met regularly with CANZ, as they did already in some other UN contexts, thus forming "JUSCANZ," pronounced "juice cans." This thoroughly confounded the UN press corps, whose computer screens seemed to be locked in to saying that the United States was always "isolated." I also tried to energize other major contributors, but with mixed success. Germany's perm rep, Gunter Pleuger, was the worst. The only time I pitied Jones Parry during his EU presidency was when Pleuger leaked internal EU discussions to India and

Pakistan in hopes of undercutting EU positions Pleuger didn't like. Of course, that also reminded me of how much of the U.S. government worked. In addition, the General Assembly's Fifth Committee, which was responsible for budget matters, was heading toward a total breakdown. Whatever agreement we might reach on an interim budget, the Fifth Committee was nowhere near concluding its regular task of examining the budget and presenting its conclusions to the Assembly. For example, the committee had jettisoned Volcker's recommendation for an external auditing capability in favor of a much weaker advisory committee, and even that was in trouble.

Work on the PBC began to come to a head on the afternoon of December 6 with an "informal" General Assembly meeting chaired by perm reps Augustine Mahiga of Tanzania and Ellen Loj of Denmark. They reported there were only two outstanding issues: the PBC's relationship to the Security Council and whether all five permanent members would be on the PBC's key "Organizational Committee." Of course, these were the two issues that mattered most to the United States, so it was not surprising they were still disputed. Interestingly, a split had developed in the G-77/NAM, as Africans figured out they had the most to gain through a strong Security Council role, which was most likely to ensure that anything actually got done. South African perm rep Kumalo endorsed the U.S. view that the General Assembly and the Security Council should act concurrently to establish the PBC, what Kumalo called the "simultaneous and identical" actions of the two bodies. China explained that there was a common Perm Five position that we should be members of the PBC's "Organizational Committee," something that Jones Parry had been taking pains to hide. The British wanted to be a Perm Five member, but they just didn't want to do anything about it. I happily supported both the Chinese and the African views, as did the Russians.

Eliasson resisted the PBC's clear subordination to the Security Council and an express role for the Perm Five, but our persistence wore him down. He needed a PBC for his and Annan's legacy list, whereas I did not, so I used his "zeal for the deal" against him, as others used it so frequently against the United States. I knew he would give in, and he did. As is often the case at the UN, the debate came down to one word in the draft resolution creating the PBC, inserting "the" before the term "permanent members," thus denoting that *all*, not merely some of them, would be on the

PBC Organizational Committee. No wonder defending the United States at the UN requires picky negotiators!

On Tuesday, December 20, the Council unanimously adopted Resolution 1645, creating the PBC, followed a few minutes later by the General Assembly. I made an "explanation of vote" stressing the PBC's subordination to the Security Council, while the perm reps from Pakistan and Egypt complained that everything associated with the PBC had been dominated by the Council. That certainly made my day.

Predictably, the PBC has done little since its December 2005 creation, but the act of creating it took up enormous amounts of time and unquestionably diverted us from real reform efforts. Moreover, creating the PBC did not buy the West an ounce of "goodwill" from the G-77, which simply pocketed it and moved on to its next demands.

In the meantime, Annan continued trying to head off an interim budget, calling Rice on December 16 to say that reform was proceeding just fine and that he wanted to send her a "compromise" on the budget issue. Rice pushed back, but Burns reported a few days later that Malloch Brown had sent him the "compromise," which he forwarded to me. The "compromise" turned out to say simply that we would "review" the budget six months into 2006, which was nowhere close to requiring another affirmative General Assembly vote before new money could be spent. I briefed Rice via videoconference on the lack of progress in New York, which she agreed was appalling, and before I could even raise the Annan "compromise," she said it was obviously insufficient. We needed an "action-forcing mechanism," which is what our interim-budget proposal was. Rice spent a lot of time shaking her head in dismay and sent me back to the struggle reinforced in my view that Washington was fully behind my approach.

As always, the EU had another fallback position (they never ran out), this one in essence expressing the six-month cut-off we wanted in budget terms rather than calendar terms. The EU proposed that the Secretariat's spending authority expire after half the 2006 budget (about $950 million) was disbursed, thus requiring a General Assembly vote to authorize expenditure of the remaining half. This "commitment cap" approach was acceptable to me, especially since the Secretariat, particularly Controller Warren Sachs, yet another Brit, working directly for Annan and Malloch Brown, had designed it, thus signaling to the G-77 that the Secretariat could live with the mechanism. We now had Annan's buy-in, and everyone knew it.

Moreover, we were now close to having sewn up EU support, considerable progress in just a short time, when the United States had stood almost alone on this issue. Nonetheless, the G-77 was in turmoil, going through endless meetings to try to reach a position on the commitment cap. Jones Parry, apparently unable to sit still, was trying to compromise again, working with Eliasson and Malloch Brown even before we knew where the G-77 would come out, proposing a nine-month cut-off (a commitment cap of three-quarters of the 2006 budget, $1.35 billion). I rejected the idea and told Malloch Brown and Eliasson to get out of the way of what were fundamentally negotiations among member governments. Malloch Brown was, coincidentally, somewhat diverted by press stories that he was receiving two paychecks for his services, which he denied.

The EU, however, was still negotiating with the G-77. I worried they would cut some kind of deal, leaving the United States isolated, but Burnham was confident the G-77 would accept the commitment cap because "we're at the brink and they have no missiles." That was true, but careful reasoning had rarely slowed the G-77. By Thursday morning, December 22, therefore, I decided it was time to break into the EU/G-77 discussions, buttressed by news that Japanese perm rep Oshima had received overnight from Tokyo firm instructions to stick with the United States. I persuaded JUSCANZ to make our commitment cap proposal $900 million, a bit lower than precisely one-half of the 2006 budget, to give us a little bargaining flexibility, mostly to limit the EU's ability to give away the store. Oshima floated our $900 million figure at a previously scheduled lunch, hosted by Canada's Alan Rock, to the amazement of many G-77ers. Egypt's clever and talented perm rep, Maged Abdelaziz, asked why the G-77 was negotiating with the EU if the EU wasn't representing the U.S. position. Of course, I had suspected Jones Parry of disingenuousness in his EU/G-77 negotiations for some time, and I now had it all out in the open. This outcome was wonderful, because I believed that the G-77 would refuse to negotiate further unless the United States was in the talks, which was exactly what I wanted.

Jones Parry replied that he was representing only the EU, but of course he would never agree to anything with the G-77 he didn't think the United States could accept. This response, of course, obscured a typical EU negotiating tactic: They would agree to something below the actual U.S. red line but say it was acceptable to them and that they were prepared to sign off on it. That left the United States in an untenable position: either continue to insist on its position and risk being isolated (a form of hell for career diplomats) or give in to what the EU had negotiated and lose important substantive ground. I was determined to break this cycle, as I had during the negotiations over the Outcome Document, and engage directly with the G-77. I started this right after lunch by addressing a meeting of the full Africa Group, the largest of the UN's five regional groups. I felt I could get a better deal for the United States, namely preserving the six-month commitment cap as an action-forcing mechanism, which was important because Annan was not letting the idea of a nine-month commitment cap die.

Now, the idea of a nine-month cap was not simply a three-month add-on to my proposal for a six-month cap. Nine months from December 31 would take us to the end of September 2006, right after the midmonth start of the next General Assembly and the arrival in New York of many dozens of heads of state, foreign ministers, and their entourages. Everyone knew that it would be next to impossible during that tumultuous period to engage in a serious debate about whether to extend the Secretariat's spending authority or risk the "crisis" of a funding cut-off. This was exactly what the proponents of the nine-month cap had in mind. A nine-month cap was, in effect, no cap at all. Jones Parry, Malloch Brown, and Eliasson all knew it, and I knew it, too, which is why I insisted on the six-month commitment cap's expiring on June 30. What this exposed, however, was yet more EU cynicism. They would force the United States to be the "bad cop," which we would do because we cared about the substance, while the EU could be the "good cop" and get credit from the G-77 for their sensitivity. Then, the EU would turn to us and expect our appreciation for "sticking with us" during the difficult fight.

The climactic meeting began at about 10:30 P.M. on Thursday, December 22, in the Secretariat's office. Stafford Neal, the Jamaican perm rep and G-77 spokesman, gave a long speech about how the G-77 didn't like the commitment cap but was reluctantly prepared to accept the nine-month figure. Jones Parry, who had been working toward this moment, remained silent, offering that perhaps Oshima or I would have something to say. Confident that another strong instruction had come in from Tokyo, I deferred to Oshima, who made the case for the $950 million, or six-month cap, generously giving up our $50 million of flexibility. The G-77 said they felt betrayed, while Jones Parry sat happily silent. I said I was just as dismayed as the G-77 that they had been led to believe the nine-month cap was acceptable to the United States, which finally began to make Jones Parry uneasy. The G-77 representatives said they had to consult with the full G-77 before any further negotiations.

On Friday morning, December 23, with a lot of Christmas plane reservations hanging in the balance, the UN was still trying to process the idea that the United States and Japan might actually hang tough, so contrary was it to the Approved Catechism that we always caved in at the end. I explained to a Western group meeting that the commitment cap was a form of "intellectual discipline," which was shortly demonstrated when the G-77 rejected the idea entirely. At this point, the EU agreed to stick with JUSCANZ, and Malloch Brown said that Annan would support the six-month cap. He even suggested the G-77 invite Annan to address them so they could hear it from him in person.

When Neal reconvened the G-77 that afternoon, he told us that the six-month cap was "a bitter pill to swallow," and they therefore wanted language in the budget resolution that would automatically grant any request from the secretary general for the rest of the 2006 commitment authority, which would, of course, mean there was no real cap at all. I said that was "a nonstarter." Why should we accept language that was the exact opposite of our position? As the discussion continued, it became clear the G-77 had no intention of inviting Annan to address them, which was unfortunate, given Annan's efforts the next year to act as if he had never agreed to the cap. We went through many more meetings, but by 6:45 P.M. the G-77 finally collapsed. The United States prevailed, having allied all the major donors to its side, and achieving a complete consensus—unanimity—in the General Assembly to approve the commitment cap. It really was Christmastime.

"We Never Fail in New York"

> I am confident John Bolton will bring peace to the world before he brings peace in his relations with the *New York Times*.
>
> —HENRY KISSINGER, SEPTEMBER 27, 2005

After an enjoyable but cold New Year's Eve at the center of events in Times Square with Gretchen and JS, thanks to an invitation by Mayor Mike

Bloomberg to join him on the stage for the ball-dropping ceremonies, and an even chillier attendance at Bloomberg's second inauguration the next day at City Hall, it was back to work.

On UN reform, that meant primarily abolishing the discredited and disgraceful UN Human Rights Commission (HRC), which the Outcome Document pledged to replace with a new "Human Rights Council." So bad was the existing HRC that in January 2003, Libya had been elected chairman by a vote of 33–3–17, with only the United States, Canada, and one other country voting "no" in the secret ballot. Most of the HRC's work focused on criticizing Israel or the United States, while real human rights abusers devoted their efforts to ensuring that the commission never took up their abuses. Unfortunately, however, before my arrival in New York, the U.S. position had become incoherent because of concessions Washington had already made. In fact, Annan and the EU were so hungry for a deal— so they could then declare another success—that I could only see a further worsening of our position. French deputy perm rep Duclos said during the Outcome Document negotiations, for example, that failure to agree on a new HRC "would be supporting the hardest-line part of the Bush administration," which would take failure as evidence that the UN as a whole was irreparably flawed. I demanded an apology, which Duclos later made, but it was a very revealing incident. State's human rights bureau was also among the most desperate to announce "success," and therefore most ready to give away the store (such as by agreeing to change the geographical distribution of HRC seats, to the disadvantage of "Western" countries, the staunchest human rights defenders). Even worse, groups like Amnesty International and Human Rights Watch were also in full retreat, agreeing to these busy EU efforts to water down our proposed improvements, all the while blaming the United States for standing in the way of "reform." Of course, as Jeane Kirkpatrick might have said, these groups "always blame America first."

Certainly, I was "standing in the way" of capitulation to the opponents of true reform. As I said to the press, "We want a butterfly. We're not going to put lipstick on a caterpillar and declare it a success." We hoped our proposals—such as reducing the HRC's size; excluding the worst offenders (those under Security Council sanctions, as Iran and North Korea would soon be) from membership; and breaking the regional group lock on selecting members from their regions—taken together, would contribute to

changing the HRC's composition. Each time one of these proposals (agreed on with the EU) was weakened or dropped it became more and more likely that a new HRC would look and act substantially like the old one. That would squander a real chance for reform, which would not come again in the foreseeable future, given how hard it had been to mount this effort to replace something as disgraceful as the existing HRC. Indeed, the entire course of the HRC negotiations stands as a classic example of what I sometimes believed to be the perm reps' motto: "We never fail in New York." Otherwise, they would have to report to their capitals that there was trouble in Paradise, which might lead their capitals to ask "why," a very unsettling thought. Accordingly, every day in Turtle Bay was a success, even if not to the outside observer, so we didn't sully our reputations as diplomats worrying about mere substantive achievements.

Against this dismal backdrop, 2006 got underway. On Friday, January 6, I was in Washington meeting with Silverberg and Mike Kozak, a State careerist now on the NSC staff who had been doing an outstanding job trying to keep his former colleagues in line with the president's policies. Coincidentally, Rice tracked me down while we were meeting, to say, "I wanted to get your opinion on what do to with the Human Rights Commission." I answered that we were already in deep trouble, and that we should not accept any more watering down of our position once negotiations resumed on January 11. Rice said, "You're absolutely right," because we had been losing the "moral high ground" by our repeated compromises, and we should refashion our strategy, which was a very nice New Year's present. Back in New York, Gerhard Pfanzelter, Austria's perm rep, and EU president during the first six months of 2006, was also surprisingly strong, saying he felt as I did that we should not settle for just anything and call it a victory.

Nonetheless, early meetings in New York reflected no changes in position since December, confirming my view that we had already given away the key issues. Moreover, in early February, international turmoil over a Danish newspaper's cartoons of the Prophet Mohammed provided reform opponents even more chance to cause trouble by raising issues of "respect" for religion. By this time, I was convinced we were going backward, but Eliasson pressed for a General Assembly vote at the earliest possible moment. I argued to the contrary, since we would be stuck well into the distant future with whatever we adopted now. Eliasson and the Europeans were having none of it, and kept proposing new compromises. A typical example

came from Switzerland's Peter Mauer. He proposed dropping our exclusion from HRC membership of any country under Security Council sanctions for gross abuses of human rights or supporting terrorism, substituting a provision that would allow expulsion of HRC members by a two-thirds vote. This was outrageous. We had already given up requiring a two-thirds vote of the General Assembly for *election* to the HRC. Now Mauer proposed to drop a complete bar against the worst offenders, offering only the illusion that we could get a two-thirds vote to throw someone off. We never fail in New York.

On Wednesday, February 15, I had the toughest conversation with Eliasson to date. After an opening twenty-minute monologue by Eliasson, I told him the United States was close to walking away from the whole wretched process because the new HRC we were about to create would be no better than the existing one. I could see Eliasson wasn't listening; he again discoursed on U.S. public opinion, so I told him to stop listening to Human Rights Watch and start reading *National Review*, although I was not sure he knew what *National Review* was. A week later, a lunch hosted by Austria's Pfanzelter with all twenty-five EU perm reps provided a most amazing demonstration of the "We never fail in New York" syndrome. All they wanted to talk about was the HRC, and their dominant concern was that, whatever emerged from the negotiation process, it had to be sold "at home." I said I wasn't prepared to do that, and that I was going to tell the truth about whatever emerged, leading Germany's Gunter Pleuger to observe that "truth" and "good and evil" were not absolutes. That was certainly true at the UN!

Eliasson's latest draft emerged on February 23. It was so bad that Annan and Jimmy Carter quickly endorsed it. By now, however, we were better organized, and the American Enterprise Institute, the Hudson Institute, and the Heritage Foundation issued a rare joint statement saying the United States should not support the draft. Incredibly, on February 26, the *New York Times* published a stunning editorial called "The Shame of the United Nations," which started out as follows: "When it comes to reforming the disgraceful United Nations Human Rights Commission, America's Ambassador, John Bolton, is right; Secretary General Kofi Annan is wrong; and leading international human rights groups have unwisely put their preference for multilateral consensus ahead of their duty to fight for the strongest possible human rights protection. A once-promising reform pro-

posal has been so watered down that it has become an ugly sham, offering cover to an unacceptable status quo. It should be renegotiated or rejected."[5] The editorial then examined what was wrong with the current state of play, and concluded: "Mr. Bolton, representing an administration whose record is stained by Guantanamo and Abu Ghraib, is awkwardly placed to defend basic human rights principles. But he also represents the United States, with its long and proud human rights tradition. We hope that his refusal to go along with this shameful charade can produce something better."

I thought that even the weakest of sisters at State would now stand with me, but I was wrong again. Crouch convened a quick videoconference DC in which everyone agreed we should oppose the draft, except State's human rights bureau, which was still in the thrall of Eliasson and the leftist NGOs. We also discussed what to do if our efforts to stop the draft resolution failed, and I urged that we refuse to participate in any such illegitimate body. Rice herself was solid, calling me shortly after the *Times* editorial to say Annan was trying to reach her. She would say we were ready for line-by-line negotiations to repair the draft, but that if we didn't get what we wanted on membership criteria, we would call for a vote and vote "no." I said those were my thoughts exactly.

On Monday, February 27, Rice's Foreign Service assistant, Steve Beecroft, called with a readout of Eliasson's last-ditch effort to persuade Rice. After "a lot of whining" by Eliasson, including attacking the *New York Times* as "very ill-informed," he said reopening the text would be "a nightmare." Rice told him that we would simply call for a vote and vote "no," which of course was exactly what he didn't want to hear. Eliasson then said that he didn't understand what the U.S. position actually was, which was further proof to me that he wasn't a very good listener. Certainly everyone else knew, even, for a change, the *New York Times*!

The Annan-Eliasson end run to Rice having failed, Malloch Brown called Burns, trying a different end run. Burns called me immediately to say he had told Malloch Brown that the entire U.S. government "are all united that this is a lousy deal," and that "you need to listen to John," which I'm sure made Malloch Brown's day. The failure of this second end run brought the EU to near panic, which they resolved in typical fashion, issuing a state-

5. "The Shame of the United Nations," *New York Times,* Sunday, February 26, 2006, p. WK 11, col. 1.

ment that, even though not entirely happy with it, they would vote in favor of the resolution. Eliasson clearly hadn't listened to Rice. He pressed forward to a vote, obviously not believing we would actually vote "no," and I suspected many others at the UN also thought we would cave in. Why not? We had so often in the past. Malloch Brown, concluding I was hopeless, called my deputy perm rep, Alex Wolff, to say that everyone was "rallying around" Eliasson's position, and that there were probably 170 or 180 votes in favor of his text. Wolff, an outstanding career Foreign Service officer, responded correctly, "Why should that make a difference?"

Eliasson repeatedly delayed the General Assembly vote in hope of a miracle, so the big day did not finally arrive until March 15. Despite Rice's firm views on voting "no," there was much gnashing of teeth inside our bureaucracy about our "explanation of vote" (EOV), as those at State who opposed our position—Rice's position, not just mine—tried to water down what we would say about it. My view, since we were taking an obviously controversial stance, was that it was only sensible to defend it vigorously and not act as though we were ashamed of it. The final EOV was weak, but our vote was "no," the word that spoke loudest all day. Cuba, along with many other human rights violators, voted in favor of the resolution, and, in its EOV, attacked the United States. I asked for the floor afterward to say that I had considered exercising a "right of reply" on behalf of the United States, but concluded, "on the other hand, why bother?" which was the laugh line of the month. Voting with the United States against the draft resolution were Israel, Palau, and the Marshall Islands, our closest friends in the United Nations.

Since its birth, the new HRC has done precisely what we predicted, performing as badly as or worse than the original. Foreign policy provides few scientific experiments, which actually permit the testing of contrary hypotheses, but withdrawal from the ABM Treaty was one, and opposing the HRC was another. Our "isolated" General Assembly vote has been fully vindicated, making it one of my proudest moments in New York. As of this writing, most of the HRC's activity has been directed against Israel, such as its June 30, 2006, decision to inscribe the issue of the Occupied Territories permanently on its agenda, just as the old HRC had done. North Korea's brutality to its entire population and the Sudanese government's brutality in Darfur have gone unchallenged.

"Reform Is Not a One-Night Stand": The Final Collapse

The UN is a target-rich environment.

—John Bolton, FREQUENTLY

The Outcome Document prescribed two principal follow-up activities on management-reform issues: the "rules and regulations review" and the "mandate review." The first, dealing with internal Secretariat management procedures, was of special interest to Annan. To me, the second was more important because it dealt with the UN's actual programs and activities, and involved real money—almost a billion dollars a year for the UN Secretariat alone. In both instances, however, little could be done without the Secretariat reports and data required by the Outcome Document. Eliasson set up yet another General Assembly working group, this one on management reform, chaired by Canada's Alan Rock and Pakistan's Munir Akram. I stressed to them when we met on November 21 that we needed the Secretariat's reports laying out the mandates and making suggestions for better management before February, since Annan hadn't yet provided them. Otherwise, neither of these important reforms could even get under way.

Annan did not present his first report, "Investing in the UN," the "rules and regulations" review, to the General Assembly until March 7, 2006. It was typical of the Secretariat's inefficiency. Demonstrating at the outset the trouble that was to come from the G-77, with Annan seated high above us in the vaguely fascist architecture of the General Assembly hall, Ambassador Kumalo of South Africa went to the podium to complain about the procedures used to transmit the report. Although Eliasson had assured us just minutes before the session began that there would be no speakers and no debate, he had been unable to resist the G-77, thus allowing Kumalo to argue that the Annan report should have gone to the Fifth Committee, the La Brea Tar Pit of past reform efforts, rather than the full Assembly. I wasn't about to leave the field with this point unrebutted, so I followed Kumalo to the General Assembly podium, even though I had no prepared remarks. We did not agree with everything in Annan's recommendations (many of which did not go nearly far enough, in my view), but I stressed that we endorsed what Annan had said about "a radical overhaul of the entire Secretariat" and a "thorough strategic refit." These were words close to

Rice's term "revolution of reform" and I wanted them locked into everyone's thinking as the benchmark against which to judge our future progress.

After this General Assembly meeting, we settled into a protracted closed-door struggle over Annan's report. We were clearly losing momentum, as Volcker stressed to me a few days later, concerned that his Oil for Food recommendations were sinking.[6] That became even likelier when Eliasson shoehorned Annan's report into the Fifth Committee, allegedly to build more "goodwill" with the G-77, but the G-77 proceeded methodically to pick it to pieces. Indeed, the G-77 had utterly intimidated the EU by threatening to force a Fifth Committee vote on Annan's report. For years, UN budget decisions had been reached by "consensus," a formula created in the mid-1980s after U.S. dissatisfaction with uncontrolled budget growth led Congress to withhold hundreds of millions of dollars in contributions. "Consensus" was supposed to mean that the United States was satisfied, but, over time, fear of "isolation" eroded our blocking power of "withholding consensus." In fact, many key budget decisions were made despite U.S. objections. During the Bush administration, because of lack of will power, there were huge increases in UN budgets, a far worse record than that of the Clinton administration, which largely adhered to the Reagan-era principle of "zero real growth" in UN budgets.

I did not fear a vote in the Fifth Committee, even though I knew we would lose overwhelmingly, for one very good reason: It would expose the charade of "consensus budgeting" for what it was, something that actually worked against our interests more often than not. Congress could then decide what its response was to the G-77's dominance in budget debates, but at least we would not be participating in a shell game of accepting "consensus" decisions that really were no such thing. In fact, this was what the EU feared more than voting itself. What would happen if Washington, or their own capitals, found out what was really happening. Think what that would do to our motto of "We never fail in New York"!

Wrangling in the windowless and often airless Fifth Committee conference room went on for days. Canada's Rock proposed that JUSCANZ

---

6. Earlier, on December 11, Louise Frechette, the first deputy SG, had resigned, largely because of her lack of management of the Oil for Food program, and in April Annan had appointed Malloch Brown to succeed her. Malloch Brown had already effectively functioned as the deputy, Frechette being invisible, so little changed in reality.

draft a letter explaining how reasonable we had all been and then solicit signatures from others, which ultimately resulted in forty-six countries signing up. Jones Parry worried that this letter might offend the G-77, but French deputy perm rep Duclos liked it. Others in the EU, however, decided they wanted to be a "bridge" between the United States and the G-77, the EU's favorite pastime in New York, which really meant they would cut a deal with the G-77 satisfactory to them, hoping that we would then fall like a ripe fruit for fear of being "isolated." I wasn't having any of it. In fact, the EU prepared a draft resolution, shared with us from within by an unlikely source, to postpone the entire issue until May, which I considered bad tactics. Even the G-77 reacted negatively to the EU's efforts at delay, with Egyptian perm rep Abdelaziz saying, "We are all trying to play tricks on each other," the issues "were clear to each side," and "we should stop playing games," statements of such clarity that they must have been painful to the EU.

On and on went the EU's efforts at delay, until finally, in the late afternoon of April 27, I said in the Fifth Committee that we were simply playing out the UN version of the movie *Groundhog Day*, endlessly reliving the same scene with the same outcome. We should either vote on the G-77 resolution tanking Annan's reform recommendations or send the entire issue back to the General Assembly (where it should have been in the first place, but for Eliasson's inability to say "no" to the G-77).

On April 28, Kumalo pressed for a vote on the G-77 resolution disapproving the Annan reforms. John Ashe, Fifth Committee chairman, and perm rep of Antigua and Barbuda, said that a vote had been called, and the large curtain on one wall of the committee room was pulled back to reveal the voting board of all 191 countries that were then UN members, which was actually a dramatic moment as these things go in UN circles. The final vote (essentially repeated in the full General Assembly on May 8) was 108–50–3, with virtually all of the industrial democracies—contributing over 90 percent of the UN's assessed budget—voting with us. Of course we were overwhelmed by the G-77's votes, their 108 supporters contributing all of 10 percent of the UN's budget, but the main point was that the reality of UN financial matters was now publicly exposed for all to see. Moreover, we had outmaneuvered the EU and forced them to follow us rather than the other way around, breaking an established UN pattern. It was a good night.

Despite the outcome on the "rules and regulations" review, which had ended in complete failure, I was still hopeful on the mandate review, especially having uncovered a ponderous UN document entitled "Regulations and Rules Governing Programme Planning, the Programme Aspects of the Budget, the Monitoring and Implementation, and the Methods of Evaluation." This tome charged the Secretariat with identifying programs that were "obsolete, of marginal effectiveness, or ineffective," exactly what the mandate review was designed to accomplish. The G-77 could hardly complain that we were simply going to do what the Secretariat—and the UN membership itself—had obviously failed to do over a sustained period. In fact, what we needed was a "zero-based budget" review, starting from the very first UN program and working right toward the present, examining everything from the ground up, to evaluate what worked and what didn't work. The UN had never done this in a sustained fashion, and it was long overdue.

I made it clear I saw the mandate review as a money-saving exercise, and that we were not going to shy away from "politically sensitive mandates," the euphemism for Arab-Israeli issues, all true examples of UN "old thinking." These "politically sensitive" mandates basically all involved economic or political support for Palestinians, in ways that not even member governments of the UN were treated. Japan worked closely with us, having many of the same "targets," programs and offices that had long been deadwood, particularly in the economic and social areas, which needed to be eliminated or at least restructured. Working as JUSKCANZ (South Korea having joined our group), we refined the list, and then started on the more hesitant EU. I made it clear to the other major contributors, such as Germany and Japan, that we needed at least some "bodies on the floor" by June 30, some mandates eliminated to prove to Congress that we had made a serious effort.

The G-77, however, emboldened by victory against Annan, now believed it had the whip hand. Akram and others essentially told us that "politically sensitive mandates" were entirely off the table, and that whatever savings might emerge would have to be plowed back into UN economic development activities (thus benefiting the G-77), with nothing being returned to UN members in the form of lower assessments. The G-77 also said that no mandates older than five years that had been renewed within that period could even be considered, an argument made up entirely out of thin air, simply to restrict the review to an inconsequentially small number of mandates. The Third World's real objective, it soon became clear, was to lift the commitment cap on the six-month budget without any conditions, particularly progress on the mandate review. Of course, once the cap disappeared, there wouldn't be any progress either, as everyone, even the EU, understood. This exercise was obviously in deep trouble, and my earlier optimism misplaced.

Confronted with the near certainty that the mandate review was headed for failure, others in the EU turned to what they saw as the only alternative: devising a fig leaf acceptable to the G-77 that would allow the EU to declare reform a success, thus lifting the expenditure cap and allowing business as usual to resume. Despite supporting us on the expenditure cap in December, the EU had lost any stomach for more trouble after the loss in the Fifth Committee.

I met with South Africa's Kumalo, suggesting that we dispense with the EU middlemen and deal directly with each other, which Kumalo liked. However, when the meeting with the entire G-77 took place on June 14, with roughly two weeks to go until the expenditure cap kicked in, I found to my surprise that the EU and Japan had also been invited. Kumalo asked me to speak first, and I explained why it was important to make significant progress on reform, and why we had favored the expenditure cap in December, reminding everyone that the General Assembly had adopted it unanimously. Japan's Oshima agreed that the cap could only be lifted by consensus, without which there "might not be money in the coffers by the end of the year." Oshima went on, "Frankly what we have here is the power of money and the power of numbers, and if one asserts itself at the expense of the other," bad things would ensue. He concluded by saying we needed "tangible improvements" by June 30 "to lift the cap by consensus." It was a good, tough speech, better than what Washington had cleared for me. Austria's Pfanzelter gave the quintessential EU speech, saying their goal was "consensus and compromise." At least Pfanzelter went on to say we needed progress in three areas (management reform, accountability, and mandate review) before the cap could be lifted.

Nonetheless, despite this effort, as the calendar moved inexorably along, the G-77 simply kept stalling. At this point, I began to think about an alternative strategy. We clearly were not going to get what we wanted: substantial reform allowing a lifting of the expenditure cap. Even worse, however, was what Eliasson and the EU were moving toward: lifting the cap accompanied by only cosmetic changes (more lipstick on caterpillars), on the back of which the EU would proclaim victory, but which would effectively be the end of reform. I thought that, starkly put, it was better to lift the expenditure cap with no reforms achieved and face that outcome honestly, regrouping to fight another day. I didn't want to lift the cap at all, and wanted to vote "no" on the resolution that would do so. This course of action would preserve our intellectual integrity, or what was left of it, and our freedom to insist on the truth, namely that real reform remained unachieved. Then, everyone could draw his or her own conclusions.

As the days fell away, the great UN meeting machine cranked up, with meetings of the regional groups, meetings in Eliasson's office, EU meetings, JUSKCANZ meetings, and on and on. Rice was traveling in Central Asia and Russia, but I kept her informed through Steve Beecroft, who relayed that she was very comfortable with my approach and believed that "we should do the right thing even if we're alone."

Late Wednesday afternoon, June 29, Ashe convened the Fifth Committee, and I gave my statement dissociating from consensus, the best I could get from State, noting to everyone again Volcker's insight about the UN's "culture of inaction." Oshima dissociated for Japan, as did Hill of Australia, and then the expenditure cap was lifted, unconditionally. Of course, the General Assembly itself still had to act, and the EU-led negotiations to find some kind of fig leaf that would provide the illusion of reform roared on. In a late-night session on June 29–30, however, India's Sen and South Africa's Kumalo agreed with USUN ambassador in charge of management and reform issues Mark Wallace that this EU effort at cosmetics was worthless, and they asked to meet with me early on June 30 to see if the United States and the G-77 could reach an accommodation. This was exactly what I had wanted, and Mark and I met with Sen, Kumalo, and Abdelaziz in the Delegates' Lounge at 9:45 A.M. We agreed there would be no more resolutions, everyone would preserve his position, and we would come back to reform later.

When we went into Eliasson's office, Kumalo explained our view that there was no point in proceeding with the Eliasson/EU resolution on mandate reform, because if he took it to the G-77, it would be "amended to death" and "take us away from management reform." He said we had to face "reality. We have run out of hours. We have to be realistic." I explained that the mandate review had been our highest reform priority, and that we didn't intend to back away from it. Nonetheless, as Kumalo had just indicated, we were nowhere close to agreement with the G-77. We should avoid further rancor and leave the picture clear as to what had been accomplished and what had not.

The General Assembly went late into the evening on June 30, but finally lifted the expenditure cap with no attendant reforms, the United States, Japan, Australia, and Canada dissociating. Once again, the brutal reality of what actually happened in New York on budget matters had been exposed, and people could draw their own conclusions whether reform had any prospect of success.

Although we all talked about continuing the reform effort, I could almost physically feel the air go out of the entire organization on June 30. In fact, although the mandate review process limped on in the next six months, nothing was achieved. No mandates were eliminated, none were consolidated, and none were reformed. The only conclusion I could reach was that efforts at merely incremental or marginal reforms in the UN system were doomed to failure, and that we needed far more sweeping reform, such as shifting from assessed to voluntary contributions, as described earlier. Whether such reforms could be enacted was highly uncertain, to be sure, but so were any lesser reforms, as our recent experience had demonstrated. At least this time, however, we had been intellectually honest, and skipped the "We never fail in New York" hymns.

So here our reform effort effectively died, stymied by G-77 opposition, Annan's ineffectiveness, and EU weakness and indecision. In a way, reform was also crippled by the State Department, and the pervasive view that "UN reform" was just simply not as important as other issues, particularly the effect of reform on bilateral relations with other countries, not to mention continuing crises. In a way, Rice herself made this point to me on April 20 in a meeting in her office on a variety of topics, when she said, "You've got not only UN reform, but Iran, Lebanon-Syria, Sudan, and only you can balance all of these." Of course, there would be more as well, particularly North Korea, but the main point was one of priorities, the balancing of which always involved competing equities and demands on scarce time and resources. The position of the State Department as an institution, however, was very clear: It liked the UN, but didn't like it enough to fix it.

CHAPTER NINE

AS GOOD AS IT GETS: THE SECURITY COUNCIL

The ignorance about the United Nations among U.S. opinion formers is profound.

—Edward Mortimer, aide to Kofi Annan, August 27, 1997

The first Security Council meeting I attended on August 4, 2005, was an "informal consultation," a private session of the Council with only Council perm reps and their staffs present. We met in a small room just off the public Council chamber, which is so well known to the public from print and television pictures. I shook hands with everyone around the room, exchanging pleasantries, as Japan's ambassador, Kenzo Oshima, president of the Council for August, congratulated me on becoming U.S. perm rep. The Council's presidency rotates among the members on a monthly basis in the alphabetical order of the members' names, just as the ambassador of each country moves counterclockwise around the horseshoe table, to the chair to the right of the one he or she sat in the month before. This can sometimes lead to strange configurations because of the formal names some countries use. During my entire time on the Council, I did not sit next to the United Kingdom, as the U.S. perm rep usually does, because we were separated by the United Republic of Tanzania to my right and the U.K.'s left. To my left during my tenure was Algeria during 2005, and Argentina during 2006.

I opened by mentioning that the last time I had been in the informal consultations room was when I'd accompanied Jim Baker, reporting on the

1997 Houston Accords on the Western Sahara. One of my goals, I suggested, might be finally to bring the long-running peacekeeping operation to a close by actually holding the referendum on the future status of Western Sahara that it had been established to undertake. There was laughter around the room, which turned out to be justified, since the fifteen-year-old effort was still struggling along unchanged when I left sixteen months later.

Into the Ditch with Security Council Reform

"Speak to me. Why do you never speak. Speak.
   "What are you thinking of? What thinking? What?
"I never know what you are thinking. Think."
—T. S. ELIOT, "THE WASTE LAND"

Compared to other UN bodies, such as the General Assembly or ECOSOC (the Economic and Social Council), the Security Council actually makes decisions that affect the real world, among which, at least in theory, could be:

- Dealing with threats to international peace and security, such as Iraq's 1990 invasion of Kuwait, the disintegration of former Yugoslavia, and more recently the threats of terrorism and the proliferation of weapons of mass destruction by states like North Korea and Iran;
- Establishing and overseeing UN peacekeeping operations and the political missions carried out by the secretary general (and a small army of "special representatives," "personal envoys" and other glorified titles);
- Initiating UN decisions on critical issues like electing the secretary general and admitting new members;

and many more. The Council's actual record, of course, was far from the ideal, as divergent views often brought it to a screeching halt. The most significant case in point, of course, was the Cold War, in which the Council played no visible role, and because of which it was largely paralyzed for over forty critical years.

The Cold War's end, with East-West gridlock disappearing, brought the prospect that the Security Council might actually take up the role envisioned by the UN Charter. Successive and very tragic failures in peacekeeping operations in Somalia, Yugoslavia, Rwanda, and elsewhere banished that notion,[1] and hopes dissipated. Moreover, the early promise that a democratic Russia might align itself with the West faded, and China continued to play its own game. Inaction, inattentiveness, and ineffectiveness all remained significant problems, since the Council in virtually every case simply reflected the external political realities, and in some cases wasn't even that positive because of the peculiar political culture that exists in the Twilight Zone at Turtle Bay. Nonetheless, in the minds of many governments, the Security Council still serves as "high table" at the UN, and is all the more alluring because they are not on it. For decades, members of the General Assembly complained that the Council was becoming more powerful, "usurping" the Assembly's functions, to the benefit of the five permanent members and the detriment of the Third World/G-77/NAM. Of course, to the extent this complaint has merit, it is because the General Assembly is even more paralyzed than the Security Council and far less able to engage in real-world activities. Over time, the Assembly has become theater, and the Council's importance increased by default, not by conscious imperialism.

Not surprisingly, therefore, calls for Security Council "reform" (a euphemism for "expansion") have been major themes in recent years, and especially during my tenure as U.S. ambassador. As with many such issues in the UN, of course, nothing really happened, proving that while theater in the General Assembly may resemble Broadway, the Council is its own little theater in the round. There were many efforts to enshrine some kind of Council "reform" in the 2005 Outcome Document, using the September Summit as an artificial deadline, but they all came to naught, since there was never agreement over what "reform" meant, let alone what to do about it. Nor did aspirants for new permanent seats ever explain what they would

---

1. For a fuller discussion of Security Council failures after the end of the Cold War, see Frederick H. Fleitz, Jr., *Peacekeeping Fiascoes of the 1990s: Causes, Solutions, and U.S. Interests* (Westport, Conn.: Praeger, 2002); Ted Galen Carpenter, ed., *Delusions of Grandeur: The United Nations and Global Intervention* (Washington, D.C.: CATO Institute, 1997); and John Hillen, *Blue Helmets: The Strategy of UN Military Operations* (Washington, D.C.: Brassey's, 1998).

The author and his parents, Jack and Ginny, at the beach in the early 1950s.

Judge Robert H. Bork, the author (then Assistant Attorney General for Legislative Affairs), and Senator Joseph R. Biden during Bork's 1987 confirmation hearings to be an Associate Justice of the Supreme Court.

The author speaks with Attorney General Edwin Meese during the 1987 Iran-contra hearings.

From left, Chief Justice William H. Rehnquist, Gretchen Bolton, Secretary of State James A. Baker III, and Chief of Protocol Joseph Verner Reed, as the author speaks just after being sworn in as Assistant Secretary of State for International Organization Affairs in 1989.

The Demilitarized Zone at
Panmunjom, Korea, during a visit
by the author on July 4, 1991.

Psychoanalyzing chads during the
2000 election recount in Palm Beach
County, Florida. From left: An unknown
Democratic lawyer; Judge Charles
E. Burton, Chairman of the County
Canvassing Board; and the author.

Justice Thomas swearing
in his law school classmate
as Undersecretary for Arms
Control and International
Security as Gretchen and
Jennifer Sarah Bolton look on.

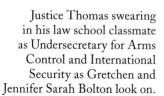

Presidents Bush and Putin greeting their respective delegations at the signing of the Treaty of Moscow in 2002; the author shaking hands with President Putin.

Georgi Mamedov, Secretary of State Colin Powell, and the author just before the signing ceremony for the Treaty of Moscow in 2002.

Cartoon from the first confirmation hearing for the UN Ambassador position, 2005.

Secretary of State Condoleezza Rice, the author, and President Bush just before the August 1, 2005, announcement of the recess appointment.

Arriving in New York.

Meeting with UN Secretary
General Kofi Annan right after
the presentation of credentials.

Addressing the Security Council.

Part of the USUN team
on the way in to a Security
Council meeting. From
left: Ric Grenell, the
USUN press spokesman;
the author, fending off the
press; Ben Chang, deputy
press spokesman; Mark
Groombridge, senior
advisor; and Ambassador
Jackie Sanders.

Japanese Ambassador Oshima and British Ambassador Jones Parry join the author in the Security Council press stakeout to discuss North Korea, July 2006.

French Ambassador de La Sablière and the author confer with Secretary General Annan on Lebanon in the Security Council chamber, July 2006.

George Clooney, Ambassador Jackie Sanders, the author, and Elie Wiesel at the Security Council's informal meeting on Darfur, September 2006.

Introducing President Bush to the USUN staff in September 2006,
with Gretchen Bolton and Secretary Rice at left.

The author addresses the General Assembly at the swearing in of incoming
Secretary General Ban Ki-moon (seated at right) in October 2006.
Outgoing Secretary General Annan is seated at upper left.

do once they achieved them. This was once again a question of process, not substance. Consequently, the issue continued to bubble along, but never precipitated a decision. If I had been able to bill at the hourly rate for partners in major Washington or New York law firms during all of the discussions I had on Security Council reform, I could have left the UN a rich man. It was also typical of the UN that so much wasted effort was spent on "reforming" the one major body that actually worked halfway decently from time to time, instead of focusing on bodies like the General Assembly and ECOSOC that served only to consume oxygen and paper.

The UN Charter listed the Council's five permanent members (the "Perm Five") in 1945, reflecting World War II's result. Although they themselves changed, their total did not. The Republic of China lost control over mainland China, fled to Taiwan, and in 1971 was replaced by the People's Republic. The USSR disintegrated and was replaced by the much smaller Russia. The United Kingdom declined from "great power" status with the loss of its colonial empire, and France, included as a permanent member by Roosevelt as a favor to Churchill, also lost its empire.[2] Another problem facing Britain and France is their slow disappearance, by their own choice, into the European Union, losing autonomy and independence in determining foreign policy. It is now practice in their Security Council speeches to say that they agree with the EU president's statement on behalf of EU members, also a regular feature taking up Council time, as the EU presidency invariably has to address us after Council members finish speaking. In fact, only the United States has remained as it was in 1945, in our case actually expanding with the admission of Alaska and Hawaii as states, while the others declined or fragmented.

The total number of nonpermanent members was six in 1945 and was expanded to ten in 1965.[3] There had been no subsequent increase, even though UN membership has grown further since the initial wave of decolonization. Nonpermanent members are elected for two-year terms, with

2. Roosevelt liked to refer to the four leaders of the World War II "United Nations" as "the Four Policemen," a concept basic to what he saw in the postwar organization. See Townsend Hoopes and Douglas Brinkley, *FDR and the Creation of the U.N.* (New Haven: Yale University Press, 1997), p. 46.
3. General Assembly Resolution 1991A (1963), ratified by two-thirds of UN members, including all of the Perm Five, in time for the first elections to the expanded Council to be held in 1965.

five new members joining the Council each year, based on a strictly adhered to pattern of geographical rotation from the UN's regional groups, as follows: two from the Western European and Others Group (WEOG, the "others" including Canada and the United States); one from the Eastern European Group; two from the Latin American and Caribbean Group; two from the Asia Group; and three from the Africa Group. One unspoken rule is that there is always an Arab member, with that seat rotating between the Asian Group and the Africa group. Thus, during my tenure, Algeria (from Africa) served in 2004–5, and Qatar (from Asia) served in 2006–7.

Deciding which countries represent the regional groups is the subject of intense debate, since the General Assembly almost always rubber-stamps regional group choices for election to the Security Council and many other UN bodies. When the regional groups cannot agree, as would happen with Guatemala and Venezuela in fall 2006, the full General Assembly decides. For many years, Israel was not in any regional group, since the Arab countries from its region blocked admittance, thus making Israel the only "permanent nonmember" of the Security Council. After repeal of the "Zionism is racism" resolution, the Europeans grudgingly admitted Israel to the WEOG, but it has still never won election to the Council.

In addition to being "permanent," the most significant Perm Five power is the veto, which allows any of them to kill a Security Council resolution, even if they stand alone, as the United States often does on resolutions relating to Israel. The veto is also a key factor distinguishing the Security Council from the Council of the League of Nations, and was the subject of intense debate in 1945. That debate continues, because the Perm Five have unassailable power to defend their own national interests. Not only can they veto substantive resolutions they dislike, they can veto amendments to the UN Charter or candidates for secretary general. The five permanent members are also the only legitimate nuclear weapons states under the Non-Proliferation Treaty, a distinction they don't often raise. Because of their unique status, the Perm Five meet frequently to discuss Security Council and other UN business, which always provokes gnashing of teeth by those who cannot attend such meetings, or who want to crash the club.

All of these circumstances led to agitation by countries that wanted to be permanent members, and thought they deserved to be, according to varying sets of criteria. As a result, there were innumerable schemes to increase the number of permanent members, and the size of the Council as a whole. I felt strongly that any increase in the Council's overall size should be minimal, since it was hard enough to get any real work done with fifteen members, and each new addition increased that difficulty not just arithmetically but probably geometrically. The United States was certainly the most concerned about maintaining the Council's (limited) effectiveness as a decision-making body. Many aspirants for permanent membership never considered the consequences of expanding the body to twenty-four or twenty-five members, so eager were they to get a chair around that horseshoe table, regardless of what would follow. I must confess, from time to time I had an "Atlas Shrugged" moment, concluding we should just let Council expansion happen, and, as we predicted, watch the whole thing slide into a ditch. But then, my sense of responsibility would assert itself, and I would revert to diligent defender of the Council's effectiveness.

Japan has the most compelling case to become a permanent member, being the second-largest contributor to the UN after the United States, a world-class economy, and increasingly willing to contribute troops and resources to UN peacekeeping operations. Unfortunately for Japan, China has no particular enthusiasm, to say the least, for Japan's candidacy. India has a claim of sorts, given its population size and rising economic importance, but it is bitterly opposed by Pakistan, which does not want its rival since birth to gain an upper hand in so important a body. Brazil wants a permanent seat, as the largest country in the Western Hemisphere after the United States, a yearning not shared by its Spanish-speaking fellow Latins such as Mexico or Argentina, which have their own ideas about who should represent Latin America. Germany, the largest economy in Europe, and the third-largest UN contributor, wants a permanent seat, which raises the interesting question of just how many permanent seats the EU should have. Former Italian foreign minister Gianni de Michelis once proposed that Britain and France resign their permanent seats, to be replaced by the EU and Japan, thus keeping the number of permanent members to five. This plan, political suicide for France and the United Kingdom, nonetheless explains why a third EU seat for Germany is utterly unrealistic.

In the months before I arrived, Japan, India, Brazil, and Germany banded together as the "G-4," trying to aggregate their various supporters into a powerful enough coalition to obtain the necessary two-thirds General Assembly majority to amend the UN Charter and make them permanent members. I never understood this strategy, because the creation of the

G-4 actually motivated and united their opponents, who were sufficiently strong to block any changes in the Security Council. This group opposing the G-4, known as "Uniting for Consensus" or informally as "the Coffee Club," made the seemingly reasonable point that major changes in the UN Charter should be achieved by "consensus" (i.e., unanimity), meaning in turn they could stop any changes they chose, whether they had a blocking one-third-plus-one in the General Assembly or not. Moreover, China, which wasn't any more enthusiastic about India than it was about Japan, could hide behind Pakistan; Britain and France, which saw their very seats in danger of eventually being lost to one permanent seat for the EU, could hide behind Italy, which was determined Germany would not get on the Council; and many others could avoid having to make a commitment to the G-4, despite intensive and often emotional lobbying in New York.

I saw how sensitive this whole question was after my initial courtesy call on China's perm rep, Wang Guangya, on August 2, my second day in New York. I had known Wang during the Bush 41 administration when he served as political counselor of the Chinese UN Mission, and he and I had been counterparts in the first days of the Bush 43 administration when I was T. I liked Wang's forthright style, and his complete command of English made him not only easy to talk to privately, but a great friend of the press, with whom he conversed easily and freely. Both before and during my tenure in New York, Wang said positive things about me to the media, which I appreciated. It tells you something that Annan's wife once asked Wang's wife why he was saying such nice things about me. At our first meeting, Wang and I readily agreed that we had no use for the G-4 proposal, but I asked if he saw any circumstances in which China could agree to a Japanese permanent seat. His answer, while complex, was essentially "no." Shortly after our meeting, Wang told the press that we were united in our opposition to the G-4 proposal, which sent the Japanese media into paroxysms, because they misinterpreted opposition to the G-4 idea as opposition to Japan. I corrected this misimpression easily with Japan's ambassador Oshima, but the incident showed how short the fuses were.

Japanese officials spent countless hours calculating compromise formulas and alternative ways to ensure a permanent seat for Japan, and were in constant contact with us in New York, Washington, and Tokyo. Japan rightly believed that without our support it had no chance of success, and that getting us on board with whatever approach they selected had to be their highest priority. I tried to persuade them that their association in the G-4 was counterproductive, because they had simply inherited all of the opponents of membership for Germany, India, and Brazil, without picking up any new supporters beyond what they already had. Moreover, concentrating on finding overwhelming support in the General Assembly (where a two-thirds vote was necessary) continually diverted Japan from its real problem, namely finding a way to overcome China's seemingly intractable opposition and likely veto. Japan's inevitable response was that if a huge General Assembly majority endorsed their candidacy, China would be "shamed" into voting to accept Japan as a permanent member, a view I found touchingly naïve.

Instead of the failing G-4 approach, I proposed a "Japan only" strategy, which would highlight the intrinsic merits of Japan's candidacy and force China to say openly whether it would actually veto a UN Charter amendment. Japan feared, with some justification, that a "Japan only" strategy would generate opposition because of the fears of Germany and others that "the train was leaving the station," and that there was really only one shot at obtaining permanent membership. For Japan to move forward alone, in this view, was tantamount to giving up for a very long time the prospects of these other countries. Accordingly, we modified the idea to a "Japan first" strategy, to make it clear that elevating Japan would not preclude subsequent positive decisions for other countries. While some Japanese officials were attracted to this idea, others, long wedded to the G-4, could not break free of their previous intellectual commitments and kept working on ingenious formulas to float the G-4 proposal off the bottom of the East River, where it was resting. Ultimately, Japan concluded that the G-4 proposal was hopeless but wanted to let it expire quietly over time, rather than making a public break from their G-4 partners. I called this approach "separation but not divorce." What it inevitably meant was that nothing much happened for long periods of time, punctuated occasionally by outbursts from other frustrated reformers, followed again by more long periods of silence. I also worked hard to explain to Oshima and others that they needed to keep in mind the two-thirds majority that would be needed in the U.S. Senate to ratify any UN Charter amendments. While there was certainly Senate support for Japan, I doubted that any of the other aspirants had nearly as much, at least in the foreseeable future.

I ultimately had the chance to explain my views directly to Japanese prime minister Koizumi at a small lunch hosted by Vice President Cheney at his residence on the Naval Observatory grounds on Thursday, June 29, 2006. Koizumi was in the United States just before the end of his tenure, and the next day Bush planned to take him to Graceland, Elvis Presley's home in Memphis, Tennessee, a long-time dream for Koizumi, a real Elvis fan. On the more prosaic subject of Security Council reform, at the VP's lunch, Koizumi greeted me on entering the VP's house by saying in English, "Ah, Mr. Bolton. You are famous!" I said immediately, "I can explain," which Cheney and Rumsfeld both enjoyed. Koizumi listened carefully to my pitch for "Japan first," but he didn't really respond, in part, I suspect, because his mind was already in Graceland.

The other G-4 members could not understand our lack of support. Ronaldo Sardenberg, Brazil's perm rep, seemed particularly disappointed, even though his long lecture to me about "democratizing" the Council seemed calculated to ensure we would continue opposing their efforts. German perm rep Gunter Pleuger blamed Japan for not being willing to jam the United States by pushing for an early General Assembly vote on the G-4 plan, or by bringing us on board. Gerhard Schroeder's electoral defeat in September 2005 brought a new perm rep, Thomas Matussek, replacing the angry, embittered, and increasingly ineffective Pleuger. At an EU meeting, Pleuger once called me "totally cynical and hard as iron," which, coming from him, was quite a bouquet. Only India's perm rep, Nirupam Sen, seemed relaxed about the lack of progress of the G-4 plan, perhaps because he sensed an inevitability for India, given its sheer size.

Another important factor in everyone's thinking was Tokyo's strong view, which Oshima frequently deployed in New York, that Japan would almost certainly reduce its assessed contribution if it could not win a permanent seat, something that it finally did for assessments beginning in 2007. I certainly did not object to this line of argument, because it exactly reflected, from the Japanese perspective, a sentiment widespread in Congress: Why were we paying so much when key elements on our agenda were constantly being ignored or rejected? When I left New York, and as of this writing, neither Japan nor any other country was any closer to a permanent seat than when this issue first started gaining attention in the early 1990s. If this book ever has a second edition, I am sure it will be true then, as well.

A Valentine for the Security Council

> Ambassador Bolton, thank you for keeping your sanity.
> —Anonymous New Yorker, September 2006

As my seat moved counterclockwise around the Security Council table, I got both physically and mentally closer to the U.S. presidency of the Council in February 2006. Having dealt extensively with Council matters during the Bush 41 administration, as well as having just had six months of experience in New York, I had lots of ideas of what to change and how to do it.

First, I simply did not think the Security Council was doing many of its jobs very well. Given all the peacekeeping operations (PKOs) in the field, the Council devoted only an insignificant amount of time to the really big-picture issues: the proliferation of weapons of mass destruction and international terrorism. I didn't expect to change that pattern in one month, but I at least hoped to shift our attention from myriads of capillary-size issues to ones of larger scope and consequence. One important way to do that was consistent with my second idea, namely that the Council had to do a better job overseeing and directing the Secretariat, both in conducting PKOs and more fundamentally in actually resolving the conflicts that gave rise to the PKOs in the first place. Too often—and I certainly include the United States as a target of this criticism—we behaved like bureaucrats processing papers: reauthorizing missions like those in the Western Sahara or Cyprus by rolling over their mandates every six months but not pressing the Secretariat to solve the underlying problems or asking the fundamental question of whether the PKOs had become a part of those problems. Third, I wanted to launch the process of selecting the next secretary general, whose term would begin on January 1, 2007, as soon as possible, in the hope of actually deciding on one in the fall, much earlier than had been the case in the past. By so doing, as will be explained more fully in the next chapter, I wanted to ensure that the incoming SG—whom we fully hoped and expected would not be a UN insider like Kofi Annan—would have an adequate transition period before actually assuming the office.

Finally, I wanted to break the increasingly stylized and formalistic way the Council did business. Not only were all public sessions done according to script—no more dramatic debates in the Council chamber as I remember from watching Henry Cabot Lodge and Adlai Stevenson in my youth—but even the "informal consultations" often consisted of delegations' reading prepared statements. Perm reps, and I did this myself, would often come in, read their statements, and then leave, letting subordinates fill their national chairs. This problem extended far beyond the Security Council. Many large UN meetings were essentially worthless, and time could have been saved by mass emailings of prepared statements to all 192 missions rather than having the meetings themselves. I was ready to shake things up. I thought I had waited a graceful period—six months is a long time for Americans—and that it was now time to act. If the others rejected my ideas, so be it, but they would not be able to say that the United States only complained and grumbled, and never tried anything new. I had a boatload of new ideas.

The first, and perhaps most revolutionary thing I wanted to do, was to start meetings on time. To me, starting on time is a courtesy to others; developing it as a habit is self-reinforcing, as is the opposite. People arrive on time in courtrooms and at plays and concerts because they know the gavel will fall or the curtain will rise at the appointed hour. Conversely, if people think meetings will start late, they arrive later and later and sure enough the meetings always begin late. On Thursday, February 2, after the customary round of bilateral consultations with Council members the day before, and after the customary buffet breakfast at the beginning of each new Council presidency, I was ready to start the first meeting on time at 10:00 A.M. I had the chimes rung in the halls outside the Council room and brought the gavel down smartly right at 10:00 A.M., to the surprise of the three or four miscellaneous other people who were in the room. I then sat there in the president's chair, waiting for others to arrive, until about ten-fifteen, when thirteen delegations had finally shown up. The custom (and there is *always* a custom at the UN) was to wait until at least fourteen had shown up before starting, but I decided to launch a new custom, and go with only thirteen.

The customary first order of business at the first Council meeting of each new month is to adopt the "program of work" for the month, much of which is known in advance because it involves the reauthorization of peacekeeping mandates or the receipt of reports from the Secretariat previously ordered by the Security Council. Those items are usually not problems, but what can sometimes provoke discussions are unexpected ideas, and I had several:

- First, I expected Senator Richard Lugar and several other SFRC members to come to New York to address the Council, which was unheard-of. It was one thing to schedule a "thematic debate," often chaired by the foreign minister of the country holding the presidency, on some topic dear to the heart of the minister. Inviting mere legislators was something different, and foreign to those with parliamentary systems rather than our essentially unique government of separated powers.

- Second, I wanted two thematic hearings, one on sexual abuse and exploitation by UN peacekeepers, and one on procurement fraud in peacekeeping operations. A recent, quite candid report by Prince Zeid, the Jordanian perm rep, had exposed the sordid issue of peacekeepers' taking advantage of the innocent people they had been sent to protect. It was a very sensitive subject: Even if we had to talk about it once, did we really have to talk about it again, and in public, of all things? On procurement fraud, the UN Office of Internal Oversight Services (OIOS) had reported that approximately $280 million out of over $1 billion of peacekeeping procurement contracts audited in the most recent six-year period had been wasted or otherwise lost. This was a gripping statistic, more than enough to wipe out the entire U.S. assessed share of 27 percent for peacekeeping of the $1 billion audited by OIOS. That alone, of course, was reason for some members to shun a public debate over it.

- Third, I wanted daily briefings by the Secretariat on peacekeeping issues, to keep the Council current and provide us with more than the usual dribble of reports. My notion was not only that we would get more information, but that Council members would become accustomed to questioning the Secretariat closely and then discussing among themselves how to resolve some of these issues and actually wrap up PKOs. I didn't envision that these briefings would be extraordinarily long, but I felt that getting into a pattern of daily meetings would actually make the Council more effective. I had written to Kofi Annan about this concept, and he had already expressed his unease to several Council members, so I knew there would be trouble over this idea.

These were my opening moves.

Almost immediately, Russian perm rep Andrei Denisov objected to all of them, as did France's de La Sablière. Fortunately, Jones Parry supported them all, and the rest of the Council was mixed. Interestingly, much of the opposition was to daily briefings, although most conceded that twice-a-week briefings made sense. I agreed to see Annan later in the day and report back. Never in my entire time at the UN was there so much opposition to a draft "program of work." We moved on to substantive issues without adopting it, just about the only time that happened. Thus is change welcomed at the UN.

I met with Annan at twelve-thirty, and it turned out he was now ready to cooperate. He suggested that the first several daily briefings focus on Haiti, with elections scheduled there for February 7. This made entirely good sense, and it would help the Council better understand the prospective challenges for the election, rather than possibly finding itself in the middle of a crisis on the seventh or eighth with little or no warning. Annan pointed out that since one crisis tended to merge into another, he foresaw the briefings evolving naturally. I convened the Council again on Friday, slightly closer to 10:00 A.M. than the day before, and established another dramatic precedent by having everyone agree that we could start with only twelve of the fifteen members present. Such dizzying change! With Annan compliant, we reached agreement on the daily briefings, although there were still rumblings of discontent, which erupted later, about my idea for three public meetings. In any event, we adopted the February program of work, yet another diplomatic triumph. The Haiti briefings actually proved quite helpful, as everyone acknowledged, although the practice of daily briefings did not survive beyond my Council presidency during the month of February 2006. Too much work.

But it wasn't all work at the Security Council. After meeting with Annan, I returned to the office of the Council president, and who should appear but Nicaragua's perm rep, Eduardo Sevilla, and his wife, escorting Miss Universe, Natalie Glebova of Canada (or perhaps it was Russia, I never got that straight) on a tour of the UN building. I was happy to show her the Security Council chamber and have the obligatory pictures taken, thinking this might well be the highlight of my presidency.

Senators Dick Lugar, Norm Coleman, and George Voinovich made up the SFRC delegation that arrived on Monday, February 6, although I had invited all eighteen committee members. I briefed them on our current state of work, and then escorted them into the Council chamber at 10:00 A.M. (precisely) to start. Lugar gave an extensive speech, and was particularly tough on Iran's nuclear weapons program. Although seven perm reps spoke, none answered Lugar directly. On the issue of Japan's quest for a permanent seat, Lugar said it was really not before the Senate at that point, and that he was happy to leave it to "my dear friend, John Bolton," which certainly got everyone's attention. Even more surprising, the three senators then held a brief news conference, the Reuters headline out of which was, "Bolton wins praise from vocal Republican critic," meaning Voinovich. That certainly got *my* attention. After meetings with G-77 perm reps and then with Chris Burnham on UN reform, I hosted a lunch for the senators and their staffs at the Waldorf residence. Protocol seated Voinovich next to Gretchen, and they had a very pleasant conversation, as everyone else seemed to as well. The press was correct that we were now making progress with Voinovich, but the clock was ticking on my recess appointment.

The next Monday, February 13 (JS's birthday), I was in Washington for Annan's call on the president, a regular visit that takes place midway between Bush's annual addresses to the General Assembly. I rode over to the White House with Rice, and she led the way into the Oval Office for the scheduled 1:05 P.M. briefing for Bush. "Bolton, you doing okay?" asked the president, as he escorted his dog Barney, who had been growling, out of the office, onto the porch. Andy Card, Steve Hadley, Mike Kozak, Dan Bartlett, and Scott McClellan were all there, but the topic of discussion was not Annan but the weekend hunting accident Vice President Cheney (who had arrived at that point) had had, and the media uproar because the press didn't think it had been promptly notified.

At one-fifteen, Annan and his entourage came in to take their appointed seats, and Bush asked, "Has Bolton been a demon up there?" Annan smiled thinly and said, "John's doing a good job," and changed the subject to reform of the UN Human Rights Commission. Bush didn't let him get very far, complaining about the HRC rapporteurs who had just issued a report critical of the Guantanamo Bay detention facility, calling it "unfair and uncalled for." "I never even knew what 'rapporteurs' were before this report," Bush joked, as Annan tried to get onto the subject of UN management reform. Many people, Bush interjected, thought that the UN was "a cushy jobs program," and that the UN needed to focus on "results not process." "Unfortunately," Bush went on, "you're dealing in a profailure world" that seemed to enjoy the "expenditure of money for the sake of spending the money." On the mandate review, Bush said "sunset 'em," meaning the mandates, which was exactly the right approach.

After Annan and Bush took a quick spin through Iran, North Korea, Venezuela, Israel-Palestine, Sudan, and Iraq, the group broke up to allow the press in for their traditional photo op, and I stood with Rice and Hadley near the president's desk, out of the way of the media hordes pouring in. Bush made a few remarks, concluding with, "And we'll continue to work closely through Secretary Bolton——Ambassador Bolton, with the Security Council and the United Nations." Rice laughed and said, "You've gotten a promotion." With the media and the UN assembly gone, Bush turned to the rest of us and said, "That sure was fun," clearly the signal it was time to leave. With that, Rice and I walked back out through the West Wing basement.

Back in New York, Annan was not so friendly. Although he had acquiesced to my plan for daily briefings, he was less happy about the public Security Council meetings on peacekeeping procurement fraud and sexual exploitation and abuse by peacekeepers. We also now learned that the G-77 wasn't happy about these meetings either. Typically, they didn't dare to say openly that they didn't want these topics discussed, but instead complained that this was more Council incursion into General Assembly territory. That argument, of course, was ridiculous, and I didn't intend to let it slow me down.

More serious was Annan's effort to tank the hearings, which he launched at the end of the monthly lunch between the Security Council and the SG, on February 16. As the lunch ended, he delivered a lengthy complaint about the two public meetings. He complained that the OIOS audit had been unfair and whined about other matters, prompting de La Sablière and Oshima to ask if the meetings should not be made private. This was a classic demonstration of the "down in the bunker" mentality that had already cost the UN so much public trust, at least in the United

States. I said I had already spoken to General Assembly president Eliasson, who had voiced no objection, and that moving behind closed doors was a mistake. Annan actually responded by saying that I shouldn't try to "intimidate" him.

That afternoon, I called nearly every Council perm rep, solidifying support for what they had all previously agreed to, namely fully public meetings. Although some obviously wished the issue would just go away, they held firm to our earlier decision. At about 6:00 P.M., Annan called me to apologize for any "misunderstanding," saying, "It's more how we discuss the matter publicly, and not that we shouldn't discuss it publicly." This wasn't even close to what he had said at lunch, but I surmised he was just trying to get out of the hole he had dug by his failed ambush. I had the Council votes to hold these meetings, which I fully intended to do. Some might characterize Annan's lunchtime sally as bureaucratic guerrilla warfare that failed. I saw it as part of a deeper problem of Annan's deviousness, but this time he had been caught.

Indeed, Annan resorted to more guerrilla warfare, preventing the undersecretary general in charge of OIOS from appearing at the Council meeting on procurement fraud, thus proving once and for all that OIOS had nowhere near the independence that a real inspector general had in the U.S. government. In the meantime, South African perm rep Kumalo wrote to say that he wanted to appear and speak on behalf of the G-77. I was happy to agree, because his participation acknowledged the legitimacy of the Council's discussing this issue—not that I thought there was any debate. In fact, this controversy over whether the two peacekeeping hearings would be public began to change my mind about the utility of public Council meetings. Whereas previously, I had worried about sensitive information leaking in public, I now concluded that the real reason people wanted private Council meetings was concern about what would happen if the media and the public saw what was actually going on. It became increasingly clear to me that we should be more public, rather than less, and the more speakers the better, whether they were Council members or not.

February 22 brought the first of the hearings, this one on procurement fraud in peacekeeping. Malloch Brown, speaking for Annan, defended the Secretariat against the OIOS audit report, but, as noted, OIOS was not permitted to speak to explain its report, a clear mistake by Annan, who looked exceedingly defensive. The other Council members gave excellent statements expressing their dismay at the extent of the fraud that had been uncovered. Oshima of Japan specifically said it would be difficult to retain domestic Japanese support for funding peacekeeping at current levels if these problems were not addressed. In a break from the rigid scripting of these events, and to everyone's surprise, I asked Malloch Brown a question about OIOS independence, which he ducked. If I had ever held the Council presidency again, I would have done more public examination of Secretariat officials, which would be good for the organization as a whole.

The hearing on sexual exploitation and abuse by UN peacekeepers took place the next day, February 23. This meeting produced more light and less heat than the one on procurement fraud, in part because no one was eager to make the procedural argument that the Security Council shouldn't be considering the issue. I stressed once again the lack of OIOS participation in this meeting, demonstrating its lack of independence from management, saying that we wanted to continue public debate on making the UN respond more fully to the problem of sexual exploitation. Both of these Council meetings were useful, but they did not have a sustained impact over time. Other Council members were uncomfortable both with pressing controversial issues and with the amount of work involved, a not inconsiderable problem for smaller delegations. The net result, however, is that the Council is not doing its job fully, not exercising oversight and control over the Secretariat, and therefore not holding it accountable. This lack of accountability has manifested itself in numerous undesirable ways and will continue to do so in the future.

In addition to our traditional "end of presidency" reception on February 28 at the U.S. Mission, I was also able to take the Security Council perm reps and their significant others to a New York Knicks–Miami Heat game at Madison Square Garden the week before. David Stern, NBA commissioner, and James Dolan, owner of the Knicks and the Garden, were our generous and gracious hosts, despite the thrashing the Knicks took. Russia's Andrei Denisov ("I love the Heat," he said) and Slovakia's Peter Burian turned out to be avid basketball fans, and China's Wang Guangya arranged a later meeting with seven-foot-three-inch Chinese basketball sensation Yao Ming. Ellen Loj of Denmark, tutored by former NBA players who joined us in the skyboxes, enjoyed her first-ever basketball game, and everyone agreed it beat the normal diplomatic cocktail reception. I certainly thought so!

Hugo the Boss Takes a Tumble

Chavez is Castro without brains.
                                —Anonymous, February 2006

As with other UN positions, Security Council seats are generally decided by the regional groups, whose choices are then rubber-stamped. Historically, the Latin American and Caribbean Group (known by the Spanish acronym "GRULAC") has been the least able to reach consensus, and their disagreements have therefore been thrown to the entire UN membership to decide. The reasons involve Cuba's perennial regional troublemaking, but also more mundane factors, such as the split between the Spanish- and Portuguese-speaking mainland countries and the largely English-speaking Caribbean island states, and the split between the small Central American states and the relatively larger countries of South America. Unlike other regions, GRULAC has never worked out a satisfactory rotation among its subregions, which has led to enormous resentment from the smaller states about South American dominance (and partially explains why Brazil, which has served nine two-year Council terms, is far from popular in UN matters in its own region). For example, in fall 2005, in the race between Peru and Nicaragua for the nonpermanent seat being vacated by Brazil, Peru won handily.

This race was by no means a big deal, although many GRULAC fights in Cold War days had considerable significance. When Cuba sought election to the Council for the 1990–91 term, the United States sought to find an opponent to stop Castro from getting both the Council forum and the possibility of obstructing real work. There were, however, no takers, and Cuba was selected. As expected, during its entire tenure, which spanned two crucial years of war in the Persian Gulf, Cuba lived up to our predictions that it would be a troublemaker. Nonetheless, as evidenced by our inability to drum up opposition to Cuba, the United States rarely prevails when it intervenes in regional group politics, especially within GRULAC, so sensitive are they to *Yanqui* interference.

Even so, the need occasionally arose for us to act, as it did when, out of nowhere, Hugo Chavez decided in late 2005 that Venezuela would oppose Guatemala to replace Argentina in the Council for the 2007–8 term.

Chavez has been described as "Castro without brains," and his interference in several elections in fragile Latin democracies showed him to be a bully and a troublemaker. We did not need him using the Council to play out his clownish fantasies. Bush himself felt strongly about defeating Venezuela, stressing in his February 13 Oval Office meeting with Annan that the Castro-Chavez connection was very troubling to the United States. When Bush asked Annan why he wasn't more critical of Chavez, Annan suggested instead that the United States "engage" more with Chavez to "defuse" the problem. I could see Bush's eyes glazing over, and he finally broke in to say, "Chavez would be a real pain in the ass on the Security Council." Then he laughed, and said, "I know I'm a pain in the ass, but at least I'm friendly."

Guatemala had already declared its candidacy, but it was a small Central American state, without a diplomatic presence in many countries, especially in Africa, and it certainly did not have Venezuela's huge oil revenues, which Chavez was not averse to spreading around to grease his way onto the Council. Moreover, Guatemala recognized Taiwan rather than the PRC, and its long-standing border dispute with Belize guaranteed it would have trouble in the English-speaking Caribbean, which was already especially vulnerable to Chavez's use of oil as leverage. On the other hand, Guatemala was an emerging democracy, while Venezuela was going in the opposite direction, and, although a UN founding member, it had never served on the Security Council, compared with Venezuela's four Council memberships, as recently as the 1992–93 term.

In New York, I met regularly with Guatemala's perm rep, Jorge Skinner-Klée, and in February 2006 we established a task force between our two missions to meet weekly to assess the ever-changing vote count. For many months, we conducted the campaign in the shadowy ways of diplomacy, making "démarches" in capitals of UN members, talking to their ambassadors in New York, and trying to line up support. Since the ultimate General Assembly vote on Security Council membership would be secret, talk was cheap. There was no way to confirm whether pledges of support were being honored, or how many pledges were made to both countries. As Skinner-Klée said he had been advised by one friendly perm rep, "Don't just take 'yes' for an answer." Moreover, there was a certain downside in too-visible U.S. lobbying for Guatemala, because we wanted to avoid Chavez turning the race into a campaign against us. Nonetheless, given the enormous stakes—the possibility of two years of Chavez sitting at "high table" in the UN—this was no time for us to be shy and retiring.

When September arrived, with Security Council elections just a few weeks after the opening of the Sixty-first General Assembly, the pace began to pick up. We tried to concentrate on high-value targets like China, with Rice speaking several times to Foreign Minister Li Zhaoxing, while I concentrated on Perm Rep Wang Guangya. On September 18, Rice was in New York for the UNGA opening and had the usual bilateral with Li. She described Venezuela as "irresponsible," noting how personally offensive Chavez was, and that he had compared Bush to Hitler. Li responded that China could not vote for a country like Guatemala with which it did not have diplomatic relations, a code for saying China objected to Guatemala's recognition of Taiwan. Nonetheless, we tried to persuade Li at least to abstain or vote for a third candidate, or at an absolute minimum not lobby on Venezuela's behalf. Rice concluded that a Chinese vote for Venezuela would be "an insult to the United States." As we were rising from the conference table, I said quietly to Rice, "That'll get their attention." She smiled and said, "Well, John, I'm just as diplomatic as you are!" A few days later, after the secretary general's annual lunch for the Perm Five foreign ministers, Rice and I found ourselves walking out with Li and Wang. Rice returned to the Guatemala-Venezuela race, reminding Li that Chavez had said she and Bush were sleeping together. This time, even the Chinese registered shock, and I thought Rice might have now found the key to rendering them inactive. We didn't see much Chinese activity as the weeks went by, but I took no comfort from that, given Beijing's neuralgia on the Taiwan issue. We urged Taiwan to do its own quiet lobbying on behalf of Guatemala among the countries that recognized it, because of the adverse impact a stinging defeat for Guatemala might have on Taiwan itself.

Fortunately, Chavez himself drove a stake through the heart of Venezuela's campaign two days later in his General Assembly speech, with a wild attack on Bush and the United States, which received wide media attention. Among other things, Chavez compared Bush to the devil, saying he could still smell the whiff of sulfur at the podium where Bush had spoken the day before. The negative reaction from many governments was not so much to the outrageous things Chavez said, but to the clownishness of his behavior, which they understood could adversely affect their national interests. His childishness proved the point we had made tirelessly, namely, that he would disrupt Security Council activity, benefiting no one at the UN except Chavez himself. Neither the United States nor Guatemala had to say much of anything, as Chavez's podiacide took its natural course.

No campaign ever goes completely smoothly, however, and we had our own bump on Saturday night, September 23, when Venezuelan foreign minister Nicolás Maduro had a run-in with Transportation Security Agency (TSA) personnel at Kennedy Airport as he was catching a flight back to Caracas. I immediately suspected a ploy, which was confirmed when we learned that Maduro had not requested the normal diplomatic courtesies that would be extended to a foreign minister. Instead, he, his wife, and his young-adult son had bought one-way tickets, in cash, very close to boarding time for their international flight, which had understandably triggered a security interest. TSA vigorously denied any mistreatment during the actual screening process, but for some unaccountable reason, the security cameras that might have verified what actually happened were not working. Nonetheless, the TSA agents on the scene spoke Spanish, and they heard Maduro yelling into a cell phone that he wanted to return to New York to hold a press conference, even though he was through screening in ample time to make his flight, escorted as he now was by Diplomatic Security agents once his identity had been established.

This was a set-up, pure and simple, and the press would determine how it played out. The Venezuelans were first out of the box, and, incredibly, some unnamed State Department spokesman was quoted as saying we "regretted" the incident. I thought this was so typical of State, assuming the United States was in the wrong even before finding out all of the facts. This played right into Venezuela's game. Many foreign diplomats have had unhappy experiences entering or leaving the United States—not that that made them different from many Americans—and it was important to avoid sympathy for Venezuela as a result of this trumped-up incident. Even if State couldn't get its act together, John McCain knew how to respond. On *Face the Nation* on Sunday morning, McCain was asked about the incident, and he said it was another reason for the Senate to confirm me. Now that's media savvy! Because the UN press corps was dispersed for the weekend, I couldn't do much until Monday morning. I went to the familiar Security Council stakeout just before the Council's meeting and described the whole affair as "Venezuelan street theater," leaving no doubt that the United States had nothing to apologize for. Fortunately, many Latin

American delegations knew the Venezuelans well enough to surmise what had actually happened, and they declined to pretend they were outraged at what the gringos had done. With that, the incident largely died.

Despite hectic campaigning, Guatemala suffered from the debilitating perception among many countries that there was no way it could prevail against Venezuela, given the amount of trade deals, cash, favors, and other goodies that Chavez was distributing. That was not what our vote count showed, because we consistently had Guatemala with a narrow but discernible advantage. Nonetheless, the perception, especially in GRULAC, that Guatemala could not stop Venezuela led to endless speculation about Guatemala's dropping out and being replaced by another candidate. Unfortunately, much of the speculation took place in State's Western Hemisphere Affairs bureau (WHA), which sent a very bad signal about our confidence in Guatemala.

The General Assembly vote was scheduled for 10:00 A.M. Monday, October 16, and by this time our joint count with Guatemala showed it comfortably ahead, with over 100 votes of the 128 needed for the required two-thirds majority if all 192 UN members voted. Nonetheless, the overwhelming sentiment among Latin Americans and Europeans was that Venezuela would win by a large majority on the first ballot, so someone was going to be quite disappointed. General Assembly voting is very low-tech, with each country writing the names of its candidates on paper ballots, which are then collected by tellers who walk the Assembly's aisles, allowing each ballot to be dropped into a locked wooden box. When all the ballots are collected, they are taken to a counting room behind the podium, and the Assembly recesses for the twenty to thirty minutes it takes for hand counting. This procedure can kill a lot of time, and that's what we immediately started in on, in a cycle that, in this first iteration, would consume three full days.

Needless to say, the General Assembly did not convene on time, and there was one other race for the Asian seat being vacated by the Philippines (which Indonesia won easily over Nepal), so the first-ballot results were not announced until just after 11:45 A.M. Guatemala received 109 votes to Venezuela's 76, with 7 abstentions, just about where we thought Guatemala would be (and 18 votes short of the two-thirds vote it needed, given that 185 countries had cast valid ballots). Diego Cordovez, a former foreign minister of Ecuador, and now its perm rep, and GRULAC chairman for

October, told me that the Latins were genuinely stunned at how poorly Venezuela had done. Others, especially Europeans, were as stunned as the Latins. I felt we were doing pretty well, hoping that the spread shown by the first vote would propel Guatemala to a two-thirds majority within the next few ballots, which was what Guatemala had been privately predicting to us.

Washington, however, was having a completely different reaction. I learned that Rice was trying to reach me (the voting results being immediately known in Washington because UN TV carried the proceedings live), and I went off the GA floor to speak with her. "When do we pull the plug?" was her question, which surprised me, since Guatemala was ahead, and indeed, moved further ahead on the second ballot, 114–74, and then again on the third, 116–70. On the fourth ballot, the last before lunch, however, votes shifted back, with Guatemala's lead decreasing to 110–75. Of course, there was no reason why any votes should have shifted backward if responsible governments had given their perm reps instructions, but that would have been untypical of the UN. I spoke again with Rice during the lunch break, urging that we needed what Germans call "*sitzfleisch*"—which means exactly what it sounds like—and a little patience. GRULAC and others would undoubtedly be chattering excitedly during lunch, and our best approach was to have Guatemala continue to press its case vigorously. Many South Americans who had backed Venezuela because of financial deals (Argentina) or leftist ideology (Brazil and Bolivia) were now in a panic they were riding the wrong horse. Unfortunately, their reaction was not to switch to Guatemala, which would have ended the agony before it began, but to find a third candidate that would allow both Guatemala and Venezuela to withdraw with their dignity intact. What really bothered South America was that some tiny Central American country might actually beat one of them, a terrible precedent.

Guatemala, however, not unreasonably, thought it was very close to victory, and Venezuela's dignity had been sufficiently stung, not to mention its disappointment at how many resources had obviously been committed unproductively, that it wasn't about to concede at this point. After lunch, we returned to the General Assembly, where the next two ballots were held, with support for Guatemala falling on both, and actually ending in a 93–93 tie on the sixth ballot. Rice called me again, now nearly shouting over the phone about what was going on. By this time, I was having a few butterflies myself, but I was convinced that a small number of delegations were simply behaving in the utterly irresponsible way that characterized much of what happened at the UN. In fact, the next day, a Sri Lankan diplomat told a USUN staffer that they had shifted their vote to Venezuela; when asked why, the Sri Lankan had smiled and said, "To see what would happen." And this was the way *serious* issues were treated! I again urged patience.

By the end of the day, on the tenth ballot, Guatemala led 110–77, exactly one vote higher in both cases than the very first vote, eight hours earlier. This was a perfect metaphor for the UN. You could spend an entire day on something, and end up exactly where you started. More concretely, I thought the first and final votes reflected delegations' real instructions, and therefore the issue was whether Guatemala could peel away the relatively small number of votes to get to a two-thirds majority, or whether the current spread was fixed.

As the delegations melted away from the General Assembly, I caucused with Guatemalan foreign minister Gert Rosenthal, an experienced UN hand, whom I knew from Bush 41 when he headed the UN Economic Commission for Latin America and the Caribbean (ECLAC) in Santiago, Chile. Because Venezuelans had been taking photos all day of me speaking with ambassadors on the General Assembly floor, thus presumably showing U.S. arm-twisting in action, we met in a basement conference room. Rosenthal, reflecting continuing confidence in their vote count, said he thought Guatemala was at its floor, and Venezuela at its ceiling, which struck me as about right. Rosenthal and I agreed he would call Belize's foreign minister to see if he could unlock the votes of the small Caribbean island states. I would call Jones Parry to see what the United Kingdom might do with its former colonies, and I also enlisted Canada to be helpful. Canada's relatively new perm rep, John McNee, worked the issue hard, but Jones Parry did next to nothing. (By contrast, de La Sablière was lobbying away at France's former African colonies, although with only mixed success.) The next morning, I called U.S. ambassadors in key Latin American countries, almost all of whom I had come to know personally over my years at State.

The second day of voting was a dreary repetition of the votes swinging in relatively narrow bands, over twelve long ballots (now at a total of twenty-two), with Guatemala consistently maintaining the lead, but not breaking through to the two-thirds vote it needed. After two days, it was clear that many countries were getting restive at the amount of time being consumed, so I suggested we take two days off to size up where things stood. Venezuela agreed only to a one-day suspension, but even this was helpful to avoid resentment building against Guatemala. While this might seem counterintuitive, since Guatemala was ahead, in the UN world resentment is actually much more likely against the country that is reasonable rather than the opposite. After all, if you can't pressure the unreasonable country, why not pressure the reasonable one? Certainly, this was a lesson Israel learned over the years. At the end of the second day, I emphasized to the press that Venezuela had just suffered ten successive and sizable defeats, twenty-one in all, and that it should withdraw in order to allow the UN to get on with its other business. Of course, I didn't expect Venezuela to listen, but I was hoping others would.

GRULAC finally decided to meet on Wednesday, our day off, but they remained hopelessly divided, as I learned at a luncheon reception at El Salvador's Mission, hosted in honor of their visiting vice president, Ana Vilma Albanez. Venezuela blamed the United States for everything, which even its supporters wouldn't swallow, but neither could they resolve how to get off the treadmill we were on. Accordingly, voting resumed on Thursday, October 19, with seven rounds in the morning, with almost no variation in the outcome, and six more in the afternoon, bringing us to thirty-five ballots altogether. Because of the Eid al-Fitr holiday at the end of Ramadan, the UN was to be closed on the coming Monday, and there was a palpable desire to take another break from the voting, enabling us to gain a reprieve until Wednesday afternoon, October 25, to everyone's evident relief. Many believed that with almost a week until the next vote, GRULAC would finally get its act together, that being defined by most delegations as Guatemala and Venezuela withdrawing, and a third candidate emerging that would win GRULAC consensus. I thought this was terribly unfair to Guatemala, since in most comparable circumstances, the trailing candidate withdrew in favor of the one leading. Unfortunately, Venezuela now had so much at stake that it was hard to see how it could exit with even a shred of dignity unless it dragged Guatemala down as well.

Bolivia, under newly elected left-winger Eva Morales, almost as much of a clown as Chavez, happily offered itself as a "compromise," but it garnered no support among the weary Latins. Rice called me the morning of Wednesday, October 25, to discuss where things stood, and told me that, earlier in the week, she had called the Chilean and Brazilian foreign ministers to urge them to resolve things. Of course, the message she sent by such calls was that we would be happy to toss Guatemala over the side, since "solving things" for Brazil and Chile meant getting both candidates out of the race in favor of a third country.

Because the General Assembly hall was being set up for a concert on October 25 (get your priorities right here, we only had business to attend to), we met in one of the UN's basement conference rooms, where the gloomy yet surly mood resembled that of a group of condemned prisoners. Venezuela's foreign minister Maduro had overcome his aversion to New York to return for this round of voting, undoubtedly because Chavez had expressed his concern that his minister's management of this exercise had not quite been up to snuff. Given the alphabetical seating arrangement in the relatively small room, Venezuela was only a few seats away from us, which at least made things a little more enjoyable, given their obvious discomfort. Earlier GRULAC meetings had again proven inconclusive, filled mostly with long disquisitions by Venezuela and Cuba about the evils of the United States and yours truly, which I wish I could have heard. (Venezuela's vice president was also attacking me publicly, calling me "the most sinister figure in the UN," which delighted me.) Sitting next to Uruguay for much of the day, I got to know their new perm rep a bit, and he seemed a perfectly reasonable fellow, which might be important if Uruguay emerged as the "compromise" candidate! In any case, six more ballots produced no movement, and we adjourned again until Tuesday, October 31.

On October 26, I went to Guatemala's Mission to meet with Rosenthal. He and Maduro had met that morning with Cordovez. Venezuela now understood clearly it could never win, and its failing effort was a tangible drain, economically and politically. Rosenthal, however, had his own domestic political problem in Guatemala, where the president had concluded there were negative political implications for Guatemala if it withdrew while it was still in the lead, as it had been for all but one vote over this long saga. Unfortunately, none of us had any idea how to break through the ceiling (and floor) Guatemala had faced from the outset.

October 31 brought six more rounds of voting, now totaling forty-seven, but no movement. Maduro and Rosenthal met the next day, and that evening Rosenthal called me to say that he and Maduro agreed they would both withdraw in favor of Panama. I felt badly for Guatemala, and for

Rosenthal and Skinner-Klée particularly, given all their efforts, but in truth Panama was a perfectly acceptable outcome for us. We had stopped a determined, well-financed effort by Venezuela, at a time when the United States was supposedly close to the nadir of its influence in the General Assembly, and basically saved the UN from itself, yet again.

Panama was elected on November 7, 2006, our Election Day, and was one of the few pieces of election news that day that brought me my cheer. Back in October, Italy and Belgium had been elected to replace Greece and Denmark, which would result in little change in Council opinion, and Panama's replacing Argentina would also not likely result in much significant change. But, in addition, Indonesia would soon take the seat held by Japan, and South Africa, in its first-ever Security Council membership, was set to swap with smaller Tanzania, both of which changes could have a significant effect on the Security Council in 2007. That, however, would be for someone else to worry about.

CHAPTER TEN

ELECTING THE NEW SECRETARY GENERAL: BAN KI-MOON IS COMING TO TOWN

I'm glad to see you still have all of your old energy.

—Kofi Annan to John Bolton at Kananaskis, Canada, June 27, 2002

Rumors about Kofi Annan's resigning because of the Oil for Food scandal were rampant at the UN when I arrived in New York, with people speculating daily about his replacement. Of course, one might ask why the United States did not force Annan from office, and why he was left to finish out his second term, which expired on December 31, 2006, a year and a half later.

Annan was simply not up to the job, but neither Powell nor Rice was prepared to push to remove him, despite his manifest inadequacies and the Oil for Food scandal. Indeed, Rice said, "I've never had a better relationship with anyone than I've had with Kofi Annan."[1] Annan was installed in a 1996 Clinton administration effort to purge Boutros Boutros-Ghali, who had never gotten along with U.S. ambassador Madeleine Albright, who took it upon herself to remove him. Ironically, I always liked Boutros-Ghali, but he had irritated Albright personally from the moment she arrived in New York. In any event, Annan was everything the Clinton

---

1. Quoted in "Another U.N. Charade," *Wall Street Journal,* Friday, September 16, 2005, p. A14, col. 1.

administration could ask for: an international bureaucrat whose very career embodied their worship of multilateralism for its own sake.

In return, Annan created problems for Clinton. He said during one of the most intense periods in NATO's 1999 air campaign against Yugoslavia, which the Security Council did not authorize: "Unless the Security Council is restored to its preeminent position as the sole source of legitimacy on the use of force, we are on a dangerous path to anarchy."[2] Even Democrats knew trouble when they saw it on that point. When I subsequently suggested to an SFRC hearing that the Senate might debate the "sole source of legitimacy" issue, Joe Biden said: "I do not think you have to worry about there being any debate on the Secretary General's statement about the sole source of [legitimacy] is the Security Council. Nobody in the Senate agrees with that. Nobody in the Senate agrees with that. There is nothing to debate. He is dead, flat, unequivocally wrong."[3]

As for the Bush administration, Annan undercut it diplomatically and proved consistently unhelpful in Iraq, both before and after the war. He said, for example, "From our point of view, and the charter point of view, it [the U.S. military action] was illegal."[4] This went well beyond Boutros-Ghali's irritating Albright, but it was the gross mismanagement of the Oil for Food program that should have caused the United States to demand Annan's resignation. The secretary general, after all, is the UN's "chief administrative officer," in the words of Article 97 of the charter, and the Oil for Food debacle was an administrative failure of the highest order. It is inconceivable that any responsible multinational corporation's board of directors would have allowed a CEO who presided over such a scandal to survive in office, but at the UN, Annan just kept purring along. There was at least one argument in 2005–6 against firing him in disgrace, namely that it was better to concentrate on picking his successor, rather than prompting what could be a huge battle within the UN with less than two years remaining in his term. Despite calls for Annan's removal by Senator Norm Coleman and

2. Reuters, "Annan Visits Macedonia to Discuss Refugees," *International Herald Tribune* (Hong Kong ed.), May 20, 1999, p. 4. col. 1.
3. U.S. Senate Committee on Foreign Relations, Field Hearing on Implementation of UN Reform, January 21, 2000, p. 69 (stenographic transcript).
4. Colum Lynch, "U.S., Allies Dispute Annan on Iraq War," *Washington Post*, September 17, 2004, p. A18, col. 1.

others, the administration decided before I arrived in New York to ride out the rest of his term, and that decision was final. It was, however, a lost opportunity to focus on reform, one that could have been put to exceptionally good use.

Given that Annan would remain in office, the conventional wisdom in New York was that the 2006 election was "Asia's turn" to assume the secretary general position for the next five-year term, a line certainly pressed by Asia Group members in an effort to make it an inevitability. This logic, of course, was flawed, since the SG position had never been conceived to "rotate," whether among regional groups, which were not themselves foreseen in the charter, or in any other fashion. Over the years, the first two SGs had come from the Western European group, Trygve Lie, 1946–52, and Dag Hammarskjöld, 1953–61; then from Asia, U Thant, 1961–71; then another from Western Europe, Kurt Waldheim, 1972–81; then one from GRULAC, Javier Pérez de Cuéllar, 1982–91. Only then had the call gone up, in 1991, that it was "Africa's turn." But, as in 1991, and as was still true in 2006, there was simply no basis for the rotation argument. In fact, because Africa had, by 2006, now held the SG position for three full terms, that in and of itself disproved the notion of regional group rotation every two terms.

Members of the Eastern European Group, moreover, had their own ideas. Conceived during the Cold War and created originally for the Warsaw Pact and a few anomalies like Yugoslavia, the group had grown much larger with the breakup of Yugoslavia and the Soviet Union. They were acutely aware there had never been a secretary general from Eastern Europe, and they rejected the idea that it was "Asia's turn" to have a second SG before Eastern Europe had even one. Several names were floated, such as Poland's outgoing president Aleksander Kwasniewski, a personal favorite of Bush's, whose term in office concluded before the next secretary general's term began, thus allowing him to step easily from one position to the other. There were also other names mentioned, but the Eastern Europeans never did settle on one candidate. Moreover, many countries from other regions argued that "Europe" had already had three SGs, and it wasn't going to get any more for a long time, no matter where on the continent they came from. Even more ominously, Russia made it clear it did not want a secretary general from the ranks of its former satellites and Soviet territories, perhaps because it would present too many painful memories of their lost empire, many parts of which were decidedly uppity, in Moscow's view. Russia concurred that it was "Asia's turn," in part, we thought, to enhance its own status as an "Asian country," albeit a poor and very lightly populated one.

The United States insisted on the best-qualified person for the job, from wherever he or she might come. I explained to the press and others, patiently and repeatedly, why the "principle" of geographical rotation didn't really exist and why it was without merit. I liked to ask as well why no one was talking about gender rotation, if "rotation" was so important, a point that usually brought discussions to an abrupt halt. The fact was, "Asia's turn" was simply the result of a 2001 political deal between the African and Asian groups for Asia to support Annan for a second term (Africa's third consecutive term), in exchange for Africa's committing to vote for an Asian in 2006. While the United Kingdom supported our view of the meritocratic principle, we could also see the practical reality that unless we could find non-Asian candidates ready to present themselves, Asia would in fact get the SG position by default.

Our behind-the-scenes focus was to encourage candidates who would take seriously the role of "chief administrative officer," and who would push forward with the *real* reform agenda. Perhaps surprisingly, there was much less interest in the job of secretary general than one might imagine, with many prospective candidates telling us directly or indirectly they simply had no desire to put themselves into the UN meat-grinder. We looked worldwide, but, except in Eastern Europe, there was essentially no interest outside of Asia, thus dramatically limiting the field of potential candidates and proving the deleterious consequences of the "Asia's turn" argument. Precisely at a time when the UN needed a truly global search, we were unable to have one. And, never forget France's insistence that candidates acceptable to them had to be fluent in French, one of the two UN "working languages," along with English. The French certainly never let us forget it.

Accordingly, the handicappers of the race, which included everyone in Turtle Bay, spent considerable time sizing up the horses. First out of the gate and the early leader was Thailand's candidate, Deputy Prime Minister and former foreign minister Surakiart Sathirathai, whom I had first met in Bangkok when I was T. Surakiart artfully locked in early endorsement by the Association of Southeast Asian Nations (ASEAN), thus showing broad support, and even more important, precluding a number of attractive candidates who did not feel they could present themselves given ASEAN's decision. Surakiart's campaign verged on the relentless, as he pushed forward in 2005 before other candidates emerged. At his invitation, we had tea at the Thai Mission in New York on August 15, and met again in the Delegates' Lounge on September 27. I listened as he described his management reform experience, and the emphasis he would give it if he became SG. He was saying all the right things, and his pitch was quite intense, because he knew that neither his candidacy nor anyone else's was going anywhere without U.S. support. Our diplomats who knew Surakiart were not high on him, characterizing him as "a rich man's son" who, according to local gossip, had once tried to bribe a college professor for a grade by giving him a Rolex. By and large, our people simply didn't think Surakiart was competent. He struck me primarily as a politician, someone for whom the art of dealing was uppermost, which would at least be a welcome change from the pious rhetoric surrounding Annan.

Sri Lanka's candidate was their former ambassador to Washington during the Clinton years (where I first met him), Jayantha Dhanapala, who was also a former undersecretary general for disarmament. Dhanapala's candidacy was a tremendous long shot. Coming from South Asia, his chances always depended on at least neutrality from India, which it displayed for quite some time, although outright support from India could have played a significant role in the race.

Dhanapala's slim chances disappeared when India's Shashi Tharoor nominated himself. Undersecretary general for public information, one of the worst swamps in the entire Secretariat, he was a well-known fiction author in India, with a personal website that did "Bollywood" proud. He was his own biggest advocate. Arrogantly anti-American in the unconscious way that was so typical of much of the "UN community," he later wrote a *New York Times* op-ed piece criticizing the United States for its inattention to cricket, saying, among other things, "Baseball is to cricket as simple addition is to calculus."[5] Moreover, as a consummate UN insider, a central element of his campaign, he was the exact opposite of the profile we were looking for. Finally, given India's aspiration for a Security Council permanent seat, and coming from a huge country, Tharoor was breaking one of the UN's unwritten conventions, namely that SGs should come from smaller fry. It was true that Boutros-Ghali had come from Egypt, but India

---

5. Shashi Tharoor, "Our Cricket Problem," *New York Times,* March 23, 2007, p. A23, col. 1.

was much larger. Moreover, Tharoor's candidacy immediately sparked interest from Pakistan, which contemplated at various times running a candidate, including Munir Akram, their ambassador. In short, Tharoor was never going to make it, although he was the last person in New York to figure that out.

Slowly, it emerged that South Korea had a candidate, too, Foreign Minister Ban Ki-moon. Ban was well known in the United States, having been posted at various times in his career as a professional diplomat in both Washington and New York. I worked closely with him during Bush 41 when South Korea achieved its highest foreign policy priority, admission to the UN, jointly with North Korea, following the 1973 model of the two Germanies, ending yet another Cold War anomaly. Ban later served as chief of staff for the South Korean president of the General Assembly, and we reconnected during Bush 43 as he prepared to move to New York to take up that position.

South Korea's 2005 strategy, implemented by Perm Rep Young-jin Choi, was to discourage discussion of the secretary general race as premature, thereby hoping to keep it fluid if Ban decided to jump in. Nonetheless, the ROK's ambitions were not entirely invisible. Ban came to New York in late August 2005, and we met at his request at South Korea's Mission, right across Forty-fifth Street from the hole in the ground that, one day, would be filled with the new USUN building. The meeting was mostly about North Korea's nuclear program and the round of Six-Party Talks scheduled the next week. Ban had other things in mind, however, including a lengthy recitation of his ideas for UN reform, which, not surprisingly, mirrored our own. I gently explained our view that we wanted "the best-qualified candidate," even if it were not an Asian, and Ban said quietly they would have something to say on the subject in the very near future.

Ban was back in New York for the General Assembly opening, and, at his invitation, I had a one-on-one lunch with him on Friday, September 15, just after Bush had departed New York. Although Ban seemed awkward advancing his own candidacy, I made encouraging noises. He had asked for ten minutes alone with Rice just before or after the regular U.S.–South Korea bilateral meeting the next day, and I said I would give her a heads-up on his intentions. In early 2006, Ban returned to New York, on his way to meetings with Rice in Washington, and we traded impressions of the state of play in the race, notably our shared views that Thailand's Surakiart, despite his early start, was basically going nowhere, and that Sri Lanka's Dhanapala was dead in the water. Other names were being mentioned (such as East Timor's then foreign minister, José Ramos Horta, a 1996 Nobel Peace Prize winner), as there would be right up until the last moment, but few seemed likely to generate much momentum. What Ban really wanted to know was what the United States would do, but I didn't know myself at that point. We had lunch again on June 1, by which time it was clear to me that Rice had a "short list" of one name: Ban Ki-moon. I didn't give that away, but I tried to be as cooperative as possible without tipping my hand. Of course, Rice had also said to me on April 20, "I'm not sure we want a strong secretary general," which I didn't reveal either.

All of this maneuvering suited me just fine, because another U.S. objective was to hold the SG election much earlier than usual, perhaps even in the summer of 2006, in order to give whomever was elected a long transition period before actually assuming office on January 1, 2007. At a January 30 Perm Five meeting, in C-209, the little first-floor conference room looking out on the East River permanently set aside for the Perm Five (to the irritation of others), we discussed the timing issue. Jones Parry and de La Sablière worried about moving too quickly, because they feared electing a new SG would undercut Annan. That wasn't my objective, although it certainly didn't bother me. Both Wang and Denisov strongly supported moving ahead early. We agreed that during the U.S.'s February Security Council presidency, we would begin consultations with the other Council members to get the process started.

This meeting demonstrated a key fact about selecting secretaries general: It is essentially a Perm Five decision, expressed through the Security Council and presented to the General Assembly. The charter's Article 97 says only that "The Secretary-General shall be appointed by the General Assembly upon the recommendation of the Security Council," which had been interpreted from the very beginning to mean that the Council nominates one person, whom the General Assembly approves. Every five years, this causes enormous heartburn for G-77 countries like Brazil, India, Egypt, Pakistan, and others, not to mention Cuba and Venezuela. Since the General Assembly is essentially confronted with a "take-it-or-leave-it" choice, some feel excluded from the decision-making. Moreover, various of the High Minded are always exhorting the UN to conduct an "open and transparent job search" with "broad consultation" and discussion, as if we were not making an intensely political decision. In plain fact, acting through both the Perm Five and the other ten Council members, all of the regions make their preferences known.

On February 8, I started separate consulations with each of the nonpermanent members in the Council president's office. This routine was often used to judge the Council's mood before moving into an actual meeting with all members present, or to try to find a solution to a problem that had the Council tied up in knots. For the Council president, it is like being a dentist, with one member after another coming in every twenty minutes or half hour until all are met. I put four questions to each one: (1) What did they think about the timing of the SG election? (2) Should we write a job description? (3) Did the next SG have to be Asian? and (4) Did we have to limit ourselves to the field of "declared" candidates, or could we pick someone else? All agreed the election should be held earlier than usual, with Japan preferring October (not surprisingly, since Japan would then be Council president), but several agreed to the summer, including Nana Effah-Apenteng of Ghana (Annan's home country), who said August or September. There was no interest in writing a "job description," the Asia's turn argument prevailed overwhelmingly, and no one had an answer to the last question.

I reported my consultations to the full Council on February 24 and met with the Perm Five immediately afterward. De La Sablière helpfully said we should begin the election process in July, noting that we couldn't wait until our target month to start, because we might find ourselves hopelessly deadlocked, as happened in Cold War days. We needed to start well in advance, to ensure that we were *no later than* our target. (Of course, July was also the next French Council presidency, the reason for his suggestion.)

In March, under Argentina's presidency, the Council agreed to begin "official" consultations in June or July. In the meantime, de La Sablière had his staff research the most recent analogous election, in 1991, when Pérez de Cuéllar's term was ending. De La Sablière had then been French deputy perm rep, Wang had been the PRC political counselor in New York, and I had been IO at State, from which we all knew one another, and had a surprisingly common view of how things had been done in 1991. All the while, the rumblings of mutiny from the likes of India and Egypt continued to grow, as they contemplated a General Assembly resolution that would "require" the Security Council to submit more than one name for the SG position. I took a "make my day" approach to that idea, and in time, it disappeared.

By this time, new names were appearing. Eastern Europe's only serious SG campaign came from Latvian president Vaira Vike-Freiberga, who was not only from the one regional group that had never had an SG, but was also female. Moreover, before the collapse of the Soviet Union, she had lived in Canada, and had been a Canadian citizen. The idea was first broached to me quietly on October 27, 2005, by Latvian ambassador Solveiga Silkalna, and we agreed to keep in regular touch, given the outside odds of a Vike-Freiberga candidacy bucking not only the "Asia's turn" argument, but the brooding Russian displeasure as well. Vike-Freiberga herself called me on November 2, and we met in New York on March 9, 2006, and on several other occasions as the campaign intensified. I said I would be more than happy to stay in touch with her quietly, given the sensitivity of any decision she might make concerning the SG's race. I would have done the same for any other Eastern European, although only Vike-Freiberga stepped up.

In early June, Malloch Brown gave a controversial speech embodying much of what we were trying to sweep away in electing a new secretary general. Before a partisan group funded by George Soros (who was also subsidizing his housing), Malloch Brown, in the words of the June 7 *New York Times*, "assailed the United States," in "a highly unusual instance of a United Nations official singling out an individual country for criticism."[6] I couldn't have said it better. He essentially criticized not just the Bush administration, but the American people for getting their news only from Fox and Rush Limbaugh, which was a typically elitist, left-wing view of the slobs in "flyover country." This petty bureaucrat obviously saw himself as floating above UN member governments, rather than recognizing he was a mere international civil servant, *their* servant, not the other way around. Malloch Brown's criticism was thus fundamentally illegitimate, quite apart from being outrageously wrong on substance, but it accurately reflected the thirty-eighth-floor view that they were not ultimately responsible to UN member governments. Annan's staff had several years earlier floated the notion that he was a "secular pope," something they actually said in all seri-

---

6. Warren Hoge, "Official of U.N. Says Americans Undermine It With Criticism," *New York Times,* June 7, 2006, p. A8, col. 1.

ousness. Being a Lutheran, I didn't even believe in religious popes, and I was absolutely determined there weren't going to be any more "secular popes" on the thirty-eighth floor.

I called Annan and told him that the speech was the worst mistake I had ever seen by a UN official. I said he should repudiate it, points I made shortly thereafter to the press at the Security Council press stakeout. I was comfortable going public because a White House staffer had told me that morning that, at a White House dinner with prominent Republicans the night before, Bush had said to them, "Bolton speaks for the American people on the UN; he understands what they really think." On my way to the stakeout, I ran into Israeli ambassador Dan Gillerman, who had been at Malloch Brown's speech. "Thunderstruck" by Malloch Brown's remarks, Gillerman had offered him a ride home "because you won't have much more work to do at the United Nations after that speech." I called several other perm reps, all of whom had reactions similar to mine. Alan Rock of Canada could only say, "What could he have been thinking?" and New Zealand's Rosemary Banks said that the remarks were "extremely dangerous" for the UN. Banks said that at a dinner the night before, as the story of Malloch Brown's remarks circulated, even Jan Eliasson had said, "It is time for Malloch Brown to shut up." That was one of my main points to the press: Malloch Brown may have been aiming at Americans, but he had hit the UN itself. Annan refused to back away from the speech, which suited me fine, because now the offensive words belonged to him as well.

By then, Fox News was beating the drums on the story, and Limbaugh was not far behind. Conservative bloggers were also on the case, as one of them, Michelle Malkin, put it in her headline: "Hey, UN: Boo-Freaking-Hoo." I flew that evening to London, landing early on June 8, and as I rode to the Park Lane Hilton, BBC Radio 4 repeatedly broadcast stories with lines like, "The UN is at odds with its top paymaster." Just as we arrived at the hotel, BBC Radio had a long interview with former senior U.K. diplomat John Weston, who clearly saw the speech as a serious mistake. The *Times* (a Rupert Murdoch paper) had a big story on page two, and the *Daily Telegraph* and the *Guardian* featured it prominently, which delighted me. I had expected good coverage, but to see Malloch Brown taken down a peg or two at home was a bonus. That evening, at about nine o'clock London time, Rice called to say, "You did absolutely the right thing" by rebuking Malloch Brown. "I was so furious," she continued, "the president was furious, Hadley was furious," she added before I could say "hello." "They were lucky it wasn't me," she continued, "because I wouldn't have been nearly so polite as you were," which was certainly nice to hear. I suspected Annan and Malloch Brown wanted to use the incident as part of their campaign to prevent my confirmation by the Senate, and to separate me from Rice if there was a way to do it. On this point, they had clearly failed. By contrast, I thought I had finally made it clear that the United States didn't want a new "secular pope" on the thirty-eighth floor, and had no intention of electing one.

Away from the sacred and back to the profane, by July 2006 we readied for the first "straw poll," an informal vote in which each Council member would "encourage," "discourage," or express "no opinion" about the four declared candidates, who were listed alphabetically: Ban, Dhanapala, Surakiart, and Tharoor. At 4:30 P.M. on July 25, in the Council's informal chamber, we excluded all Secretariat personnel, including the translators. Only two people per delegation were permitted in the room, in what turned out to be a vain attempt to keep the results of the straw poll private. De La Sablière gave out UN pens, so that each of us would be writing in the same color; I joked that they should all be given back for budget purposes, although I noticed some perm reps kept theirs for souvenirs. I voted Rice's inclination, because IO's instructions were incoherent, and waited with the others for de La Sablière to read out the results of each secret straw ballot. Ban and Tharoor led with 12 and 10 "encourage" votes respectively, with Dhanapala and Surakiart trailing badly (4 and 5 respectively). The actual votes appeared in the press within hours. While I was happy about Ban, I was amazed that Tharoor had done so well.

August all but disappeared in New York, as it so often does, with many people on vacation. There was widespread speculation that both Dhanapala and Surakiart would withdraw, and that other candidates might now be induced to enter. As it turned out, both of them stayed in, although they never achieved vote totals that gave them a chance at success. I would have bet money that Pakistan would offer a candidate, whether Munir Akram or someone else, given that Tharoor was one of the two leading candidates, but that did not happen, for reasons that were never very clear. Surprisingly, in mid-August, another candidate did jump in, only informally at first, that being Prince Zeid of Jordan, who was highly regarded for his candid report on sexual exploitation and abuse by UN peacekeepers. Nonetheless, Zeid did not exactly come from the part of Asia that China and Japan likely had in mind when they said "Asia's turn," and Zeid's Swedish mother and lovely British wife probably weren't the "profile" that Beijing and others had in mind. Moreover, with Boutros-Ghali, another Arab (even if nominally in the African Group) having been secretary general only ten years before, I didn't see the "Asians" really letting this happen. Even so, I liked Zeid and respected him, and I knew that Jordan's king Abdullah had personally raised the issue with Bush, perhaps more than once. As Zeid himself liked to say jokingly, it helps when your cousin is the king.

Russia's new perm rep Vitaly Churkin and China's Wang prevented further straw polls until September, and even after Labor Day when vacations were over, which put us dangerously close to repeating the patterns of earlier elections and going right to the end of the year. I struggled to understand what was on their minds, because earlier they had been advocates for proceeding more quickly, and now even Jones Parry and de La Sablière, who had been more hesitant, were concerned that we were falling behind schedule. We finally agreed to hold two more straw polls, the first on September 14.

I decided it was time for a private sit-down with Wang to discuss what China and the United States really wanted, which we did on September 13. We agreed to tell each other how we had voted in the first straw poll, and I said we voted to encourage Ban and discourage the other three. Wang said he voted to encourage all four, to support the "Asia's turn" argument, which he thought would also lead to instructions to support Zeid in the next poll. Interestingly, Wang did not think Pakistan would enter unless Tharoor's vote rose substantially, which Wang did not expect. After discussing the others, Wang said flatly that China liked Ban. Here, I thought, the rubber was meeting the road. Wang and I agreed to talk after the next straw poll.

On September 14, the Security Council took its second straw poll. This time, Ban had a commanding lead, 14 votes to "encourage" and only 1 to "discourage." Tharoor stayed at 10 "encourage" votes, Surakiart unaccountably rose to 9, Dhanapala fell further to 3, and Zeid gained only 6, coming in fourth despite speculation that he might finish second or third. Ban's showing was nearly conclusive at this point, and the only question was whether the sole "discourage" vote came from a permanent member and might turn into a veto. Wang immediately told the press that Ban had finished first, and even though he didn't give out the exact vote totals (which

Council members had all agreed we would not do), the press interpreted Wang's enthusiastic report as meaning China favored Ban. I personally suspected that the "discourage" vote came from Japan, given diplomatic tensions between the two countries, and I decided that I would talk to Oshima to persuade him to have Tokyo change his instructions to be supportive.

Vike-Freiberga called the day after the straw vote, and I filled her in on what was happening, stressing to her that it was now or never. She said she did not want to wait until arriving in New York, but preferred to declare her candidacy on Latvian soil, which she did. I congratulated her on the direction of her thinking, saying that sometimes you could achieve your objectives without necessarily prevailing, but like the expert politician she was, she fired back, "No one likes a loser." Vike-Freiberga arrived in New York over the weekend and campaigned vigorously, but there was no way of knowing whether it was making any difference. Later in the day on Friday, Zeid called, quite discouraged at the outcome, saying that Greek perm rep Dimis Vassilakis had tried to talk him into withdrawing, and telling the press that the Security Council should wrap up this issue in September. I assured Zeid that we were not trying to influence his decision whether to stay in or withdraw one way or the other, at which point Zeid said he had to get off the telephone because his cousin, King Abdullah, was calling.

Rice met with China's foreign minister Li on Monday morning, September 18, and I filled her in beforehand on my conversations with Wang about Ban. She was quite pleased, and she and Li in effect sealed the deal on Ban at the end of their bilateral, which Wang and I each quickly followed up. I had yet another lunch with Ban, and we started off discussing the straw polls. Ban believed the one "discourage" vote he had received came from Ghana's Effah-Apenteng. He reasoned that the "discourage" ballot had also voted to "encourage" Tharoor, but had expressed no opinion on other candidates. Ban speculated that Tharoor was Annan's man (an insider who he hoped would not trash his "legacy," such as it was), and that Effah-Apenteng was trying to help Annan. I said both Wang and I thought it was Japan, but Ban said he had already spoken with Oshima, who flatly denied it. I made a mental note to myself that I still needed to talk with Oshima. I stressed to Ban that we needed to bring this process to a conclusion, sooner rather than later, before Tharoor or others could figure out a way to disrupt it. Ban agreed he would have the ROK delegation begin pressing this point in their lobbying.

Ban also said he had had a "surprising" conversation with U.K. foreign secretary Margaret Beckett (who had succeeded Straw) and Jones Parry, in which Jones Parry said that Britain considered the UN Department of Political Affairs (DPA) to be "its" slot. Ban said he had not responded. Of course, I knew that Jones Parry really considered it "his" position, which he very much wanted when he stepped down as perm rep in 2007, so I decided to lay out for Ban some of our thoughts on changes we wanted once he took office. One item high on my list was that the new secretary general should request the resignations of all high-ranking UN officials, above the rank of assistant SG, to clean house, much the way an incoming U.S. president can remove his predecessor's top appointments. That didn't mean that all would have to depart immediately, or that some might not be retained, but a call for resignations would send a clear signal that change was coming. Ban seemed to get the point.

Ban's comments about his unpleasant conversation with the Brits also explained why Jones Parry had suddenly grown nervous about speeding along to finish the selection of the next secretary general. I reported all of this to Rice at the Waldorf that evening, right before her meeting with the other Perm Five foreign ministers. She said that Beckett and French foreign minister Douste-Blazy both made strong arguments for slowing down, but no one else had seemed interested. Lavrov said that Vike-Freiberga was never going to be SG, and no one said anything negative about Ban. Nor was Surakiart mentioned, but a military coup in Thailand a few days before had ended his candidacy for all practical purposes. In any case, Rice persuaded the ministers to hold another straw ballot on September 28, which greatly distressed Jones Parry and de La Sablière when they heard it.

They turned to another tactic, resisting differentiating the ballots between permanent and nonpermanent members. The Council's mood was strong to have different-colored ballots to see which, if any, of the Perm Five were willing to reveal that they would consider vetoing any candidate. I wanted differentiated ballots, because it would show that all of the candidates other than Ban had at least one veto (ours), and that some would have several. Wang and Churkin agreed with this assessment. In a meeting with only the five perm reps, Churkin asked de La Sablière and the British deputy perm rep (Jones Parry being on vacation again) point-blank whether they had a new candidate, or whether they expected a new one to

come out of the woodwork. De La Sablière gave the game away immediately by saying, "The minute we elect a new SG, Kofi is dead," which certainly sounded good to me. The Brits and the French were beginning to
realize that the gravy days with Annan, where they dominated top positions
in the Secretariat, and where their EU networks predominated, were over.
The Perm Five meeting ended without a decision, and we went out separately to meet the circling press. They knew exactly what issue we had been
discussing, and since I happened to walk out with Wang, I put my arm
around his shoulder and said, "On this issue, China and the United States
see eye to eye." I loved it.

On September 28, in a straw poll with undifferentiated ballots Ban
dropped to a 13–1–1, vote, which I took to be either Britain or France moving away from "encourage" to slow him down. I asked Jones Parry how he
thought this tactic was going to get them into Ban's good graces, and he just
gritted his teeth. Everyone else in the race also lost "encourage" votes, a new
candidate from Afghanistan (former finance minister Ashraf Ghani) received only three, and Vike-Freiberga received seven "encourage" votes to
finish third, a credible showing for a late entrant.

The next day, I met with Oshima, urging him to reconsider Japan's "discourage" vote on Ban, which he did not deny to me. I urged Japan to support Ban, so that we could wrap this up, and so that Japan would not be
isolated, an argument I knew would appeal to a career diplomat. I called
Rice on Saturday, September 30, just before she left on a Middle East trip,
to tell her that things might start moving very quickly, and she said only,
"You handle the tactics any way you think appropriate."

Oshima told me Monday morning, October 2, that their new prime
minister, Shinzo Abe, would be traveling to Beijing and Seoul that week.
He wanted to postpone any formal vote for secretary general until after
Abe's trip, which I said I would try to help arrange. With the differentiated
straw poll coming up that afternoon, I took it that Japan could not yet vote
"yes," but might at least shift to "no opinion," which was in fact what happened. The vote showed Ban now leading with 14 "encourage" votes, and
only one "no opinion" vote, which we could see was not from a permanent
member. Afterward, I moved for a quick formal vote in the Council, on
October 9. Wang flatly told the press outside the Security Council room
that Ban would be the next secretary general; I was a little more restrained,
but there was no doubt the race was over. Several of the other candidates,

sensing the end, withdrew, including Tharoor, whose exit was teary and dramatic, as doubtless his term as SG would have been.

The Security Council's formal vote on October 9 turned out to be more than a little anticlimactic, given that North Korea had tested a nuclear weapon the day before, setting off another intense diplomatic battle, but we were all determined to bring the SG race to a close. The vote was in fact unanimous, adopting Resolution 1715, and by then all of the other candidates had formally withdrawn. Of course, the General Assembly still had to vote, and I succeeded in setting that vote for the end of the week, just to eliminate any possibility that troublemakers might be lying in wait.

On Friday, October 13, I had yet another one-on-one lunch with Ban Ki-moon, this time in his suite at the Intercontinental Hotel, right across Forty-ninth Street from the Waldorf. Ban said he thought he would not resign as ROK foreign minister until mid-November because of the problems North Korea was causing, which was understandable but which would substantially reduce his transition time. I stressed that we wanted Ban to enjoy flexibility in his appointments, and that our absolute prerequisite was cleaning out the incumbent top officeholders, in order to give him space to put his new team together. He would never have a better opportunity than right at the outset of his tenure, and he should especially understand he did not have to be bound by the existing organization chart. For example, he should consider combining various departments, such as Political Affairs and Peacekeeping, and then splitting the new entity into separate geographical regions.

I told Ban he did not have to "balance" each and every personnel decision. He should consider the politics only of the total pattern of his appointments, but he seemed already to have convinced himself he needed to appoint a woman from the Third World as deputy secretary general. In fact, I would rather have a tough-minded manager from the G-77 than one of the High Minded from the Valhallas of Europe, and stressed again that he had to emphasize qualifications, or he would find himself overwhelmed by political concerns. I said that the United States wanted either Peacekeeping Operations (DPKO) or Political Affairs (DPA), and suggested that Japan or Germany take Management, given their large contributions. This was a lot to absorb, especially just a few moments before the General Assembly's formal election, but I was confident Ban was listening carefully.

The General Assembly meeting proceeded uneventfully, as cooler heads prevailed to persuade Venezuela and Cuba not to disrupt the meeting. Representatives of the various regional groups spoke, and I spoke as representative of the host country. My favorite line was my last, "Expressing our appreciation for the work of [Annan's] top team of advisers, who will also be moving on to new challenges," which produced chuckling all around the hall. Ban gave a modest speech, recalling the help that the United Nations had provided South Korea at the time of the 1950 North Korean invasion, without which, of course, there wouldn't be a South Korea. He also talked about reading a letter his young schoolmates had written asking the UN to help another small country under attack, obviously referring to the Hungarian Revolution of 1956, which was actually quite moving. I pointed out to the press the contrast between the success story of South Korea, which had just seen one of its citizens become UN secretary general, whereas the impoverished North Korea was testing nuclear weapons.

Ban visited with Bush in Washington on October 17, meeting Hadley in the West Wing, which allowed the president to slip in informally. Most of the meeting was on North Korea, but Abrams relayed to me the next day that, after Bush congratulated Ban on his election, Ban said he hoped to focus on democracy issues and human rights. Bush then said that Ban "should get rid of the [senior] staff" at the UN, and specifically "get rid of Malloch Brown," whom he called "anti-American," and "appoint your own people." "You should want to change the entire management culture," said Bush, because "the UN is not well run. . . . The UN doesn't believe in consequences," said Bush, "just rhetoric." Bush pushed specifically for an American to head DPKO and stressed how hard it was to justify the annual American contribution with so many problems in the organization. There was no doubt Ban had heard the message from "the highest level," as they say. Now the only question was what he would do about it.

A few days thereafter, Burnham announced his resignation, effective November 15, to return to investment banking in New York. I was sorry to see him go, but he had long since planned this departure, and his forthright announcement made it plain what we expected from everyone else, not that there was any great rush to the Secretariat's doors. This was a part of the entitlement mentality we were striving to break, and the sound of people digging in at their offices, hoping to ride out the transition, showed just how serious the problem was, and how hard Ban Ki-moon's task would be.

When Burnham's resignation was officially announced, I issued a statement praising his work, concluding, "We expect many other senior UN officials to transition out as well, and we thank all of them for their service."

On January 16, 2007, Ban visited Washington again, this time to meet with Bush in the Oval Office. His early days were already marked with controversy, as several of his reorganization schemes were rejected before they were even fully debated, and others were scaled back, due to the intense G-77 lobbying against them. I suspected Ban's task would be harder than even we had predicted, and the real question was whether he would sink into the swamp of the UN's "culture of inaction" or withstand it and perhaps even overcome it. On that issue, we can only await further developments.

CHAPTER ELEVEN

SECURITY COUNCIL SUCCESSES ON NORTH KOREA

It is a maxim founded on the universal experience of mankind, that no nation is to be trusted farther than it is bound by its interest; and no prudent statesman or politician will venture to depart from it.

—GEORGE WASHINGTON, NOVEMBER 14, 1778[1]

While the Six-Party Talks wandered aimlessly, North Korea did not rest. Starting in summer 2006, likely encouraged by the weakness of our negotiating strategy, the North took several provocative actions. The first occurred in July when it fired off a volley of missiles, and the second was in October when it tested a nuclear device. This time, however, the American response did not come in the Six-Party Talks, but in the Security Council. For the first time in my six years in the Bush administration, I had the opportunity and the policy leeway to go after the DPRK the way I wished I had been able to do from the start. Unconstrained by the baggage of the Six-Party Talks, joined by a strong and determined ally in Tokyo, and without any interference or even much involvement from State's Bureau for East Asian and Pacific Affairs, we went after the DPRK hammer and tongs, diplomatically, of course.

---

1. Quoted in Joseph J. Ellis, *His Excellency, George Washington* (New York: Alfred A. Knopf, 2004), p. 123.

North Korea Goes Ballistic

Fireworks on Tuesday, the Fourth of July, 2006, started early, at about 2:45 P.M. when the Ops Center called to say that North Korea had fired a rocket from their east coast Kittaeryong base, seemingly timed to coincide with the launch of the space shuttle *Discovery*. In rapid succession, more missiles were launched from the DPRK's east coast, toward the Sea of Japan, payloads, ranges, and targets all unknown. The North fired seven missiles in all, one of which was a long-range Taepo-Dong 2, which blew up forty-two seconds into flight, following a trajectory that would have taken it over Japan, toward Hawaii. Another off-course missile landed close to Russia, which we thought might grab their attention. After the first shot, I immediately called Japanese perm rep Kenzo Oshima and learned that he was unaware of the missile launches. I also called de La Sablière and Jones Parry to alert them in case we decided to call for an emergency Security Council meeting that evening. Japan's initial reaction was surprisingly serene, but the level of agitation rose with each successive shot, as I could tell in my near-continuous phone calls with Oshima, who by 5:00 P.M. was in his office for easier communication with Tokyo.

In the preceding days, the media, especially the Asian press, had been filled with rumors that the DPRK was about to break its 1999 moratorium on missile launches from the Korean peninsula. The moratorium, announced after the 1998 Taepo-Dong shot that landed in the Pacific east of Japan and caused a near panic there, had been a significant propaganda coup for the North because of its peaceful appearance. In reality, however, the moratorium never truly constrained North Korea's ballistic missile program, both because the North itself continued to do everything except conduct actual test launches and because of its extensive ballistic missile cooperation with Iran, which was using the same basic missile technology. Given the possibility of an imminent DPRK launch, the United States had already been preparing a draft sanctions resolution before the actual launches, which we modified to take account of the multiple DPRK shots.

The DPRK launches created a potentially dispositive moment to show that the Six-Party Talks had run their course, and I was determined to exploit it. Rice convened a conference call at about 6:15 P.M., having spoken with Bush and Hadley. For that night, they wanted our response to be low-key, saying we were consulting in the Security Council, which we were certainly already doing. I explained the state of play in New York, and as I was doing so, was interrupted by a call from Oshima. He said that Japan's Security Council was meeting in the prime minister's office as we spoke, and that he expected to hear imminently whether they wanted an emergency Council meeting that night. I returned to the conference call to give this update, and Rice asked that I alert her as soon as we knew something one way or the other, since she planned to call several foreign ministers that evening. Oshima called at about 8:25 P.M. to say that Tokyo had decided the Council should meet Wednesday morning, after which I called de La Sablière, since France was Council president in July, to tell him that we were appropriately accommodating Japan, which had the most at stake from a threatening North Korea.

On Wednesday, there was a secure interagency videoconference call at 7:00 A.M. Rice began by saying that ROK foreign minister Ban Ki-moon had been "very strong," referring to the DPRK's "deepening isolation" and its "threat to regional and international security," concluding "no more business as usual." Foreign Minister Taro Aso of Japan was "also very strong," and Rice "had to rein him in a bit," which bothered me. I wanted Japan out front on the Security Council resolution, not being reined in by us. Rice said China's foreign minister Li was "disappointing," saying, "We should hope for calm" through meetings, and "not escalate the issue." Rice responded, "I didn't stay up to midnight to talk about future meetings, but about the North Korean launches." To us, she stressed, "We've got a China problem." I reported again on developments in New York, and others chimed in with additional steps being taken, including sending Jim Kelly's successor, EAP assistant secretary Chris Hill, to the region. Hadley observed twice that we should assess why our current North Korea policy had not succeeded, which he ascribed to allowing the Six-Party Talks to become negotiations rather than using them to pressure North Korea. Hadley was right, but no one in EAP really ever thought the Six-Party Talks were intended for anything other than negotiations! Rice designated Crouch to chair an interagency working group, and I called him right after the videoconference to say I was worried that EAP would try to maneuver us away from sanctions and back to the Six-Party Talks. He agreed and asked that I keep him posted regularly on developments in the Security Council.

At the July 5 meeting of the Security Council, Oshima gave a very strong statement, saying we would circulate a resolution and asking to meet and discuss it that afternoon. I spoke in support, as did others, significantly including Effah-Apenteng of Ghana and Basile Ikouebe of Congo (Brazzaville). Wang then spoke, and "the China problem" emerged into full view, compounded by Russian perm rep Churkin's backing him. Wang wanted to reprise what the Council had done after the 1998 North Korean missile launch, which was to issue a press statement, the weakest possible response (below Council resolutions and presidential statements). I answered that this was different from 1998, stressing the nuclear weapons issue and the combined threat posed by the DPRK seeking both nuclear weapons and a long-range ballistic missile capability. There was no way we would follow the 1998 precedent, which itself had been pathetically weak, and typical of Clinton's North Korea policy. After the Council meeting ended, Oshima, Jones Parry, and I appeared together at the press stakeout for a photo op, demonstrating we were all on the same wavelength. During the day, I was constantly on the phone with other perm reps, lining up support for our draft and comparing notes with Oshima on how things were going. Not only was a strong resolution essential, but so was speed. If the Council dillydallied, as it did too often, even a strong resolution at the end would not have the profound effect I wanted.

Back at USUN, I immediately called Crouch and Joseph, and we agreed not to water down our draft resolution—which essentially prohibited all missile-related sales to and from North Korea—to satisfy China and Russia. Otherwise, the text could die a death of a thousand cuts, which was our typical pattern of negotiation. If China and Russia abstained on a tough resolution, so be it. The resolution would pass anyway. If either were to veto, that would demonstrate that the Security Council had not been up to the job, freeing us to do what we chose to do outside the UN. So be that, too. In a 4:00 P.M. videoconference, Joseph reported on "defensive measures" being drawn up, and I explained events in New York. In particular, we now also had "a Russia problem," Churkin frantically complaining that our draft resolution was "an extreme, extreme thing." Nonetheless, Crouch repeated what he, Joseph, and I had agreed earlier, namely that we were not going to compromise the text just for abstentions by China and Russia. No one disagreed. Nonetheless, Burns made several troubling comments about "not interfering" with the Six-Party Talks. It was not our resolution that was "interfering," but North Korea's missile launches, a point EAP had trouble processing. Afterward, I called Joseph and found him equally troubled. He repeated what he had said before, namely, "I'm not long for this job," given the weakness of both our DPRK and our Iran policies.

On Thursday, July 6, Oshima and I agreed we would try to put the draft to a vote the next day, which, under the Council's practices, meant we had to circulate a "final" text that evening so that everyone would have twenty-four hours' notice of what was to be voted, and to get appropriate instructions from their capitals. Because these "final" drafts were printed with blue ink, the colloquial expression for setting up a vote was to say "we're putting this in blue today," with a vote the next day. Unfortunately, however, the Brits were now slowing us down with a host of legal niceties, as Jones Parry kept saying that "legislation" had to be written precisely. This was a good encapsulation of the "global governance" mentality I so disliked, because if the Council were "legislating," then in fact we were behaving like "lawmakers," a point critical to understanding subsequent disputes on both North Korea and Iran. At a minimum, however, the British scriveners were opening the possibility of delay, thus inviting Chinese and Russian obstructionism, which was not long in coming. Crouch told me that Bush's phone calls with Hu and Putin had been inconclusive on a Security Council resolution, but Bush had said to Hu, "The great Chinese people have been slapped in the face by North Korea," which was certainly designed to get Hu's attention. Crouch believed China really was agitated with the DPRK, although they clearly weren't giving that impression publicly.

By midday, however, Oshima was now very worried about abstentions by China and Russia, and he asked that we meet with Jones Parry and de La Sablière. Since Rice was solidly in favor of a vote the next day, I saw no reason the four of us should not meet. This was a mistake. The meeting was a debacle. Jones Parry and de La Sablière worried that the resolution was too strong, not as it might affect North Korea, *but as it might affect their efforts to deal with Iran's nuclear program* (described in the next chapter). They worried about offending Russia and China so much over North Korea that it would make them less cooperative on Iran, as if to date the two of them had shown the slightest cooperation on Iran anyway! Given how weak the European position already was on Iran, and their unwillingness to pressure Iran, and thereby risk creating dispositive evidence of the already-evident failure of their diplomatic efforts, this was not only bad news, it was simple appeasement. Even worse was that Japan, obviously infected by Britain and France, now wanted to spend more time working on China and Russia.

When I reported this setback to Washington, Crouch responded, "Fuck these guys, they are completely worthless." Even worse, French national security adviser Maurice Gourdault-Montagne was telling Hadley at that very time that de La Sablière's instructions were to support not a resolution, but only a presidential statement, which was a substantially weaker outcome. All of this, the French explained to Hadley, was to avoid a confrontation with Russia and China before upcoming July meetings on Iran. The European approach thus created a vicious circle: Their weakness on Iran produced weakness on North Korea, which only encouraged Iran's boldness, producing a weaker response from the Europeans, abetted by EAP's weakness on North Korea, and so on. It was like competitive devaluations of national currencies. Rice was furious when she heard about this and called me to say I should pull Jones Parry in particular aside and ask him, "What the hell are you doing?" because that was certainly what she was going to do when she called Beckett, Douste-Blazy, and Aso that evening. Having seen what Britain and France would do when we asked for their support on North Korea, where they faced no threats, had no strategic interests, and had no trade ties, there was little doubt how they would behave in any coming crisis with Iran, where the opposites were true. Neville Chamberlain was alive and well in New York.

Fortunately, on the evening of July 6, France shifted. Gourdault-Montagne called Hadley again to say that now France *did* want a tough resolution on North Korea, because without one "all is lost on Iran." That was better. Hadley said if I didn't "see a French attitude adjustment" on Friday, I should call Gourdault-Montagne myself, since he would be in New York that day. Calls to London produced similar good news, namely that the concerns Jones Parry had raised about our draft were not shared at 10 Downing Street. The bad news came Friday morning when Burns called to say that Rice had agreed with Lavrov the night before to postpone going into blue to give the Chinese a chance to bring the North Koreans around. Lavrov had been Russian perm rep immediately before becoming foreign minister, and he loved showing off his UN bargaining skills, through which he constantly flummoxed other ministers unfamiliar with the jargon or the minutiae. I thought this was yet another example, especially since it was

180 degrees from what Rice and Hadley had specifically said to me just the afternoon before.

I spoke several times with Rice on Friday, and she said she completely understood my logic on the timing of a vote, which she certainly had no intention of postponing past Monday, which was better than what I had feared. Rice arranged another conference call on Saturday at about 4:30 P.M. with the usual suspects: Hadley and Crouch from the NSC, and Burns, Joseph, and me from State, and others as well. Rice said she wanted to tell us about the "unpleasant" conversation she had had with Chinese foreign minister Li. The Ops Center had previously briefed me on the call, as they typically did, reporting that Li had repeatedly blamed the entire crisis on Japan's aspiration for a permanent seat on the Security Council! "I was pretty raw with him," said Rice, asking if China would veto the current draft. "If we have no other choice, we will," Li replied, basically also threatening the end of the Six-Party Talks. Rice then asked us, "Do we believe they would veto? What would be the effect of going ahead, and what about timing?" Knowing what Rice's counselor Philip Zelikow was prepared to say, I let him go first. He argued that we should accept a veto if we had a credible post-veto strategy, which he thought we did, and noted the political costs of showing weakness and bowing to China's threat. Rice said China was leaving us with no choice except to be prepared to go outside the Security Council to deal with North Korea our own way. I said there was a substantial chance the Chinese were bluffing, but whether they were or not, we needed to push ahead.

Nonetheless, over the weekend, in a series of seemingly continuous Perm-Three-plus-Japan meetings, Jones Parry and de La Sablière worked away at postponing any vote where there was a risk of a Russian or Chinese veto or abstention. At 10:30 A.M. Sunday, July 9, in yet another Perm-Three-plus-Japan meeting, Oshima reported on a Li-Aso conversation, from which Japan concluded that China's veto threat was serious. They believed China felt cornered and was not handling itself well. De La Sablière gave his readout of the Li-Douste-Blazy call, in which Li had said, "China would have no choice but to use its right of permanent membership," meaning a veto. There was no doubt the Chinese DPRK veto threat more deeply worried the British and the French because of Iran. Rice convened another conference call at 1:00 P.M., showing that our resolve was flagging as well, and said we should agree to see what a Chinese delegation led by Deputy Foreign Minister Wu Dawei, then visiting Pyongyang, came back with. If the result was the *status quo ante* (resuming the missile moratorium and returning to the Six-Party Talks), we would have no need to go ahead with the resolution. I was stunned at this reversal, meaning that, after all we had been through, we would accept the *status quo ante, the original Chinese position*. I pitched proceeding with the vote on Monday, July 10, because simply returning to the *status quo ante* got us nothing, and further delay risked bleeding away votes we already had. Rice wasn't biting, and no one else spoke in support of my view, so it was left to me to tell the Japanese we wanted a further delay in the vote, just as Russia and China had been asking. One positive note was that Rice stressed that we tell the Chinese that the DPRK was causing a "crisis" in Sino-American bilateral relations, which was certainly fine with me. Interestingly, Hadley asked Rice if she had spoken to Bush, and she said she had not.

When the Perm-Three-plus-Japan convened at 5:00 P.M., Oshima reported that Wang had instructions to vote "no," which de La Sablière confirmed. China would not accept that the Council would invoke Chapter VII of the charter (the only portion under which "legally binding" decisions could be made, said the lawyers); would not agree that the DPRK launches were a "threat to international peace and security" (a quotation from the charter that Perm Five lawyers always insisted on); and would not accept any kind of sanctions. All of this meant a resolution with no teeth. The other four cosponsors on the Council arrived at about five-thirty, and Jones Parry and de La Sablière made every argument they could think of in favor of a presidential statement (PRST), all for fear of a Chinese veto of a strong resolution. "Even lemmings had to stop and think before a vote," Jones Parry pleaded, but Peter Burian of Slovakia responded that we could not be for unity at any price. I stressed that making China stand in the sunlight and pay a price for the veto was an important factor we had to emphasize in their internal calculations. By then, the French and British were pounding on only one note—Iran, Iran, Iran—and the meeting broke up inconclusively. That evening, Rice had another call with Li, who again simply tried to blame Japan. Rice responded, "Don't ever tell me again that Japan is the problem." She said that the "difficult impasse" we faced would have "consequences" for the bilateral relationship, and that she could not understand why China was not stronger with North Korea, especially given the

DPRK's "slap" to China. She concluded by telling Li, "This [the Six-Party Talks] is the one big project that China has embarked upon, and it's a failure," saying it was "high time China [either] did something" or supported our resolution.

At 7:15 A.M. Monday, I waited for another secure videoconference, scheduled to begin as soon as a meeting between Bush, Cheney, Rice, Hadley, and Crouch concluded. Rice and Hadley didn't appear on the screen until nearly 8:00 A.M., however, meaning the meeting with Bush had gone much longer than expected. When our conference call did begin, it was clear things had shifted again, this time back in the right direction. Rice asked me about developments in New York, and I stressed that the idea of a PRST rather than a resolution hadn't died yet. I was still resisting, with which Rice emphatically agreed. She had been "hashing things over" with Bush, who now wanted "to put the ball squarely in the Chinese court." They had to "deliver" on the Wu mission, or we were taking the draft to a vote whether or not they continued to threaten a veto. If they did veto, then there would be "other consequences" in the bilateral relationship, which was the right approach. By "deliver," the president meant not just a return to the missile moratorium and the Six-Party Talks, but the implementation of the September 2005 joint declaration from the talks (which has gone nowhere), meaning the dismantling of the nuclear programs. How long we were actually prepared to delay a vote was not clear, but I was so happy with the substantive outcome Rice directed that I suggested we just say we were evaluating things day by day, and she quickly agreed. We were back on track again.

On Monday, we had one of several Perm-Five-plus-Japan meetings during this crisis, a very unusual case of inviting a country outside the Perm Five to attend one of our meetings, but obviously warranted in these circumstances. Wang still had no news to report on Wu's mission in Pyongyang. Oshima made clear that, while he would be disappointed by a Chinese veto, that would be their decision, and they would bear the consequences. I agreed with Oshima. Wang said that China opposed the resolution no matter what happened with Wu's mission. Moreover, while China wanted good bilateral relations, said Wang, his voice rising and angry, "Good bilateral relations are not *given* to China." Even more emotionally, he said, "Our vote comes from Beijing, not from Tokyo or Washington. We are a sovereign nation, and our vote will be the same whenever it comes [i.e., negative]." Oshima said, reasonably, that if China planned to vote "no" whatever the result of Wu's visit, then he wanted a vote today, and he asked Churkin how Russia would vote. Churkin said he didn't have instructions, which I doubted. When Wang and Churkin left, I said to Jones Parry and de La Sablière that it was time to stop discussing a presidential statement; the entire thing had become a time-consuming, unproductive detour away from a tough resolution. This time, the message sank in, as did the reality. I called Crouch at about 1:00 P.M., mostly to find out what Bush had said in the meeting before the morning videoconference, given Rice's tougher approach. "The reason we were where we were this morning," Crouch said, "was the man who gave you your job in New York."

On Tuesday, July 11—now one full embarrassing week after the DPRK missile shots—there was a substantial shift in our favor. Russia circulated its own resolution, clearly meaning the idea of a presidential statement was dead, which Wang said he could support, albeit unhappily. Russia's draft was nowhere near acceptable, but this was still an important improvement. On the other hand, Iran was slowing us down, there were no reports from Wu Dawei's mission, and time was dragging. On July 12, Rice called from Paris, where she was attending Iran meetings, to stress that Russia should want a vote, veto or not, before the G-8 Summit in Russia over the weekend, because the leaders would not want to have the issue unresolved. Of course, we also had war breaking out in Lebanon, which, in its own peculiar UN-centric way, pushed the Security Council to finishing with the DPRK before turning to Lebanon. Later that morning, Wang asked me into a small conference room near the Security Council for a quiet conversation. Wu was returning to China on Friday, a day or so ahead of schedule, because he was getting nothing from the DPRK, he said, and Wu would report directly to Hu, just before Hu left for St. Petersburg. I interpreted this meeting as Wang's looking for a way to avoid having to cast a veto. When the Perm-Three-plus-Japan met that afternoon, Oshima said China was now "desperate" and that the Wu mission had become "embarrassing," which we both also saw as China's trying to get out of the veto box it had built for itself.

By Thursday, July 13, we learned that Wu was already on his way back from the DPRK, empty-handed. The day was filled with other business, including casting my first veto on a very unbalanced resolution critical of Israel, but the Perm-Five-plus-Japan met again at the U.S. Mission early that evening, grinding our way through the text. By and large, we got what we wanted, confirming how Oshima and I saw the tactical situation, but several key points remained unresolved. On Friday morning, however, the Russians and the Chinese, having obviously heard from their capitals overnight, began to walk back from what we had agreed. As that meeting broke, Rice called from Russia for a status report, this time agreeing with Oshima and me to push for a vote on Friday or Saturday, even if it meant a Chinese veto.

The major issue remaining was whether the resolution would use the phrase "acting under Chapter VII," which along with several other buzz phrases, was what Perm Five lawyers liked to have in resolutions said to be "legally binding." Of course, many resolutions, even those authorizing the use of force, as in the 1950 Korean conflict, had not used the buzz phrases, but the lawyers were legal formalists who wanted the words for protective comfort. Russia and China caused this entire debate by arguing that the phrase "acting under Chapter VII" was a sneaky way of authorizing the use of force, which was utter nonsense. Nonetheless, they knew exactly what they were doing, overriding their own lawyers in an effort to weaken the DPRK and Iran resolutions. Personally, I couldn't care less what we did with the phrase "acting under Chapter VII," or the entire Potemkin Village idea that Chapter VII resolutions were "legally binding," or any more "binding" than any other Council resolution. In any event, Rice was also prepared to give way on a reference to Chapter VII, although I wasn't telling anyone that. After two contentious Perm-Five-plus-Japan meetings, at which we failed to resolve the issue, Oshima said, "Then we are at the end of our discussions, and we must agree to disagree. . . . My country is threatened," and "prepared to face the consequences" of a Chinese veto. Wang was emotional again, saying, "I accept your challenge. My president asked me to avoid [a veto], but he said, 'If you need to use it, use it.'"

On Saturday, July 15, at 8:45 A.M., Rice had another conference call, starting with my explaining where things stood in New York, and with Rice stressing that she wanted this wrapped up before the Bush-Hu meeting in St. Petersburg the next day. China's foreign minister Li shared that view, saying "our young colleagues in New York" (meaning Wang and me) needed to conclude things. I'm sure Li's phrasing must have amused Rice. I pressed my view that we were overwhelmed by legal formalism, and that our excessive hangup over particular words was getting in the way of our basic objective, namely something we could conclude was truly binding on

North Korea. I said, "What we want is a binding resolution, and we don't absolutely have to say 'abracadabra' to get it." That was all Rice needed to hear, immediately agreeing, and saying we had to give up the "theological" approach to these issues, given that this was to be the first Security Council resolution on North Korea since 1993, and a "big victory."

Nonetheless, we were in fact caving in before the threat of a Chinese veto. I called Oshima to tell him the bad news. At our last Perm-Five-plus-Japan meeting, Oshima had said he wanted to know how Russia and China would vote if we accepted the "special responsibility" compromise language we had been discussing. Wang and Churkin both said they would go along with it, with Wang saying that the draft resolution was "a political decision by the Security Council," which, of course, is what I believed anyway. We then had to wait for Koizumi's decision. Given the time differences, the G-8 leaders' dinner had already begun in Moscow, and time dragged on until the word came back from Koizumi that Japan could accept the compromise formula. With that, we had our precious unanimity, and de La Sablière presented the final text as a "presidential" draft, which meant all Council members agreed with it.

The Council convened at 3:45 P.M. and adopted Resolution 1695. Both South and North Korea spoke, and the DPRK response was a wonder to behold. It was long and contained extensive attacks on the United States and Japan. After delivering it, the DPRK representative ostentatiously rose from his chair and walked out of the chamber. Given that kind of performance, I broke from the script and asked for the floor to reply. I noted that this was a historic day, with the unanimous passage of Resolution 1695, but that North Korea had set a world's record, rejecting it within forty-five minutes of its adoption. I also said that I could respond to what the DPRK had said about the United States, but borrowing a line I had once used against Cuba, I asked, "On the other hand, why bother?" In its speech, Japan referred to the text as "legally binding." I did not, because State's lawyers were in the full tizzy mode by this point. Their final, Solomonic conclusion was that I should not say the text was "legally binding" in my speech, but I could say so when answering press questions, which I later did. Although the press had extensive coverage of Resolution 1695, the Council immediately left it behind to turn to the war in Lebanon.

North Korea Goes Nuclear, and We Prevail Again

Indeed, North Korea all but dropped off our radar screen until mid-September, when the Asian press began speculating about an imminent North Korean nuclear test. On Tuesday, October 3, the DPRK announced it was going to test, and I thought this might provide an opportunity to do something endlessly discussed at the UN but rarely practiced, namely "preventive diplomacy." Oshima, Security Council president in October, agreed, so I raised the matter that morning. (I also thought that a test would allow us to argue that North Korea should be suspended or expelled from UN membership, but State was never able to swallow that possibility.) The only solace conservatives found in the North's test was that, finally, it would be impossible for the EAPeasers to continue their solicitous approach to the DPRK. Of course, this optimism proved to be completely unfounded. In fact, Hadley's first reaction, according to Joseph, was to send Hill to Beijing to talk to North Korea. Talk about rewarding bad behavior!

I urged the Council to brainstorm *before* the crisis, as the advocates of "preventive diplomacy" were always telling us, and not react reflexively, but that proved impossible. De La Sablière said, "We . . . have to define a strategy and discuss how the Council has to react, but first we must issue a statement." I couldn't make that up. When we met on October 4 to consider the DPRK nuclear threat, we first spent one hour and fifteen minutes discussing the situation in Guinea-Bissau, a clear demonstration of Council priorities and instinct for the capillary. Even worse, when Oshima raised the DPRK agenda item, there was no one on the list requesting to speak, and a long silence after he opened the floor! All the endless jabbering over the years about how well-suited the Security Council was for "preventive diplomacy" had brought us to this point: silence in the face of a nuclear threat. I did not want to speak first, but I wasn't going to let the whole thing collapse, so I suggested we demand that North Korea withdraw its threat and verifiably eliminate its nuclear programs, or Chapter VII would follow. I concluded that this was the greatest threat the Council had faced during my tenure as U.S. ambassador, which was followed by another long silence, until Oshima took the floor in his national capacity and gave a strong statement. Others then spoke, but it was perfectly apparent that we didn't have the collective will to engage in "preventive diplomacy," or in fact do much else except await developments. It represented a total failure of the Council.

The inevitable then happened, as I learned on Sunday, October 8, at about 10:15 P.M., when the Ops Center called to say the Chinese had just informed Embassy Beijing that the North intended to test imminently. We learned later that the DPRK had told the Chinese in Pyongyang they anticipated a yield of about four kilotons, which was quite small, about a quarter of the yield of the bomb dropped on Hiroshima. I called Oshima, who hadn't heard anything, but said he would check with Tokyo. When the test actually occurred, we tried to sort out the conflicting information coming in during an 11:15 P.M. conference call among State and the NSC. One reason for the confusion was that the yield was so low, well under half a kiloton, that seismic information alone could not verify that the explosion was nuclear rather than non-nuclear. Thus, the statement Bush planned to issue on Monday morning would refer to the DPRK's "claimed nuclear test" until we could be more certain. In the meantime, Rice had a conference call with Ban, Li, Aso, and Lavrov, in which Ban told her that South Korea was cutting off humanitarian assistance to the North, an important first step, indicating that even the Roh Moo-Hyun administration understood that North Korea was way over the red lines this time.

Rice called me at 8:30 A.M. on Monday, and I urged that we go directly for a sanctions resolution, especially since another test could not be ruled out, and she agreed. When North Korea came up in the Security Council at 10:20 A.M. (after approving Ban as secretary general), I circulated Bush's statement and explained the elements of a draft resolution we would circulate shortly, including broad prohibitions on WMD and missile materials, an explicit inspections provision, an arms embargo, and a prohibition on selling luxury goods to the DPRK. Jones Parry and de La Sablière were supportive, while Wang and Churkin were very circumspect. They were on defense, and no one opposed the idea of an explicit Chapter VII sanctions resolution. I reported back to Rice that we were well launched, and she said Bush and Putin had had a very good conversation, with Putin acknowledging that what we did on the DPRK would have an effect on Iran. Bush agreed, saying this was yet another reason to be tough on the North. The Perm-Five-plus-Japan met that afternoon, and Oshima and I distributed our respective draft resolutions, with Japan's tougher than ours in several respects. Churkin and Wang both said they wanted something similar to the Iran-related Resolution 1696, showing just how deleterious our set-backs on that resolution had been, although both said they did not have any real instructions yet. I reported again to Rice at about 5:00 P.M., and although happy with the way things were going, she recognized it could come completely unstuck on Tuesday when Russia and China had instructions. What this really showed was the advantage of moving quickly to take advantage of the shock value of the DPRK test.

Unfortunately, by the time Wang received his instructions on Tuesday, the shock had obviously worn off in Beijing. He had an exhaustive list of changes amounting pretty much to eliminating every important aspect of our proposed sanctions regime. Beijing didn't like the centerpiece of our draft, the provision to inspect cargo entering North Korea, blessing as it did our PSI authority; they didn't want to cover North Korean illicit activities other than proliferation, such as counterfeiting and narcotics; they didn't want an arms embargo; they opposed our prohibition on "luxury goods"; they didn't like requiring regular reports; they certainly didn't like the broader Japanese economic sanctions; and on and on and on. For all of our thanks to China for years of "effort" in the Six-Party Talks, what China was really prepared to do—even in the face of a DPRK nuclear test, another slap in China's face, in Bush's words—was precious little. The extent of China's opposition surprised even France and Britain, which finally realized that if China and Russia wouldn't agree on a tough resolution in circumstances like these, there was no chance of anything meaningful on Iran, in which case their entire effort at Iranian diplomacy would be ineluctably revealed as a complete failure. I saw the problem and the potential differently, hoping that a tough resolution against North Korea could ratchet us back up from the mush that the Perm Five political directors were agreeing to on Iran (as described in the next chapter), and get to something that might actually have a real-world impact.

The only glimmer of light was that Wang asked to meet with me alone, saying that State Councilor Tang Jiaxuan's Thursday visit to Washington was quite important even though the trip had been scheduled before the DPRK nuclear test. On Wednesday, Wang went to Washington to brief Councilor Tang, in advance of his Thursday meetings (which were to be followed by a Tang visit to Moscow). Despite China's opposition, I still thought we could get a resolution by Friday, which Oshima strongly endorsed, to keep the pressure on despite the stalling from China and Russia, the shock having definitely worn off. Rice agreed with me that Friday was the day to go for a vote, when I spoke to her late Wednesday afternoon, especially since she was planning to leave for Asia early the following week.

Instead of dealing with North Korea, we spent large parts of Tuesday and Wednesday dealing with a temper tantrum Russia was throwing over Georgia, including attacking the United States for linking certain visas Russia wanted to Russia's agreeing to a change in the text of a resolution renewing the UN observer mission in Georgia (UNOMIG). State bureaucrats in Washington had done this entirely on their own, as if running their own foreign policy, and as if we didn't have a major crisis going on with North Korea. Although our Georgia position was correct on the merits, it was evidence that no one was looking at the big picture in Washington. What I most objected to was not that State had helped the Georgians, but that they had given Churkin a club to beat the United States with in New York, which he was happily doing. At one point, Jones Parry tried to smooth things over, saying he looked forward to more discussions, to which Churkin snapped back, "I wouldn't hold my breath."

Following a Thursday Security Council session on Georgia, I did take the Council through our DPRK sanctions draft, saying we planned to put it in blue that afternoon and vote on Friday. Wang and Churkin were still stalling, using Tang's Saturday meetings in Moscow and saying they had no further instructions. At this point, I didn't have a readout of Tang's meetings in Washington earlier in the day, which meant that they certainly had not been bell-ringers. We had six cosponsors by that point, and expected two more, so all the signs were that the nonpermanent members were still behind a swift and strong Council reaction to the DPRK test. I continued to believe we were in a very strong position.

Between the DPRK test and the ultimate adoption of Resolution 1718, Jones Parry counted twenty-three Perm Three or Perm Five meetings (plus Japan in all cases). But the most significant meeting of all was a one-on-one I had with Wang Thursday afternoon, when he pulled me aside to tell me China's latest thinking. He said Foreign Minister Li was somewhere near the China-DPRK border, meeting with "people close to the Dear Leader," that Tang would be in Moscow on Saturday, and that ROK president Roh would be in Beijing on Friday. Wang wanted the vote on Monday, which I told him was out of the question. Then he got to the real point, which was that even if we insisted on a Friday vote, there would be no veto, which was about 179 degrees different from China's approach in July after the missile shots. Wang said they were still debating whether to abstain or vote "yes," but we clearly had the whip hand. China did not want a public tiff over this resolution, which at least showed a good sense of public relations. I filled Oshima, Jones Parry, and de La Sablière in immediately, and they fully understood the significance of Wang's remarks.

I called Rice with the good news that there would be no Chinese veto, and then returned to the French Mission for another Perm-Five-plus-Japan meeting, at which we seemed to be going nowhere. At one point, to rebut the Chinese and Russian point that we should refer to a specific article of the charter, I threw my well-worn copy of the UN Charter on the table and said, "I hate comparing this thing to the U.S. Constitution," but I explained that the president typically never invoked a specific clause of the Constitution, instead relying generally on his executive authority. One of the French staffers later scooped up that copy of the charter to keep as a souvenir of the meeting, because he was so delighted at what I had done. As it turned out, there was actually a reason to keep a souvenir, because, with remarkable ease, we did solve both the "threat to international peace and security" and the Chapter VII issue. Wang agreed to combine the "threat" language with another preambular paragraph, thus giving us an unambiguous finding that the nuclear test constituted a threat, much better than Resolution 1695, on the DPRK missile launches, or Resolution 1696 on Iran's nuclear program.[2] We also agreed quickly to de La Sablière's proposal to say, "Acting under Chapter VII and taking measures under Article 41," which sacrificed nothing and did get us a clean reference to Chapter VII, all of which made our lawyers very happy. Given how intractable these issues had seemed for so many months with both Iran and North Korea, this was remarkable progress, and gave me hope we might even bring the Europeans along for comparable language on Iran (but only briefly, as the next chapter will describe). One of State's lawyers was so amazed with these developments that, referring to my recent nomination for the Nobel Peace Prize, he wrote of the language we had obtained, "I think this is really, truly remarkable—this should win the Nobel Prize for Security Council negotiating."

---

2. The final preambular paragraph read, "*Expressing* profound concern that the test claimed by the DPRK has generated increased tension in the region and beyond, and *determining* therefore that there is a clear threat to international peace and security."

Nonetheless, we then ran into a brick wall of opposition from Russia and China on the inspection provision (later embodied in paragraph 8[f] of the final resolution). Even with this issue unresolved, however, I believed we could now realistically look for a vote, not on Friday, but on Saturday, which I informed the press waiting outside the French Mission when our meeting concluded. Later that morning, the Security Council adopted the Georgia resolution, which, after Rice had spoken with Lavrov, dropped the phrase Russia had objected to, a concession much noted by the Japanese press and others. Afterward, I took the Council through our latest DPRK draft, noting there were still areas of disagreement but saying we expected to put the text in blue and vote on Saturday. In fact, at a Perm-Five-plus-Japan meeting following the Council consultations, Wang raised the possibility of a "presidential text," meaning one that, in effect, all fifteen Council members cosponsored. Although Wang was still objecting to the inspection paragraph, this showed that China was very close to giving in even on that point. He clearly believed that a "presidential text"—the ultimate symbol of Council unity—would make it difficult for Japan or the United States to claim a "victory," or for commentators to declare a Chinese "defeat," thus allowing China to minimize the political sting of this resolution.

No sooner had we almost resolved China's objection, however, than Russia unaccountably developed major problems both with the inspection provision and with the specific WMD materials barred from sale to North Korea, where we had used standard lists from the Nuclear Suppliers Group (NSG) and other antiproliferation regimes. When we met later in the day, it was clear Russia was concerned less with North Korea than with Iran, where they feared a similar resolution would definitely crimp Russian sales to the mullahs. That was fine with me, but I worried that France and Britain might collapse before this new intransigence, as they would later over the Iran resolution itself. Wang seemed as surprised as we were at the new Russian concerns, further proof that Moscow was worried about Iran, not the DPRK. We let the Russians and the Chinese leave to have a Perm-Three-plus-Japan meeting, and I said I wasn't compromising anymore. Oshima, Jones Parry, and de La Sablière all agreed: We would put the draft resolution in blue, not negotiate, and see on Saturday if Churkin was bluffing.

On Saturday, October 14, the Perm-Three-plus-Japan met at 9:30 A.M. in Room C-209, not knowing whether we would bring the issue to a close or whether we were headed for a train wreck. I still believed China was basically prepared to accept the text as it stood, but Russia was much harder to predict, and more prone to last-minute theatrics (or hysterics, depending on your perspective), a specialty Sergei Lavrov had perfected during his years as perm rep in New York. Although the Perm Five were supposed to gather at 10:00 A.M., Churkin called to say that he would be late, not a good sign. I went off to find Wang, who was having a cigarette in the German Lounge. He said President Hu would be going to bed in Beijing around noon our time, and that he had until then to make a final recommendation on the Chinese vote. When Churkin arrived, he and Wang caucused separately, while Jones Parry, de La Sablière, and I agreed that if we could get China and Russia to agree to the NSG and Missile Technology Control Regime (MTCR) lists, we could take a slightly more flexible position on the Australia Group list (chemical and biological weapons). With that change, and a purely cosmetic change on the inspection provision, we were ready to go to a vote.

While waiting for the Secretariat to do the necessary clerical work, Churkin approached me in the Council chamber to say that Russia would in fact vote "yes." He also said he had a message "from Sergei personally" that "Iran will not be this easy." I never doubted that. Churkin also said that Lavrov's meetings with Tang in Moscow had moved China from an abstention to a "yes" vote, which was, of course, essentially the opposite of what Wang was telling us, namely, that Tang had shifted the Russians. As Wang had suggested the day before, the draft was presented as a "presidential text," and the vote on Resolution 1718 was therefore unanimous. I called Rice at Camp David after the vote, and she observed wryly, "It takes a nuclear weapon to get the Security Council to move this quickly." Wang and I also posed for a photo together, and Colum Lynch of the *Washington Post* asked us what had "closed the deal." I responded "good diplomacy," and Lynch answered, "That might be true, but it's not a good quote," which tells you everything you need to know about the media mind-set at the UN. Needless to say, my quotation did not appear in the *Post*'s pristine pages.

After the unanimous vote on Resolution 1718, the DPRK delegate said that they "totally reject" the resolution, calling the Security Council's action "gangsterlike" and "coercive," and accused the United States of having "manipulated" the Council. If only. Then, yet again, the North Koreans walked out to show their contempt. I took the floor to say that this second walk-out was the contemporary equivalent of Khrushchev pounding his shoe on his desk in the General Assembly, which upset Churkin and a few American liberals, but brought many positive comments during the following week. Bush chaired an NSC meeting on Monday morning, which I attended by secure video. There was a lot of conversation about how China would treat Resolution 1718 and whether they would inspect along the North Korea border. Bush asked correctly, "Isn't this what PSI is all about?" Rice was preparing for her imminent departure to Asia, and she stressed that her intentions were not simply to "restart" the Six-Party Talks. Bush responded that China was "coming our way," and that we "should see if the squeeze [on North Korea] works," because "China will have to call Kim's bluff." I found this all very encouraging. In fact, the peripatetic state councilor Tang traveled shortly thereafter to Pyongyang, where he met with Kim Jong-il, prompting the South Korean press to report that Kim had apologized to Tang for the nuclear test. This piece of propaganda gained such currency that the Chinese Foreign Ministry itself, the following week, had to put out a statement that Kim had done no such thing. In fact, the appeasement-minded ROK minister of unification actually had to resign over this incident, showing that there were limits even for the Roh Moo-Hyun government.

Epilogue: The Munchkins Win on North Korea

> The North would clearly prefer to negotiate with softer and inexperienced Americans.
>
> —JAMES R. LILLEY, FORMER U.S. AMBASSADOR TO SOUTH KOREA AND CHINA, NOVEMBER 9, 1998[3]

In retrospect, I wished two things about our Security Council counterattacks: that we had done it previously in the Six-Party Talks, and that we had continued to do it after I left the administration in December 2006. Strong diplomacy in the Security Council produced two tough resolutions. Weak diplomacy in the Six-Party Talks has allowed North Korea to consolidate

---

3. James R. Lilley, "New Rules in Korea," *Newsweek,* November 9, 1998, p. 19, col. 1.

and solidify its nuclear posture and taken the United States down the same road as the failed 1994 Agreed Framework. Indeed, in many respects, as of this writing, we are simply repeating the mistakes of 1993–94, despite the administration's promising start in exactly the opposite direction.

The Six-Party Talks resumed in Beijing on December 18, producing an agreement announced on February 13, 2007, in which North Korea once again promised to give up its pursuit of nuclear weapons in exchange for tangible economic and political benefits. Analytically so similar to the 1994 Agreed Framework that Clinton administration alumni praised it, this deal let North Korea escape from the corner where we had put them by Resolution 1718's sanctions and our Treasury Department's aggressive efforts to impose tough economic pressure on the DPRK for its illicit money-laundering through international financial institutions. The February 13 agreement is what Powell would have loved to try in 2001 before Bush pulled him back from "leaning too far forward" on his skis, and was a sad and disappointing outcome for those who had fought hard for the principles Bush had repeatedly advocated publicly. It came even after the revelation of yet another UN scandal—"Cash for Kim"—in which UN funds were deposited into DPRK bank accounts, with the ultimate use of the funds seemingly under the control of the DPRK rather than the UN.[4] Ban Ki-moon responded immediately by saying he would order a UN-system-wide external inquiry, which was exactly the right thing to do, and the UN Development Program closed its programs in the DPRK. Whether anything will actually change at the UN as a result remains to be seen.

The February 2007 deal was radically incomplete: It did not deal with North Korea's existing stockpile of nuclear weapons; it did not deal with their uranium-enrichment program; and it contained no verification provisions whatsoever, except for the prospect of the IAEA returning to Yongbyon, perhaps the least important place for inspectors given our own national technical capabilities to observe North Korea. EAP's bureaucratic opposition to verifying North Korea's "commitments" could easily take up a full chapter, and at least shows they got one thing right: Any effective verification scheme—a scheme that the United States should insist on—would

---

4. See Melanie Kirkpatrick, "United Nations Dictators Program," *Wall Street Journal*, January 19, 2007, p. A15, col. 1, and "U.N. Cash for Kim," *Wall Street Journal*, January 19, 2007, p. A14, col. 1.

be completely rejected by North Korea, thus tanking any prospects for a negotiated settlement. This is why the bureaucracy and South Korea's government are so worried about even the mention of verification, which, done right, would lay waste to their fantasy of negotiating North Korea out of its nuclear weapons.

Moreover, the agreement opened the prospect of taking North Korea off the United States' list of state sponsors of terrorism, without any commitment to resolve the issue of Japanese and South Korean abductees; it held open the prospect that our very effective financial sanctions and law-enforcement activities against DPRK financial transactions would be lifted; and, worst of all, it enmeshed the United States in a miasma of continuing negotiations through "working groups" that would chatter on endlessly, which was exactly what EAP had been seeking since the Clinton administration. This approach legitimized North Korea and allowed it to buy more time through the prospect of negotiations that the bureaucracy would fight to protect, never recognizing that the passage of time during negotiations was not cost-free to the United States. Every day that went by with North Korea free to continue to work on its WMD and ballistic missile programs was a day the North could make more progress, and a loss to the United States. Time is not on our side when dealing with rogue state proliferators, which North Korea surely knows, but which State's bureaucracy manifestly does not.

Nonetheless, the state of play at this writing is that the permanent government has triumphed over Bush, or at least over his principles. This is a far cry from the Bush who said to Putin at Camp David in October 2003 that Kim Jong-il was "like a baby who throws his food on the floor," so that the adults come around to pick it up, whereupon the baby throws the food on the floor again. "We should all say the same thing," said Bush, "let the food stay on the floor." I doubt that Bush's personal views ever changed, but he was either not confident enough to continue to insist on them or distracted by political attacks that increased with the loss of the House and the Senate in the 2006 congressional elections, Iraq, and the growing turmoil now associated with the end of two-term administrations. Moreover, the departure of many "hardliners" was like eliminating players from the defense team in football. Eventually, even a bureaucratic offense could start scoring once the defense's numbers dwindled.

Our historical experience tells us that North Korea will never give up its nuclear weapons voluntarily, and that it is only a matter of time before their cheating is exposed, at which point one hopes that Bush will repudiate this charade that the Risen Bureaucracy has perpetrated. In fact, the only true way to resolve the DPRK nuclear weapons problem is the reunification of the Korean peninsula, which one hopes will come sooner rather than later. If I were Kim Jong-il, I would not be optimistic. Just as the Italians once dealt with Mussolini, and the Romanians with Ceausescu, one day the North Korean people may have the chance to deal with Kim Jong-il. His death will be dirty and contemptible, like his life and his regime, and it will be exactly what he deserves.

CHAPTER TWELVE

IRAN IN THE SECURITY COUNCIL: THE EU-3 FIND NEW WAYS TO GIVE IN

Our dear imam ordered that the occupying regime in Jerusalem be wiped off the face of the earth. This was a very wise statement.

—MAHMOUD AHMADINEJAD, OCTOBER 26, 2005

Powell Fades to Rice

You're not going to believe what I just did.
—COLIN POWELL, NOVEMBER 17, 2004

Following Bush's November 2 victory in the 2004 presidential election, the EU-3 presented their latest proposal to Iran, hoping they could obtain Iran's critical threshold decision to suspend all enrichment and reprocessing activities. We heard consistently from them, especially UK foreign secretary Jack Straw and and UK political director John Sawers, that it was essentially a done deal, only a few points to resolve, making progress nicely, wrapping up the last details, and so on. In fact, we heard this right up until November 11, when I spoke to Sawers, who said with great fanfare, "The Iranians will announce in one hour" that they would accept a new agreement with the EU-3. Iran was also sending a "side letter" dealing with "one or two issues" where "they will put in their interpretation," meaning the

EU-3 would simply follow its own interpretation. I said that sounded like a problem. Sawers, happy as could be, said it was not; in fact, Iran was sending a letter to el Baradei as we spoke, affirming the suspension and inviting IAEA monitors to verify it. I asked Sawers if he had Iran's side letter; he did, but he declined to send it to me.

A few hours later, the Brits called Jim Timbie on my staff to say that, having now read the Iranian "side letter," they were asking Iran not to announce the "deal," but to hold off until at least the next day. Interestingly, by then the Brits said France and Germany were against any "side letter" at all, which meant they were firmer than the Brits! One point in Iran's side letter indicated that Iran needed just a little more time to run the conversion facility at Esfahan, because it couldn't be shut down quickly. This, of course, was nonsense, because such plants are designed precisely to shut down quickly in case of an accident. By now we had a copy of the side letter, which contained a number of other problematic points, such as a time limit on negotiations and IAEA resolutions, suggesting to me there was no real meeting of the minds and perhaps no deal at all, despite Sawers's optimism. Sawers called at about 1:40 P.M. to say EU-3 ambassadors in Tehran would respond to the side letter that evening, which should wrap things up. I asked why he was so confident, and he said the EU-3 ambassadors all thought the side letter had only been necessary to get the hard-line mullahs on board, which was now accomplished. Even though Blair was in Washington, he and Bush discussed Iran only briefly. Powell told me Bush was reluctant to say publicly exactly what he thought of the latest EU-3 deal with Iran—not much—because he had just rejected Blair's request that we convene a Middle East peace conference or appoint a special Middle East envoy.

Despite Sawers, the Brits told us later that their man in Tehran didn't want to deliver the EU-3 response because he thought it would scuttle the deal! Finally, Iran announced on November 14 it was accepting the deal and would suspend enrichment and reprocessing on November 22. Hossein Mousavian, Iran's chief nuclear negotiator, also announced: "Europe will support Iran's joining the international group of states possessing the ability to manufacture nuclear fuel" *once the suspension ended.* Ali Larijani, then Supreme Leader Khamenei's representative to Iran's National Security Council, said Iran's diplomats had given away "a round pearl" and only gotten a "bonbon" in return. Rouhani had a press conference, announcing,

"It's no problem if Iran wants to start uranium enrichment. Based on the agreement, it is said that the Europeans will support Iran to become a member of the fuel-cycle club." What a deal! The EU-3 assured us they had pressed Iran to stop making such statements, as if that would solve the problem. Even they admitted Iran had clearly not made a strategic decision to give up the pursuit of nuclear weapons.

On Monday, November 15, 2004, Powell opened his staff meeting by announcing he was resigning as secretary of state, departing at the end of Bush's first term. He then left for the White House, and Armitage continued the meeting. I was surprised there was no applause or other show of support when he left, but perhaps the news was just too shocking. It definitely consumed a lot of time the rest of the week, although Powell himself left on a previously scheduled trip to Latin America. During a stop to refuel at Manaus, Brazil, in the middle of the Amazon tropical forest, Powell decided to talk to the press. Armitage told me Powell spoke at some length about intelligence on Iran's efforts to weaponize their nuclear capability and to fit it into warheads consistent with their ballistic missile efforts. I was stunned, but even more stunned when Powell himself called, starting off by saying, "You're not going to believe what I just did." I am rarely speechless, but I was then. Powell said someone asked about information recently released by Iranian dissident groups, particularly whether A. Q. Khan supplied weapons-design information. Powell said sometimes the dissidents were right and sometimes not, and the next question was specifically about delivery systems. For whatever reason, he began discussing information we had recently received, getting in deeper and deeper. He said, among other things: "I have seen some information that would suggest they have been actively working on delivery systems. . . . You don't have a weapon until you can put it in something that can deliver a weapon. I'm talking about what one does with a warhead. We are talking about information that says they not only have missiles, but information that suggests they are working hard about how to put the two together."[1]

I was delighted. First, I hadn't done it. Second, I thought this was exactly the kind of intelligence we needed out in public to show exactly what Iran

---

1. Secretary Powell's remarks to the press in the airport lounge in Manaus, Brazil, en route to Santiago, Chile, November 17, 2004, http://www.state.gov/secretary/former/powell/remarks/38357.htm.

was up to. Now that Powell had spoken, I could refer without qualm to his press conference in the jungle and let reporters draw their own conclusions. Third, this information came as the EU-3 raced hell-bent toward the latest "agreement" with Iran, and I asked Sawers about it in one of our conversations. It was plain he couldn't have cared less what the intelligence said, and he quite likely doubted it as well, not that he had taken the time to be briefed on it. In fact, he was almost defiant in ignoring it, so concerned was he not to be accused of overstating what he knew, because of intelligence failures on Iraq. Here is proof that diplomats, like generals, tend to fight the previous war, avoiding mistakes they made the last time by making mistakes in the opposite direction. Inaction in the face of the risks posed by Iran's activities does not amount to "playing it safe" and avoiding the pitfalls of Iraq. It means instead rolling the dice on the good faith of the mullahs, a truly desperate gamble with the highest stakes for our innocent civilian populations, and those of our friends and allies like Israel. This sort of weaponization information was precisely one of the red lines I had previously asked Sawers and Ehrman about, which he had said would mean the end of negotiations with Iran. In the end, of course, it meant no such thing, proving what I always believed, namely that these negotiations were really an EU-3 effort to prove they were different from the United States, and that Iran was not Iraq. Now that Powell had made at least some of the intelligence public, however, it was far harder for Sawers or anyone else to sweep it under the rug.

Our immediate problem was that the timing of this latest EU-3/Iran deal, right before the November IAEA board meeting, aborted yet again our efforts to get a referral to the Security Council. Even worse, the EU-3 would make a sustained effort to have the BOG endorse their deal, and they were already beavering away, although we, the Aussies, and the Canadians wanted something tougher. While the EU-3 had enough spine to resist us, they melted before a persistent Iranian whining campaign, weakening their own draft considerably. I had one brainstorm, which was to report *the deal* to the Council (thus getting it there by hook or by crook), not that I thought the EU-3 would accept this, but hoping a little asymmetrical bargaining would brace them against their inclination to surrender. Fortunately, Iran came through for us once again, proposing at the last minute to keep twenty centrifuges up and running "for experimental purposes," an idea el Baradei quickly endorsed. This was so far off the deal that I hoped even the EU-3 might reject it, but no, they started immediately looking for a compromise. The risk of "experimental" centrifuges, of course, was allowing Iran to resolve remaining technical problems, thus providing them with the knowledge they could operationalize far from IAEA inspectors, utterly without their (or our) knowledge. De Laboulaye and Sawers clearly understood this point, but the Germans did not.

So "close" did the EU-3 think they were that a call was arranged between Straw and Rouhani on November 26 to wrap things up, but word came back from the Brits that the call had not gone well. At this point, feeling there was little to lose, I asked Sanders in Vienna to push for a Security Council referral, supported by Australia and Canada, much to the chagrin of the increasingly tongue-tied EU-3 perm reps. How many times can you say you have a deal and not produce it before you begin to realize maybe you don't have a deal? Powell asked Straw what was happening and told me Straw now seemed resigned to a Council referral. "Jack, they're doing it to you again," Powell had said, which was certainly true. Incredibly, however, the EU-3 once again changed their IAEA board resolution, downgrading their deal with Iran from a "legally binding" agreement to a voluntary suspension. This EU-3 self-loathing of their own deal had to provoke hilarity in Tehran, and I certainly wasn't going to save the EUroids from themselves. We detailed our objections to the resolution in an "explanation of vote" that was nine single-spaced pages long, the most important line of which was that we still reserved all of our options about convoking the Security Council. The resolution, another opportunity missed, was adopted on November 29. Iran played its role perfectly, announcing that suspension would last "months not years," until the end of negotiations with the EU-3, when the carrot trucks rolled into Tehran. By late December, the press reported that Iran continued conversion work at Esfahan. This was hardly consistent with the "deal," so I sent a letter to Sawers, de Laboulaye, and Schaeffer asking their reactions, thinking I might send them a letter every time we saw a violation by Iran, just so the EU-3 knew we were watching. I expected we would have a thick file very quickly.

Rice started off her tenure as secretary of state following a tough line on Iran. By late February 2005, however, she began to wobble, largely because of Nick Burns, newly installed as undersecretary for political affairs, State's number-three job. Burns quickly renewed an earlier relationship with Sawers and was his faithful conduit into State. Rice told me on February 25, "We are thinking of making some adjustments in the Iran policy on the

World Trade Organization and airplane spare parts, not to help the Europeans, but to avoid our being blamed as the party responsible for the collapse of the EU-3/Iran talks. The Iranians have done a good job of painting us in the corner, and we need to get out." This reasoning was misguided, since it was the EU that had painted itself into a corner and now wanted to pull us in as well. I couldn't believe we were back on the airplane parts issue, having killed it earlier when Straw first raised it. Joseph's nomination to replace me had been announced by then, and I started to fade away. I was nonetheless struck when Philip Zelikow, Rice's counselor, told me on February 28 that Burns would handle the Iran issue, and Joseph would not. I immediately passed this to Joseph, who professed not to be worried, given his close relationship with Rice at the NSC in the first term. If I needed confirmation about the wisdom of my leaving, however, there it was. Burns's coup was one reason Joseph was unhappy almost from the day he started in T.

By this time I was on my fourth letter to the EU-3 political directors on Iranian violations of their deal (this one on continued construction of the heavy-water production facility at Arak), and we were still writing tough speeches for Sanders to give at the March 2005 IAEA board meeting. I was also encouraged that Rice's public comments were still tough on referring Iran to the Security Council, so I hoped she was trying only to make a tactical and not a strategic policy shift. In any case, I was then deep in my confirmation battle for the USUN position, paying less and less attention to many things that had previously occupied so much time. Unfortunately, the big shift, much applauded by the EUroids, came on March 11, when Rice publicly endorsed the EU-3's negotiating efforts, in exchange for a "commitment" from them to go to the Security Council if those efforts failed. Of course, that's what the EU-3 had assured Powell they would do in summer 2003, when they initiated their fruitless negotiations with Iran. Part of the shift also allowed el Baradei to get his third term as IAEA director general, which was a mistake, but which was probably already foreordained by Powell's lack of enthusiasm for our campaign against el Baradei before he left office.

The EU-3, the United States, and the Security Council Flunk on Iran

> The European doctrine of managed globalization envisions a world of multilateral rules that will supersede U.S. power.[2]

Once again, however, Iran came through, as I knew it would, helping my efforts to get to the Security Council. In May 2005, because the EU-3 carrot trucks had not rolled into Tehran, Iran threatened to resume conversion and enrichment. In June, Ahmadinejad was elected president, bolstering the hardliners and undercutting their "smiley face" public diplomacy in New York. Thus, when I arrived at the UN in August, Iran itself had again changed the political dynamic of getting a Security Council referral. In my first courtesy calls, French deputy perm rep Michel Duclos said without qualification that he expected to see Iran in the Council by the end of August. Jones Parry was pessimistic, worried that Russia and China would block anything we tried to do.

Here, I encountered the most paradoxical EUroid argument of all, namely that the *threat* of going to the Security Council was more important than the Council's actually *doing* anything. This argument, which Jones Parry made repeatedly, took it for granted the Council was not likely to do much once it took up an issue, so it was therefore best not to ask that it do anything, thus preserving the threat intact. Of course, this analysis assumed that the targets of such "threats" were so witless they couldn't figure out the threats were ultimately hollow. More crucially, and ironically, it shared the view of the UN's staunchest critics, namely that the Council was largely ineffective. The difference was that the High Minded of the world didn't want anyone else—perhaps especially the critics—to see the proof of their skepticism. By contrast, I thought you could never know how effective the Council could be unless and until you actually tried to have it act, thus following through on the threat. If the Council then worked effectively, so be it. If it did not, as in the case of Iran, so be that. It was then on to other ways and means at our discretion outside the Council to solve the problem. This

---

2. Rawi Abdelal and Adam Segal, "Has Globalization Passed Its Peak?" 86 *Foreign Affairs* 103, p. 105, (January–February 2007).

last step especially worried the High Minded. Once we turned to solutions not involving the Security Council, the magic was broken, and the great unwashed might never return to the UN's hollow cathedral.

In any case, the EU-3 concluded they needed an IAEA resolution calling on Iran to "return" to the "suspension" it had "agreed to," and they worked away frantically yet again in Vienna to save their "deal." On August 11, the IAEA board passed another weak resolution, pushing matters off until September when another el Baradei report was expected. Even worse were reports from Washington. Fred Fleitz, formerly of my staff, now working for Joseph, told me that Joseph was depressed about Rice on both Iran and North Korea, saying, "I've never seen her like this before." On September 15, 2005, when I was back in Washington, Joseph told me unhappily that Rice was listening to Hill on North Korea, and to Straw and Burns on Iran, and certainly not to him on either. And still more bad news came in early November, when Joseph said, "I'm isolated, and J.D. [Crouch] and I are very limited in what we can do," noting the widespread impression that Hadley, although now national security adviser, still acted like Rice's aide.

At the September IAEA board meeting, we counted over twenty votes to refer Iran to the Security Council, but the EU-3 were unwilling to break "the spirit of Vienna" by forcing a vote, especially without Russia and China. Despite every EU-3 effort, on Saturday, September 24, the IAEA board had no alternative to a vote if it was to have any further role. The EU text, finding Iran in noncompliance with its NPT obligations, but not explicitly referring it to the Council, prevailed by a vote of twenty-two "ayes" (including India, importantly), one "nay" (the irrepressible Venezuela), and twelve abstaining (including Russia and China). We thus broke "the spirit of Vienna" before the final confrontation at the IAEA over referral to the Council, so we at least had that particular bout of angst out of the way. One might well ask how one could find Iran in "noncompliance" with its NPT obligations (the diplomats' way of avoiding the dreaded word "violation") *without* referring it to the Council, but after two years of slogging we had at least gotten this far.

That, however, meant little. Once the September IAEA board ended, Vienna returned to somnambulance to wait for the November board, as if Iran would put its nuclear program on hold for two months. On October 26, Ahmadinejad reminded us exactly what the problem was by saying Israel should be "wiped off the map." Jones Parry and I decided the Security

Council should issue a presidential statement on such an obvious flouting of the UN Charter (a member calling for the elimination of another member), but, in our October 28 consultations, Russia and Algeria objected because there was no appropriate agenda item under which to raise Ahmadinejad's remark. This, of course, was nonsense. For their benefit I drew a little map of the Middle East, held it up in the consultation room, and then erased Israel. I suggested that this qualified Ahmadinejad's statement for inclusion under the long-standing agenda item on "the Middle East," and my silver-tongued oratory carried the day. Algeria and China then said, however, they needed instructions, meaning we ended up issuing only a "press statement" that attracted no attention whatever, as Russia, China, and Algeria knew would be the case.

In November, again at the EU-3's request, we sought no IAEA referral of Iran to the Security Council. In December, I had lunch with Crouch in the White House mess, and he confirmed what Joseph was saying about decision-making at State. Crouch thought Joseph would stand it perhaps for a year, but not much longer. As for Crouch, he said he was Rice's deputy's deputy, and there was little he could do without more support from above, which reminded me why I was happy to be at USUN. Outside observers were seeing the same phenomenon not only with respect to Iran, but more generally. As the leader of one group said to me, in very short order I might be "the last Republican left standing" at State. Rice, they concluded, had been captured.

On January 10, 2006, the Iranians reverted to form by breaking IAEA seals at the Natanz enrichment facility and resuming "research" work. With that, the EU-3 finally concluded it was time to go to the Security Council, just over two years after they should have done so. Even Russia unhappily agreed, showing the impact of Iran's unambiguous public resumption of enrichment-related activities. Iran threatened to block IAEA inspectors if it were referred to the Council, reinforcing even the EU-3's conviction that it was futile trying to bargain. The EU-3 foreign ministers, on January 12, called for an emergency meeting of the BOG, which Rice echoed. Coincidentally, Angela Merkel, the new German chancellor, in Washington for her first meeting with Bush, said that Iran had "crossed a red line" by its recent actions, raising hopes that Schroeder's defeat might mean a more determined German foreign policy. Media coverage of the decision to seek a Council referral was heavy. Especially gratifying was a report by CNN's

Chris Burns: "After two years of talks and little to show for it," he said, "it was hard for the Europeans to admit defeat." Yes indeed.

Both Annan and el Baradei immediately took steps to prevent any referral. Annan called a meeting of the Perm-Five-plus-Germany to describe a call with Ali Larijani, now Iran's chief negotiator. When Duclos said Annan's public remarks had been unhelpful, Annan lost his composure, as he did remarkably often when challenged by mere member governments, physically shaking, saying things like, "I won't be lectured to," and "I know how to do my job." El Baradei suggested that Iran be allowed to keep a "pilot scale" enrichment facility, an idea closely resembling the "research" exception we had earlier rejected, just as we did this one, not that it slowed el Baradei down. He refused to supply a supplemental report on Iran, which the EU-3 and the United States had sought in time for an emergency BOG meeting scheduled for February 2. (Instead, we received a report from IAEA staff, which in many respects turned out to be more helpful, since it was not subject to el Baradei's typically heavy editing in favor of Iran.) Iran was also spinning out propaganda, including a willingness to consider a Russian proposal on enrichment, which Rice unfortunately endorsed, thus implying legitimacy for "peaceful" nuclear activities by Iran even as it violated the NPT by seeking nuclear weapons.

The Perm Five foreign ministers plus Germany had dinner on January 30 in London, as Iran threatened to put Israel into a "permanent coma" if Iran were attacked (an unsubtle reference to Sharon's coma, after his massive stroke). The ministers agreed that the February 2 IAEA board would refer Iran to the Security Council, which, inexplicably, would take no action until after the March BOG meeting. The IAEA board voted to approve the referral on Saturday, February 4: twenty-seven in favor, three opposed (Syria, Venezuela, and Cuba), and five abstaining (Algeria, Belarus, Indonesia, Libya, and South Africa), yet another blow to "the spirit of Vienna." The *New York Times* called it "the climax of a two-and-one-half year campaign by the Bush Administration," which "also signals the failure, at least for now, of the two-and-a-half year strategy of France, Britain and Germany that was based on the premise that Iran could be coaxed into" giving up its nuclear program.[3] On script, Iran said it would cease "voluntary

---

3. Elaine Sciolino, "Nuclear Panel Votes to Report Tehran to U.N.," *New York Times,* Sunday, February 5, 2006, p. A1, col. 5.

compliance" with the Additional Protocol and press ahead with uranium enrichment.

Merkel spoke again with Bush and, among many other things, discussed Iran, during which Bush explained the difficulty of our having direct bilateral talks. Merkel said that "There is a widespread wish in Europe to have the U.S. in a direct relationship with Iran." Bush responded: "But then we'd become the bad guy. We can't really resolve these issues if we are in the lead; if we are in the lead, the EU will retreat . . . and blame us for any problems." He continued, "Especially if I am the negotiator, many in the EU will not support whatever the U.S. position is, and will say we are being unilateralist again, and too tough." Merkel answered ruefully, "Yes, you are criticized if you negotiate, and if you don't."

That about summed it up.

Having worked out a draft Security Council presidential statement (PRST) with Britain and France (giving Iran fifteen days to suspend enrichment activities), we scheduled a Perm Five meeting for Thursday, March 9. De La Sablière handed out the draft PRST, and we adjourned. On Friday, our one-hour-and-a-half Perm Five meeting can be described simply: Russia and China would not engage in line-by-line negotiations. We met again on Monday, and the Brits and French had a weaker draft, retreating and compromising out of habit. I read from a *New York Times* story quoting former Iranian negotiator Rouhani:

> But in a remarkable admission, Mr. Rowhani suggested in his speech that Iran had used the negotiations with the Europeans to dupe them. . . . "While we were talking to the Europeans in Tehran, we were installing equipment in parts of the facility in Isfahan, but we still had a long way to go to complete the project," he said. "In fact, by creating a calm environment, we were able to complete the work on Isfahan." As a result of the negotiations with Europe, he added, "We are in fact much more prepared to go to the U.N. Security Council."[4]

---

4. Elaine Sciolino, "Showdown at U.N.? Iran Seems Calm," *New York Times,* Tuesday, March 14, 2006, p. A8, col. 1.

The article also said, " 'The most important promise' the Europeans gave Iran, he said, 'was that they would stand firm against attempts to take this case to the UN Security Council.' " While the EU-3 denied this last remark, they were deeply embarrassed by Rouhani's comments, although not enough to change course.

During the week of March 13, we had two "informal informal" consultations of the full Council at the French Mission, basically trying to keep the nonpermanent members informed, and influence them against the Russian/Chinese intransigence. At one point, when I explained why the Parchin explosives facility was something Iran wanted to hide, Tanzania's Mahiga thanked me and said the Iranians listened carefully to every word I said, and that "they are scared stiff of" me, which was good news. The Perm Five political directors were constantly talking, continuing to water down the draft PRST, while we remained largely at rest in New York. On March 22, we had another Perm Five meeting, after which I spoke with Rice, who was in the Bahamas, attending a meeting of the region's governments. She seemed confused that what she was hearing from me was so different from what she was hearing from Burns. This divergence led Silverberg to say to a colleague in IO, "John is interested in substance and Nick is interested in style."

Rice decided that we should finish the PRST before a Perm-Five-plus-Germany foreign ministers meeting on March 30, which we did; the text was read out on March 29.[5] As I hoped, on March 30 Iran rejected the PRST, demonstrating why we should have gone right to a Chapter VII sanctions resolution. The March 30 foreign ministers meeting turned out to be inconclusive. By April 11, we were hearing from the IAEA that Iran had enriched uranium to reactor-grade levels, meaning their 164-centrifuge cascade worked, news to greet el Baradei as he arrived in Tehran on yet another of his pilgrimages.

The Perm-Five-plus-Germany political directors continued their discussions of the follow-up resolution, especially the deconstruction of Chapter VII, and the slide toward rendering Council resolutions even less comprehensible. Jones Parry, de La Sablière, and I met on May 3, and I told them that the United Kingdom and France were deviating from three points the Perm Five legal advisers had agreed upon for what constituted a

---

5. Statement by the president of the Security Council, S/PRST/2006/15, March 29, 2006.

"mandatory" Council resolution, namely an express reference to a "threat to international peace and security," the phrase "acting under Chapter VII," and the use of the word "decides" in a resolution's key operative paragraphs. While Russia and China were flatly wrong in asserting that even a simple reference to Chapter VII was a covert way of trying to authorize the use of force, I fully understood why they pursued this course. I was mystified why France and Britain acquiesced in it. These were the two weakest of the Perm Five, and yet they were the ones most willing, even eager, to water down the purport and strength of Security Council actions. As in the North Korea discussion, I did not consider these words and phrases magical. I knew Rice didn't care, but our lawyers did, and the press understood these incantations were important. Accordingly, to back away from them precipitously signaled weakness, especially if we did so before even proposing our own language! Here, we came to what really bothered the French and British. Jones Parry summed it up by saying, "I am so tired of having to go out in front of those damned cameras and explain why we gave up on this or conceded on that." How's that for a reason?

The Brits and the French introduced a modestly improved draft resolution in the Council on May 3, one of the first meetings for Vitaly Churkin, the new Russian perm rep. De La Sablière stressed that we wanted the resolution passed promptly, so that the expected thirty-day waiting period for Iran to comply would expire before the next IAEA board meeting in mid-June. Since I had no expectation Iran would comply, that meant we would start on a sanctions resolution by mid-June. Nonetheless, in subsequent Perm Five meetings, Russia and China stalled, meaning that the odds of finishing the text before the foreign ministers met on Monday, May 8, diminished rapidly. I had been scheduled to go to my first-ever Kentucky Derby that weekend, but the trip disappeared in the fog of our negotiations. Jones Parry was also in disarray, Straw having just been canned as foreign minister, perhaps because his endless repetition that force against Iran was off the table had finally irritated Blair enough to fire him. De La Sablière and Jones Parry suggested a Saturday "informal informal" Council meeting, which the nonpermanent members agreed to only reluctantly. In fact, the Council's North-South divide had been exposed at a staff-level meeting on the draft resolution the day before when Congo's staffer said, "Why do we care about nuclear weapons?" Indeed. Although the Saturday meeting ended inconclusively, de La Sablière once again stressed helpfully that we should vote on the resolution the coming week.

As we waited for Rice to arrive in New York on May 8, Bush received a long, stream-of-consciousness letter from Ahmadinejad. I thought we should ridicule the letter, which Tony Snow, newly on board at the White House, agreed to, but Rice did not. The Perm-Five-plus-Germany dinner that evening turned out to be one of the great debacles of the entire Iran matter. The foreign ministers spent two hours alone before dinner, agreeing to a two-track approach: continuing to pursue a Chapter VII resolution, while also allowing the EU-3 to present a new package of carrots and sticks to Iran. This approach had been discussed among the EU-3 political directors and Burns in March, but I thought we had killed it, since it showed weakness to Iran at precisely the point we should be showing strength. Yet here it was again, this time accepted by Rice. What the ministers actually decided was unclear, since Lavrov said he had no intention of agreeing to either a Chapter VII resolution or sanctions. Of course, given that position, there was little chance that the "sticks" would contain Council sanctions, or at least not effective ones. It also meant negotiations on the Chapter VII resolution would come to a complete halt, which they did. With the EU-3 rushing back to the negotiating table, there was no way Russia or China would allow negotiations on a Council resolution to proceed.

I was sick about the implications of this deal, which delayed our "mandatory" resolution for the rest of May, all of June, and almost all of July, and with the text ultimately adopted (Resolution 1696) being substantially weaker than the one we had been drafting in early May. This was the first time I thought seriously about not staying as the UN ambassador past the end of my recess appointment, so distressed was I about the ministers' deal. It not only cost us a nearly three-month delay, but essentially eliminated whatever international momentum we had gathered toward applying real pressure on Iran, momentum we never entirely recovered. Rice advocated a "bold approach," with lots of carrots, a flashback to Powell's comments at the September 2004 G-8 dinner, and she accepted that the resolution could expressly disavow the use of force, an utterly gratuitous concession, for which we received nothing in return. The EU-3 thought their renewed negotiations would take thirty to forty days to see if they would be productive. I knew this was a wild underestimate, and, as it turned out, was less than half the actual amount of time consumed by this frolic. I called Joseph with the news, and he said immediately, "It's a surrender." Crouch said he believed Rice had briefed Hadley earlier, not that Hadley had bothered to tell Crouch, a concise example of how the interagency process had evaporated in the second term. Even the EU's Javier Solana, who attended the dinner, said to me the next morning that he felt "a sense of disarray" from what had come out of the meeting. I wanted to respond, "Join the club."

After a lunch in Rice's honor the next day, I tried to claw back the damage done. Rice was explicit that the delay inherent in this new tactic did not bother her, so long as we passed the Chapter VII resolution before the June IAEA board meeting. She thought the total delay before we came back to discussing our current draft resolution would be *ten days or less,* which I knew was a complete fantasy, as just described. She was also not worried by the media perception, and almost certainly Iran's, that we were talking about a package only of carrots, not a package of carrots and sticks. (If there were only one phrase I could ban from State's lexicon it would be "carrots and sticks," which is too often a substitute for real strategic thinking.) So strong was the carrot perception that one reporter flatly asked Joseph when he would be resigning. I was just glad they weren't asking me. I was floored by how indifferent Rice was to the potential consequences of what she had agreed to. Worse, she said, "The Iranians must understand that we're really prepared to isolate them through sanctions," which was in fact the precise opposite of what we were doing. Even the French, at the staff level, were surprised that Rice had agreed to this outcome. Churkin understood exactly what had happened, practically crowing to the press over the next several days that the EU-3 and the United States had caved in on Iran. I wasn't in a mood to dispute him.

The action shifted to the Perm-Five-plus-Germany political directors, as they put together a "package" that was predictably very heavy on carrots and very light on sticks. I was happy to be out of it, but I knew we would inevitably be back at the Council after Iran—yet again—refused to give up uranium enrichment. Nonetheless, there was little I could do until the carrot effort crashed once more. I was cheered by Crouch's telling me that in one Bush-Merkel telephone conversation, the chancellor said, "I like your ambassador at the UN more than I like mine," which I hoped was not damning with faint praise. I heard another report of that conversation to the effect that Merkel said, "I understand your UN ambassador much better than my own. I've been thinking about having your ambassador represent Germany." Now, that would have been something!

Rice called me to an uneventful meeting on May 23, as the political directors were meeting in Paris, which allowed me to compare notes in person with Joseph, who was still quite discouraged. He did say that DoD was joking that the EU's new motto was "speak softly and carry a big carrot," which was the best we were doing for laughs. There was good news, as Iran called the latest EU-3 effort, even before it was completed, "offering chocolate and walnuts for gold." I supposed there was some unknown Iranian candy bar referred to there, but at least the negative implication came through.

The worst news came on Tuesday, May 30, 2006, when I learned of the decision that the United States would actually join in direct talks, along with the EU-3, Russia, and China, if Iran were to agree to suspend enrichment. Rice scheduled a dinner in Washington at the Watergate's Aquarelle restaurant, with Hadley, Burns, Joseph, and me, to tell us this, or at least to tell me, and to decide which conservative journalists we were to call to spin them about how wonderful the decision was. Joseph had prepped me over an open phone line Monday, saying, "Nick is beaming broadly," which told me all I needed to know. Crouch said that he, Hadley, Dan Bartlett, Jim Wilkinson, and others were all concerned, but that Rice and Burns were unswayed. Rice had spoken to Bush at Camp David over the weekend, and the way ahead was apparently clear. I asked Crouch what reaction the White House press types anticipated, and he said, "The press will spin it as weakness, and the base will go crazy." In the meantime, Zoellick was resigning as deputy secretary, opening an extended vacuum with no deputy, which Rice allowed Burns to fill. I asked Abrams if there was any possibility at the dinner that I could change the direction in which we were headed. "Just listen," he advised, because Rice's mind was made up. Rice saw that the EU-3 effort was near collapse, and she reasoned that we had to intervene to save it, exactly as at the start of the second term when she shifted policy! Of course, what we should have done was watch the EU-3 effort slide beneath the waves, and then get on with serious efforts to stop Iran's nuclear weapons program.

I saw Rice one-on-one at 5:15 P.M., and she told me what she would say the next day about joining the EU-3 negotiations, and her explanation, as Joseph, Crouch, and Abrams had all forecast. Rice wanted to remove Iran's excuses for not confronting the likely consequences of its continued nuclear efforts, and, in Lenin's phrase, she wanted to "sharpen the contradictions" for Iran in reviewing the alternatives now before it. Bush had called Putin with the change of policy, said Rice, and Putin had said that he would now be supportive on sanctions, a promise I did not fully believe. Obviously, this was a done deal, so I followed Abrams's advice and said nothing. I wandered back to Joseph's office (my old office), and we sat for a while in silence. I asked why we were having dinner now that we all knew what was up, and Joseph said he thought it was mainly to make sure he and I were "okay with the decision."

At the Aquarelle, as Rice arrived, Robert McNamara walked up to her and said, "I'm a Democrat, but I think you're wonderful." In response, for my appetizer, I ordered carrot soup. Only Joseph noticed, suppressing a chortle. We soon got down to handing out assignments to call conservative commentators, all of which fell to Joseph and me. While we were at the table talking, Bush called Hadley on his cell phone. During their brief conversation, Hadley said he had reached Cheney in Wyoming and had passed on the decision. Hadley gave the phone to Rice, who named the happy attendees at our dinner party, and then said she had spoken with Kissinger, Baker, and Powell, with Powell spending the bulk of their conversation discussing Iraq. Rice asked what I thought would happen in the Security Council if Iran refused to suspend enrichment, which was a near certainty, so I said we should move immediately for Chapter VII sanctions, stressing that as long as discussion of the EU-3 package was proceeding, we were at a dead stop in New York, and had been. The dinner ended at about 8:40 P.M. The carrot soup did not cheer me up. The crab cakes I ordered made me feel better.

I flew back to New York the next morning, and, as we had agreed, called Iranian perm rep Zarif between calls to the conservative writers on my list. They couldn't believe what they were hearing. Neither could the Iranian, who originally scheduled a meeting with me, and then canceled it on Tehran's orders. I was finally having fun again, so I called Zarif directly. He came on the line and said, "Hello, Ambassador," to which I replied in truest diplomatic fashion, "Hello, Ambassador, thank you for taking the call." We were off to a good start, that certainly being the way Burns would have described it. I said I had hoped to meet him at the UN to give him a document (the public statement Rice was about to make), but I understood he was not able to do so. He said that was right, so I said, "Well, I am under instructions to deliver this to you, and you are under instructions not to meet, so what are we going to do?" We agreed I would deliver the statement to him, and that we would each make it clear in subsequent press comments we had not actually met. He probably needed that more than I did! I later described our discussion as "courteous and businesslike." Groombridge, who had joined my staff at USUN, took the document to Iran's Mission, donning wrap-around sunglasses to better fit the part, and I handed it out at an already scheduled 11:00 A.M. Security Council meeting. When I called Crouch later to ask him what the overall picture looked like, he said, "Our enemies love it," and, "our friends are skeptical or irritated," which was the reaction I had received in my press calls. Israel didn't like it, but it had no choice but to swallow hard and accept it.

In press interviews that day, particularly a live appearance on Neil Cavuto's show on Fox News, I gritted my teeth to try to defend Rice's announcement without hopelessly compromising myself. I noted that we still had red lines, such as the requirement that Iran suspend enrichment before we would meet with them, and that they didn't have forever to respond. I had very much in mind what Crouch had told me earlier, namely that Bush had said to Rice, "Don't make me look weak," which of course is exactly what I thought this announcement did. I suspected Bush knew it, too. To my amazement, I learned the next day that Rice, Burns, McCormack, Gunderson, and Wilkinson had all watched the Cavuto interview in her office, and, fortunately for my job tenure, had liked it. Hadley also liked the Cavuto interview, and he called to talk generally about the reactions. Hadley had spoken to the renowned Islamic scholar Bernard Lewis, and thought him not as negative as he might have been. That was not what my former AEI colleague and T staffer Dave Wurmser, now on Cheney's staff, later told me, saying Lewis had complained about Burns's being in charge of Iran policy. Lewis told Wurmser that Hadley responded that both Burns and Bolton were in charge of Iran policy, which was truly false advertising.

The Perm-Five-plus-Germany foreign ministers met in Vienna on June 1, and agreed on the carrot recipe for Iran, but said only that if Iran rejected it, "Further steps would have to be taken in the Security Council," which was so vague it was no surprise even Lavrov could agree to it. The *New York Times* characterized it the next day as: "Package of Terms (No Sanctions Included) for Iran."[6] Burns, in fact, sent Joseph a note saying that

---

6. Thom Shanker and Elaine Sciolino, "Package of Terms (No Sanctions Included) for Iran," *New York Times*, Friday, June 2, 2006, p. A12, col. 1.

we should not refer for the foreseeable future to "sanctions" against Iran, but only "consequences" if Iran didn't suspend enrichment. This was laughable and proved the cover-up was on. In fact, Lavrov had not moved at all in opposing sanctions. Rice said on three Sunday talk shows on June 4 that she wasn't going to get into details, which would have been painfully brief, on the "consequences" side, but stressed that the possibility of the United States' talking with Iran was not a major departure, but simply an extension of the shift made at the outset of her tenure at State in explicitly endorsing the EU-3 negotiating effort. That was true, but I was surprised that she would admit it publicly, since it made the policy entirely her own. Solana delivered the package of carrots to Iran in Tehran in early June, with the ministers having agreed we would seek Security Council sanctions if the Iranians didn't respond by June 22.

The ministers' June 22 "deadline" came and went, with Ahmadinejad saying on June 21 that we would get Iran's answer on August 22, the end of a month on the Moslem calendar, and not before. After a series of Perm-Five-plus-Germany political directors meetings, during which we were at rest in New York, the EU-3 essentially agreed we wouldn't press Iran for a definitive answer before Ahmadinejad's deadline. They also agreed to Russia's insistence that when we returned to the Security Council it would not be to seek sanctions, but only to make the suspension of uranium enrichment mandatory on Iran. Actual sanctions would have to wait until later.

Rice called me from Paris on Wednesday, July 12, at 7:35 A.M., saying, "We have resolutions coming out of our ears," which was certainly true, given our work in response to North Korea's July 4 missile launches. Later that day the Hezbollah-Israel war started, so we were busy. On Tuesday, July 18, we had a Perm-Five-plus-Germany meeting, which de La Sablière opened by handing around the slightly modified May "suspension" draft, explaining all the changes the EU-3 had already made to try to satisfy Russia and China (a long speech indeed), and said he hoped we could move quickly, given how close we had been in May. Churkin thanked him for distributing the text and said he would report it to Moscow to receive instructions. Wang's deputy said basically the same thing, and then we all sat there and looked at each other for a while. All three EUroid delegations looked as if they had just had the wind knocked out of them, saying, in effect, "But our foreign ministers have already agreed to this!" Unswayed, the Russians and Chinese just sat there. We met again the next day, and Churkin handed out his rewrite of the EU-3 draft, which pretty well gutted it. The EU-3 perm reps again looked as if they had been slammed in the gut. Ironically, much of the language Churkin wanted to insert came from the July 12 foreign ministers statement, drafted by the political directors, so it was impossible to reject something they had already agreed on.

On Monday, July 24, we had a Perm-Three-plus-Germany meeting, including Germany's new perm rep, Thomas Matussek. (The Perm Five foreign ministers and political directors had met so many times with their German counterparts on this issue that we were "late" in so doing in New York mostly because none of us had wanted to include Matussek's predecessor.) It was clear to me that neither Jones Parry nor de La Sablière any longer cared what the draft text said, and I didn't really either, so long as it had a clear deadline, no later than August 31. If we could at least get that, we had one more chance to make a stand in the Council, and if we failed, no one could say we hadn't tried. With that, on Monday, July 31, by a vote of 14–1–0, we adopted Resolution 1696, with Qatar voting "no" because they wanted to wait until Ahmadinejad's August 22 deadline before doing anything. At least we hadn't succumbed to that humiliation.

Of course, Ahmadinejad followed his own schedule in any event and responded to the EU-3 offer on August 22, as he always said he would. He was nearly as incoherent as in his earlier letter to Bush, but the bottom line was clear: Iran was not suspending its enrichment activities. In a kind of *Readers' Digest* version, Ayatollah Khamenei, Iran's real *el Supremo*, also said publicly that Iran had no intention of giving up its nuclear program, and Iran denied IAEA inspectors access to the large underground facilities at Natanz where industrial-scope enrichment could take place. Although Joseph and I wanted to move quickly once we had Ahmadinejad's answer, Burns, as usual doubtless reflecting Sawers's views, said this might not actually be a complete response. Fortunately, Bush took a hard line at a press conference that morning, which I followed with the press throughout the day. More troubling was that Rice was watering down our draft sanctions resolution on such subjects as international credit and air travel on the grounds that we didn't want to penalize the Iranian people. Of course, these restrictions and several others would have a disproportionate impact on the Iranian elite, whom we were trying to target, so Rice's wobbliness even before we circulated a draft text to the EU-3, let alone Russia and China, was worrisome. In the meantime, I was also trying to set up a meeting with the EU-3 in New York, but Germany's Schaeffer told Matussek not to hold even preliminary meetings until Resolution 1696's August 31 deadline had passed.

Astonishingly, on August 22 we issued no statement on Ahmadinejad's response, and Crouch told me early on August 23 that Bush and Rice were meeting at 8:55 A.M. on what to say. The final statement was a muddle, a sharp contrast to Bush's remarks at his August 22 press conference. Crouch and Joseph were disconsolate because they had not even had a chance to weigh in. There was nothing about prompt action in New York, which had been my priority. Incredibly, France was tougher, with Douste-Blazy saying it was "now or never" for Iran. Rice called at around 7:00 P.M. to say she didn't want to circulate anything in New York until we had had a chance to talk to the EU-3, which of course was exactly what we would accomplish by circulating a text that would contain only sanctions ideas that foreign ministers and political directors had been hashing over for months. Rice asked how hard I thought it would be to get the sanctions resolution adopted, and I said it would be very hard indeed, given the track record to date. That clearly took her aback, and I wondered for the umpteenth time what Burns was telling her. Rice also said that Solana would be having more meetings with Iran in the next few days, which could be important in convincing the EU that Iran wasn't going to give in and suspend its uranium enrichment. I thought exactly the opposite, namely that it would impel the EUroids on to more negotiation and less work on the sanctions resolution.

The next day, Rice spoke to Lavrov, on vacation in Siberia, who said, in light of Iran's inadequate response, he was willing to talk about sanctions but not yet discuss a sanctions resolution. Somehow, Rice was encouraged by this call, but I didn't understand why. On Friday, August 25, Solana said publicly that he had already spoken twice with Ali Larijani, head of Iran's Supreme National Security Council, since Ahmadinejad's response, and they would talk further in Brussels on August 31. The consequence of these delays was not only that we were stalled on a sanctions resolution, but that Iran's work on its nuclear program continued while we fiddled. Proving the point, on August 26, Ahmadinejad formally opened the Arak heavy-water production facility. Proving the point further, Larijani postponed his meeting with Solana until Wednesday, September 6, in Berlin, a venue he probably thought even more congenial than Brussels. Worse, Sawers said our proposed sanctions were too broad and should be trimmed back, a tactically obtuse way to enter negotiations with Russia and China, which were only too eager to trim them back further. Joseph described himself as "frustrated" and "flabbergasted," and I judged he was closer to resignation than ever.

Thus, when August 31 came, I wondered how to say with a straight face we were taking a tough line on Iran. Fortunately, the IAEA issued a brief but devastating report, one of the most helpful it ever issued, making clear that Iran was still actively obstructing the IAEA's work, and still trying to perfect uranium enrichment. On September 3, Annan met with Ahmadinejad, and happily reported that Iran was ready for a "solution" to the nuclear problem. Indeed! Even Annan conceded, however, that the next steps were in the Council, not that we were doing anything toward that end. Larijani canceled a series of meetings with Solana, and their one brief encounter was unproductive. Two weeks after our "deadline," and several months after what should have been the real deadline, we were still spinning wheels. Rice, in New York for the General Assembly opening, had dinner with Solana on Sunday, September 17, arguing that Iran was stalling, a point she also made the next day in her meeting with Chinese foreign minister Li Zhaoxing, concluding, "If Javier [Solana] can't produce something this week," we would move ahead with sanctions. Solana ultimately had to tell the Perm Five foreign ministers on Monday, October 2, that his meetings with Larijani had gone nowhere. Lavrov, however, still insisted that sanctions were premature.

The EU-3 circulated their own draft sanctions resolution on October 17, which Burns had agreed to, without telling Crouch, Joseph, or me. Their text was, of course, weaker than what we had been working on, and it included Rice's agreement to an EU-3 idea that we make it clear in the sanctions resolution that it did not apply to the Bushehr facility, which would delight Russia and Iran. Of course, Rice had been soft on Bushehr since the administration's earliest days, so her acceptance of the EU-3 view was not really surprising. Crouch said he had asked Burns, "When John praises this resolution to the press, what is his answer to the question, 'What current nuclear activity will this resolution stop?' If the answer is, 'Nothing,' don't we have a problem?" This was an excellent question. Burns had no answer, in part because the question didn't matter to the EU-3 (or, therefore, to Burns) and in part because Burns just didn't know much about the mechanics of enriching uranium or weapons production (neither did any of the other political directors except Russia's Kislyak, a Cold War arms negotiator). I tried to push back some of what Burns had agreed to, but the EU-3 were still of the view that preemptive concessions to Russia would speed the process of reaching agreement on a resolution, which I thought was delusional. It would only encourage the Russians to seek more concessions, which is exactly what happened. I had earlier handed out a cartoon that summed it all up, showing Ahmadinejad almost buried in a pile of paper, with the caption reading, "I can't find my enriched uranium under all of these notes from the UN."

Rice met with Lavrov in Moscow on Saturday, October 21, and at least made clear to him that Russia should not ship fuel rods to Bushehr. The Perm-Three-plus-Germany met in New York the next day, just as Iran fired up its second long centrifuge cascade, enriching UF_6 and thereby showing just what Iran thought of all of these negotiations. I urged that we take a tough and broad position on travel bans for top Iranians, naming several of the worst proliferators (a position weaker than what I wanted to take, but I was constrained by Rice's earlier decision); include a prohibition on Bushehr at least for bargaining purposes; and omit a huge carve-out the Germans wanted for existing contracts, a position I called "sanctions without pain." The EUroids were divided among themselves on these and many other substantive points, such as how far to abase ourselves in the text on our willingness to lift sanctions at some point, with France taking a position relatively close to ours. The EU-3 were obviously unhappy with all of these disagreements, and the next day, Jones Parry and de La Sablière said the EU-3 political directors had instructed them to roll back even the relatively modest changes they had agreed to the day before, retreating to a much weaker text. Of course, all these discussions were taking place before we had even shown a draft to Russia and China.

To make matters worse, the EU-3 then circulated their weaker draft, which finally caused Rice to explode. Silverberg said to me, "She's never talked to me like that in all seven years I've known her." As it turned out, Rice was angry because she did not know the state of play on the negotiations, Burns was out of the country, and Silverberg took the hit. By this time, the usual round of media stories was beginning to appear about a split between the EU-3 and the United States, many of them sourced to anonymous diplomats complaining about the hard line I was taking. I was also sure that Rice would not like the *Wall Street Journal* editorial entitled "Secretary of State El Baradei."[7] Silverberg called both Joseph and Sanders (who had joined USUN in February 2006 as our ambassador in charge of Security Council issues) in distress both at the pounding she had taken and that Burns had not come to her defense, even though she said she had kept him fully posted. "I do everything through Nick," she had said over the phone, almost in tears, to Sanders. Joseph doubted that Rice understood that Burns's multiple concessions over the past several months had boxed her in: "She won't look at the reality that Burns screwed this up; everyone else realizes it, but she does not."

The EU-3 were confident going into our October 26 Perm-Five-plus-Germany meeting that they were very close to agreement with Russia. However, Churkin, rapidly translating from his instructions in Russian, gave his "general and preliminary" reactions. In his twenty-minute speech, Churkin basically trashed the entire EU-3 draft resolution, saying expressly it did not represent what ministers and political directors had agreed, didn't include any of Russia's suggestions, and would only back Iran into a corner. The Chinese deputy perm rep basically agreed, although, mercifully, he was brief. The EU-3 tried for about twenty minutes to pick up the pieces and start a paragraph-by-paragraph review of their text, but the Russians and Chinese would not agree.

As Churkin and I left the British Mission at the same time, knowing that the press was waiting outside, Churkin said to me, "Let's go out together and denounce the text!" I was very tempted. This was what Lavrov might have had in mind when Rice had said to him back in September that "our two perm reps seem to be working well together," and Lavrov had replied, "Yes, they tease each other, but in a very constructive manner."

After such a productive session, the Perm-Five-plus-Germany perm reps did not meet again until Friday, November 3. Churkin and Wang hadn't moved an inch. I suggested that we let our political directors get together again, so they could agree on what they thought they had agreed to, which caused mutterings among the EU-3, and led Churkin to quip, "But John, you have always said we should carry the burden here." It was hilarious. Churkin stressed his argument that there had been serious disagree-

---

7. "Secretary of State El Baradei," *Wall Street Journal,* Thursday, October 26, 2006, p. A18, col. 1.

ment among the political directors, and that Russia and China were not just making up their recollections about what political directors had actually done. Instead of going back to political directors "to re-establish what they previously agreed to," Churkin said, "Why not do our jobs here?" The EUroids simply did not know what to say in the face of this sustained assault. Jones Parry asked hopefully, "Can we take the discussions any further now?" which was greeted with silence, and the meeting ended.

On Tuesday, November 7, we met at the French Mission, no more productively than the last meetings. Given our election results, it was clear to me that things were only going to get worse, as Russia took heart from the Republican loss of control of the House and Senate. De La Sablière said the EU-3 wanted a legally binding resolution, and that "despite John's vigilance," they had tried to take Russia's difficulties into account. He was at least remarkably candid, complaining to Churkin that "we have not been rewarded" for the EU-3's efforts to "water down" the language "to make Russia's life easier," and that the EU-3 were "disappointed you have not acknowledged this move." After over an hour, literally no one had anything to say, and the meeting ended. On and on the Perm-Five-plus-Germany meetings went. On November 9 and 13, we made little progress, with both the EU-3 and Russia agreeing that political directors should speak again by phone to see if they could resolve these differences. By this time, I suspected that even Jones Parry and de La Sablière were saying to themselves that the political directors had made this bed, and now they could lie in it. I filled Joseph in, sensing that his mood remained very unhappy. " 'Clintonian' is the only word for this," he said sadly. "You have even more depressing news than I do," I said lightly, but Joseph responded gloomily, "That's because I'm closer to the source."

Ahmadinejad announced on November 14 that Iran was planning to install sixty thousand centrifuges at Natanz, and that the world was prepared to accept Iran as a nuclear power. Burns called at about 7:10 P.M. to report that the political directors' conference call had not been successful, and that he and Kislyak had almost gotten into a brawl over the phone. Both Sawers and Kislyak suggested, at separate points, that they have another in-person meeting of political directors, but Burns said he had resisted, insisting that the "action" remain in New York. How thoughtful. I was sure Nick was busy with many other very important matters, and certainly busy enough to avoid news stories about "failures" on the Iran front. Accordingly, on November 15, we had our sixth Perm-Five-plus-Germany meeting of this series, at which it rapidly became evident that we weren't going anywhere. I suggested, as I had to Burns, that we refer all of this back to foreign ministers. Of course, the other possibility was to force a resolution to a vote and see what Russia would do in the crunch, but the EU-3 were still nowhere near ready for that. The EU-3 were now resisting the United States more strongly than they were resisting Russia. Sawers flew to Moscow in late November to meet Kislyak to discuss their latest concessions, but reported that Kislyak had simply been dismissive. Why compromise when your opponents are giving things away so rapidly? One French staffer wrote an email about the French perception of Sawers's pilgrimage to Moscow: "Kislyak pockets elements in his favor and rejects everything else. No idea of what comes next except my holiday."

On December 6, in Paris, Perm-Five-plus-Germany political directors met again, looking to give Russia almost anything in order to get a resolution. By this time, my imminent departure was public, and Bob Joseph had told Rice that he was leaving the administration no later than February. The only hope now was that if the Security Council could impose some sanctions, no matter how weak and ineffective, Iran would freak out, perhaps withdrawing from the NPT or expelling IAEA inspectors, and we could once and for all expose what they were up to. Given how watered down the draft resolution now was, however, it looked increasingly as if Iran would simply live with it, because it would cause no particular hardship to them.

In December, after my recess appointment expired, the trend downhill continued. What the Russians essentially wanted, and what they substantially achieved, was to distinguish between "illicit" proliferation-related transactions by a given entity and "licit" nonproliferation activities. This, of course, turned what should have been an exercise in imposing economic pain on the entire entity (and on Iran for proliferation) into an exercise in bean counting, with Iran holding the beans. This would weaken the proposed sanctions not only against Iran, but also against others, because it drove a huge conceptual wedge into the entire sanctions rationale. The changes in the draft Iran resolution had an immediate effect on North Korea, where our Treasury Department's successful efforts to squeeze Banco Delta Asia were similarly parsed, ignoring the reality that the entire DPRK government was a criminal enterprise. Treasury was livid over the developments in New York, but it was irrelevant. Secure in the knowledge that the once-fearsome interagency process now barely existed, Burns simply ignored Treasury.

Ahmadinejad responded on December 11 by opening a conference in Tehran to discuss whether there had been a Holocaust in Europe during World War II, promising a reasoned debate on both sides. By late December, staffers from the EU-3 missions in New York were complaining how badly things were going, as the draft resolution continued to weaken. During all of this time, and with all of these concessions, however, the Russians never once indicated that they would actually vote in favor of the text, once they got what they wanted. The *Wall Street Journal* correctly editorialized that a weak resolution might be worse than no resolution at all,[8] but resolution there would no doubt be. It finally came on Saturday, December 23, with the unanimous adoption of Resolution 1737. One last time: "We never fail in New York." I was happy to be back in Washington getting ready for Christmas.

The entire EU-3 effort was premised on the view that they could handle an "axis of evil" member better than we had handled Iraq, and that Iran could be talked out of pursuing nuclear weapons. Our support for the EU-3 thus perversely enabled their effort to make us look bad, with the far more dangerous consequence that Iran gained almost four years of additional time to perfect an indigenous capacity throughout the entire nuclear fuel cycle, leaving us all in a far more vulnerable position than when we started. During 2007, Iran continued its inexorable process of perfecting all of the requisite technologies, toying with the IAEA and its inspectors and the EU-3, despite more Security Council resolutions and more negotiation efforts by the EU-3. Israel's ambassador Dan Gillerman once described the state of play quite well in a speech to the Security Council, saying that Ahmadinejad was denying the existence of the Holocaust, even while "preparing the next one." The fact is that Iran will never voluntarily give up its nuclear program, and a policy based on the contrary assumption is not just delusional but dangerous. This is the road to the Nuclear Holocaust.

---

8. "Who's Tough on Tehran?" *Wall Street Journal,* Thursday, December 21, 2006, p. A16, col. 1.

CHAPTER THIRTEEN

DARFUR AND THE WEAKNESS OF UN PEACEKEEPING IN AFRICA

What shall we do tomorrow? What shall we ever do?

—T. S. ELIOT, "THE WASTE LAND"

The UN's greatest potential as the Cold War ended seemed to be in peacekeeping. Successes in Namibia, bringing it to full independence under majority rule, and Mozambique, helping to end a debilitating post-colonial civil war, were positive signs, marking the actual end of conflicts. Other operations failed. Somalia, for example, disintegrated into anarchy and became a base of operations for terrorists and pirates. Sub-Saharan Africa's first secretary general, Kofi Annan, placed considerable emphasis on Africa, but by the time of my arrival in New York, stasis had replaced success.

The concentration of the Security Council's work on Africa is staggering. In mid-2005, there were eight continuing African peacekeeping operations, out of a total of seventeen worldwide, plus three continuing "political" operations, and countless emissaries and temporary missions. By October 2006, shortly before I left New York, there were eighteen operations with 80,976 military and police personnel, and 15,000 civilians serving worldwide,[1] and the prospect of a further, substantial increase if the UN

---

1. "United Nations Military, Police Deployment Reaches All-Time High in October," press release PKO/152, November 10, 2006.

ever established a peacekeeping presence in the three Darfur provinces of Sudan. These last figures do not include the UN's political missions, which, depending on how one counted them, totaled approximately eighteen worldwide by the end of 2006.

In 2006, for example, the Council passed a total of 87 resolutions, of which 76 dealt with specific conflict situations. Of those, 46 addressed African conflicts, while only 30 dealt with conflicts elsewhere, meaning that African resolutions amounted to 60 percent of the total worldwide output. Similarly, there were 59 presidential statements in 2006, of which 48 addressed specific conflicts, and 29 of them, approximately 60 percent of the worldwide total, concerned Africa. As tragic and homicidal as Africa's conflicts have been, however, there is no serious argument that 60 percent of the aggregate threat to international peace and security is concentrated on that continent, not when compared to the global proliferation of weapons of mass destruction and international terrorism. The Council concentrates on Africa for a variety of reasons, and one could make the argument that this concentration was justified if problems in Africa were actually being solved. The unfortunate reality, however, is that the UN is both ineffective in Africa and inattentive (and often ineffective) to more pervasive problems elsewhere.

While UN peacekeeping efforts are complex and defy easy generalization, the concentration on Africa is no accident. Especially in his second term (2002–6), Annan pushed relentlessly to increase UN involvement there, including retaining a UN presence in countries after an operation was concluded. The UN Secretariat complicated matters further, with confused and overlapping mandates for the Department of Peacekeeping Operations (DPKO) and the Department of Political Affairs (DPA), rather than integrated political and military operations organized on geographical lines (as I proposed to incoming secretary general Ban Ki-moon in late 2006). Former European colonial powers are all too willing to lead a new interventionism in their former colonies, helpfully financed largely by others, to show their High Minded "concern," and to maintain at least some of their past influence. As is too often the case in "humanitarian" affairs, actual performance is less central than demonstrating "compassion." It has not been, and still is not, politically correct to ask if the UN is actually solving the problem at hand, prolonging it, or perhaps even exacerbating it. Africa needs a concept for "graduation" from peacekeeping operations, which many African diplomats recognize, to reassert its abilities to resolve its own problems. This is politically difficult to advocate at the UN, less because of what it says about Africa than for what it says about the True Believers' view of the UN. Whether Annan's departure will make a difference on this score remains to be seen.

How and why the promise of UN peacekeeping was blunted in the post–Cold War era is beyond what I can treat here, but the African experience demonstrates many of the reasons for the continued failure. Those who know it best are Africans themselves, many of whom are in private despair over the UN's ineffectiveness and urged me on in my efforts to resolve the political disputes that had given rise to peacekeeping operations in the first place. They understood better than anyone else that the price of continued stasis was all too evident in the conflict regions' unattractiveness to international trade and investment, the risk of future political and military instability, and the individual fear and uncertainty felt by often-innocent peoples enmeshed in the conflicts. Unfortunately, however, in the UN culture, solving problems is less admired than avoiding responsibility or laying blame, a culture that exists in both the Secretariat and the Security Council. Indeed, the Council is as much or more at fault, having over the years abdicated much of its political and military authority and judgment to the Secretariat. The Council creates peacekeeping operations and then rolls over their mandates year after year, without exercising the leadership necessary to solve the basic conflicts, rather than simply to freeze them. I decided to try something different, but the battle against the prevailing status quo culture proved more difficult to overcome than even I had believed.

The main event—or better stated in the UN context, the missed opportunity for a main event—was Darfur. This region fell into crisis after extensive efforts, led by the Bush administration, to resolve Sudan's long-standing North-South civil war appeared to end successfully. Whether that settlement will hold remains unresolved, but even as its implementation got under way, tragedy had come to the fore in western Sudan. In 2003, government-backed Moslem militia forces known colloquially as "janjaweed" killed, raped, and displaced black Moslems, launching what Secretary Powell, on September 4, 2004, was the first to call "genocide."

Darfur was the worst example of the UN's inability to address critical problems in Africa, but there were enough others to form a pattern. Progress in ending these conflicts need not be impossible, but progress will not occur, in my view, unless the Security Council and the Secretariat place a higher value on resolving problems rather than simply massaging them. The examples that follow are incomplete, given the magnitude of the UN's activity in Africa, but they are sufficient to demonstrate the problem.

Ethiopia-Eritrea

An early peacekeeping crisis in my tenure came on October 4, 2005, when the Security Council convened hastily at 5:00 P.M. to deal with Eritrea's order grounding helicopter flights over its territory by UNMEE, the UN Mission in Ethiopia and Eritrea. The flight ban would substantially impair UNMEE's ability to operate, since many of its observation posts were in remote locations in these Horn of Africa countries, and could only be reached in a timely way by air. Most admitted that Eritrea had acted out of frustration that Ethiopia had refused for over three years to comply with the December 2000 Algiers Agreement between them. That agreement was intended to settle the disputed boundary between the two countries created after Eritrea declared independence, providing for arbitration through a neutral Eritrea-Ethiopia Boundary Commission (EEBC), the results of which both parties agreed to accept as binding. The Security Council first created UNMEE in Resolution 1312 to monitor a cease-fire between the two sides while they negotiated in Algiers, and then continued and enhanced it thereafter in Resolutions 1320 and 1430. By 2002, the EEBC had completed its work delimiting the boundary, which should then have been demarcated physically. Ethiopia, however, was dissatisfied with the outcome and simply refused to allow the EEBC's demarcation work to proceed, thus causing over three years of stalemate. The UN just watched.

Neither the Ethiopian nor the Eritrean government would win any popularity contests, and I certainly had no favorite, but it seemed to me Eritrea had a point: Ethiopia had agreed on a mechanism to resolve the border dispute in 2000 and was now welching on the deal. I thought the Security Council, after over three years of watching the grass grow, should now determine whether both parties were still prepared to adhere to their commitments. If so, then demarcation should proceed, or if not, it was time to terminate UNMEE, which was simply propping up Ethiopia's flat violation of its commitments. That, of course, was not the way Annan and the

Secretariat saw the situation. Neither did many Council members, who focused like laser beams on Eritrea's interference with UNMEE's operations rather than on the underlying dispute. Eritrea was unquestionably interfering improperly in UNMEE's operations, but as a way to get our collective attention in the only manner a small, impoverished country knew how, by biting the UN's ankles. So, instead of dealing with the real problem, Annan and the Secretariat wanted to bite Eritrea back, but only with words, of course.

I thought that instead of responding at the capillary level, we should use Eritrea's action, which I certainly did not defend, as a pivot point to raise the underlying issue to the Council's attention. Then, we could either move to resolve it or determine that the underlying reason for its creation, the agreement between Ethiopia and Eritrea, no longer existed, at least *de facto*. In effect, UNMEE was now part of the problem, as Eritrea's manipulation of its operations demonstrated. I said in the Council consultations that UN peacekeeping operations should not have eternal life, and that addressing this issue should be a central element of "UN reform." This caused a lot of heavy breathing, but I was heartened that the SG's special representative for Ethiopia-Eritrea, Joseph Legwaila of Botswana, said, "I just hope people wake up and realize it is important we should deal with the [border] stalemate decisively to make sure it ends." Unfortunately, the Council continued to dither, fearful that if it actually tried to stand up to Eritrea, the whole of UNMEE might be shut down. At one point I had a USUN staffer say at a Council experts' meeting that the headline so far was "Eritrea Faces Down Security Council." Characteristically, British deputy perm rep Adam Thomson responded protectively that such a statement was "wounding" to the Council, as indeed true statements often are.

To be sure, the reaction of the State Department's Africa bureau (AF) was initially not much better. AF had slumbered for three years right along with the Security Council, having endless meetings with Ethiopia and Eritrea but making no progress. The thought of terminating UNMEE was as heretical to AF as it was to other governments, since UNMEE's existence enabled them to say that *someone* was addressing the problem, even if ineffectively, thus laying off responsibility elsewhere. In fact, AF's attitude was highly typical of State's bureaucracy, which usually considered its own country or regional issues more important than larger policy questions such as UN reform or WMD proliferation. UNMEE, like many other UN operations, was a substitute for real action, a crutch, and my talk of kicking away the crutch was not greeted enthusiastically at first. Unexpectedly, however, AF's assistant secretary, Jendayi Frazer, endorsed my view that we should use the crisis precipitated by Eritrea to try to resolve the border dispute and not simply let it fester forever. Unfortunately, things moved slowly. Only on November 23 did the Security Council adopt Resolution 1640, which demanded that Ethiopia accept the boundary commission's decisions as binding and allow it to demarcate the border.

Nothing happened. Accordingly, and predictably, Eritrea decided to bite another ankle, demanding that UNMEE expel all U.S., Canadian, European, and Russian military observers, another affront to the UN's sensibilities. To me, this was simply further proof that UNMEE was now part of the problem, a pawn in the Ethiopia-Eritrea dispute, not an effective tool in resolving that dispute. Still lost in the capillaries, however, Annan again vented against Eritrea. As before, I wasn't defending Eritrea, whose singling out of countries it thought partial to Ethiopia was hardly winning it friends, but the myopia of the Secretariat's response was just as troubling. If Eritrea was effectively withdrawing its consent to the peacekeeping operation, it was entitled to do so, especially since Ethiopia had already effectively withdrawn its consent for three years by obdurately refusing to comply with its freely undertaken obligation on border demarcation. Instead, Annan proposed that UNMEE operate only on the Ethiopian side of the border, which would have effectively rewarded Ethiopia's three years of intransigence by implicitly placing all of the responsibility for the current flap on Eritrea. Moreover, the idea that UNMEE in its present parlous condition was a deterrent to either Ethiopia's or Eritrea's resorting to force, if they deemed it in their interest to do so, was obviously misplaced. Despite grim Secretariat predictions about hostilities being imminent, none occurred. By now, France, Japan, and several other Council members had begun to agree with my point that whatever redeployment we might consider for UNMEE, it had to be decided in the context of the overall boundary dispute, and whether UNMEE still had a long-term role.

By mid-December, DPKO's military professionals leaned toward withdrawing UNMEE entirely, but Annan, viewing this as a personal defeat for his vision of ever-greater UN peacekeeping operations, especially in Africa, tried to stop them from pursuing their logic. At a December 21 Council meeting, I stressed that Eritrea had effectively withdrawn its consent for

UNMEE to operate, meaning that a fundamental prerequisite for UNMEE's deployment had ended, and that we had to consider complete withdrawal, perhaps after thirty days' notice to both sides to see if they came to their senses. De La Sablière immediately agreed with my analysis, and, as I had, rejected the idea that UNMEE's continued presence somehow amounted to a "preventive deployment" that would deter hostilities. Most other Council members also moved very close to my position, leaving only Jones Parry defending Annan's view. No one seemed to understand the collateral point that neither Ethiopia nor Eritrea was likely to get serious about listening to the UN, after close to five years of taking it for granted, until they realized that the UN might actually be about to depart.

Events took yet another turn in early January 2006, when AF's Frazer decided to make a major effort to push Eritrea and Ethiopia to demarcate the border. To give her some operating space, she asked that we basically freeze UNMEE in place for thirty days. She also said she would have agreed to terminate UNMEE long before had Burns not insisted we maintain it. I knew where that came from: Malloch Brown, on Annan's behalf, fearing another UN "failure," had gotten to Burns on an issue with which Burns had little involvement and no knowledge. Frazer fully understood that if the countries themselves were not prepared to implement their own agreement, UNMEE had no role to play. I explained Frazer's proposal to the Security Council on January 9, saying that she didn't plan to "solve" the problem, but to implement the solution Ethiopia and Eritrea themselves had previously agreed upon, namely implementing the 2002 boundary commission decision. I stressed we didn't expect this initiative to last forever; we would insist on progress from the parties, or we would terminate it. In the meantime, we should leave UNMEE's status unchanged for thirty days, at the end of which I would report again to the Council where things stood, and we could decide how to proceed. Since no one else had the slightest idea what to do, the "U.S. initiative" was easily endorsed. No one backed Annan's December options for UNMEE's redeployment, which was important, so Frazer's effort would not be undercut before it even started.

For reasons I never understood, however, Frazer reversed course, and asked in early February to reopen the 2002 EEBC decision, which she had concluded was wrong, and award a major piece of disputed territory to Ethiopia. I was at a loss how to explain that to the Security Council, so I didn't, simply asking in February for another thirty-day extension of the UNMEE status quo while the "U.S. initiative" continued. No one had anything to say, and certainly no one had any other ideas, so it was agreed. There followed a number of fruitless EEBC meetings and short-term extensions of UNMEE. One EEBC meeting, in London, consisted largely of Ethiopia's American lawyer talking to Eritrea's American lawyer, which even most Council members recognized was a charade. Still, the Council took heart that "at least they agreed to meet again," a refrain I heard countless times at the UN from diplomats looking for any "progress" so we could uphold our motto, "We never fail in New York." On May 31, I finally pushed through a reduction in UNMEE force levels from 3,400 to 2,300, over fierce resistance from Jones Parry, despite what staffers in his own mission told us were clear instructions from London to support our preferred level of 1,500, and even though the UNMEE force commander agreed he would not be impaired at all even by a reduction to 1,800. While this force-sizing issue was hardly earth-shattering, it exemplified the rocklike opposition at the UN to acknowledging any problems with UN operations, or any questioning of the absolute centrality of a UN role.

Still, nothing happened with the "U.S. initiative," nothing happened on the ground between Eritrea and Ethiopia, and nothing much happened in the Security Council. On September 26, 2006, as we considered the latest proposals for a short-term extension of UNMEE's mandate, I said that our meetings had become yet another UN version of the movie *Groundhog Day*. Even Annan's latest report finally described the situation as "untenable." Nonetheless, as I left the UN, the "*Groundhog Day*" approach prevailed, and the Ethiopia-Eritrea border dispute was no closer to resolution than it had been since 2002.

Sudan

My first contact with Sudan came while I was still undersecretary, and involved the EU's pursuing its long-term objectives by confronting the United States with a lose-lose proposition, which we promptly lost. The EU has little or no capacity to project strategic strength, but when following its own theology, it is as committed to the faith as the people who built the cathedrals and churches all over Europe, which few of their descendants now attend. Although religious influence in Europe seems confined to the extraordinary number of holidays for saints' days, for many of the High Minded the older devotions have been replaced by the pursuit of global governance, and in particular the International Criminal Court (ICC), discussed in Chapter III. More important, especially in the case of Sudan, the EU's pursuit of its ICC objectives was repeatedly and cynically designed to put the United States in an impossible position, with only unpleasant and inconsistent alternatives, in the hope and expectation that we would acquiesce in progress for the ICC in order not to frustrate other important American objectives.

In September 2004, faced with what Powell called "genocide" in Darfur (based on two hundred thousand to four hundred thousand estimated killed and 2.5 million displaced), a term the EU avoided, the EUroids responded in typical fashion, not by doing anything about the oppressive regime in Khartoum, but by getting out their wig boxes and preparing to go to court. They proposed that the Security Council create a "commission of inquiry" to investigate the atrocities committed in Darfur, an obvious preliminary to referral to the ICC. Ironically, when the Rome Statute creating the ICC was drafted, the EU tried to keep it separate from the UN system, repeatedly rebuffing Clinton administration efforts to tie it more closely to the Council. Now, however, facing adamant opposition from the Bush administration—or at least some parts of it—the ICC was in trouble, and the EU wanted to use the Council to bolster its work. By early 2005, with my nomination as UN ambassador held up, the EU got their way, as the Council adopted a referral to the ICC, on which the United States abstained. In part, this was a gesture to the EUroids, which they cynically pocketed, knowing they had a precedent they could and would use against us later. We should have voted "no," insisting on actually doing something about Darfur rather than pretending that this referral would have the slightest effect on any of the combatants in the continuing Darfur tragedy. If anything, two years after the referral, the ICC's involvement has made things worse in Sudan by stiffening Khartoum's resistance to a UN peacekeeping force.[2] Moreover, there were legitimate alternatives to using the ICC, such as cre-

---

2. Stephen Rademaker, "Unwitting Party to Genocide," *Washington Post,* Thursday, January 11, 2007, p. A25, col. 2.

ating an ad hoc international tribunal, with limited jurisdiction, as in the case of the Khmer Rouge's atrocities in Cambodia.[3]

The EU's real attitude emerged in late 2005 as the EU made it clear it would not continue its funding levels for the African Union peacekeeping force in Darfur (AMIS, the African Union Mission in Sudan). AMIS had done little to improve the situation, since it was not mobile, not well-equipped, and riven with political conflicts among its member states. ("Very weak on the ground" was the way the Nigerian perm rep put it during a meeting with Annan in May 2006.) Instead, Annan and the EU had decided it should be replaced by a UN force, largely, I suspected, because a UN force would receive assessed contributions from all UN member states, meaning 27 percent from us. No one said that publicly, but everyone knew it. Moreover, there was widespread concern that the conflict would widen, since Sudan was supporting rebel groups inside Chad against the government there, and Chad was reciprocating on the Sudanese side of the border.

France started out very skeptical of a UN takeover of Darfur, largely because it foresaw an endless drain for peacekeeping troops, which might in turn exhaust traditional sources for such troops and prevent them from being deployed to higher priorities for France, such as Côte d'Ivoire, a former French colony. France warmed considerably toward a UN force, however, when the risks rose for the pro-French government in Chad, also a former colony, where regular French forces were actually deployed to protect the regime. One area where we found common ground with France was insisting that the UN Secretariat provide the Council with several options for accomplishing the UN takeover of peacekeeping operations in Darfur, something Annan and DPKO resisted, but de La Sablière and I finally pushed through. Not only was our approach simple common sense, but it represented a reassertion of Council authority and supervision over the Secretariat, especially on the military side, which we needed to do more of.

In February 2006, using the U.S. presidency of the Security Council, we tried for as much progress as possible on Darfur, with mixed success. The Pentagon offered up several military logisticians to the UN, whose salaries and expenses we would continue to pay. We hoped to make the Secretariat's work more realistic, and not entirely dependent on U.S. capabilities to get

---

3. See David B. Rivkin, Jr., and Lee A. Casey, "Darfur's Last Hope," *Washington Times*, February 4, 2005, p. A19, col. 1.

UN forces into Darfur and supply them while they were there, not to mention rescuing them if things went badly. The Secretariat resisted mightily, based on a 1997 General Assembly resolution the G-77 had pushed through, limiting the Secretariat's ability to accept such "free" assistance. One would be hard pressed to come up with something more inane, although Annan was able to do so. While resisting our offer to supply military planners, which all agreed DPKO needed, he called publicly for U.S. participation in the actual peacekeeping force, which he knew full well was not a possibility. This was entirely theatrical, as Annan tried to have it both ways: tweaking us and playing to the G-77, and not accomplishing a single thing to actually solve the problem in Darfur. In fact, we supplied substantial amounts of information on Darfur to the Secretariat (involving such matters as terrain, weather, and local infrastructure), without which it could have done no effective planning at all.

Rumsfeld was acutely aware of the risk that U.S. forces would be drawn into Darfur on the ground, if only because UN or AU forces might get themselves in a fix and need someone to extract them, which only we would be capable of doing. I met with Rumsfeld and a few of his aides at the Pentagon on March 8 to brief him on developments in New York, and he stressed that Bush had repeatedly made it clear to him that he wanted no American forces involved except for limited logistical assistance. This conversation showed the competing pressures on Bush, on the one hand from people like chief speechwriter Michael Gerson, who wanted to do something muscular in Sudan because it was the "moral" thing to do, and on the other hand from people like Rumsfeld, who wondered how "moral" it was to risk even more Americans' dying far from home in a conflict in which our national interests were remote, to say the least. With the 1993 experience in Somalia still a fresh memory at the Pentagon, our military was concerned about ambiguous or conflicting responsibility for "command and control," which became ever more vital as the situation on the ground became more dangerous.

Moreover, the Security Council's African members also began to go slow on shifting control from the AU to the UN, insisting that AU decisions must come first, with the Council following. The AU continued its authorization for AMIS to conduct the Darfur operation, postponing an early 2006 hand-over for six months. Fortunately, the AU, under intense EU and U.S. pressure, did not succumb to the normal rotation pattern for its chairmanship, under which, incredibly, Sudan would have taken over for 2006, but instead chose Congo Brazzaville (in part because Congo was joining the Security Council for two years in 2006 as a nonpermanent member). Perhaps even more incredibly, however, the Arab League then decided to make Sudan its head for the next year, giving Sudan both international prominence and increased clout. Although the AU decision was positive, the Arab League outcome showed just how divided the AU would remain, with the split between North Africa and Sub-Saharan Africa evident for all to see.

In fact, for many weeks in early 2006, the AU-led peace talks in Abuja, Nigeria, the AU's last effort to reach a peace agreement, hoping to replicate the earlier success in ending the North-South civil war, seemed to be going nowhere. Khartoum said there would be no UN activity in Darfur, even just for planning, until the AU peace process had come to a conclusion, although a UN assessment mission might actually have facilitated the Abuja talks by helping to elaborate what a UN mission could do. Efforts to have the Security Council adopt sanctions against several individuals for their misconduct in Darfur ran into enormous difficulties, especially from China, which was defending its oil interests there by protecting Sudan's government. Ultimately, on April 25, we prevailed, but imposed sanctions on fewer individuals than we wanted, in Resolution 1672, adopted 12–0–3 (Russia, China, Qatar). All the while, the situation in the region remained dismal, deteriorating to the point where Sudan-backed rebel groups made a dramatic attack on N'Djamena, the capital of Chad, in mid-April, nearly ousting Idriss Déby, the French-backed ruler.

The AU's self-imposed deadline for the Abuja process was April 30, and a few days afterward, the parties did in fact conclude the much heralded "Darfur Peace Agreement" (DPA) with considerable outside assistance. Deputy Secretary Bob Zoellick spent several days in Abuja at the end of the negotiations, and knowing Zoellick, I had no doubt he was a major factor in pushing the talks to a conclusion. Whether the DPA would work, of course, was an entirely different matter. Right from the outset, Khartoum refused to provide any cooperation to DPKO's efforts to get planners and logisticians on the ground in the Darfur region, to understand better what a UN peacekeeping force would need in order to function. Even so, Bush wanted action. Crouch told me as the talks in Abuja were still grinding along in early May that "the guy down the hall" was expressing frustration about getting the Security Council to say something clearly on Darfur. Rice, of course, strongly endorsed so doing, although it pained the Brits and the French to hear it, the Brits because they hadn't thought of it, and the French because they constantly worried that the potentially large force required for Darfur would drain from or constrain other African operations more important to France.

On Monday, May 8, Bush, Rice, and Zoellick made one of the strangest White House announcements I have ever seen, starting around 11:45 A.M. as the three of them filed into the Roosevelt Room, looking as collectively unhappy as one could imagine. I watched the television in the German Lounge, and I was struck that Bush's "thank you" to Zoellick for his efforts on Darfur, especially at Abuja, was completely perfunctory. I wondered if something had gone awry in their earlier Oval Office meeting, an impression that was reinforced later in the day when Alex Wolff heard from a D staffer that Zoellick had been added to the White House meeting as "an afterthought." As best we could tell, Zoellick thought he should have been sent to New York to address the Security Council at the ministerial-level meeting we had been arranging in anticipation of "success" at Abuja, a thought that must have been a complete nonstarter for Rice. Watching the three tense faces on the television screen, I wondered if this was the last straw for Zoellick, whose resignation had long been rumored and ultimately was announced a few months later. I was not privy to all, or perhaps even many, of the details, but no one believes Zoellick enjoyed his time as deputy secretary very much, or his relationship with Rice.

Rice arrived in New York later that afternoon, a visit actually previously arranged for other, unrelated meetings, involving Arab-Israeli affairs and also Iran, with Perm Five foreign ministers attending. These other events allowed many ministers to attend the Council meeting on Darfur as well, and others came attracted by the prospective media spotlights. We started at about 2:00 P.M. on May 9, and several ministers, Rice included, peeled off in less than an hour, since the entire affair was largely a photo op to show we were "doing something" about Darfur. A week later, on May 16, after many fits and starts, and much opposition by Russia, China, and Qatar, the Council unanimously adopted Resolution 1679, endorsing the DPA and setting the stage for a transition from AU to UN control of peacekeeping in Darfur. Russia and China were concerned about our invoking Chapter VII, reprising the endless battles on that issue described in earlier chapters, but gave way on this resolution because they feared being exposed and isolated on a subject as sensitive as Sudan. This was an object lesson in what could be achieved by signaling that the United States was prepared to insist on a Council vote on a text we wanted, whether we had "unity" in the Council or not. Our willingness to risk a display of disunity actually enhanced the likelihood that the outliers would fold, which they did, thus creating "unity" on the stronger resolution that we wanted. By standing firm, rather than showing weakness, we actually did achieve the best of both worlds. I thanked Churkin for Russia's support, and he laughed and said, "Only for you, John!"

Nonetheless, Khartoum, in many ways large and small, publicly and privately, was already making it clear it had no intention of accepting a UN peacekeeping force in Darfur, no matter what the DPA or the Security Council said. As if things weren't complicated enough, in early July, we faced the bizarre issue of controversial comments on a personal blog that the SG's special representative in Sudan, a former Dutch minister of development, Jan Pronk, had been happily writing. In his latest effort, he allowed as how the DPA was in serious trouble—true enough, but it was unacceptable for a UN official to be saying so on the Internet. I thought it was outrageous enough that an international civil servant had his own personal blog. As with Malloch Brown's various bloviations, it showed that many senior UN officials simply did not think they were accountable to anyone. Pronk was already controversial, and was also the subject of an internal UN investigation for alleged improprieties with staff, so the "nonrenewal" of his contract (Heaven forbid anyone get fired at the UN!) was actually a small blessing.

On more serious matters, Sudan continued to resist a UN peacekeeping force, despite Annan's rosy predictions to the contrary. U.S. and British efforts within the Perm Five to agree on a resolution to "rehat" the AU force in Darfur into a UN operation bogged down by mid-August. Bush, as I was quietly informed from time to time, still wanted something to happen, although it was not clear whether the rest of his government was paying attention, especially with Zoellick gone and no one else pushing the issue as assiduously as he had. I didn't much like our draft resolution as it then stood, but Jones Parry and I agreed nonetheless on August 16 to circulate a joint U.K.-U.S. text as soon as possible, just to see if we could kick-start the Council into action. Effah-Apenteng of Ghana, the Security Council president, suggested we invite Sudan's foreign minister to address us at the end of August and have him explain why his government was being so uncooperative, which was at least worth trying. The meeting came on August 28, but Sudan stiffed us, and the Organization of the Islamic Conference and the Arab League, which Effah-Apenteng also invited, made only brief statements, obviously hoping to glide through this meeting without causing waves. Although this had been largely a waste of time, at least we could say we had checked the box of trying to talk with Sudan at a high level and continue pressing to move on the "rehatting" resolution that week, before the end of Ghana's presidency.

To that end, Jones Parry and I convened another Perm Five meeting after the Council meeting concluded, trying to overcome the basic objection from China and Russia—which were unabashedly fronting for Sudan's government—namely, their insistence that Khartoum had to approve any UN peacekeeping activities in Darfur. A traditional UN peacekeeping operation entailed consent of all the parties, as to which there was nothing exceptional, and in the case of Darfur, there was no country—no matter how High Minded, and despite endless posturing by some—that was actually prepared to fight its way into Darfur. That said, "consent by the Khartoum government" was a thinly veiled euphemism for never handing over to the UN, which I knew Bush simply would not accept. Jones Parry saw the same reality, and we wrestled with ways to avoid allowing Sudan to kill the idea, without being unrealistic about what UN members were actually prepared to do (as opposed to what they talked about incessantly). By August 30, the next-to-last day of Effah-Apenteng's presidency, we had settled on a formula for the Council to explicitly expand the mandate of the existing UN force in southern Sudan to encompass Darfur, and say the Council "invites the consent of the" government of Sudan to that end. This formulation ducked the issue of what would happen if Khartoum declined to give its consent, and therefore, like so many UN compromises, didn't resolve anything. What it did allow, finally, was a vote on the "transition" from an AU to a UN force in Darfur. Wang nonetheless continued to take a hard negative line on our draft, but I sensed Russia and Qatar were ready to throw in the towel and vote "yes," if for no other reason than that the draft left the key issue unresolved until a future date.

In fact, China tried to delay a vote, which told me immediately they did not want to veto, and probably did not even want to abstain and thus be visibly defending Sudan's government, which indicated precisely we should move quickly to a vote, which we did the next day, August 31. Khartoum was saying publicly it planned to attack rebel groups that had not signed the DPA, and it was building up its military forces in and around Darfur, which also meant there was actually some need to move quickly before Khartoum created new facts on the ground. Accordingly, I was disappointed on August 31 when Resolution 1706 was adopted, 12–0–3 (China, Russia, Qatar abstaining), given the signs we had seen the day before. I asked Churkin what had happened, and he said the Chinese had worked hard in Moscow and overturned the Russian Mission's recommendation that they vote "yes," which led Jones Parry and me to wonder what had happened to *our* embassies in Moscow, which had been instructed to press the Russians hard. At bottom, however, the split vote did not bother me, since it provided yet another example that, on an important issue, the League of Nations–like obsession with the "unity" of the Council would not stand in the way of our pushing for a vote when we felt it important. Of course, since we avoided the toughest issue, the hardest work was still ahead of us.

In the meantime, another unique UN moment came on September 14, when I chaired an "Arria-style" meeting of the Security Council on Sudan in a UN basement conference room. These kinds of meetings, named for the former Venezuelan perm rep who invented the concept, were ways for NGOs and others to speak to Security Council members without having an actual Council meeting. During the summer, representatives of Elie Wiesel and George Clooney had approached USUN about our hosting an Arria-style meeting, with them as the principal speakers, and I had agreed, figuring that their appearance would be enough of an attention-getter it might give us momentum we were otherwise completely lacking. Lots of celebrities came to the UN, but I never saw anything like the mob scene for Clooney, from press and UN staff alike. A few months before, Clooney and I had both been guests at *Newsweek*'s table at the annual White House correspondents' dinner in Washington, at which nearly every female in the Washington Hilton's huge main room had asked for his autograph. The UN visit was much the same, thus once again providing humility lessons, and therefore character-building, for the rest of us. Wiesel and Clooney both gave strong statements on Darfur, followed by silly and somewhat offensive comments by a Qatari staffer representing Qatar, basically saying Darfur needed doctors not movie stars. Clooney had a surprisingly good put-down in response, saying he had heard the Qatari's compliment about his acting skills, but then his earpiece had gone dead and he hadn't heard anything else. Weisel also subsequently nailed the Qatari, saying his credibility on Darfur would have been much better if he had admitted the threat of Islamic terrorist groups like Hezbollah. Churkin later objected several times to the Weisel-Clooney meeting, deriding it as a media show, which just signaled to me the Russians were probably wondering how they could put together something similar on an issue of interest to them.

The days passed, and Resolution 1706's implementation, the supposed "transition" from the African Union to the UN in Darfur, went nowhere. Rice pressed Chinese foreign minister Li hard during their September 18 meeting at the General Assembly's opening, but Li simply repeated that Khartoum's consent was necessary, as if a little Chinese pressure couldn't have gotten Sudanese president Omar Hassan al-Bashir to say "yes" fairly easily. Rice pressed the point, saying Bashir "needs to understand he will not have China's protection on the Security Council." Li was silent, showing he fully understood. Pronk, who had not yet departed, added to the fun, saying that the DPA was "in a coma," and "should be on life support," which was pretty much what he had said earlier on his blog, and was even truer than the first time. Now the problem was not Pronk, but Annan, who responded typically to Sudan's obduracy, by working on ways large and small to surrender to Khartoum's demands, thereby undermining Resolution 1706. The AU voted on September 20 to extend the mandate of its Darfur force until the end of 2006, but that simply postponed the reckoning, given that no one expected the AU's performance to improve. Annan's answer was what he called "AU plus," under which the UN would bolster its support for the AU, but not effect a complete hand-over. This was a muddled idea, showing weakness in the face of Khartoum's opposition, which could only encourage them further. Moreover, the risks for both the AU and UN forces potentially involved were substantial, given the danger of confused "command and control" relationships as in Somalia in 1993. I knew exactly how the Pentagon would react.

Supporting Annan's proposal, Malloch Brown was in the news again, criticizing Bush and Blair for "megaphone diplomacy" on Sudan. This was yet another assault by a supposed international civil servant against democratically elected leaders, which was not only illegitimate but harmful to what we were trying to do in Sudan. I urged Jones Parry to defend Blair, but, probably agreeing with Malloch Brown, he wouldn't. Perhaps Brits never liked Theodore Roosevelt's "bully pulpit," but I told the press Malloch Brown had to apologize. Within days, he backed down, calling Bush and Blair "moral stalwarts on what needed to be done," further proving the wisdom of not allowing the United States to be used as a well-bred doormat at the UN. Bush's impatience with the UN increased as well, and he appointed former AID administrator Andrew Natsios as his special envoy on Sudan (in effect, giving him the Sudan role of the departed Zoellick), saying, "The United Nations should not wait any longer," before getting into Darfur.

Sudan gave its answer to the UN's collective confusion in early October, in a diplomatic note from Sudan's perm rep, emphatically rejecting Resolution 1706, adding: "In the absence of Sudan's consent to the deployment of UN troops, any volunteering to provide peacekeeping troops to Darfur will be considered as a hostile act, a prelude to an invasion of a member country of the UN." Copies of this letter, an obvious effort to intimidate potential troop contributors, were sent to many countries, including members of the Security Council, but not to the United States. When I first learned of the letter on October 5, I saw clearly it required an immediate and forceful response before its intimidating effects really began to spread. I called Jones Parry to suggest we jointly recommend an emergency meeting of the Council, but his limp-wristed response was, "This is the wrong time for the U.S. and U.K. to be in the lead on something like this." I said, "You sound like Malloch Brown," ironically, since this was now three days after Malloch Brown had *recanted* his earlier criticism of Bush and Blair. I wasn't going to wait around for the Brits, so I called Crouch to tell him my plans, and specifically that we would seek a Council presidential statement rejecting the Sudanese letter.

A Security Council meeting was scheduled for 11:30 A.M., and I didn't have to do much more than read the offending passage from Sudan's letter, which most other Council members had received, to make the point. Churkin objected to discussing the letter, saying only a member of the Council who had actually received it should have the right to raise it, and that the United States was "reading someone else's mail." That Orwellian point was immediately put paid by at least eight Council members who said they had received Sudan's letter (one of whom had quite naturally given us a copy). Churkin, Wang, and Jones Parry all made it clear they didn't really want to do anything about the letter, Wang saying we had been rushed into adopting Resolution 1706, and now we were being rushed into doing something about the letter. Other members of the Council were much more irritated. Effah-Apenteng disagreed we had been rushed into anything on Resolution 1706 and responded sharply to Wang's call for patience, saying, "While patience is a virtue, so is preventing the loss of innocent human life." He also said we should "treat the letter with the contempt it deserves," and was echoed by Mayoral of Argentina, who said the Council "should not tolerate these threats," which "run contrary to the conduct of responsible nations." Mayoral said he took the threat very seriously, since Argentina already had troops in the UN operation in southern Sudan, and his first thought on reading the letter had been to wonder if those troops were now in danger. Tanzania's Mahiga agreed with this assessment, and the Danish deputy perm rep asked, correctly, if we shouldn't insist that Sudan immediately withdraw the letter, in writing.

By the afternoon, the flurry we had created grew more interesting, when Sudan's ambassador to Washington went to the State Department to say their perm rep's letter did not in fact represent "the true position" of Sudan, and it should be considered "null and void." This hasty effort was Sudan's defense against the presidential statement we were proposing, and showed yet again the advantage of responding fast and hard when attacked. I said to the press, "They popped off. We stood up. They backed down." The matter ended without a PRST because we were soon diverted by North Korea's nuclear test, but we had made our point. Pronk, however, also kept popping off on his blog, and in late October Khartoum expelled him from the Sudan, thus effectively ending his mission, which was what we had been trying to do earlier.

More significantly, Annan accelerated his efforts to convince the Security Council to back away from Resolution 1706, having the Secretariat summon the Council to a meeting in their offices to discuss options. Summoning all of my Protocol Indignity, which I knew how to do after years at State, I said I would not attend such a meeting unless it were held in the Council's consultation room, and sent only a staff notetaker instead. I had no intention of backing away from or undermining Resolution 1706, and especially no intention of colluding with Annan in so doing. Even though I knew the mattress mice in Washington were moving in that direction, reflecting the anxiety they were hearing from Britain and other EU types, I figured when they were ready to concede, they could send me an instructions cable. I didn't plan on surrendering—to the Sudan of all places!—until the order arrived in my in-box. I was especially worried by a pernicious Annan idea for "joint command" of the Darfur peacekeeping force, which was exactly the kind of mushy formulation that caused the United States such tragedy in Somalia in 1993. The Brits seemed to be buying into this potential debacle, so I called Crouch and Eric Edelman at Defense to urge them to get the interagency process working to abort this idea. Rumsfeld tried to make the point at a principals' meeting on Tuesday, November 7—ironically his last such meeting, although neither he nor any of the rest of us knew it at the time—but he felt that no one had really focused on what he was warning about.

As if we didn't have enough problems, Jones Parry decided he wanted to lead a Security Council mission to an upcoming November AU meeting in Addis Ababa, which worried us because of the mixed message such a mission would convey. With Annan in full retreat on Resolution 1706 and the rest of the Council at best divided, this was hardly the time to be doing anything that could further weaken whatever was left of our position. On November 10, after a three-hour debate, news that even Annan didn't like the idea of a mission (because it would distract from his *own* trip to Addis Ababa) finally helped derail the Jones Parry idea, still leaving us, however, the problem of Annan's weak posture. By this time, however, there didn't seem to be anyone paying attention to the issue at high-enough levels of the State Department to make any difference, and NSC staffers told me that the risk of Rice's signing on to Annan's idea was high.

Sudan was not budging from its position that Resolution 1706 was a threat to its sovereignty, and Foreign Minister Lam Akol told a Secretariat assessment team that " 'transition' [to a UN force] is off the table." Jones Parry gleefully told me that Burns had agreed to a "joint command" in Darfur, and wondered why I was holding out. I could only grit my teeth, although I was tempted to say, "Because I am apparently the only one who remembers Somalia." Natsios said after the AU meeting that Sudan had until January 1 to accept the "agreement" worked out there, which was essentially Annan's "AU plus" idea, or we would go to "Plan B," which was never defined. By January 1, however, nothing had changed. Whether it ever will in fact remains to be seen.

Expressing their disdain for all this diplomatic maneuvering, Sudanese

forces and the janjaweed started yet another new round of military operations in mid-November. In a November 28 letter, Sudan's president
al-Bashir contended the Addis Ababa agreement gave full command and
control even of a "joint force" to the AU, and said Sudan would have veto
power over any "foreign elements," just as a few of the high points. One
could not say that this approach completely rewrote the November "deal,"
because that deal was nearly incoherent to begin with, but even at that
al-Bashir was not finished. In spring 2007 he made it clear he was still renegotiating the November deal, which would, inevitably, further delay a UN
deployment, doubtless exactly what al-Bashir wanted.[4]

Côte d'Ivoire

A civil war in the former French colony of Côte d'Ivoire occupied an in-
credible amount of Security Council time during my tenure, usually with
France and Annan asking to increase the number of UN peacekeeping
forces deployed there. Cease-fires between the government and the rebels
who held the northern half of the country repeatedly broke down, and tensions always seemed to be high, at least in France's view. The north is
largely Moslem, with many noncitizens from neighboring countries, while
the south is largely Christian and animist, with a critical dispute turning on
eligibility to vote in future elections. Moreover, even in the half of the country held by the government, there were deep political divisions. France did
not like incumbent president Laurent Gbagbo, and Côte d'Ivoire perm rep
Philippe Djangoné-Bi once explained to me it was because Gbagbo was
trying to open up the country to reduce the control France had exercised
since nominal "independence." Before I arrived in New York, we had more
or less supported whatever the French proposed, for reasons I never understood. There was no U.S. interest at stake, other than the annual 27 percent
assessment for the UN peacekeeping force (UNOCI), which, since 2003,
essentially supported a separate French force, approximately four thousand
strong, keeping the government and rebels apart.

In January 2006, for example, a round of violence apparently initiated

---

4. Warren Hoge, "Egypt Refuses U.N. Request to Help Sway Sudan Leader," *New York
Times,* Sunday, March 25, 2007, p. YT11, col. 1.

by Gbagbo against his opposition in the south spun up Annan and the French, who contended there had been a breakdown of law and order, and we therefore needed more peacekeepers. The U.S. defense attaché in Abidjan, by contrast, said, "The last thing we need here is more troops." In a Council meeting on January 19, I opposed increasing the number of UN peacekeepers, arguing that our micromanagement of the country's internal situation had so fragmented military and political responsibility there that it was no surprise we were running into trouble. Moreover, the "crisis" was a good example of incremental rather than strategic decision-making by the Council, which did not address how to resolve the underlying problem. Although we addressed the immediate issue by "borrowing" a small number of UN peacekeepers from Liberia and imposing sanctions on several individuals responsible for the violence, the basic problem was ignored, as usual.

This flare-up over Côte d'Ivoire also provided an opening for one of my reform ideas, reviving the UN's Military Staff Committee (MSC). Consciously modeled after the U.S.-U.K. joint staff arrangement in World War II, the MSC was to "advise and assist the Security Council on all questions relating to the Security Council's military requirements."[5] The MSC consists of the chiefs of staff of the Council's five permanent members, which could in turn invite the participation of other members on issues where they might be helpful. Reflecting the UN's overall paralysis in the Cold War, the MSC was stillborn and rarely met even at the general-officer level, much less at the chief-of-staff level. For the same reasons, the charter's provisions for agreements between the UN and its member states for the supply of combat forces also never moved off the charter's parchment. Over time, even the military planning function shifted away from the Council into the Secretariat. Not only did this migration increase the influence of the secretary general at the expense of the Council, it tended to exclude the United States disproportionately, to the benefit of France and the United Kingdom. These and other European nations felt far more comfortable working in the UN's bureaucracy than Americans, except those who were already True Believers.

I wanted to reinvigorate the MSC, to claw back responsibility for military affairs that had drifted into the Secretariat, and thereby increase U.S.

---

5. UN Charter, Article 46, Section 1.

influence. I knew the Pentagon was on board because they justifiably worried that they were the ultimate rescue squad for the UN when it found itself in trouble, and they had long sought greater opportunity for more sensible planning. I pursued the idea in Perm Five meetings and found that Russia and China were very enthusiastic, as they were generally about strengthening Perm Five cooperation. De La Sablière had mixed views, remembering the importance of Perm Five cooperation during the late eighties and early nineties in dragging the UN out of its own Cold War ashes. On the other hand, and prodded by Jones Parry, who was death on the idea of reviving the MSC, de La Sablière also knew that the EU was bureaucratically far more adept than we. In fact, the head of DPKO was French, and very much part of the EU network at the UN. Jones Parry likely saw my idea for what it was—an effort to increase U.S. influence—and opposed it precisely because an increase in our clout would inevitably decrease that of the EUroids. In essence, nothing came of my effort. Ostensibly, the Brits said that they were worried that resurrecting the MSC would offend the sensitivities of others who were not on the MSC, prompting me to ask Jones Parry why he was so embarrassed by the Charter's own words?

None of the Council's extraordinary level of attention to Côte d'Ivoire seemed to change the situation in the country, and by late October, France was pushing a Security Council resolution it said was vital to adopt by October 31 to avoid chaos. De La Sablière explained that a one-year deal, extending the term of President Gbagbo, but also providing the authority under which Prime Minister Charles Konan Banny, the French favorite, operated, expired at that time. There were supposed to have been elections, but the Gbagbo-Banny power struggle had prevented them. The African Union attempted to sort things out in a statement on October 17, but internal AU compromises resulted in the communiqué leaving the critical question—the political relationship between Gbagbo and Banny—ambiguous. France's draft resolution was clearly written to tilt things in Banny's direction, reducing Gbagbo to figurehead status. Such provisions, by definition, therefore, went beyond the confused AU agreement, contrary to France's normal mantra of deferring to the AU and obviously again reflecting France's intense inclination to micromanage internal Ivoirian affairs to its advantage. I didn't mind breaking loose from deferring to the AU, which often, as in the case of Sudan, tied our hands, but neither did I see any compelling reason to be picking winners and losers inside Côte d'Ivoire, a view shared by many Africans, at least in what they said privately.

Paris was obviously highly spun up, however, as de La Sablière proclaimed that France viewed the matter with such concern that it might well pull its four thousand troops out of the country if the situation weren't resolved by October 31, so concerned were they about a possible collapse of the security situation and the attendant risks to the French forces. The Security Council convened at France's request at about 4:45 P.M. on Monday, October 30, with time obviously running short before the supposed expiration of the current *modus vivendi*. De La Sablière said that all three African members of the Council supported France's draft resolution, which he characterized simply as an endorsement of the AU's October 17 communiqué. I asked to hear specifically from all three African Council members on whether they agreed or disagreed that the French text was different from the AU communiqué, and if they answered that France's draft was different, I wanted to know whether they nonetheless supported it, as de La Sablière had said. I thought this was a "no-lose" proposition, and it produced a considerable period of silence, since everyone understood the implications of what I was asking. Although I had told only de La Sablière, my still-informal instructions were to abstain, and the Russian and Chinese comments foreshadowed they were likely to abstain as well, which would leave France's resolution, even if it passed, with three permanent members on the sidelines. Jones Parry supported de La Sablière, even though FCO in London had informed our embassy that their position was essentially the same as ours.

Effah-Apenteng of Ghana finally stepped in to say that the French text was different from what the AU had said, but that France's changes were necessary to remove the "ambiguity" in the AU statement, which was, of course, another way of saying we were renegotiating it. Tanzania's Mahiga conspicuously said nothing at all, but he did not seem happy. Things were obviously not moving in France's direction, and de La Sablière observed ominously, "One day, we will look back and remember this meeting since, with respect to Africa, the Council has always listened to the SG, its African members, and France." Of course, that summed up nicely for me exactly what was wrong with things. On learning of this discussion later, Rice reacted correctly, saying France was "overreaching," which was just what I needed to hear. There were further discussions that evening and on the morning of October 31, but no discernible progress in deciding what to do.

France asked for a Council meeting at 4:00 P.M. on October 31, obviously hoping to jam its draft through. In the meantime, Washington was melting down again because EUR was worried that France's feelings might be hurt if we abstained, which in turn worried Burns. De La Sablière said it was "absolutely necessary for us to act today." I countered by saying we should at least take until the end of the week to see if we could sort things out. Nearly everyone else also asked for a delay, and de La Sablière began to get more exercised, insulting the Tanzanian deputy perm rep for not knowing what his instructions were. In fact, Tanzania had now switched from supporting the French draft to an abstention, thus breaking "unity" among the African Council members and infuriating France, which the Tanzanian deputy perm rep happily announced to everyone else, apologizing with excessive politeness for not understanding French well. We recessed in disarray, but out of nowhere, after about thirty minutes of milling around, de La Sablière concluded that the deadline was not actually October 31, but November 1, based on a rereading of the year-old agreement. Nobody wanted to argue with that small miracle, so we adjourned for the evening for the usual diplomatic receptions and dinners.

This delay was fortunate for me, because Burns convinced Rice to change her position to support the French resolution, which news he happily passed on to the French ambassador in Washington. Silverberg and Frazer, who had been arguing for an abstention, were simply cut out thereafter, and Silverberg told Sanders over the phone that Burns had delivered a "blame America first" lecture to her for upsetting the French. I called Frazer, who said, "I agree with you 100 percent," and that Burns had no idea what he was doing in the middle of this African issue. Ironically, on November 1, de La Sablière agreed to all the changes we wanted before I had to back down, and Resolution 1721 was unanimously adopted that day. Whether any of this affected events on the ground in Côte d'Ivoire was unclear. In early March 2007 President Gbagbo announced a new agreement with the northern rebel forces leading toward elections, but there had been many such agreements since the civil war broke out, all of which had foundered.

Somalia

Since the failed UN operation on Somalia in 1992–93, the country was largely ungovernable, and had in fact come apart. Much of the territory around Mogadishu and the south was controlled by rival warlords, and the territory of "Somaliland," a separate former colony, had declared its independence from the rest and was actually doing quite well on its own. Somalia's anarchy was an attraction for terrorists, especially after the fall of the Taliban in Afghanistan, and Islamic fundamentalists made strong gains among many of the Somali factions. Fighting began to intensify in spring 2006, with the "Islamic Courts Union," the vehicle of the fundamentalists, advancing. By late September, other governments in the region, notably Kenya, began to worry that all of Somalia (outside of Somaliland) might fall to the ICU, bringing us yet another haven for terrorists, along the lines of the Taliban model in Afghanistan. The immediate issues were whether to relax the long-standing arms embargo, so that an outside peacekeeping force could more explicitly help the "Transitional Federal Government," which was the only real alternative to the Islamicists as an organizational framework, and whether to endorse a peacekeeping force by regional neighbors.

After weeks of discussion, mostly between London and Washington, the Security Council adopted Resolution 1725 on December 6, modifying the arms embargo enough to allow a peacekeeping force to deploy, under the command of the regional Intergovernmental Authority on Development (IGAD). Continued military success by the Islamic militias, however, prompted intervention by Ethiopia in late December, which in fairly short order, due to the support of American air strikes, routed the militias, thus giving the Transitional Federal Government a chance to establish itself. How long the Ethiopian intervention could continue, and how successful the IGAD intervention would be, beginning with the deployment of Ugandan troops in March 2007, remained to be seen. One thing was certain: The UN's role had been and remained minimal.

Western Sahara

Because of my work in Bush 41 and then with Jim Baker on the Western Sahara, I had a particular interest in trying to wrap up this fifteen-year-old peacekeeping operation, and in giving the residents of the territory the referendum on its future status they had long been promised. Morocco initially agreed to a referendum—that was, after all, what the "R" in MINURSO, the Spanish acronym for "Mission of the United Nations for the Referendum in Western Sahara," stood for—but consistently blocked taking the steps necessary to conduct it, such as voter identification and registration. This was a clear example of the limitations of UN peacekeeping, which Sudan's government was demonstrating contemporaneously in Darfur, namely that there simply was no chance of success if any of the actual parties to a dispute dug in their heels and refused to cooperate. In that sense, at least with respect to UN operations directly affecting them, almost every UN member has a kind of veto, not just the Security Council's Perm Five. This is undoubtedly why the UN so often resembles the League of Nations in its achievements.

I met repeatedly in 2005–6 with the perm reps of Algeria and Morocco, both of whose countries were quite satisfied with the status quo in the territory, but for essentially opposite reasons. Morocco is in possession of almost all of the Western Sahara, happy to keep it that way, and expecting that *de facto* control will morph into *de jure* control over time, giving it both territorial breadth consistent with its historical concept of the "proper" size of Morocco and access to possible natural resources and fishing rights. Morocco's alternative to a referendum was "autonomy" for the territory, which meant effectively keeping it under Moroccan control. Algeria, the main supporter for the POLISARIO (the political and military vehicle for the Sahrawi rebellion), tens of thousands of whose refugees lived in camps near Tindouf in southwestern Algeria, liked having the threat of POLISARIO action against Morocco, but found the threat more useful than the actual prospect of renewed hostilities. In fact, unresolved tensions between Morocco and Algeria, unrelated to the Western Sahara, were a major factor in the dispute, not that anyone talked about them very much. Peter van Walsum, a retired senior Dutch diplomat with extensive UN experience as a former perm rep, and Baker's replacement as the SG's personal envoy for the Western Sahara, tried repeatedly in 2005 to see if any Council member, especially the United States, planned to pressure Morocco to adhere to its many commitments to hold a referendum. He found that none were willing, except Algeria, which of course Morocco would ignore.

One of the high points of my tenure at the UN came when van Walsum briefed the Security Council on April 25, 2006, explaining that "international legality" (the World Court having rejected Morocco's claim of sovereignty over the Western Sahara) was in conflict with "political reality" (Morocco's control over almost all of that territory), and that the Council had to find a compromise. Although many countries could not conceive of a conflict, let alone a "compromise" where "international legality" might give way to mere "political reality," I was delighted that someone had at least spoken the unspeakable, even though his logic cut against the Sahrawi position. If only others were as forthright as van Walsum.

Since it was clear that Morocco had no intention of ever allowing a referendum, there was no point in a UN mission to conduct one. Instead, and typically of the UN, MINURSO seemed well on the way to acquiring a near-perpetual existence because no one could figure out what to do with it. Accordingly, consistent with my fundamental notion that the Security Council should try to find a real resolution to the underlying problem, I suggested terminating MINURSO and releasing the Sahrawis from the cease-fire they had agreed to in exchange for the promise of a referendum. If Morocco didn't like that prospect, then let it get serious about allowing a referendum. If not, then the Council should admit its failure and get out, or at least not become another part of the problem by locking in a status quo that could go on indefinitely. Otherwise, MINURSO seemed a perfect example of costly UN peacekeeping operations that were not promoting resolutions to conflicts, but prolonging or even complicating them.

The biggest obstacle to my approach was, as usual, the State bureaucracy, joined unusually by the NSC's Elliot Abrams. They accepted Morocco's line that independence for the Western Sahara—which nearly everyone thought the Sahrawis would choose in a genuinely free and fair referendum—would destabilize Morocco and risk a takeover by extreme Islamicists. This was why the administration had rejected the last "Baker Plan" in 2004, and why Baker finally resigned as the SG's personal envoy after eight years of trying to resolve the issue. I wondered what had happened to the Bush administration's support for "democracy" in the broader

Middle East, but there was no doubt here that stability for King Mohammed VI trumped self-determination. In practice, it meant that State was always open to plans for "autonomy" for Western Sahara, which Morocco, at regular intervals, promised to produce, and invariably never did, at least not until after long delays. I engaged in a number of frustrating and unsuccessful efforts to find support for the referendum elsewhere in the U.S. government, but failing to do so, Abrams and I agreed to convene a meeting at State on June 19, 2006, to see if he and I could come up with a common strategy. If so, we knew that the bureaucracy, having no alternative ideas, would endorse it.

I explained my view to the meeting, which had over thirty attendees, which was that MINURSO had failed in its central mission to conduct a referendum and was now actually an obstacle to Morocco and Algeria dealing with each other and the continuing fact of tens of thousands of Sahrawi refugees; that in the absence of someone with Jim Baker's status, the UN had essentially no political role to play; and that Morocco was never going to agree to a referendum where independence was a real option. Abrams stressed stability in Morocco, but said that if Morocco came out with a "true" autonomy plan, he could support terminating MINURSO. I still thought the reverse was true, namely that neither Morocco nor Algeria would get serious until they saw MINURSO about to disappear, and I never believed that Morocco would tolerate "true" autonomy. Nonetheless, during this one-hour meeting, we had stretched the limits of the bureaucracy about as far as we could, and I made at least some progress on the idea that eliminating MINURSO would not impede the search for a solution, but might actually be the only way to achieve one. Other than Abrams and me, all of the representatives from the rest of the bureaucracy wanted to defend the status quo. At this rate, of course, MINURSO would have perpetual life, and this was the United States that couldn't figure out what it wanted to do, let alone the UN!

In fact, in March 2007 Morocco promulgated yet another "autonomy" plan, with no provision for a referendum, and the Sahrawis rejected it yet again. This could well go on forever. The Security Council has gone back to sleep.

Conclusion

This review amounts to a snapshot of UN peacekeeping weakness in Africa during my time in New York. Among those operations not covered, there are additional failures, some conflicts that remain unresolved, and a few that may well emerge as successes. In Liberia, for example, the UN peacekeeping operation was essentially static when I arrived at USUN, with newly elected president Ellen Johnson Sirleaf taking office in January 2006. On the other hand, in the Democratic Republic of the Congo (DROC), what appeared to be a successful electoral process in 2006 may fall into disarray, a fate that could yet again befall Liberia. In the DROC, the first round of nationwide elections in April were without major disruptions, as were the runoffs on October 29. There was intermittent fighting among forces loyal to the major candidates even after the victor, Joseph Kabila, was inaugurated in December. His opponent, former rebel leader Jean-Pierre Bemba, fled the country after further fighting in March 2007, but both former candidates retain the military capability to resume hostilities, suggesting that the election has not resolved the underlying problems, a pattern true of many of the peacekeeping operations touched on here in greater detail. Moreover, allegations that emerged in May 2007 of UN peacekeepers' engaging in "gold for guns" transactions, indicate the continuing frailties of the UN's own capabilities.

My experience with UN peacekeeping projects in Africa shows that even a region that purportedly held the strong personal interest of the secretary general, that was represented by a powerful regional group that always possesses at least three votes on the Security Council, and in which the need for humanitarian assistance predominates, the UN's record remains disappointing. In less favorable circumstances, whether pursuing WMD proliferators like Iran and North Korea, or dealing with equally real threats to international peace and security like the continuing assault on Israel, we know from direct experience what the Council's limitations are. Thus, the UN has difficulty with high-profile, high-risk international issues, and it also has difficulty with low-profile, low-risk issues, which doesn't leave much room for optimism at either end or in the middle.

CHAPTER FOURTEEN

ISRAEL AND LEBANON: SURRENDER AS A MATTER OF HIGH PRINCIPLE AT THE UN

John Bolton is right. This place is a mad house.

—FRENCH PERMANENT REPRESENTATIVE JEAN-MARC DE LA SABLIÈRE,
OCTOBER 31, 2005

UN involvement in the complex contemporary Middle East over the years has been sporadic and incomplete, fortunately so, in my opinion, given the pervasive anti-U.S., anti-Israel attitudes at the UN. During my time in New York, the Middle East spotlight shone mainly on Lebanon and the Occupied Territories, building to the crescendo of the Israel-Hezbollah war in July–August 2006 and its troubling aftermath. Obviously, Iran's nuclear and ballistic missile capabilities also deeply concerned Israel, as did Iran's funding of terrorist states like Syria and terrorist groups like Hamas and Hezbollah. Moreover, as it had for decades, Israel faced constant assault on its interests in both the Security Council and the General Assembly, which also troubled me greatly.

From the very creation of Israel as a state, it has been mistreated at the UN, the most flagrant example of the UN's capacity to distort reality. During the Cold War, Israel's closeness to the United States made it a target of Soviet propaganda in the battle for influence in the Third World. The Soviets abetted the combination of the Arab dismay at Israel's very existence and widespread anti-Americanism they were stirring up and the international left's hatred for America and its vigorous system of political and economic liberty. When the Cold War ended in American victory, existing attitudes at the UN didn't change, and in some senses became worse. Now, there were no longer two superpowers for the Third World to play off against each other, accumulating goodies in the process. With only the United States, whose interest in the UN had been tenuous at best for years, the goodies were harder to come by, and kicking Israel was one of the few enjoyable pastimes left. With so few other options for entertainment or political gain, the game became more intense, even after the repeal of "Zionism is racism." Trying to achieve political gains, "facts on the ground" at the UN, became more important than real facts on the real ground in the Middle East, which not only diverted attention from the central issues but made them harder to resolve by introducing so many irrelevancies.

Democracy Versus Terrorism in Lebanon

> It's strange for me to say it, but this process of change has started because of the American invasion of Iraq. I was cynical about Iraq. But when I saw the Iraqi people voting, eight million of them, it was the start of a new Arab world.
>
> —WALID JUMBLATT, LEBANESE DRUZE LEADER

I'd barely gotten settled in New York when, on August 17, 2005, I paid one of my first courtesy calls on Terje Roed-Larsen, a Norwegian diplomat with a propensity for speaking his mind. This was always a source of delight to me, and trouble at the UN for others so inclined. Larsen, president of the International Peace Academy and a Middle East expert, greeted me by saying he was the second-most-hated man at the UN (after yours truly), joking that my "proposal" to eliminate ten floors from the Secretariat building was too modest. After the pleasantries, we got down to business concerning Roed-Larsen's other role, the SG's special representative for Resolution 1559 (adopted September 2, 2004), which called for all Syrian forces to leave Lebanon, the disarming of all militias (such as Hezbollah and Palestinian groups), and fully restoring Lebanon's sovereignty over its territory. The Council adopted Resolution 1559, cosponsored by France and the United States, very narrowly, 9–0–6, barely obtaining the charter's required nine votes. The six abstentions included Russia, China, and both Moslem nonpermanent members, Pakistan and Algeria, clear indications of trouble ahead.

Lebanon, of course, wanted to cast off not only Syria's military occupation, but also Syria's long-standing effort to extinguish Lebanon as a country and absorb it within "Greater Syria." Syria essentially ignored Resolution 1559, confident that the slim vote margin made it impossible for the Security Council to do anything more definitive. The political calculus changed entirely, however, with the February 14, 2005, assassination of former Lebanese prime minister Rafik Hariri, which brought the anti-Syrian feelings of most Lebanese people into the open and into the streets. Within a month, Syrian president Bashar al-Assad ordered his forces to withdraw, and on April 7, 2005, the Council adopted Resolution 1595, creating an "Independent International Investigation Commission" (IIIC) to help Lebanon investigate Hariri's murder. Outside assistance was necessary because of Syria's thorough infiltration of all aspects of Lebanese law-enforcement and security institutions. Without the IIIC, Syria would simply stonewall and pronounce the crime unsolvable, and the dramatic terrorist effect would ultimately suffocate the "Cedar Revolution" that had erupted spontaneously after Hariri's murder. The IIIC's chief investigator was Detlev Mehlis, a respected German prosecutor, generally seen as tough and impartial, who had, in a previous assignment at home, concluded Libya was responsible for the 1986 bombing of West Berlin's La Belle Discotheque, which had killed two U.S. soldiers. Roed-Larsen wanted to use an upcoming IIIC report to get very tough with Syria, which was certainly fine with me, and he also wanted to explain privately the difficulties he'd had with Kofi Annan and Annan's advisers, notably Lakhdar Brahimi, former foreign minister of Algeria.

Briefing the Security Council on August 25, Ibrahim Gambari of Nigeria, undersecretary general for political affairs, emphasized Syria's lack of cooperation with the IIIC. We had a draft press statement designed to increase the pressure on Syria, which France's Duclos proposed afterward. Reflexively, Russia and Algeria objected to citing Syria by name, as if there were dozens of other countries that had previously occupied Lebanon, had the motive and the capability to conduct terrorist assassinations there, and were also not cooperating. The statement ultimately said: "The members of the Council reiterated their call on all States and all parties, especially those who are yet to respond adequately, to cooperate fully in order to expedite the work of the Commission."[1] I am sure Syria felt duly pressured by *that* display of eloquence and clarity. I said to the press I wanted to provide "the American translation" of the statement, which I did, nailing Syria directly for failing to cooperate. I received more coverage than the Council's statement, which demonstrates why clarity should mean more than it does at the UN.

On September 20, during the General Assembly opening, Rice invited me to attend a meeting of the "Quartet," one of Colin Powell's mistakes, perhaps created when he wasn't paying attention. It was intended to work on the Middle East peace process, and consisted of Russia, the EU, the UN, and the United States. Only America had the clout to do anything constructive, but the other three could cause a lot of mischief. It was particularly inappropriate to have "the UN" as a member, since all the other parties were UN state members, as were most of the chief disputants. How the UN could therefore contribute much I never understood, especially given the Secretariat's decidedly anti-Israel bias. This Quartet meeting focused on Israel's recent withdrawal of settlers from the Gaza Strip, and included as principal participants Rice, Lavrov, Annan, and—the EU being the EU—three people: Jack Straw (Britain being EU president); Javier Solana, the EU high representative for the common foreign and security policy; and Benita Ferrero-Waldner, EU commissioner for external relations, all three of whom were accompanied by their own squadron of aides. Out of this entire mélange, there were only two principals representing actual states: Lavrov and Rice. No wonder this group couldn't accomplish much, which was fortunate for the United States and Israel.

Significantly for Lebanon, the Quartet's hardest issue to resolve was its own final statement (a statement being the *sine qua non* of a successful meeting in UN-land and diplomacy generally) on armed groups such as Hamas participating in the upcoming Palestinian elections. The United States proposed that the Quartet say: "Those who run for or serve in elective office should not support or engage in armed activities outside the control of the state, for there is a fundamental contradiction between such activities and the building of a democratic state." Although this language

---

1. Security Council Press Statement on Work of Commission Investigating Killing of Former Lebanese Prime Minister, SC/8482, August 8, 2005.

would actually help Abu Mazen, the Palestinian Authority leader, as he tried to disarm Hamas, there was a sharp debate, which Rice seemed to be winning. Unaccountably, however, she suggested the Quartet call Abu Mazen to see if he could accept the language, which befuddled me, since she had already confidently said he would like it. Why risk a different answer? Then, Lavrov returned to a point he had raised earlier but dropped, namely, that the Quartet's language should be more "aspirational"; Rice suggested adding the word "ultimately," which effectively robbed the statement of all contemporary impact on the imminent elections. By this time, everyone was on the phone to Abu Mazen, agreeing to delete the sentence entirely from the Quartet's statement. Instead, Annan would express it as his view in the subsequent press conference, as if that would have anything like the significance of Russia's actually signing on to it. Both the word "ultimately" and the call to Abu Mazen were Rice's suggestions, and both were unforced errors, as they say in sports.

On October 12, shortly before the Mehlis report, Ghazi Kanaan, Syria's interior minister (basically, the chief of police), and formerly for many years the head of Syria's security forces in Lebanon, committed suicide by blowing his brains out. He likely knew everything worth knowing about people and events in both Lebanon and Syria. Mehlis had interviewed him only a few weeks before, which provoked enormous speculation that Kanaan had died in "an assisted suicide" to prevent him from talking further. Although many U.S. experts concluded it really was suicide, Kanaan had not led the kind of life in which suicide was an option. Life in Syria and Lebanon was hard, and so was death.

We received the Mehlis report itself on October 20, and I had Mehlis to breakfast at the Waldorf the next morning. He struck me as a low-key, professional, authoritative individual, whose conclusions were likely to be solidly supported by the evidence. He believed the Lebanese were regaining self-confidence, but he stressed repeatedly they were still insecure, especially about the risk of Syria's returning to Lebanon and taking reprisals against anyone who had engaged in "anti-Syrian activity." He said that the Syrians were not cooperating at all and asked if I would object to his making corrective suggestions to the Security Council. I said I would not, and then asked Mehlis directly if he thought Syrian president Assad was involved in Hariri's assassination. He smiled and said, "Yes, of course," which was why he believed Syria would never cooperate fully. To do so would mean "the death of the regime," explaining why Assad refused to be interviewed by the IIIC. "Assad is talking to the press, why can't he talk to me?" was the way Mehlis put it. The only alternative was to increase international pressure on Syria, because Syria was "the key" to finishing the investigation and reaching final conclusions. Mehlis accordingly saw no hope of the IIIC's concluding by December 15, when its mandate expired. Mehlis would not stay beyond that date due to his wife's fears that the constant assassination threats he received might actually come to pass, which was certainly understandable, but it left us in a quandary about his replacement.

Later that day, at the Reagan Library in California, President Bush announced that Rice would convene a ministerial-level Security Council meeting on Lebanon on October 25, less than a week away, followed (at least in State's planning) by a Council resolution, and then another resolution on Roed-Larsen's next report, to be issued a few days later. I thought all of this was fantasy, which it proved to be by the end of the day, as others came to the same conclusion. Unfortunately, this scheduling by remote control by people in Washington who had no clue about what went on in New York was a constant irritant, to which I simply stopped paying attention. Worse actually than the second-guessing on scheduling, though, was the absence of any concern about the *content* of these resolutions that State was so busily queuing up. That bore the unmistakable mark of Undersecretary Nick Burns and State's obsession with process over substance.

Mehlis gave his public briefing to the Council on October 25, Rice's idea for a ministerial-level meeting having dissipated by then, and the briefing was very low-key, more so than his written report, which was unfortunate. Mehlis at least made it very clear that the IIIC was under considerable threat, and everyone understood that he personally was at risk. Mehlis also stressed that Lebanon should establish its own judicial authority to handle the trial of the crime, thus implicitly rejecting the idea that only some international tribunal would be up to the job. In the closed Security Council session that followed, I stressed that we were at a critical point, with the restoration of Lebanese sovereignty and security in the region at stake. I also emphasized that the Council's credibility was at a critical point because the Syrians were manifestly not heeding either Resolution 1559 or Resolution 1595. The French were always neuralgic about linking the two resolutions, which I could never understand, since they both addressed the issue of Lebanese independence from Syrian domination. Moreover, de La

Sablière worried that Mehlis's briefing had been weak, and given the importance of our earlier collaboration, France's hesitancy made it impossible for us to join the issues in a strong press statement. Part of the problem was that Mehlis had a prosecutor's natural, justified disinclination to reveal his hand before trial, a disinclination that would only grow as the trial actually drew nearer.

By definition, Syrian obstructionism meant the IIIC could not fully complete its work, which was doubtless exactly what Syria had in mind, and why sweet reason wasn't going to bring it around. A government prepared to murder its opponents wasn't suddenly going to turn over voluntarily the very evidence that would bring it down, as Mehlis stressed during our breakfast meeting. After the other Council members spoke, Mehlis responded, providing a telling anecdote. In discussing the lack of Syrian cooperation, he said that he had asked the Syrians for their files on Hariri, and they had said they had no such files. Everyone broke out laughing, including Algeria's Baali, who was sitting next to me at the Council table in our alphabetical order. He whispered that the Syrians probably even had a file on him, not to mention the mountains of paper they would have had on a former Lebanese prime minister. The Syrians' claim about the files proved exactly how brazenly Syria was stiffing the IIIC.

Fortunately, a flap over the editing of the Mehlis report did not obscure its central point, namely that there was high-level Syrian involvement both in Hariri's assassination and in obstructing the IIIC investigation. The editing controversy turned on whether Annan had forced Mehlis to weaken the report, deleting key information concerning Syria's role in the assassination and subsequent cover-up, and was ignited when the UN's electronic version of the report showed the tracked changes, which very clearly indicated what had been redacted and what had not, an important caution for all who use word processors. Despite *pro forma* denials by Mehlis and the SG's spokesman, almost the entire UN press corps believed that the editing had been at least as extensive as shown by the tracked changes, and perhaps even greater.

The real issue was how tough our response to Syria's obstructionism would be. France was adamantly against imposing sanctions, and to box us in, Foreign Minister Douste-Blazy made this point publicly in Paris on October 24. France worried that Russia, Syria's protector, would react negatively, thus splitting the Council, but the split was already apparent to all.

State's NEA bureau supported France. By contrast, Rice wanted to take a harder line, which I supported. Still, I was more confident in public than I was in private, telling the press stakeout that it was "true confessions" time for Syria, implying that real penalties would follow if Syria were not forthcoming.

Later on October 25, I talked to de La Sablière about the critical issue of sanctions against individuals, especially whether sanctions would apply only against suspects in the Hariri assassination or also against those who were obstructing the IIIC investigation. The French were nervous about the latter category, afraid that too robust a resolution "would sink the ship" by alienating Russia and others. Many in Washington wanted to go after obstructers as well as suspects, which suited me, but Washington also wanted a ministerial-level meeting soon to present a unified response to Syria, so I pointed out to Hadley in a conference call that suspects were almost certainly also obstructers. We needed to decide whether we wanted to circulate a resolution and have ministers meet in less than a week, on October 31, or whether we wanted sanctions against individual obstructers. Framed that way, the question was easier to answer, since Washington wanted the flash and glitz of a ministerial meeting more than a protracted debate, especially with France, over sanctions. I wouldn't have come out that way, but I needed to cut through yet another endless interagency discussion and get a decision. With that, I called de La Sablière to say that we would agree to target sanctions only against actual suspects in the Hariri assassination, and, accordingly, we circulated our draft resolution.

Rice called on Friday as we were working away, and I said we were still aiming for a ministerial on Monday, October 31, to vote on the resolution. Rice said she was now inclined to confine the meeting to the Hariri assassination, rather than covering the next Roed-Larsen report. I said that would make things more manageable with France, which she accepted.

That afternoon, in informal consultations, de La Sablière and I took the other members through the text, listening to a laundry list of Algerian objections from Baali, who was obviously following Syria's party line. There were many other criticisms, but I saw no chance of a Russian or Chinese veto, which was what most concerned me. We went through a few more contortions, and then put the resolution in blue, in time for a Monday vote, even though we knew Russia still wasn't satisfied because of the references to possible sanctions against Syria if it did not cooperate with Mehlis and the references to Syrian interference in internal Lebanese affairs. We heard that evening that Algeria, China, and Russia were all signaling they planned to abstain, but I thought they were bluffing.

I filled Rice in on Saturday. De La Sablière was nervous, asking for a Perm Three meeting at 3:00 P.M., at which he argued we should give up a preambular paragraph calling on Syria to renounce terrorism, as well as drop the reference to future sanctions against Syria if it did not cooperate with Mehlis, in exchange for a firm Russian commitment to vote "yes" on the resolution. I didn't see any reason to give in now, but de La Sablière asked if he could present the idea to Denisov as a purely French idea, which I said I would not object to. On Sunday, the three of us met again, and de La Sablière said that Denisov was now raising other issues. Lavrov, the former perm rep, fresh from seven years' experience in New York and ready to go to work yet again on his ministerial colleagues, did not want any further negotiations until the Perm Five foreign ministers' dinner that evening.

Rice called me after the dinner, joking "that was fun," meaning, of course, the exact opposite, and she explained the many changes Lavrov wanted, including those on future sanctions against Syria, most of which she had apparently agreed to. Lavrov had said he needed further instructions overnight from Moscow, which was undoubtedly not true, given that he brought with him all the authority he needed. Perhaps he had had a flashback to his perm rep days, forgetting he was now foreign minister. I thought it more likely he just wanted time to see if he could think of further changes to squeeze out of us. The ever-considerate Perm Five foreign ministers had agreed that their perm reps would meet Monday at 7:00 A.M. at the French Mission, which was fine for me, an early riser, but debilitating for those who did not follow Benjamin Franklin's rules about when to go to bed and when to rise. So hard was it for the French that there was no one at their mission at 7:00 A.M., so I went to Jones Parry's office, which was in the same building, to wait them out. We finally got started at about 7:35 A.M. De La Sablière reviewed the changes ministers had agreed to the night before, and asked if Russia and China would now vote in favor. Denisov said he thought that additional changes had been agreed to, which Rice may have mentioned to me, but which I wasn't entirely sure about. I decided to object to them, leaving Denisov to say he would need to go back to Lavrov for further instructions. We agreed to meet again at 8:45 A.M.

After the Russians and the Chinese left, I called Rice to say Russia was asking for more than had actually been agreed to the night before. I said that if they continued to insist, we would tell the rest of the Council at 9:00 A.M. what we were in fact prepared to accept, and call the Russian bluff: Let them abstain if they felt they had to. Rice agreed, and off we went to the UN, for our eight-forty-five Perm Five meeting. By eight-fifty, Denisov was still on his cell phone with Lavrov, so we explained to the other Russians and Wang that we were prepared to vote on what we had discussed earlier, which Wang said he could agree to, thus putting a bit more pressure on Russia. Unfortunately, Denisov went in the other direction, saying he wanted a favorable reference in the resolution to "Syrian cooperation with Mehlis, which would, of course, have been science fiction. I said "no" and called Rice, who, happily, said she would veto any resolution with a positive reference to "Syrian cooperation" with Mehlis. We convened informal Council consultations at about 9:30 A.M., with Wang saying China was prepared to vote "yes," forcing both Denisov and Baali to play for more time, saying they still needed instructions from their ministers, who were, of course, all of a couple of blocks, not many time zones, away.

We adjourned for them to get instructions, and then we learned Douste-Blazy had told Lavrov he was willing to say something nice about "Syrian cooperation" with Mehlis, and Straw seemed similarly inclined. I stood in the hallway to meet Rice as she arrived and took her aside to explain what was happening, and we then found the French and the British to get them to pull up their socks. By this time Lavrov had finally shown up, apparently concluding he had caused enough chaos for one morning, and agreed to language imposing a clear commitment on Syria to cooperate with the IIIC, without saying anything about past "cooperation." De La Sablière, Jones Parry, and I then rushed off to explain what was up to the nonpermanent members, which was the point at which de La Sablière concluded we were in a madhouse.

The Council convened in public session at 11:00 A.M., and with eleven foreign ministers present, unanimously adopted Resolution 1636. The resolution required UN member governments to freeze the assets of suspects named by the IIIC or Lebanon and prevent them from entering or transiting their territory, and also specifically required Syria to detain suspects named by the IIIC, a direct slap. After the ministers and others spoke, Syrian foreign minister Farouk Sharaa gave a long Stalinist-style response to what the Council had just done, leading Rice to pass me a note that said

"Syria is all muscle and no brain." The next day, I spoke with J. D. Crouch at the NSC, who told me that he had said at a staff meeting with respect to Resolution 1636, "John was brilliant, but he was outshone by the Syrian foreign minister," which was hard to argue with. Bush sent me a handwritten note the next day that read, "Congratulations on passing the Syrian Resolution by 15–0 (nothing better than a landslide). Now perhaps the Syrians will get the message."

Just two days later, on November 2, Roed-Larsen briefed the Security Council on his report on the implementation of Resolution 1559, saying that Syria's resistance continued to impede Lebanon's ability to assert its full sovereignty and disarm militias supplied by Syria. As with Mehlis's report, Annan had heavily edited Roed-Larsen's, although we did not know the specifics. It would have been quite useful to follow up Resolution 1636 with a resolution on Roed-Larsen's report, but the British and French were both doing a lot of heavy breathing about "overloading" the Council, and would not agree, especially given what Annan had eliminated from Roed-Larsen's "final" report. Accordingly, after Roed-Larsen's briefing, my main objective was to "reinsert" what Annan had edited out, especially the scheduling of Lebanese elections for a new president, to get rid of Emile Lahoud, the Syrian Quisling still holding the job. This was critical under Lebanon's complex constitutional structure, within which the president had significant power and the new Parliament, while freely and fairly elected, was constrained because the election process was still incomplete. Also subject to Annan's editing were passages in which Roed-Larsen had pointed out the still-significant presence of Syrian intelligence operatives in Lebanon, even if its uniformed military had largely pulled out. Moreover, not only was Syria not halting the flow of arms into Lebanon to groups like Hezbollah and militant Palestinian refugee militias, it was all but openly supplying them. Finally, Syria was flatly refusing to take even basic steps to establish normal diplomatic relations with Lebanon, because to do so would mean acknowledging precisely what Damascus did not want to acknowledge, namely that Lebanon was an independent country. Roed-Larsen gave good answers to these questions, which laid the groundwork for a tough resolution against Syria if I could just persuade France and Britain to lean forward a little bit.

Mehlis went back to work in Lebanon, asking again within days of his return to interview Assad and other high-level Syrian and Lebanese officials. This request sent the Syrians into orbit, especially since Mehlis wanted to interview many witnesses out of the country, where they would be subject to less intimidation. By November 11, Mehlis had at least interviewed Lebanese president Lahoud, which must have been interesting, since Lahoud denied any involvement in the Hariri assassination. Syria's next ploy was to involve Annan, in the hope that his ever-ready instinct to compromise, so foreign to the mentality of a prosecutor like Mehlis, would aid Syria's obstructionist efforts. On November 2, I conferred with de La Sablière, and we both called Annan, urging him to reject any Syrian effort to insert him between them and Mehlis. Our calls seemed to work, since the Syrian proposal to make Annan a middleman disappeared.

In the meantime, Israeli politics were getting more complicated. Sharon decided to leave Likud and form a new party and a new cabinet, a decision still reverberating today. And, on November 21, in an eerie foreshadowing of what was to come in July 2006, Hezbollah launched a substantial attack, including missile and mortar fire, across the Blue Line, the border between Israel and Lebanon, in the Sheba Farms region, with subsequent Israeli aerial retaliation. I thought the Security Council should issue at least a press statement strongly condemning the Hezbollah attacks, so I spoke with Israeli perm rep Dan Gillerman. We agreed this was worth a major effort, but that we would not support any statement equating Israel's act of self-defense with the initial Hezbollah attack, the instinct infusing most other UN delegations. This was an early test for me in the continuing struggle against "moral equivalency," one of the UN's worst diseases, exemplified here as the view that an act of aggression and a response in self-defense had the same moral implications. It was also a struggle against the State Department bureaucracy, many of whose members shared the "moral equivalency" disease. I believed that if all we could get from the Security Council was a bucket of mush, it would be better to have no press statement at all, which was another kind of diplomatic heresy. The feeling that the world was waiting breathlessly for the Council to say something about this or that event was pervasive at the UN, often expressed self-importantly by governments—saying slowly and in a deep voice, "The Council must pronounce itself." I simply did not agree from a cost-benefit perspective, and, to paraphrase our mother's advice, "If you can't say something useful, don't say anything at all."

By the morning of November 23, we had agreement on a draft press statement, which, for the first time ever, criticized Hezbollah by name for its attack across the Blue Line. Just as I thought we were close to adopting the statement, Jones Parry popped up, supposedly on instructions from his ministers, and also supposedly representing the EU (the Brits being EU president at the time), with language criticizing Israel. My staff was worried we would be the only ones opposing Jones Parry's language, in which case I said I would be perfectly happy with no press statement at all. Interestingly, when Jones Parry offered his language and I rejected it, France, Denmark, and Greece all sat silently, giving the lie to the idea that this was an EU position. I told the press afterward that including a specific criticism of Hezbollah was a significant victory, which, in the tiny world of the UN, it was indeed.[2] We had a related flap on November 30 when I questioned Undersecretary General Gambari about his meeting with Hezbollah on a recent trip to the Middle East, asking him what steps he had taken to ensure that the meeting was not seen as legitimizing terrorism. Gambari, obviously nonplussed by the question, answered in generalities, obviously having never been called on the issue before. A UN staffer later snottily told a USUN staffer that they were outraged the United States would question the "right" of the Secretariat to meet with whomever they wanted. These people obviously had a lot to learn, starting with the fact that they worked for member governments, not the other way around.

Press statements were indeed the locus of considerable trench warfare in New York, and another battle followed a week later over what Russia's Denisov, the Council's November president, would say at the annual "International Day of Solidarity with the Palestinian People," a decades-old, anti-Israel propaganda exercise. It will come as no surprise that there was no "day of solidarity" for the Israeli people, or the American people, or anyone other than the Palestinians, the tip of the spear at the UN against Israel. We worked to ensure that Denisov's statement was not offensive to Israel and the United States (I claim nothing more than that), but the real news out of the 2005 Day of Solidarity was a map of the region, prominently displayed in this meeting on the UN's premises, which showed no

---

2. Security Council Press Statement on Incidents Along Blue Line Separating Israel, Lebanon, November 23, 2005, SC/8563: "The members of the Council expressed deep concern about the hostilities, which were initiated by Hizbollah from the Lebanese side, and which quickly spread along the entire Blue Line."

state of Israel. The Hudson Institute's Anne Bayefsky spotted the map and was apparently the only one attending the festivities who thought it in any way out of the ordinary. We discovered that the map belonged to the Palestinian UN "observer mission," which is where I suggested it be returned (rather than being stored at the UN, as it had been for many years), and that it not make any further public appearances at UN events. A better outcome would be the end of the entire propaganda exercise, but we were nowhere near achieving that result.

Sadly, on December 12, reality intruded again with the terrorist assassination of Lebanese journalist Gibran Tueni, a prominent anti-Syrian activist, yet another in the string of such murders, the most prominent being Hariri's. Bush issued a statement all but accusing Syria directly, since there was little doubt who had ordered the hit. We and the French immediately tried to have the Security Council issue a presidential statement, although we spent a lot of time trying to persuade the French Mission not to come in too low. The Council finally agreed to "condemn in the strongest terms" Tueni's murder, and we at least said that he was a "patriot who was an outspoken symbol of freedom and the sovereignty and political independence" of Lebanon, which clearly implied that he was anti-Syrian.[3] On the same day we received the final Mehlis Report on the Hariri assassination and were expecting a formal letter from Lebanese prime minister Siniora asking that the IIIC mandate be extended so that its investigation could continue.

I met with Mehlis the next day, just before his final briefing to the Council, and asked him if he had a problem with expanding the IIIC's mandate to cover the other assassinations in Lebanon, which he said he did not. Thus, I was surprised, as was de La Sablière, when Mehlis gave a more negative answer when asked the same question in the Council meeting. I suspected that the Secretariat had gotten to him, and indeed, the more I thought about Mehlis's decision to leave, the more convinced I was that it was irritation with the Secretariat as much as anything else that led him to decide to return to being a prosecutor in Berlin. He was particularly unhappy with the Secretariat's slow pace in picking his successor and was prepared to do whatever was necessary to ensure there was no hiatus in the

---

3. Statement by the President of the Security Council, S/PRST/2005/61, December 12, 2005.

investigation, which the Secretariat's foot-dragging was threatening. As with the PRST on the Tueni assassination, we had been pounding away on the French to strengthen the resolution we were drafting that extended the IIIC mandate for six months, to come down harder against Syria's obstructionism, and to be more explicit about expanding the IIIC's mandate to cover the other assassinations, as Siniora had finally requested. The French were too cautious and too afraid that Syria would stir up a negative reaction in the Arab world. Even though France was excellent at taking credit for being Lebanon's great friend, in my experience it was usually the United States that pushed the envelope furthest on behalf of Lebanese democracy.

French national security adviser Gourdault-Montagne called Hadley to argue against broadening the IIIC mandate to cover the other murders, and Hadley said we would revisit our position, which astounded me. Annan was also against expanding the mandate, which spoke for itself. If we were right that Syria was behind these killings, expanding the investigation would help expose the links by demonstrating similarities among the assassinations and uncovering evidence applicable to more than one killing, thus strengthening the overall case against Syria's murderous efforts to maintain control over Lebanon. Our dilemma in New York was that while we wanted strong statements in the resolution about Syria's lack of cooperation, thus laying the basis for future sanctions, we were coming quickly to the end of the IIIC's existing mandate, which we obviously had to extend. Time was not on our side, because the imminence of the mandate's expiration weakened our bargaining position. Fortunately, Mehlis made a strong pitch that there would have been no Syrian cooperation without Resolution 1636. He stressed that Syria was still obstructing his work, such as by arresting the relatives of witnesses he wanted to interview and threatening at least one journalist working at the UN, further examples of the unsubtle way Syria, the Al Capone of the Middle East, did business.

France was still nervous that our draft resolution was too strong, and Gourdault-Montagne repeatedly called Hadley urging that we back off (the French having obviously given up on persuading me, or even Jones Parry, who this time was hanging tough, for some reason). Gourdault-Montagne stressed the importance of Council unanimity, and why we should therefore be more accommodating to Russia, China, and Algeria, a mind-set the NSC's Elliot Abrams correctly called "surrender as a matter of high principle." Unfortunately, the Lebanese government was not being

terribly helpful, saying it wanted both strong language and Council unanimity, which was understandable although impossible. De La Sablière,
Jones Parry, and I agreed we would try one more time with Denisov before
pushing for a vote on December 15. Baali had told me that Russia was not
as upset about pressuring Syria or extending the IIIC's mandate as about
feeling left out of the drafting process, and was instead asserting its prerogatives as a Perm Five member, an important insight. De La Sablière and I
concluded that if we satisfied Denisov, then Baali and Wang would not
raise any additional objections. Seeing that we were close to a deal, de La
Sablière and I met again with Denisov at 12:30 P.M. He pleaded that he had
no instructions from Moscow, so the three of us agreed to meet again that
afternoon.

I went off to meet former president George H. W. Bush, who was arriving at the UN for Annan to announce his appointment as special envoy for
relief concerning the devastating earthquake that had recently struck Pakistan. Former U.S. chief of protocol during Bush 41 Joseph Verner Reed,
now a UN undersecretary general, and I waited for Bush in the lobby by the
Secretariat entrance, and he rolled in just after 3:30 P.M. We went up to
Annan's conference room on the thirty-eighth floor for a briefing, then
down to the press area for Annan to announce the appointment. Bush 41
took a number of questions, including one asking if he had any advice for
me as his successor as U.S. perm rep. Bush smiled and declined to give any
advice, saying instead, "He has my full confidence and, what's more important, has the full confidence of the president."

After walking Bush 41 back to his motorcade at the Secretariat entrance, I returned to the Security Council area at four-thirty, only to find
Denisov still on the phone with Moscow. Fortunately, at four-forty-five, he
came back into the consultations room with a thumbs-up, and shortly
thereafter we unanimously adopted Resolution 1644, which extended the
IIIC's mandate and authorized it to assist Lebanon to investigate the whole
gamut of political assassinations, although Denisov explained at length
how unhappy Russia was. We finished just before 7:00 P.M., which made
everyone, including the press, happy, since they could now all scurry off to
Christmas parties.

Literally on the last day of 2005, former Syrian vice president Abdel-
Halim Khaddam, now in exile in Europe, said publicly that Assad had
threatened Hariri shortly before the assassination, a key element of the

Mehlis reports. Khaddam continued his antiregime activities into the new year, which indicated more trouble for Assad's regime than many had previously thought. Unfortunately, at French insistence, Rice and Hadley agreed to the idea that we would produce only a PRST rather than a resolution on Roed-Larsen's next report, which we did on January 23, and over Annan's resistance to saying anything that might upset Syria or Hezbollah. Two days later, in Washington, I explained to Rice at some length how unhelpful Annan had been on this issue, especially the obstacles he had thrown in Roed-Larsen's way, which troubled her greatly, as it should have.

The Ground Shifts: Sharon Sidelined and Hamas Victorious

Sharon's massive stroke on January 5 threw Israeli politics into disarray. Further compounding the already-complex Middle East situation was Hamas's overwhelming victory in the January 26 Palestinian elections, something our Middle East "experts" had completely missed coming down the road. The ramifications of both developments were enormous for Israel and the region, and their impact on the UN was also important. One immediate question concerned funding for the Palestinian Authority (PA), which the United States planned to terminate once Hamas, a terrorist organization, took control. We wanted the UN to move funding away from a Hamas government as well, but ran into enormous opposition from Annan, the UN bureaucracy, and the Europeans, who could hardly conceive of such a thing. Because State's NEA could also barely conceive of a funding cut-off, our efforts at the UN were episodic and not very effective. There was a related question of UN contact with Hamas officials—leaders of a terrorist organization—and as my earlier exchange with Gambari demonstrates, there was considerable Secretariat neuralgia over the idea that the UN should refrain from dealing with terrorists. The United States did follow that policy, for example, by ensuring that General Keith Dayton, our "security coordinator" between Israel and the PA, would have no further contact with Palestinian security forces reporting to any Hamas member of the PA cabinet. This was the real answer to Powell's famous question, "Who else am I supposed to talk to?" in January 2002, at a Principals Committee meeting, after it became clear that Arafat was completely complicit in the Iranian shipment of weapons to the Palestinians on the *Karine-A*. Sometimes, the answer is, "Silence is golden."

In the meantime, I met on February 10 with Serge Brammertz, Mehlis's successor as head of the IIIC, in the Security Council president's office (since the United States was then president). Brammertz, a Belgian, had roused worries in some quarters that he was questioning work Mehlis had done, but I concluded that he was simply concerned with the transition from investigative activities to the actual preparation for trial, although only a few arrests had been made. Brammertz was pursuing a number of "new" areas of investigation as a necessary preparation to rebut what defense attorneys might later try to do to create "reasonable doubt." He seemed to have no basic disagreement with Mehlis's underlying rationale that the highest levels of Syria's government were involved in the Hariri assassination. Brammertz was more low-key than Mehlis and less inclined to talk to the press, but I did not detect in this or subsequent conversations that he was any less determined than Mehlis to follow the evidence on Hariri wherever it might lead. In fact, he was more supportive than Mehlis had been (or than Annan had allowed Mehlis to be) of expanding the IIIC's cooperation with Lebanese investigations into the other assassinations of anti-Syrian figures.

On March 14, there was an incident in Jericho, where Israeli forces attacked a Palestinian Authority "jail" that held suspected Palestinian terrorists, in the presence of British and U.S. observers. The Palestinians had dismissed the observers, who departed under protest, but prudently, since they judged their own safety to be in jeopardy without PA support. Once the observers were gone, the PA clearly intended to release the terrorists (one of whom was accused of assassinating an Israeli cabinet minister), which the Israelis had no intention of allowing. Qatar, fronting for the Palestinians, wanted a presidential statement on the attack, stressing the completely false implication that Israel had struck in collusion with the United States and the United Kingdom (not that it would have bothered me if it were true). Israel was clearly justified in preventing the suspected terrorists from being released and had ample grounds to move when it did. We stood firm against a PRST, despite the possibility that the Qataris might transform the draft into a resolution, which we would then have to veto. The Arab League members in New York finally faced the Palestinians down, and the issue went away.

Hamas, however, was clearly going to be a problem at the UN, as when their new "foreign minister" addressed the Council for the first time on March 30, accusing the United States of great crimes against the Arab and Moslem peoples. I responded by saying that "gratuitous slander is an inauspicious way to begin" his tenure, which was probably more diplomatic than necessary. More trouble came on April 11, when Qatar, again fronting for the PA and the Arab League, proposed a PRST extremely critical of Israel for retaliating in the Gaza Strip against a Qassam rocket attack. Qatar pressed especially hard to adopt the statement on April 13, which was Passover, meaning no Israeli diplomats were around. I said I didn't mind working on religious holidays, despite the absence of Israelis, but I wanted to be clear that in the future no one else could ever raise a religious holiday as an excuse for the UN not to do something. That produced a deafening silence and mass confusion about what the Council's "rule" was about working on religious holidays. It turned out that there was no rule, except who could evince the most angst about not having a holiday to stall something they didn't like.

When we discussed the draft PRST, the United States was almost completely isolated, worrying de La Sablière that our position would subsequently complicate the way the EU-3 wanted to deal with Iran's nuclear weapons program. Since I thought the real difficulty on Iran was the weakness of the EU-3 position, I did not find his argument persuasive. Quite agitated, the Qataris noted that the Council was 14–1 in favor of the text and urged that it should simply be adopted, ignoring the convention that PRSTs are adopted unanimously, besides ignoring our veto right. What many really wanted to do, however, was blame the collapse of the PRST on the United States, which for them was almost as much fun as actually issuing a PRST lambasting Israel. I avoided the ambush by saying we were perfectly prepared to continue negotiating, and the back-and-forth went on for most of the day. The Qataris then changed course and asked for an open meeting of the Council to discuss the Israeli "attack," which I opposed by saying that the Council was not an exercise in group therapy (although for many UN members that is precisely what it is). Because this was a procedural question, there was no veto available to us, and the open meeting was in fact scheduled for Monday, April 17.

Simultaneously, we had proposed a press statement condemning yet another terrorist attack in Tel Aviv, which the Qataris attempted to turn into a general discussion about what was wrong in the Middle East (mostly meaning Israel). I told my staff, again, that if we couldn't get the right kind of press statement on the terrorist attack, I would be happy with no statement at all. In fact, I questioned whether we should *ever* expend any effort in the future on such exercises, given that the Council was apparently unwilling or unable to address reality rather than propaganda. If the Council was determined to deal itself out of Middle East issues, so be it. The result: no Qatari PRST on Gaza, and no press statement on Tel Aviv. The Council did not "pronounce itself," and amazingly to some, the world moved on.

By April 19, Roed-Larsen's latest Resolution 1559 report was out, and very significant because he twice specifically mentioned not only Syria's negative role in Lebanon, but also Iran's. The Iranians, of course, went through the roof. Roed-Larsen explained to me at length how he had worked to prevent Annan from editing these two references out of his draft, which didn't surprise me in the least. Having gotten only a PRST in response to Roed-Larsen's last report, this time I pressed even harder for a resolution, which the French agreed to. Unfortunately, they did not want to criticize either Hezbollah or Iran by name, part of the "We never fail in New York" syndrome of never asking for more than what you can assuredly get. Worse still, Lebanese prime minister Siniora was importuning us not to name either Hezbollah or Iran, which showed just how fragile his position was. I agreed with de La Sablière on a phrase admonishing "concerned states and other parties," an unfortunately typical example of UN-speak, but one that we could say made clear that Syria, Iran, and Hezbollah were all covered.

As it turned out, however, the real dispute with others in the Council was our effort to pressure Syria into exchanging full diplomatic representation with Lebanon and demarcating their border, steps that might not sound significant, but that went to the most fundamental question, namely Syria's acknowledging that Lebanon was in fact an independent country. Some members felt we were interfering in bilateral relations, so we made minor wording changes to satisfy them, without detracting from the fundamental objective of leaning on Syria. We had certainly isolated Russia and China, making China especially uncomfortable, right after we had just squeezed them on the Sudan sanctions resolution. I thought we could bring both of them around, but, as Churkin said to me, "I can't pull a rabbit out of a hat two days in a row." On May 17, Resolution 1680 was thus adopted

13–0–2, with both Russia and China abstaining to protect Syria. More positively, on June 14, Resolution 1686 unanimously extended the IIIC's mandate for another six months, showing that at least on that score, Russia and China were still on board.

Gaza, however, was tense, as Palestinians kidnapped and held hostage an Israeli soldier, provoking Israeli retaliation and the inevitable Security Council meeting, this one on June 30. I urged that the quickest way to end the crisis was to release the Israeli, an approach seen as unreasonable only at the UN. I also made it clear that the Security Council had "limited credibility" and that we should not "provide evidence for those who say it is all talk and no action." (As we were leaving, de La Sablière, an amateur sketch artist, showed me a drawing he had done during the debate of Israeli foreign minister Tzipi Livni saying, "John for president," but he wouldn't give it to me!) Israel demonstrated it thought Hamas was responsible for the kidnapping on July 1 by shelling the offices of the new PA prime minister, Hamas's Ismail Haniya. Not surprisingly, the Palestinians decided to torque things up in New York by pressing for a Council resolution to condemn Israel. As I reflected on how to respond, thinking of the endless difficulties in achieving "fair" or even accurate presidential statements, I concluded this might just be the pivot to stop the fruitless and frustrating negotiations we engaged in during these exercises. First, I wasn't at all sure that Qatar, the PA, and their Arab League allies could even muster the nine affirmative votes they would need to pass a resolution, given the initial Hamas kidnapping. Second, I didn't see what benefit would accrue to the United States by intense work to make a resolution marginally less objectionable, thus ironically making it easier for some of our "friends" to support it, perhaps thus reaching the nine or more votes for passage (and making us look marginally more *un*reasonable when we vetoed it). And third, a quick, sharp veto might help change the climate at the UN, making it clear we weren't content to keep playing the same old games.

Whatever the Arabs were planning, they didn't do it quickly. Dan Gillerman said there had been stories in the Arab press that day criticizing the Arab perm reps in New York, saying I intimidated them, and that the Arab League needed to toughen them up, so I didn't expect the silence to last for long. Late on Wednesday, July 5, Qatar finally circulated a draft so extreme that one USUN staffer described it as "an Arab 'Hail Mary' pass." This was what I needed, so I explained to Gillerman we had no intention of haggling over this draft to make it "more balanced," although we both had little doubt that the EUroids were just chomping at the bit to be "helpful" and "bridge the differences."

Just such an effort was underway at the "new, improved" Human Rights Council in Geneva, where the anti-Israel forces had forced a "special session" and were hammering home yet another critical resolution. It passed with twenty-nine in favor and eleven against, with the Western Group all voting "no," except for Switzerland, repugnantly abstaining. Five other countries also abstained, including sadly, Mexico and South Korea. This was behavior typical of the former Human Rights Commission, and veterans assured me you could tell no difference whatsoever between what happened at the new HRC and what would have happened at the old HRC. This was precisely what I had predicted, and why I argued so strongly not to put lipstick on the caterpillar.

Undeterred by their embarrassment in Geneva, the EUroids joyously continued negotiating Qatar's draft resolution, succeeding to the point that it was only very unreasonable rather than wildly unreasonable. At this point, I was frankly paying more attention to responding to North Korea's missile launches, when Hezbollah attacked across the Blue Line into Israel, kidnapping two soldiers and killing three, and firing numerous rockets into Israel, targeting civilian settlements. Israel's Defense Force (IDF) answered with punishing force. De La Sablière told me that Rice (in Paris for Perm Five and G-8 ministers' meetings) had agreed to keep the Hamas and Hezbollah kidnappings separate, which I hoped was untrue, given the timing. Annan's first reaction was to send a Secretariat mission to the region, which would accomplish little until the parties themselves were good and ready to stop the fighting, but which, given the anti-Israel bias infusing the Secretariat, would keep the UN in the spotlight and generate negative propaganda. Unhelpfully, the French began circulating a draft PRST welcoming Annan's move.

The Qataris pushed for a vote on their draft resolution on Thursday, July 13. Rice's first instinct was to see if we could delay until after the vote on North Korea's missile launches, but I didn't see that a U.S. veto on the Gaza resolution would have any impact on the North Korea resolution. On Thursday afternoon, de La Sablière convened the Council (France being president) for a vote on Qatar's resolution, which lost 10–1–4 (the "1" being the United States veto and the "4" being Denmark, Peru, Slovakia, and the

United Kingdom). This was my first veto, and I was very happy to cast it against the misbegotten Qatari draft. I also gave a very tough speech, which included a line I had long wanted to deliver, in this case a shot against Alvaro de Soto, a Secretariat official with a long reputation of anti-Americanism now involved in Middle Eastern affairs: "The 'policies' of the United Nations are determined by its member governments, not by officials of the Secretariat, whatever their personal views." [4] Gillerman gave a very good speech, describing "terror" as the "occupying power" in the Middle East, not Israel.

The next day, Friday, the Council accepted the inevitability of Annan's Middle East mission, which consisted of Vijay K. Nambiar of India, who knew little about the region, and the two current SG special representatives, Roed-Larsen (on Resolution 1559) and de Soto (for the region generally). Abrams emailed me, "This will be a top contender for 'most useless trip of the year.' " Syria refused to allow Roed-Larsen in, to which I said that if Roed-Larsen couldn't go, none of them should. Annan wanted to bend to Syria, but we prevented this act of UN self-abasement. The mission departed, but not for Syria.

Terrorists Strike and We Muddle

In the meantime, the IDF was definitely "doing something" in Lebanon, although its precise objectives remained unclear. One disturbing piece of news was Abrams's reporting that Israel was speculating about who would fill the security vacuum in southern Lebanon after these hostilities, until the Lebanese Armed Forces (LAF) were able to take up that burden. This was a curious question to ask *after* launching military action, and strongly implied that Israel did not plan to stay long in southern Lebanon once its mission, whatever it was, was accomplished. This confusion unfortunately played into the hands of others, like Annan, who also wanted a new inter-

---

4. De Soto proved his anti-American bias in his final report on leaving the UN in June 2007, in which he characterized the Quartet as dominated by the United States and questioned whether the UN should remain part of it. On this, de Soto and I agree at least partially: I would be happy if the entire Quartet disappeared. See Harvey Morris, "UN envoy blasts US for pro-Israeli agenda," *Financial Times,* Thursday, June 14, 2007, p. 3, col. 3.

national force, but one very different from what Israel likely had in mind. After all, the UN Interim Force in Lebanon (UNIFIL) had been there since 1978 and hadn't filled the "security vacuum" that Hezbollah had actually been filling very much to its own satisfaction. UNIFIL had the limited rules of engagement typical of UN peacekeeping operations, essentially allowing the use of force only in its own self-defense. As a result, it had done little to assist the Lebanese government in restoring its sovereignty in southern Lebanon, as specified in Resolution 425 of 1978, even after Israel fully withdrew its forces in 2000. There was no chance that Annan or the Secretariat could even begin to conceive the kind of muscular force that would actually be necessary under Israel's concept, and yet Annan (not to mention the G-8 leaders in St. Petersburg on July 16) was using words very similar to the ones Israel was using. This was a prescription for confusion, and therefore trouble.

Worse still, introducing a security force quickly, whether the one wanted by Annan or the one wanted by Israel, undoubtedly required a cease-fire, which Israel very clearly did not want. I could see a train wreck coming. Meanwhile, the Secretariat was briefing the Council and the press as if Israel's main objective was to level UNIFIL rather than Hezbollah. This bias was decidedly unhelpful, since many nonpermanent members were vehemently in favor of the Council's "pronouncing itself," and the risks to UNIFIL provided many opportunities for pronouncing, although as a matter of basic logic Hezbollah's initial attack was the real cause of risk to UNIFIL, not Israel's exercising its right to self-defense. Greece's deputy perm rep even said expressly that "pronouncing" was important "to take the pressure off the Council," which was certainly one embarrassing way to look at the world. France, as Council president, was pressing to "do something," although this was directly contrary to President Chirac's comment in St. Petersburg that "Israel needs time to crush Hezbollah." That sounded like something Bush would say, and rightly so. "This represents a new level of hypocrisy for France," said Abrams, but we both recognized that State's bureaucracy was also agitating to "do something," which we worried might infect Rice.

One way France was unhelpful was in acceding to Annan's request to "brief" the Security Council in a public session on Thursday, July 20. Of course, it was difficult to resist the secretary general's request for such a briefing, but this one had more to do with publicly pressuring the United

States than any desire to convey information, which could be done just as easily and more efficiently in a closed session. Moreover, Annan's three-man team, back from the region, was to brief publicly on Friday, but Annan didn't want to wait that long. Sure enough, Annan called for "an immediate cessation of hostilities," which was clearly directed against Israel. Repeated U.S. statements made clear we weren't interested in yet another Middle East cease-fire that would simply return us to the *status quo ante;* we wanted to make real progress in the region, intending that it would be lasting, for a change. The UN, however, wanted a cease-fire, and didn't have the culture for long-term solutions. If the United States wouldn't accept a cease-fire, how about a "cessation of hostilities," which Annan kept trying to spin as something different, but which we weren't buying, at least at that point. Annan concluded that "the Security Council must speak with one voice in the coming days," a not-so-veiled reference to us as Israel's greatest friend on the Council. I responded to the media after the meeting by asking how a democratic state like Israel could have a cease-fire with a terrorist group. Annan never answered my question.

In the consultations after Annan's public remarks, almost every Council speaker called for a cease-fire and criticized the IDF's "disproportionate use of force," another favorite way to bash Israel. The argument was that Hezbollah had "only" kidnapped and killed a few IDF soldiers, and that Israel's response was "excessive." I later asked the press if Israel's response had to be limited to killing and kidnapping an equal number of Hezbollah troops, or if America's response to Pearl Harbor should have stopped after inflicting casualties on Japan equal to ours on December 7. The "disproportionate use of force" argument was nonsense and missed the point that the threat to which Israel was acting in self-defense was Hezbollah's very existence, not simply the immediate incident that triggered the exercise of that right. I was also acutely aware that Israel was being used as a surrogate target for the United States, where the "disproportionate" use of force was the way we conducted the business of war, once we were compelled to use force, preferring a swift resolution rather than allowing a drift into attrition.

Rice arrived in New York Thursday evening to receive a briefing from Annan's Nambiar-led mission to the Middle East at the Waldorf on Friday, July 21, before they briefed the full Council. I spoke to Abrams in Washington beforehand and said I was increasingly nervous about all of the flapping around at State. Abrams responded, "I can tell you unequivocally:

Bush is not flapping." This was important, since NEA assistant secretary David Welch, "nearly hysterical," on Thursday had phoned Israeli ambassador to Washington Danny Ayalon about getting humanitarian relief into Lebanon before the Friday briefing. Rice called me to her suite at 8:15 A.M. to say she wanted a non-UN force to fill the "security vacuum" in Lebanon once Israel withdrew, with the largest troop contributor in command, which she thought could be France, Turkey, or Italy. Unfortunately, there was still no real understanding of how or when this force would deploy, or how it related to the cease-fire everyone else was demanding. Rice said all these issues would be discussed next Thursday in Rome, after she visited the Middle East on Sunday. To make the point we were on shaky ground, I gave Rice a *USA Today* cartoon showing two cats, "Hezbollah" and "Israel," clawing each other, as a haughty poodle, labeled "UN," entered. The caption read: "In Marches Fluffy." She smiled.

Nambiar, de Soto, and Roed-Larsen started their briefing at 8:30 A.M. in Suite 35H, the usual meeting room on secretary of state visits, laying out their plan to end hostilities. Nambiar intended to convey much the same information to the full Security Council at 10:00 A.M. That struck all of us as a bad idea, because describing such a UN plan, which elaborated on what Annan had forecast the day before, was not what Rice needed just as she left for the region. Roed-Larsen got the point and immediately suggested the UN troika redraft what they planned to say. Rice's abbreviated briefing thus served a useful purpose almost in spite of itself. She headed back to Washington, and her final words to me about the Security Council were, "Let them talk, just not do anything," which sounded right to me.

Postponed until 11:00 A.M., the Council didn't convene until 11:25 A.M. because we waited for Undersecretary General for Humanitarian Affairs Jan Egeland to show up. Egeland, a High Minded Norwegian who criticized the United States reflexively for its "insufficient" responses to humanitarian tragedies, apparently was too busy to arrive on time, despite numerous calls to his office. The Council chamber was as full as I had ever seen it in the delegates' and the public sections. Nambiar gave both the regular monthly briefing on the Middle East and a summary of his trip, a pale shadow of what Annan had said the day before, although he too called "urgently" for a cessation of hostilities. In his typically self-important way, Egeland announced he was appearing "on behalf of the humanitarian workers of the UN system," not that anyone had asked him to. He blamed almost everything on Israel, par for the course from the High Minded. Gillerman took a lot of the punch out of Egeland's grim portrait of Lebanon's humanitarian situation, and out of the calls for a cease-fire, by saying Israel would support "humanitarian corridors," through which relief supplies could be safely transported. Fortunately, after this meeting, Rice's trip to the Middle East froze activity in the Council for at least a few days.

In response to a second incident of Israeli fire hitting a UNIFIL position, this time killing four, Annan accused Israel of "apparently deliberately targeting" the UNIFIL post. By contrast, he had said nothing comparable about Hezbollah, which consistently endangered UNIFIL by firing rockets from very near their posts, in effect using UNIFIL as a shield. Annan calmed down after talking with Israeli prime minister Olmert, who said Israel would investigate the incident, but the Secular Pope was obviously getting tetchy that no one was listening to him. One of the four UNIFIL dead was Chinese, prompting China to demand a PRST condemning the IDF attack. China's first draft was harsh and completely unacceptable, but on Wednesday, July 26, Wang showed me a more-restrained draft, which still characterized the incident as a deliberate Israeli attack. We agreed to keep talking, but the news was filled with reporting that Rice's Rome meeting with other foreign ministers had broken down in disagreement. This was far from accurate, but the media hype was that the United States was "isolated" on the cease-fire question, which I knew would spin up NEA and not be pleasing to Rice.

With the bad news from Rome as background, the Council received a briefing on the UNIFIL incident, followed by a highly charged diatribe from Wang, followed in turn by the usual lynch-mob rhetorical excesses against Israel. I felt that the Secretariat was cynically using the deaths of the four UNIFIL soldiers to push for what Annan had wanted for some time, namely a cease-fire, so I intervened to say that any PRST had to be focused on the precise issue at hand, the deaths of the peacekeepers, or it would be very hard to reach agreement. I then left for Washington for my second confirmation hearing, which was necessary if I were to be confirmed before my recess appointment expired in December.

By the time I returned to New York, a modest PRST had been agreed to, but we faced a more troubling issue: The Secretariat was trying to schedule a "force generation" conference for "security" in southern Lebanon after IDF withdrawal. This was under way even though there was still no agreement on what the force's mandate would be, or its rules of engagement, reflecting the confusion that had attended this idea from the very outset. Lebanon's problem was Hezbollah, and the only answer was someone prepared to use force to disarm the terrorists and restore order until the LAF was able to take over, whenever that might be (and no one knew). However, the Secretariat and many others at most wanted an "enhanced UNIFIL," with modestly stronger rules of engagement, but not actually doing anything more than the kind of patrolling UNIFIL had done with little effect for over twenty-five years. I saw no point in asking troop contributors to come forward until we could tell them what the mission was. In addition, a clone of UNIFIL would simply return us to the *status quo ante,* and be a clear retreat from the United States' often-expressed view that we did not want a business-as-usual cease-fire, followed by more Hezbollah attacks across the Blue Line a few months later.

Despite an understanding I'd worked out with the French that neither of us would circulate any resolutions without prior agreement, they circulated a text on Saturday without warning us or even the Brits. When I called de La Sablière to ask why he had proceeded without advance notice, our conversation actually uncovered a more troubling disagreement concerning the "replacement force" we had been talking about for some weeks in a confused fashion. France, said de La Sablière, now did *not* want it to have "enforcement authority," basically meaning they wanted a traditional UN peacekeeping operation with very narrow rules of engagement, rather than what we had envisaged—a deployment of "real armies" prepared to use force to disarm Hezbollah and otherwise fill the "security vacuum." France now wanted a political solution among all the parties to the Lebanon conflict before agreeing to a force or deploying it, in effect giving Hezbollah the ability to veto any agreement if it didn't like the look of the force that would follow the IDF's withdrawal. France's unexpected shift put the United States in a very difficult position, and it seemed to have come directly from Chirac himself, yet another Chirac reversal.

At 8:45 A.M. on Sunday, July 30, I learned that Annan wanted a Security Council meeting because an Israeli air strike at Qana in southern Lebanon had caused numerous civilian deaths. While this loss of life was undoubtedly tragic, Annan's move was yet another ploy to increase pressure on the United States and Israel to accept a cease-fire, a cynical maneuver to force the media to deploy their clichés about an "unusual Sunday session" of the

Security Council. With France in the presidency, and their predilection for following Annan's directives, the meeting was inevitable. It started later that morning, with Annan in full High Minded mode. He admitted he knew only what the government of Lebanon had told him (there being no UNIFIL personnel anywhere near Qana), and he had not spoken to Israel, but off he went. We must "condemn this action in the strongest possible terms," calling for—surprise!—"an immediate cessation of hostilities" due to the "moral outrage throughout the world" because both sides (moral equivalency, you see) had "committed grave breaches of international humanitarian law." The speech and its bromides made clear that this was a massive Annan publicity grab, using all the same points he had used against Israel since the outset of the war. He directly criticized the United States, saying the Council should "put their differences aside," obviously meaning the United States should recede from its position, and concluded by chiding the Council for its inaction, saying that the authority and standing of the Council were at stake, and that we had to act, et cetera. Very dramatic, very good press for Annan, and all of it pure theater.

Rice had been planning to travel from Israel to Lebanon, but when Prime Minister Siniora refused to see her, she decided to return to Washington. Combined with the negative reporting on the Rome meeting, this constituted serial media pounding on Rice, which, I heard from those traveling with her, had been greatly discomfiting. In the meantime, on her instructions, her counselor Phil Zelikow informed the French in Paris that the United States could accept a "suspension of offensive operations," or so de La Sablière told me during the morning's consultations. Since Israel was on the offensive, that was, as a practical matter, not so different from Annan's call for an "immediate cessation of hostilities," and de La Sablière was using that convergence to make my life difficult. Hadley and Burns called to learn what was happening, and I asked what Zelikow was up to. Hadley insisted that Zelikow was just "brainstorming" and did not reflect Rice's position. Burns said Zelikow was "completely out of bounds," but I pointed out that de La Sablière had told half of New York what he was saying, and I said eighteen days into the war, this might not be the best time to be "brainstorming" with a bunch of foreigners.

That afternoon, de La Sablière concluded that he couldn't see any formulation of a PRST on the deaths at Qana acceptable to both the United States and Qatar, so when the Council reconvened at about 4:40 P.M., there was doom and gloom, which I tried to lift by stressing again that we were perfectly prepared for a PRST along the lines of the one issued after the deaths of the UNIFIL peacekeepers. We were not, however, going to agree to a cease-fire or a flat condemnation of Israel. De La Sablière then read from an AP story that Israel had agreed to a forty-eight-hour bombing halt, although no reason was given, and Annan, who had joined us, jumped in to say that even that was a basis from which we could start toward a permanent cease-fire. I wasn't about to let that happen, so de La Sablière said we should recess again while he tried further approaches to a text. While we were milling around, Burns told me that Rice, calling from Israel, said we were having a bad day (meaning, of course, Rice had had a bad day, with her trip to Lebanon canceled), and that we should try to settle on some kind of PRST without further delay. In fact, I stuck by the cease-fire language that the foreign ministers had agreed to at the Rome meeting ("calls for an end to violence"), which was innocuous, and said that until ministers decided to move away from that language, we weren't going anywhere in New York. We ended the day with a final text that was plain vanilla, but at least it did not produce any lasting damage.

After yet another Council meeting, on Monday, July 31, during which Tanzania's deputy perm rep leaned over and asked me why the Arabs kept having meetings at which Gillerman had a chance to explain the Israeli position so effectively, de La Sablière asked me to come back to the Council presidency office for a one-on-one chat. He believed the conceptual gaps between our two positions on Lebanon might be unbridgeable, but he did agree to my suggestion that we at least try to lay out the differences side by side to get a better idea. Of course, to do that I needed a cleared draft of our resolution, which was still not ready, although people in Washington had been working on it for weeks. Burns said Rice (now flying back to Washington) was eager to come to New York by the end of the week for a ministerial-level Council meeting to vote on the text, but he was somewhat at a loss to explain how I was supposed to get to that point without an approved text to discuss.

Rice called me twice from her plane. I explained that France wanted an immediate cease-fire and believed that the international force should not have enforcement authority, since any deal had to have the complete political agreement of Lebanon, Israel, and Hezbollah. This also implied, for France, a "two-step" process, the first being the cease-fire, the next being the creation of the new international force. We had resisted this approach, wanting to wrap everything into one resolution to help achieve the "sustained" solution we wanted. This was the fundamental conceptual difference between us, which Rice said was "very helpful" to hear, as if she had not previously heard it. She also wanted any new international force to be tied to implementing Security Council Resolution 1559, to minimize Syrian and Iranian interference, and she wanted an arms embargo, so Hezbollah did not reload. I stressed I needed a cleared draft in New York, which she said she would get wrapped up as soon as she arrived in Washington.

The next day, August 1, Rice called at about 9:30 A.M. to say that, having looked at the draft resolution that had been endlessly masticated by the bureaucracy, she wanted to change it. She planned to break the in-house logjam, which was good news, but she revived Zelikow's idea of a "suspension of offensive operations," which led me to wonder if perhaps Zelikow hadn't really been doing Rice's bidding after all. Rice had also spoken with France's Douste-Blazy about his Monday trip to Beirut, where he found Siniora strongly opposed to any international force other than a traditional UN peacekeeping operation and opposed to any cease-fire not based on an "exchange of prisoners" with Israel (meaning exchanging the Israeli hostages for Hezbollah terrorists long held by Israel). Incredibly, Douste-Blazy had even gone to Tehran to meet with the Iranian foreign minister, and found him hard and uncompromising (*quelle surprise!*). No one knew exactly what Iran's responsibility was for Hezbollah's attack, but I certainly suspected that Hezbollah's paymaster was deeply involved in the military activity.

De La Sablière and I met at the French Mission at 10:00 A.M. to continue our discussion, although I had little to say except that the idea for "suspension of offensive operations" was in fact back on the table. De La Sablière said that he thought there had to be some mention in any resolution of the disputed Sheba Farms territory on the Golan Heights, which Lebanon claimed, but that everyone else thought was Syrian land under Israeli occupation, and the "exchange of prisoners," all of which suggested that France, the former League of Nations mandatory power in Lebanon, was simply acting as Siniora's mouthpiece. In the meantime, the French draft resolution was the only game in town until we got our act together. Interestingly, Abrams, who had been on Rice's trip, said she believed she'd had a political agreement to resolve the fighting "before Qana," but that the bombing had thrown everything into disarray by preventing her from going to Lebanon. Neither he nor I believed this was an accurate reading.

As our position eroded, I heard that Annan's chief of staff, Malloch Brown, was saying "sanity" had broken out in the Bush administration, which really meant that we were shifting yet again toward the position of France and other EU countries. Malloch Brown was also again in the news, in a *Financial Times* interview urging the United Kingdom not to be seen as so closely tied to the United States on this war, which was just as illegitimate as his earlier comments about the United States. I pressed Jones Parry to say something publicly in response, but he declined to do so, although he was obviously embarrassed that his boy in the Secretariat had been popping off so indiscriminately.

The ultimate irony was that toward the end of the following day, August 2, de La Sablière called to say he wanted future meetings on the draft text to be between just the United States and France. He felt this was important so that whatever we finally came up with would not be seen as an "Anglo" text and would get a better reception in the Middle East, since everyone else was waiting to see what the two of us did. When Jones Parry complained to me about it several times, I referred him to Malloch Brown. It was also fortunate in other ways, because Washington seemed more confused on the war than on anything I could remember.

Gillerman told me emphatically on August 3 that Jerusalem was quite concerned about the draft resolution. Israel did not want a "cessation of offensive operations," whatever that actually meant, only to find itself pinned down in southern Lebanon until a new international force was created. This was an inherent problem of France's "two-step" approach, and was one reason why we had rejected it until Rice had changed her mind. The bigger problem, of course, was Israel's initial strategy to rely on a new international force to cover its exit from Lebanon, after decades of believing that no international force could really provide the protection Israel needed. That afternoon, de La Sablière and I and our teams met for three and a half hours, plowing through the draft resolution, making considerable progress on many side issues, and also at least understanding each other better on our main differences. One of our key assumptions during this conversation was that France would be the major contributor to any new international force, and therefore quite likely its commander, an assumption turned upside down the next day when Gourdault-Montagne told Hadley that France would not take the lead. Ironically, France said that, without the United States and the United Kingdom in the force, it wanted only a "fair share" with other "real armies," as opposed to traditional UN peacekeepers. This new position had come directly from Chirac, although we did not fully understand what was motivating his reluctance.

I met again several times with de La Sablière on Friday, August 4, feeling by the afternoon that I could go no further until Washington finally decided what it actually wanted in a resolution. I was "saved" when de La Sablière told me that Siniora had rejected what we had written so far, and that he could not meet further until he had new instructions from Paris, to which delay I graciously (and happily) agreed. When partial instructions arrived, they included the direction to agree to the phrase "full cessation of hostilities." This was just a shadow away from the "immediate cease-fire" Annan had wanted from the outset, and a long, long way from "no cease-fire without a political solution," our original objective, from which we had been in headlong retreat ever since Rice's trip to the region. By the end of the day on Friday, de La Sablière and I had resolved all but the two most important issues: how to describe the "cessation of hostilities" (on which point France and the Arabs thought they were making a huge concession by not demanding an immediate, unconditional Israeli withdrawal) and how to handle the return of the kidnapped Israelis and the Hezbollah prisoners long held by Israel (which France insisted be addressed equivalently, and which I continued to reject). By this time, however, Israel was in turmoil, because what we were agreeing to did not in fact resemble our original position. As I told Gillerman, however, and as he reported back to Jerusalem, if Israel was dissatisfied, Livni needed to call Rice, or Olmert needed to call Bush. I certainly wasn't making up the U.S. position in New York.

This being Friday, of course, what really concerned most other delegations was whether they would be able to go to the Hamptons for the weekend. At about 6:30 P.M., Rice called to say we should accept the French formulation on the "prisoners" issue (essentially implying simultaneous release of the Hezbollah terrorists and the kidnapped Israelis). We should also accept the French formulation for "cessation of hostilities" if we could make it clear that only Israeli *offensive* operations would cease, and that their ability to engage in self-defense would not be impaired. I immediately called de La Sablière, who, needless to say, was elated by this news, and with the additional news that Rice wanted to reach agreement on Saturday, which Burns had been telling me. I had said that would be impossible without major concessions by us, which I suppose we had just made. The one thing these changes reinforced, however, was the legitimacy of the IDF's being in southern Lebanon, and its ability to conduct *defensive* operations, which I thought was critical. Even so, as inexplicably as it was relying on an international force, Israel seemed determined to pull the IDF out as soon as possible, or even sooner.

I called Hadley at 6:00 A.M. on Saturday, August 5, to fill him in. He called me back at 7:15 A.M. to say that Gourdault-Montagne believed we had reached agreement, and that we should put the text in blue later that day, which made Gourdault-Montagne very happy since he had just arrived in Provence, having driven late the evening before from Paris to start *les vacances*. I called Gillerman to read him what Rice had agreed to, so that he could call Jerusalem in case they wanted to appeal to Bush or Rice. At about 10:20 A.M., I spoke with Rice and Hadley, both by this time on Air Force One with Bush, flying to Crawford, and summarized where we stood, conveying Gillerman's unhappiness with the latest draft. De La Sablière and I met again in midmorning to put the final touches on the draft and agreed that we would circulate it at 1:00 P.M., asking for an informal Council meeting at 3:00 P.M. to explain what we had come up with. Hadley called at 1:00 P.M. to say Israel was now concerned that the provision for an arms embargo on Lebanon would be ineffective. Ironically, we were also hearing from the Secretariat that enforcing or even monitoring the embargo would be too difficult for poor UNIFIL, which suggested Israel's assessment was dead accurate. I certainly had no faith in the existing UNIFIL, but as of Saturday, there was still at least a possibility of some international force other than a "blue helmet" force.

Of more immediate concern was Siniora's call to Rice informing her that he wanted to make it more explicit that the LAF would deploy into southern Lebanon as the IDF withdrew. This would have been an excellent idea six years earlier, rather than allowing Hezbollah to take control of the territory when the IDF unilaterally withdrew the first time. For Rice, however, a possible move by Lebanon meant we now had to put more pressure on the French to deploy as part of the "international force." Significantly, Rice did not say that Siniora objected to anything else in the draft text, although the Lebanese and Arab missions in New York were already going ballistic, presumably based on what they were hearing from the French about the latest text. I suggested to Rice during this call that she reconsider coming to New York for the vote on this resolution, given the odds that it would come apart once we tried to implement it. Rice appreciated this view, but made it clear she would be there when the resolution was adopted.

By 3:00 P.M., we were prepared to start informal Council consultations, but Qatar asked for a delay to get its instructions. Israel announced publicly that it could accept the resolution, which displeased the French greatly because of the likely Arab counterreaction. When we started at three-thirty, de La Sablière took the other members through the text, suggesting expert meetings later on Saturday and Sunday, with the prospect of adopting the text on Monday. Jones Parry, after taking a shot at the United States for "causing" three weeks of inaction by the Council, nonetheless praised the resolution, stressing we had "made an effort to maximize the chances that the resolution will actually be implemented," which was true. Ghana's Effah-Apenteng, president of the Council in August, called for experts' meetings over the weekend, and we adjourned. Annan, who had returned from a Caribbean trip (what a time to be away from New York!), asked to see de La Sablière and me afterward, to express the concern he had heard from Putin, namely that Israel considered everything "defensive," and that the resolution would therefore be ineffective. Annan also worried about a Beirut meeting of Arab League foreign ministers on Monday, which just reinforced my belief that we should adopt this text, as problematic as it was, as soon as possible before it began to unravel. I called Rice at around 5:30 P.M. to brief her, and to warn about the Monday Arab League meeting, and found she was still focused on prodding France to deploy into southern Lebanon.

On the Sunday, August 6, talk shows, Rice pressed for a Security Council vote in the next day or two. That afternoon, I went to see de La Sablière at his mission, and he said Chirac had just called Blair to complain that the draft was not friendly enough to Lebanon, especially on the "prisoners" issue. I found this hard to believe, since Rice had essentially agreed to something very close to what France had been pushing. It was clear, however, that France was nervous about actually implementing the resolution, perhaps motivated by growing concern about deploying French troops into Lebanon. The rest of the Perm Five arrived at 3:00 P.M., as requested by Russia, and Churkin said they were getting "strong signals" from Siniora that he didn't like the text, specifically that its adoption would mean civil war and his murder. Churkin asked that we hold off action until after the Arab League meeting on Monday, and, to my amazement, de La Sablière immediately agreed. After more palavering, it was clear the United States was the only Perm Five country that objected to waiting for the Arab League to meet on Monday.

De La Sablière and I met at the French Mission at 9:00 A.M. on Monday, and he said that France was trying to find changes to the Saturday draft that would not modify "the nature of the resolution in its main elements," but would leave it "friendlier to the Lebanese," thus aiding Siniora, who needed "the perception we've been listening and taking into account" his concerns. He had a series of amendments he said were "close to, but not over, your red lines," starting with Sheba Farms. There, the French wanted to have Annan study all possible options, which was only slightly better than Siniora's idea for the UN to take control of the territory, a nonstarter from my perspective. We then learned that the Arab League had decided to send a delegation to New York to negotiate directly with us. We should be pleased by this visit, we were told, because the Arabs might simply have rejected the draft outright, and the Security Council would be gridlocked. This alternative actually looked better and better to me.

In a series of confused conference calls with Rice, Hadley, and others during the day, it became clear that we were abandoning the central element of our original position, which was a truly robust international force, and sliding into accepting a plussed-up UNIFIL, hoping that did the trick. I met again with de La Sablière at 3:00 P.M., and most of our discussion revolved around the Lebanese cabinet's decision to deploy fifteen thousand LAF troops into the south "as the Israeli army withdraws behind the Blue Line." I handed over a paper Washington had sent with language that would create the new international force in the current resolution, but de La Sablière now seemed more focused on assuring that any new force had the government of Lebanon's consent and that the force's role was to assist Lebanon, not to "enforce" anything on its own. For that reason, he did not at all like the more muscular mandate our draft proposed, even though we had left out Chapter VII (which we were getting very good at), and even though our joint Saturday text tacitly envisioned a Chapter VII force in the second step. More important, our understanding not to address disarming Hezbollah in the first step would not even be addressed in a second resolution, leaving open for me the issue whether the Security Council would ever address it. This was another major departure from where we started, without even a glimmer of an idea how to get back to it. That evening, with Rice and Hadley both back from Crawford, we had another long, confused discussion about where we were. As a career Foreign Service officer once said, if the American people knew how we formulated policy, they would be after us with pitchforks.

On Tuesday morning, de La Sablière said France thought the Lebanese decision to deploy fifteen thousand troops was important, and that "building on this announcement" made sense because it could also solve coordinating the timing of the IDF's withdrawal as the LAF and the international force deployed. Although our latest idea was overloaded, with too many difficult elements to pass at once, France's main difficulty was the risk that the international force would find itself engaged in "peace enforcement," which they just didn't want to do. In a 12:40 P.M. conference call, Rice made it clear that an "enhanced UNIFIL" was what we now wanted, which would surely make France happy, but which represented the triumph of hope over experience. The afternoon was consumed by a public Council meeting with the Arab League delegation, consisting as advertised of Amr Musa, Sheikh Hamed bin Jasem bin Jabr al-Thani, foreign minister of Qatar (referred to by us as "HBJ"), and Sheikh Abdullah bin Zayed al-Nahyan, foreign minister of the UAE, and current chairman of the Arab League. This was all theater, as were most formal meetings of the Council and other UN bodies, since we certainly were not negotiating anything.

After the public performance, we had a private one in Room C-209, where the Arab Leaguers (along with Lebanon) met with the Perm Five. De La Sablière correctly tried to resist this meeting, because he knew its only purpose was to jam France and the United States. De La Sablière was generally unhappy, largely because of the way the Arabs were trashing our Saturday draft, but I was of no solace to him there. The Arab League/Lebanon/Perm Five meeting was utterly incoherent, although Amr Musa, himself a former Egyptian perm rep (before becoming foreign minister) was more than ready to go through our Saturday draft line by line to tell us what was wrong with it. I told Musa that experts had been through three hours of Qatari amendments on Sunday, and I had no great desire to sit there and do it again. De La Sablière heartily agreed, saying the Arabs had to be more practical given the reality of the Israeli military presence in southern Lebanon (although, of course, there were no Israelis in this crowded room). HBJ, sensing the Arab League was not winning friends or influencing people, agreed we should simply adjourn. I kept HBJ and Qatari perm rep Nasser back after the others left to say what I thought they already understood, that another meeting like the one we just had would be disastrous for their efforts, not to mention their relations with the United States.

Rice spoke with Olmert on Wednesday morning, August 9, and Olmert agreed Israel would accept an "enhanced UNIFIL" in lieu of a "real army" under Chapter VII, and that an "enhanced UNIFIL" would be enough to enforce the arms embargo. I had feared we would end up with UNIFIL again from the first time I heard the idea of a "new international force." Now, here we were. Rice assured Olmert that we would hold firm against pressure for even a token IDF withdrawal before the new force deployed, which seemed to be all that Israel needed. Nonetheless, we both knew that France had not yet accepted that point. At 9:30 A.M., I met again with de La Sablière, who complained that France had taken a huge risk by cosponsoring the Saturday draft with the United States, knowing that Lebanon didn't like it, but even they had been surprised at the negative Arab reaction Now, without some kind of initial IDF withdrawal, he would have to break off discussions and report to the Security Council that we were in disagreement. So doing, of course, allowed France to pander to the Arabs and get out of the hole they had dug by agreeing to the Saturday draft (not that I liked that text, but for opposite reasons). As I told de La Sablière, going back to the other Council members was tantamount to inviting them into the negotiations, which we both knew could move the text so far toward the Arab side that the United States would veto it, causing untold trouble for what was left of the Council's credibility. I didn't tell de La Sablière my real concern was that we would fold and not veto even a terrible French text, given that I already had instructions to concede on almost everything that concerned the French (although the instructions were silent on timing).

The Israelis finally decided to expand their Lebanon operations north to the Litani River, leaving me wondering what had taken them so long. I was even more surprised to learn that the Israeli cabinet vote on the move had been divided and came only after a six-and-one-half-hour meeting. By this point, I had begun asking who the LAF was more likely to be loyal to, Hezbollah or the government of Lebanon. This question produced, to say the least, a wide range of answers, but was critical to whether the LAF in its current state could really bring stability to southern Lebanon absent a much stronger international force than "enhanced UNIFIL."

Rice was pushing hard for a Security Council vote on Friday, which might or might not have something to do with the expected Israeli move toward the Litani River, and which of course we could always achieve by giving in. We had another Perm Five meeting at 9:15 A.M. Thursday, with de La Sablière saying candidly that France would not do again what they had done with the Saturday draft, namely endorse something Siniora did not support. This was more difficult than it might seem, since, as Churkin pointed out, Siniora was saying different things to different people, prompting de La Sablière to quip, "He's Lebanese, isn't he?" Churkin also raised the idea of a seventy-two-hour "humanitarian truce," which was never going to go anywhere, but which complicated our efforts for the rest of the negotiations, while giving Russia a propaganda bonanza. After several more meetings in New York and conversations with Siniora, it became clear that our last hopes for a Chapter VII mandate were finished. Rice was prepared to give up on Chapter VII because Annan told her, in a conversation I had not previously been aware of, that we could write language for "enhanced UNIFIL" that would be an effective substitute, which I thought was delusional. Unfortunately, we were in full retreat now, which wasn't helped by Rice's saying that she wanted to come to New York on Friday even if the vote were not until Saturday, which would signal our avid pursuit of almost anything to vote on, thus further weakening what was left of our bargaining leverage.

Annan wanted to convene the Security Council that evening, which in the current atmosphere of near panic in New York (not to mention State) would be a disaster, but in three separate telephone calls, Rice urged me to agree. I came as close as I ever did in government to refusing a direct order, telling her that such a meeting would be the equivalent of our committing diplomatic suicide if we wanted any of our position to survive. To my relief, she finally relented. The Israelis were extremely unhappy, as Rice told me when she called again at about 7:15 P.M., saying that Livni had said, "You've given away the cease-fire, you've given away Chapter VII, you've given away Sheba Farms, now tell us why we should sign on to this resolution?" Not a bad question, but there we were.

De La Sablière and I met again on Friday morning, August 11, making at least a small modification on Sheba Farms in Israel's direction, as well as a few other minor changes, and I thought that was it. Rice wanted more clarifications on the question of Israeli withdrawal, which were well taken, and which de La Sablière accepted unhappily.

Just before the Council's afternoon meeting, I got nervous that the Arab League might be drifting away. I went searching for HBJ, and found him in the small conference room off the German Lounge. He was very gracious, saying he was dealing with Siniora, trying to fend off the remaining Hezbollah objections over such things as the opening of ports and airports in Lebanon once the cessation of hostilities kicked in. I agreed to stay nearby, which I did for close to an hour, answering questions HBJ was getting, and at one point talking to Siniora directly. We had an informal consultation of the Council at about 3:45 P.M., as de La Sablière and I explained the final text. We were unable to go to an immediate vote, however, because the Chinese said they still needed instructions, and for that the sun had to rise in Beijing. We finally started around 7:00 P.M. with a unanimous vote on Resolution 1701, followed by national statements, and concluded by about 9:10 P.M. Whether it would last and whether it would work were unpleasant questions no one wanted to address, especially given all of the unhappy concessions we had to make along the way. I declined repeated requests by Sean McCormick to do television interviews to defend the resolution, leaving it to Burns, who was only too eager to do so.

Events in the region moved quickly, with first the Lebanese cabinet and then the Israeli cabinet agreeing to the cease-fire. We immediately ran into a disagreement over what troops would join the "enhanced UNIFIL," and who would command it. France, finally at the crunch point, on Chirac's direct order, offered to contribute only two hundred troops, far less than expected. Chirac feared they would be at risk from Hezbollah, which explained in hindsight why France had jettisoned our original concept that the new international force would actually enforce the cease-fire and the arms embargo and disarm Hezbollah. France's contribution later increased, but with Italy as the largest troop contributor, an Italian would be the new force commander when the current commander's tour ended. Siniora suggested troops from several Islamic counties, most of which did not have diplomatic relations with Israel, an obvious potential problem, but one the obtuse Annan refused to understand. I advised Livni and Gillerman, over lunch in the Delegates' Dining Room on August 16, to push back hard against any troop contributions from countries with which Israel had a problem, which they had already started doing. The issue took months to resolve.

As time dragged on, it became increasingly clear there was not going to be another resolution to disarm Hezbollah, that the arms embargo was not being enforced, that Hezbollah was rearming, and that "enhanced UNIFIL" looked and acted much like the existing, ineffective UNIFIL. Although armed Hezbollah formations did not reappear in southern Lebanon, no one doubted that Hezbollah supporters were being rearmed and resupplied, or that Hezbollah's political presence was returning. Although rocket attacks against Israel did not resume, Hezbollah's explicit threat to Lebanon's government actually increased after the war, since its mere survival in the face of Israel's threat to destroy it made Hezbollah appear victorious. Street demonstrations and threats of violence against Siniora and his supporters grew increasingly frequent, as did Hezbollah's political efforts to undermine Lebanese constitutional procedures in many other ways. The plain fact was that no one was prepared to contemplate the use of force to disarm Hezbollah if it did not do so voluntarily: not the democratically elected government of Lebanon, not Israel, not France, not the United States, and most certainly not the Security Council. So, this gang of armed terrorists continues to exist threatening both Israel and freedom in Lebanon.

Whether representative government can survive in Lebanon, and Syrian and Iranian influences kept out, remains very much in doubt, despite the summer war between Israel and Hezbollah and despite Resolution 1701. Contrary to everything we had said at the outset of the hostilities, the net result, over a year later, appeared yet again to be just another Middle East cease-fire, with no dispositive change in the situation on the ground, which was, if anything, somewhat less favorable to Israel, and certainly less favorable to democracy in Lebanon, than before.

To demonstrate this point, the Arab League used another shelling incident in the Gaza Strip to try to embarrass Israel in the Security Council, occasioning my second veto, which I was happy to cast, on Saturday, November 11. The Arab League clearly was not interested in negotiations over the incident. In fact, they almost hoped for a veto so they could raise the issue in the General Assembly, where they would win overwhelmingly, and where the United States has no veto. I thought this was an easy case, but

NEA's bureaucrats, this time spun up about continuing Hamas-Fatah negotiations to form a Palestinian "unity government," twisted in every possible direction to find a way to support Qatar's draft resolution. Even more troubling, Rice was in doubt about what the United States should do right up until Saturday morning, when the vote was scheduled, this after four days of intense work on the issue following the shelling. As one senior official put it, "Condi is pissed off, and blames the Israelis" for putting her in a difficult position. Thus, although the immediate problem was averted through our veto, the longer-term prospects were troubling. With less than a month to go until my departure, the indecision over whether to cast a veto was a fitting example of what I thought lay ahead. For Israel and Lebanon, it meant more of the same, as far as the eye could see.

CHAPTER FIFTEEN

RECESSIONAL

The tumult and the shouting dies;
The Captains and the Kings depart.

—RUDYARD KIPLING, "RECESSIONAL" (1903)

I thought about a second shot at confirmation almost from the day of my recess appointment, but I didn't do much besides daydream about it until well into my tenure at the UN. I suffered under the illusion that perhaps my performance in New York might make a difference to a large number of senators, so I concentrated simply on doing my job. It was easy to get lost in the job, with activity boiling away on so many fronts, right up until the UN finally broke for the Christmas holiday at the end of 2005. During that intense, five-month period, I had conversations with many senators, including George Voinovich, all in a perfectly business-as-usual manner, which I did not excessively analyze, interpreting them simply as indications that my situation was neither better nor worse than before. Voinovich was especially interested in UN management reform, the new UN Human Rights Council's inadequacies, and the UN's role in Kosovo, which he did not think was going well. These were important issues, and I was perfectly content to discuss them with him and others. I first raised the question of what would happen when the recess appointment expired with Brian Gunderson, Rice's chief of staff, on Thursday, December 29, when I was in Washington for Christmas. He agreed to have State's lawyers look into the various options, including pressing for Senate confirmation, a second recess appointment, or being named "acting perm rep" under the Vacancies Act.

The Lugar-Coleman-Voinovich trip to the UN in early February 2006 was obviously helpful. News reports to that effect were reinforced by the conclusions of State's lawyers that, even without Senate confirmation, there were indeed several ways for me to continue as perm rep once the recess appointment expired at the end of 2006. I mentioned this planning exercise to Rice on February 13, as I rode with her to the White House for the Bush-Annan meeting, explaining that I was seeing Rove afterward, and she said, "Great," asking that I keep her informed. Later, as Rice and I walked off to separate meetings, we ran into Josh Bolten, who said, "Thanks for the Nobel Prize nomination!" referring to my recent nomination by Per Ahlmark, a member of Sweden's parliament and former deputy prime minister, for my nonproliferation work. (Bolten and I had had our names confused so many times, dating back to the early 1980s, that it was a wonder *he* hadn't received the nomination!) There had been press reports on the subject, prompting Rove to greet me with his typical irreverence: "You've been nominated for the Nobel Peace Prize by a Swede? What's gone wrong with you?" Rove and I discussed the obviously critical issue of Voinovich, there being no sign of any weakness in any other Republican vote, and what Voinovich's support in the SFRC would mean: a favorable vote in the committee and a changed dynamic on the Senate floor, where a Democratic filibuster now seemed much less likely.

In any case, until Voinovich was ready to switch, there was little point in trying to generate any other confirmation-related activity, other than quiet preparations. I knew that one of Voinovich's concerns, as he had told me in 2005, was Richard Holbrooke's promise to stay in close touch with Voinovich after his contested nomination in the late nineties was approved. Voinovich had accordingly released his hold, and Holbrooke was confirmed. Afterward, Voinovich never heard from Holbrooke again, and he was so angry he didn't want to be burned twice. I discussed the issue with Rove, Norm Coleman, and a number of other senators, but we found no satisfactory solution. At one point we thought several senators might act as "guarantors," to reassure Voinovich that I would honor my commitment to stay in touch, unlike Holbrooke, but Voinovich demurred. By then, May was fading into June 2006. Given election-year dynamics, with Democrats likely shutting down Senate confirmations in anticipation of big gains in

November, I worried we were running out of time. Lugar understood the timing problem, agreeing we had a very narrow window. He also agreed, once we decided to go for a committee vote, that there was no need for further hearings, since I had testified several times before the SFRC while at USUN, including in late May. Then, simply anticipating expected Democratic insistence on a hearing, Lugar decided it was inevitable, which stretched out the schedule and gave the opposition more time for obstruction. In the meantime, we heard from perm reps in New York that senators like Voinovich and Hagel were calling them and other foreign diplomats and Secretariat officials, asking about my performance. I wondered how that would look in full public view. Fortunately, the perm reps who received calls—or at least those who told me about the calls—were positive.

Even as I was working toward confirmation, however, a contrary line of thought was in my mind, precipitated by Rice's May 8 dinner with the Perm-Five-plus-Germany foreign ministers, at which she had sidelined our Security Council drive for sanctions against Iran. For the first time, I wondered if it was not time to leave the administration, so distressed was I at the havoc caused to our sanctions diplomacy, and for what it revealed about the overall drift of our policy. Not since Powell's surrender on Iran at the September 2004 foreign minister's dinner in New York had I been so depressed. One meeting alone is not cause to resign, although the State Department could turn any grand strategy into an endless list of process points—go to this meeting, make this phone call, sit next to this person, and so on, *ad infinitum*. This was a mentality that trivialized policy analysis, because making a fuss over a mere "process point" could always be made to seem an overreaction, which it often was in the big picture. The May 8 dinner was bad enough, but also on my mind was the large and growing list of wrong directions and mistakes elaborated in the preceding chapters on Iran, North Korea, the Middle East, and others.

Nonetheless, we still worked away in preparation for another confirmation effort if Voinovich changed his mind, with numerous senators pressing him. On Wednesday, July 19, however, Coleman, in one of our many conversations, said he still wasn't getting a definitive answer. Voinovich had tried to reach me earlier that day, and surmising he was calling with bad news, I wasn't eager to return the call. Because of scheduling difficulties our offices agreed I should call Voinovich at his home at 8:30 P.M., which I did, slipping out of a dinner at the Regency Hotel in honor of Danny Ayalon,

Israel's departing ambassador to Washington. I was amazed when Voinovich told me he would have an op-ed piece in the *Washington Post* the next morning entitled, "Why I'll Vote for Bolton," parts of which he read to me over the phone. Voinovich also planned a press conference later that day to amplify the message, which showed he had given careful thought to his decision and its roll-out. His switch now made impossible any argument that opposition to the nomination was bipartisan. I was confident that if we could just get the nomination out of the SFRC death trap, a floor vote was likely and would be positive. Rove called the next morning and said, "I love it when a plan comes together," a line from the now-expired television program *The A Team*, and many senators called as well.

Lugar scheduled a confirmation hearing for Thursday, July 27, before which we were already laying preparations for the next stage. All the Republicans were on board, including, for future reference, Lincoln Chafee, who told Deb Fiddelke of the White House staff on July 26, "I voted for him once, and I'll vote for him again." Republicans including Voinovich, Coleman, Kyl, and McCain were talking to Democrats, among whom they discerned little appetite for another filibuster. In fact, Democratic leader Harry Reid released Democrats up for election in November from any obligation to vote along party lines, which was obviously encouraging. AIPAC's Howard Kohr told me that many Democrats, even those opposed to the nomination, agreed it was a mistake to "change horses in midstream," so the real issue was whether we could get the nomination to the floor for action before the August recess. I feared that if things drifted into September, the likelihood of anyone getting confirmed, even noncontroversial nominees, was slim. In any case, I was pressed by events in New York and did little preparation for the hearing, figuring that "campaigning as an incumbent" was the best answer.

The confirmation hearing itself was a snoozer. I thought that the Democrats just didn't have their hearts in it this time. Voinovich actually announced he had spoken to a number of other perm reps in New York, and that their comments had been significant in his decision to support the nomination. He urged other senators to make similar calls. Moreover, for the first time, I was able to get out the full story on the NSA intercepts, explaining the "minimization" procedure that resulted in U.S. names not being explicitly included. I also stressed that I had no personal reason to withhold either the names or the intercepts themselves from review by senators, although I noted carefully the equities the intelligence community had at stake. Finally, I described publicly for the first time the 2005 negotiations between Chris Dodd and the White House, and how close we had come to agreement, including the meeting among Dodd, Biden, and myself in Biden's office. All this demonstrated to anyone interested that the issue was neither as mysterious nor as complex—nor as important—as Dodd would have liked everyone to believe. Even Dodd, in describing the earlier negotiations, made what could have been an important concession by saying that he would be satisfied if an appropriate member of the Senate Intelligence Committee reviewed the intercepts, rather than himself.

Toward the end of the desultory questioning, the hearing room's ceiling sprang a large leak, on the Democratic side of the dais, and the committee staff rushed around putting trashcans under the downpour. The hearing adjourned at about 1:00 P.M., after only three hours, a real anticlimax. I headed back to New York, plunging again into the Hezbollah-Israel war and our faltering Iran efforts. Reports from the hearing were uniformly positive, and on the Sunday talk shows on July 30, Senator Chuck Schumer of New York, chairman of the Democratic Senatorial Campaign Committee, said that he thought a filibuster was "unlikely." In fact, within a few days, the only Democrat who seemed to have any inclination to resist an up-or-down floor vote was Dodd, and we were already working on what we might be able to do even there. All of this was to no avail, however, because at the August 2 SFRC business meeting, the Democrats exercised their right under committee rules to postpone a vote on my nomination until the next meeting, which was not until September. I feared this was all that Dodd needed, given Democratic expectations for the 2006 elections, as the Democrats shut down the Senate.

The most immediate question was when the SFRC business meeting would be held, since the tentative date, September 12, conflicted with Chafee's primary in Rhode Island, where he faced a close race against a conservative challenger. Every instinct was to schedule the SFRC meeting before the primary, which Lugar ultimately did, picking Thursday, September 7. During the August recess, I called many senators, briefing them on the frenetic activity we had just been through, with Resolutions 1695 (North Korea), 1696 (Iran), 1701 (Israel-Hezbollah), and later, 1706 (Darfur), touching base, but also ensuring there weren't any hidden problems. There were positive signs with Democrats. Connecticut's Joe Lieberman said he would support me, both on the nomination and on any cloture vote, an especially significant act of courage since he had been defeated in the Democratic primary and was running for re-election as an Independent. Ben Nelson of Nebraska told me expressly, as he had in 2005, that he would vote for me and for cloture if need be. Diane Feinstein of California, after I briefed her on Resolution 1701, said, "Good work, Ambassador," and given her close relationship with Rice, I thought this significant. I also had positive calls with Senators Pryor of Arkansas and Boxer of California, and several Democratic members of the House of Representatives. In August, one of them called Harry Reid, who said he didn't think the Democrats would filibuster because, in Reid's words, "Our Jewish friends don't want one." Reid did say that "we may take some time," which we interpreted to mean that Reid might put the Republicans through the exercise of a cloture vote in order to burn up floor time, which we reported to the Republican leadership. Schumer was also strongly against a filibuster: He was "not a man deliberating" on the issue, as it was relayed to me. Biden's staffers also thought a filibuster unlikely, saying they had searched vigorously during the August recess for any derogatory information on me they could find, and, sadly for them, nothing turned up.

Even with their earlier comments to the White House, everyone remained nervous about Chafee and Chuck Hagel, so I asked Jim Baker to call them, which he did in late August. Baker said he explained to Chafee he had been responsible for bringing me into the Reagan White House, and added, "There were almost as few moderates in Washington then as there are now. John may not always agree with us, but he's done a damn good job." Chafee didn't say much of anything other than, "I'm delighted to hear that you brought John into the government," but Baker interpreted Chafee's relative silence to mean that he didn't have any particular concerns with me personally. If he'd had any, Baker reasoned, as did others when I told them of the conversation, Chafee would have raised them to hear what Baker had to say.

Indeed, Chafee's staff was telling the White House at the time of Baker's call that he had a particular person he wanted to be nominated for a Rhode Island federal district court judgeship. Lugar's chief of staff, Ken Myers, told Fiddelke and Jeff Bergner, now in charge of legislative affairs at State, and an old friend, that Chafee told Lugar directly that if the administration would commit to making that nomination, he would support mine. While I knew from long experience there would be no deal based on a judgeship, I thought this was further proof that Chafee had no problem with me as such. The real issue now was what deal there was to cut, and how much leverage Chafee had over the White House because of my nomination. For a senator facing a tough primary and a tough re-election race in November, I thought this was a curious set of priorities, unless he had already concluded he was destined to lose, but wanted to help a friend on the way out the door. Republican Whip Mitch McConnell talked to Chafee in early September, basically telling him that real senators didn't try to pull off judgeship deals such as the one he was suggesting. Chafee hemmed and hawed, which meant to me McConnell was making progress. At one point, McConnell, who was generally thought to be the best person to work on Chafee, said to me, "You never know, although why he would do anything other than support you in terms of his primary is beyond me."

As for Hagel, Lou Ann Linehan, his long-time top aide, was telling people that we should not worry about Hagel's reluctance to commit publicly to vote for me again: "It's not Bolton; it's the whole situation," she would say, because Hagel was unhappy with so much of what the Bush administration was doing. I finally decided to call Hagel directly, after teeing up some preliminary soundings. Baker spoke with him and reported back to me, laughing, "You're okay, but you need to tell him you're through writing articles critical of the UN." I thought that was pretty funny, too, but Baker went on to say that I should stress that I was enjoying the job and being productive, although it was unclear to me why I had to say so. Bill Timmons, a pillar of the Washington lobbyist corps, said Hagel told him he liked me personally, but that other ambassadors had said I came on "too strong" at the UN. On September 5, I spoke to Hagel for about twenty-five minutes. He started in a worrying way, saying he wasn't going to talk to the press about our conversation, although he had no objection if I did. He then said that the UN was a "hothouse up there," and "not anchored in reality," but he was troubled by "phone calls he had received in the last few months" from other UN ambassadors. I went through the litany of recently passed major Security Council resolutions (1695, 1696, 1701, and 1706), and he said it was "a good inventory of what you've produced and accomplished." He continued that "the pressure will continue to grow on you because of where you are," and he wanted "to make certain that you and I understand the importance" of the UN ambassador's role. After some further discussion about the deficiencies of the administration's hard-line Middle East policy, Hagel said, "I'll support you."

At about 7:00 P.M. on Wednesday, September 6, the day before the SFRC business meeting, Coleman called to say that the SFRC vote was canceled because Chafee was still not on board. He thought White House legislative director Candi Wolff would have already called me, which she had not, so I called her. She had just come from a Frist-McConnell-Lugar-Coleman meeting, at which they had assessed that Chafee was paralyzed with fear because of his September 12 primary. They decided Lugar would simply postpone Thursday's SFRC meeting and all the pending nominations until the next week, to avoid highlighting the Chafee problem. The most likely scenario, she said, would be to have the business meeting on September 12, the day of Chafee's primary, or perhaps the day after, thus giving him a reasonable excuse why he couldn't be in Washington, so he wouldn't have to vote one way or the other. I went back to the Waldorf and called Steve Rademaker, formerly assistant secretary for arms control and now Frist's foreign policy adviser. He, too, was in the earlier strategy meeting, and said the problem was that Chafee was melting down, given how close his primary might be. At 8:00 P.M., Fiddelke reported that Chafee had agreed the SFRC should meet on September 12, which at least was something. Nonetheless, here we were, yet again, with a last-minute problem, and no particular strategy. Having myself worked with both Voinovich and Hagel, I wondered why I had left Chafee entirely to the White House, but it was too late for second-guessing.

The next day, however, Chafee experienced another meltdown, believing he could win his primary only by voting against the nomination, apparently on the theory that this would attract independent voters to participate in the Republican primary, saving him from his opponent, who had endorsed my nomination. In fact, the RNC had included a question about my nomination in a recent poll showing that Rhode Island voters were utterly uninterested, no matter how Chafee voted. Then, unaccountably, Lugar decided to go ahead with the SFRC meeting that day and push the other nominations through, thus making it plain for all to see that there was a problem in my case. As it turned out, my nomination did not come up at all in the meeting, surprising the Democrats, and no new date was scheduled. Instead, McConnell would meet with Chafee on September 13, the day after the primary, to see what was on his mind, and the next likely SFRC business meeting would be September 19. Fiddelke spoke to Chafee, and he said the judgeship and his bill on breast cancer were still on his mind, and, as to my nomination, "All of this is interconnected." That meant Chafee was still in bargaining mode. I asked how Chafee was still eluding the combined weight of the White House and the Senate leadership, although it was an increasingly academic question, and the answer always was, "It's Chafee." The only good news was that the press uniformly ascribed the delay in the vote to Chafee's upcoming primary, but I had no doubt that Dodd and others knew weakness when they saw it and therefore turned their efforts to reinforcing Chafee's nervousness.

Then came yet another twist. Chafee wrote Rice a letter, which he released to the press, tying his hesitation on my nomination to our Middle East policy, which he thought was too pro-Israel. Steve Laffey, Chafee's Republican primary opponent, immediately issued a press release criticizing Chafee for indecisiveness, showing Chafee couldn't avoid the issue simply by ducking the vote, which one might have thought was obvious. Moreover, if there were anything Chafee could do to remind pro-Israel Democratic senators why they should oppose a Dodd-led filibuster, this was it. That weekend, I was in Nebraska to give a speech and attend a University of Nebraska football game, and I ran into Hagel. He was very gracious and seemed genuinely determined to help, saying the idea for Chafee's Middle East letter was his, and that he would speak again on Monday with Chafee. Hagel thought much of the problem lay with the administration's "mishandling" of Chafee, citing several phone calls Chafee had made to Rice that she had not returned. Back in Washington, people were working on Rice's response to Chafee's letter, defending the administration's Middle East policy and strongly endorsing me, which could give Chafee a way out of his dilemma, if he really wanted one.

Chafee won his primary on September 12 but announced he was not immediately returning to Washington, meaning that his McConnell meeting was off. Rice signed the letter to Chafee and called him, but incredibly only congratulated him on winning his primary. She did not raise the matter of my nomination because she thought it "inappropriate." Given this missed opportunity, I wondered again whether I should stay at USUN, by confirmation or otherwise, or leave the administration. RNC chairman Ken Mehlman called Chafee to underline the importance of party solidarity, as the party had stood with Chafee in his primary. Mehlman reported that Chafee wanted to be assured we could avoid or break a filibuster; he wanted the answer to his letter to Rice on the Middle East; and he wanted his judgeship, all of which at least indicated Chafee was still open to supporting me. The McConnell-Chafee meeting was now scheduled for Tuesday, September 19, and everyone urged that we simply sit still and allow that meeting to happen, even though the Senate adjournment target of September 29 was agonizingly close at hand. McConnell and Chafee did meet, but it was, yet again, inconclusive.

Bush was in New York for the General Assembly opening, conducting bilateral discussions and also attending special events, such as a traditional meeting with the staff of USUN, which presidents and secretaries try to do on their visits to embassies around the world. On the morning of September 20, while we were in a holding room before the USUN event, I thanked Bush for all his support during this long process, especially now with Chafee. I thought at first he was about to respond with exactly what he thought of Chafee, but he just said, "It's all just politics, but that's nothing new in Washington, is it?" I repeated how much I appreciated what he had done personally, and he responded, "You just keep doing what you're doing, and we'll get it done." Bush received a warm greeting from the USUN staff and their families, and a very strong response when he said he was working hard to get me confirmed, followed by something like, "I know there are people who don't agree with me on that, but that's just too bad." While Bush chatted and shook hands with everyone, I thanked Josh Bolten again, and he said, "This is not your fault, and it's for the good of the country, so we're happy to do it." Bolten also said they thought Chafee might be trying to call Bush directly, which they were looking forward to.

Voinovich was pitching in as well. He called me on September 20 to report that Chafee had just told him his real problem was our Middle East policy, and specifically our lack of vocal opposition to Israeli construction on the West Bank. Voinovich made a strong case that I was doing well, working closely with Rice, and reflecting U.S. policy, which Chafee accepted, although noting I was "too tied in with the Jewish community." Voinovich tried to explain that this was a positive, since the "community" would take bad news from me, and he thought Chafee understood. Rice spoke again with Chafee, telling me it was "a good call," and that things were "going to come out okay," since Chafee seemed positively inclined toward me. There were "a few things for Rhode Island" Chafee told her he wanted, but our team was encouraged by the call. Then, Bush spoke with Chafee, making a very strong pitch on my behalf, but Chafee was, unusually, quite aggressive in telling Bush what he wanted in return, not a good sign, in my opinion.

McConnell was also still trying with Chafee, but he couldn't get anything definitive out of him. The SFRC agreed to schedule another business meeting on September 26, the outer limit to have any prospect of getting the nomination through by September 29, and Josh Bolten and McConnell continued their efforts at persuasion. They were unsuccessful, so Coleman tried again on September 26 (the SFRC meeting having been canceled). Coleman called that evening as I was on my way to Mayor Mike Bloomberg's annual reception at Gracie Mansion for the General Assembly opening, describing the conversation with Chafee as "surreal." Chafee kept repeating, "Can't this wait until after the election?" He complained that Rice's response to his letter on Middle East policy had really not addressed his concerns, nor had their subsequent conversation. Many other Republican senators, including McCain, also kept trying, one telling Chafee, "A hell of a lot of us broke our asses getting you through that primary," with no effect, and one coming away "shaking his head at why Chafee couldn't understand why the vote needed to be before the November election." Another concluded, "Chafee just can't make up his mind." On a happier note, Arlen Specter, at the National Press Club, answered a question on me by saying, "I'm for him. I think he's done a good job. He's smart, he's industrious, and he's cantankerous, and those are three good qualifications."

As had been evident for some time, however, the prospects for confirmation were slipping away through Chafee's indecision, and the likely November outcome was hardly encouraging. Accordingly, I had closely followed deliberations on "Plan B" for another recess appointment or something comparable and arranged to see Cheney in the West Wing on September 28. He was—how to put it?—unhappy with Chafee. We discussed what to do if the Senate did not act during the expected lame duck session after the November election, and I said the key issue was whether Bush and Rice wanted me to stay on as UN ambassador after the present recess appointment expired. Cheney seemed surprised, and said, "There's no question about that, based on what I've heard the president say. I'll raise it with him again." We discussed the various options, such as a second recess appointment or using the Vacancies Act, and I stressed that if there were no action in the lame duck Senate, which seemed likely, we should have a decision as soon as it ended. At noon, I met Rice, and we first discussed Chafee. She was incredulous Chafee was not satisfied by her response to his letter on the Middle East. I said we needed to consider what to do in the absence of a Senate vote, and whether I should stay on in New York, and Rice said, smiling, "Oh, come on, I'm not tired of you yet." I called Crouch the next day, who said Bush was "very concerned" that Chafee was not following up on commitments at least to vote me out of the SFRC, which was a wrinkle I hadn't heard before. I never thought Chafee had committed to anything, which is certainly the way he behaved. In any case, the Senate went into recess for the election early in the morning of September 30 with no further action.

As the election approached, the White House worked on "Plan B," in order to be ready depending on the outcome on November 7. That outcome was as bad as many predicted, with Republicans losing control of both the Senate and the House. While we were all recovering, Bush fired Rumsfeld the day after the election. The Republican congressional reaction was outrage: If Rumsfeld was to be made the sacrificial lamb, why wait until *after* the election? Rumsfeld had offered to resign several times already, and had been very loyal to Bush, so making him walk the plank on November 8 looked to many simply like cratering to the new Democratic majorities before they were even sworn in. More parochially, I wondered what Rumsfeld's going over the side meant for me, and the conclusions one could draw were not very happy ones.

Chafee got his walking papers on November 7 as well, and I knew Bush would call him shortly to extend his condolences. Before that happened, however, Chafee held a news conference on November 9, basically saying he was happy Republicans had lost the election, wasn't sure if he would stay in the party, and by the way, the results had convinced him not to vote for me. So much for the White House's postelection efforts at confirmation, and any chance the lame duck Senate session would take action! Even the day before, when McConnell had spoken yet again to Chafee, the only subjects discussed had been the judgeship and Chafee's desire for the administration to hire at least some of his soon-to-be-unemployed staff, which showed a certain amount of chutzpah given what he did the next day. Ironically, even Chafee's home-state newspaper, the *Providence Journal,* was complimentary, in its own way, about my performance, saying, "Oddly, he has done pretty well. . . . Mr. Bolton has been a competent Ambassador [and] should be allowed to stay on."[1] By this time, the press was full of stories about the White House and the new Democratic Hill leadership looking forward to "bipartisan cooperation," which I knew was a charade. The inevitable futility played out in my own case, as Republicans urged confirmation, while Dodd called for my nomination to be withdrawn, hardly a sign the two sides were even close to agreeing on what "cooperation" meant.

I thought hard about what might lie ahead if the administration resorted to "Plan B" and concluded it was better to leave when the recess appointment ended, upon the Senate's adjournment for the year, than to try to hang on. First, I didn't like the direction of our policy on too many issues, particularly Iran, North Korea, and Arab-Israeli issues. With Rumsfeld's departure, and the loss of his strong voice and sound opinions, things would only get worse. I judged that I could likely accomplish more from a philosophical perspective outside the administration than inside, and that this was the cleanest time to make the break. There were important policy issues to frame in the already under way 2008 presidential campaign, and there was obviously no way to affect that process locked into an increasingly lame duck administration. Second, if the administration did give me a second recess appointment, or used the Vacancies Act, it would simply give the Democrats a club to beat the administration with, and it would be only a matter of time before the administration folded. What if the SFRC under Democratic leadership simply refused to process any new State nominees until I departed? Why even give them that opportunity? Third, by simply leaving at the natural end of the recess appointment, I wouldn't actually have to "resign" from the administration, which struck me as the most gracious way to depart, as quietly and with as little fuss as possible under the circumstances. It would also thereby be clear that it was my decision to leave, and not the administration's, but not in a critical way. I didn't want to make unnecessary trouble for Bush.

Friends gave me advice on both sides of the question, some arguing I should get out before the continuing collapse of the administration's policies dragged me down with it, others arguing I had to stay in to continue to

---

1. "Bolton Did a Good Job," *Providence Journal,* Wednesday, November 29, 2006, p. B1, col. 1.

fight the good fight, as the numbers of real conservatives in the administration dwindled. Although the advice was conflicting, both viewpoints rested on the same analytical perception, namely that the administration was in disarray on foreign policy, their major difference being the assessment of the costs to me personally of staying rather than going. During this time, nearly three weeks following the election, I was consulting with staff lawyers and others on the specifics of what "Plan B" would look like. While helpful, they were obviously not decision-makers, and I was hearing nothing from the White House about the direction of its thinking.

Having reached my decision, I met again with Cheney, in the early afternoon of November 30. I told him I had decided to leave when the recess appointment ended, explaining my reasons, and specifically that I hadn't spent a month in Florida in 2000 to see foreign policy go in the direction it was heading. He asked that I "not pull the trigger until we get back to you," and I agreed, pointing out that I should send the letter notifying the president of my intention to step down the next day. After leaving Cheney's office, I signed an already-prepared letter to Bush, dated December 1, and then caught the USAir Shuttle at Reagan National. By the time I returned to Manhattan, Josh Bolten had called and asked that I not send the letter until after the last Senate lame duck session was over. I said I should send the letter before the Senate even came back into session, because no one should be expending any further resources under the false impression we still thought confirmation was possible. Rove called me the next day, Friday, December 1, and I made the same point to him on timing. Neither one tried to talk me out of leaving, which was fortunate for both sides of the conversation. Rice had been out of the country with Bush, and I was not able to reach her on Friday, so I went ahead and had my letter delivered both to her office and to the White House. Bolten called back to say that he hoped that the letter would not become public until after the lame duck session, and I urged again that no one on the Hill or elsewhere be allowed to expend any further effort on something that was obviously not going to happen.

What the White House really wanted to do was work on a roll-out strategy to make my departure public, which I told Bolten was perfectly all right with me. Gretchen and I flew down from New York on Monday, December 4, by which time the roll-out strategy had already commenced. Bush issued a very nice statement, which I thought would eliminate press speculation about policy differences within the administration. That was certainly my intention in trying to make a "gracious" exit, a policy I followed for as long as I could after leaving the government.

We were scheduled to meet Bush in the Oval Office at 3:00 P.M., but meetings on Iraq delayed it until three-thirty. While we waited in a small room in the West Wing basement, Hadley came in and said, "This is bad. This is bad. This is bad." I didn't say anything. When we did arrive at the Oval Office, Bush gave Gretchen a hug and asked, "You're not angry with me, are you?" I said I was not, and Bush said, "Well, I'm angry," and said various unkind things about "that ungrateful senator," meaning Chafee. Bush, who was joined only by Hadley and Josh Bolten, thanked me for the job I had done in New York, and I thanked him for all his support during the confirmation process. We talked for slightly over twenty minutes, during which time Bush asked, "Is there anything we can offer you? You can have anything," which was generous if overstated, but I declined. We talked about our daughters' respective experiences at Yale, and Bush asked if JS had had a hard time because of me. I told the recent story of how, in a simulation in her Grand Strategy course, she had been chosen to play the White House chief of staff, which Bush thought appropriately humorous. The press mob was then allowed in to photograph the scene, and Bush made some very friendly remarks. The White House press office asked beforehand if I also wanted to say anything, but I declined. We then left the White House and took the next shuttle back to New York. The White House roll-out strategy was complete, and my exit was gracious, so we both had what we wanted.

I returned to Washington on December 5 to meet with Rice. She asked if I might be interested in accepting the counselor's job, which Zelikow had recently vacated, and I declined. She didn't ask if I had any ideas who my successor should be, and, accordingly, I didn't offer any. That evening, Bush hosted a farewell dinner in the White House family quarters for Annan, which was a painful affair, given everything that Annan had done during his tenure to undercut the United States and Bush in particular. Since I was still in my gracious mode, however, I gritted my teeth and went along. While we were waiting in the basement lobby to go up to the family quarters, a White House staffer told me that, during their September visit to New York, the Bushes had vaguely offered an invitation to a farewell event at the White House for the departing SG, and that Annan's office had harassed them unmercifully since then to schedule something, hence this dinner. Annan had submitted, as his preferred guest list, Madeleine Albright, Richard Holbrooke, Ted Turner, and Tim Wirth, but none of them were there. While we were still waiting, Sally Quinn, wife of former *Washington Post* editor-in-chief Ben Bradlee (two more Annan guests), came up to me and said, "I see you're like my husband: forgotten but not gone." I had never met her before. I knew I was going to like this dinner. I liked it even more when it was over.

For the next several days, I did the usual departure routine, speaking to the USUN staff, thanking them for all of their hard work, calling senators and others to thank them for their support over the past two years. In previous departures from government service, I had found the exit process difficult, since, for all of the aggravation, the opportunity to affect public policy so directly was hard to lay aside. This time, however, after some initial qualms about my decision to exit, I was actually looking forward to leaving, which surprised me somewhat. The unhappiest moment came on December 8, when I learned that Jeane Kirkpatrick had died the day before. I had thought of doing a few "farewell" things on this next-to-last day of the recess appointment, but decided not to for obvious reasons, substituting instead a moment of silence at my last USUN staff meeting that morning. The Senate adjourned for the year on December 9, and the recess appointment as UN ambassador concluded. After a few more weeks to wrap up bureaucratic obligations, my government career ended. As the Edith Piaf song goes, *"Je ne regrette rien."*

CHAPTER SIXTEEN

FREE AT LAST: BACK TO THE FIRING LINE

Mon centre cède, ma droite recule,
situation excellente, j'attaque!

—MARSHAL FERDINAND FOCH, 1918

After nearly six years of service in the Bush administration, I had many ideas on what we did right and what we did wrong, and lessons to be derived for the future, a few of which I cover in this chapter. While in the government, it is almost impossible to step back from the press of events, reflect on what you're doing, and make course corrections except on an incremental basis. As the saying goes, the urgent crowds out the important. Nonetheless, our 2008 national elections will be extraordinarily consequential, involving critical choices on national security. These choices will certainly be far broader than the course we should pursue in Iraq, despite our current preoccupation and the preferences of some politicians to have that issue alone predominate. The proliferation of weapons of mass destruction, and especially North Korea and Iran; the unsettled Middle East, with manifold threats to our friends and interests, such as Israel, democracy in Lebanon, and the region's oil and gas reserves; Russia's renewed aggressiveness, and its quest for renewed superpower status; and China's large and growing demand for energy and its rapidly increasing military budgets and capabilities are among the immediately recognizable problems.

Moreover, we cannot ignore the EU's proclivity to avoid confronting and actually resolving problems, preferring instead the endless process of diplomatic mastication. In certain circumstances, this approach may have its uses, but for the EU, it is essentially now their solution to everything. This decline in European will and capacity is matched by the related phenomenon, beloved by many Europeans, of using multilateral bodies for "norming" both international practice and domestic policy, a development that, over time, most profoundly threatens to diminish American autonomy and self-government, notions that to us spell "sovereignty." It is clear that the United Nations remains unreformed. Whether it is in fact unreformable remains to be seen, but the EU's almost invariable proclivity to turn to the institution makes this question of far more than academic interest.

Finally, as we have seen in the preceding pages, our own Department of State has serious cultural problems that must be addressed with even greater urgency than the UN. Succeeding secretaries of state have ignored reforming the department, leaving it essentially to run itself, which has only allowed the problem to fester and grow, to the point where our capacity to advocate American interests in foreign affairs is now severely impaired. This issue may never rise to the level of a campaign stump speech, but it is no less important for the next several presidents and secretaries.

The Next Generation of Threats to America

Russia and China have been active WMD proliferators over the years. Russia's close relationship with India, and China's with Pakistan, were undoubtedly key factors in the development of the Indian and Pakistani nuclear and ballistic missile capabilities, a case study in how competitive proliferation works. Fortunately, the Cold War was not rife with more such examples, but since its end, the problem has certainly grown worse. Iraq under Saddam Hussein, North Korea, and Iran have all benefited from varying levels of Chinese and Russian support in their WMD and ballistic missile programs. Others, such as Cuba, Syria, and Burma, have benefited as well, although the spread of technology and the existence of proliferation networks like that of A. Q. Khan of Pakistan mean that Russia and China are now not the only sources of critical proliferation technology and materials.

What led Russia and China to engage in this dangerous behavior? And what should be its long-term implications for our respective bilateral relationships and international peace and security? The central problem is that neither Russia nor China has fully internalized our understanding that proliferation represents a significant threat. To be sure, they may lip-sync the appropriate words in the Security Council or in foreign ministers' communiqués, but they do not act in a manner consistent with these declamations. To be fair, many Europeans and others have not fully internalized this reality either, as the futile effort to impose meaningful sanctions on Iran demonstrates: Sanctions without pain are not sanctions at all. The hard truth is that we must all be prepared to forgo the short-term gains of selling WMD-related, advanced technology and dual-use items to dangerous governments in order to enhance our longer-term security prospects. The United States correctly views such "lost profits" as investments in future security, and not actual losses. Until Russia, China, and the EU fully accept this view, the risks will continue to grow.

Why is America already so strongly of this view while others are not? The EU's members are mixed in their performance on proliferation, some far stronger than others. Their inadequacies stem from their mercantilist economic policies and their inability to see dangers just over the horizon. Continued work by the United States can mitigate the problem, but can never fully solve it as long as many Europeans live in the happy illusion that they have passed beyond history and are secure in their comfortable EU "space," terrorist attacks in London and Madrid, assassinations in the Netherlands, and riots in Paris notwithstanding. Extrapolating from the EU's increasing authority over its member states, the EUroids view "conflict resolution" through the prism of "global governance," hoping to resolve disagreement through consensus and negotiation, thus misreading their own bloody last century and other contrary historical evidence. Perhaps their changing demographics, such as shrinking "European" birth rates and increased immigration from North Africa and the Middle East, will register with them at some point, but not yet. Others share the EU's problem, such as Brazil and India, but these states, too, are capable of greater watchfulness, with the continued exertion of U.S. leadership and example.

Although the United States will have an increasing number of issues on which we disagree with "Europe," as the EU likes to call itself, none is so important as WMD proliferation. The EU's weakness and self-absorption are manifest in many ways, but no other has such immediate and direct implications for America's own security. In its external foreign policy, the EU's approach is ever more globalist, statist, bureaucratic, legalistic, and passive (and far too often pacifist), an approach that many on the American left would be delighted to adopt for our country as well. This self-identification with "Europe" has characterized our Eastern Establishment for decades, as exemplified by the "global test" theme of Senator John Kerry's 2004 presidential campaign and by the *New York Times* editorial page on a daily basis. It represents a strain in American thinking, distressingly strong at the State Department and among the High Minded, that is both seductive and debilitating, offering as it does the same comfortable view of stability and security beyond history where so many Europeans today happily slumber.

The cases of Russia and China are more complex. At its start, the Bush administration believed that Russia's feelings of insecurity, especially from Islamic terrorism, provided a basis for closer cooperation against common international threats. We established a new strategic framework on offensive and defensive weapons and started what seemed to be promising joint efforts against terrorism and proliferation. Nonetheless, Russia felt it was not brought rapidly or fully enough into Western security structures, although it rejected repeated efforts by our Department of Defense for closer cooperation in such fields as missile defense. Moreover, Putin, for his own domestic reasons, moved decisively against increased political and economic freedom inside Russia, actions themselves precluding closer Russian integration into Western alliances, or even more basic relations of trust and confidence. Accompanying these troubling changes in Russia's domestic policy was a renaissance of its great-power aspirations, manifest in a number of unhappy policies respecting the former Soviet empire (what Russia calls the "Near Abroad"), the Middle East, and especially Iran and North Korea. Some of the factors underlying the effort to bolster Russia's status date to czarist days (Russia's never-ceasing effort to obtain access to warmwater ports), and some have more recent foundations, such as regaining as much as possible of the lost Soviet empire.

In some respects, Russia's policies are based on a form of racism, a view that North Koreans and Iranians are not capable of mounting truly serious threats to Russian interests. I saw this many times in comments from senior Russian officials, not openly or crudely stated, but apparent nonetheless. In addition, as with the EU, economic and commercial considerations rate high for Russia. The Bushehr nuclear plant in Iran will bring Russia an estimated $1 billion, and the construction of up to five additional nuclear facilities could produce up to $10 billion by some current estimates, along with potentially lucrative contracts for nuclear fuel supplies and related services. Iran has been a prolific consumer of high-end advanced conventional weapons, also paying in hard currencies, which sales Russia desperately needs to reduce the per-unit costs of its own military rearmament. North Korea figures in Russia's commercial calculus, but mainly because North Korea represents a land transport route into the far more attractive South Korean market Russia desperately wants to access. Finally, many Russian leaders are motivated by an atavistic desire to stick their thumb in America's eye in the Middle East, payback for the lost commercial opportunities they had in Saddam Hussein's Iraq, and desire for a greater license to meddle in affairs as they routinely did during Soviet days. In the Far East, they seek to constrain not only the United States, but also China, which Russia sees looming over its Far Eastern territory, hungry for both the natural resources and the vast stretches of underpopulated land.

The Bush administration has lost whatever illusions it had about the direction of Putin's Russia, and it is certainly hard now to find much that is encouraging in the direction of either Russia's domestic or its international policies. Its protection of Iran in the Security Council is nothing short of a flashback to the Cold War, and the intense competition for geostrategic and ideological advantage that the Cold War represented. And for the United Nations, as with North Korea, the struggle forecast yet again the prospect, perhaps the likelihood, of gridlock in the Security Council, and the consequent marginalization of the UN as a whole. Despite the straight-line regression in Russian policy, however, our efforts to turn Russia around cannot diminish. There are still at least a few sound thinkers in Moscow, and they provide at least some reason to believe all is not yet lost. Russia is far more at risk from a nuclear-capable, ballistic-missile-equipped Iran than the United States or even the EU at this point. Moreover, if the extremist clerics ruling Tehran were ever to give nuclear devices to terrorist groups, one set of claimants would undoubtedly be Islamic terrorists inside Russia, who have already brought their terrorism to the streets, theaters, and subways of Moscow itself.

At a minimum, however, we must not give way to Russia's general insistence on watering down sanctions efforts. The case of Iran is particularly instructive, offering as it does both the collapse of European will and the determination and the corrosive effects of a cynically resurgent Russian view of its own importance. The debilitation starts with the EU-3, who water down their own policies to the lowest common denominator, usually Germany's, and then insist we can go no further without bringing Russia and China on board. Since Russia is determined to protect its potential markets and other interests in Iran, that means that the policy is watered down even further, ultimately to the level represented by Security Council Resolutions 1737 and 1747, sanctions resolutions so weak that Iran feels perfectly free to ignore them. Even worse, Iran is able to undertake low-cost experiments, such as capturing and exploiting as hostages British and American service members and civilians, essentially without fear of reprisal. The United Kingdom responds, as its Foreign Office always wants to do, with a "softly, softly" approach, while leaking to the press that "harsh" statements by President Bush are making their task more difficult. Given this British/EU approach, it is hard to see what incentive Russia has to alter its behavior in the direction we seek. If anything, it actually encourages further Russian regression in its broader foreign policy toward a Soviet-era approach.

China, by contrast, has both improved and slipped backward during the Bush administration, in large part due to the effective use of sanctions against some of China's major trading companies. China's outward proliferation activities, especially in ballistic missiles, but also in the nuclear area with Pakistan and Iran, have been driven largely by commercial considerations, especially for those companies controlled by the People's Liberation Army, which often operates independently from the "political" authorities in Beijing. Every time a Chinese entity has been sanctioned, China has reacted angrily, demonstrating that the sanctions have gotten their attention. Even though the activity prompting the U.S. sanctions is routinely denied, the impact has been unmistakable. Although far from adequately or completely, China has taken some steps during the last several years to curtail these sales, and further progress may be possible.

In the case of North Korea, Chinese objectives stretch back for millennia. Fundamentally, China likes a divided Korean peninsula, likes having North Korea as a vassal and a buffer state between its forces and those of the United States and South Korea, and very much fears the collapse of the Kim Jung-il regime. This policy is widely divergent from what should be the U.S. view, which is that the DPRK regime itself is the source of the problem, which will disappear only when the regime itself disappears. To date, China has been completely unwilling to apply sufficient pressure against North Korea to make it renounce its nuclear ambitions, for fear of collapsing the regime itself. There are two reasons, one short-term and one long-term. First, China fears a wave of Korean refugees across the Yalu River, with its attendant destabilizing political and economic consequences. Second, China fears the loss of the DPRK itself, given that South Korea and American forces would undoubtedly move to fill the security vacuum that the DPRK's implosion would entail. In such an event, we would have an enormous and immediate interest in locating and securing North Korea's nuclear weapons and programs, lest elements of the disintegrating command structures carry these valuable—and salable—assets away with them. For China, the humanitarian problem, though real and potentially quite large, is in fact only transitory, while the change in the balance of power implied by Korean reunification is much more serious. Nonetheless, reunification is inevitable, as it was for Germany. China must be confronted with this reality, and with the need to have it made a higher and more direct priority in the bilateral Sino-American relationship.

Beyond the special case of North Korea (to which Russia has nothing comparable, except perhaps Belarus, or other parts of the "Near Abroad"), China cares about oil and natural gas. Its large and growing demand for energy has been and will increasingly be a major driver of its foreign policy, leading it to seek assured sources of supply around the world. China's solicitude for undesirable and threatening governments like those of Iran, Sudan, and Burma can be explained in large measure by its desire to support governments that can help China achieve its broader objective of energy security. Iran, as one example, has skillfully played this Chinese interest to its advantage, and has also had considerable success with countries like India and Japan, which also rely extensively on external sources for oil and natural gas. China itself is fully aware of the risks of dependence on external energy sources, as its efforts to expand domestic nuclear energy demonstrate, reminding us, incidentally, why the United States should also once again be turning to nuclear power to supply our energy needs. But for the immediate future, before nuclear energy can even begin to make a dent in China's energy needs, pressure to seek foreign oil and natural gas will be critical to China's economic growth, and requires long-term attention from Washington.

Both Russia and China are intent on rebuilding or expanding their military capabilities. A vigorous and sustained revitalization and transformation of Russia's military from its trough at the end of the Cold War has been a primary objective for Putin, and by all available evidence, it is well under way, overcoming entrenched resistance by the uniformed bureaucracies. So important was this transformation that Putin moved Sergei Ivanov, one of his closest personal and political friends and allies (dating from their time in the KGB), from the post of national security adviser to make him minister of defense and directed him to assume direct control over the project. Ivanov has been rewarded with promotion to deputy prime minister and is a candidate to succeed Putin himself. China is undertaking a substantial increase in defense expenditures and is expanding its strategic offensive weapons arsenal. It has successfully tested an antisatellite capability, which could well frustrate U.S. intelligence and early-warning systems as well as defeat our nascent missile defense program. Of immediate significance, Beijing has positioned over a thousand missiles aimed against Taiwan, lest Taiwan's vibrant democracy shows signs of moving toward *de jure* independence.

These Russian and Chinese efforts are a long way from the Cold War, but they are also far from insignificant and bear close monitoring. Other major players are already responding, as Japan, for example, moves closer to becoming a "normal" nation in meeting its own burdens of self-defense. For now, Japan's leadership believes that the best way to accomplish this objective is to remain under the U.S. nuclear umbrella and to strengthen our mutual defense ties, such as in missile defense efforts, which we should obviously support. Weakness on our part, however, will only encourage those segments of Japanese opinion arguing that Japan should move in a more independent direction, toward acquiring its own nuclear weapons capabilities. India is expanding in both the nuclear and ballistic missile fields, with or without U.S. cooperation, as well as enhancing its long-range naval capabilities, partially in response to China, but partially as an expression of its own growing and more confident role in South Asia and beyond. Japan and India already see what we should be seeing, namely China's emergence as a politico-military as well as economic power, and are acting accordingly.

Rogue states and terrorist groups, and even "responsible" nations, are carefully watching what happens with Iran and North Korea, and whether we succeed in shutting down their nuclear weapons programs. There is no doubt that failing to eliminate these two high-profile threats will induce others to follow the same path, with every prospect that they, too, will succeed, absent some dramatic change in international trends. This should be unsettling in the extreme. While no state or combination of states currently poses a serious *military* threat to the United States, military threats are not the most immediate consequence of WMD proliferation. They may become so as a resurgent Russia or China dramatically expands its military budgets and other capabilities, such as antisatellite warfare. Today, however, weapons of mass destruction are primarily weapons of terror, designed to hold hostage innocent civilian populations as targets of blackmail and coercion. Retaliation, and even the threat of annihilation, will not be sufficient to deter or dissuade terrorists who seek salvation in their own suicide, as in the September 11 attacks. Nor can "assured destruction" be calculated, as it was in Cold War days with the Soviet Union, to restrain the likes of Kim Jong-il or Ahmadinejad, just as Hitler in his last bunker was hardly capable of acting according to "rational" calculations.

Moreover, it is wholly insufficient to argue that because countries like Israel, India, and Pakistan have already achieved a nuclear weapons capability outside the Non-Proliferation Treaty, we can accept that others may also possess such weapons. That logic necessarily shreds the NPT itself, which was always an incomplete and therefore inadequate protection. The NPT is not the issue, but the logic and emotion of proliferation that now drive states nominally committed as non–nuclear weapons states applies all the more starkly as the number of nuclear aspirants grows, since almost all states have more than one enemy. If antipathy to the three non-NPT nuclear weapons states is an excuse (four if one now counts North Korea, which has withdrawn), there is simply no end to nuclear proliferation. Nor, unpleasant as it is for some to handle, are all nuclear states equal from the U.S. perspective. An Israel with nuclear weapons is not the same as an Iran so armed, just as the United Kingdom with nuclear warheads was not the same as the Soviet Union during the Cold War. Defending America means reducing the number of nuclear weapons states overall, if for no other reason than to reduce the threat of banditry, but it also means keeping perspective that some risks and threats are greater than others.

Here is where the tragedy of events in Iraq after the overthrow of Saddam Hussein weighs most directly on the conduct of American foreign policy. Iraq's continuing civil war has led many in the United States and abroad to conclude that the decision to overthrow Saddam was incorrect, with the obvious implication that toppling other rogue regimes, such as those in Iran or North Korea, would also be a mistake. As bad as the situation in Iraq may be, however, this conclusion badly misreads reality. Bush administration policy on Iraq divides analytically into two very separate questions. First, were we right to overthrow Saddam Hussein? Second, has our policy since the overthrow been correct? Although public opinion in the United States overwhelmingly answers the second question in the negative, properly so for many reasons, the turmoil in Iraq tells us nothing about the answer to the first question. Saddam's regime itself constituted a threat to peace and our security, whether or not imminent, and that alone was a compelling justification to eliminate it. What we did afterward will be a matter of debate for years, and there is a compelling argument that we should have handed authority back to the Iraqis as soon as possible and let them see if they could sort things out among themselves, rather than embroiling the United States in internal controversies that in some cases have endured for centuries.

Our strategic interests in Iraq have always been to ensure that it is not a WMD threat or a base for terrorism. Overthrowing Saddam accomplished the first objective far into the future, and achieving the second did not and does not require much of what we did in the over four years following Saddam's ouster. The risk of conflating the two separate points—regime change and its aftermath—is that many conclude that the postoverthrow violence undercuts the initial decision to change the regime in Baghdad. This erroneous and pernicious view, if widely accepted, would constrain or eliminate our ability to use military force or to work through other means to change regimes in places like Tehran and Damascus, for all the wrong reasons. This is certainly not to say that regime change or using military force are preferable ways to proceed, and clearly they are not the first options. But for rogue states like Iran and North Korea, nuclear weapons are the ultimate trump cards, which is why they show no evidence whatever of making a strategic decision to give up the pursuit of such weapons. Absent any such evidence, and therefore any basis to believe that a rogue state can be talked out of its nuclear weapons program, regime change and military force must remain as credible options. Indeed, in both Iran and North Korea, one or the other may well be required sooner rather than later. We cannot allow our recent history in Iraq to persuade us to the contrary.

Nor can we allow the unhappy state of affairs in Iraq to dissuade us from the continuing struggle against Islamic terrorism, in the Middle East, Afghanistan, or any place it arises. A major conceptual problem in this war is our failure to call it what it is, which is surely not a "global war on terrorism," however evocative that title may be. As much as the United States deplores the terrorism of Basque ETA separatists or Northern Irish extremists, they are not our focus. When President Bush decried "Islamofascism," a cumbersome but accurate description of the problem, the High Minded criticized him, and he backed away. But Al Qaeda and its jihadist allies, and even those who simply emulate Al Qaeda's methods without formal affiliation, clearly warrant this description, which will suffice until a better one emerges. Their worldview, whether for Sunni or Shia extremists, is unmistakably totalitarian, based not on ideology, as were the last century's totalitarian regimes, but on theology. This brand of totalitarianism has rarely been seen in the West, at least since the Renaissance. As bad as this theological fascism is for those who suffer under it, the United States and its allies face their own immediate threats not just in Iraq, but in the continuing threat to the United States, and to Israel and other close friends and allies. While those threats have not produced a dramatic attack inside the United States since September 11, 2001, recent indictments for conspiracies against the Sears Tower in Chicago, Fort Dix in New Jersey, and John F. Kennedy Airport in New York all show that the danger is real. It can never be repeated enough that the havoc the terrorists have already caused would grow exponentially if they acquired weapons of mass destruction.

Because of its location, Israel experiences the terrorist threat almost daily, facing Hamas, Hezbollah, and other Islamic terrorist groups, not to mention being within range of Iranian missiles. Hamas has now seized control of the Gaza Strip, fracturing the Palestinian Authority, leaving the "former terrorists" of Fatah now in control of the West Bank; Hezbollah is close to overthrowing Lebanon's democratic government; and Syria is increasingly under Iran's control. Given this reality, there is no rationale for the United States to pressure Israel into "peace agreements" with its remaining Arab neighbors, or to believe that "dialogue" on such issues will have any material effect on the Middle East's numerous other conflicts. Even if Ahmadinejad got his fondest wish, and Israel disappeared, these conflicts would continue unabated. Towering above all, of course, is the Iranian nuclear threat, a truly existential one for a nation as small and as close to Iran as Israel, whose willingness to use military force in its own self-defense has rarely been questioned. Israel's own internal political disarray, which most knowledgeable observers believe is the most confused ever in the history of the Jewish state, simply complicates an already untenable diplomatic environment. Of course, Israel's own government for its own reasons may decide to make concessions in various negotiations, and bear the consequences, but the United States has no interest in precipitating such decisions. In fact, as we await the unfolding of new French president Sarkozy's foreign policy, there may actually be cause to believe that the EU's position will grow closer to that of the United States and be more supportive of Israel than in many years, another reason for Israel not to lower its guard prematurely.

Afghanistan is still not completely free of the Taliban, and most believe that Osama bin Laden and his top aides and Taliban remnants still remain hidden in the border regions between Afghanistan and Pakistan, where they continue their war against the West. NATO should be doing more to finish off these remnants, both for the immediate benefits of so doing and for the collateral political and propaganda effects that destroying this theological Führer would bring. Musharraf's regime in Pakistan is itself continually on unsure footing, and a coup or assassination attempt could well put secure command and control of Pakistan's nuclear forces in real jeopardy. A coup by Islamofascists would be their quickest, most direct way to put nuclear weapons in the hands of terrorists. Even a failed coup risks the seepage of some of Pakistan's nuclear arsenal into terrorist networks. However dissatisfied some may be with Musharraf's democratic credentials, his regime's stability may be one of the greatest sources of Israel's security from a terrorist attack with nuclear weapons.

What all of this says is that history has not ended for the United States, or any other country, for that matter. Mortal adversaries still exist; many long-standing, natural allies are still (or have become) fainthearted; and considerable, and often difficult, foreign policy and defense work still remains to be done. Defending and promoting our interests and values requires, among many other things, much more effective American diplomacy, diplomacy not limited to the channels and procedures defined by others, and which is very clear about the utility of the various options that are open to us.

"There Is No Such Thing as the United Nations"

In particular, more effective U.S. diplomacy must avoid the trap of channeling all or most of our efforts through the UN system. Our independence by definition means we must decide ourselves where, how, and when our interests will be protected, even if the ever-growing propensity of the EU and others is to dial Turtle Bay. UN organizations, funds, and programs can be useful instruments of our foreign policy, but they manifestly cannot be the only or even the preferred instruments. They are only options among many others, and any resort to them has to calculate the costs as well as potential benefits of using them. Unilateral American action (Grenada, Panama), bilateral alliances (U.S.-Japan), multilateral defense alliances (NATO), ad hoc military coalitions (Persian Gulf Wars One and Two), regional organizations (OAS), and enforcement coalitions of the willing (Proliferation Security Initiative) are all legitimate and potentially effective alternatives. In the marketplace for international problem solving, the UN has a lot of competition, as well it should. America should choose the instruments that serve its interests best and not assume that those interests are invariably the same as those of the EU or any other bloc.

For almost all Americans, these sentiments are neither controversial nor offensive. Many, however, disagree, taking offense that anyone would describe the United Nations as an "instrument" of any national foreign policy, and most certainly not that of the United States. These are the true believers, the High Minded elite who worship at the altar of the Secular Pope. Of course, all 192 nations pursue their national interests at the UN—seeking to use it as an instrument of their foreign policy—but only the United States is criticized for it. Even those who are not vergers for the High Minded, however, have ample practical reasons to channel increasing decision-making authority into the UN system, especially if part of their agenda is to circumscribe U.S. global power. I include in this category not only those seeking to influence traditional matters of foreign affairs, but also the increasing category of "global governance" advocates who hope to transfer areas of authority traditionally left to national government to supranational bodies, or to constrain nation-states through "norming," effectively tying their hands. Issues like family planning and abortion, the right to keep and bear arms, environmental policy, the death penalty, and many others, even taxation, are now being dragged into the international arena, often with the support of the U.S. left. They have found themselves unable to prevail in a fair fight within America's system of representative government, so they now seek international forums to argue their positions, where their collectivist proclivities find greater sympathy among foreign governments and NGOs.

Most important, it is inherently untenable that America submit to any decision-making process in which it is simply one nation with one vote among 192 "equal" nations. There is nothing "equal" about them except the diaphanous idea of "sovereign equality" that no one outside the UN pays the slightest attention to. There is no doubt that the one-nation-one-vote principle—as fraudulent an analogy to real democracy as has ever been made—completely dominates UN program, budget, and management decision-making, almost entirely to the detriment of the United States. Moreover, the General Assembly, the specialized agencies' governing bodies, and lesser lights of the UN system (such as the Human Rights Council/Commission) have also attempted to assert authority in a variety of ways, especially through "norming" efforts that increasingly cover areas of traditionally "domestic" public policy. Unfortunately, we cannot tarry here long enough on this critical issue. In fact, however, the UN Charter confers potential power only on the Security Council, where the five permanent members are protected by the veto.

As we have seen, there are really two aspects of "UN reform," one concerning management and one concerning "governance" and policy-making. On management, I conclude from my experience that incremental efforts at reform are inherently incapable of producing significant and lasting change. Even as we battled unsuccessfully to adopt just a few of the Volcker Commission's proposals in response to the Oil for Food scandal, new problems such as "Cash for Kim" emerged. Tellingly, as with many failed reform efforts, this example deals only with accountability and transparency, and not at all with *effectiveness,* which ultimately has to be the measure for any program or body. A program can be utterly transparent and completely ineffective, and that is not our goal. If we cannot even achieve transparency at the UN, despite what I hope is not immodest to say were Herculean efforts, we have no hope of ever achieving greater effectiveness. The entrenched support for existing ways of doing business by too many

UN members is too strong to overcome, and the temptations for corruption, favoritism, mismanagement, laxity, and "looking the other way" are too great to allow one to expect a different result.

Moreover, at least in current circumstances, "UN reform" is not worth the costs for the State Department's permanent bureaucracy, which is busy tending to its client countries and bilateral interests. For State's regional bureaus, problems of "norming" are simply not issues that matter, and there is accordingly no motivation whatsoever to lobby their respective countries to shift their positions, especially when doing so might distract from more "pressing" bilateral issues. My personal efforts on "UN reform" go back to 1989, and Congress tried even earlier by withholding U.S. contributions, as did President Reagan by withdrawing the United States from UNESCO. Since the mid-1980s, almost nothing significant has changed. Surely, over twenty years of failed effort at "reform" (pressed in Republican administrations with more vigor than in the Clinton years) is enough for us to conclude that we have tried long enough with an incremental approach.

Accordingly, I conclude only one UN reform is worth the effort, and without it nothing else will succeed: Voluntary contributions must replace assessed contributions. If America insisted it would pay only for what works, and that we get what we pay for, we would revolutionize life throughout the UN system. There is simply no doubt that eliminating the "entitlement" mentality caused by relying on assessed contributions would profoundly affect UN officials around the world. As noted in Chapter V, UN agencies that are now voluntarily funded—like WFP, the high commissioner for refugees, and UNICEF—tend to be effective and transparent, thus providing clear lessons for the remainder of the UN. To argue otherwise would ignore the experience of market-driven imperatives throughout human history, which is really what switching to voluntary contributions would mean. If member governments providing resources were not satisfied with the outcomes produced by their UN contributions, they could shift their funds elsewhere, thus providing a "market test" for effectiveness. If non-UN programs or agencies proved more effective, the UN would quickly feel the consequences. Without doubt, moving from assessed to voluntary contributions would take an enormous effort, but even widespread debate about doing so would have a positive effect. Congress should immediately signal it wants to move in this direction and should communicate its sentiments directly to foreign parliamentarians, as well as letting the executive branch explain it diplomatically. Let the global debate on voluntary contributions begin, and let Congress drive the debate. State's bureaucracy may even follow!

In the meantime—and it may be a long time, given the magnitude of the change to voluntary contributions, and the magnitude of the opposition we will face—we need to deal with the UN as we find it. In at least one short-term respect, we may have some breathing space with the installation of Ban Ki-moon as secretary general. Of all the candidates to succeed Annan, I thought he was the least likely to wake up at some point during his five-year term concluding he was God's gift to humanity. Annan's acolytes did neither him nor the UN any good by postulating the SG as the Secular Pope, and Annan's embrace of the idea did none of the rest of us any good either. For at least a short period of time, Ban has the opportunity to press for reforms before the enormous inertia of Turtle Bay overtakes him, and the United States should encourage him to do so. We should not overestimate what even a "reformist" SG can do, but neither should we underestimate what inattentive management can allow to happen, as the Oil for Food scandal so graphically demonstrates. This is fundamentally an issue for member states, and that means the United States. Specifically, until we achieve a system of voluntary contributions, we must be prepared in the interim to withhold funding from UN activities we consider illegitimate, such as the Human Rights Council.

The larger issue of "reform," however, is UN governance, which really translates into U.S. influence in the organization. From a purely Platonic perspective, debate on UN governance can last forever, but what must matter most to the United States is how any change will affect our interests and our clout (minimal as it currently is). That is why the United States can and should support Japan for permanent membership on the Security Council, as we have since Nixon's presidency. However, if that is not achievable, we would be better off with no change in the Council's composition than with changes that result in potentially doubling the number of permanent members and expanding the Council beyond the point where it can function effectively. In fact, there are few structural changes that will improve America's situation within the UN system, and even if there were, the odds of achieving them may be impossible, as the failed battle to reform the HRC so vividly demonstrates. In fact, moving to voluntary contributions will do more to increase American influence, as well as to promise the greatest opportunity for increased UN effectiveness, precisely because the withdrawal of U.S. funding also implies diminished U.S. involvement. If other countries want our funding and our presence, they can have it, but only under circumstances of appropriate U.S. influence. If others do not like this trade-off, they are of course free to put their own money where their preferences lie, and we will direct our resources elsewhere.

Many of the real UN governance problems are not due to UN organizations as such, but to the political environment that has developed in the world's "UN cities" over the decades. In New York, Geneva, Vienna, and elsewhere, the very existence of UN governing bodies and agencies has created its own distinctive cultures, which, like other rent-seeking bureaucracies, have become part of the resistance to increased effectiveness and U.S. influence. Most basically, the existence of "permanent missions," especially in the Manhattan media hot house, itself fosters a UN-centric culture, the cumulative effects of which cannot be overestimated. "We never fail in New York" is a direct consequence of this culture, abetted by the notion of a "trade union of perm reps," often invoked to explain why "we" needed to stick together against one perceived threat or another to our status and authority. The culture in the UN cities has broader effects as well, such as continually reinforcing the preference to resort to the UN. Even personnel assignments for diplomats of UN members contribute to the problem. Almost every nation views a UN posting as a premier assignment for both junior and senior diplomats, so that the inculcation of the UN culture reaches deep even into distant foreign ministries. For the United States, by contrast, New York is unattractive for the Foreign Service. It is not treated as "foreign," and thus has few of the financial or other incentives of overseas assignments, and is actually quite disadvantageous financially, especially for Foreign Service officers with young families, because of New York's high living costs.

Moreover, the EU's propensity to replicate its bureaucratic and diplomatic culture in New York is a large, growing problem. Although we are familiar with the G-77/NAM desire to use the UN to leverage larger transfers of financial resources, these efforts, after years of repetition, are easy to withstand for any U.S. administration with even a little spine. The G-77/NAM priorities are almost entirely material, and no longer driven by an ideological agenda, as they often were during the Cold War. The EU agenda, by contrast, is more complex and sophisticated and involves remaking UN institutions into replicas of the deadening Brussels bureaucracies, which are far removed from democratic control, and ever more devoted to decreasing the authority of nation-states. Brussels thus sees itself as post-Westphalian, above and beyond the nation-state, a model for the rest of the benighted planet, and therefore wants to clone itself elsewhere. The UN is a critical venue to achieve full transformation of the EU's institutional form and governance style into global governance, and especially to whip the still unrepentantly Westphalian United States into line. After all, if the EU can make it in New York, it can make it anywhere.

For the United States, the more immediate problem, and one more immediately solvable, is the EU's constant effort to be the broker in all UN disagreements, including those the EU itself has caused. This EU desire to be the middleman—the bridge—stems not from altruism but from a carefully calculated objective of increasing its influence at the expense of other blocs, and particularly at the expense of the United States. Unfortunately, in diplomacy generally, we have a disturbing tendency to give way to the EU—Iran's nuclear weapons program being the most prominent current example. (We give way in other cases as well, such as pleading with China to host the Six-Party Talks on North Korea, which indicates yet another troubling tendency developing at the State Department.) The EU's bargaining style, as recounted in many cases in this book, is first to achieve its own objectives, which are often quite minimal, and then to leave us hanging well short of *its* goals, all the while taking credit with both the G-77/NAM and the United States for its prodigious diplomatic "bridging" efforts. All of this is usually facilitated by the twenty-five EU members' singing the same tune, although there are also certainly examples where internal EU disagreements hobble or even destroy their effectiveness. In the UN, at least, we can only hope for more of the latter. Instead of allowing or encouraging this EU shell game, the United States should deal directly with the G-77/NAM more often, cut the deal we want, and marginalize the EU, thus also frustrating their global governance agenda. In fact, through JUSKCANZ, we have the makings of a Pacific counterweight, in UN circles at least, to the EU, and we should use it more often and more effectively.

As for the G-77/NAM coalition, our continuing objective should be to break their fragile unity at every opportunity, until these blocs disappear on the ash heap of history. The NAM has never answered Moynihan's fateful question: "Given the end of the Cold War, what are you nonaligned about?" Nor will they ever, because there is no answer. In fact, differences within the G-77/NAM can and will continue to grow, creating fissures we should enlarge at every opportunity. Moreover, within the regional groups there are also wide divergences we can use to our advantage, all on condition we don't talk about it too openly. To this day, the one factor that can unify the G-77/NAM is the opportunity to oppose something the United States wants. It is worth fracturing the G-77/NAM, but we can do it at leisure, once we have dispensed with the larger problem of creeping EU-ism.

A Cultural Revolution for the State Department

The United Nations is my client.

—DEAN RUSK, SUCCESSOR TO ALGER HISS,
PREDECESSOR OF YOURS TRULY, C. 1947[1]

No one disputes that we need to be represented internationally by the finest State Department we can assemble. Unfortunately, over the decades, a culture has emerged at the department that not only does not represent us as effectively as it could and should, but that has in many respects acquired a mind of its own. At least when it comes to Republican presidents, many at State are determined to formulate their own policies, regardless of what the elected president might want to pursue. There are a variety of reasons why this culture has emerged over the years, but one underlying factor is that successive secretaries of state have not paid adequate attention to what has been going on beneath the high policy they concentrate on. This may be understandable, given the pressures of the office, but we are now long past the point where this neglect can be allowed to continue. It is not enough to

---

1. Rusk succeeded Hiss as the State Department's director of special political affairs in March 1947, a position equivalent to assistant secretary of state. This office is the lineal ancestor of the Bureau of International Organization Affairs, or "IO," which I headed in Bush 41, described above. See Thomas J. Schoenbaum, *Waging Peace and War: Dean Rusk in the Truman, Kennedy and Johnson Years* (New York: Simon & Schuster, 1988), p. 157. (" 'The United Nations is my client,' [Rusk] would say when Acheson or Lovett grumbled about his eagerness to involve the U.N. in almost every question of foreign policy.")

disparage the Foreign Service, as Rich Armitage used to do by calling it the "Foreign Circus." The department's culture must be changed, and changed soon. While there are any number of proposals to reorganize and restructure the State Department, its problems are not going to be corrected by moving around lines and boxes on an organizational chart, but only by a cultural revolution.

The ideal civil servant is one who faithfully pursues the policies of the incumbent administration, respecting the democratic legitimacy that comes from the president's election. The president is, of course, the *only* person in the executive branch with such electoral legitimacy (the VP being an adjunct of the president). To state the obvious, no one in the permanent bureaucracy is elected by anyone. Obviously, the president does not determine the details of each and every policy, but the president's senior appointees carry his policy messages to the diverse departments and agencies, and, working with career professionals, implement them, seek necessary legislative changes, and otherwise do what is necessary to carry them into practice, modified as necessary by the factual circumstances they confront. This model, however, does not describe what happens at State, where too much of the permanent bureaucracy thinks it is responsible not just for implementing policy, but for setting it, no matter what the president of the moment thinks, certainly not if that president is Republican. Consider the following reasons.

First, political opinion among State careerists is overwhelmingly Democratic and liberal. This ideological coloration is in part due to self-selection at the entry level, and in part due to acculturation over years of employment at State, from forces both inside the bureaucracy and outside, especially from the High Minded in academia. I well remember the day after the 2004 election when State's cafeteria might as well have been hung with black crepe, so gloomy was the mood after Bush's victory, and the contrast with the 1992 election, where people were all but drinking champagne for breakfast. In fact, there *are* at least some conservatives within the career Civil- and Foreign-Service ranks at State, but they are few and naturally reticent to reveal themselves given the harm that can befall their careers. There are also careerists who are exactly what they should be: civil servants who follow the policy directives of the administration that is in power, and do so vigorously and unapologetically. In fact, almost all those who have come out of the closet to make their conservative views known, to their credit, follow this proper paradigm of government professionals, not allowing personal philosophies to override the direction taken by the department's political leadership. I must confess that it took me years of my own government service to appreciate, let alone prize, these qualities of the prototypical civil servant, but I see it now as an endangered species that desperately needs protection. Unfortunately, the lack of sufficient conservatives and true civil servants allows the predominant liberal bias free rein. These liberals include many with whom I have differed on both policy formulation and execution, and whom I have taken to task in these pages. My criticisms do not suggest that they resist the policies of conservative Republican administrations because of corrupt or illicit motives or incompetence. Instead they don't follow the policies simply because they don't want to, they don't believe in them, and—perhaps most important—they can get away with it. Even when some try to lip-sync the words, and some liberal bureaucrats honestly try, they perform inadequately, because their hearts just aren't in it, and because they yearn for the Restoration of the High Minded.

Second, the Foreign Service regularly observes the way foreign policy is formulated in most other countries, where the permanent bureaucracies really do predominate, passing policy on to transient and typically compliant political ministers, who often do little more than read the talking points careerists hand them. After all, in London, for example, they don't call such careerists "the mandarins of Whitehall" for nothing. In Europe, there is little popular input into foreign policy formulation, and in autocratic regimes, popular opinion is easily disregarded. European diplomats typically react with horror to the populist pressures brought to bear in America by economic interests, ethnic groups, powerful members of Congress, and others who affect policy making, let alone opinionated cabinet secretaries and their appointees. In fact, "political" appointees in most foreign ministries are few and far between, certainly compared to the U.S. tradition. Many at State in the Civil as well as the Foreign Service yearn for the autonomy of EU ministries, far from the madding crowd, and some do more than just yearn. They know how to use Washington's multifaceted levers of power, leaking to philosophically congenial members of Congress and the media, and thereby carrying on the ideological struggle well outside of traditional bureaucratic corridors.

Third, presidential ineptitude cannot be ignored. Counterproductive or lackluster appointments squander the executive's most effective tool for overcoming bureaucratic inertia. "Personnel is policy" is not just a slogan; it is a fact. Presidents and secretaries of state who see senior officials as interchangeable have only themselves to blame when they are either captured by the permanent bureaucracy or unable to move it where they want it to go. Too many key appointments go to people who don't know what the policy is, don't care about it, or are too timid to stand up to the bureaucracy even if they actually know what they should be doing. State's permanent bureaucracy is smart and subtle in its ability to "capture" political appointees—by both seduction and intimidation—and mold them to its will, as Powell's entire tenure and careerist influence over Rice demonstrate. Jim Baker's tenure, of course, demonstrates the opposite. Another classic example is co-opting political appointees to fight the bureaucracy's age-old turf fights, rather than pursuing their president's philosophical and policy objectives, thus capturing the energy and intelligence of the political officials for the bureaucracy's agenda rather than the president's. "Battle fatigue" among political appointees is another factor that should not be ignored by the White House, although too often Republican administrations act as though the problem does not exist.

A bureaucracy without sufficient political leadership cannot be used effectively. Led inadequately or inattentively, State's careerists will simply continue doing what they want to do, as the case of North Korea demonstrates. Even beyond this phenomenon, there are still other problems confronting even the most disciplined political leadership at State, if conservatives ever put one in place. Here, we find the heart of the cultural problem. Different and analytically quite separate from ideology, it nonetheless magnifies and at times disguises the bureaucracy's philosophical biases. To be sure, these State Department deficiencies exist in other ministries of foreign affairs, which may at times, fortunately, be the only thing that keeps us afloat diplomatically.

1. The most serious of State's cultural deficiencies is one that the permanent bureaucracy not only recognizes but has named: "clientitis." The term means excessively advocating the interests of the country or region for which an official is responsible (as if a lesser amount of such advocacy would be acceptable, or even natural!). Unfortunately, even the label chosen for the problem shows that the bureaucracy does not

really understand it. The problem is not "excessive" advocacy for Country X, but the fact that the bureaucracy doesn't know who the real client is, let alone how vigorously to represent it. The "client" is not France or Europe or whatever, but the United States. If "clientitis" were actually the problem, it would mean excessively advocating the interests of the United States, something State is rarely accused of. A novelist could not have written a more precise statement of the department's wrongheadedness than Rusk's comment about the UN, quoted at the head of this section, and this from a future secretary of state, no less! "Clientitis" permeates the "functional" bureaus at State (economic affairs, nonproliferation, refugee affairs, and so on) as well as the regional bureaus, although their parochialism favors international organizations and treaties rather than foreign countries. Thus, for many careerists dealing with nuclear issues, criticism of the IAEA or the NPT for being inadequate or incompetent is the equivalent of heresy, whereas protecting "their" agencies and treaties is holy writ.

2. "Moral equivalency," a disease of the sophisticated, is especially prevalent among EUroid diplomats, and is highly contagious, frequently spreading to State's permanent bureaucracy. It involves equating actions or policies that are fundamentally different, thus allowing the High Minded to criticize or distance themselves from both, thereby adopting a satisfying tone of moral superiority. For example, Palestinian terrorist attacks and Israeli defensive responses are equated, both contributing to "the cycle of violence" in the region, and both should be condemned. Iran's drive for nuclear weapons is in response to excessive American efforts to isolate the mullahs, and both should suspend their policies to allow EU diplomacy to resolve the problem. The list is almost endless. In its most poisonous version, as in the example of Iran, the United States is the cause for the overwhelming bulk of the world's problems. According to this narrative, *we* provoke the disreputable behavior of rogue states and other undesirables, who, left alone by us, would have remained friendly and docile. If only our conduct were corrected, other countries would comport themselves with sweet reason as well. Jeane Kirkpatrick called this the "blame America first" syndrome, and it is rampant at State. One of the worst consequences of moral equivalency is the enervating effect it has on America's own diplomats. If all positions are, in essence, "morally

equivalent," how can one justify advocating one's own so vigorously at the expense of other, equally "legitimate" views?

3. "Mirror imaging" is related to moral equivalency, but is perhaps an even more widespread operational problem, involving the inability to see that representatives of other countries do not bargain on the same terms as our diplomats. Consider: You are a U.S. diplomat who is reasonable, moral, practical, and, importantly, a sophisticated woman or man of the left, as are almost all foreign diplomatic colleagues you encounter. You can see both sides of an issue, and you can find reasonable grounds for accommodation, surely, with even the most obdurate "interlocutor," a word almost as prized at State as "nuanced." Unfortunately, however, not everyone on the other side of the table is your mirror image. If your "interlocutor" thinks you are a limp-wristed, weak-kneed, morally degenerate envoy of a decaying civilization, his priorities are likely to be very different from yours. In fact, if the person opposite is not your mirror image, you are poised to be taken advantage of, and will perhaps not even be aware of it. A classic example was Jones Parry during the December 2006 negotiations with Russia over Iran: "Please, if we have nothing to give, then how will we make progress?" he said at one point. There is an urban legend among U.S. negotiators about a Cold War–era Soviet diplomat who used to open his conversations with Americans by saying, "What have you got for us today?" Indeed. Moreover, many cultures, perhaps most, are more patient than ours, and more obdurate, perfectly content to prolong negotiations if they are not getting what they want. The "mirror imaging" problem leads our diplomats to conclude that the failure to reach agreement must be our fault, and must therefore be resolved by further concessions.

4. Most fundamentally, State careerists are schooled in accommodation and compromise with foreigners, rather than aggressive advocacy of U.S. interests, which might inconveniently disrupt the serenity of diplomatic exchanges, not to mention dinner parties and receptions. There are no "Stonewall Jacksons" in the Foreign Service Hall of Fame. Smoothness and stability in diplomatic relations are prized despite the negative consequences such stability often entails. Officials throughout their careers are rewarded for reaching agreements, and quickly, with far less emphasis on evaluating what the agreements ac-

tually say. "Unity" in the Security Council on draft resolutions, for example, is given pride of place in our efforts, rather than concentrating on the substance of the resolutions themselves. Too often, diplomacy becomes the objective, rather than simply one of many tools for achieving an objective.

Straight talking is too often subordinated to accommodating foreign sensitivities, as if American sensitivities do not matter, or, even worse, are slightly embarrassing. So, for example, one never says another government has "violated" a commitment, only that it is in "noncompliance" with the commitment, or even "apparent noncompliance." Over and over again, we give foreigners the benefit of the doubt, a syndrome whereby we negotiate with ourselves before we even show up at the bargaining table, watering down our position in advance, thus helpfully making it easier for the foreigners to water it down even further. These are some of the consequences of the supremacy of process over substance. Another is the surprisingly short time horizons in State Department decision-making, which inevitably sacrifice policy and philosophical considerations. This is what, over time, produces senior Foreign and Civil Service officers who exemplify the culture, not as flawed individuals who aren't tough bargainers, but as individuals who carry out what they have learned throughout their careers. This is not a question of personalities, but of a defective, self-perpetuating culture.

An implicit foundation of the accomodationist school of diplomacy is that diplomacy itself doesn't cost anything. Under this theory, it never hurts to negotiate with adversaries, since, compared to the alternatives, talking provides the potential only for benefits, without risk. If diplomacy were truly always costless, this argument would have force, but in fact the selection among alternative courses of action in international affairs, as in life itself, always entails benefits *and* costs. The costs of engaging in diplomacy are many, including: legitimizing outlaw regimes and giving them political acceptability and increased opportunities for propaganda and disinformation; reducing economic and political pressures that may be difficult to sustain during negotiations, especially protracted ones; and the signal sent of potential future weakness. Moreover, there is the long-term, cumulative cost of weak and ineffective bargaining, of always "coming in too low" in bargaining positions, as State consistently does. The effect of this weakness is analogous to the impact on airline costs of eliminating just a few pounds of weight from each flight. Over millions of route miles, the aggregate savings can be huge. In diplomacy, the cumulative cost impact over decades of weak American efforts must be frighteningly high.

Most costly of all, however, is the factor of delay. By consuming time, diplomacy provides an adversary the most precious of resources, more valuable than any other because it is not for sale. This can involve time for the United States and its allies to grow complacent; time for an opponent to ready its defenses or prepare its offenses; time to perfect its weapons of mass destruction; or even just time to think. Nowhere is delay more costly in contemporary terms than in WMD proliferation, where time is often the critical component in determining whether a proliferation effort will succeed or fail. Obviously, diplomacy's benefits in many contexts will outweigh its costs, but it is a grotesque mistake to believe that diplomacy never has costs.

Very few at State, of course, would admit to any of this. Almost all would emphatically deny it. But it is the *actions* of the permanent bureaucrats that matter, not their rhetoric. Moreover, these cultural defects do not mean that there exists at State an incurable weakness of character or capabilities that prevents a cure. Many careerists are as tough as they come, and anyone who has ever engaged in an internal turf struggle with State bureaucrats knows the true meaning of street fighting. Instead of fighting with ourselves, however, in a circular firing squad, we should be directing our energies against our foreign adversaries, which we are certainly not now doing adequately. This cultural problem is solvable, although we need to understand that, because it developed over decades, it will take decades to cure. Criticism from the outside alone will not remedy the problem.

Most basically, from the first day of training through the last session of career counseling, root-and-branch changes are needed, a "cultural revolution in diplomatic affairs." Diplomacy should come to mean *advocacy*. Advocacy for American interests must be the priority, not compromise and conciliation for their own sake. Disagreement with foreign friends or adversaries is not itself distasteful, nor simply an unpleasantness to be overcome as rapidly and quietly as possible without regard to substantive outcomes. Disagreement reveals underlying issues that should be resolved consistently with our own interests, and it is those interests that should determine how we proceed. "Argument," which lawyers do all the time, but which diplomats shy away from, is neither unpleasant nor disagreeable, but actually critical to making the case for the interests we are advancing. "Compromise" should involve mutually satisfactory outcomes, not having to accept unsatisfactory outcomes on some issues as the only way to achieve our objectives on others. Litigators are prized for "going to the wall" for their clients. We need that same resolve in our diplomats, and we can get it by creating the right incentives and training.

This cultural revolution is not insuperably difficult, but it will require intense and sustained attention from State's "seventh floor," and from the White House. Changes need to be made in the incentives and rewards system, with different paths to promotion and career development. This panoply of interlocking institutional changes must be overseen by the secretary's top lieutenants, and not be left to "the system" itself to administer. One important change in career patterns would be assignments in private business (not just sabbatical years at universities, which would only make the current culture even worse), where techniques in aggressive negotiation to reach mutually advantageous outcomes are prized and not derided. Success in making these changes at State, however, is critical, and long, long overdue. Otherwise, the United States will continue to go into international organizations, conferences, meetings, and negotiations—bilateral or multilateral—crippled from the outset. Reform of the State Department is critical to advancing American interests more effectively, and we need it now, before it is too late.

For myself, in or out of government, I have no intention of leaving the firing line. The 2008 elections are close, and getting closer, and the High Minded sense victory. Their incessant pounding against the Bush administration, including that directed personally—and quite intentionally— against many of its leading figures, such as Cheney, Rumsfeld, Wolfowitz, Feith, and Libby, and the departure of others such as Crouch, Joseph, and Rademaker, have left administration foreign policy in something like free fall. While that certainly enhances the risk that more mistakes will be made before the end of Bush's second term, there is a larger risk as well, namely that wherever Bush ends up, the American left will try to characterize that as the outer extreme of acceptable "conservative" foreign policy, deriding other views as beyond the Pale. This form of historical revisionism, so frequently successful, cannot be allowed to succeed again.

As a veteran of the Goldwater campaign, of course, I saw it all long ago. Win or lose in one election or another, I am not going away. As Senator John Kyl said to me at one point during the 2005 confirmation battle, when the assault on me was in full swing, recalling campaign advice he had once received, "You have to consider yourself like a big gray battleship that will take a lot of hits. The important thing is to keep moving and keep firing." Gray may not be my best color, but I certainly plan to follow Kyl's advice and keep moving. And keep firing.

INDEX

Index

Oil for Food program
  and American opinion about UN, 206
  and Annan, 172, 173, 174, 203, 204, 205,
    209, 221, 226–27, 240*n*, 273, 274
  and calls for Annan's resignation, 273, 274
  Coleman's investigation of, 172
  and Outcome Document, 205
  and reform of UN, 221–22, 226, 240, 442,
    444
  Volcker report about, 173, 174, 203–4, 206,
    209, 211–13, 222, 226–27, 229, 240, 244,
    442
OIOS. *See* Office of Internal Oversight
    Services, UN
OLC. *See* Office of Legal Counsel
Olmert, Ehud, 397, 403, 408
OMB (Office of Management and Budget),
    202, 224
Onassis, Jackie Kennedy, 17
OPCW. *See* Organization for the Prohibition
    of Chemical Weapons
OPEC (Organization of Petroleum Exporting
    Countries), 21
Organization of American States (OAS), 441
Organization for Economic Cooperation and
    Development (OECD), 21
Organization of the Islamic Conference, 355
Organization for the Prohibition of Chemical
    Weapons (OPCW), 95–97
Orr, Robert, 214, 215
Ortega, Daniel, 189
Oshima, Kenzo
  and Bolton's first Security Council meeting,
    246
  and election of Ban as secretary general,
    285, 287
  and Japan's assessed UN contribution, 254
  and North Korea, 292–95, 297–305, 307,
    308
  and reform of UN/Security Council, 231,
    232, 243, 244, 252, 253, 260, 262
Outcome Document
  finalizing the, 216
  negotiating and drafting the, 198–216, 232
  and reform of UN/Security Council, 220,
    222, 223, 234, 239, 248
  and September Summit, 196, 217
  as validation for Annan's "In Larger
    Freedom," 221
Özal, Turgut, 39

Pakistan
  and arms control, 92
  and BWC Verification Protocol, 92
  and China, 430, 434
  earthquake relief efforts in, 386
  and election of Ban as secretary general,
    278, 279, 283, 284
  and Lebanon-Syria relations, 373

  and next generation threats to America, 430,
    434, 437, 440
  nuclear/ballistic missile program of, 430,
    434, 437, 440
  and Outcome Document, 199, 214
  and PBC, 229, 230
  Powell-Bolton visit to, 69
  and reform of Security Council, 251, 252
  Taliban in, 440
Palau, 238
Palestine, 260
Palestinian Authority (PA), 374, 375, 387,
    388, 389, 391, 439
Palestinians
  and culture of State Department, 451
  and definition of terrorism, 208
  disarmament of, 372
  elections for, 374–75, 387
  International Day of Solidarity with,
    383–84
  and Iran, 388
  Israeli relations with, 31, 208, 260, 387–93,
    412, 451
  in Lebanon, 372
  and Lebanon-Syria relations, 381
  and reform of UN, 242
  as refugees, 372, 381
  See also Hamas; Palestinian Authority; PLO
Pan Am 103 bombing, 127
Panama, 271–72, 441
Parchin (Iran weapon testing facility), 157, 325
Paris, France
  PSI Core Group meetings in, 125–26
  riots in, 431
Patten, Chris, 116
Patterson, Anne, 195, 215
Peace Building Commission (PBC), 206,
    213–14, 225–26, 227, 229–30
peacekeepers, UN
  exploitation by, 257, 260, 262, 283
  "gold for guns" transactions of, 370
Peacekeeping Operations (DPKO), UN
  Africa as focus of, 341–42
  Bush's comments about, 289
  in Côte d'Ivoire, 361–65
  and election of Ban as secretary general, 288
  in Ethiopia-Eritrea, 344–48
  failures in, 248
  and functions of Security Council, 247
  in Lebanon, 394, 401
  number of, 341–42
  and procurement fraud, 257, 260, 261–62
  and reform of Security Council, 251, 255,
    260, 261–62
  in Somalia, 366
  in Sudan/Darfur, 342, 343–44, 348–61
  in Western Sahara, 247, 267–69
*Penn Central Transportation Co. v. City of New
    York* (1978), 17

ABOUT THE AUTHOR

John Bolton was appointed by President George W. Bush as United States permanent representative to the United Nations in 2005 and served until his appointment expired in December 2006. He also served as undersecretary of state for arms control and international security affairs from 2001 through 2004. Bolton is an attorney and has spent many years of his career in public service, holding high-level positions in the administrations of Presidents Ronald Reagan and George H. W. Bush.

PHOTO CREDITS